Northwestern University
STUDIES IN *Phenomenology &*
Existential Philosophy

Phenomenology and
the Social Sciences

Edited by

Phenomenology and the Social Sciences

VOLUME 2

MAURICE NATANSON

NORTHWESTERN UNIVERSITY PRESS

EVANSTON   1973

Contents

VOLUME TWO

[ix]

x   /   *Contents*

PART V

Phenomenology and History

Phenomenology and History

Gerhard Funke

HISTORY, THE SCIENCE OF HISTORY, AND THE PHILOSOPHY OF HISTORY

1. HISTORY IS MADE UP of both what has occurred and what is occurring at present. It designates what takes place for man in the worlds of nature and culture. In general, history deals with the occurrence-nature of what befalls man as the recollecting of what has occurred.

If history is understood *objectively* as the simple temporal connectedness of occurrences, and *subjectively* as the narrative presentation of these occurrences, then clearly the term "history" has reference to every natural and spiritual happening; it can concern itself with purely natural happenings just as correctly as with cultural happenings. A universal history of nature (Kant) and a history of the cosmos (Laplace) are just as conceivable, then, as a history of biological species (Darwin) or a universal evolutionary history (Spencer).

Yet, if history, in accordance with the etymology of the German word *Geschehen* (*scehan*), designates an *event* [*Ereignis*], or whatever, in coming to pass, abruptly breaks in on man, then "history" must signify whatever comes about in an essentially eventful manner; [1] this mode of occurring becomes significant for

Translated from the German by Roy O. Elveton.
1. K. Keuck, "Historia: Geschichte des Wortes und seiner Bedeutung in der Antike und in den romanischen Sprachen" (Dissertation: University of Münster, 1934), pp. 78 ff. See also Jacob and Wilhelm Grimm,

[3]

human destiny precisely because something is consciously known to be meaningful. In this case, the authentic sense of history is to be found solely in the meaningful events of human life, and is not coextensive with everything that happens within the context of life. Happenings that occur abruptly and eventfully are determined by the way in which they come to pass, and not by the mere fact of their occurrence. Hence specific historical happenings are eventful in this sense, and in this sense alone: they are fortuitous occurrences. "History" in different compounds (for example, *anasciht = eventus, missesciht = fortunae asperitas, insciht = prodigium*) takes on the meaning of "event," or "chance occurrence," [2] and signifies the eventful and fortuitous coming-to-pass of an occurrence.

Since the beginning of modern times, history taken narrowly has referred to actual happenings in the sense of human deeds (the *res gestae*), and has simultaneously included in its reference the narration of such happenings (the *expositio rerum gestarum*); the happenings themselves appear to have significance for a social totality. Hence the concept of history is used both subjectively and objectively.[3] These contrasting senses of history are found not only in conjunction with universally relevant events but also on lower levels, in reference to incidents that are only relatively important.

The concept of ἱστορία or ἱστόρημα, quite generally employed with reference to "history," has, with the passage of time, lost its original meaning of "inquiry," "exploration," or "knowledge won through intuition."[4] On higher levels it has become so thin as to designate merely "scientific presentation," and on lower levels it

Deutsches Wörterbuch (Leipzig: Hirzel, 1854–); English translation from 4th ed. by John Francis David, *An Etymological Dictionary of the German Language* (London: Bell & Sons, 1891); and F. Kluge, *Etymologisches Wörterbuch der deutschen Sprache* (Strasbourg: Trübner, 1883), s.v. "Geschichte."

2. J. Hennig, "Die Geschichte des Wortes 'Geschichte,'" in *Deutsche Vierteljahrschrift für Literatur und Geistesgeschichte*, XVI, no. 4 (1938), 511 ff. See also P. E. Geiger, "Das Wort Geschichte und seine Zusammensetzungen" (Dissertation: University of Freiburg im Br., 1908), pp. 18 ff.

3. Diefenbach's *Vokabular* (1482) defines "History or happening = thing, *historia, res gesta.*"

4. Herodotus 1.1. Bodin uses the term *"historia"* in the sense of *"contemplatio"* in his work *Methodus ad facilem historiarum cognitionem* (1566), English translation by Beatrice Reynolds, *Method for the Easy Comprehension of History* (New York: Octagon Books, 1966).

signifies only "simple narration." The so-called objective concept of history labels insignificant occurrences "incidents" or "stories." A more significant event is an *acta* or *res gestae*. The subjective concept of history speaks of "history" in unimportant contexts, and of *narratio* or *expositio rerum gestarum* in more important contexts.

Bodin's expression, *"historia id est vera narratio,"* the point of departure for the modern interpretation of the word "history," signifies both inquiry (*vera* narratio) and narrative presentation (vera *narratio*).[5] History as a science is then construed as *"historia vel vera narratio hominis rerum, tam praeteritarum quam presentium,"* and designates *"quicquid omnium ubique rerum cognovimus, quae fiunt, quae nostro vel alieno sensu haurimus."* Hegel draws these two aspects together:

> In our language history unites both the subjective and the objective aspects, and signifies both the *historiam rerum gestarum* as well as the *res gestas*, the narration of history as well as the happenings, deeds, and occurrences themselves. The unity of these two meanings must be seen as belonging to a higher order than that of mere external coincidence, and we must therefore hold that the narration of history emerges simultaneously with authentically historical deeds and occurrences: there is an internal and common basis that throws them up together.[6]

Both the science of history and the philosophy of history are concerned with "historical phenomena," but they have different questions and problems in mind; thus it must first of all be made clear what the precise concern of the science of history is. The material object of the science of history cannot be simply happenings as such. The science of history is not concerned with the entire course of the world and with everything that occurs. Nor is there a direct correlation between the objective aspect of this universal process and the subjective aspect of the exploration, investigation, and explanation of this process in its totality. Even if such a history were to be established in both its subjective and objective aspects, a universal "history of nature" could not be put together without a certain selectivity and a point of view

5. Cf. Hennig, "Die Geschichte des Wortes 'Geschichte,'" pp. 511 ff., and Bodin, *Method*, chap. 1, pp. 15–19.

6. G. W. F. Hegel, *Philosophie der Weltgeschichte* (1830), I, p. 144 (my translation).

from which to make choices; thus it could not be carried out without a culturally conditioned acceptance of relevant factors.

If it is correct to view "nature" as a cultural concept which varies with changes in cultures, then the "history of nature" and the "history of culture" belong together. In a more restricted sense, "history," considered objectively, refers to the eventful coming-to-pass of the world of man alone—the world that rests on free decision, achievement, and determination—along with the cultural, social, economic, and political processes and changes that are part of it. Considered subjectively, "history" is the conscious laying-hold of just these events and processes. History is customarily spoken of in this sense,[7] but usually with the addition that such a laying-hold is for the first time truly historical when its report is factually correct ("how it actually happened") and free from subjective embellishments (seen "without prejudice").

From this discussion the following definitions result:

"History" is the potential object of historical description; or, in other words, it is the historical process, the historical state of a culture itself (Voltaire).

"History" is the factual content of the historical description. It is that aspect of events that is known and evaluated by the science of history (Bernheim).

"History" is the writing of history. It is the presentifying reconstruction of events, which subjectively brings to life the processes and motives themselves (Croce).

Here we are not considering "history" either in the sense of a specific course of instruction or as a historical survey. The historical-scientific discipline of "history" presents the evidence for history as that which has taken place. The *fides historica* is here dependent on methodologically correct investigation. But methodological confidence necessitates first critical reflection regarding the possibility of historical knowledge and historical presentation; at the beginning of the modern period, for example, Bodin's *Methodus ad facilem historiarum cognitionem* (1566) appears at the same time as the investigation *De recto historiarum judicio*. When we speak of historical certainty, we refer to the certainty that the science of history is in a position to achieve.

---

7. R. Rocholl, *Die Philosophie der Geschichte*, I (Göttingen: Vandenhoeck & Ruprecht, 1878), p. 1.

The development of man as a social being is generally treated as a special object of the science of history. The writing of history as a narrowly factual account (in logography, records, and chronologies), as a pragmatic-didactic exercise, and as an exploration of origins and developments all attest to this. The earliest type of historical writing is the simple sequential enumeration of historical occurrences in their "natural" temporal order. The pragmatic writing of history [8] attempts to fasten on the motivations of historical personalities or to ascertain the moving forces of events in order to hold up the lessons of the past to the contemporary world and to posterity in the form of practical conclusions. It is history *"quae simul instituit lectorem quae ipsi in vita civiliutilia vel noxia sectanda vel fugienda sunt."* The apodictic writing of history, which always relates facts and aims to uncover and demonstrate the necessity of historical happenings, follows the same tendency. In the developmental writing of history, historical events are investigated causally, and their development is presented, not as a simple spatial or temporal succession, but as a tightly knit chain. Here, preeminently, the principle *historia vitae magistra* holds; we are to become (once more) prudent and (forever) wise through historical experience.

Only man has history in the authentic sense. The thoughtful investigation and ascertainment of this history is pursued by historical inquiry through the empirical study and criticism of sources. The writing of history in the authentic sense is the presentation and discussion of the significance of this history. Taken together, historical inquiry and historical writing form the science of history. Hence the now classic definition: the science of history is that science which investigates and presents the temporally and spatially determined facts of man's development, which development takes place through man's activities (individual as well as typical and collective) as a social being, within the context of psychophysical causality.[9] Events that are part of universal history and those belonging to particular and specialized histories, events relating to mankind as such and those relating to particular peoples, states, or collectivities, as well as events involved in select aspects of man's political, social, cultural, economic, and personal achievements—all these make

8. Polybius *Histories.* 2. 56 and 3. 31.
9. E. Bernheim, *Lehrbuch der historischen Methode* (Leipzig: Duncker & Humblot, 1894), p. 9.

up the factual content of the science of history. The historical, then, includes:

(1) all experienceable individual processes which have actually taken place within the objective order (the process of history itself);

(2) those nonempirical (though disclosed through the facts themselves) presuppositions in the objective order that bear a relation to actual occurrences (historical conditions); and

(3) those moments within the subjective order which bear a relationship to the historical facts (historical truth).

2. If philosophy, in comparison with the firmly established individual sciences, is not to be regarded as the science of what is truly not worth knowing, then we must state what philosophy actually achieves. Philosophy must cover an area which would otherwise be undiscovered and incapable of being explored except through philosophy itself. When we think back on the origins of philosophy, it becomes clear that philosophy, in contrast to myth and religion, is the scientific preoccupation with reality in general. Such scientific, foundational work naturally begins by directing itself toward that which is nearest, and only later does it attempt to draw the more distant into its inquiry. Philosophy's increasing distance from the world is thus in principle immanent to the discipline itself.

Of course, as soon as the appropriate method has been found for treating a specific domain of objects, and as soon as the limits of this domain and its objects can be clearly differentiated from those of other fields of inquiry, then the domain in question achieves independence, separates itself from the general scientific concern, and can be classified as a well-grounded individual science. Thus a continuing process of emancipation has separated the world that belongs to the mundane scientific disciplines, that has been built up by the individual sciences, from the general attempt to achieve scientific mastery of the pregiven world. What is left for philosophy is what, in accordance with the above definition, is not ripe for becoming part of an individual science, and yet is not thereby lacking in importance altogether. The process of the growing independence of the individual sciences cannot in principle be completed. During the past two hundred years we have seen how psychology, sociology, and logic have successively become separated from philosophy when the delimitation of their field of inquiry and the discovery of their own methods have been achieved, and when they have been able to maintain their own particular rights and claims.[10]

Philosophy, thus construed, will always be the science of those objects of a higher order which lie remote from the developed objects of the individual sciences; [11] it is the science, therefore, of those objects in the broadest sense which, in any particular direction, still refer back to something else—objects which are prior to what is immediately given and which, in any case, are not to be found on the surface of that thinking which is directly in the service of life-interests. Accordingly, it is not surprising that, in the process of its historical unfolding, philosophy has become more and more subtle—so subtle, in fact, that it seems commonplace to say that philosophy no longer addresses itself to the educated man of common sense.

But although this is said repeatedly, it is nonetheless incorrect. The course of scientific endeavor cannot be turned back, and it is just as impossible to cast philosophy back into some form that it possessed at one time.

Generally, philosophy is the procedure which seeks to secure a foundational presentation of things in one single step. When the nearest objects in the world and their obvious external characteristics have been parceled out to the various individual sciences, then the further questioning and seeking for the presuppositions and conditions under which these objects stand is left for philosophy. Thus philosophy does not simply establish and prove knowledge, nor does it merely recognize knowledge as possible; philosophy questions what must be acknowledged when something like knowledge is presented in a given case, and hence under what presuppositions it stands. Moreover, philosophy does not simply verify, describe, and classify beings and happenings as mere givens; it is also compelled to clarify what precisely are appearances, in their nature as appearances, what is the nature of happenings as occurrences, and what "is" the being of entities. Philosophy thus seeks the meaning of appearance in itself; it is

10. G. Funke, *Beantwortung der Frage, welchen Gegenstand die Philosophie habe oder ob sie Gegenstandlos sei* (Mainz: Gutenberg Buchhandlung, 1965), pp. 5 ff.

11. G. Funke, *Phänomenologie: Metaphysik oder Methode?* (Bonn: Bouvier, 1966), pp. 5 ff.

not concerned merely with the meaning of this or that particular appearance, or the meaning of appearances in their totality.

In brief: philosophy continually faces questions which are not problems for the individual sciences that are concerned directly with determinate objects.[12] The mathematician is not concerned with the essence of number; the biologist accepts life, and the phenomena associated with life, and does not seek to determine the nature of life per se; the historian acknowledges as self-evident that there are other appearances besides those belonging to the realm of nature, appearances equally delimitable, but historical in nature, with which he works. It is not incumbent on him as historian to seek the essence of the historical or of historicity.

But there can be no question that everything which in the individual sciences is acknowledged as self-evident and non-problematic (and this holds for "history" as well) can be seen as problematic from another point of view. To permit what is otherwise taken as self-evident to become a problem is certainly the unique characteristic of philosophy. Knowledge cannot stop at the point where the individual sciences begin; rather, it must carry its investigations beyond those points which the individual sciences simply use as fixed and unquestioned points of departure. Naturally, there *need* be no philosophers, and it is therefore not *necessary* for one to pass beyond the currently accepted self-evidences of life and of the individual sciences to seek their more distant presuppositions, conditions, and grounds. Yet such questions can be raised; and when they are, they will eventually uncover coherent structures which require the delimitation of their content and the establishment of appropriate methods for dealing with them. When such methods are found, it is likely that the region thus constituted will once again proclaim its autonomy and fall away from philosophy as an independent discipline. In principle this process is endless. However, it must also be said in principle that this process reveals the reason why the adequate completion of philosophy's task must be understood as a process of constant stripping away of what is worldly and increasing subtlety. It is not that contemporary thinkers are unable to express themselves so that the man on the street can understand them.

12. J. E. Heyde, "Über die Bedeutung von gr. φιλοσοφία und lat. *philosophia*," in his *Wege zur Klarheit* (Berlin: de Gruyter, 1960), pp. 153–75.

On the contrary, the problems that philosophy alone is capable of raising today are just those problems that can be meaningfully posed only in relation to determinate, historically unfolded conditions. Husserl's thesis is that in the twentieth century philosophy can be pursued only as phenomenology. It is a mistake to think that healthy human reason (itself quite valuable as a conditioned appearance) is sufficient by itself to grasp, simply and correctly, the results of the most subtle thought of the past two or three thousand years. No one could seriously believe that he could acquire the contemporary epoch-making results of mathematics and physics without fulfilling the conditions necessary to follow these results: here the multiplication tables of common sense simply do not suffice. It is equally invalid to assume that one can discover a "royal path" to philosophy, as if simple self-reflection, or reflection on "what man thinks," already constitutes a sufficient entrance to philosophy. To say this is to undervalue the accomplishments of scientific endeavor, on which philosophy's subsequent reflection is based.

It is also true that good will, friendly interest, and beautiful "general thoughts" are of no help in philosophy.[13] As in every other science, in order to understand the problems philosophy involves, those preconditions must first be fulfilled which permit one to think in terms of the discipline. The fulfillment of such preconditions is of course possible, but the contrast between philosophy and things closer to our normal apprehensions remains. Fulfilling the conditions is possible only by indicating what domains are left to philosophical investigation today and by uncovering the paths leading to the thorough exploration of these domains. In any case, philosophy is not the simple creation of general thoughts about God and the whole world, as one is led to believe by the phrase "this is my philosophy" (a phrase which means only "this is my opinion"). Personal and subjective opinions are just as out of place in philosophy as in other sciences; philosophy deals strictly with questions of foundations and of more extensive examination of foundational connections and coherencies. Finally, philosophy is not an aesthetic and loose discussion of everything imaginable, but rather the attempt to dis-

13. See Edmund Husserl, "Philosophie als strenge Wissenschaft," *Logos*, I (1911), 289–341; English translation by Quentin Lauer, "Philosophy as Rigorous Science," in *Phenomenology and the Crisis of Philosophy* (New York: Harper & Row, 1965), pp. 71–147.

close as worthy of questioning something that has not yet emerged as a problem. When it is undertaken radically, philosophy sets in operation the process of successive regressive questionings whereby the phenomena themselves can finally be comprehended in their nature as phenomena, which is to disclose them precisely within a phenomenology. The mind strives to know how, why, and what something is, and cannot, therefore, forever remain with dogmatic pronouncements. Hence, even where at first everything appears to be clear, philosophy raises further questions—in this case, for example, questions with respect to the nature of the historical.

Now it appears to be quite clear that man, as a mundane appearance, is also a historical being, and that, being subject to change, he develops differently in different times. It thus becomes obvious that, in addition to those natural appearances that are simply present, there are other appearances that are explicable only with additional effort. They are distinguished from all known natural objects by the fact that they owe their origin to man. Because they are not simply given in a natural manner, the laws of their formation, and indeed the question of whether there are such laws, must be clarified. Clearly not every occurrence is instantly constitutive of history. If that were the case, the historian would be quickly finished with his work and would attend to what concerns him, possessing an unclear preconception of those things that would count as "historical objects." Yet no matter how legitimate the procedure followed by the scientist of history may be, it is fair to ask how well founded is his preconceived concept of history.

At this point questions arise which indeed require clarification. A philosophy of history could locate itself here. It would have to ascertain what a historical phenomenon is in comparison with natural appearances. It would also have to explain what role man plays in history, and whether it is indeed a question primarily of examining the free actions of human activity, or of displaying man as a natural physiological-biological being. A philosophy of history would eventually have to look into the issue of human responsibility, an issue that can be considered only when the existence of something like freedom is presupposed.[14]

14. Historical-methodological and historical-metaphysical questions in this sense have been treated in the twentieth century by the Windelband-

3. At the beginning of modern times, Pico della Mirandola, a philosopher of the Italian Renaissance, made a statement concerning the dignity of man that seems to agree in an extraordinary way with contemporary thought. Pico gave an account of the creation of the world and maintained that God, after the completion of his work, desired that there be someone having reason in order to view the beauty and greatness of his work. Thus God arrived at the creation of man, to whom he said the following:

> We have given to thee, Adam, no fixed seat, no form of thy very own, no gift peculiarly thine, that thou mayest feel as thine own, have as thine own, possess as thine own the seat, the form, the gifts which thou thyself shalt desire. A limited nature in other creatures is confined within the laws written down by Us. In conformity with thy free judgment, in whose hands I have placed thee, thou art confined by no bounds; and thou wilt fix limits of nature for thyself. I have placed thee at the center of the world, that from there thou mayest more conveniently look around and see whatsoever is in the world. Neither heavenly nor earthly, neither mortal nor immortal have we made thee. Thou, like a judge appointed for being honorable, art the molder and maker of thyself; thou mayest sculpt thyself into whatever shape thou dost prefer. Thou canst grow downward into the lower natures which are brutes. Thou canst again grow upward from thy soul's reason into the higher natures which are divine.[15]

Here we find something which is emerging once more in our own day as an *opinio communis:* man is condemned to freedom. Man is his own freedom, and is nothing apart from it. For Pico (as, later, for Herder), man has not chosen this freedom for himself, just as Heidegger and Sartre claim. Yet since freedom has been given to him, he is unable to separate himself from it. Everything that he does or does not do is a result of his freedom. It was in this sense that Herder maintained that man was the first being of creation given over to freedom and intended for freedom. Man's being was not that of an unfailing machine in the hands of nature; he was the aim and goal of his own creative

---

Rickert school. See W. Windelband, *Geschichte und Naturwissenschaft* (Strassburg: Heitz, 1893), and H. Rickert, *Die Grenzen der naturwissenschaftlichen Begriffsbildung* (Tübingen: Mohr, 1896).

15. Pico della Mirandola, *On the Dignity of Man,* trans. Charles Glenn Wallis (1486; New York: Bobbs-Merrill, 1965), pp. 4–5.

process. It is precisely this freedom that man realizes in history; it is in history that man becomes what he is, and therein lies his greatness and his risk. Herder goes on to say: consider how much nature ventures when it entrusts reason and freedom to so weak a creature! The balances of good and evil, of truth and falsity, depend on man's choice. Without the hypothesis of freedom "history" cannot be explained.

When man chooses, he introduces developments which would not have taken place, or would have occurred differently, if he had not acted. This does not mean that the actions themselves do not unfold within the otherwise thoroughly known course of nature. But the fact that such acts occur *hic et nunc* introduces an element that is irreducibly unique. Thus if it is correct to say that history presents a domain of appearances that are founded and determined through the introduction of freedom (that is, abruptly and eventfully), then man does not simply possess history, but is a thoroughly historical being.[16]

Let us cite an example, following it with a comment from Aloys Müller. A mathematician discovers an important theoretical relationship, a new mathematical principle. He writes an article about his discovery, which he would not have done had he not discovered this particular principle. Other things would also not have taken place had he not made the discovery: the post office would not have been busied with sending the article, the compositor would not have set the type, and so on. What has caused these occurrences to have taken place?

The cause is clearly the fact that reflection on this principle occupied the thought of a particular scholar at a particular time, and brought him to a resolution to write an article. The emergence of this thought into the temporal world and the formation of the scholar's intention has affected many physical and psychical processes. According to Müller, the decisive question here is whether this emergence can be explained in terms of natural laws.

Without a doubt, such an explanation is not possible. Natural laws hold for physical and psychical processes. Those processes in our example that are purely natural are completely dominated by natural laws. But the laws are silent when it is a question of

16. A. Müller, "Ontologie der Geschichte," in *Einleitung in die Philosophie* (Bonn: Dümmlers, 1926), pp. 43 ff., 47 ff.

the introduction of a quite different order into connections sustained by nature. Laws do not permit us to deduce what particular thought will enter into the temporal world, nor do they permit us to deduce the specific individual to whom the thought is to occur, nor the time and context of its occurrence. Most often it is a question of greater or less probability. For example, we can state with some certainty that simple factual knowledge accompanies perceptions. But even in these simplest cases, the exact time at which knowledge occurs and the scope of such knowledge cannot be foreseen with absolute certainty. In any case, what takes place in the case of such knowledge would also be unintelligible from the viewpoint of natural laws.

From this it follows that only those processes that cannot be understood on the basis of natural laws are historical. Of course many elements within such processes can be explained by the natural sciences, but the natural sciences cannot grasp why this particular occurrence takes place here and now, because it comes to pass without laws. Such occurrences must have their own science—and this is the science of history. Its objects are manifestly temporal and without laws. Doubtless "history" contains uniformities that in some way result from the regular structures of natural processes. These are not historical uniformities, but natural uniformities that refer to an invariable "psyche" and can be derived from determinations of class, race, and numbers. Clearly natural categories do forcefully intrude on the historical in this way.[17] This, however, does not mean that nature and history are essentially identical, nor does it imply that "nature" itself is not an interpretational schema.

Thus both the natural sciences and the historical sciences study individual processes belonging to the temporal world. The natural sciences study those individual processes that can be understood in terms of more universal processes (that is, in terms of laws); and the historical sciences study those processes which are also individual but which remain unintelligible from the standpoint of law. Now the science of history, for its part, must seek its own understanding of its objects; it cannot simply posit them. It would not be a science at all if history simply reiterated "something has just taken place, and now something else, and now something else again." The science of nature finds

17. *Ibid.*, p. 44.

understanding through laws. How does the science of history find understanding? By placing itself within the ends and aims posited by man. The understanding that belongs to the natural sciences is the understanding of laws; the understanding proper to the so-called historical sciences is the understanding of ends.

The processes that are affected through the hypothetical principle of free human action are immeasurable. It is simply impossible, in principle, for the science of history to register all actions that gain entrance to the realm of natural processes. It must make selections, and this is in fact the procedure it follows. Through his freedom, man adopts a stand with respect to the requirements of his environment, and comes to change this environment in its quasi-natural givenness by acting on the demands put on him by his situation (Rothacker, Toynbee). Man continually transforms nature into culture (Gehlen) by the sum of his interventions. Each human interpretation that is manifested sets forth a framework that is constitutive for man's interventions and is hence "historical." [18] Man is historical because he is an active being condemned to freedom. He is historical continually and solely within the dimension of significations that he himself practices, and thereby within the culture that has been produced by him. If the historian were actually able to register an indefinite number of actions, he would still distinguish a select number of them as important. But if we are to preserve the historian's scientific character, this selection cannot be the result of an arbitrary choice. Through the combined effectiveness of evaluational standpoints, what can be called culture, or cultural values (such as religion, science, the state, art, language, and so on), takes its place alongside the natural world; the science of history presents only those occurrences that are important for such cultural values and that bear a direct relationship to them. It is the accent of significance that is decisive. For this reason we also term the historical sciences the "sciences of culture." Naturally these formal observations are not prejudicial toward some eventual value-system.

18. The challenge-response schema is found independently in E. Rothacker, *Geschichtsphilosophie* (Munich and Berlin: Oldenbourg, 1934), and in A. J. Toynbee, *A Study of History*, Vols. I and II (New York: Oxford University Press, 1948); the point of departure from man as an active being is emphasized by A. Gehlen, *Der Mensch* (Berlin: Junker und Dunnhaupt, 1940).

At this point a broader perspective opens before us. The science of history (or the science of culture) is the only science whose objects are free from laws. All other sciences stand in contrast to it by virtue of their objects, which are determined by laws. However, all objects thus determined have something in common vis-à-vis the objects of history, which can be expressed by saying that they all have structure. Structure and lawfulness are intimately connected. Thus, there is no structure to world history, or to any partial history, if it is true that history and historical objects cannot dispense with freedom and free intervention. If history necessarily involves freedom, then history cannot make use of structure in the sense of the natural sciences.

Three types of processes are found intermixed in mundane history. First, there are psychical and physical motivational processes, which include the operations of the three elementary human drives toward mastery, satisfaction, and possession. It can be noted here that such processes also involve causality. Second, historical occurrences also involve a teleology. The psyche appears as a totality, and every process related to a totality is teleological. This holds for particular entities and relationships between entities, for the individual psyche and the supraindividual totalities of peoples and races, and perhaps also for the totalities of groups and classes. In this connection one may think of such processes as the inner development and emergence of the historical spirit of a particular epoch [Zeitgeist], life-style, or culture. Third, one must also accept purely spontaneous occurrences. In a broad sense, all authentically historical processes that can be characterized as examples of the intervention of freedom are spontaneous. In a more limited sense, spontaneous happenings are those abrupt and eventful historical upheavals, of greater or lesser significance, that are oftentimes associated with particular personalities. These spontaneous events determine the nature of mundane history as it is usually understood. Both causative and teleological processes can be described as historical processes only in a limited sense insofar as they are involved along with these spontaneous events.

Thus mundane history remains the field of decisions continually effected by individuals which constitute a "second nature" alongside the natural order, and finally present the totality of the transformed natural order as culture. As a science, history will of course not attempt to describe all factually present free and responsible behavior as constituting a response to the human situation, but will exclude behavior that adds nothing to definitively posited goals and their contexts.

The question concerning which point of view is to be decisive for this synthesis of historical occurrences is one whose answer cannot be derived from any natural law, and hence cannot be universally binding. It is neither predelineated in the plans of some divine providence, nor prefigured in a Platonic world of ideas. The establishment of judgmental criteria is itself historical and is accordingly subject to change.[19] For this reason, it is not surprising to hear the admonition that history must be continually rewritten. This follows from the fact that the synthesizing of actions, with the required selection and combination in accordance with a guiding idea, is itself a historical product, a historically underivable event.

Just as an individual bears the responsibility for what he permits his life to become (wherein his refusal is also a decision), so also the historian is responsible for the point of view on which he bases his selection. Once again the question arises whether or not historicism represents the last word.[20] With this question, however, one is still within the domain of "mundane history."

THE THEORETICAL STARTING POINT

IF ONE OF THE TRADITIONAL TASKS of philosophy is that of "saving the phenomena," that is, not simply taking them as *facta*, but seeking to comprehend them in their facticity, then such a philosophy, starting from the given, must lay broad foundations and uncover the logical and historical conditions that are actively at work in the emergence of phenomena. That a particular phenomenon comes to appear in a particular manner is determined by its associated preconditions, in the absence of which the appearance could not be what it is. And if the phenomenon and its coming-into-appearance are different, the difference

19. Heinrich Barth discusses the problem of knowledge as a problem of decision in "Philosophie der Existenz," *Jahrbuch der schweizerischen philosophischen Gesellschaft*, II (1942), 31 ff.
20. K. Heussi, *Die Krisis des Historismus* (Tübingen: Mohr, 1932). Compare his historical observations (pp. 22 ff.) and his systematic ones (pp. 38 ff.).

implies a difference in the constitutive conditions for their possibility.

1. Accordingly, "history" is not to be understood solely in the mundane objective sense as "world history," "cultural history," "history of morals," and so on, but also as the temporalizing of transcendental conditions for appearances in general (thereby including such appearances as "world history," "cultural history" and "history of morals"). If it is correct to say that classical and modern philosophy has occupied itself with mundane history, its metaphysical implications and its eschatological extrapolations, without paying attention to the transcendental conditions for such an examination, then the question concerning the relationship between philosophy and history must be raised anew. Clearly the progress of events in the mundane historical sciences is one thing, and the constitutive conditions for their occurrence in consciousness, and hence the conditions for their being given, is another.[21] Now if, in accordance with its etymology, philosophy is not *doxa* but *epistēmē*, then, in the case of its relationship to history, philosophy is not a "philosophy of history" or a "history of philosophy," which simply ascertain mundane relationships and objective relations. Philosophy is a science that regards history as a phenomenon. Philosophy is the science of "transcendental philosophy," and it thus stands as the universal disclosure of the conditions, presuppositions, and foundations encountered in the domain of the historical.

Just as "nature" presents a constitutive structure of the understanding whose meaning and implications rest on the foundation of constitutive conditions belonging to and composing it alone, so also does "history" signify a unity of meaning whose objective existence refers back to moments of the constitution of meaning through which history can present itself "as it is" and can itself become an "appearance." If, following the traditional model of transcendental philosophical investigation, one terms the conditions and presuppositions (the constitutive ground) of that

21. Edmund Husserl, "Vorlesungen zur Phänomenologie des inneren Zeitbewusstseins," edited by Martin Heidegger as a special volume of the *Jahrbuch für Philosophie und phänomenologische Forschung*, IX (1928); English translation by James S. Churchill, *The Phenomenology of Internal Time-Consciousness* (Bloomington, Ind.: Indiana University Press, 1964), pp. 63–64 (hereafter cited as *PIT*).

which is objective or mundane "subjective" and "transmundane" (i.e., "transcendental"), then in principle this traditional model manifests itself as transcendental philosophy, or as a philosophy of subjectivity. "Transcendental subjectivity" categorizes the totality of presuppositions and conditions for such things as appearances in general. Only insofar as philosophy, in principle, continually seeks presuppositions and conditions is it "radical," and only as the radical investigation of foundations is it science. An object is always given within a determinate "how" of its coming-into-appearance; it is never given "in-itself."[22] As a mundane givenness, it is a constituted formation of the apprehending consciousness.[23] On its side, the experience that the so-called objectivity of natural phenomena and the objectivity of historical events are moments of significance belonging to a genetic apprehension of these appearances is a transcendental experience, which has its *historical place* by virtue of the precise meaning it possesses, and also *grounds* historicity in a deeper sense. The phenomenality of the phenomena, the coming-into-appearance of appearances, and the constitutedness of the constituted are not simply nothing—even when nothing mundane or objective is thereby intended and nothing usable transmitted.

If "objective time" and "objective world" are constituted in a consciousness that brings the transcendental conditions for such intentional meanings to givenness, i.e., to appearance (and thus to evidence), then this consciousness itself is the ground for such objective and mundane beings within the manifold variety of its temporalizing process—a consciousness which can only be called time-constituting.[24] There are no appearances apart from a coming-into-appearance, and wherever something comes to appear as something, there consciousness must be as well. In consciousness the "subjective" and "transcendental" presuppositions for the "objective" and "consciousness-transcendent" come to givenness, and only thereby can philosophy be provided with a foundation. The philosophy that investigates the temporalizing process of such a consciousness arrives at this subjectivity through an "interiorizing reflection," and if it proceeds thus methodologically, it is then "phenomenology," the foundation-laying for the tem-

22. *Ibid.*, pp. 47, 100–101.
23. *Ibid.*, pp. 63–64.
24. See H. Hohl, *Lebenswelt und Geschichte* (Munich: Alber, 1962), pp. 14 ff.

poralizing of phenomena, and as such it is a "method," that is, a distinctive attitude of thought.[25] A so-called metaphysics of spirit and of nature remains possible only in terms of the immanence of transcendental consciousness, and hence on the foundation of manifested subjectivity.[26] There is no "myth," "logos," or "transition from myth to logos," no "naïve," "sophisticated," "habitual," or "scientific" world other than within the relevant intentions of a factual and readily apparent attitude and interpretation. Everything, each so-called worldly entity and each ego that attributes such worldly entities as present to itself and perceived and valued by it, presents a moment within an interconnectedness of intentions;[27] that is, the mundane ego is constituted in its historicity just as is any other mundane object—it is constituted in *cogitationes* in the broadest sense, in attitudes, interpretations, and achievements.

The ego-pole and the object-pole of a specific *cogitatio* are experienced in thoroughly different ways. Husserl's principle holds true: "The world, however, never is a thinker's experience. To refer to the world may be an experience, but the world itself is the object intended."[28] Equally, in the immediate co-knowing involved in an intentionally fixed experience, the ego-pole reaches givenness without thereby becoming "objectified." Knowledge of the world or of objects finds its correlate in such co-knowing (knowledge as *syneidēsis* and *conscientia*). As a substratum of habitualities,[29] the ego, although it occasionally emerges in connection with a consciousness of the world or of affairs within the world, is yet not constituted as an object of this world. This is indicated by the fact that in the apprehension of the world and its objects, a distinction can be made, since the time of Hus-

25. Edmund Husserl, *Die Idee der Phänomenologie: Funf Vorlesungen* (1907; The Hague: Nijhoff, 1950); English translation by William P. Alston and George Nakhnikian, *The Idea of Phenomenology* (The Hague: Nijhoff, 1964), p. 19.
26. *Ibid.*, p. 47.
27. See Eugen Fink, "L'Analyse intentionelle et le problème de la pensée spéculative," in *Problèmes actuels de la phénoménologie*, ed. H. L. Van Breda (Paris: Desclée de Brouwer, 1952), p. 76.
28. Edmund Husserl, *Logische Unterschungen* (Halle: Niemeyer, 1900–1901); English translation by J. N. Findlay, *Logical Investigations* (New York: Humanities Press, 1970), II, 568 (hereafter cited as *LI*).
29. Edmund Husserl, *Cartesianische Meditationen* (The Hague: Nijhoff, 1950); English translation by Dorion Cairns, *Cartesian Meditations* (The Hague: Nijhoff, 1960), § 32, pp. 66–67 (hereafter cited as *CM*).

serl's *Logical Investigations,* between sensory content and interpretational structure, a distinction that corresponds to the distinction between sensual *hylē* and intentional *morphē* in Husserl's
Ideas I.[30] However, not only does experience in the widest sense
convey knowledge of the world, objects, things, and special contents, but along with such performances and coinciding with
their intentional-constitutive achievements, we experience an ego
as experiencing, as returning to previous experiences and antici-
pating experiences to come, an ego as living in continual habit-
ualizings, an ego that concretely experiences itself as a "substratum of habitualities," inseparable from its intentional acts.[31]

The problem of the formation of habitualities is a historical
one, just as is the problem concerning the formation of factual
references. That is, there is an objective genesis of concrete consciousness, in which all these achievements are enacted and
maintained as a permanent repository, a genesis that is present
along with the constitution of all variety of intentionalities and
with the achieving transcendental spontaneity.

It can be said that "man is a person as the subject of intentionality" [32] only when it is presupposed that an ego, as a substratum of persisting habitualities to which return can be made,
can be genetically constructed through the performance of intentional acts. The intentionality that characterizes consciousness
and constitutes the essence of transcendental subjectivity becomes manifest and transparent in man. Consciousness is continually attending to things, or to the world as the totality of
things. Yet the world and its objects present themselves only as
the intended correlate of consciousness; apart from this they
possess no (Platonic) independent being, nor can consciousness
find a path to them that leads away from consciousness itself.
One form and possibility for such a consciousness, in which reflection continually reaches back to prior meaning-constituting
achievements, was almost completely ignored by Husserl.

If the person is the true subject of intentionality, which in
turn is that by which man first becomes a person,[33] then, to avoid

30. See I. Fisch, "Husserls Intentionalitäts- und Urteilslehre" (Dissertation: University of Basel, 1938), p. 14.
31. *CM,* § 30, p. 65.
32. Edmund Husserl, Ms A V 10, p. 104; and according to Hohl,
Lebenswelt und Geschichte, p. 16, also A V 9, p. 10 (all such references
are to the Husserl Archives at Louvain).
33. See Husserl, Ms A V 7, p. 64.

circularity, we must clarify how this is possible. If "world," "earthly life" and "life-world" are to be understood as primordial meaning-formative achievements belonging to intentional consciousness, then the process of becoming a person is not simply one intentional performance in addition to countless others. Quite the contrary: all these primordial meaning-creations provide the occasion for the genesis of a person, which emerges as one with these intentional achievements. It is correct to say that "life, originating out of the richness of intentionality and making possible life's intentional relations, creates its own time: history"; [34] but it must then be added that the achievements of ongoing intentional objectification are retained by their being co-known as intentional, so that the ego knows at any moment that it is itself responsible for particular achievements which it has indexed as "new," "familiar," "surprising," "expected," "unexpected," and so on. This is possible only when an inner temporalizing process is at work that contains the preconditions for the formation of the time-horizon present in the realm of the objective and mundane. Before we can speak of a goal-directed series of acts in the objective realm, and hence before we can say that a particular series of facts forms an objective relationship, the question of the formation of the very principle of relatedness must be transcendentally clarified.

If they are taken to present a set of related meanings, objective historical relationships refer back to the meaning of the formation of relatedness itself. Here "history" is a preeminent phenomenon since in general objective historical connections can be comprehended only within the context of the primordial formation of relatedness. This, however, is the case where the *now* of an intentional perception does not simply expire, but transforms itself into something that has passed, a "has just been," a "no longer present," and hence is to be found in the genesis of an internal time-consciousness. [35]

Here we must speak of a "hypothesis" in a quite primordial sense: only under the presupposition of the genesis of a consciousness that temporalizes itself as a unity and whose course parallels that of intentional achievements can the problem of history be unfolded.

34. Hohl, *Lebenswelt und Geschichte*, p. 16.
35. *PIT*, pp. 100 ff.

2. Transcendental consciousness, with its characteristic "transcendence in immanence," is in principle "externalizing" by virtue of intentionality. When it is operating, it posits and fills horizons of possible object apprehensions. It also presents an "externalization" when an ego speaks of itself as "I, this person," for this phrase sets forth an equally intramundane constitution. If transcendental subjectivity refers to the totality of preconditions for every possible apprehension, then the phrase "I, this person" is constituted within a self-apprehension that has its own conditions. The entire complex of such constitutions refers back to still earlier achievements wherein what is constituted is disclosed as that which has been given meaning, but this is only evident for a consciousness that persists and is conscious of relationships. A "radically incarnate consciousness" [36] is always intentional and horizon-forming. But that it is so is perhaps consciously known through repeated reflection and corresponding regress. Yet such a reflective regression is in turn only possible where consciousness forms a relation, not where consciousness merely indicates an "atomism" of isolated individual intentions. The fact that consciousness is itself "one" and can relate itself to itself and to its previously enacted achievements through reflection presupposes the antecedent temporalizing of this consciousness as the temporalizing of relationships, and therefore its genetic historicity.

The basic problem of a phenomenology of historicity is this: with every phenomenon, whether it is an ethical norm, a dogma, or an entire science, one must return from the structure in question back to its intentional being and significance. "It is always necessary to reflect on the original meaning of that which has come to be established." [37]

Everything that appears must, as the product of a "subjective" achievement, have a historical beginning: that is, its meaning must originate with the emergence of its constitutive conditions. Husserl adds: "To 'understand' a cultural fact means to be conscious of its historicity, and to take it as something that not only occurs 'in' history, but as something that is historical

36. The term is singled out by A. de Waelhens; see "Die phänomenologische Idee der Intentionalität," in *Phaenomenologica* II (The Hague: Nijhoff, 1959), 137.
37. A. Diemer, *Edmund Husserl* (Meisenheim: Hain, 1956), p. 351.

through and through." [38] But the historicity of all objective knowledge in the natural and spiritual domains does not represent the sole form of historicity. For according to Husserl, "consciously known along with all knowledge and comprehension of cultural affairs is the fact that they are results, that is, they are structures that derive from human creativity." [39] Only when this "knowing along with" is present are so-called objective time and objective history no longer taken as self-evident and naïvely accepted as factual appearances "in" which something can take place, and only then does the ground of temporalizing become present, rendering all historical dogma impossible.

Therefore, we must clearly distinguish so-called historical time, within which something comes to pass, from the temporalizing of the conditions for the possibility of such "historical" frameworks. To draw this distinction is also to distinguish reflection on intramundane "historical" (traditional) relations from that continuing "co-knowing" of the subjective conditions for everything objective (including the objectivities of the intramundanely given).

Once again, following Husserl, we must point out two viewpoints to be taken into account. (1) Just as the individual cultural form has its tradition behind and within it, so the very presence of the cultural as a totality "implies" the entire cultural past.[40] This means that history is "nothing other than the vital movement of the coexistence and the interweaving of original formations and sedimentations of meaning." [41] (2) "Every consciousness in a unitary sense (as a constituted immanent unity) is at the same time necessarily also unity of consciousness of the objective to which it 'refers.' But not every consciousness is itself time-consciousness, i.e., consciousness of something 'temporal.' " [42] An act of judging, thinking, or presenting may last for a shorter or longer period of time, but what is judged, thought

---

38. Edmund Husserl, "Die Frage nach dem Ursprung der Geometrie als intentional-historisches Problem," ed. Eugen Fink, *Revue internationale de philosophie*, I (1938–39), 220 (my translation); cf. the English translation by David Carr, "The Origin of Geometry," in *The Crisis of European Sciences and Transcendental Phenomenology* (Evanston, Ill.: Northwestern University Press, 1970), p. 370.
39. "Origin of Geometry," p. 370; quoted in Diemer, *Husserl*, p. 352.
40. "Origin of Geometry," p. 371.
41. *Ibid.*
42. *PIT*, p. 124.

about, or presented is neither short nor long, neither more nor less enduring.[43] By contrast, the second synthesis following the performance of intentional acts can be viewed as follows: the *cogitationes* not only communicate a meaning that belongs to a particular state of affairs, but the very enactment of the *cogitatio* makes it possible that "the ego grasps himself not only as a flowing life but also as *I*, who live this and that subjective process, who live through this and that cogito, *as the same I*." [44] A historical consciousness in the authentic sense is present only when such a "centralizing ego" emerges.[45] It is one-sided to describe transcendental genesis by observing only the spatial intramundane perspectival relationships pertaining to the constitution of objects. There is a transcendental genesis that is at one with the intentional constitution of affairs and of object-evidences, for the *cogitationes* bring "new and abiding properties" to the ego, precisely those properties involving relations of persistence. This means that the endurance and unity of consciousness with respect to intentional-constitutive acts sets forth a foundation-laying synthesis and is thereby the historical event *katexochen.*

Regarding the concrete (mundane) ego, we must find out what it is without which it *cannot* be concrete. It can be concrete "only in the flowing multiformity of his intentional life, along with the objects meant—and in some cases constituted as existent for him—in that life." Corresponding to and accompanying these intentional processes is the formation of history, and clearly, "in the case of an object so constituted, its abiding existence and being-thus are a correlate of the habituality constituted in the Ego-pole himself by virtue of his position-taking." [46]

With the initiation of intentional processes the first "historical" and eventfully transpiring result, which is not itself intentionally aimed at, is this: "I exist for myself and am continually given to myself, through experiential evidence, as '*I myself.*' " In its role as a foundational synthesis this historical temporalizing "is true of the transcendental ego and, correspondingly, of the psychologically pure ego; it is true, moreover, with respect to any sense of the word ego." [47]

43. *Ibid.*, p. 125.
44. *CM*, § 31, p. 66.
45. *Ibid.*, § 32, p. 66.
46. *Ibid.*, § 33, p. 68.
47. *Ibid.*

Without this "historical" synthesis of the concrete ego there could be no subsequent reflective disclosing. To be sure, a regressive reflection will continually attempt to clarify what is pregiven, but such reflection is unthinkable and "groundless" without the synthesis of historical temporalizing that takes place in the genesis of relations. Thus it is clear to Husserl that "the problem of *explicating this monadic ego phenomenologically* (the problem of his constitution for himself) must include all constitutional problems without exception." [48]

Once we have attained "genetic phenomenology," [49] we are at the level of encompassing and non-divisive foundations. Foundational relations in general depend for their discovery on the prior establishment of something like relationship *per se,* which follows from the formation of the ego as a "unity of consciousness." Such a "unity of consciousness" is the presupposition without which constitutive regressive questioning in the domain of so-called objective-historical facts and relations cannot be pursued. For the unavoidable point of departure is the ego, which "as the persisting ego, is determined by this abiding *habitus* or state." [50] And this *habitus* is the sediment of a prior synthesis, the formation of a historical unity.

It is naturally correct to say that "the *a priori* conditions for *a priori* structures and ideal formations lie in what man, once he has understood himself as a rational animal, recognizes as his eternal nature"; [51] but in this context we must not forget that, "by his *own active generating,* the Ego constitutes himself as *identical substrate of Ego-properties,*" and that it also constitutes itself "as a 'fixed and abiding' *personal Ego.*" Indeed, throughout all modifications it preserves "an abiding style with a unity of identity throughout all of them: a 'personal character.' " [52]

This "historical" character of the structure of consciousness is unavoidable and cannot be ignored. Here the formation of invariance presents the first problem for a phenomenology of the historical.

The first persisting invariant element in the being of the world and necessarily belonging to it is: I myself as a person, a man, a

48. *Ibid.*
49. *Ibid.,* § 34, p. 69.
50. *Ibid.,* § 31, p. 67.
51. "Ursprung der Geometrie," p. 225 (my translation).
52. *CM,* § 32, p. 67.

body, together with the spatio-temporal externality surrounding me, and as continually affirming the existence of other persons. . . . No matter how I transform one world into another, through such variations I always have a possible world as the world of my possible ego; in every possible world that I can conceivably constitute I am present thereby as a human being, not as actually human, but as one variation among my possibilities. Thus in a certain respect I am invariant within this universe of possibilities.[53]

Thus before history becomes a phenomenon within the world with "objective" time and objectively measurable time-relationships, it is the temporalization of consciousness with a determinate and unified style, a "personal character," and a connectedness of "habitualities."

3. A victory of phenomenology as "science" over phenomenology as the history of self-developing consciousness is incorrectly claimed for the "logicism" of Husserl's *Logical Investigations,* or for the "ideational abstraction" and "eidetic reduction" in the first volume of Husserl's *Ideas.*[54] The problem of history is the problem of universal foundations: more precisely, the philosophical problem of universal foundations leads directly to the problem of history. In this regard, several works of Husserl must be viewed together: his *The Phenomenology of Internal Time-Consciousness* (1905–28), the *Cartesian Meditations* (1931–50), *The Crisis of European Sciences and Transcendental Phenomenology* (1936–1954) and "The Origin of Geometry" (1939). In these works the principle is established that temporality is no longer an unimportant and empirical accidental factor in contrast to transcendental structures, but is rather an essential character of consciousness as it becomes transparently aware of its unity.[55]

53. Diemer (*Husserl,* p. 362) refers to Ms B III 1, pp. 3, 12.
54. As against Paul Ricoeur, "Husserl et le sens de l'histoire," in *Revue de métaphysique et de morale,* LIV, nos. 3–4 (1949), 282 ff.; English translation by Edward G. Ballard and Lester E. Embree, "Husserl and the Sense of History," in Paul Ricoeur, *Husserl: An Analysis of His Phenomenology* (Evanston, Ill.: Northwestern University Press, 1967), pp. 143–74.
55. Cf. L. Landgrebe, *Phänomenologie und Metaphysik* (Hamburg: Schröder, 1949), pp. 74 ff.; and Hans Wagner, "Kritische Betrachtungen zur Husserls Nachlass," *Philosophische Rundschau,* I, nos. 1–2 (1953), 94 ff.; English translation by R. O. Elveton, "Critical Observations concerning Husserl's Posthumous Writings," in *The Phenomenology of Husserl* (Chicago: Quadrangle, 1970), pp. 204 ff. See also Hohl, *Lebenswelt*

It must still be pointed out that, despite all attempts to connect the problem of history in phenomenology with the problematic of the life-world,[56] the "life-world" does not comprehend what its achievement is and what this achievement makes possible. The consciousness that uncovers the meaning of the relationships in the life-world is itself no longer a consciousness within the life-world. In opposition to all historicizing and etymologizing tendencies and all attempts to use primordial relationships as the key to discovering appropriate comprehension and understanding, we must emphasize that the comprehension of structures and the understanding of constitution is not just a simple knowing of intentional acts or experiences that runs along with such acts, but is something that can be disclosed only through a *post eventum* regressive reflective analysis and with the aid of the most diverse clues. The consciousness that is within the life-world cannot achieve what a later reflection, itself an eventful occurrence, can achieve.[57]

As a matter of fact, for Husserl temporality is the invariant element within transcendental subjectivity,[58] and that which is intrinsically "first" in terms of the historical "is our present [*Gegenwart*] as a living time that is lived through [*lebendig durchlebte Zeit*]." [59] Since transcendental subjectivity does not become transparent to itself other than within a lived-through present, the historicity of consciousness—if later forms of experience in the mode of reflection achieve more by way of insight than earlier forms—becomes an eminently essential moment. It is not the early forms of consciousness from which the most important information is to be expected, but the temporalized and more encompassing later forms to which "reflections on reflection," or reflections on the natural attitude, belong.[60]

und Geschichte, p. 78; and W. Brüning, *Geschichtsphilosophie* (Stuttgart: Klett, 1961), pp. 141 ff.

56. The Mexico Philosophy Conference in 1963 devoted a special symposium to the life-world problematic in this sense. See *Symposium sobre la noción Husserliana de la Lebenswelt* (Mexico: Universidad nacional autonoma de Mexico, 1963). In addition, see the work of Landgrebe (1949, 1952, 1963, etc.), Hohl, *Lebenswelt und Geschichte,* and G. Brand (1955, 1971).

57. Funke, *Phänomenologie: Metaphysik oder Method?* pp. 136–65.

58. Husserl, Ms B III 1, p. 3.

59. "Ursprung der Geometrie," p. 222 (my translation).

60. Cf. Theodor Litt, *Einleitung in die Philosophie* (Leipzig: Teubner, 1933), pp. 11 ff.; and H. Hohl, *Lebenswelt und Geschichte,* pp. 49 ff.

Accordingly, our task must be to set aside the abundant prejudices of the life-world that operate within investigations into the phenomenon of history, and to return to those investigations which alone can be justified in terms of transcendental relationships. History, seen as the temporalizing of consciousness, is by no means a mere secondary appendage to philosophy, but rather provides the best way of approaching philosophy's problematic.[61]

The question of the historicity of consciousness conceals the problem of the relativity of knowledge, and this problem must now be developed from our general phenomenological starting point. Let us relate this issue to Husserl's thoughts concerning the "origin of geometry." Husserl states:

> We understand [geometry's] persisting manner of being: it is not only a mobile forward process from one set of acquisitions to another but a continuous synthesis in which all acquisitions maintain their validity, all make up a totality such that, at every present stage, the total acquisition is, so to speak, the total premise for the acquisitions of the new level. Geometry necessarily has this mobility and has a horizon of geometrical future in precisely this style.[62]

The view set forth here will permit us to develop clearly the historical problematic from a phenomenological starting point.

The "mobility" Husserl maintains geometry "necessarily" has forces on us a decision with respect to the "historicity" or "eternality" of truth. If consciousness is truly "historical" and if geometry is a historical product, then, given such historicity, we must ask wherein this achieving consciousness grounds the universal validity and the requisite universally binding character of geometrical propositions. If, on the other hand, "geometry" in its systematic unity is the internal connectedness of geometrical forms, then in fact the question of the history of the formulation of these relationships immanent within the content is only an empirical and historical question, and as such is only partly relevant.[63]

The traditional understanding of science which Husserl the logician took from the nineteenth century contends that scientific truths (geometrical propositions) hold with necessary universality. Husserl, the radical transcendental phenomenologist who

61. Ricoeur, "Husserl and the Sense of History," p. 152.
62. "Origin of Geometry," p. 355.
63. Cf. Brüning, *Geschichtsphilosophie*, p. 143.

posed the problem of foundations in a universal way, had to understand the noematic meaning and unities of meaning of intentionally operative acts as forms of constitution and had to go back to those noetic achievements in which they reach givenness (evidence), even though this very procedure historicizes transcendental conditions for the possibilities of things insofar as things come into appearance only with the emergence of a consciousness that is polarized into intentional contents. This means that no phenomena "exist" without becoming phenomenalized in determinate experiences, and that geometrical phenomena "exist" only in noeses, which are the conditions for the coming-into-appearance of such phenomena. Husserl criticized the traditional interpretation of scientific theory when he emphasized the fundamental incorrectness of the "separation in principle between epistemological elucidation and historical . . . elucidation, between epistemological and genetic origin." Equally incorrect is the limitation of the concepts "history," "historical clarification," and "genesis" to the fact of the simple emergence of an appearance.[64]

As is the case with everything that is given to consciousness, "geometry" can only be understood when we have been made aware of its historicity; however, this means that *every* cultural meaning and unity of meaning must be taken as something "that not only occurs 'in' history, but is historical through and through."

When the transcendental conditions for the possibility of an appearance are such that the appearance can occur only in the noetic-noematic correlation as a result of the unfathomable temporalizing of consciousness, then a "historical a priori" belongs to the very essence of appearances. However, the "historical a priori" will not compromise the claim to universal validity raised on behalf of scientific knowledge if we advance the hypothesis that transcendental subjectivity and its self-expression through intentional achievements do not come into appearance "haphazardly," but "systematically"; that is, transcendental subjectivity must be understood as the *"ratio in the constant movement of self-elucidation"* [65] and such an understanding of it is in turn possible only in terms of historical temporalizing.

64. "Origin of Geometry," p. 370.
65. Edmund Husserl, *Die Krisis der europäischen Wissenschaften und die transzendentale Phänomenologie, Husserliana* VI, ed. Walter Biemel (The Hague: Nijhoff, 1954), p. 273; English translation by David Carr (cited in n. 38 above), p. 338 (hereafter cited as *Crisis*).

Only when the general structure of reason is held to be teleological [66] can we trust that the historical emergence of specific rational achievements and a rational system that progressively manifests itself in these rational functions are not contradictory, and that—*sit venia verbo*—there exists a "pre-established harmony" between the factual step-by-step achievements of knowledge and the unopposed advance of this knowledge from a given historical context to further horizons. In brief: we can maintain the existence of a "historical a priori" and yet exclude "historical relativism" [67] if we can say of reason's living achievements "that without them the objects and the world would not be there for us and that the former exist for us only with the meaning and the mode of being that they receive in constantly arising or having arisen out of those subjective *accomplishments.*" [68] If the factual operations of reason form a rational system, then the historicity of these meaning-bestowing achievements will not permit the acceptance of a self-subsistent pregiven domain or a "historical" relativizing of truth. Whether or not they *will* form such a system cannot be anticipated by an open, or in other words historical, system. The requirements of a phenomenological interpretation and analysis are thereby made manifest. One can speak of a rational system, of a universally valid rational synthesis, of the "conscious life of the subjectivity which effects the validity of the world" [69] only if such rationality actually makes its appearance. Since man is a historical being we can state with certainty:

> We also have, and know that we have, the capacity of complete freedom to transform, in thought and phantasy, our human historical existence and what is there exposed as its life-world. And precisely in this activity of free variation, and in running through the conceivable possibilities for the life-world, there arises, with apodictic self-evidence, an essentially general set of elements going through all the variants.[70]

This essentially universal content is *"ratio* in the constant movement of self-elucidation" only to the extent that it makes an appearance. Since Husserl's philosophy can be a rational one only if

66. *Ibid.*, p. 341.
67. "Origin of Geometry," pp. 373 ff.
68. *Crisis*, p. 160.
69. *Ibid.*, p. 151.
70. "Origin of Geometry," pp. 374–75.

consciousness—by virtue of its presupposed thoroughgoing his-toricity—reveals a rational system in terms of which it manifests itself, the unfolding of such a consciousness is philosophy itself as an activity that attempts to render the rationality of things transparent. If this has not been seen by traditional philosophy, phenomenology, which concerns itself with such relationships, is the proof for its actuality.[71] Such a phenomenology is "historical" in a twofold sense.

THE HISTORICAL MOTIVE

PHENOMENOLOGY'S UNDERSTANDING OF HISTORY is con-ditioned by two thetically posited presuppositions, which for Husserl do not have the status of hypotheses. The first precondi-tion for all further understanding is this:

> We are what we are as functionaries of modern philosophical humanity; we are heirs and cobearers of the direction of the will which pervades this humanity; we have become this through a primal establishment which is at once a reestablishment [Nach-stiftung] and a modification of the Greek primal establishment. In the latter lies the *teleological beginning,* the true birth of the European spirit as such.[72]

Husserl stresses a *universal* direction of the will which dis-tinguishes European mankind and which, historically, is taken up, grasped, appropriated, and modified in accordance with its original historical establishment. The relating of the timelessly universal and the historically particular is here achieved through an interpretational device that states that the genuinely "uni-versal" can only be the teleological tendency present in what occurs. Hence the historical unfolding of the historically pregiven original endowment and the establishment of a proposed end. "To every primal establishment [Urstiftung] essentially belongs a final establishment [Endstiftung] assigned as a task to the histori-cal process." [73]

If we are to posit a "historical a priori," then this a priori (and every a priori) must have meaning only as an essential a priori,

71. *CM,* § 41, p. 86.
72. *Crisis,* p. 71.
73. *Ibid.,* p. 72.

and thus it must have universality.[74] The only meaningful way to posit an a priori for the historical such that it is constitutive of the historical in general is to posit an impetus in history toward the establishment of some proposed end. The historical is stamped with the particular meaning intended by the notion of teleological being, for the sole universal carried by the delimitation of the historical is that of the purposive assignment of some end. Thus a phenomenological view brings together the universal (the time-lessly valid) and the particular (the historically given) by posit-ing a universal reason that becomes transparent in particular historical evidences, in which the "innate a priori" or the "uni-versal logos of all conceivable being" is historical in its very being, and whose rational structure is brought to evidence (qua self-givenness) insofar as an all-encompassing reason becomes his-torically actual. For "all the rationality of the fact lies . . . in the Apriori." [75] Since reason must be presupposed a priori for all rational clarification, the proof of this a priori rests on the emer-gence (indeed, the *universal* emergence) of this reason. Cor-respondingly, the historical motive for a phenomenological in-vestigation of "history" lies in this: that the most radical and fundamental (i.e., going to the deepest roots and seeking the most extensive implications) rationalization of the factual is "his-torically" not forthcoming. The crisis of consciousness which has occurred in the various foundational crises of the sciences (those that can truly be called "sciences") propounded by the European spirit, results from the fact that the rationalization of historical reality in accordance with the a priori of reason has been neglected. Yet the recognition of this neglect already bespeaks the eventful emergence of reason. Insofar as phenomenology is con-cerned with documenting this neglect, phenomenology has a "historical mission" and will provide documentation relevant to the accomplishment of this mission that is part of its historical beginnings.

1. The exposition in *The Crisis of European Sciences* [76] can only serve as an "introduction to phenomenological philosophy"

---

74. Edmund Husserl, *Formale und transzendentale Logik* (Halle: Niemeyer, 1929), p. 219; English translation by Dorion Cairns, *Formal and Transcendental Logic* (The Hague: Nijhoff, 1969), p. 248 (hereafter cited as *FTL*).
75. *CM*, § 64, p. 155.
76. Cf. Hohl. *Lebenswelt und Geschichte*, p. 19.

(as the subtitle of Husserl's book states) when the clarification of this crisis is followed by some indication of its solution, a solution to be looked for from "transcendental phenomenology." The mere description of the causes of such a crisis does not by itself suffice as a justification for an entirely new and decisive philosophy that steps forward with important claims. The "crisis of European sciences" and "transcendental phenomenology" are so closely interconnected that the inquiry that discovers the crisis and renders it comprehensible (phenomenological reflection on foundations) is at the same time a judgment which, through its understanding of the crisis, has freed itself from a naïve preoccupation with the causes of the crisis. It does not thereby claim (either justly or unjustly) any particular dignity, but in its critical questioning it "is" both a new emergence of universal clarity-seeking reason *and* an eventful new elevation of reason to higher levels.

When we speak of a "crisis," the decision that can turn the situation in another direction is also an issue in our discussion; yet this decision can only follow from a more radical reflection on determining presuppositions. If we can say that the "European sciences" are passing through a crisis precisely at this historical moment, then we can also say that the resolution of this crisis is itself a historical task.[77]

"Authentic historicity" and "truly universal validity" are the basic questions for a phenomenological philosophy of history, and such a philosophy can be "saved" only when change and necessity can be brought together without contradiction. It is not sufficient to say that the universality of absolute spirit "surrounds everything that exists with an absolute historicity, to which nature is subordinated as a spiritual structure"; [78] the very form of

77. Husserl treats this theme in his Vienna Lecture, "Die Philosophie in der Krise der europäischen Menschheit" (1935, published in *Krisis*, pp. 314–48); in the Belgrade essay "Die Krisis des europäischen Wissenschaften und die transzendentale Phänomenologie," *Philosophia*, I (Belgrade, 1936, reprinted in *Krisis*, parts 1 and 2); and in the *Beilagen* published in *Krisis*. The latter also contains an account of the most important facts relating to the history of these texts (pp. xiii ff.). In addition to the English translation of the *Krisis*, Carr's volume also contains translations of the Vienna Lecture, "Philosophy and the Crisis of European Humanity," pp. 269–99, and of a select number of the *Beilagen;* and, in the Translator's Introduction, a brief discussion of the history of the texts.
78. Vienna Lecture, p. 298.

science and of the scientific spirit must itself be historicized, and in such a way that factual human culture becomes a consistently carried forward self-reflection whose principal structure cannot be anticipated. Reflections on life-world relationships, the sciences grounded within the life-world, and the absence of questions regarding the connectedness of all historical knowledge up to the present are all embodied within the process of reflection itself, and all continually involve advance beyond previously attained viewpoints. This insight is apodictic, and hence "scientifically" relevant, not when the forms currently part of the observations of the natural or human sciences are posited, with irresponsible naïveté, as self-evident ("timeless," "true in themselves"), but when the "subjective" origins of all "objectivities" have been successfully disclosed through a radical (going back to the roots) reflection. Only then does human knowledge take on "the form of a universal philosophy which grows through consistent apodictic insight and supplies its own norms through an apodictic method." [79]

The universality and necessity spoken of here is the discovery of the conditions for the possibility of something by recourse to "subjective" origins. Yet "universality," "necessity," and "validity" can be maintained only through the universal, necessary, and valid presupposition of a rational (and universally rational) structure for reality. The self-reflection of reason that appears in "historical" stages is accordingly continually working toward the increasing rationalization of the world, and every sort of foundational critique advances this process further. Now insofar as philosophy possesses this character of a continuing and reiterative reflection on foundations, philosophy *is* "*ratio* in the constant movement of self-elucidation." If philosophy were to stop the critical process and become a fixed dogmatism, foregoing any account of the subjective origin of the objective sciences, it would fall into a forgetfulness of origins. The present crisis of European man results from this forgetfulness, and this crisis can be alleviated only when the uncritical fixation on determinate stages of the historical process of becoming conscious is overcome.

Only "when the task is brought to consummate clarity and thus to an apodictic method" [80] will the crisis be at an end. The

79. *Crisis*, p. 16.
80. *Ibid.*, p. 72.

crisis consists in this: the radical foundation-laying process has broken off at some point, making possible an almost boundless pluralism of positions, a pluralism that permits each position to lay claims for itself with total naïveté and to draw from its convictions justification for every type of intolerance. Now that philosophy which reflects most deeply on the conditions for the possibility of things is the philosophy that supplies its own norms. The transcendental phenomenology manifested in repeated regressive reflections claims to function precisely in this way. The apodicticity of its procedure consists in acknowledging the necessity and universality of a teleological tendency and a universal task that can only be completed "historically." Evidence for this is to be provided in fact (i.e., "historically"), and this evidence is the actual carrying out and hence the "historical" realization of this thoroughgoing rationalization. Transcendental, reflective, and radical-regressive phenomenology is thus not one philosophy among others; it is the disclosing enactment of the true aims of reason. Origin, enactment, and end are so closely related that each is, for man, a "historical" event that emerges within concrete frameworks and situational contexts, so that man's taking up *and* advancing the endowment of reason gives expression to the universal tendency toward self-reflection through repeated critical insight and verifies the teleological character of the presupposed *ratio* in actuality. The universally necessary is historical when the universal and necessary is a (teleological) "tendency," for the realization of this *telos* belongs to history. On the other hand, such a realization is necessary in the case where the universal is not *factum* but *faciendum,* and the universal that is not (or not yet) *factum,* but is in process, is *ratio.* Its historicity does not stop short of relativizing specific positions and concepts: it posits the universal and the necessary which, with apodictic certainty, remain "historical" and never pass into mere "history" (that is, "what has simply passed"). In brief, the universal and necessary character of the structure of reason lies in its ongoing and open, critical capacity to surpass itself, its ability to pose and then dissolve metaphysical positions, and its nature as a constant process of being "on the way" as expressed in its methodological ends.

2. Where phenomenology remains a "method" in this sense and does not transform itself into a dogmatic metaphysical

38 / *Phenomenology and History*

"system," it lays itself open constantly to a continual self-reflection. To this extent its task can be termed a thoroughly "historical" one. But it is historical in the authentic sense in that it masters the fact of history itself (the "tradition") in a continuing critical understanding by setting out the subjective presuppositions present in every historical manifestation (whether "spiritual" or "natural"). If self-reflection can achieve this, and if historically emerging phenomena in all ontological regions can in this way be understood with radical philosophical certainty, then human reason, in achieving such ever-widening certainty, can be identified with philosophy understood as phenomenology.[81]

The unfolding of the "historical a priori" constitutes the very life of human reason: the "systematic *unfolding of the all-embracing Apriori* innate in the essence of a transcendental subjectivity (and consequently in that of a transcendental intersubjectivity)." [82] If transcendental subjectivity contains the totality of conditions for the possibility of things, then the factual (and, within determinate frameworks, concretely necessary) conditions can only be shown from the point of view of what is actual. However, insofar as "showing" always employs correlative relationships, such as *intentio* and *intentum, cogito* and *cogitatum, noesis* and *noema, praxis* and *pragma,* the hypothetically acknowledged rational character of the whole, the "universal logos of all conceivable being," is "constituted" only *for* reason and with the *actualization* of reason, and hence only within historical temporalizing.

It has often been said with respect to the text of Husserl's *Crisis* and its indication of the crisis in the sciences "resulting from the forgetting of the foundational being of the world" [83] that a "return to history" is necessary to overcome this crisis. If this means that we should replace the scientific experiences of a later (post-Galileo) age with original experiences in the domain of the life-world, in order to clarify the crisis in the sciences by viewing the foundational relationships that exist among them, we are then guilty of evaluating too highly the mundane historical investigations of the problem of the life-world.

Husserl's broadly based investigations exploring the genesis

81. *CM,* § 64, pp. 152 ff.
82. *Ibid.,* p. 155.
83. Hohl, *Lebenswelt und Geschichte,* p. 21.

of the "objective sciences" [84] clarify the relationship between the life-world and the world of science. Since so-called "rational objectivism" (or "physicalistic objectivism")—the position of modern science since Galileo—misapprehends its own origins, it leads to a crisis in the twentieth century insofar as it posits something in-itself that is actually a constituted meaning-formation. According to Husserl, the self-misapprehension in scientific interpretations consists in equating the mathematized world of idealities with the intuited and immediately experienced world of perception. A world of abstractions takes the place of the world as it is naturally experienced, and thereby all inquiry becomes directed at "objective truth," "objective reality," the "objective world," and hence an "objective world view." The more forcefully this objectification is pursued, the more quickly does the intuitively given and vital experienced world disappear behind idealizations; but at the same time the opportunities offered by anticipated "empirical regularities of the practical life-world" become more workable.[85]

The mistake made by this entire "objectivistic" attitude is to forget subjectivity, for the dominant idea for us is that the life-world constitutes the forgotten basis of meaning for the idealizing and objectifying exact sciences, and that it already bears its meaning content within itself and does not first receive it through an *ex post facto* synthesis.[86]

In this respect, the fundamental problem is this: only from the point of view of the life-world and its meaning content do the sciences receive *their* meaning and justification. This means that scientific consciousness is not a synthesis (in the Kantian sense) through which form (and meaning) is given to formless material, but, as precisely formulated by the objectivistic and idealized attitude of the modern sciences, it is a consciousness that simply clarifies meaningful relationships that are already given. Clearly, with the universal application of the phenomenological procedure to the analysis of the constitution of meaning, the positing of such a life-world once more entails a return to the meaning-bestowing achievements that lie behind the meanings that are now given precisely within the life-world. A so-called phenome-

84. *Crisis*, pp. 52 ff.
85. *Ibid.*, pp. 43 ff.
86. Cf. Hohl, *Lebenswelt und Geschichte*, p. 21. See also L. Landgrebe, *Der Weg der Phänomenologie* (Gütersloh: Mohn, 1963), pp. 41 ff.

nology that would be satisfied simply with what is given here and would omit further questions of genesis and constitution would be a metaphysics of the life-world.[87] However, for a truly phenomenological point of departure a fixed dogmatism is only a springboard for regressive questionings in which formative relationships are to be clarified; it is entirely provisional and is to be constantly surpassed by reiterated critique.

Every dogmatic metaphysics of the life-world is methodologically inadequate, in that one discovers relationships in the life-world only by carrying out a critique of a given position that takes as its point of departure the world as it is scientifically delineated, and when the position of the life-world is reached this critical evaluation of positions is silenced. It is not at all self-evident that the life-world involves questions of ultimate and unsurpassable relationships and that lying before us are primordial foundations that must be accepted in their immediacy.

If phenomenology is the "science of origins," the "source" of all true knowledge and the "foundation for all philosophical methods," [88] then it confirms its true nature not only when, proceeding as a picture-book phenomenology, it discovers life-world relationships and describes them, but also when it leads back to processes of meaning-formation. Reflection on what in principle belongs to philosophy cannot be obscured by fascination with life-world relationships. The following text must be cited in opposition to all life-world metaphysicians: "To the radicalism of phenomenology belongs its beginning as the self-reflection of the one who philosophizes." [89] Such self-reflection is only truly real when it becomes practical, and it becomes practical only in practice; and its practice *is* the application of the phenomenological method.

One cannot sensibly utter the sentence "science is a function of a theoretical interest that itself belongs in the subjective sphere," [90] and then not take the life-world relationships on which

87. G. Brand, H. Hohl, and L. Landgrebe, influenced much more strongly by Heidegger than by Husserl, continue the metaphysical orientation begun by Eugen Fink, H.-G. Gadamer, and M. Müller.
88. Husserl, *Ideen III: Die Phänomenologie und die Fundamente der Wissenschaften*, Husserliana V (The Hague: Nijhoff, 1952), chap. 3, pp. 80 ff.
89. Husserl, Ms B I 10/XIII (1932), p. 1.
90. Husserl, *Ideen II: Phänomenologische Untersuchungen zur Konstitution*, Husserliana IV (The Hague: Nijhoff, 1952), p. 375.

the sciences rest in a similar manner, for they are also present in consciousness as a function of a certain interest.

Phenomenology is "historical" only when it is a universally applied "method" of reiterated regressive questionings of the conditions for the possibility of things; it can be methodological only by continually bringing forth historical proof that it is devoted without qualification to the constitutive conditions of what is given. Its metaphysically accentuated (quasi-naïve and dogmatic) positional starting points can at best set forth a provisional metaphysic whose hidden requirements of correction, control, and critique can become shown with appropriate self-reflection.[91] If it is characteristic of empirical sciences to observe and describe the pregiven real world within the context of a "naïve praxis," [92] this naïve praxis is forbidden to transcendental phenomenology, which must remove itself necessarily, universally, and comprehensively from "the naïveté of the natural and positive-scientific life."

The reiterated regress can be broken off only on one condition: "the demand to accept no knowledge that cannot be accounted for by originarily first principles, which are at the same time matters of perfect insight—principles such that profounder inquiry makes no sense." [93] And yet, if this requirement is acknowledged as appropriate, then from the viewpoint of the problematic as developed thus far it surely follows that it cannot be correct to hold the so-called primordial life-world relationships as decisive, for in the apprehensions belonging to the life-world no transparent principles are discovered beyond which we cannot question.

The life-world apprehension does not "know" whether such principles lie before it, nor does it "know" whether they are ultimate and primordial. Consciousness can attain such knowledge only through the universal application of a self-reflection that does not simply disappear when it reaches the immediately given, but reflectively questions beyond it. The view belonging to the life-world does not notice that the apprehensions achieved in "naïve praxis" are as a matter of fact "life-world" apprehensions. Only subsequent reflection can communicate the fact that naïve achievements are at issue when it is a question of life-world

91. Funke, *Phänomenologie: Metaphysik oder Methode?* pp. 57–59.
92. Husserl, Ms B I 9/X, p. 32.
93. *FTL*, p. 4.

enactments, a fact that is not known by the attitude located within the life-world itself. The process of rationalization is "historical" in the bad sense when it carries its clarifying questioning back to the establishment of life-world beginnings, but does not make it apparent that this process itself is not naïve in the way the life-world is. The process of rationalization indeed reaches backwards, but it is itself in each case a newly initiated present, and from this point alone is the past (the "historical") better understood in terms of the "historical" temporalizing of new forms of consciousness—that is, reflection—than it has understood itself. This reflection, in accordance with the "principle of all principles,"[94] puts forth a mode of demonstration peculiar to itself and possesses its justification in itself, deriving it from no other form of demonstration.

The problem of "historicity" is unfolded in its most basic form when no one factually emergent form of demonstration leads back to any other, but each remains standing as an actual "new" possibility for consciousness. Only in surpassing old self-evidences are new positions possible, and the self-evidence of the life-world relationships, as that of the connections occurring in the scientific world of idealities and objectivities, becomes questionable when a reflective critique is initiated. Hence truly historical consciousness, that is, the consciousness that first emerges in historical temporalizing, is reflective-reiterative consciousness. Here too assertions can be found that explicate and express determinate givens, assertions that are thereby "an *absolute beginning* called in a genuine sense to provide foundations, a *principium*."[95]

3. It cannot be correct to interpret the "return to the life-world" as having the same significance as a return to "transcendental subjectivity."[96] The setting aside of the self-evidence or self-evident validity of the objective-scientific view occurs only through reflection, and is *not* the result of a new "naïve

94. Husserl, *Ideen I: Allgemeine Einführung in die reine Phänomenologie, Husserliana* III (The Hague: Nijhoff, 1950), § 24, pp. 52 ff.; English translation by W. R. Boyce Gibson, *Ideas: General Introduction to Pure Phenomenology* (New York: Macmillan, Collier Books, 1962), pp. 83 f. (hereafter cited as *Ideas* I).
95. *Ibid.*
96. Hohl, *Lebenswelt und Geschichte*, p. 22.

praxis" exercised within the mode of understanding belonging to the life-world. Husserl correctly saw that "the proper return to the naïveté of life—but in a reflection which rises above this naïveté —is the only possible way to overcome the philosophical naïveté which lies in the [supposedly] "scientific" character of traditional objectivistic philosophy." [97] The "praxis" within the life-world may be naïve, but this fact is not itself established by this attitude; it is first accessible only through a surpassing that does not belong to the life-world, a surpassing effected by making the life-world transparent by means of conscious and reiterated reflection. It would be a "phenomenological naïveté" if one did not see new possibilities of intentional understanding in the reflective nature of consciousness, instead of always orientating *all* possible modes of exhibiting meaning, including the mode of reflection, according to the model of sensible intuition.

The rejection of a true reiterative and critical reflective phenomenology by the school of life-world metaphysicians who turned from Husserl to Heidegger bypasses the "principle of all principles." A consciousness cannot be called "historical" if truly *authentic* relationships are continually sought in simple, historically past beginnings. Such beginnings are decisive only when, in relation to some kind of presumed logical consciousness that remains identical, they permit an easy and clear depiction of the structure that prefigures the nature of such a consciousness. However, if the logical function of consciousness (the constitution of meaning and the rendering of meanings evident) is "historical" in itself, then the "historical" beginnings of the achievements of consciousness are to that extent largely irrelevant for a comprehensive understanding of these achievements; for the initiating life-world modes of disclosure that belong to naïve praxis indeed point out and bring into appearance all things, but they do not indicate that it is a question of the "subjective" constitution of "objectively" understood relationships. The understanding of these relationships presupposes an attitude of consciousness that leaves this original naïveté behind and does not seek understanding in origins that are past (and hence "historical" in this sense), but instead enters into "historical temporalizing," or the attitude of reflection. The "transcendental reduction to essences" cannot occur within naïveté, and the en-

97. *Crisis*, p. 59.

trance into "the realm of the mothers of knowledge" is not to be found in the praxis of the life-world.[98]

It is surely not the "essence" that is produced, but the "consciousness of the essence." But we can only speak of "essence" by means of mediating ("constitutive") consciousness, and if we are to take the presentation of the "historicity" of consciousness in all earnestness, we must concede that "an originally-giving consciousness of an essence (ideation) is in itself and of necessity spontaneous."[99] However, what is the meaning of spontaneity when "life-world metaphysics" and "etymologizing" philosophy locate everything decisive and essential in "historical" beginnings? Either unforeseeably "new" and original modes of disclosure, arising in "historical temporalizing," bring hitherto unencountered *intenta* into appearance, which in that case are co-constituted with these modes of disclosure and the current "logical" communication thus raises itself above "historically" earlier possibilities of demonstration, or this is not the case at all, and to speak of the logical historicity of consciousness[100] is to speak nonsense.

The "historical" time of mundane history can be divided into two clearly distinguishable epochs: a prehistorical or "early" time, when man lived quasi-naturally within traditionally determined communities and where his world was a mythical one,[101] and a philosophical time in which man, "through self-objectification," appears as "the bearer of reason."[102] If the "principle of all mythologies" is tradition, then the "principle of philosophy" must be freedom. It is a "historical" event of the first order when man no longer lives naïvely and no longer shifts responsibility away from himself. Life within the relationships of the life-world also has its truth, but it lacks knowledge of itself and knowledge *that* it is "subjective." To break away from the "historically" predetermined paths of tradition manifests freedom, and the reflective and critical attitude toward oneself hence becomes a symbol of freedom. If we now "postulate a truly human development of mankind," this is conceivable only on the basis of "autonomous

98. *Ibid.*, pp. 152–53.
99. Husserl, Ms B I 21/IV, p. 17.
100. Cf. Husserl's sketches for an idea of a "concrete infinite historicity" in *Krisis*, pp. 500 ff.
101. Husserl, Ms B I 21/IV, p. 38.
102. Husserl, Ms K III 18, p. 29.

freedom." [103] The epochs of mundane history are dependent on the historicity of consciousness.

The transcendental modification of this consciousness is then manifested in philosophy, and the first break in history is followed by the entrance of the critical attitude "against all familiar and foreign traditions," an attitude that is found wherever we meet with the distinction between men who judge as common men bound to a tradition (*doxa*) and men who live out of knowledge (*epistēmē*).[104]

The most historically relevant event for mankind is the emergence of theoretical man who is possible only on the basis of a "historical" change of transcendental consciousness. Husserl states that the theoretically interested man suppresses every particular personal interest; he directs himself toward the truth that is independent of the changes of such interests; he concerns himself with beings free from traditionally defined prejudices; he lives as theoretician "in an unholy state, for instead of fearing the gods, he asks if they exist and what they are, and what justifies the belief that they are such-and-such." [105]

Now if the philosopher is the most radical theoretician whose basic aim is to demand and achieve justification for the givenness of what is given, then his theoretical achievement is eminently "practical," for the adoption of such an attitude takes away the value of many "historical" opinions as pregiven truths; truth can now be found only in the evidences offered by foundational relationships, and hence only on the basis of the new attitude of consciousness made possible by the "historicity" of consciousness.

If philosophy has until now been determined by the traditional and has not recognized the "historicity" of transcendental consciousness, then the crisis of philosophy (as also the crises of those sciences that are essentially determined by this philosophy) is a sign of the absence of self-understanding. For philosophy can only be philosophy of consciousness, and it will understand itself to be that only when it continually relates the achievements issuing from consciousness back to their ground. In this way philosophy will be what it can be only through the constant performance of radical self-reflection. Such reflection, however, sus-

103. Edmund Husserl, "Die Idee einer philosophischen Kultur," *Japanisch-deutsche Zeitschrift für Wissenschaft und Technik* (1923), p. 46.
104. Husserl, Ms E III 3, p. 7.
105. Husserl, Ms B I 21/IV, p. 14.

pends the popular twentieth-century slogan "back to the object!," for the essential question concerns the achieving subjectivity from which issues all experience in the widest sense. In this sense, with reference to the historicity of consciousness, *the great turning point in the history of philosophy is the turn to transcendental philosophy inaugurated by Descartes and Kant.*[106] For this reason the "greatest of all revolutions must be characterized as the transformation of scientific objectivism . . . into a transcendental subjectivism." [107]

Critical-analytic phenomenology is truly suited to its time insofar as in its reiterative-reflective function it pushes the processes of regress and reduction to explore the conditions for the possibility of the given; for it is then a philosophy which, through critical questioning, preserves and maintains the "historicity" of consciousness. If this is what phenomenology actually is, then to it falls the decisive task of resolving the present "historical" crisis: phenomenology is the critical consciousness of the present age. Man and world designate a "particular transcendental structure of transcendental subjectivity," [108] and no philosophy other than transcendental phenomenology bears witness to this structure. The "unholy state" of theoretical-critical man is that of the philosopher who has adopted a "historically" new attitude of consciousness.

The final problem facing a transcendental phenomenology oriented toward the historicity of consciousness must be the question concerning the historicity of truth. If "objectivity" is a subjective mode of constitution, then "objective truth" is dependent on such constitutions. The critical reflection that uncovers this constitution hence cannot lay claim to objectivity in this sense; it possesses another, transcendental, truth. The nature of this truth must now be revealed and must make its appearance in new "foundation-laying" discoveries.

This can take place only with a transforming realignment of man's entire life in ordering the foundations for these functions "in philosophical culture," which will occur "in the community of investigators bound to each other in philosophical striving and advancing *in infinitum* in history." This community of investigators is made up principally of Europeans and the rest of truly

106. *FTL*, § 100, p. 255.
107. *Crisis*, p. 68.
108. Husserl, Ms A V 14, p. 15.

"human" humanity insofar as they pursue the "universal criticism of tradition, life, and the world of life in its infinitude." [109] The prejudices of the life-world and of the scientific and objectivistic attitudes lead to a fixed dogmatism and to an attitude of intolerance, for with them a subjective individual view is taken for something in-itself. The process of uncovering the subjective origins of *all* positings of the in-itself suspends the claim to exclusive validity made by "historically" emerging positions *and* the claim to objectivity (that is, the claim that it is a question of the in-itself). This suspension itself represents an act of freedom, for the very act of consciousness in here and now critically elevating itself above simple acceptance of the self-evident validity of its own position cannot itself be "derived" from any source.

Man's often-postulated freedom manifests itself in this theoretical attitude, which originates in a radical self-reflection on one's own achievements. At some time in man's historical life reason will become the universal critic of those "world views that have grown out of historical prejudices and superstitions, and will also become the critical judge of possible systems of values and aims together with their claims to universal validity." This rational consciousness of humanity is not a *factum* but a *faciendum*. Its historicity rests on the historicity of transcendental subjectivity, a subjectivity which will also bring into evidence those meaningful claims to truth that are part of this new arrangement and that refer to these new phenomena and new entities.

> The truly existent not only comprises the world of facts, but also includes the world of values and their guiding normative principles, the world of practical ends and formations of ends, of possible guiding forms of ends and means in general, and thus of normative principles over-all. The logos thus becomes the guiding spirit of a human life and its world that is to be completely transformed,[110]

and precisely therein, in the unfolding of such a life, lies the "historical" task of phenomenology as the philosophy of a radically transcendental consciousness, a task whose mastery will make manifest, evident, and *existentiell* the "historicity" of transcendental subjectivity.

109. Husserl, Ms B I 21/IV, pp. 15, 16.
110. *Ibid.*, p. 17.

EGO, CONSCIOUSNESS, EVENT, AND PHENOMENOLOGICAL EGOLOGY

THE EGO AND THE LIFE of consciousness that remain as
a residuum after the performance of the phenomenological reduction are not part of the world.[111] This does not mean that
phenomenology's investigations turn away from the world. Phenomenology uncovers no self-sufficient second world, and its goal
is not to demonstrate the existence of a world "beyond" this one.
Ego and *cogitatio* are not extramundane because they form a
world distinct from the world of the natural attitude, but because
they *constitute* the world. Phenomenology is therefore the analysis of intentionality and constitution.[112] The residual consciousness is not substantial; it does not appear as a *hypokeimenon*
whose accidents would then be appearances, feelings, and so on.
Thought is not the successive unfolding of variable circumstances
within a secret dream-life. Thinking is always a thinking of
something and is therefore "content-full." That which is thought
about is what it is only as one pole of an experience or as an act
of consciousness in the broadest sense. The correlation between
cogito and *cogitatum* cannot be suspended.[113]

To be an ego and to understand oneself as such does not mean
to concern oneself with a part of the world; nor does it mean to
withdraw back into one's personal and characteristic inner life,
which itself is already the product of a constituted self-interpretation combined with the views of others. To understand oneself as
ego means to have discovered the *ego cogito cogitatum qua
cogitatum*. In the *cogitatio*, the transcendental ego is what it is
only in relation to its intentional object.[114] It is the task of
phenomenology to lay bare the intentional experiences of consciousness as achievements of the constitutively functioning ego,
to make use of the entire realm of intentional objects as clues for
regressive constitutive questionings, and to explicate the phenomena of the formation of objective meaning and of the origin

111. Cf. *CM*, § 12, pp. 27–29.
112. Cf. *Ideas* I, pp. 373 ff.
113. *Ibid.*, pp. 188 ff.
114. *CM*, § 15, pp. 35 ff., and § 21, pp. 50–53.

of the "world" in general.[115] With the performance of the phenomenological reduction phenomenology finds itself within transcendental subjectivity, for all mundane facts and all regional-
ontological essences refer back to the transcendental ego as their
ultimate and necessary point of reference. Turning to extramundane transcendental subjectivity is not a turning toward the
irrational, but rather an abiding with the world in order to comprehend it from the standpoint of spirit [Geist].[116] A genuinely
phenomenological description is the description of the egological
life of consciousness, and this entails "seeing" how the ego constitutes its cogitatum in the cogitationes. "How" the cogitatum is
constituted is not itself a part of the world, but is premundane.
Thus transcendental phenomenology is concerned with the experience [Ereignis] of spirit that "gives" itself in the bipolar
noetic-noematic form. Ego here means simply subjectivity, or the
totality of subjective presuppositions for everything objective.

The two guiding thoughts of phenomenology are undoubtedly
the theory of reduction and the theory of constitution.[117] In general, constitution here refers to every original relationship between ego and world and, more specifically, between the ego and
everything mundane (or structured) that is met up with in the
world. All attempts to comprehend aspects or parts of the world
refer to the transcendental ego. In particular, to grasp the constitution of the "world" as it is founded on the ego means to learn
to see the constitution of meanings, values, relevance, and existence.[118] The theory of constitution is a theory for the investigation
of meaning, and the constitution of meaning lies not only in the
apprehension of objects but also in authentic self-understanding,

115. Eugen Fink, "Die phänomenologische Philosophie Edmund Husserls in der gegenwärtigen Kritik," Kantstudien, XXXVIII, nos. 3–4 (1933),
344; English translation by R. O. Elveton, "The Phenomenological Philosophy of Edmund Husserl and Contemporary Criticism," in Phenomenology of Husserl, p. 95.
116. Eugen Fink, "Was will die Phänomenologie Edmund Husserls?"
Die Tatwelt X, no. 1 (1934), 31.
117. Fink, "Phenomenological Philosophy of Husserl," p. 102.
118. Edmund Husserl, "Nachwort zu meinen Ideen," Jahrbuch für
Philosophie und phänomenologische Forschung, XI (1930), 550 (my
translation); cf. English translation as Author's Preface to Ideas I (the
page on which the present quote appears is part of a small section of
the "Nachwort" that was not translated; all further references are to the
English ed.).

where it is not simply a matter of "observing" something mundanely pregiven, including myself (as "person," "anthropological subject," etc.), but of attesting to an imperative or "ought" [*Seinssollen*] that is not pregiven. That which cannot be derived from any other mundane entity and which comes into appearance in an eventful way must be called an authentic "ought." And what in an authentic sense ought to be is what has become manifest— the real. Stated differently, the nontheoretical understanding that is occupied and engaged with things discloses meaning to itself. If it does not wish to remain a description of regional ontological essences, phenomenology must not ignore the historical. Constitutive regressive questionings are concerned not only with what is constituted, but also with the constitution itself. Constitution, however, is the coming-into-appearance of meaning or the self-genesis of what cannot be derived, i.e., of that which comes to show itself through itself. The thought of a demonstration that comes solely from the affairs themselves contains the following definition: the emergence of what cannot be derived is an event [*Ereignis*]. When we concern ourselves with "the things themselves" and take the concept of things or affairs quite broadly to include every constituted unity of meaning, then we must also take up the question of constitution itself as an eventful emergence. In the precise sense (as underivable and without reference to what is previously given) the "eventful" is the emergence of the projective spirit and of consciousness, whose comprehension takes place through various modes, when this spirit and consciousness give themselves and understand themselves as projective in the content-full noematically polarized *cogito*. This eventful self-understanding, bound up with noematically polarized noeses, also constitutes a being without thereby involving an anticipation of this eventfully transpiring understanding.

The "world" has its being naturally as something entirely determinate, with a meaning that can be apprehended intersubjectively. Determined in this way, this being requires an absolute consciousness as the ultimate origin of the bestowal of meaning.[119] So-called phenomenological idealism does not deny the reality of the world or the reality of this or that structure of the world. It does strive to discover the meaning of the world. The world's existence cannot be disputed, but it is precisely this sense

119. *Ideas* I, pp. 130–31.

of indisputability that requires clarification.[120] Meaning is "given" with experiences. Yet nothing justifies our speaking of non-intentional experiences, for this would mean that such experiences are concerned with nothing. We can, however, distinguish between transitive and intransitive experiences.[121]

The constitution of meaning is also present where experiences are not intentionally related to intersubjectively constituted beings but to a "thrown being" of the nature of Dasein, who is alone concerned with these experiences. Here a being is constituted that is nonderivative and for whom it is not a question of other beings but of its own being. The being of this being would be the constitution of meaning, the latter being a name for the functioning of transcendental subjectivity.

1. The transcendental ego is not something that can be seized directly apart from the coming-into-appearance of phenomena. It is not a "givenness," a "primordial fact," or something that "exists in-itself." Rather, it is simply that which possesses the sense of "absolute being." [122] As such, absolute being is nonderivative, so that phenomenology becomes the philosophy of that constituting spirit which alone cannot be traced back to some other being.[123] To speak of "being" without permitting a determinate meaning to become attached to it is just as misleading as to speak of the "absolute" and then to attempt a clarification or grounding of this absolute.[124] It follows from this that the meaning of the transcendental ego can only manifest itself in its constituting function. Taking into account its moments of determinateness and nonderivability and its a priori and premundane nature, such an appearance lies only with "spirit," which is never empty and is always nonderivative.[125] Thus we speak of the "world" as a constituted meaning or as a unity of meaning.[126] There is no doubt

120. Cf. Gaston Berger, The "Cogito" in Husserl's Philosophy, trans. Kathleen McLaughlin, with an Introduction by James M. Edie (Evanston, Ill.: Northwestern University Press, 1972), p. 74.
121. Alexander Pfänder treats this distinction in Die Seele des Menschen (Halle: Niemeyer, 1933), pp. 29 ff.
122. Husserl, "Nachwort," p. 21.
123. On this see Theodor Litt, Mensch und Welt (Frankfurt, 1948), pp. 153 ff.
124. Cf. Berger, The "Cogito," pp. 107 ff.
125. Cf. Litt, Mensch und Welt, pp. 293 ff.
126. CM, § 41, p. 84; Edmund Husserl, Pariser Vorträge (The Hague: Nijhoff, 1963), pp. 21 ff.; English translation by Peter Koestenbaum, The Paris Lectures (The Hague: Nijhoff, 1964), pp. 20 ff.

that the constitution of meaning extends beyond the intersubjective constitution of meaning. It lies in so-called *"existentiell* understanding" and "self-evidence" which is meaningful in itself without being touched by intersubjectivity. Thus not only projected meaning but also the projection of meaning itself belongs to the domain of the phenomenological investigation of constitution. For there is both a constituted meaning, which as constituted and pregiven is accessible to a "universal observer," and a meaning which, though not preconstituted and therefore not intersubjectively accessible, yet remains meaningful even though it should only appear in "engagement," which is itself never meaningless. In brief, meaning lies not only in what is logically possible, in what can be conceived, and in the already present-to-hand, but also in the actually possible [*Realmöglichen*] and conceptually unforeseeable. If phenomenology is the analysis of intentionality and constitution, it is then bound up with the actually possible in a particular way. And if transcendental subjectivity is what it is in continuous evidences or constitutions of meaning,[127] then it itself has meaning and presents a unity of meaning. The problem of history in the transcendental phenomenological sense is not that of mundane history, but of the constitution of the transcendental ego itself. Here autogenesis is historical in a primary sense.[128] Is it also intentional?

We must see whether experiences such as anxiety and care are nonintentional. Certainly the enactment of these kinds of experiences does not primarily constitute something that can be encountered intersubjectively. This, however, does not eliminate the possibility that a particular being constitutes itself as a unique unity of meaning in the enactment of anxiety and care, namely, as a being whose own being is an issue for itself. Anxiety and care constitute a being of the form of "Dasein," the sense of whose being is made up of the being-an-issue-for-itself. Whenever, as for Heidegger,[129] "Dasein" designates a being as a unique unity of meaning, this being has its own forms of disclosure through which it "gives" itself, "constitutes" itself, and becomes "trans-

127. Cf. *CM*, § 23, pp. 56–57, where Husserl speaks of "transcendental constitution," "reason," and "unreason."
128. Cf. *CM*, § 30, p. 65: "The transcendental ego inseparable from the processes making up his life."
129. Cf. Martin Heidegger, *Sein und Zeit* (Halle: Niemeyer, 1931), pp. 41 ff.; English translation by John Macquarrie and Edward Robinson, *Being and Time* (New York: Harper & Row, 1962), pp. 65 ff.

parent" to itself or "understands" itself. Thus it naturally belongs to the meaning of anxiety and care that they cannot be taken over by someone else but belong precisely to the one who now "exists" them, just as it explicitly belongs to the meaning of the being of nature that it be "objective," that is, that it can be experienced intersubjectively and is not capable of being intended solely by one individual. It is then not misleading to speak of a phenomenology of existence. The title designates nothing other than the phenomenology of the constituting spirit that cannot be derived from anything pregiven and that cannot be found as a part of the world.

If every being is to be analyzed in terms of those intentions that constitute it, then this holds equally for beings of the form of Dasein. And if Dasein is uniquely disclosed through anxiety and care because its own being is an issue for it and because its being is not accessible in general, then the phenomenon in question here is not an intersubjectively given and intersubjectively constituted meaning that we can simply adopt. Rather the phenomenon that discloses itself here is of a peculiar sort: the coming-into-appearance of a spirit that projectively constitutes mundane entities. Its function is demonstrated only in its manifestation, and the self-understanding in terms of which it attests that its being is an issue for itself in its performings, constitutings, and projectings is uniquely constituted in anxiety and care. This means that the being for whom its own being is an issue is an understanding Dasein, where understanding is the "understanding of meaning." Phenomenology primarily has to do with being as a constituted unity of meaning. However, with the enactment of performed intentional-constitutive achievements phenomenology also seizes the phenomenon-being of phenomena, in the sense that this being is the event of spirit. Hence all objectively constituted and intersubjectively accessible mundane appearances are phenomena, and so also is the appearance of beings which possess the form of understanding and are self-disclosing in crisis and *kairos;* here phenomena are the coming-into-appearance of the being that constitutes mundane entities, the spirit and consciousness that become self-conscious of their premundane constituting function in its modes of interpretation. Phenomenology thereby becomes the doctrine of crisis, *kairos,* and *katastasis.*

Husserl's *Logical Investigations* oppose the view that the ego is a mundane substance that bears psychological states. In *Ideas I* Husserl maintains that the ego cannot be seized mundanely and that we cannot say anything about its nature and properties. Ego and intentions belong together: however, only the manner in which intentions "point themselves out" can be described.[130] The "ego" in part designates a mode of being and not a particular being, and also in part designates transcendence of a unique sort within intentionality that cannot be compared to the transcendence attributable to the intended "noematic pole" of an intentional act. The ego is not given as something constituted (and hence transcendent within the immanence of consciousness), but it "is" its constituting. For the empirically thrown ego, *character* and *habit* are constituted on the basis of the ego's historically mundane situation and its relational contexts, and these traits show themselves in the form of a horizon. In this way, the ego takes on some similarity to an object (though an object with a unique structure). Thus the ego as a *"Gestalt," "man," "person,"* and so on is not identical with the transcendental ego which is the source of all acts, including acts of self-interpretation. The intentionality belonging to the acts of transcendental consciousness has nothing to do with the "activity" of a personal, human, and psychological (mundane) attitude. Just as the "passivity" of receptive consciousness (which is not "nothing") refers back to the transcendental *cogito*, each activity appropriate to the practical will presupposes the self-disclosure of the pure ego. "Passivity" signifies a withdrawing, neglecting, or aimless distancing from the achievements issuing from the ego; it is a remaining fixed to what is mundanely given. The mundanely given, however, is what it is only for an intentional consciousness; this is recognized by the forms of both active *and* passive genesis.[131] It shows itself to be nonmundane precisely in this regard.

It remains to clarify in what sense the transcendental ego with its *cogito* is the origin of acts. Undoubtedly, the answer is that the ego affirmatively "posits" itself and temporalizes those "determinations," "positions," or "theses" that serve as the point of departure for each meaningful identification that achieves its completion in the evident synthetic constitution of an "object." In evidence the toward-which and the from-which of subjectivity

130. Pfänder employs this expression in his psychological investigations. See *Die Seele des Menschen*, pp. 326 ff.
131. *CM*, § 38, p. 77.

become transparent. The ego signifies the freedom of consciousness, the fiat that lies within it,[132] and evidence must be its expression. Original having-in-evidence is an ego-ray [Ichstrahl]. This means that thought does not present itself as a realm wherein the ego freely wanders in manifesting its freedom. On the contrary, the manifestation of freedom lies in the fact that something has meaning. The doctrine of evidence suspends the mundane opposition between theory and praxis, activity and passivity, for evidence-giving intentionality is the enactment of premundane (pretheoretical and prepractical) freedom.[133] Furthermore, if thought, which as such is always meaningful (whether it is a question of appropriating objects or of the understanding care for the being that is in each case mine), is to be the manifestation of freedom, then it is also free with respect to itself. This means that it is not a thinking about something pregiven, but rather originative thought. Every object-directed thinking shows itself to be accompanied at the same time by the evidence of that which it intends—it is conscious-being [Bewusst-sein]. In the act of intending, consciousness of what is not pregiven remains consciousness of what it is—i.e., intention. It is present in constituting self-consciousness as something nonmundane. Thus we can say that subjectivity is determined by both intentionality and self-consciousness. Self-consciousness is also intentional, but not as if there were an intentional reflective directedness toward the function of consciousness as such. The intentional nature of self-consciousness lies in the fact that it witnesses to its free constituting function in the autogenesis of immanent time-consciousness.[134] Time is the form of being [Sein] in historical life.

Time-consciousness and self-consciousness belong together in the constitution of duration and succession in which the moments of time are identified, recognized, and remembered. The analysis of the constitution of immanent time-consciousness runs counter to any theory of time that transforms "succession," "duration," and so on into mere contents of consciousness, as is the case with the traditional theory of time (Brentano). The relationship between transcendental subjectivity on the one hand and activity

132. Cf. Emmanuel Levinas, En découvrant l'existence avec Husserl et Heidegger (Paris: Vrin, 1949), § 11, "Le Moi, le temps et la liberté," pp. 40 ff.
133. Ibid., pp. 40–41.
134. Ibid., p. 41. Cf. Husserl, Ms B III 1, p. 90.

or passivity on the other is clarified along with the constitution of immanent time-consciousness, which removes any basis for speaking of constitutive transcendental phenomenology (and, along with it, fundamental ontology) as a "must-less activism." [135]

The origin of all consciousness is (according to Husserl) the phenomenological "primordial impression" [*Urimpression*]. In the "impression" as such there is both an original passivity and an original "spontaneity," and yet each impression is continually an impression of a determinate meaning. Primordial consciousness [*Urbewusstsein*] is consciousness of the intentionally constituted condition of evidence: the immediately present sets forth the first event of spirit. Here spirit as intentional is with itself in immediate presence. A pure presence naturally knows no connections, and thus each impression vanishes. What is "present" loses actuality and relevance, and is at best retentively held fast by a new present that takes its place, and so on. The retention in question itself sets forth an intention by means of which what remains firmly grasped here as the limit of what is past can be thought, and thereby stands open to further actualizations of memory. The interweaving of intentions, retentions, and protentions constitutes duration, which is the taking up once again of what has been previously given, the actual present evidence, and anticipation. Spirit [*Geist*] is free in retentively holding fast, just as it is free in the intentional primordial impression; it is, furthermore, a protentional power relating to protentions that cannot be anticipated. Accordingly, time is not an "external" givenness that is foreign to consciousness. Time presents the condition in terms of which mundane entities can be thought of as such, and this means that the intentional, retentional, and protentional achievements of consciousness constitute "time." In this way, each objective occurrence in time and each mundane historical process finds its grounding. The constitution of time expresses freedom, just as the transcendent and noematically polarized intentionality expresses freedom. Of course time does not "give" itself in the same way that the constituted objects of intersubjective experience give themselves. No primordial subject [*Ur-Subjekt*] stands behind "time," bringing its various moments together and unifying them into one objective and universal time. On the contrary, time is constituted nonobjectively by the free intentional

135. Cf. Barth, "Philosophie der Existenz," p. 36.

achievements of each individual subject and its stream of consciousness, and this excludes such subjects constituting time for others. Concepts such as "flow," "course," and so on can be used in a general sense only with reference to intersubjective constitutions and with the aid of analogies.

Phenomenological time, which must be distinguished from objective time and which does not coincide with Bergson's "pure duration," [136] does not present the form of a stream of consciousness that would be one mundane given among others. All intentions that are immanent within the stream of consciousness (such as "impressions," "sensations," "apperceptions," and so on) are not to be viewed as psychological realities which need only be described (in the manner of the first Husserlian school) phenomenologically. Rather are they primary achievements of premundane subjectivity which is not a being [Seiendes], but is more akin to being [Sein]. Here it is clearly seen that the antinomy of spontaneity and passivity is suspended at the level of spirit manifest in intentions, as is shown by the paradigmatic example of the primordial impression. The "present" is what is evident and given in intentions. With the retentions and protentions involved in the abrupt appearance of the primordial impression, the present is a first emergence of spirit where spirit posits itself and comes to possess itself, that is, where spirit is a free projection. Already at this level of "impressions," "sensations," and "perceptions" where intentionality itself, directed toward the external object, seems spread out through time and thus appears as a psychic content (and where the traditional epistemological passivity is quite at home), the emergence of meaning can only be ascertained in conjunction with the constitution of meaning. Time is therefore qualified solely through its contents, which share in the rhythm of time without thereby creating time.

"Spirit" is the inner meaningfulness of thought and the freedom of insight [Einsicht]. This freedom fulfills itself in time. Time has no preexistence before spirit and does not engage spirit in a mundane "history" in which it could perish. This means that historical time is constituted time, and history as such can be clarified only by thought. If the meaning of the abstract world of science refers back to the world of the "transcendental aesthetic" (in Kant's sense), and hence to the concrete everyday world of

136. Cf. Levinas, En découvrant l'existence, p. 42.

all possible attributes, then this concrete world constitutes itself in immanent time as the world of culture and of history, the time of self-comprehending consciousness and freedom. This self-comprehension poses a problem.

2. Man is not truly himself when he remains with the simple affirmation of the Cartesian *cogito*. Correctly understood, this *cogito* is human only when it has first discovered itself to be reason (i.e., freedom). Stated in another way, the *cogito* is human only when it reveals that the *ego cogito* is always the *ego cogito cogitatum qua cogitatum*. If it is to be free, the ego must be explicated as the center of evident achievements, and these are the achievements of the constitution of meaning. The being of the ego as spirit or thought is authentic only when it discovers and understands itself as such. Hence phenomenology manifests a concern for man's self-understanding as the center of reason's achievements, and endeavors to disclose universal reason as it belongs to man as such by virtue of his very meaning.[137] The object of every thinking, its *cogitatum,* belongs to the sphere of the immediately evident. Thus from the very start the "world" has "objective" existence in this sense of being constituted in intentionalities. The *cogito's* self-certainty indicates the situation of a spirit that does not discover itself as one being among others. Spirit's knowledge of itself and of its freedom is involved because relationships to the "outside" have been suspended. The *cogito* indicates a situation in which spirit exists as origin. Certainty is not the index for a knowledge of objects, but for the situation of being conscious [*Bewusst-sein*]. It is made up of the perfect agreement of what is intended and what is given in immanent perception.

We may note in this connection that this exceptional state of affairs exists only for an ego and a stream of experience in relation to itself. Immanent perception is possible only in such a case.[138] However, this coincidence presents a mode of being of consciousness wherein consciousness is at its own disposal in what is given in the present. In the absolute evidence of the *cogito* as such the freedom of consciousness, made present in what is actually intended, points to original reason as the consti-

137. Cf. Husserl, "Die Krisis der europäischen Wissenschaften" (Belgrade ed.), p. 92.
138. *Ideas* I, pp. 111–12.

tution of meaning. The evident consciousness enclosed within the *cogito* is identical to the enactment of the freedom of spirit itself. Evidence and knowledge appear as modes of being of spirit, for true knowledge and knowledge of the truth are freedom.[139] In this sense there is knowledge only insofar as there is self-consciousness. Uncertainty concerning the "external" world rests on the fact that there can be no pure experience of something objectively given, but only a perspectivally adumbrated one that can be endlessly modified. Every new experience can in principle serve to cancel the knowledge achieved up to that moment, at least in the sense of essential variations. The uncertainty of "external experience" is based on the uncertainty of the present, i.e., on the essential openness of the present to the future. When the givenness of a "state of affairs" belonging to external experience is declared to be absolute, spirit has then passed beyond its own possibilities, and thereby estranges itself from its own freedom. Spirit must seize each transcendence in its true meaning (that is, as constituted) through the immanence of what it possesses at the moment. Constitution takes place within the self-temporalizing life of consciousness. This means that nothing can invade consciousness from the outside and that everything must take its point of departure from it. It follows from this that transcendental idealism has no aim other than to make explicit every kind of being that an ego can present to itself.[140] A philosophy of pure meanings thereby opposes the man dogmatically imprisoned within the "natural attitude." [141] Yet it is not a question of assigning a privileged status to the question of meaning, but rather of viewing everything within the framework of the question of meaning.[142] The correspondingly radical change of attitude consists in this: that the question concerning the existence of "affairs" [*Sachen*] that supposedly lie at the foundation of "meanings" is to be given up as entirely illegitimate. No affairs are to be posited and subsequently appointed as bearers of meaning which could then be made intelligible by means of the achievements of consciousness or by an appeal to

---

139. Cf. J. E. Heyde's investigations concerning the "Relativität der Wahrheit," *Grundwissenschaft*, XII, nos. 1–4 (1933), 34.

140. *CM*, § 22, p. 54.

141. For the problem of dogmatism, see Erich Rothacker's *Die dogmatische Denkform in den Geisteswissenschaften und das Problem des Historismus* (Mainz: 1954), no. 6, pp. 240 ff.

142. Berger, *The "Cogito,"* pp. 73 ff.

forms of understanding of a Kantian nature. Transcendental subjectivity bestows no meaning on a preexistent affair. No "affairs" or "things-in-themselves" are present to transcendental phenomenology, and an experience within a preempirically structured space is as impossible as the "incorporation" into consciousness of matters of fact that are foreign to it.[143] Hence there is no pregiven matter to which a subsequent meaning is granted. Phenomenology recognizes the traditional dualism of matter and form only in a very limited sense. The distinction is but a relative one for phenomenology, as can be seen with respect to Husserl's interpretation of "intentional meanings" and "material *hylē*." [144]

The question arises as to what can be accomplished by such a system of meanings that rests on nothing. Can one speak of "meaning" and "sense" without also accepting the existence of "essences," "entities," and "affairs" to which meanings are related, or without positing subjects that preside over the comprehension of meaning? If phenomenology demands a new attitude, it will undoubtedly bring forth no arguments against realism and will use none of the arguments of traditional idealism. It will not remove itself from concrete events even though it puts itself at a distance from realism.[145] We do not lose being [*Sein*] when we take the foothold offered by an investigation of sense and meaning, even though the realm of meaning is larger than the realm of being. "Having a meaning" does not serve to point out any particular mode of being, but "being" is a "meaning." Accordingly, being should not be selected as the point from which all else is to be viewed, and the position of phenomenology is not limited by this specification, but passes beyond it. The philosophy of being is itself founded on a transcendental phenomenology that takes the form of an "egology." This egological phenomenology is to be understood as the universal unfolding of transcendental subjectivity manifested in purely egological and intersubjectively initiated performances, wherein the innate a priori or "universal logos of all conceivable being" comes to expression. Together with egology, transcendental phenomenology, as the disclosure of subjectivity's achievements, is "the true and *genuine universal ontology*." [146] This ontology is not to be taken simply as

143. *FTL*, p. 232.
144. Berger, *The "Cogito,"* pp. 75–76.
145. *Ideas* I, pp. 152 ff.
146. *CM*, § 64, p. 155.

a formal and empty one, but is a material regional ontology that includes all eidetic being possibilities. "Everything conceivable" is included within the realm of the actually possible [*Realmögli-chen*]; not only what is intersubjectively given and accessible, but also the situation-bound contextual possibilities of being. What is "conceivable" and not already given is what ought to be, and to that extent appears with a certain preeminence. Thus the conceivable does not simply show itself as what has already been given, but also as what will be enacted in the sense of self-commitment and self-declaration. And it can also be said that within the realm of the actually possible what ought to be is what is conceivable and preeminent, and that what ought to be in the full sense is what comes to light in projects and hence is the eventfully and historically emergent, which, as a genuinely actual possibility, is the real [*das Wirkliche*]. A teleological trait thereby holds sway in consciousness.

The "universal concrete ontology" taken up by phenomenology would also be the intrinsically first science carried out by means of absolute groundings.[147] However, knowledge lies not only in knowing what has been projected, but also in the enactment of projects. Meaning is found not simply in the constituted appearance, but in the constituting coming-into-appearance as well. According to Husserl:

> In respect of order, the intrinsically first of the philosophical disciplines would be "solipsistically" reduced "egology," the egology of the primordially reduced ego. Then only would come intersubjective phenomenology, which is founded on that discipline; moreover it would start with a generality that at first treated the universal questions, and only subsequently would it branch out into the apriori sciences.[148]

This sentence emphasizes the intersubjective character of intentional objective investigation, as well as the nonintersubjective character of the self-interpretation manifested in crisis and *kairos* and grounded solipsistically in the "moment," in self-understanding, and in co-knowing. This self-testifying engagement is "historical," for it cannot in principle be anticipated: it is not pre-given but is eventful. We can say that "the intrinsically first

147. Cf. *CM*, § 64, "Concluding Word," pp. 151 ff.
148. *Ibid.*, p. 155.

being, the being that precedes and bears every worldly Objectivity, is transcendental intersubjectivity: the universe of monads, which effects its communion in various forms," [149] if we understand the being of this intersubjectively constituted universe of monads as one that is itself insightfully constituted in egological experience. The world of the natural attitude, of intersubjectively accessible nature, of objective cultural goods, and of mundane history is a world that reaches back to the achievements of this monadological community which itself, not pregiven, refers back to its constitution in pure egological subjectivity. Egology is thus the domain of the ego that is not a part of such a community and is not intersubjective, and it is also the domain of the unforeseeable eventfulness or manifestation of transcendental subjectivity.

If it is the "pure ego" which, as the intrinsically first being, discloses itself through itself in co-knowing, then this means that the entire field of consciousness, together with all of its unities of meaning, is constituted by the ego. It reveals itself with the emergence of mundane beings and whenever something eventfully transpires in consciousness. This intrinsically first being is present originally in the purely egological and solipsistic (and hence truly prephenomenological) sense in the *kairos* of decision by means of its self-commitment to the projectively known aim that takes precedence (i.e., the aim possessed in evidence); it is furthermore present in concerned being where this ego is an issue for itself; and, finally, it is present in the constitution of intersubjectively accessible objects. In the light of Husserl's *Cartesian Meditations*, there can be no doubt that phenomenology, which has to do with phenomena as constituted appearances, is first possible only on the basis of the egological unfolding of subjectivity, that is, on the basis of the coming-into-appearance of phenomena. The fact that every "something" or "totality of meaning" exists for transcendental subjectivity, and is what it is as constituted by and for this ego, in no way limits our view to what can be seized intersubjectively. What turns out to be an indispensable and privileged relevance for the "natural attitude" of the intersubjective, objective, realistic, and naturally constituted does not, however, completely hide pure egological constitutions. The phenomenality of the phenomenon is not a

149. *Ibid.*, p. 156.

phenomenological givenness, but makes up the content of absolute and nonderivative egological evidence.[150] "Egological evidences," "ontological thoughts of being," [151] and so on are aimed at intersubjectively in subsequent enactments, although they thereby come into appearance in a modified form and are no longer what they were in their original enactment as eventful occurrences. According to their very meaning they are incapable of intersubjective clarification and objectification. This uniqueness is quite compatible with the general thesis of phenomenology, which states that every mode of being, including every being that can be characterized as transcendental, has its own particular constitution.[152] Thus if we are to speak meaningfully of a phenomenon's coming-into-appearance as distinct from its presence-to-hand, an event presents itself differently than the "given," the "fulfilled moment" differently than the "objective temporal series," the "personal situation" differently than the "physical field." [153] In each instance, "meaning" is present and hence also transcendence in immanence, although in uniquely different ways. The "historical," as well as the "natural," belongs to the *universum* of true being (that is, to the universe of constituted unities of meaning). However, we shall not inquire here into the mundane phenomenon of history, for which a certain degree of intersubjective understanding is in principle possible, but rather into the pure egological achievements that lie within transcendental subjectivity's coming-into-appearance in its self-projectings, achievements which are thereby preeminently eventful or historical. According to Husserl:

Every imaginable sense, every imaginable being, whether the latter is called immanent or transcendent, falls within the domain of transcendental subjectivity, as the subjectivity that constitutes sense and being. The attempt to conceive the universe of true being as something lying outside the universe of possible consciousness, possible knowledge, possible evidence, the two being

150. Cf. Fink, "L'Analyse intentionelle," pp. 70 ff.
151. Cf. Eugen Fink's essay "Zum Problem der ontologischen Erfahrung," in *Actas del primer congreso nacional de filosofia*, III (Mendoza, 1949), 733.
152. Cf. *CM*, § 41, pp. 83–85.
153. Cf. Paul Tillich's investigations of *logos* and *kairos* in *Kairos*, I, Zur *Geisteslage und Geisteswendung* (Darmstadt: Reichl, 1926), pp. 23 ff.

related to one another merely externally by a rigid law, is non-sensical.[154]

What in each case emerges as my own also has meaning. Thus egology necessarily stands alongside phenomenology, just as the fulfilled *kairos* stands alongside objective time. Here too the a priori, or the "logos of all conceivable being," unfolds itself, and only by including egology can we speak of a "universal concrete ontology." If transcendental phenomenology passes beyond the traditional eidetic regional ontologies by its inclusion of egology, it does so not in order to eliminate them, but in order to ground them. Only thus can transcendental phenomenology take on the name of a "concrete ontology" and present itself as the concrete logic of being. In this sense, constitution is not only "bestowing" in the sense of informing, but is also truly creative. The problem of creativity is bound up with the problem of the ego's achievements in bringing to light evidences. Here our use of language falters: we speak of a "productive creation," of an "active fulfilling," or of a thematically operating unconscious activity.[155] In all such cases it is primarily a question of an objectifying constitution. Despite these examples, we must continually keep in mind that we can only use analogies, and that we cannot truly speak of a "creating," "producing," "making," and so on. Transcendental subjectivity does nothing, for every active comportment and every action takes place in the world; they are mundane occurrences, and as such are constituted as a part of the world. What transcendental subjectivity "achieves" is to be understood analogically. This understanding also constitutes meaning. Constitutional investigation is present in the description of the universal structures of possible modes of consciousness, which are thereby preconstituted and intersubjectively accessible; and alongside the communicable experience of an object and also belonging to possible modes of intentional consciousness is the egological ("*existentiell*," "pragmatic")[156] concern-for-the-being-of-the-ego-itself

---

154. *CM*, § 41, p. 84.
155. Cf. *Die Krisis*, § 73 (not in Carr trans.); cf. *FTL*, pp. 180, 34.
156. Cf. the section concerning "Pragma ou corrélat intentionel de l'agir" in Paul Ricoeur's *Le Volontaire et l'involuntaire* (Paris: Aubier, 1963), pp. 195 ff.; English translation by E. V. Koҥák, "The 'Pragma' or Intentional Correlate of Acting," in *Freedom and Nature: The Voluntary and the Involuntary* (Evanston, Ill.: Northwestern University Press, 1966), pp. 209 ff.

which is disclosed in every witnessing and is to be made into the ego's authentic and appropriate possibility. Within the nonobjectively polarized enactments of anxiety and care there is constituted a being of a unique sort; namely, a unity of meaning that cannot be apprehended intersubjectively, and to whose very meaning belongs a witnessing to itself in uniqueness and singularity, in situation, and in *kairos*. [157]

3. Phenomenological constitution is surely equivalent to intentional evidence. Through the ages, the "intended" has been reduced to the pure *cogitatum* on the one hand, and on the other hand "pure intending" has been reduced to the *cogito*. If we are then to speak of being and nonbeing, such expressions do not relate to "things-in-themselves," but to constituted meanings. The "object" displayed or intended in determinate acts then possesses the evident character of an existent or nonexistent object, of something that has explicit being or has a canceled or suspended being. Thus intentionalities are continually present "which, as acts and correlates of 'reason,' essentially producible by the transcendental ego, pertain (in exclusive disjunction) to all objective senses." [158] We must speak of reason where meaning is present. We can thereby resolve the question of whether or not meaning is present only if meaning is something accessible intersubjectively (and therefore objective and general). It is clear that "existence," in the sense that refers to a single being within a situation for whom its being is an issue in the fulfilled moment of decision, is intersubjectively comprehensible and thus represents an "objective meaning." However, this implies nothing as to whether the existing itself, as a "critical" or "decisive" giving evidence for, can be subsequently reenacted. Enactment and reenactment, the event that arises from itself and reflection on what thus eventfully transpired, have different meanings.

"Existence" and "transcendental ego" are hence continually referred to inauthentically and understood when only a general observation is employed. Just as with the achievement of free "constitution," only the enactment of "existing" can make comprehensible what "existence" and "transcendental ego" are. Meaning also lies in the abruptly eventful, unforeseeable, and nonre-

157. The ego is to be taken, then, as the identical pole of experiences. Cf. *CM*, § 31, p. 65.
158. *CM*, § 23, p. 57.

peatable (without its very nature being transformed) self-testifying, without making the phenomenon-being of the phenomenon something objective and intersubjective. The eventful coming-into-appearance of evidence in the fulfilled moment, with its specific character of eventful-being, must, in principle, elude the universal observer. Yet it does not fall outside the framework of the flowing, achieving life of consciousness that gives itself only through evidences. The evidence for determinate, nonobjectively polarized enactments consists in the fact that within this life of consciousness the concern is not for any being [*Seiendes*], but for the being of the achieving ego itself. And this understanding sets forth a unique constitution of meaning.

We must adhere to the following:

> The ego constitutes himself for himself in, so to speak, the unity of a "history." We said that the constitution of the ego contains all the constitutions of all the objectivities existing for him, whether these be immanent or transcendent, ideal or real. It should now be added that the *constitutive systems* (systems actualizable by the Ego), by virtue of which such and such objects and categories of objects exist for him, are themselves possible only within the frame of a genesis in conformity with laws.[159]

This is the authentic history, a history of spirit who thinks beforehand [*vor-denkt*] thoughts of being ("existentials," "categories"). The ego constitutes itself as nonderivative in the constitution of objective, intersubjective, and monadically shared unities of meaning that are intentional evidences. The historical event *katexochen*, the truly ontological achievement, is the achievement of the transcendental ego in constituting mundane entities.[160] The meaning of event includes the fact that *what* it brings and signifies can be communicated, but that what makes up the eventful coming-into-appearance can only be experienced in its own unique instance. We speak of being and of nonbeing and their modal variations only on the basis of achieving intentions:[161] is this also the case for eventful-being? This would mean that here too an achievement of the transcendental ego is present, though an achievement that is, in accordance with its very meaning, bound up with crisis and *kairos*, i.e., with witness-

159. *Ibid.*, pp. 75–76.
160. Cf. Fink, "Zum Problem der ontologischen Erfahrung," p. 739.
161. *CM*, § 23, p. 56.

ing and not with mere observation. To this extent, pure phenom-enological philosophy will be preceded by a " 'solipsistically' re-duced 'egology,' " which alone does not take up the phenomenon just as a present appearance, but as an appearance in its coming-into-appearance.[162] In short, it renders the phenomenon accessible as project, since it is this that "gives" the ego as it understands itself. The emergence of meaning is thereby what is authentically historical. Mundane history is solely concerned with constituted occurrences that are relevant from different points of view; as the "history of philosophy" it can also concern itself with the ordering, subsequent reenacting and understanding of the consti-tution of ontological meanings, i.e., with the repristination of "ontological experience."[163]

As philosophical and historical writing, the history of philos-ophy, if it is to be meaningful, reenacts thoughts concerning be-ing which the transcendental ego has freely projected. Such thoughts "are" only in authentic reenactment, in which they are constituted as phenomena.[164] Egology is nothing other than the solipsistic evidence gained in the co-knowing of nonderivative intentions. But the having-in-evidence of the noematic pole of an intentional act is still only the occasion for a having-in-evidence of the meaning of the ego itself. The free projecting of noemati-cally polarized noeses constitutes the ego's innermost possibility of being, so that within such self-witnessing the ego comes to appear as what it is. If the ego forms itself into a unity of mean-ing within the unity of a history that is constituted by it, a history for the transcendental ego is possible only on the basis of the constitution of an inner unity within the consciousness of time. However, this history is neutral with respect to whether or not what is constituted in eventful achievement is intersubjectively accessible. History in the authentic sense of "event" is the emer-gence of intentionalities or constitutions in general. The primor-dial phenomenon is the coming-into-appearance of evidence, whereby what can be called mundane history in its specific form can first begin.

162. Cf. Barth, "Philosophie der Existenz," p. 31.
163. Compare in this regard B. Croce's position in his theory concern-ing the writing of history: *Teoria e storia della storiografia* (Bari: Laterza, 1917); English translation by Douglas Ainslie, *Theory and History of Historiography* (London: Harrap, 1921).
164. Cf. Fink, "Zum Problem der ontologischen Erfahrung," p. 738.

This means that from the very start the transcendental ego constitutes itself as "historical" with uniquely different intentions through the nontransitive constitution of immanent time-consciousness. What is eventful about this constituting achievement of the ego lies in the fact that, as constituting, this ego is not dependent on something previously given, and it thus preserves the character of something original. This holds precisely for the authentic sense of the "historical" in general, so that the truly eventful as such can never be intersubjectively constituted. The reflection of a "universal spectator," for whom my innermost being is inaccessible, transforms the eventful into something pregiven, general, and objectively accessible, into a "historical object" which he seeks to approach with traditional objective methods. The universal spectator thereby effects the mundanization and denaturing of the historical. To the extent that it pursues the analysis of objective intentionality and constitution, phenomenology is oriented toward the "appearance" as an objective unity of meaning. It thereby discloses the constitution of the regional eidetic sciences and the empirical sciences. Egology, which emerges prephenomenologically as the first philosophical possibility, deals with the transcendental ego that is an appearance only in the sense of a coming-into-appearance, and hence insofar as it stands in the truth. This is the case in disclosing thoughts concerning being [*Seinsgedanken*], in the evidence of the phenomenon-being of the phenomenon, and in a co-knowing that runs along with temporalization.

Consciousness and Historicity as Origin

In speaking of phenomenology and egology, we encounter a fundamental difference between the "premundane" and the "mundane." We can only treat constitution analogically using mundane terminology. Constitution sets forth a relation between the extramundane constituting ego and the "world," where the "world" and the intended *cogitatum* (traditionally called the "transcendent") also include what is noetically actual. "Being," "nonbeing," "worldly being," "eventful being": all these meanings have a specific sense. If the nonobjective transcendental ego cannot be characterized in terms of being, nonbeing, or

worldly being, and if on the contrary these three are only moments of meaning constituted by the transcendental ego, then
this ego itself can only be defined by the moment of constitution,
a moment when it is not a question of some other being (itself
dependent on the ego's determination of meaning), but of the
ego itself, which is the evidence belonging to thinking, the life
of consciousness, the stream of experience in its entirety. Constitution designates achievement in the sense of the advent of
meaning within a unity of meaning.[165] To put it another way,
constitution is another name for intentionality and for the relation to a *cogitatum* that can be either something objectively
given or the nonobjective concern for the ego itself. The evidence
grasped in theoretical observation and in practical behavior
manifests constituting achievements of the ego; in this having of
evidence we find no mundane methodological construing of evidence, no demiurgic fabrication, no mystical creation *ex nihilo*.
The categories of receptivity and spontaneity do not extend this
far.[166] As premundane, constitution is not otherworldly.[167] The
problem of constitution only indicates the fact that it is possible
to analyze and describe a series of phenomena or individual
noemata and lead them back to corresponding *noeses* in accordance with their very possibility and their eidetically universal
form.[168] Constitution is then only the unfolding of the transcendental ego. Yet, even though the ego is neither passive nor active
in the mundane sense, it does permit itself to be characterized
as creative, if by this we understand either that the ego allows
meaning to be viewed noetically-noematically, or that the ego
attests to the presence of meaning. However, both the letting
something be viewed and the attesting have the basic sense of
revealing. For if "being" and its modal variations are determinations of meaning belonging to the transcendental ego, then there
"is" simply nothing before the ego's constituting activity and its
evidences. It is the transcendental ego that presents origins. And
if the origin is what cannot be derived from something else, then
the original achievement of the ego is consciousness. The relation
of the ego to what is intended and to what can be seized as

165. Cf. here the works of Charles Serrus, in particular "L'Oeuvre
philosophique d'Edmund Husserl," *Etudes philosophiques*, II (1930), 127.
166. Cf. Berger, The "*Cogito*," p. 103.
167. Fink, "Was will die Phänomenologie Edmund Husserls?," p. 30.
168. *Ideas* I, pp. 386–87.

cogitatum is a relation of a unique sort: it is a knowledge relation in the true sense.

This does not mean that this knowledge relation is the same as the mundane knowledge relation, or the laying hold of something that exists, where what is indeed adequately constituted lies before the "disinterested observer." The knowledge relation is part of another form of evidence. Here we must return to the principle of immediate evidence, i.e., of the total absence of presuppositions, where everything is handed over to the standpoint that "gives" what is there.[169] Correspondingly, phenomenology and egology can easily recognize what nontheoretical and nonobjectifying experiences involve with respect to the meaningful and the original. We must recognize explicitly that the "position" of a feeling, a valuing, and the like can be submitted in its full particularity to intentional analysis. Thus it is self-evident that for this reason the moral, aesthetic, and emotional possess their own originality. They are grounded in regions that belong to them alone, regions that can be correlated with a special constitutive phenomenology.[170] When we speak of phenomenology here, we express the fact that the intentional objects of value-intentions, duty-intentions, and feeling-intentions are intersubjective in principle and are accessible to intersubjective intentional analysis.

History as a mundane phenomenon can be handled in the same way. History as an event in the authentic sense, i.e., as the temporalizing of what cannot be anticipated, repeated, or seized universally, and as the content of the fulfilled moment, uniquely occurring within its context and situation, can only be grasped egologically; that is, it can only be grasped within those evidences that uniquely belong to each instance. The autogenesis of the ego as such grounds the subsequent possibility of our speaking of the "ego" constituted as a "part of the world" (as "man," "rational animal," a "unique project of nature," or as a "defective" and inferior being), so that it can become the object of mundane history. History in the egological sense is the self-attesting of the transcendental ego within the emergence of intentions and evidences. Once again, the eventful coming to pass, *katexochen*, is the temporalizing of spirit.

169. *LI*, II, § 1, "Introduction," pp. 263 ff.
170. *Ideas* I, p. 390.

1. All "achievements" or "acts" that are different in terms of the meanings they intend are not of equal importance. Certain particular intentions can be absent without the intended object thereby disappearing completely. Of course, one intention that cannot be absent in intersubjective constitutions is the thesis of being [*Seinsthesis*], the primordial belief [*Urdoxa*]. Here "belief" should not be taken to mean a belief in something purely imaginary; it is rather a belief in being in the sense of the *natural* thesis concerning being. This primordial belief is also to be found where one would at first not expect to find it. This can be shown with the example of moral valuation.[171] Here the intended (*cogitatum*) is the originally moral, and the moral is truly understood when life is led in correspondence with it. The essence of "value" is not grasped through a theoretical gazing on something, but is truly given in a manner appropriate to our consciousness (and thus as phenomenal) only in the performance of an "advancing toward" and a "pursuing" of an end, or in accepting responsibility.[172] Naturally, what is intended by a value-intention can be at the same time an "object" of aesthetic evaluation, practical judgment, and so on. The real issue here, however, is this: moral valuation as such is constantly accompanied by a doxic thesis, for a task presented to the will with its accompanying components of stress and stimulation is essentially nothing other than a totality of acts which, not being actual, are to be realized. Thus, what appears as an "ought" constantly implies this thesis of being. In all acts of this sort a "polythetic" constitution is present.[173] Such acts are specified through the "aesthetic," "affective," or "moral" position because there is a particular intention of that nature. Yet they are never present without a doxic thesis or a belief in being. It is precisely here that the fundamental intuitive and theoretical character of phenomenology can be found. The question remains, however, whether the primordial belief and thesis concerning being that is in force for phenomenological intentional analysis and eidetic ontological description is also to be adopted in this sense for egology.

Doxa signifies that something is pregiven, that it is constituted as either real or ideal, and that as a result it is in principle accessible to intersubjective validation through subsequently re-

171. Berger, The *"Cogito,"* p. 80.
172. Cf. *Ideas* I, pp. 305–6.
173. Berger, The *"Cogito,"* p. 80.

enacted and corresponding intentions. Being [*Sein*] as consti-
tuted-being is accessible to fundamentally theoretical intentions,
and thus it is also open [*offenbar*], where this openness possesses
its own specific mode of demonstration. Opposed to being as
open and pregiven there undoubtedly is "standing-in-the-truth."
Here the phenomenologically primordial belief is not enacted,
and this belief accordingly reveals itself as a moment of meaning
belonging to a specifically phenomenological *ontological* constitution. In this case, it belongs to intersubjective, objectifying,
and eidetic intentions, and not to those that can be termed "egological" and which present true origins. Ego, *kairos*, and crisis
belong together because they all designate the event of constitution.

It is not necessary to devote particular attention to the theoretical (primordial doxic) aspect of the phenomenological attitude and its doxic thesis, since it is not the "phenomenon" of
phenomenology that we are investigating, but the phenomena
belonging to constitutive phenomenology. Of course, the objectivity of what is encountered in special intentions as "moral,"
"aesthetic," "sentimental," and so on, is oftentimes only potentially objective, yet the primordial belief is itself also implicit in
potentialities. Indeed, it must be present, for it alone guarantees that evidences "hold." Therefore, in whatever manner an
act constitutes its object, it constitutes it within a doxic attitude,
so that what gives itself in this way can be encountered without
always having to be actual. The doxic *cogito* is actually objectifying.[174] However, the autogenesis or self-constitution of the transcendental ego (transcendental subjectivity), which is eventful
temporalization and which results along *with* those constitutions
that are themselves objectively polarized and doxically objectified, is not distinguished from the constitutions accessible to
particular objective phenomenological intentional analyses by
the fact that it is *not* intentional (i.e., possesses *no* meaning),
but by the fact that for it this primordial *doxa*, this belief in a
being that can in principle be encountered, is absent. The essence of transcendental subjectivity is not objective, and as a
result it is not something pregiven and co-constituted by the
doxic thesis, but rather the constitution of being and beings

174. *Ideas* I, pp. 305–6.

[*Seiendem*] in thought. It may also be expressed thus: only if the doxic thesis that applies to all phenomenological constitutions does not hold for the autogenesis of transcendental subjectivity can we speak of a prephenomenological egology, and of the ego as not constituted in the sense of something objective. What is disclosed in constitution is one thing, and the constituting disclosure itself is something entirely different. Truth as the disclosedness of what has come to light is one thing, and the truth of what comes to light in constitution—the "standing-in-the-truth"—is something entirely different. This is the case where "true" designates the disclosedness of being, and where "being" is a moment of meaning belonging to constitution.

The following statement naturally holds true phenomenologically: the ego does not stand over and against a reality that is simply to be described and observed; entities are first constituted within the *cogito*'s life of intentional acts where the primordial *doxa* necessarily belongs to the constituting intentions, so that, from the point of view of the subject, what emerges as *doxa* (a belief in being) comes into appearance noematically, as existence.[175] This statement does not hold true with respect to egology. The self-constitution of consciousness that follows from the temporalizing of objective noematic doxic constitutions does not constitute this ego or consciousness as an entity, but as pure "concern for the ego itself." This indicates the primordiality and nonderivability that holds only for thought or for being that is conscious. A possible "bearer" of *cogitationes* is first "posited" in and through such *cogitationes*. The primordial *doxa* is not in force for the achievements of the transcendental ego, for what is at issue is this ego itself. It does not constitute itself in the manner in which all mundane constitutions take place; it constitutes itself as premundane. Constitution itself is premundane, and the autogenesis of the transcendental ego is the temporalizing of the premundane. Just as being belongs to what is mundanely constituted as phenomenon-being, so to the constituting itself there belongs self-eventfulness as the coming-into-appearance of the phenomenon. Viewed egologically, "phenomenon" is the same as "projecting," "attesting," and "achieving," that is, the streaming life of consciousness with *all* its evidences, including

175. *Ibid.*, p. 274.

those evidences belonging to its co-knowing. These are the phenomena which must be acknowledged as clues leading back to the functioning ego. According to Husserl:

> The *universe of subjective processes*, which are the "really inherent" consciousness-constituents of the transcendental ego, is a universe of compossibilities only in the universal *unity-form of the flux,* in which all particulars have their respective places as processes that flow within it. Accordingly even this most universal form, which belongs to all particular forms of concrete subjective processes (with the products that are flowingly constituted in the flux of such processes) is the form of a motivation, connecting all and governing within each single process in particular. We can call it furthermore a *formal regularity pertaining to a universal genesis,* which is such that past, present, and future, become unitarily constituted over and over again, in a certain noetic-noematic formal structure of flowing modes of givenness.[176]

The originally constituted time-consciousness that is not found beforehand makes objective temporal statements and objective history possible. The constituting time-grounding intentions of transcendental subjectivity (which themselves reveal this subjectivity as nonbeing, meaning-disclosing, and flowing) present "standing-in-the-truth" as evidence of the ego. From the viewpoint of what is constituted, this "standing-in-the-truth" designates something objective. The *egological* phenomenon that is designated is the projecting of the project. And, when taken as the theme of constitutive questioning back to origins, what is projected becomes the *phenomenological* phenomenon. Projecting thought, however, cannot be shared intersubjectively precisely because it is projecting. Thus the ego is essentially "historical" in achieving its constitutions, while the mundanely historical lies within the realm of what is constituted. Mundane thought is determined by transcendental consciousness.

Projecting thought is truly historical (that is, eventful) because as thought it is nonderivative. Its achievements cannot be anticipated, for this would contradict its very meaning, and it would already in each case have entered into appearance with the anticipation. Thus it is not pregiven. Accordingly, it can be said that in constituting and intending, and hence in the original achievements of the transcendental ego, what is attested to is

176. *CM,* § 37, p. 75.

that which is not already in being but ought to be. Therefore
what becomes manifest primordially in constitution is not being
[*Sein*] and the belief in being [*Seinsglaube*], but what ought to be
[*Seinsollen*]. The authentically actual (that which truly works to
some effect) are those *cogitationes* in the widest sense that do
not permit the ego to be seen as a constituted appearance but
present the phenomenon in its coming-into-appearance. Herein
lies the "ontological experience."

The positions of realism and idealism (in their traditional
forms) present meaningful answers to the question of the nature
of being, but are here left behind. Both positions remain at the
level of mundane argumentation, whereby "being" as such does
not become a problem, i.e., where being does not come into view
as a constitutive moment of meaning belonging to the intentional
egological life of consciousness. Only where this *is* the case, and
thus only where the constitutive questioning back to origins does
not stop short, does the transcendental ego emerge as not mundane. The achievements of this ego are evidences which, in their
appearance-being [*Erscheinungsein*] and in their coming-into-
appearance, can be phenomena and can therefore exhibit and
point to meaning in each case. The theory of constitution maintains only that it is possible to analyze and describe phenomena
of all sorts in their horizons and with respect to their structure
in infinitum.[177] Here too the absurd is seized in its evidence and
in terms of its meaning. The intentional objects of acts continually have the evident character of being or nonbeing (i.e.,
being that has been canceled or struck out). The turning of attention toward these constitutions means the enactment of intentions belonging to a higher level. What is first given is worldly
in the vulgar sense. The logical, the moral, the aesthetic, and the
traditional objects of metaphysics come next; then follow "objective space," "objective time," "nature" in its entirety, the
"world," and so on, and finally "animal being," "man," "soul,"
"body," "social community," "culture," and the like.[178] Mundane
history also belongs here. The authentically historical in the sense
described (i.e., as origin and eventful transpiring of what ought
to be) and as a phenomenon of a higher level is not met with
here. The nonderivability of spirit manifested in evidences shows

177. *Ideas* I, pp. 386–87.
178. *CM*, § 64, p. 154.

that these evident achievements, which are *cogitationes* in the widest sense, occur eventfully.[179] The eventful advent of evidence shows not only the nonderivability of the constituting ego, but also its self-determination as "thought" and consciousness. The *essence* of constitution is just what is achieved in the act of constituting, and constitution without recourse to something given is intuition. It is the evidence within the *kairos* itself. It can only be said of the intuitively evident that it "gives" itself originally.

2. Truly "original" self-giving means that, in intuitive evidences, something is intended and constituted that arises solely from the evidence itself. This is the case with the functioning ego in its achievements, where the ego is solely an issue for itself. Thus what is evident and manifest in intentions and constitutions is the historical event in the authentic sense, and the "essence" of the transcendental ego is historical achievement or unforeseeable constitution. Through constitution, an objectifying bestowal of meaning is achieved, and in constitution the transcendental ego is disclosed as preobjective. The flowing life of consciousness achieves its concept: it is consciousness *of* something. The sole actuality of the noetically-noematically polarized stream of consciousness is thereby realized: that consciousness as achiever is what it ought to be. The "ought to be" shows itself as the actually possible and therewith as the real [*Wirkliche*]. To this extent (analogically) we can speak of transcendental subjectivity's standing-in-the-truth.[180] This connection can be clarified by what follows.

Since transcendental phenomenology strikes out from a determinate given that serves as a clue for the constitutive questioning back to origins, the constructive achievements that are to be questioned regarding history are the achievements that pertain to occurrences as events. Nonderivability belongs to the meaning of the eventful, and to the meaning of what is nonobjectively constituted belongs the intentional relationship to that being which is in each case an issue for itself. In the authentic sense, therefore, the historically eventful occurrence is the manifestation of the intentionally constituted thinking of the ego, which, with its self-determination as constituting, displays

179. Cf. Litt, *Mensch und Welt*, pp. 168, 293, *et passim.*
180. Regarding "analogical speech" see Berger, *The "Cogito,"* p. 77.

the authentic "ought to be." Thus everything depends on the evidence belonging to the fulfilled moment, whose "fulfillment" consists of the disclosure or evidence of what ought to be. Hence the fulfilled moment is not to be thought of apart from standing-in-the-truth, that is, apart from the achievement of the conditions constituted by the ego itself. The kinds of evidences bound up with intentions, constitutions, and achievements all witness to projective thought. Where thought is not the ascertainment of what is given or the analysis of something already constituted, it is then itself project; it does not aim at beings but at what ought to be. Thought itself projects the conditions that determine it. If the meaning of the transcendental ego is to be "formative of meaning," then the *cogito* is never without its *cogitatum*. A *cogitatio* that is not intentionally directed to what is pregiven can only be termed projective when it permits a view of what ought to be or when it brings to the fore that which has the status of preeminence. The appearance of evidences cannot be anticipated, and thought cannot be taken away from others. The eventful is bound up with the fulfilled moment, and as a nonrational breaking in of spirit every act of understanding is an event in this sense. Every truly constitutive bestowal of meaning, such as is present in the understanding of affairs, of others, and of self, is, as an achievement of spirit and thought or of the *ego cogito cogitatum*, historical and nonderivative. Spirit, thought, and so on, however, always have the form of consciousness.

In each case evidences pertain to a determinate ego whose self-possession is static, but lived dynamically within the flow of evidences. Accordingly, this ego is not the theme of mundane descriptive phenomenology, for it has to do with the phenomenon as a constituted unity of meaning. "Egology" belongs to transcendental subjectivity, for each breakthrough of spirit (that can be subsequently ascertained as having occurred "at a given moment," "in a particular situation," or "within a specific context") is not an intersubjective event, but only an egologically witnessed phenomenon. This means that spirit is at work when and where it wills; spirit is free, and in its modes consciousness is also free.

Traditionally, phenomenology is the intentional analysis of objectively constituted spirit, involving in every case, thanks to the primordial *doxa*, the abiding meaning of "what is" that is always intended as "existent." Egology, however, *sit venia verbo*, would be the phenomenology of the constituting spirit, and hence of the transcendental ego in a coming-into-appearance that cannot be anticipated. Understanding and evidence are therefore the authentically historical events that emerge with intentions. It is thus not surprising that, when the meaning-unity "affair" is taken as a point of departure for constitutive regressive questionings, constituting achievements are pointed up other than those displayed by regress from such meaning-unities as "history," "event," and the like, where no preconstituted objectivity is in question. This means that ontological experience is projective and that ontic experience lays hold of something. In both cases meaning is involved. Of course something is "meant" when we speak of "subjectivity," "constitution," "intentionality," "what ought to be," "crisis," and so on. It is not correct to say that what cannot be demonstrated as a phenomenon in the sense of an objective appearance is simply nothing. Just as the phenomenon-being of the phenomenon is not a phenomenon in the objective sense, or just as intentionality itself does not present such an appearance (without thereby being simply "nothing"), so also is it the case with respect to subjectivity or the transcendental ego. In these cases one can say that they present a theme for a thetically speculative delineation.[181] This makes it clear that there is a difference between the domains of what is ontically constituted and ontological constitution,[182] between knowledge and the co-knowing of temporalization.

At first it appears certain that not only "objects" in the vulgar sense but "everything" that "gives" itself as objectively accessible is constituted, and that we can in this way designate what, generally speaking, is the mundane.[183] This includes man as a thinking being, as a psychophysical unity, as a soul, as a cultural and communal being, and so on.[184] The transcendental ego also constitutes itself in its enactments, not as an objectively existent being, but as manifest within the continuously streaming flow of evidences that is here conscious of itself. This means that "the ego is himself *existent for himself* in continuous evidence; thus, in himself, he is *continuously constituting himself as existing.*
. . . The ego grasps himself not only as a flowing life but also as

---

181. Cf. Fink, "L'Analyse intentionelle," p. 70 and throughout.
182. It is above all Eugen Fink who emphasizes this distinction; see "Phenomenological Philosophy of Husserl," pp. 130–31.
183. *Ideas* I, pp. 202 ff., 388–89, 244–45, 264, 265–66.
184. *Ibid.*, p. 389.

I, who live this and that subjective process, who live through this and that *cogito, as the same I*" [185] In each case we speak of the constitution of a meaning that need not be "objective." Something objectively constituted can be disclosed, but the being-disclosed itself is not in turn disclosed as something objective—and yet it is not nothing. The question concerning the meaning of being is therefore dependent on the event of the bestowal of meaning, on thetic determination, on thinking the original thoughts of being, on consciousness within the various modes of its unfolding, or on whatever else this is to be named. Viewed in this way, "nothingness" and the fact of "history" are also constituted, and here constituted does not mean "categorially formed" in the critical sense, or "categorially construed" in the Neo-Kantian sense, but "determined in terms of its meaning."

Together with the question of the meaning of history, there also lies before us the corresponding task of disclosing that meaning which the phenomenon at issue contains by implication. Thus the question "what is the meaning of history?" parallels the question "what does it mean to have a body?" or "what does the being of the alter ego signify?" [186] In brief: what "nongiven" elements must be posited in order that "X" may have this or that meaning? Where it is a question of the eventful as such, where the event is the clue for a corresponding regressive questioning (and where the issue does not concern this or that "event" as a mundane occurrence), what is to be found out by the questioning must be the constituting itself and not what is constituted. Here there is an intention of a higher order. We can only make something of the intention when something is achieved in it that belongs to its necessary conditions. Here recourse to what is given is broken off, for what is achieved must be what stands in question (and what appears here as "posited"). Therefore, where the meaning of the eventful or of coming-into-appearance is an issue, it is not a matter of *what* appears in this or that particular case, nor is it a matter of *what* transpires. What is intended is the meaning of event itself, of occurrence, of self-witnessing, and here only egological experience in the sense of projecting what is intended is possible. [187] A subsequent reflection

185. *CM*, § 31, p. 66.
186. Cf. Berger, *The "Cogito,"* p. 85.
187. Cf. Fink, "Zum Problem der ontologischen Erfahrung," p. 739.

already sets forth an intention that is different from that of the projective enactment itself. Accordingly, the authetically historical is not "man," "culture," "society," or "class," for in each case something mundane and constituted is presented. The authentically historical is the transcendental ego, or transcendental subjectivity as such, the constituting subjectivity that makes such inquiry and speech possible. This also includes our speaking of a "creative intuition." [188]

That being whose meaning includes nonderivability, the *nulla re indiget ad existendum,* absoluteness, and "having-its-own-self-as-an-issue" is spirit, which comes to light in intuitions and evidences, and shows itself in co-knowing (as *conscientia*). It temporalizes itself, and for this reason its meaning is "achievement," "nonobjectivity," "historicity." The question of history and historicity must also follow on the basis of egology and not on a mundane descriptive phenomenology that investigates the domain of what is intersubjectively constituted. As a result, we cannot set up a doctrine of essence for our inquiry. The emergence of evidences in determinate constitutions and intentions (which are not of interest to us here with their objective content) also makes up the self-disclosure of transcendental subjectivity. Concrete and mundane historical events are unimportant in terms of their particular meaningfulness. They draw their meaning from the events of spirit, reason, and consciousness.

Knowledge and Appearance as Event

Any individual "piece" of the world has implications of meaning that go beyond what is actually given. In precisely this way the mundane being of this piece of the world, its phenomenality and its objectivity, reach beyond its immediate content. This does not prevent what is intended from being itself an accessible meaning-content. It is accessible to the ego: "universal and eidetic self-explication signifies mastery of all the conceivable constitutive possibilities 'innate' in the ego and in a transcendental intersubjectivity." [189] Among these intersubjective possibilities are communicable interpretations of meaning—of

188. Cf. Berger, *The "Cogito,"* in which he returns to this problem in great detail (pp. 85 ff.).
189. *CM,* § 64, pp. 153 ff.

"existence," "event," and so on. Now what is intended by these comprehensible concepts has a unique status. An intending is present here, in the unique sense of an intending of that which achieves conceptual understanding in the intending itself. We note correctly that to "intend" an intention, to "speak" about language, or to "understand" a concept in each case presents the "event" that is meant by the intending, speaking, comprehending, or, in short, by the "thinking." [190] The constitution of transcendental subjectivity designates the event *katexochen* because here a "coming-to-the-world" is present. If every object, every piece of the world, has, qua intentional object, its horizon that refers to other constituted objects,[191] then such a horizon must be absent from the transcendental ego which, in accordance with its meaning, is an "origin." According to its very meaning the transcendental ego is not primarily *cogitatum*, but *cogitatio*, even though it can investigate itself as *cogitatum* in all investigations where it encounters itself within the reflective attitude. Thinking about the transcendental ego is, then, not an original thinking when this ego is itself thought of as something constituted. From this it follows that only the projecting itself can justifiably be spoken of as the "essence" of transcendental subjectivity. There can be no basis or aid for foreseeing such an achievement, and precisely herein lies the sense of the egological phenomenological meaning of "letting be seen," of "intuiting," and of "showing." This must constantly arise from the "affairs themselves." As constituted, the "affair" is nothing apart from the intentional achievements in which the nonobjective *katexochen* (transcendental subjectivity) reveals itself. Here it is certain that by the eventfully historical we mean an achievement of the ego, and in this respect it is not to be questioned that on the one hand the coming-into-appearance of a constituted object can be intersubjectively accessible (and thus phenomenon qua appearance), and on the other hand the projecting itself can be called a phenomenon only in its coming-into-appearance. The being of the phenomenon is something different from the phenomenon itself.

The self-initiated advent of phenomena in general is purely egological and transcendental. Whether an intending, intuiting, imagining, understanding, conceptualizing, or knowing is present

190. Cf. Litt, *Mensch und Welt*, pp. 293 ff.
191. *CM*, § 19, pp. 44 f.

is in each case bound up with the achievement of the subjectivity in question, and, in general, can be grasped intersubjectively and phenomenologically only *post eventum*. An egological phenomenological example can clarify this. We speak of "others" and associate a specific meaning with this term. The meaning of the "entirely other" is its subjectivity, and subjectivity is precisely that element whose authentic being cannot be apprehended reflectively.[192] The subjectivity of the other cannot actually be given. Hence the meaning of the "other" is such that I cannot reach the other in the authentic sense of his being the origin of his own being. I can grasp the other as "man," as "soul," as a psychophysical being, or as the center of constitutive acts, but I cannot grasp him in his subjectivity. What he truly is is not manifest and disclosed as something existent, but is something that manifests itself and temporalizes itself as "historical." The being of an existent can be grasped if it is totally encompassed by what is revealed and constituted. It cannot be won insofar as it is origin, achievement, or subjectivity, or insofar as it reveals itself only within the function of what these analogical concepts designate, wherein it projects the presuppositions for such designations. The meaning of subjectivity can be specified and treated intersubjectively, but nothing is thereby said concerning subjectivity *in* its coming-into-appearance. To place the "subjectivity" or the "existence" of "others" before oneself is to be this subjectivity oneself.[193] This is not possible. The meaning of subjectivity as achieving can come to light only in achieving what makes up the concept of subjectivity, i.e., in taking subjectivity in hand. We must therefore distinguish the truth of an assertion about something that is pregiven from the achieving of conditions that are definitive for "standing-in-the-truth."

1. Thus subjectivity is a being of a unique sort. It *is* historically. Husserl spoke of the paradox of human subjectivity, "being subject for the world and at the same time being an object in the world." [194] After the enactment of the phenomenologi-

192. *Ibid.*, § 60, pp. 139–41.
193. Cf. Bergson's statements in *Zeit und Freiheit* (Meisenheim, 1949), pp. 153–57; cf. English translation by R. L. Pogson, *Time and Free Will* (New York: Macmillan, 1959).
194. *Crisis*, § 53, pp. 178 ff.

cal reduction, "subject-being" cannot mean "psychological subject," for everything mundane has been bracketed, including all
characteristics such as "human being," "being with a soul," and
so forth. Nor does "subject-being" designate a process in man's
soul; it has the meaning rather of viewing the world, the "objective," in its entirety within a pure "correlative attitude" as the
pole of constitutive achievements so that it becomes something
uniquely "subjective." [195] To the mundane as a noematic pole of
meanings or as a correlative transcendental phenomenon belongs the manifold of intentions and subjective acts in which the
mundane is constituted. These can be brought into view by a
transcendental reflection, becoming thus themselves intended
and questioned as to their essential nature, only when, qua subjective modes of givenness, they become points of departure for
constitutive questionings back to origins. The constitutively functioning "subjective modes of givenness" themselves become
themes for essential investigations. Just as what had previously
been named "object" within the naïve attitude now becomes a
particular (constituted) subjective moment, so now, speaking
analogically, the constituting subjective modes of givenness become the "objective-subjective" that is to be traced back to something subjective at a higher level. "Within the epochē a universal
concept of the subjective encompasses everything: ego-pole and
universe of ego-poles, multiplicities of appearance or object-
poles and the universe of object-poles." [196]
    Man is not only a subject for the world in the psychological
sense, but as a psychological being he is himself constituted in
a specific sense, and is thus an object in the world. As such, man
is a phenomenon in the usual sense, and as such a phenomenon
he also serves as a clue for reflection and constitutive questioning that draws this world-possessing ego-pole into view as something constituted, and hence as something "objective-subjective."
However, we can justifiably ask whether "transcendental subjects, i.e., those *functioning* in the constitution of the world," are
actually "human beings." If our talk of subjectivity is to be truly
meaningful, then subjectivity itself must have a constituted
meaning. It, then, is a "phenomenon," and each ego "is considered purely as the ego-pole of his acts, habitualities, and

195. *Ibid.*, pp. 182, 179.
196. *Ibid.*, p. 179.

capacities."[197] The radical questioning back to origins, beginning from no matter what clue, does not lead back ultimately to one ego among many, but in each case to an individual and primordial ego and its achievements, a constituting ego to which the intending of "others," the "thou," and the "intersubjective community of monads" can belong. The final ego, therefore, is the ego as ego-pole of all transcendental life, the primordial ego, or the ego of the epochē.[198] It can be said with reference to transcendental subjectivity that what serves as the condition for its essential determination at the same time belongs to what is to be determined.[199] That is, the ego constitutes itself as historical: it is transcendental subjectivity.

Egology has to do with this constituting subjectivity, whose very meaning is that of its functioning. Subjectivity constitutes itself in evidences as functioning, and this makes up its autogenesis. The nonderivability of the primordial constituting ego signifies that it is what its meaning expresses, not as a preconstituted given, but within the constituting enactment itself, so that it posits or achieves that which makes up its meaning. The fact that in its original constituting life this ego at the same time projects an original sphere of objects which is thereby also "primordial,"[200] and which, as an achievement, is an eventful "appearance" of the intentional ego that announces itself with "self-consciousness," the "perception of what is other," and the "apprehension of the thou," is here of lesser interest to us. Phenomenology can subject this entire object-sphere to an eidetic ontological description that will always culminate in intentional analyses. Egology treats this ego in its phenomenon-being, i.e., in the projection of origins. The origin, however, is thought as achieving: it is consciousness in all its modes. What is meant here is held fast by the terms "intuition" and "evidence." For egology, the problem of origins is bound up with the problem of knowledge. Here it is not a question of the emergence of phenomena within the surveying glance of a universal observer who fastens on what is preconstituted.[201] There is no such mere mundane historical course for egology. The eventful coming-into-ap-

197. *Ibid.*, p. 183.
198. *Ibid.*, p. 184.
199. Cf. *CM*, § 38, pp. 78–79.
200. Cf. *Crisis*, p. 183.
201. Cf. Barth, "Philosophie der Existenz," p. 32.

pearance of something not yet pregiven lies in the fact that something is projected that is subsequently accessible to the intersubjective view as its meaning and concept. As "phenomenon," the subjectivity of the ego signifies "event," "project," "achievement," or the becoming evident of an interpretation anticipated in and through projects. The achievement that posits itself for what it is (i.e., as unforeseeable) through its functioning is consciousness, co-knowledge, thought. Where it is a question of the primordial and original ego, the essence of the transcendental ego is to be "self-projective."

The creative intuition of which phenomenology speaks [202] designates a presentification of a phenomenon projected in constitution (and not pregiven in intuitive evidence) that could also be a phenomenon of co-knowledge. "Phenomenon" here designates an eventful-being in a particular sense: the coming-to-presence of constitution in its constituting. A constitution of meaning is also present here insofar as the ego, in its functioning as ego-pole for transcendental achievements, projects itself on the occasion of primordial constitutions in intentions, protentions, retentions, and so on.[203] In egology, "phenomenon" signifies the constitution that is itself "appearance as event," or "being in time." Naturally, the achievement that posits conditions (and which is to this extent "anticipatory") and that is analogically termed "event" cannot be the "entrance of the projected future into a present appearance," [204] since it is constitutive of temporality. The eventful signifies the meaning of an act. This implies that we are not concerned with the abrupt emergence of something pregiven on some imaginary plane that awaits discovery and which as such is already open to some future experience. We are concerned with constitution and everything that it achieves, and it achieves not only the formation of the objective meaning belonging to the noematic constitution of objects in the broadest sense, but also the constitution of objective time with its past, present, and future.

The ego signifies the nonreal, nonactual, nonanonymous, and ideal premundane pole of constitutive performances. The ego is not the "bearer" of natural and previously sketched out processes

202. Cf. Berger, The "Cogito," p. 79.
203. Crisis, p. 160.
204. Barth, "Philosophie der Existenz," p. 32.

in the realm of phenomenal occurrences, but at most signifies "being in time" itself, if we completely exclude from this the sense of "object-being," a sense which, as something constituted, cannot stand as an origin. It is possible to designate objects as temporal only because constituting consciousness temporalizes itself. Beings "are" in time only insofar as this self-temporalizing consciousness also permits the determination of being to arise from itself. To speak of "being in time," then, is possible only with reference to the functioning ego. This "being in time" is not an existent object. As nonderivative, what is at issue for it is not a previously constituted being, but its own being. The ego does not project itself on what is already given, but is actively intentional, and from this there emerges an intramundane givenness. The ego discloses itself through its achievements as premundane. This disclosure itself, as self-constituted, is not to be seized with mundane categories of being. The being of transcendental subjectivity must therefore be combined with the character of the nonderivative. Constitution is present in the form of the creative intuitions of the intentional life of consciousness, and these do not imply what already "is," but what ought to be! Accordingly, "event" refers not to this or that event, but to what is specifically self-achieving and nonderivative, and this is thought in the form of meaning-bestowing intentionality, which does not fabricate or produce the world, but gives the world as phenomenon. Everything that is constituted in a worldly mode, everything that can be encountered as noematic pole, receives the meaning of being something existent, and constitution itself "is" the "ought to be." Thus the content of egology is the being of the ego itself as the "ought to be." What the "ought to be" is for an ego nonderivative in its functioning and, as nonderivative, necessarily also "thinking," is easily stated: it must be a projective thinking in the sense of projecting the thought of being [*Seinsgedanken*] itself, and therefore it is a transcendental consciousness. The creative intuition is not a personal certainty regarding what has been, but the evidence for what is not pregiven and "ought to be." *What* it is that is not pregiven and constituted in thought thereby proves itself to be something of preeminence [*das Vorzügliche*]. Thus the constitution of the transcendental ego documents what ought to be. History in the mundane sense reports the event of the coming-into-appearance

of phenomena (phenomena which manifest the actually possible) from the point of view of what is constituted.

2. For transcendental phenomenology, "constituting," "intending," "self-attesting," "becoming manifest," "caring and concerned preoccupation with" all pose epistemological problems.
Where both "being" and "nonbeing" are included as moments of
meaning, we cannot inquire into the being of the constituting
that constitutes *every* meaning. Its meaning lies in the liberating
disclosure of what is at issue for it. However, thought is concerned with what is evident, and this can serve as the clue for
intentional analytic inquiry into origins and for the revealing of
self-understanding. We also encounter the "circle of understanding" in speaking of creative intuition in relation to the constituting achievements of transcendental subjectivity, though here it
is transferred to what is manifestly evident as such, and is to be
taken as documentation of the actually possible in the authentic
sense. What holds for Dilthey's hermeneutic also holds true in
general: the full concretion of the "inner" experiential relationships accessible to reflection can only be grasped through the
manner in which they have expressed themselves in objectifications. Psychological reflection and historical observation are
bound to each other. The objectifications must be referred back
to the "inner" reality that is expressed in them, and this "inner"
reality is comprehensible only by the way in which it expresses
itself and by the particular "procedural mode that runs through
the expression." The necessary circularity of understanding has
its basis in this reciprocity.[205] Of course, the transcendental ego
is not to be understood in our context as an "objective idealism." [206]

We can now formulate our thoughts more concisely. The
phenomenon-being of transcendental subjectivity as coming-into-
appearance is a mode of knowledge or thought insofar as the
ego is what it "is" only in knowledge and thought. Therefore
every "understanding" and every "intuition" naturally belongs

205. Cf. L. Landgrebe, *Philosophie der Gegenwart* (Bonn: Athenäum-
Verlag, 1952), p. 106.
206. In the sense, perhaps, of Rothacker's investigations in *Logik
und Systematik der Geisteswissenschaften* (Munich and Berlin: Oldenbourg, 1927), pp. 52 ff.

to knowledge. With regard to the actual and nonderivative achievement of subjectivity, every manifestation in the projection of something not pregiven is not tied down to beings. A mundane ought (a "duty," etc.) is self-evidently a constituted part of the world. The authentic "ought to be" cannot be pregiven, but is visible solely in the meaning-constituting project that has its own confirmational structure. What is thus projected is only *post eventum* accessible to intentional analysis,[207] an analysis which, using the clue provided by a mundane ought, seeks the correlative achievements of consciousness. Here also the primordial is the self-projecting transcendental that makes itself known in achieving the *conditions* for the subsequent apprehension of being, and not in the apprehension of being itself. For this reason our task does not end with directing the reflective glance toward the transcendental ego, but must go on to view the present achieving of transcendental subjectivity itself. Egologically (and hence with reference to the achieving of presuppositions) no objective truths become visible; rather, something objective becomes constituted through the achieving of presuppositions as standing-in-the-truth, which then becomes a pregivenness for an apprehending consciousness. Transcendental subjectivity constitutes itself in projectively bringing something to the fore, for the epistemological character lies in this "drawing to the fore," and nonderivability lies in projecting. Both characteristics belong to the enactments of thought and its differing grades of consciousness. Finally, transcendental subjectivity constitutes knowledge *as* decision, and allows neither knowledge to rest on decision nor decision to rest on knowledge. Projective thought decides beforehand what "is." Transcendental subjectivity itself is not thereby included within this "is" that is constituted in the thinking of being [*Seinsdenken*] as a domain of truth lying before the objectifying view and intersubjectively accessible. As knowing constitution, the creative intuition that makes its appearance in the achieving of presuppositions (because it is not tied to pregiven beings) is continually at work, and in functioning as knowing it is a constitution manifesting what ought to be. Just as there is no such thing as an empty intention, so also there is no such thing as empty thought. To

---

207. Concerning *logificatio post eventum* see T. Lessing, *Geschichte als Sinngebung des Sinnlosen* (Munich: Beck, 1921), §§ 27–29, pp. 46 ff.

speak of achievements with reference to transcendental subjectivity without positing correlative *cogitata* is an absurdity. Correspondingly, the eventful emergence of what is "given" to the naïve realistic viewpoint takes place within the evidences of transcendental subjectivity precisely in and through its functioning transcendentally. Thought is the thought of origins, and to this extent the phenomenon here is present in its phenomenality.

If phenomenology is to be concerned with the "affairs themselves" so that they reveal themselves as what they truly are, then in effect we have said that ultimately we cannot turn to what is mundane, for mundane objects do not show themselves for what they truly are: constituted objects. They not only refer to other objects by means of various implications of meaning, but in their evident presence they are bound up with corresponding achievements of the life of consciousness, without themselves disclosing this connectedness. This means that the "affair itself" is never simply an "affair" but is constantly related to consciousness. Stated differently, it is a phenomenon in the sense of a mundanely constituted unity of meaning. If it belongs to the meaning of phenomenology to display the affair as it presents itself and within the limits in which it presents itself, then for *this* phenomenology one can simply remain alongside the constituted object, for this phenomenology describes the "object" and investigates eidetic regional ontologies and the individual sciences. The affair-being, however, is not seen by this phenomenology, and is therefore not a self-evident fact that shows itself as such. What we have here is a problem of validity.[208] Yet problems of validity are such only for consciousness; and whoever inquires into the affairs themselves must also inquire into the essence of consciousness. Now if phenomenology's concealed meaning is to hold as valid only what shows itself as it is,[209] then, paradoxically enough, the true "affair" is *transcendental subjectivity*. Only transcendental subjectivity is not bound to anything subsistent that appears within determinate horizons and with determinate implications that always refer to other beings and, accordingly, to a being within immanence. The corresponding achievements of transcendental subjectivity are not con-

208. Cf. *Paris Lectures*, pp. 6 ff.
209. See Heidegger's analysis of "logos" and "phenomenon" in *Being and Time*, pp. 49–50. See also the concept of "genesis" in *CM*, § 37, pp. 75–77.

cerned with something transcendent within immanence, but with this immanence itself. Such achievements, when they can be seized, are seized in co-knowledge.

The "affair" that shows itself as it is in a genuine sense and that achieves what it is, is transcendental subjectivity as constitution and thus as the phenomenon that is an event. This means that a thinking that lives in evidences is one that is not primarily situated on the plane of theoretical universal observation, but on the plane of positings. Insofar as a thinking that is not dependent on the world projects itself, what is at issue for it in its constituting is thought and consciousness itself. It is the authentic and self-demonstrating "affair"—it can only be understood in terms of itself [aus sich heraus]. This, however, is precisely what is meant by standing-in-the-truth, by the achieving fulfillment of conditions for something. Knowledge of affairs in the mundane realm requires the thesis of being. That which is truly self-demonstrating, however, is alone the autogenesis of transcendental subjectivity in its constituting. The being-relatedness [Seinsbezogenheit] of thought that lies before every naïve attitude is here an ought-relatedness. The evidences of the transcendental ego that temporalizes itself in its achievements give proof of the "fulfilled moment" that, precisely because of projects, can be designated as kairos. Here phenomena are eventfully "true," i.e., manifest, and a disclosing is self-demonstrating in the authentic sense when it issues from the transcendental ego. To this kairos belong speculative determinations that follow "historically."

Now transcendental phenomenology will not overlook or pass over "egology," [210] even when the domain of the mundane objective appears at first to be its proper concern. Undoubtedly the life of the transcendental ego springs into view directly as constitution of the world. At this point the so-called "existentiell problems" do not yet unfold themselves.[211] Even the meaning of "existence" and "existing," or of "existence in its existing," [212] is to be understood from the viewpoint of the problem of transcendental knowledge. The orientation toward the objective concepts of knowledge and of static theoretical truth is surrendered

210. Cf. Husserl's investigations of "time as the universal form of all egological genesis" in CM, § 37, pp. 75–77.
211. Cf. Berger, The "Cogito," pp. 89–90.
212. Barth, "Philosophie der Existenz," p. 31.

when knowledge is taken to mean evidence for what ought to be and what is not pregiven. However abstract and indifferent the term "project" may seem, a "knowing and thoughtful projecting" is the projecting of something that takes precedence. What ought to precede cannot in general be anticipated, but is historical.[213] Nor does the term "meaning" simply designate a unity of meaning that can be encountered as something at hand; rather it designates the instituting of meaning in intentional actualization, and hence a coming-into-appearance. The investigation of meaning and the analysis of intentionality do not stop short of primordial thinking; the Husserlian egology, as the doctrine of the arising of appearance due to the projective achievement of intuition, becomes the doctrine of the authentically historical occurrence. The act-character of transcendental intentions expresses this. Transcendental subjectivity shows itself to be premundane in the constituting and actual coming-into-appearance of evident intuitions that are constantly intuitions of something, and, as such, are determinative of the facts that will be accessible to mundane historical observation. This achieving constitution, this phenomenon-being in coming-into-appearance, provides the sense of everything egological.

Now if one moves in principle from the "given" that presents a structure of meaning to the constructive achievements of consciousness, then the unity of meaning now in question is the transcendental ego itself, together with all the achievements that constitute it in what it shows itself to be (namely, as non-objective origin). Reflection on this origin as well as on the non-objective *katexochen* thereby remains within the mundane realm, and similarly intentions, intuitions, and imaginings (and thus acts or experiences in the widest sense) can be intersubjectively designated as posited meaning-bestowing achievements. However, the fact that we can speak of intuitions, intentions, and imaginings in this way has an achieving projection as its presupposition. We can accept the following hypothesis: transcendental subjectivity binds itself to the life of acts as such, *not* in a manner that renders this life accessible in an epistemological and reflective fashion, but in such a way that this life comes to appear as "historical" in the authentic sense, as documentative of crisis, *kairos*, and ethos, as founding consciousness, time, and

213. *Ibid.*, pp. 35 ff.

world, and as witnessed to and coming-into-appearance in un-foreseeable *cogitationes*, wherein an original co-knowing cannot be denied. World-structures are here progressively understood in the measure of their relating back to an *ego cogito* whose non-derivative achievements present a systematic unity of reason.[214] Phenomenology thereby surpasses regional eidetic ontologies by bringing together the various unrelated elements given to naïve observation, or by understanding their specific meanings within the context of achievements relating to the continuing unfolding of reason. Egology returns completely to origins, and hence it returns not to any specific constituted meaning as a clue, but to the constitution of meaning itself as achievement. Here we must apply concepts such as "reveal," "disclose," "autogenesis," "pro-ject," "coming-into-appearance," and "standing-in-the-truth," but only after they have been stripped of their mundane sense. Each evidence has its own manner of demonstration and its own place in the manifold of constitutions.[215]

This is not to say that nothing can be said about transcen-dental subjectivity, or that we must adopt an attitude of silence before something mystical and ineffable. Nor does it mean a lapse into mundane discourse. The phenomenological reduction gains a release from both a mystical "other world" and the mun-dane as such, and as residuum there remains only the coming-into-appearance of the transcendental in evidences. Of course we cannot avoid speaking in analogies in treating this theme, where the aim of the discourse is to suggest what is intended so that the individual's own enactment can perhaps be achieved without simply taking over something from someone else. The explica-tion of meaning and a fulfilling self-givenness [216] can be taken away from no one, and they present a unique mode of actualiza-tion through which a historical moment can be fulfilled. The function of transcendental subjectivity in forming syntheses is uniquely characterized when nothing "comes from without." [217] Thus the formation of meaning takes place only in the spiritual realm, which designates the sphere of intentionalities as such. The unity of meaning is an "intuited" unity, and is not a unity produced by a "practical creativeness" nor a mundane givenness

214. *CM*, § 64, p. 155.
215. Berger's inquiries aim in this direction: *The "Cogito,"* p. 90.
216. *CM*, § 62, pp. 150–51.
217. Berger, *The "Cogito,"* p. 93.

posited as the "pragma" of a willing,[218] it is the functioning that makes up the streaming life of consciousness witnessed to by actualizing performances,[219] and, since it understands itself in this way, it is to be understood as the premundane and authentically historical.

EGOLOGY AND TRANSCENDENTAL KNOWLEDGE

NOTWITHSTANDING THEIR TRADITIONAL DESIGNATIONS as "transcendental idealism" and radical "transcendental subjectivism,"[220] egology and transcendental phenomenology present themselves as distinct from each other. Moreover, in this instance knowledge of something distinct is at the same time a distinct kind of knowledge. The use of the terms a priori, transcendental, knowledge, absolute, immanence, synthetic, experience, ego, reality, being, and constitution should not lead one to draw the hasty inference that such terms serve as representations of older idealistic thoughts. The "a priori" is not only what in Kantian terms logically precedes experience, remaining inaccessible to experience and independent from it; it appears here as a formal or material a priori of essence. Moreover, since there is a categorical intuition in addition to sensory experience, there is no opposition between experience as such and the a priori. The a priori has meaning only as an a priori of essence.[221] Likewise, the "transcendental" is not opposed to the "empirical," but only to the "mundane." Here the transcendental is not bound up with a Kantian formal a priori, but is a unity of meaning of a unique sort. Thus "transcendental subjectivity" does not mean "consciousness in general," but simply "ego."[222] This ego constitutes itself in its *cogitationes*, so we can unequivocally state that I can reclaim myself "as the pure ego, with the pure stream of my *cogitationes*,"[223] though these must not be of an objective kind. Knowledge, then, in the transcendental sense, is not to be interpreted as "ways of knowing objects" as the critical philosophy

218. Cf. Ricoeur's *Freedom and Nature*, pp. 209–10.
219. *Ideas* I, pp. 353 f., 230 f.
220. *CM*, § 62, p. 150, and *Crisis*, pp. 97 ff.
221. *FTL*, pp. 248 ff.
222. *CM*, § 20, pp. 47 ff.
223. *Ibid.*, p. 21.

interprets it. Nor does it give itself on the basis of a transcendental reflection. Rather "gives" is itself a reality, that of the authentic "affair" itself, namely, the system of a priori that emerges in evidences. This means that "this system of the all-embracing Apriori is therefore to be designated also as the systematic *unfolding of the all-embracing Apriori* innate in the essence of a transcendental subjectivity (and consequently in that of a transcendental intersubjectivity)—or as the systematic unfolding of the *universal logos of all conceivable being.*" [224]

The Kantian transcendental experience is never "absolute," for it attains no thing-in-itself, and knowledge presents only an infinite task within the framework of the categorially ordered domain of reality. By contrast, the phenomenologically constituting achievement of the ego, which is such only in the *ego cogito cogitatum,*[225] is absolute in the sense that everything that appears remains the constitutive achievement of this *cogito* that unfolds itself *in infinitum,* that is dependent on no other being (worldly or otherworldly), and that gives itself as self-demonstrating. It thus belongs to the very meaning of this *cogito* that only its own being is an issue for it: its free constitution of the unity of consciousness, of the world as the totality of unities of meaning, and of time as the universal form of egological genesis.[226] If the "world" is understood to be a phenomenon within the ego, then the traditional problem of transcendence is solved by the formula "transcendence in immanence." [227] This means that the transcendent names the nonreal noematic pole that belongs as a correlate to the actual *cogitatio;* this noematic pole makes up a piece of the world (even if only in the sense of a constituted unity of meaning) and is naturally also transcendent to the individual consciousness in the psychological sense. To what is constituted belongs "soul," "I," "you," "within," "outside," "consciousness," and so on, all of which show themselves as they are in original evidence in the absolutely reduced ego of transcendental subjectivity.[228] For their part, transcendence and immanence gain meaning only as constitutions belonging to the extramundane

224. *Ibid.,* p. 155.
225. *Crisis,* pp. 170 ff.
226. *CM,* § 37, p. 75.
227. *Crisis,* p. 82.
228. *Ibid.*

(but not "otherworldly") ego from whose achievements nothing is to be exempted, not even its achieving of itself, as the autogenesis of the self-temporalizing consciousness shows.

The paradox of human subjectivity as both subject for the world and object in the world is resolved by the phenomenological egological distinction between "we as human beings, and we as ultimately functioning-accomplishing subjects." [229] One may contend that syntheses are present here, and this is correct on the assumption that this does not refer to synthetic judgments a priori in the Kantian sense that can be discovered in the results of the exact natural sciences or in the sciences in general on the occasion of transcendental reflection.[230] Under phenomenological analysis these sciences show themselves to be attempts at interpretation, and hence are the result of constitution. But these interpretations thereby gain a specific importance, for as attempts at interpretation they themselves refer to "affairs" which ought to be the givens of a pretheoretical interpretation. It is therefore necessary to isolate a "natural world–concept" and a "life-world," for syntheses in the authentic sense are to be understood as "identifications" and scientific syntheses form only part of such possible identifications.[231] The identification lies in the *cogitatum*. This means that it is found in the *ego cogito cogitatum* or in the intentional enactment of reason.

Now what is constituted has a primarily objective meaning. If "world," "soul," "man," "you," "I," and the like are made the objects of constitutive questioning back to origins, then a higher level analysis would make it perfectly clear that we must have constant recourse to the "absolutely unique, ultimately functioning ego." In terms of this ego everything that has "meaning" is comprehensible as "phenomenon," and belongs in the world as constituted pole.[232] However, since the transcendental life of consciousness, even though itself a condition for phenomena, is extramundane, the meaning of transcendental subjectivity, which, in the case of autogenesis, is that of "event," cannot be objective and can lie only in constitution itself as constituting. Reason in

229. *Ibid.*, p. 182.
230. *Critique of Pure Reason*, trans. Norman Kemp Smith, 2d ed. (New York: Macmillan, 1964), Introduction.
231. *Crisis*, pp. 121 ff.; *CM*, § 18, p. 41.
232. *Crisis*, pp. 186 ff., 183.

its broadest sense is the "structural form belonging to all transcendental subjectivity" as such.[233] Each experience is therefore rational and is related to unities of meaning. The experience of the ego, however, is projecting. It is not built on the dualism of sensible receptivity and formation in accordance with the understanding. Egological achievements are nonderivative intuitions, and thus experience is the unfolding of reason. For phenomenological correlativism there is nothing that does not refer to constitution and thus to the achievements of reason; given its very concept, there is nothing that can be excluded from reason. The analysis of the phenomenon, which is both the phenomenon as appearance as well as the phenomenon in its achieving coming-into-appearance, shows that there is no primacy of pure theoretical reason.[234] The constitution of the world and the autogenesis of transcendental consciousness contain meaning. Although "being," "nonbeing," and all their modal variations are constituted meanings, we still speak in a comparative manner of a unique "mode of being" that belongs to this rationally unfolding ego, but then we speak of it only in the sense of a substratumless and extramundane "actualism" or "intentionalism," where the transcendental ego remains inseparable from its experiences.[235] However, it must also be noted that transcendental subjectivity (in contrast to all traditional "realistic" and "idealistic" interpretations) presents a concrete reality which can be seized immediately and which, though not worldly, is original and possesses no similarities to a logically "pure" consciousness. We are not transcendental subjectivity by virtue of the fact that we are "human beings" or any other mundanely constituted being, but only by virtue of our projective-functioning.

The self-evidence of our rationality as human beings must be clarified. The method requires "that the ego, beginning with its concrete world-phenomenon, systematically inquire back, and thereby become acquainted with itself, the transcendental ego, in its concreteness, in the system of its constitutive levels and its incredibly intricate [patterns of] validity-founding." [236] Egology is the unfolding of this transcendental subjectivity in its achieve-

233. *CM*, § 23, p. 57.
234. This is meant to counter Berger's statements; see *The "Cogito,"* p. 100.
235. *CM*, § 30, p. 65.
236. *Crisis*, p. 187.

ments themselves. Phenomenology is concerned with the exposition, articulation, and analysis of what is constituted.[237] The ego possesses a unique way of being actual. The principle, which can be formulated in opposition to a naïve ontology, that "reality is manifold" holds good throughout.[238] Transcendental subjectivity, which determines and constitutes the sense of "being" and "nonbeing," is not itself simply nothing, but points to its own form of reality which is meaningfully described by such terms as "constituting," "intending," and "achieving." Transcendental subjectivity shows itself to be real without being "substantial" in the sense of an entity [Seienden]. "Transcendental" no longer designates a special way of observing the givenness of the world with reference to its a priori elements,[239] but instead points to the being-outside-of-the-world that is constitutive of what ought to be.[240] We can only speak here of a philosophy of being when the phenomenon-being of transcendental subjectivity is viewed as "event," and therefore as manifestation of the "ought to be." The reality of constituting subjectivity is the origin of everything phenomenal. The terms "real" and "reality" are to be stripped of every mundane meaning for reality extends beyond being qua presence-at-hand [Vorhandensein]. Eidetic ontology and the static phenomenology oriented toward the object continually proceed from a concrete genetic egology.[241]

> For indeed whatever occurs in my ego, and eidetically in an ego as such—in the way of intentional processes, constituted unities, Ego habitualities—has its temporality and, in this respect, participates in the system of forms that belongs to the all-inclusive temporality with which every imaginable ego, every possibility-variant of my ego, constitutes himself for himself.[242]

Such an ego, however, is not "conceivable" in an intersubjective anticipatory viewing. Its "conceivability" lies rather in its actuality, which sets forth that which is genuinely and actually possible and is thereby the "event" of thinking and conceiving. The con-

237. Ibid.
238. Cf. Müller's Einleitung in die Philosophie, p. 32, and Mensch und Welt in ihrem irrealen Aufbau (Bonn: Dümmlers, 1947), pp. 34 ff.
239. Berger, The "Cogito," p. 102.
240. Eugen Fink, "Das Problem der Philosophie Edmund Husserls," Revue internationale de philosophie, I, no. 2 (1939), 226–70.
241. CM, § 37, pp. 76–77.
242. Ibid., § 36, pp. 74–75.

ceivable is solely that which demonstrates itself in the achieving project in terms of what it signifies itself to be. This is the historical phenomenon *katexochen*. Furthermore, constitution is not a Kantian "construing." [243] There is no mundanely active construing at work here, even when knowledge of the self signifies a self-temporalizing.[244] The meaning of constituting remains simply "having in evidence" (and in this sense also "understanding"). And evidence is self-givenness in the widest sense, including both phenomenological objectivities and egological engagement. Transcendental subjectivity is thereby "the *ratio in the constant movement of self-elucidation.*" It is the nonderivative achievement of the actually possible. Evidences are those achievements that are self-demonstrating, and hence the transcendental ego must be characterized by reason, *ratio*, and thought precisely because of this character of a self-enabling being-responsible-for. Reason also makes up the essence of the mundane ego, which grasps itself in a certain sense as constituted, whether it is called a "unique project of nature" (Gehlen), a "thrown project" (Heidegger), a being "condemned to freedom" (Sartre), or a "sinful nothingness" (K. Barth). The self-objectification of transcendental subjectivity in its constituting life and in its self-understanding "as being in being called to a life of apodicticity" [245] refers back to achievements of thought, *ratio*, and reason that are bound up with the manifestation of what ought to be. According to Husserl, only because man is a rational ego can he understand himself as a teleological being in terms of what ought to be, since just this rational achievement of presuppositions itself, and hence the evidence belonging to what ought to be, "holds sway in each and every activity and project of an ego." [246] Historical occurrences are not to be taken ontically, but ontologically. Of course, traditional "ontologism" and "criticism" at first present dogmatic standpoints concerning the clarification of the world insofar as they proceed simply from "intuition" and "construction." [247] They too must be questioned as something mundane if the reduction is to succeed in placing everything intramundane

---

243. Cf. the investigations of P. Lachièze-Rey in *L'Idéalisme kantien* (Paris: Alcan, 1931), pp. 57 ff.
244. *CM*, § 23, pp. 56–57.
245. *Crisis*, p. 340.
246. *Ibid.*, p. 341.
247. Cf. Berger, *The "Cogito,"* p. 105.

in doubt. Only the "conscious life of the subjectivity which effects the validity of the world" cannot be reduced, the subjectivity which at the same time sets forth metaphysical clarifications.[248] Only the evidence of the correlational bond between the life of consciousness and the noematic can justify the thesis regarding the self-giving of consciousness, i.e., the intuition that is "transcendental experience." [249] This, as the eventfully transpiring, is *the* historical phenomena. For:

> The bare identity of the "I am" is not the only thing given as indubitable in transcendental self-experience. Rather there extends through all the particular data of actual and possible self-experience—even though they are not absolutely indubitable in respect of single details—a *universal apodictically experienceable structure* of the Ego (for example, the immanent temporal form belonging to the stream of subjective processes). Perhaps it can also be shown, as something dependent on that structure, and indeed as part of it, that the Ego is *apodictically predelineated,* for himself, as a concrete Ego existing with an individual content made up of subjective processes, abilities, and dispositions—horizonally predelineated as an experienceable object, accessible to a possible self-experience that can be perfected, and perhaps enriched, without limit.[250]

In the *cogito* we see "how the ego constitutes himself, in respect of his own proper essence, as existent in himself and for himself." [251] Intuition as a particular mode of consciousness bestows meaning through fulfilling self-demonstration.[252] It manifests the actual concern of transcendental subjectivity. This concern that makes up the essence of transcendental subjectivity discloses and confirms itself within the "circle of understanding" in accordance with the clue offered by the constituted meaning, which continually serves as the point of departure for mundane reflective observations. From this constituted meaning that has being, especially being of an objective sort, a regressive questioning can be taken up concerning those acts that make possible that which is actually possible. Not consciously known beforehand, these acts demonstrate in their coming-into-appearance

248. *Crisis*, p. 151; Fink, "L'Analyse intentionelle," p. 84.
249. *Crisis*, p. 153.
250. *CM*, § 12, pp. 28–29.
251. *Ibid.*, § 41, p. 85.
252. *Ibid.*, § 62, pp. 150–51.

what ought to be, and only thus can "teleological being" be maintained as the general structure of reason.[253] Precisely because of its intentional intuitive life of consciousness, the extramundane ego is never "empty," and for this reason the formula *cogito ergo sum* is too narrow and must be replaced by the *ego cogito cogitatum*.[254] On the other hand, this ego is not to be viewed as something conclusively constituted and therefore mundane, as is the case with such determinations as *"si fallor sum"* (Augustine), *"volo ergo sum"* (Maine de Biran), *"amo ergo sum"* (Amiel). As thus mundanely constituted, the ego is not questioned further. The ego is extramundane, without thereby being any less concrete, insofar as "world," "beings," and "objectivities" first emerge with evident experiences. In each instance we ourselves are extramundane in our own understanding enactments, not as constituted as such-and-such, but as ego-poles, i.e., as proving ourselves in constituting.[255] What is at issue here is temporal constitution which, as it is not pregiven, points out the genetic achievement of the flowing life of consciousness. The entire egological life consists in achieving the presuppositions for what cannot be anticipated, and is thus a standing-in-the-truth. Scientific philosophy has but one task:

> that of inquiring consistently and exclusively after the *how* of the world's manner of givenness, its open or implicit "intentionalities." In displaying these, we must say to ourselves again and again that without them the objects and the world would not be there for us and that the former exist for us only with the meaning and the mode of being that they receive in constantly arising or having arisen out of those subjective *accomplishments*.[256]

As achieving, the egological projecting is not a comportment vis-à-vis existing possibilities, but is a making possible [*Ermöglichung*]. It is this making possible that is historical and that concerns us here. It is not a question of this individual constituted unity of meaning having this or that character, but of the projecting of phenomenality as such. To this extent the achievement of the transcendental ego in the *cogitatio* is also the conception of being, the absurd, nothingness, and so on.[257] Only

253. *Crisis*, p. 341.
254. *CM*, § 14, p. 33, and *Crisis*, p. 170.
255. *Crisis*, p. 171.
256. *Ibid.*, p. 160.
257. Fink, "Zum Problem der ontologischen Erfahrung," p. 739.

with this achievement emerges the "affairness" of the affair, the being of beings, and the phenomenality of the phenomenon, and similarly, the historicality of what occurs, which thereby becomes a phenomenon of a nonobjective sort, i.e., "the ontological project is the sole path to ontological experience." [258] Each egologically evident phenomenon indicates the *kairos*, and consciousness is always historical in composition as the event of the unforeseeable comprehension of meaning. After it has become unfolded, understanding is the innerworldly "hypothetical, analytic, and critical phenomenology," "historical" in its achievements and "archeological" in its starting point, which is the confirmation of the operative transcendental subjectivity.

258. *Ibid.*, pp. 740 ff.

Intentionality and the
Method of History

Donald M. Lowe

HISTORICAL SYMPATHY is the understanding of meaning
in context. Such understanding is a form of consciousness of the
past, which I wish to describe in terms of its intentionality. This
article is, therefore, a study of the method of history from the
phenomenological standpoint.[1]

[i] HISTORICAL UNDERSTANDING

SYMPATHY FOR THE PAST is the trademark of the practicing historian. We all try to capture the past *wie es eigentlich*

1. The problem of the understanding of meaning in context has been
dealt with from the standpoint of intellectual history, or the history of
ideas, in a number of worthwhile articles. See A. O. Lovejoy, "Reflections
on the History of Ideas," *Journal of the History of Ideas,* I (1940), 3–23;
A. Edel, "Context and Content in the Theory of Ideas," in *Philosophy for
the Future,* ed. R. W. Sellars, V. J. McGill, and M. Farber (New York:
Macmillan, 1949); J. Higham, "Intellectual History and Its Neighbors,"
Journal of the History of Ideas, XV (1954), 339–47; J. C. Greene, "Objectives and Methods in Intellectual History," *Mississippi Valley Historical
Review,* XLIV (1957–58), 58–74; J. R. Levenson, "Historical Significance,"
Diogenes, XXXII (1960); and Q. Skinner, "Meaning and Understanding
in the History of Ideas," *History and Theory,* VIII (1969), 3–53. From the
standpoint of phenomenology, there are many relevant studies, such as
those of Edmund Husserl, Martin Heidegger, Paul Ricoeur, and H. -G.
Gadamer on historical consciousness, Max Scheler and E. Stein on sympathy, and Alexander Pfänder and Alfred Schutz on meaning. My purpose
here, specifically, is to provide an intentional description of historical sympathy, which therefore differs from Fritz Kaufmann's "The Phenomenological Approach to History," *Philosophy and Phenomenological Research,*
II (1941–42), and L. E. Shiner's "A Phenomenological Approach to Historical Knowledge," *History and Theory,* VIII (1969), 260–74.

gewesen. Yet each generation of historians must reexamine to its own satisfaction the perennial question: How do we know the past? The old answer passed on to us assumes that there is a past, which we can recapture within the framework of chronological narrative. But there are several unjustified assumptions in that answer. (1) The statement "there is a past" is ontologically contradictory. The problem of time-consciousness cannot be understood at all, unless we realize that the past was, the present is, and yet the present recedes cumulatively into the past, as each successive future becomes another present. So what is time? And, assuming that it is a continuum of some sort, what is the relation between past and present? (2) If we ignore the problem of time raised by the first assumption, we must then assume that the historian, though never outside of time, can acquire a time machine in his mind enabling him to project himself back to a previous era, and that somehow, if he lives with his sources long enough, he will come into possession of this time machine. This is not a satisfactory methodological explanation of historical sympathy. (3) Nor can we simply assume that chronology is an adequate framework for reconstructing the past. As any historian knows, chronology in itself tells us nothing. In historical reconstruction so much depends on our definition of a period and our selection of what we believe to be relevant within that period. A different definition and selection would produce a different chronology of the past.

Let us instead approach history from the standpoint of temporality, that is, viewing time as endured experience. History is not the past. We must distinguish between the two: the past was; history is. History presupposes a past; and the historian with his perspective from a present attempts to understand a past. It is the historian who, in reviewing a past, endows that past with significance for his own present. As long as there is a future which will become a present, the prospect of another viewing of that past remains open. Yet, that past was, once upon a time, a living present for its subjects, whose future was still undisclosed. It is this "presentist" aspect of that past which the historian must recapture.

Leonard Krieger once characterized the historian's effort as follows:

> The historian has developed a faculty for moving both backward and forward through time. If he moves forward in time together

with his historical agents in order to recreate . . . the conditions as these agents came to see and feel them—he also moves backward in time to his historical agents from the conclusion of their action in order to create . . . knowledge of the conditions which must have prevailed upon and within the agents unbeknownst to them.[2]

This faculty for moving backward and forward through time, which I shall call reflexive time-consciousness, is fundamental to any historical understanding of meaning in context. The world which the subject faces in his living present is always prospective, with its future still undisclosed; whereas that world as reconstructed by the historian through the benefit of hindsight is always retrospective. The difference between a prospective knowledge and a retrospective knowledge of the same situation is not merely quantitative; it is perspectival and temporal. And the historian must sense that difference, and at the same time hold on to both temporal modalities of knowledge. The intuitive presence of this reflexive time-consciousness distinguishes good works of narrative history, and especially biography, from poor ones.

Nevertheless, the problem of understanding meaning in context is usually neglected, both by analytical philosophy of history and by the behavioral sciences. The criterion of analytical philosophy is logical and empirical. The behavioral sciences study the observable behavior of man. Each method presupposes a nonperspectival, nontemporal standard of objective knowledge. Hence the elucidation of the perspectival and temporal elements in historical understanding is beyond their provinces.[3]

2. "The Horizon of History," *American Historical Review,* LXII (1957–58), p. 72.
3. Concerning the relation between temporal perspective and knowledge, see D. F. Pears, "Time, Truth, and Inference," in *Essays in Conceptual Analysis,* ed. A. Flew (London: St. Martin's, 1956); D. Schon, "Rationality in Retrospective and Prospective Deliberation," *Philosophy and Phenomenological Research,* XX (1959–60), 477–86; F. Kümmel, "Time as Succession and the Problem of Duration," in *The Voices of Time,* ed. J. T. Fraser (New York: Braziller, 1966). Concerning the methodological problems of behavior, see Charles Taylor, *The Explanation of Behaviour* (London: Routledge and Kegan Paul, 1964); Erwin Straus, *The Primary World of Senses,* trans. Jacob Needleman (New York: Free Press, 1963); and Maurice Merleau-Ponty, *The Structure of Behavior,* trans. Alden L. Fisher (Boston: Beacon Press, 1963).

For such elucidation, we must return to an older discussion. R. G. Collingwood spoke of the outside and the inside of a historical (as distinct from natural) event. The inside is the process of thought, which the historian can understand by the reenactment of past thought in his own mind. Ultimately, therefore, all history is the history of thought.[4] Similarly, Max Weber spoke of explanatory understanding (*erklärendes Verstehen*), as distinct from direct observational understanding. In explanatory understanding, we seek the meaning an actor attaches to his act in terms of his motive, and we rationally explain the motivation by placing the act in an intelligible and more inclusive context of meaning.[5]

In one sense, Collingwood and Weber were both concerned with the understanding of meaning in context. Collingwood's "outside" of an event and Weber's "inclusive context" are both variants of Krieger's "knowledge of the conditions which must have prevailed upon and within the agents unbeknownst to them." And Collingwood's "inside" of an event and Weber's "motive" are variants of Krieger's "conditions as these agents came to see and feel them." However, neither Collingwood nor Weber entirely succeeded in describing the reflexive time-consciousness involved in historical understanding.

Collingwood was correct in emphasizing the reenactment of past thought in the historian's mind, and describing it as a form of active, critical thinking. But he missed the crucial distinction between thought and reenactment, which is more than the mere difference between the original context of a thought and the present context of its reenactment. It is a distinction in temporal modes of perspective. The past within which that thought first occurred was for its original thinker a present, with its future still unknown, that is, open. But for the historian that present has become a past, with its immediate future already accomplished, that is, closed. There is a fundamental difference between intended meaning facing an unknown, open future and reenacted meaning enclosed within a known, determined past.

4. R. G. Collingwood, *The Idea of History* (Oxford: Oxford University Press, 1946), pp. 213–15.
5. Max Weber, *The Theory of Social and Economic Organization*, trans. A. M. Henderson and T. Parsons (Glencoe, Ill.: Free Press, 1947), pp. 94–95.

It is this distinction in the temporal modes of thought that Collingwood missed.[6]

Weber, in his discussion of explanatory understanding, was concerned with the relation between motive and context. Motive is a complex of subjective meaning, which we understand within a more rational context of objective meaning. Weber associated the rational with the objective and opposed both to the subjective. Yet subjective meaning is what he wanted to understand. To the extent that the larger context of meaning is rational and objective, there is no methodological problem involved in its construction. As for subjective meaning, Weber fell back upon his pure or ideal type. But the ideal type is also a rational objectification. Thus, he arbitrarily equated the rational, objective meaning of an ideal type with the ongoing intended meaning of a subject. In other words, he made no distinction between the imputed retrospective meaning of an ideal type and the intended prospective meaning of a subject.[7] This is the weakest link within the entire *Verstehen* sociology of Weber. It is because of this weakness in his conceptualization of meaning that Weber, in his historical studies, always emphasized typology at the expense of the temporal, historical dimension.

Reflexive time-consciousness is the crucial faculty which makes possible any historical understanding of meaning in context. My criticism of Collingwood and Weber is that both the reenactment of past thought and the search for the objective context of meaning reduce, rather than elucidate, that faculty. This failure is due to the contradiction between their nontemporal

---

6. In "Some Perplexities about Time," *Proceedings of the Aristotelian Society*, New Series, XXVI (1926), 135–50, Collingwood contrasts the present as being real from both past and future as being ideal. For him, the distinction between the real and the ideal undercuts the temporal continuum of past-present-future. Therefore, he cannot make real distinction between past and present within the continuum of reflexive time-consciousness. My criticism is that, within his philosophical framework, as laid down in *An Essay on Philosophical Method* (Oxford: Clarendon Press, 1933) and *An Essay on Metaphysics* (Oxford: Oxford University Press, 1940), Collingwood fails to justify the possibility of historical understanding. For a good discussion of what he means by "all history is the history of thought," see L. O. Mink, "Collingwood's Dialectic of History," *History and Theory*, VII (1968), 3–37.

7. See the criticism of Weber in Alfred Schutz, *The Phenomenology of the Social World*, trans. G. Walsh and F. Lehnert (Evanston, Ill.: Northwestern University Press, 1967), pp. 25–31.

presuppositions and the thoroughly temporal character of historical understanding. There is a relationship between perspectival standpoint and the content of knowledge. Since historical understanding is founded on reflexive time-consciousness, it can only be clarified methodologically if one begins by describing time-consciousness. For this reason I believe that phenomenology, in its clarification of consciousness as the framework for knowing the world, can aid historiography to advance beyond Collingwood and Weber in the discussion of the method of history.

In the next two sections, I shall borrow Edmund Husserl's description of the intentionality of consciousness and Alfred Schutz's analysis of double motives within consciousness. After that, the discussion will turn to the historical understanding of meaning in context.

[2] THE INTENTIONALITY OF CONSCIOUSNESS

MAN IS IN THE WORLD, not as an opaque object, but as a living conscious subject. The world appears to him by means of his consciousness.[8] The dialectic between the conscious subject and his world is unique, and must be preserved in any adequate study of man as a being.[9] Objective, behavioral study of man reduces the meaningfulness of that consciousness; and subjective study, i.e., subjective idealism, ultimately ends in the solipsism of a Leibnizean monad.

How then to study man, without falling into either objective reduction or subjective solipsism?[10] For man, consciousness is the privileged realm, the ground from which all experiencing, distinguishing, and meaning become possible. It is, therefore,

8. "One, [consciousness] is empirically *contained* in the world as psychical correlate of an organism. Two, it is *awareness of* the world as transcendental correlate of the real. Consciousness, in brief, is clearly both psychical (empirical) correlate of a body and transcendental correlate of the real" (H. M. Chapman, "Realism and Phenomenology," in *Essays in Phenomenology*, ed. Maurice Natanson [The Hague: Nijhoff, 1966], p. 84).
9. See the approach along this line of Peter Berger and Thomas Luckmann, *The Social Construction of Reality* (Garden City, N.Y.: Doubleday, 1966).
10. This is the theme of Husserl's "Philosophy as Rigorous Science" (1911), trans. Quentin Lauer, in *Edmund Husserl: Phenomenology and the Crisis of Philosophy* (New York: Harper & Row, 1965), pp. 69–147.

epistemologically prior to any distinction between subject and object, mind and nature. Hence we must start with the immanent clarification of our own consciousness. Yet, such clarification is not behavioral, in the sense that there are available observational studies of both human and animal consciousness as objective acts.[11] Rather, it must be self-reflexive, in the sense that we clarify consciousness by means of our own consciousness. This possibility is what Husserl described as the phenomenological standpoint of bracketing the world.

Man is in the world; yet the world is for his consciousness. We start with the natural standpoint of man living in the world. We then withdraw from the natural standpoint into our consciousness, thus adopting the phenomenological bracketing. From the bracketed standpoint, we seek to clarify the structure of our consciousness. With that insight, we then return to reconstitute the world as a *Lebenswelt*, revealing its transcendental intersubjectivity. The circle of withdrawal from the world, self-reflexion of consciousness, and reconstitution of the life-world seeks to elucidate the real-life dialectic between man in the world and the world for his consciousness. The phenomenological clarification of consciousness is the preparatory ground for the reconstitution of the life-world. It is crucial to understand that this is Husserl's unifying theme; and centering around this theme there is a continuity in the development of Husserl's thought, from the Göttingen period (1901–16) when he was concerned with the structure of consciousness, to his later periods when he sought to reconstitute the life-world. The clarification of consciousness and the reconstitution of the *Lebenswelt* by means of that clarified consciousness—these are the two poles of Husserl's thought.

Husserl himself described his effort, in 1931, as follows:

I, who am here reflecting upon myself, become conscious that under a consistent and exclusive focusing of experience upon that which is purely inward, upon what is "phenomenologically" accessible to me, I possess in myself an essential individuality, self-contained, and holding well together in itself, to which all real and objectively possible experience and knowledge belongs, through whose agency the objective world is there for me with all its empirically confirmed facts, in and through which it has for me at

11. See the distinction between human and animal consciousness as pointed out by Aron Gurwitsch in *Studies in Phenomenology and Psychology* (Evanston, Ill.: Northwestern University Press, 1966), pp. 89 ff.

any rate trustworthy (even if never scientifically authorized) essential validity. . . . Continuing this self-reflexion, I now also become aware that my own phenomenologically self-contained essence can be posited in an absolute sense, as I am the Ego who invests the being of the world which I so constantly speak about with existential validity, as an existence which wins for me from my own life's pure essence meaning and substantiated validity. I myself as this individual essence, posited absolutely, as the open infinite field of pure phenomenological data and their inseparable unity, am the "transcendental Ego"; the absolute positing means that the world is no longer "given" to me in advance, its validity that of a simple existent, but that henceforth it is exclusively my Ego that is given (given from my new standpoint), given purely as that which has being in itself, in itself experiences a world, confirms the same, and so forth.[12]

In other words, this exclusive self-reflexion brackets out the natural standpoint of man in the world, and concentrates, from the phenomenological standpoint, on man's consciousness. In this phenomenologically bracketed consciousness, leaving aside the connexion between consciousness and the world of the natural standpoint, I discover a meaningful field. It is one wherein my essential individuality is the center, or, in other words, my ego as subject. And there is a bracketed "world" of immanent appresented objects, whose "existence" depends on me and has meaning for me. Of course, these immanent objects exist solely for my consciousness, and therefore are not exactly the same as objects in the world of the natural standpoint. The relation between the egological subject and the immanent objects for his consciousness is not intersubjectively real, but subjectively intentional. Here we fall back on the original meaning of the word *intentio*, a directing of the mind toward.

Consciousness is always in flux, always going through a succession of mental phases. Yet, within this succession there is the identity of the apperceived object; it is through the multiple phases of consciousness that I identify the object. The problem of identity within the stream of consciousness can be answered by the *noesis-noema* correlation. For each perceived object within my consciousness, I can distinguish between acts of per-

12. Edmund Husserl, author's preface to *Ideas: General Introduction to Pure Phenomenology*, trans. W. R. Boyce Gibson (New York: Macmillan, Collier Books, 1962), p. 11.

ceiving as such (noesis) and the data of the perceived (noema). Within the flux of consciousness, there is a succession of noetic acts of perceiving; but these noetic acts intentionally converge on one single noema of the apperceived. It is this noesis-noema correlation of our intentional acts which makes it possible to establish the identity of an object within the flux of consciousness. This is, of course, not an explanation, but rather a description of how a subject perceives an object. Intentionality is thus the noesis-noema correlation characteristic of our consciousness. It is in this sense that we may speak of intentionality as consciousness of something.[13]

I have tried to summarize briefly what Husserl meant by the intentionality of consciousness. Consciousness as flux presupposes temporality, and within this flux there is the possibility of identity. Identity and temporality are not antinomies; rather, they require each other. A mere instantaneous phase in itself can have no identity, nor can a succession of phases per se, without identification, lead to a sense of duration. But, together, identity and duration become possible for consciousness.

After this brief discussion of the noesis-noema correlation of consciousness, we can now turn to consider the problem of the temporality of consciousness, which should throw light on the historian's faculty of reflexive time-consciousness.

Husserl, in his lectures on *The Phenomenology of Internal Time-Consciousness* (1905–10), gave a phenomenological analysis of temporality. Like any phenomenological clarification, this involved the bracketing out of the time of the world and an inward self-reflexive clarification of the immanent time-flow of consciousness. In this way, the internal constitution of time-consciousness can be made clear as the basis for our experiencing of intersubjective time.[14]

The central problem in the study of time-consciousness, or temporality, is the duality of the now moment. "Since a new now is always presenting itself, each now is changed into a past, and

13. The foregoing two paragraphs are based on Husserl's *Ideas*, §§ 32, 36, 84, and 92; see also Aron Gurwitsch, "On the Intentionality of Consciousness," in *Studies in Phenomenology and Psychology*.

14. Here Husserl is not concerned with the study of natural, physical time, nor the analytical argument about the unreality of time. Instead, in the tradition of Augustine's *Confessions*, Book XI, he is describing that time-consciousness in the subject which makes possible all other senses of time.

thus the entire continuity of the running-off of the pasts of the preceding points moves uniformly 'downward' into the depths of the past." [15] Yet it is from within the now moment that there emerges a sense of duration. We cannot be conscious of the now moment but only of what has just been. This consciousness takes the forms of primary remembrance, or retention, and secondary remembrance, or recollection.

However, we neither retain nor recollect pure, empty time phases in themselves. Rather, we retain or recollect an immanent object through a series of now phases. An object is presented in our consciousness within the horizonal field of the time-phase. Though we can shift our attention from presented object to time-field, we can never entirely separate the two. That is, it is not possible to attend to object without time-field, nor to an empty time-field without object. Rather, within our consciousness there is an intentional interplay between presented object and time-field.

In actual perception, an object is presented and retained within a series of now phases; whereas, without perception, an object can be freely recollected within a similar series of successive now phases. Both retention and recollection are intentional acts, and time-consciousness results from the intentional acts of retaining and recollecting presented objects within time-flux. This time-consciousness is not a mere "running-off" downward into the depths of the past, but a continuum. "The now changes continuously from retention to retention. There results, therefore, a stable continuum which is such that every subsequent point is a retention for every earlier one. And every retention is already a continuum." [16]

Because of the correlation between presented object and time-field, in any intentional act the object is appresented as a noematic unity within a flux of time-phases:

In the stream of consciousness we have a double intentionality. Either we consider the content of the flux with its flux-form . . . or we direct our regard to intentional unities, to that of which we are intentionally conscious as homogeneous in the streaming of the flux. . . . The stream of lived experience with its phases and

15. Edmund Husserl, *The Phenomenology of Internal Time-Consciousness*, ed. Martin Heidegger, trans. J. S. Churchill (Bloomington, Ind.: Indiana University Press, 1964), p. 50.
16. *Ibid.*, pp. 50–51.

intervals is itself a unity which is identifiable through reminiscence with a line of sight of what is flowing. . . . The attentive perception of this unity is an intentional lived experience with variable content. . . .

With the second intentionality, I do not pursue the flux of the field . . . ; rather, I direct my attention toward what is intended in every field and in every phase which the field has as a linear continuum. Every phase is an intentional lived experience.[17]

Consciousness is thoroughly intentional and temporal. This intentionality can shift its focus from the noematic unity of the presented object to the flux of time-phases, and back again. This is what is meant by the double intentionality of the stream of consciousness.

Intentionality, with its correlate of internal time-consciousness, is the foundation on which Husserl subsequently sought to reconstitute the life-world. We live in and become aware of our world in a thoroughly intentional, temporal manner. Any description of that world must bring out its intentional, temporal structure. In the fifth Cartesian Meditation (1929–31),[18] Husserl described how, after the phenomenological bracketing, intentional consciousness remains as a thematic field with the ego, the subjectivity, as its center. Within this thematic field, the ego primordially experiences itself as psychophysical corporeality, with the center of its location *here*. This is the ego's private world. However, within this egological field, the ego can intentionally experience other corporeality, with its location *there*. The ego experiences that corporeality as another ego, and attributes to it its own ego-centered field; this is the foundation for all intersubjective experiencing. The life-world as transcendental intersubjectivity is that real world wherein all egos participate.

There are certain problems concerning how it is possible to constitute ontologically a transcendental intersubjectivity out of the intentional experiencing of the private ego.[19] Fortunately,

17. *Ibid.*, pp. 157–58.
18. Edmund Husserl, *Cartesian Meditations*, trans. Dorion Cairns (The Hague: Nijhoff, 1960), pp. 89–151.
19. See Eugen Fink, *Problèmes actuels de la phénoménologie*, ed. H. L. Van Breda (Brussels: Desclée de Brouwer, 1951); Alfred Schutz, "The Problem of Transcendental Intersubjectivity in Husserl," *Collected Papers*, Vol. III, *Studies in Phenomenological Philosophy*, ed. I. Schutz (The Hague: Nijhoff, 1966). This line of inquiry has been profoundly pursued by Maurice Merleau-Ponty in *Phenomenology of Perception*, trans. Colin Smith (New York: Humanities Press, 1962).

they are not directly pertinent to this paper.[20] For our purpose, the important insight is Husserl's characterization of the life-world as an ongoing transcendental intersubjectivity. It is not an objective, quantitative world of nature, but a cultural-historical world which surrounds each of us. "Each man understands first of all, in respect of a core and having as its unrevealed horizon, *his* concrete surrounding world or *his* culture; and he does so precisely as a man who belongs to the community fashioning it historically." [21] This world has as its internal coherence each subject's conscious intentional experiencing of human feeling, motivating, and acting.

[3] Meaning in the Life-World

The social theory of Alfred Schutz centers on the study of the life-world as an ongoing intersubjective community. This theory is a development of the phenomenological standpoint of Husserl. "Our everyday world is," according to Schutz,

> from the outset, an intersubjective world of culture. It is intersubjective because we live in it as men among other men, bound to them through common influence and work, understanding others and being an object of understanding for others. It is a world of culture, because, from the outset, the life-world is a universe of significations to us, i.e., a framework of meaning [*Sinnzusammenhang*] which we have to interpret, and of interrelations of meaning which we institute only through our action in this life-world. It is a world of culture also because we are always conscious of its *historicity*, which we encounter in tradition and habituality, and which is capable of being examined because the "already-given" refers back to one's own activity or to the activity of Others, of which it is the sediment. I, the human being born into this

20. "Here we shall not pursue the question whether the problem of intersubjectivity must not first of all be made the theme of an 'ontology of the life-world purely as the world of experience'. . . . It can, however, be said with certainty that only such an ontology of the life-world, not a transcendental constitutional analysis, can clarify the essential relationship of intersubjectivity which is the basis of all social science" (Schutz, "Transcendental Intersubjectivity in Husserl," p. 82).

21. Husserl, *Cartesian Meditations*, p. 133.

world and naively living in it, am the center of this world in the historical situation of my actual "Now and Here"; I am the "null point toward which its constitution is oriented." That is to say, this world has significance and meaning first of all by me and for me.[22]

The clarification of this life-world cannot depend on an objective rational system. Instead, Schutz seeks to bring out the intersubjective structure of meaning embedded in the ongoing life-world. "It is the meaning of our experience and not the ontological structure of the objects which constitutes reality."[23] Clarification of the meaning-structure of the life-world is possible on the basis of Schutz's thesis of the reciprocity of perspectives. The reciprocity is not a physical change of location, but an intentional interchange of standpoints within meaningful communication. This exchange of perspectives is central to Schutz's phenomenological social theory. Thus his study of the meaning of the everyday world is based on Husserl's concept of the intentionality of consciousness.

In Schutz's analysis, I do not live in an objective, quantitative world: that world is an idealized scheme, based upon the presuppositions of objective, scientific reason. I really live in a common-sense, everyday world, which has meaning for me precisely because I am at its center, surrounded by horizonal fringes. I am the null point, its *here* and *now*, projecting into the horizon beyond. This is the arena of action for me. But my world was given to me at birth, which was my only absolute determinant. It provided me with a specific cultural and historical point of departure. My life then has its history; I am now the sedimentation of my pasts. Together, my birth and my life constitute a biographically determined situation, which is itself the basis for meaningful action. At each moment in my life, I have available from my pasts a stock of knowledge, made up of typifications of the common-sense world. I anticipate, project, and act

22. Alfred Schutz, "Phenomenology and the Social Sciences," *Collected Papers*, Vol. I, *The Problem of Social Reality*, ed. Maurice Natanson (The Hague: Nijhoff, 1962), p. 133.
23. Schutz, "On Multiple Realities," *ibid.*, p. 230, while quoting from Husserl, *Ideas* § 55: "In a certain sense . . . we may even say that *all real unities are 'unities of meaning.'* Unities of meaning presuppose . . . *a sense-giving consciousness,* which on its side, is absolute and not dependent in its turn on sense bestowed on it from another source."

in terms of generalized typical expectations, until I discover something which contradicts the expectations. The stock of knowledge at hand is the means available for my project of action, and it is constantly being reconfirmed or modified as I continue to participate in life. Knowledge as a set of typifications is thus a historically and socially derived cultural phenomenon.

From my location here, I have a purpose at hand, which provides me with a system of relevance by which to reorganize my stock of typified knowledge. This is how I project action in the world. It is from my perspective. But that world is populated by my fellow men. With some of them I enter into direct, face-to-face relations. These are my consociates. I look upon my consociate, from my location here, as being situated there. In social interaction, I assume that he has his purpose at hand and his organizing system of relevance, and that his perspective, though located there for me, is his here location. And I fully assume that he can intentionally understand my perspective as being my here location. This is the reciprocity of perspectives at the basis of every intersubjective communication.

This direct, face-to-face relation is the fundamental form of intersubjective understanding of meaning; there is always the intentional projection of myself into the perspective of another. Understanding of meaning, therefore, cannot be the same as my experiencing of meaning for me. It is an act of intentional reciprocity. This face-to-face intersubjective communication of consociates is the model for all other indirect, nonpersonal relations of intersubjectivity. Within my world at present, there are many with whom I do not enter into personal relations, though it is always possible for me to do so. These are my contemporaries. The world of contemporaries is for me one of impersonal understanding in the present. There were also predecessors in the past with whom I can never enter into any personal relations. That world of predecessors is for me an understanding of subjects in the past. Finally, there will be successors in the future, and my understanding of them is anticipatory. Understanding of each of these three worlds of indirect experience is a variant of the understanding of consociates. The increasing degree of anonymity and impersonality, from contempories to predecessors to successors, produces a correspondingly greater dependence on typification. But, more important, my understanding of each of these impersonal worlds is modified by a different modality of time-consciousness: present, past, and future.[24]

Meaning and understanding are intentional categories which operate within time-consciousness. According to Schutz,

> Even a superficial examination makes it clear that the problem of meaning is a time-problem—not a problem of physical time . . . but a problem of historical time. The latter is always a passage of time, filled, to be sure, with physical events yet having the nature of an "internal time consciousness," a consciousness of one's own duration. It is within this duration that the meaning of a person's experience is constituted for him as he lives through the experience. Here and here only, in the deepest stratum of experience that is accessible to reflection, is to be found the ultimate source of the phenomena of "meaning" [*Sinn*] and "understanding" [*Verstehen*]. This stratum of experience can only be disclosed in a strictly philosophical self-consciousness.[25]

Meaning resides within the immanent time-consciousness of the subject, with its horizonal interplay of retrospection and prospection. Understanding is the approximation of the meaning in one conscious subject by the intending consciousness of another, made possible by the reciprocity of perspectives in the present, or between a present and a past, or in anticipation of a future. Thus both meaning and understanding are thoroughly immersed in the different modalities of time-consciousness. Any intersubjective study of meaning and understanding must employ concepts which can disclose the temporal modes of intentional consciousness.

Schutz's analysis of the meaning of motive and action for the subject can be examined in terms of the different modalities of time-consciousness.[26] Using Husserl's concept of the double intentionality of consciousness as both the flux of now phases

24. The foregoing three paragraphs are based on Schutz's "The Dimensions of the Social World," *Collected Papers*, Vol. II, *Studies in Social Theory*, ed. Arvid Brodersen (The Hague: Nijhoff, 1964). The genius of Schutz's language is that his analytical concepts are derived from the intentional structure of social intersubjectivity, rather than from any systematic societal objectification. Meaning, always subjective and perspectival, has to be derived from the intentional level, and not the objectification, of social reality.

25. Schutz, *Phenomenology of the Social World*, p. 12.

26. The following discussion of motive and action is based on *Phenomenology of the Social World*, chap. 2; see also "Choosing among Projects of Action," *Collected Papers*, Vol. I.

and the appresentational unity within the flux, Schutz distinguished between undifferentiated ongoing experience and discrete meaningful experience. The former is the flux of experiencing from one now phase to the next, whereas the latter is a reflexive glance directed at experience from a subsequent vantage point. It is this intentional retrospection within an ongoing consciousness which endows experience with meaning. For meaning is a retrospective act of intentionality. Yet action is an emergent activity, filled with protention, directed toward the future.

The interplay between retrospection and prospection in a project of action can be clarified by distinguishing between act and action. What is projected in consciousness is the act, which becomes the goal of action; action is then the execution of a projected act. The goal is realized at the end of a course of action when the act has been carried out. Action itself is empty, unthinkable without the act projected as the goal. But in the project of an act, that act is fantasied as having been completed, or as Schutz would say, in the future perfect tense (*modo futuri exacti*). Once the action has begun, the actor's experience is enlarged through time; what was projected now comes to be displaced by what is experienced. When the action is completed, the act, with its action-course behind it, is different from the projected act, with its action-course not yet undertaken. Since meaning is the intentional gaze of the ego directed to experience within consciousness, "the meaning of an action is different depending on the point in time from which it is observed." [27]

Within consciousness, with its sediments of experience and its horizons of retention and protention, an act provides its own intentional unity. It defines a meaning context within which the actor is motivationally related to his project of action. The motive, by which the actor is intentionally related to his act, can be clarified in terms of two temporal modes. As the actor faces his act as a project, his immediately conscious motive is a prospective expectation, a "let's go" voluntative fiat. This is his in-order-to motive. The in-order-to motive relates the actor to his project of action in terms of prospective intentionality. On the other hand, at each moment in the course of an action and well

27. Schutz, *Phenomenology of the Social World*, p. 65.

after its completion, the actor can always take a backward look at himself, and relate the projected act to his past. This reviewing is his because motive. The because motive relates the actor to his project of action in terms of a retrospective intentionality. "The in-order-to motive explains the act in terms of the project, while the genuine because motive explains the project in terms of the actor's past experience." [28]

The in-order-to motive is the immediately conscious expectation of the actor in relation to his project of action. It is this motive which explains to the actor himself, at the moment when he faces his project, the meaning of that act to him. It is therefore always subjective and specific. On the other hand, the retrospective because motive varies according to the vantage point from which the actor tries to relate the project of action to his past experience. From each different vantage point, his retrospection of his past will vary, and therefore the because motive will vary. The because motive is still subjective, in the sense that it is the actor himself who is undertaking the retrospection. But it is also possible for others to explain his act in terms of his past experience, and these others will have an entirely different set of vantage points. Hence, the because motive can be both subjective and intersubjective; it is, moreover, never static, but always changing with changing vantage points. Thus, the in-order-to motive of an act is always subjective and specific, and must be recaptured exactly as it was; whereas the because motive is both subjective and intersubjective, and provides for perspectival variation and growth within a larger context of social reality.

To understand the meaning of an act, we must understand the double motives of the act from the standpoint of the subject, and clarify those motives in terms of their temporal modes, both prospective and retrospective, in order to bring out the temporal dynamics of meaning. This approach to the study of meaning in social intersubjectivity is possible through the reciprocity of perspectives, which is founded on the intentionality of consciousness as analyzed by Husserl. The above discussion is summed up in Schutz's simple statement: "We come to the conclusion that social things are only understandable if they can be reduced

28. *Ibid.*, p. 91.

to human activities; and human activities are only made understandable by showing their in-order-to and because motives." [29]

[4] THE UNDERSTANDING OF MEANING IN THE PAST

WE NOW RETURN TO CLARIFY the historical faculty of
reflexive time-consciousness on the bases of Husserl's description of the intentionality of consciousness and Schutz's analysis
of double motives. There is a dual level of subjective time-
consciousness operating in the historical understanding of meaning in context. To be truly sympathetic, the historian has to
recapture the ongoing prospective time-orientation of the world
of his subject as the subject faces an unknown future. But the
perspectival vantage point of the historian places him later in
time than his subject, enabling him, through benefit of hindsight, to view the world of his subject in a light unknown to the
latter. Historical understanding is precisely this act of prospective sympathy within retrospective hindsight, possible only
through the faculty of reflexive time-consciousness. Thus, history
is neither antiquarianism, which lacks a sense of retrospective hindsight, nor propaganda, which lacks prospective sympathy for the past.

The content of history is the subject in his life-world.
This world is the ongoing intersubjectivity; it is not an objective
world. Objectification results from the effort to analyze the life-
world in conformity with the model of knowledge prevailing in
the natural sciences. The more we attempt to explain the life-
world in objective terms, e.g., behaviorally, the more we reduce
the intentional level of that world. The human world *can* reveal
its meaningfulness, if we are willing to approach it on its own
terms. It includes both the subject in his world and the world
for his consciousness. It is an ongoing field for existence, with
the subject at its center. Yet this life-world is an intersubjective,
not a monadic world, with as many centers as there are subjects
in it. Each center offers a specific thematic orientation in the
world as a horizonal field for existence. From this center, the
subject casts light upon certain aspects of his world, while others
remain in shadow. This stance is his relation to the world.

29. Schutz, "The Social World and the Theory of Social Action," *Collected Papers*, II, 13.

The subject faces his world as an ongoing reality. It offers a past as well as a future for his consciousness. His consciousness is both perspectival and intentional: perspectival, in the sense that it stems from the subject's being-in-the-world, and it cannot comprehend the totality of his sedimented cultural-biographical past nor disclose the entirety of his present; intentional, in the sense that within his here-and-now located consciousness the subject perceives his world and undertakes projects of action. There is a dialectic between a course of action which involves the subject in his world, and the subject's consciousness of that action from the projection of an act to the completion of its action-course. Action per se has no meaning. It is the projection of his act, from anticipation to actualization, which enlarges the subject's awareness of his being-in-the-world and is the source of meaning.

> Meaning . . . is not a quality inherent in certain experiences emerging within our stream of consciousness but the result of an interpretation of a past experience looked at from the present Now with a reflective attitude. As long as I live *in* my acts, directed toward the objects of these acts, the acts do not have any meaning. They become meaningful if I grasp them as well-circumscribed experiences of the past and, therefore, in retrospection. Only experiences which can be recollected beyond their actuality and which can be questioned about their constitution are, therefore, subjectively meaningful.[30]

As the subject faces his world, he undertakes projects of action. His prospective awareness of his world is the context for his in-order-to motives. However, that world can be viewed and re-viewed retrospectively, from subsequent vantage points, by both the subject and the historian. Each viewing detaches that world from the prospective consciousness of the subject, and adds cumulatively to the retrospective consciousness of the world. This is the retrospective context for the understanding of the subject.

We have here, implicitly, the methodological procedure for the operation of historical understanding. Historical understanding is the re-presentation of the prospective consciousness of the subject within the retrospective consciousness of the historian. The methodological analysis of historical understanding con-

30. Schutz, "On Multiple Realities," p. 210.

sists of two steps: First, how is the life-world presented to the prospective consciousness of the subject as an ongoing reality, or in other words, what is the subject's prospective meaning context? Second, how does the historian re-present the subject in his life-world, how does he provide the retrospective interpretational context for the understanding of the subject? [31]

The life-world as an ongoing field for existence appears to the prospective consciousness of the subject as three interacting zones, extending from the ego as thematic center into the distant horizon. These zones are (1) perspective, (2) symbolic order, and (3) institutionalization. Each zone is made up of a subsystem of typifications, culturally and historically derived. The life-world appears in the subject's consciousness in terms of the noesis-noema correlation of these three zones. [32]

By *perspective* I mean the subject's stance in relation to his world. This is more than a point of view; it is his way of per-

31. "In such a case the answer to the question 'What does this social world mean for me the observer?' requires as a prerequisite the answering of the quite different questions 'What does this social world mean for the observed actor within his world and what did he mean by his acting within it?' (Schutz, "The Social World and the Theory of Social Action," p. 7).

32. From the standpoint of social science methodology, there are other triadic categorizations of the social world, such as language, thought, and culture, or personality, culture, and society. These categorizations may appear similar to mine, but there are fundamental methodological differences. First, these other categorizations are based on objectification of the social world, whereas my categorization, following the insight of Schutz, is derived from the phenomenological standpoint of how prereflective consciousness anticipates the world in terms of three zones of intersubjective typification. See Schutz, "Concept and Theory Formation in the Social Sciences," and "Phenomenology and the Social Sciences," both in *Collected Papers*, Vol. I. Second, in other categorizations, one of the three categories is usually analyzed in depth, while the other two are assumed to be constant; or the three are comprehended in terms of an external norm of objective rationality, for example, the functional analysis of social structure by Talcott Parsons; or, finally, as Marcel Cohen admitted in his "Social and Linguistic Structure," *Diogenes*, XV (Fall, 1956), 38–47, the relations of the three become problematical. The virtue of my triadic categorization is precisely that none of these three categories can be studied in itself, since each can be clarified only in relation to the other two, and all three are correlated in terms of the intentionality of the subject's internal time-consciousness. In a sense, George H. Mead's study of *Mind, Self and Society* (Chicago: University of Chicago Press, 1934) has been highly instructive, in that Mead studied successively each of the three categories in terms of the other two. And, in spite of his pragmatic-behavioral background, Mead's *Philosophy of the Present* (Chicago: Open Court, 1932) approaches the phenomenological clarification of time-consciousness.

ceiving himself in his world. From this stance the world reveals a future for him. Hence, it is his mode of prospection. Moreover, behind the subject's perception of his situation in the world there is a sedimentation of personal and biographical growth as well as of historical and cultural inheritance. The subject is what he is because of his past. Yet that past does not determine him; rather, it defines the boundary of his possibilities. Perspective can be described as that prospective intentionality which emerges from the subject's past and projects him into the future. Thus, within his consciousness, the subject can be only perspectivally aware of his perspective. This seemingly convoluted relation between the subject's perspective and his consciousness is not a contradiction, but an individualized structure relating the subject's past and his future.

Symbolic order is the intermediary zone of the subject's lifeworld, between perspective and institutionalization. The symbolic order is the truth of and for the subject. Within it, the subject perspectivally anticipates his future. He believes this symbolic order to be timeless; and as such it is a framework of meaning for him. Nevertheless, symbolic order is thoroughly within time. It came from behind the subject's own past; it relates his past to his present; and it is, in turn, affected by the subject's prospection into the future. This is the transcendent-immanent duality of symbolic order for the subject. It is the immanent self-illumination of the subject's life-world; yet, for it to be truly illuminating, the subject has to believe that it transcends his world. Precisely because of this duality, the symbolic order comprehends and penetrates the subject's life-world, and endows that world with meaning for him.[33]

33. My concept of an ongoing symbolic order resembles somewhat Eric Voegelin's concept of a cosmion: "Human society . . . is as a whole a little world, a cosmion, illuminated with meaning from within by the human beings who continuously create and bear it as the mode and condition of their self-realization. It is illuminated through an elaborate symbolism, in various degrees of compactness and differentiation. . . . The self-illumination of society through symbols is an integral part of social reality . . ." (*The New Science of Politics* [Chicago: University of Chicago Press, 1952], p. 27). However, there is a fundamental difference between Voegelin's cosmion and my symbolic order. Voegelin, starting with certain Aristotelian-Christian assumptions, insists that some cosmions possess anthropological (in the case of the Greek) and soteriological (in the case of the Christian) transcendent validation. For me, the method of history has to be based entirely on the intentionality of consciousness, regardless of Aristotelian anthropology or Christian soteriology. Hence,

Institutionalization is the outermost zone of the subject's life-world. The subject is born into a set of intersubjective relations. These are the preestablished typifications through which he perceives others, and himself in relations with others. These relations already define for him certain modes of temporal orientation: they are personal relations with consociates in the present, and impersonal relations with contemporaries in the present, with predecessors in the past, and with successors in the future. To the extent that these relations have meaning for the subject, they reinforce his time-consciousness. Institutionalization is never static, since the subject, in his participation in relations with others, lives out and revises these preestablished relations. Institutionalization is the foundation for both perspective and symbolic order, and thus I situate it as the outermost zone of the subject's life-world.

Each zone of the life-world is a partial typification of temporal reality—perspective as prospection within time, symbolic order as comprehension of change, and institutionalization as stabilization of time. None of the zones is isolable, since each depends on and affects the other two. The three zones are presented to the internal time-consciousness of the subject. Together, they constitute for him a field for action. From his center, the subject can thematically direct his attention from one zone to another.

However, the three zones are not presented equally to the consciousness of the subject. If the world appears relatively institutionalized to the subject, his symbolic order is more likely to be accepted as transcendent and universal, and his perspective correspondingly taken for granted. On the other hand, if he perceives his world as a de-institutionalizing one, the subject might fall back on his symbolic order to fill that vacuum, and he might become much more aware of his own perspective. In addition, a new symbolic order might emerge to challenge existing institutionalization and perspective. No one can be equally conscious of all three zones.

The life-world is for the subject an intentional field. From the center of his world, he approaches the three zones by means

----

my concept of symbolic order is a thoroughly immanent one, though the subject may believe his symbolic order to be transcendent, and that belief has real consequences for him. In other words, the concept of a symbolic order is meaningless without a subject who mediates it, intentionally, with reference to his perspective as well as to the institutionalization of his world.

of his in-order-to motivation, on the basis of which he formulates his project of action. He anticipates that the immediate outcome of the projected act, when carried out, *will have* approximated his original in-order-to purpose. However, the subject cannot anticipate any approximation unless, for the time of his project-ing, he places his awareness of the life-world in the past tense. Then, on the basis of his retrospection of the world as a stabilized continuum, he can anticipate his projected act in the future. The three zones become intentionally the noematic referential system for the noetic act of in-order-to prospection. Thus, the time orientation for the formulation of a projected act is in the future perfect tense. The in-order-to motive is the meaning of the projected act for the subject within the context of his pro-spective awareness of his world.

We have shown how the life-world is presented to the on-going consciousness of the subject. The historian can recapture that world, *wie es eigentlich gewesen,* as the subject's meaning context, by focusing upon the subject's prospective awareness of the three zones in terms of his in-order-to motivation. There is no methodological problem involved in such a presentation, except that, obviously, the historian must have available the personal writings of the subject as the primary documentation for this presentation.

We now come to the second step in our methodological analysis of historical understanding: How does the historian, with his benefit of hindsight, *re-present* the subject in his life-world, how does he provide the retrospective interpretational context for the understanding of the subject? For an intersub-jective re-presentation from the retrospective standpoint of the historian, what is required is not a rational objectification, but what Schutz called constructs of the second degree:

> The thought objects constructed by the social scientists, in order to grasp this social reality, have to be founded upon the thought objects constructed by the common-sense thinking of men, living their daily life within their social world. Thus, the constructs of the social sciences are . . . constructs of the second degree, that is, constructs of the constructs made by the actors on the social scene. . . .[34]

34. Schutz, "Concept and Theory Formation in the Social Sciences," p. 59.

From his own location, here and now, the historian retrospects the historical world of the subject, there and then. He does this by re-presenting the three zones of the subject's life-world in reverse order, from the outside in. It is a retrospection from the outermost zone of institutionalization, via symbolic order, to the innermost zone of perspective, i.e., from the intersubjective to the personal. The historian must be aware throughout that he is undertaking constructs of the second degree, in order to interpret the constructs of the first degree within that life-world.

The historian can re-present *institutionalization* as a sedimented intersubjective structure for meaning.[35] The subject is born into an existing culture of relationships, which possess a history prior to his appearance, and which define his situation for him. The growth of the subject is a process of internalizing these relations, so that he can have consciousness in his world. There can be neither perspective nor symbolic order without institutionalization as the outermost zone of the life-world. Yet, institutionalization is not a discrete, unchanging objective structure. Perceived by the subject as external relationships, it is maintained and revised by the typified intentional feeling, motivating, and acting among the subjects indwelling within it. Institutionalization is thus the perceptual framework for the subject's perspectival quest for meaning within symbolic order. It should be clarified in terms of the intersubjective perceptual values embedded in it.[36]

The historian can re-present *symbolic order* as an intersubjective referential system for meaning. It is the subject's truth, by which he comprehends change. Symbolic order is never a logical system, and should not be distorted as rational philosophy. Rather, it is the relatively coherent articulation of symbols and values by which the subject can legitimate, i.e., rationalize, his world. Each order has certain underlying presuppositions, and each symbolizes its world at a slightly different

35. See Berger and Luckmann, *Social Construction of Reality*, pp. 45–85, for the concept of institutionalization.

36. I have in mind a recent pamphlet of Clifford Geertz in which he describes certain cultural-symbolic relations in Bali in terms of the Balinese conceptualization of person, time, and conduct. Through this approach one can understand "the way in which a people perceive themselves and others, the way in which they experience time, and the affective tone of their collective life" (*Person, Time, and Conduct in Bali*, Yale University, Southeast Asia Studies, Cultural Report Series, No. 14 [1966], p. 2).

level, whether mythic or rational, transcendent or immanent. Therefore, symbolic order is a referential system, to be thought out by different perspectival standpoints within it. It is the conscious mediation between externalized, or intersubjective, institutionalization and internalized, or personal, perspective.[37] Embedded in symbolic order are key concepts by which the subject can perceive his world. They are the perceptual correlates between personal perspective and intersubjective institutionalization. These key concepts, historically derived and varying from culture to culture, can be brought out and analyzed.[38]

The historian can re-present *perspective* as the subject's structured approach to meaning within his life-world. Perspective is always situational and embodied. It is situational in that the subject was born into an existing institutionalization and symbolic order, and his growth involves the internalization of these in his consciousness. It is embodied in that the subject is always an embodied being sensing and feeling in the world.[39]

37. Such an approach to the study of symbolic order is different from both the linguistic relativity approach of the Sapir-Whorf hypothesis, and the structural analysis of Lévi-Strauss. For the former, see B. L. Whorf, *Language, Thought, and Reality,* ed. with intro. J. B. Carroll (Cambridge, Mass.: MIT Press, 1956), and H. Hoijer, ed., *Language in Culture* (Chicago: American Anthropological Association, Comparative Studies of Cultures and Civilizations, no. 3, 1954); for the latter, see Claude Lévi-Strauss, *Structural Anthropology,* trans. C. Jacobsen and B. G. Schoepf (New York: Basic Books, 1963), and the criticism by G. Lantéri-Laura, "History and Structure in Anthropological Knowledge," *Social Research,* XXXIV (Spring, 1967), 113–61. Instead, I have in mind Maurice Merleau-Ponty's "On the Phenomenology of Language," in *Signs,* trans. and intro. Richard C. McCleary (Evanston, Ill.: Northwestern University Press, 1964); see also P. F. Lewis, "Merleau-Ponty and the Phenomenology of Language," *Yale French Studies,* XXXVI–XXXVII (1966), 19–40. A self-contained linguistic structure does not reveal a semantic world of meaning. Language is a system of available signs. On the basis of language, speech emerges as an intentional correlate of the signifying and the signified. Speech is unthinkable without a speaker, with his in-order-to motive at hand.

38. Here I have in mind B. Snell's philological analysis of key perceptual terms in archaic Greece, in his *The Discovery of the Mind,* trans. T. G. Rosenmeyer (Cambridge, Mass.: Harvard University Press, 1953), chap. 1.

39. "Every external perception is immediately synonymous with a certain perception of my body, just as every perception of my body is made explicit in the language of external perception. If, then, as we have seen to be the case, the body is not a transparent object, and is not presented to us in virtue of the law of its constitution . . . if it is an expressive unity which we can learn to know only by actively taking it up, this structure will be passed on to the sensible world. The theory of the body

Perspective is, therefore, never an abstract, rational viewpoint. It is the subject's individuality, by which he orients himself in the intersubjective world. Perspective is the mode of prospection of an embodied subject, within the framework of his institutionalization and symbolic order.

The retrospection of a life-world, by means of the internal time-consciousness of the subject or of the historian, is always undertaken from a perspectival standpoint other than the here and now of the subject's ongoing reality. The retrospective standpoint approaches the subject's world as being there and then—another place, another time. This perspectival variation leads us, in our retrospection of a life-world, to flatten it out by detaching it from the reality of its ongoingness. It appears in retrospection to be much more structured and rational, i.e., de-temporalized, than it actually was. But the life-world is a thoroughly temporal reality. We live in time, in the sense that we are surrounded by an ontological Time. But we cannot intuit ontological Time directly; it is meaningless, and cannot be characterized. Instead, within a life-world time is institutionalized, symbolized, and prospected. Thus, in our retrospection we can bring out explicitly how time is institutionalized, how it is symbolized, and how it is prospected. This task is undertaken by the relatively new historical and anthropological study of time, which attempts to determine the meaning of temporal institutionalization, temporal symbolization, and temporal prospection for the subject.[40] This effort can compensate for the inevitable

---

image is, implicitly, a theory of perception. We have relearned to feel our body; we have found underneath the objective and detached knowledge of the body that other knowledge which we have of it in virtue of its always being with us and of the fact that we are our body. In the same way we shall need to awaken our experience of the world as it appears to us in so far as we are in the world through our body, and in so far as we perceive the world with our body. But by thus remaking contact with the body and with the world, we shall also rediscover ourself, since, perceiving as we do with our body, the body is a natural self and, as it were, the subject of perception" (Merleau-Ponty, *Phenomenology of Perception,* p. 206). See also C. A. van Peursen, *Body, Soul, and Spirit: A Study of the Body-Mind Problem,* trans. H. H. Hoskins (London: Oxford University Press, 1966), chap. 10; Erwin Straus, *Primary World of Senses;* and F. J. J. Buytendijk, "The Phenomenological Approach to the Problem of Feelings and Emotion," in *Feelings and Emotions,* ed. M. Reymert (New York: McGraw-Hill, 1950).

40. E.g., S. G. F. Brandon, *History, Time and Deity* (Manchester: Manchester University Press, 1965); Geertz, *Person, Time, and Conduct in Bali;* J. Needham, *Time and Eastern Man,* Royal Anthropological In-

flattening out of temporal reality in our retrospective re-presentation.

The historian can re-present the subject in his life-world by portraying the three zones of typified reference. The clarification of each zone depends on the other two; and the three together constitute the retrospective interpretational context for understanding the subject. The interpretational context is not a system of explanation derived from an extrinsic model, whether psychoanalytical or functional. It is a construction of the second degree, based on the first degree constructs of the subject. All concepts within this interpretational context ultimately refer back to the consciousness of the subject. The context is therefore constitutive rather than extrinsic, intersubjective rather than objective, re-presented with the benefit of hindsight. Thus, the interpretational context is the subject's lived-through context, extending beyond even his own retrospection. It is the framework for the subject's consciousness, and yet is derived from his consciousness. This is not tautology, but hermeneutics.[41]

We have shown, methodologically, how the three zones of the life-world can be presented from the standpoint of the subject as his here and now, and re-presented from the standpoint of the historian as being there and then. In the former case they constitute the prospective meaning context for the subject, and in the latter case they form the retrospective interpretational context for the understanding of the subject. The prospective meaning context is the subject's ongoing consciousness of his world. His project of action in this context anticipates meaning. The retrospective interpretational context is the lived-through (i.e., from anticipation to actualization) consciousness of that world, within which the meaning of the subject's acts emerges. The life of a subject is thematically a biography of his projects.

Meaning is the sense given by our consciousness to lived experience. But this sense-giving can be undertaken in anticipation, i.e., *modo futuri exacti*, as well as in retrospection. An-

stitute, Occasional Papers, No. 21 (1965); S. Toulmin and J. Goodfield, *The Discovery of Time* (New York: Harper and Row, 1965).

41. This is in accord with the existential-phenomenological approach to psychology and psychiatry. We understand man's quest for meaning in terms of the intentionality of his consciousness. See Joseph Lyons, "Existential and Phenomenological Psychology: A Selective Bibliography," in *Existential Psychology*, ed. Rollo May, 2d ed. (New York: Random House, 1969).

ticipated meaning is the in-order-to purpose of a specific project, whereas retrospected meaning is the lived-through implication of an act within the broad stream of our consciousness. Prospective meaning projects us into the world; retrospective meaning is the cumulative consciousness of involvement in the world. Meaning, therefore, is that intentional correlate between the subject in his world and that world for his consciousness. To the extent that our method of history hermeneutically describes the dual, that is, prospective and retrospective, contexts of a world, we can bring out the multiple dimensions of meaning.

[5] PROSPECT: FOR A HISTORY OF PERCEPTION

WE CAN UNDERSTAND MEANING in the past because history is the re-presentation of the prospective consciousness of a subject within the retrospective consciousness of the historian. Historical consciousness presupposes reflexive time-consciousness, the reciprocity of perspectives, and the duality of meaning in terms of the double motives. All of these are intention categories, which can be clarified by phenomenology.

I believe that this intentional analysis of the method of history has renewed the tradition of historical sympathy by providing it with a phenomenological foundation. This foundation makes it possible to overcome the Collingwoodian problem of how to rethink past thought, as well as the Weberian problem of the objectification of subjective meaning.

The approach advocated here is neither the history of ideas nor psychoanalytic history. It is intentional, in its emphasis on the consciousness, both prospective and retrospective, of the subject in his life-world. Within the framework of a phenomenology of the social world, the understanding of meaning in the past calls for a history of perception.

PART VI

Phenomenology and Political Science

A Critique of the Behavioral
Persuasion in Politics:
A Phenomenological View

Hwa Yol Jung

> Two roads diverged in a wood, and I—
> I took the one less traveled by,
> And that has made all the difference.
>
> Robert Frost, "The Road Not Taken"

INTRODUCTION

THE AIM OF THIS PAPER is not so much to show how, as
Ludwig Wittgenstein once described his mission of philosophizing, the fly can get out of his bottle, as to show, hopefully, that it
is indeed caught in a bottle. The title is taken from Heinz Eulau's
book *The Behavioral Persuasion in Politics*,[1] in which, even
though political behavioralism is a protean movement, he attempts to spell out the over-all family resemblance of its various
aspects and to formulate the general principles of the behav-

1. *The Behavioral Persuasion in Politics* (New York: Random House,
1963). See further "Political Science," in *A Reader's Guide to the Social
Sciences*, ed. Bert F. Hoselitz, rev. ed. (New York: Free Press, 1967), pp.
129–237; "Tradition and Innovation: On the Tension between Ancient and
Modern Ways in the Study of Politics," in *Behavioralism in Political
Science*, ed. Heinz Eulau (New York: Atherton, 1969), pp. 1–21; "The Be-
havioral Treatment of Politics" and "The Behavioral Movement in Political
Science: A Personal Document," in *Micro-Macro Political Analysis* (Chi-
cago: Aldine, 1969), pp. 148–65 and 370–90; "Political Behavior," in
International Encyclopedia of the Social Sciences, ed. David L. Sills (New
York: Macmillan, 1968), XII, 203–14; and Introduction to *Political Be-
havior in America: New Directions*, ed. Heinz Eulau (New York: Random
House, 1966), pp. 3–13.

134 / *Phenomenology and Political Science*

ioralist approach to political science and his own philosophy of man (that is, to define the behavioralist "paradigm"). A true critique, to be sure, is not and ought not to be merely a negative enterprise of mere faultfinding. Its aim should be "to sort out" or assess the scope and boundaries of the conceptual framework under consideration. As a critique this paper has a twofold purpose: on the one hand, it attempts to define the limitations of political behavioralism, and, on the other, it suggests an alternative, phenomenological way of coping with those limitations. In so doing, both political behavioralism and phenomenology are treated as philosophies of political science.

By phenomenology, I mean the philosophical movement which was developed in Europe by Husserl and which by now represents a far broader geographical and ideological spectrum than when it was first initiated. In this paper, I rely heavily on what is known as the "second school" of phenomenology, "existential phenomenology," which attempts to synthesize the philosophical insights of Søren Kierkegaard and those of Husserl.[2]

2. For a body of literature relevant to my critique of political behavioralism, see particularly the following: Edmund Husserl, *The Crisis of European Sciences and Transcendental Phenomenology*, trans. David Carr (Evanston, Ill.: Northwestern University Press, 1970); Martin Heidegger, *Being and Time*, trans. John Macquarrie and Edward Robinson (New York: Harper, 1962); Jean-Paul Sartre, *Being and Nothingness*, trans. Hazel E. Barnes (New York: Philosophical Library, 1956), and *Critique de la raison dialectique*, Vol. I (Paris: Gallimard, 1960); Maurice Merleau-Ponty, *Phenomenology of Perception*, trans. Colin Smith (New York: Humanities Press, 1962), *The Structure of Behavior*, trans. Alden L. Fisher (Boston: Beacon, 1963), *The Primacy of Perception*, ed. James M. Edie and trans. William Cobb et al. (Evanston, Ill.: Northwestern University Press, 1964), and *The Visible and the Invisible*, ed. Claude Lefort and trans. Alphonso Lingis (Evanston, Ill.: Northwestern University Press, 1968); Paul Ricoeur, *Fallible Man*, trans. Charles Kelbley (Chicago: Regnery, 1965), *Freedom and Nature*, trans. Erazím Kohák (Evanston, Ill.: Northwestern University Press, 1966), and *Freud and Philosophy*, trans. Denis Savage (New Haven, Conn.: Yale University Press, 1970); John Wild, *Existence and the World of Freedom* (Englewood Cliffs, N.J.: Prentice-Hall, 1963); Alfred Schutz, *Collected Papers*, 3 vols. (The Hague: Nijhoff, 1962–66), *The Phenomenology of the Social World*, trans. George Walsh and Frederick Lehnert (Evanston, Ill.: Northwestern University Press, 1967), and *Reflections on the Problem of Relevance*, ed. Richard M. Zaner (New Haven, Conn.: Yale University Press, 1970); Erwin W. Straus, *Phenomenological Psychology* (New York: Basic Books, 1966), and *The Primary World of Senses*, trans. Jacob Needleman (New York: Free Press, 1963); Maurice Natanson, *Literature, Philosophy, and the Social Sciences* (The Hague: Nijhoff, 1962), and *The Journeying Self* (Reading, Mass.: Addison-Wesley, 1970); Calvin Schrag, *Experience and Being* (Evanston,

For existential phenomenologists, phenomenology is a descriptive enterprise which explores the different regions of human existence, the meaning of man's placement in the world. "Existential phenomenology," Paul Ricoeur concisely states, "makes the transition between transcendental phenomenology, born of the reduction of everything to its appearing to me, and ontology, which restores the question of the sense of being for all that is said to 'exist.'" [3]

In discussing political behavioralism and its critics, Eulau studies three fundamental questions: (1) the nature of the knowledge of political things, (2) the basic unit of political analysis, and (3) the nature of value in the theory of politics.[4] So far, the center of the controversy between the supporters and the opponents of political behavioralism has focused on the third issue. I shall, however, shift the center of this inquiry to the first issue. Indeed, the first issue encompasses the second and the third, for the most basic ingredient in politics is the "political *behavior*" of man, since politics is a system of behavior and "value," in turn, is a political thing.[5] The focal point of the issue involved in this paper thus belongs to the philosophy of political science, which reaches beyond a narrow identification with the analysis and justification of its logic and language.

The three aspects of Eulau's inquiry are not, strictly speaking, scientific questions: they are questions of philosophy, of which epistemology is only a part. Those political scientists who *talk about* these issues, regardless of their persuasion, are in fact turning to philosophy. For political science as a purely empirical discipline cannot deal with these questions. Strictly speaking, phenomenology is a philosophy, whereas political be-

---

Ill.: Northwestern University Press, 1969); and *Patterns of the Life-World: Essays in Honor of John Wild*, ed. James M. Edie, Francis H. Parker, and Calvin O. Schrag (Evanston, Ill.: Northwestern University Press, 1970). For a comprehensive survey of the development of phenomenology, see Herbert Spiegelberg, *The Phenomenological Movement*, 2 vols., 2d ed. (The Hague: Nijhoff, 1965).

3. *Husserl: An Analysis of His Phenomenology*, trans. Edward G. Ballard and Lester E. Embree (Evanston, Ill.: Northwestern University Press, 1967), p. 212.

4. "Tradition and Innovation," p. 3.

5. For a phenomenological critique of the behavioralist conception of value, see the author's forthcoming paper "The Place of Valuation in the Theory of Politics: A Phenomenological Critique of Political Behavioralism," *Journal of Value Inquiry* (1974).

havioralism claims to be a science. Nevertheless, political behavioralism, as "ism" suggests, is a philosophical approach to the study of politics. To talk about the nature of political behavioralism is not "doing science" but "doing philosophy," or else (to use a term fashionable in modern philosophy) it is engaging in "metaempirical" or "metascientific" activity. Curiously enough, however, political behavioralists (including Eulau) are rarely willing to admit that they are engaged in philosophical discourse, for the reason, I suspect, that they regard philosophy as an exclusively normative discipline. As Stanley Cavell rightly observes, philosophy is shunned or is considered esoteric not because a few men guard its knowledge, but because most men (including, I might add, political behavioralists) guard themselves against it.[6] On the other hand, phenomenology is not simply a methodology: it is also a complete philosophy of man and of social reality. Phenomenologically speaking, moreover, philosophy is not so much a particular body of knowledge as it is "the vigilance which does not let us forget *the source of all knowledge*."[7] By the same token, the philosopher is not a possessor of knowledge but rather a perpetual beginner, taking nothing for granted; for him everything is in principle questionable.

Eulau has recently been called a "revisionist" in the behavioralist camp.[8] Perhaps he is a revisionist when he avows that there is a continuity between the "tradition" and political behavioralism. He is "more cautious in his claims and more aware of the difficulties than are most behavioralist political scientists,"[9] but his modest claims, of course, make him no less a crusader for political behavioralism.

First, unlike David Truman, Gabriel Almond, Robert Dahl, and David Easton, Eulau claims neither "revolution" nor total victory for recent political behavioralism; nor does he write a tearless eulogy for the death of the old science of politics. Instead, without fanfare, he uses the modest terms "renaissance" and "innovation." For him political behavioralism represents a mixture

6. *Must We Mean What We Say?* (New York: Scribner, 1969), p. 22.
7. *Signs*, trans. Richard C. McCleary (Evanston, Ill.: Northwestern University Press, 1964), p. 110 (italics added). See also Aron Gurwitsch, *Studies in Phenomenology and Psychology* (Evanston, Ill.: Northwestern University Press, 1966), p. 68.
8. Dante Germino, *Beyond Ideology* (New York: Harper & Row, 1967), pp. 190–91.
9. *Ibid.*, p. 191, n. 5.

of continuity with and discontinuity from the tradition; the tension between the two is symptomatic of scientific growth. As "renaissance" means to "look both forward and backward," Eulau claims to leave the door open for "the dialogue between the hinterland of tradition and the frontiers of innovation in the study of politics." [10] Unlike Dahl, who confidently wrote an "epitaph for a monument of a successful protest" (that is, the behavioralist approach),[11] Eulau believes that "the behavioral approaches in politics will continue as separate and distinct—unless, of course, there is an unpredictable failure of nerve." [12]

Second, Eulau views science as an additive body of knowledge based on "the canons of scientific method" and with an infinitely open future. The growth or progress of science is made by increment rather than, as Thomas Kuhn suggests,[13] by revolution. So the scientific spirit corresponds to the "progressive" spirit of liberalism. Eulau's caution against "reified" conceptualizations (for example, Easton's and Morton Kaplan's "general systems theory") favors the Baconian inductive view of science, since Eulau is inclined to believe that in scientific endeavor there is no real substitute for the painstaking, piecemeal "crucible of empirical research." The aim of theory is to provide analytical tools that facilitate empirical research.

Third, Eulau is methodologically self-conscious. But although his "personal document" about the "Young Turks" is a very un-

10. "Tradition and Innovation," p. 19. See also *Behavioral Persuasion in Politics*, pp. 7–8, and "Political Science," pp. 172–73. On the other hand, however, he is critical of William T. Bluhm's work, *Theories of the Political System,* 2d ed. (Englewood Cliffs, N.J.: Prentice-Hall, 1971), for the reason that it is "a clever if malformed attempt at juxtaposing certain classical and contemporary writers that failed to be convincing because, in stressing continuities, it neglected to take account of the profound discontinuities that make for a very conspicuous separation of the ancients and moderns" ("Political Science," p. 178).

11. Dahl writes that "it [the behavioral mood] will gradually disappear. By this I mean only that it will slowly decay as a distinctive mood and outlook. For it will become, and in fact already is becoming, incorporated into the main body of the discipline. The behavioral mood will not disappear, then, because it has failed. It will disappear rather because it has succeeded. As a separate, somewhat sectarian, slightly factional outlook it will be the first victim of its own triumph" ("The Behavioral Approach in Political Science: Epitaph for a Monument to a Successful Protest," *American Political Science Review,* LV [December, 1961], 770).

12. "Behavioral Treatment of Politics," p. 150.

13. *The Structure of Scientific Revolutions,* 2d ed., rev. and enl. (Chicago: University of Chicago Press, 1970).

scientific account of that scientific movement, it must not be overlooked: there is always an autobiographical element in every intellectual journey, scientific or otherwise. Eulau means to be "persuasive." By definition, persuasion (*per-suadere*) is an emotive appeal to induce a person or a group of persons to admire one set of qualities rather than another.[14]

Fourth, Eulau explicitly acknowledges the *differentia* between what is human and what is merely natural when he says: "The behavioral persuasion in politics is concerned with what man does politically and the meanings he attaches to his behavior." [15] For both phenomenology and political behavioralism, then, the starting point of the analysis of human behavior is the *meaning* (or a set of meanings) that the actor attaches to his action. For every thinking and acting has a meaning for the human subject: man is condemned to meaning in politics, society, and history. This thesis of Eulau's is the essence of the phenomenological approach to the human and social sciences. One of the main criticisms made by this paper, however, will be to show that the a priori method and the presuppositions of political behavioralism that are based on the philosophy of the natural sciences are incompatible with and do injustice to the understanding of the meaning structure of human behavior and social reality. Unlike the logical and behavioral positivists who define scientific or empirical knowledge according to the procedures of the natural sciences, especially physics, Alfred Schutz proposes a challenging idea that "the particular methodological devices developed by the social sciences in order to grasp social reality are better suited than those of the natural sciences to lead to the discovery of the general principles which govern all human knowledge." [16]

14. Charles L. Stevenson says in *Facts and Values* (New Haven, Conn.: Yale University Press, 1963), p. 32: "A 'persuasive' definition is one which gives a new conceptual meaning to a familiar word without substantially changing its emotive meaning, and which is used with the conscious or unconscious purpose of changing, by this means, the direction of people's interests."

15. *Behavioral Persuasion in Politics*, p. 5. Cf. Schutz, *Collected Papers*, Vol. I: *The Problem of Social Reality*, ed. Maurice Natanson, p. 59: "The world of nature, as explored by the natural scientists, does not 'mean' anything to molecules, atoms, and electrons. But the observational field of the social scientists—social reality—has a specific meaning and relevance structure for the human beings, living, acting, and thinking within it."

16. *Collected Papers*, I, 66.

In phenomenology and political behavioralism the psychological view of man has led to an emphasis on individual behavior as the basic unit of analysis. Both approaches start from the method of individualism rather than from that of sociologism. However, like psychological behaviorism, political behavioralism as a philosophy opts for what is externally observable or what is "public" by rejecting the intended meaning (usually labeled as "private") that the actor attaches to his action, including value as an existential norm. Although it is extremely rare to find reference to phenomenology in the literature of political behavioralism, Eulau mentions the term "phenomenological" once, very vaguely, as he juxtaposes the public, accurate, and firsthand observation of political behavioralism with the private, inaccurate, and secondhand observation of phenomenology.[17] Political behavioralism as a scientific method abandons the relevance of the vast universe of experiential data of everyday life simply as "subjective" or "private" and thus unscientific and unempirical. On the other hand, phenomenology is a philosophy which justifies the raw, original data of experiential meaning as the foundation of all theoretical activity. To be meaningful, the models of political man as abstract constructs cannot ignore the meaningful world of political actors. Phenomenology denies neither the concept of "objectivity" nor that of "science." It denies only scientism, the doctrine which insists that the only valid methods of science are those of the natural sciences, and "methodolatry," the prior requirement that scientific investigation must first start with a methodology which tends to tailor facts to fit method. The real question is not whether the science of politics is possible but only in which direction it must move. Running counter to the facts of human experience, scientism and methodolatry commit themselves to too narrow a view of the human sciences, which must take account of man (including the scientist) as a unity of complementary poles of subject and object.

In the following pages, I propose first of all to describe the structure of human behavior and, in so doing, to assess critically the behavioralist conception in terms of the intentional framework of phenomenology. Second, I shall attempt to show that, in its effort to build the exact, rigorous science of politics, political behavioralism breeds conceptual reductionism. In contrast, the

17. "Political Behavior," p. 208.

rigor of phenomenology as a philosophy consists in showing that objective knowledge presupposes the preobjective life-world. As the political theorizer himself is an active participant in, rather than merely a passive spectator of, this life-world, political theory is to be regarded as a human project and an intersubjective enterprise. In this sense, a philosophy of political science is and must be also a philosophy of the political world. Third, I shall argue that political behavioralism is unaware of the body as the subject of both knowing and acting (that is, both the knower and the actor as embodied beings). As mind is to body, so is conceptual knowledge (or symbolic meaning) to preconceptual knowledge (or felt meaning). As mind and body are inseparable, so are thought and feeling. Moreover, the phenomenology of the body is a critique of artificial reason and points to the inherent limitation of political behavioralism as a scientific analysis of human behavior.

THE STRUCTURE OF HUMAN BEHAVIOR

AN UNDERSTANDING of what political things are must precede a possibility of the knowledge of them. What then are political things? The answer to this question cannot just be taken for granted. For Martin Heidegger, the question of "What is a thing?"[18] is bound up with a series of metaphysical questions. What complicates the matter further in our inquiry is the adjective "political." Since the political thing is nonetheless a thing, we ought first to ask: What are things? There are both natural and human things. Natural things are flowers, trees, rocks, mountains, water, air, earth, etc., things of nature, free from the handiwork or cultivation of man. Human things are cultural artifacts, the products of human labor or man-made objects (tools or instruments), such as pipes, bells, hammers, abaci, computers, schools, highways, natural languages, mathematical and logical symbols, government, etc. To use a phrase of Marshall McLuhan's, they are all "extensions of man." Thus the question "What is a human thing?" leads to the most fundamental question: "What is a man?" or, to put it more existen-

18. *What Is a Thing?* trans. W. B. Barton, Jr., and Vera Deutsch (Chicago: Regnery, 1967).

tially. "Who is man?" For the lack of a better term, I shall call the total being of man the "ontology of man" or, as Heidegger describes it, man as "Being-in-the-world" (*in-der-Welt-sein*).[19]

Paul Valéry pointed out that all politics, even the most simple and crude, implies an idea of man and of the world.[20] Eulau's political behavioralism also raises the basic question of man, beginning with the idea that "the root is man" and ending with the idea that "the goal is man." The behavioral persuasion in politics considers the "analysis of man" and human behavior as its central theme of investigation. Its aim is not to formulate a normative philosophy of man, which Eulau explicitly rejects, but rather to shift the focus of political research toward psychological man and his behavior and away from the institutionalist approach. The behavior of a person or a group of persons rather than "events, structures, institutions, or ideologies"[21] has become the center of attention in behavioralist political research.

Eulau rejects early psychological behavioralism (that is, "the physiological stimulus-response psychology of behaviorism") as having "little in common with" modern behavioral inquiry. Whereas early reflexiology exorcised mental phenomena from the social sciences, modern behavioral science

> is eminently concerned not only with the acts of man but also with his cognitive, affective, and evaluating processes. "Behavior" in political behavior, then, refers not simply to directly or indirectly observable political action but also to those perceptual, motivational, and attitudinal components of behavior which make for man's political identifications, demands and expectations, and his systems of political beliefs, values, and goals. "Behavioral" is, therefore, preferable to "behavioristic," and I shall use it in the dynamic sense.[22]

Political behavioralism, then, as Eulau depicts it, rejects nothing out of hand. If it rejects nothing, it is a ubiquitous technique, which seems to be the reason why Eulau uses the term "political behavioralism" synonymously with "political behavior." However,

19. See *Being and Time,* particularly pp. 78 ff.
20. *History and Politics,* trans. Denise Folliot and Jackson Mathews (New York: Pantheon, 1962), pp. 103, 241.
21. *Political Behavior,* ed. Heinz Eulau, Samuel J. Eldersveld, and Morris Janowitz (Glencoe, Ill.: Free Press, 1956), p. 3.
22. Eulau, "Behavioral Treatment of Politics," p. 151.

the term is rather misleading, because political behavioralism as a scientific method is only one way, not the all-encompassing way, of analyzing political behavior. There are ways of treating political behavior either "behaviorally" (scientifically) or "non-behaviorally" (nonscientifically)—for example, phenomenologically. In order to keep his scientific method intact, the behavioralist must identify his notion of behavior with overt behavior. Specifically, in order to conserve quantitative measurement, observation, and empirical testability, covert phenomena (what Eulau calls "mental" phenomena), such as intentions, beliefs, motives, feelings, and values, must be either translated into the "observable contexts" or inferred from overt behavior or from what Felix Oppenheim calls the "behavior event." [23] Thus behavior *is* really overt behavior or only the external indications of action. So-called "private" and motivational phenomena are reduced to "public" and observable events or the external components of action.

It is no mere accident that "consciousness" is a forbidden word for political behavioralists as well as for psychological behaviorists. But consciousness ought not to be treated as if it were a philosopher's myth or fable. Is consciousness just "a ghost in a machine"? Robert Lane and Karl Deutsch are two eminent political behavioralists who are willing to use the term "consciousness." [24] Lane uses consciousness in the narrowly defined sense of "sensitivity," "awareness," and "discernment," in contradistinction to "knowledge" or "intelligence." Though Deutsch criticizes mechanism for leaving no room for consciousness (or will), in mapping out his cybernetic geography of man he treats consciousness as an analogue to the purely internal processes of any electronic network: it is "a collection of internal feedbacks of secondary messages. *Secondary messages* are messages about changes in the state of parts of the system, that is, about primary messages. *Primary messages* are those which move through the system in consequence of its interaction with the outside

23. *Dimensions of Freedom* (New York: St. Martin's, 1961), p. 16.
24. Lane, *Political Thinking and Consciousness* (Chicago: Markham, 1969), pp. 312 ff., and Deutsch, "Mechanism, Teleology, and Mind: The Theory of Communications and Some Problems in Philosophy and Social Science," *Philosophy and Phenomenological Research*, XII (December, 1951), 185–223, which has been incorporated in his *The Nerves of Government* (New York: Free Press, 1966), in chaps. 2, 5, 6, and 8.

world." [25] Both Lane and Deutsch agree that consciousness is something internal; it is sensitivity or the internal feedback of secondary messages. Thus they are unaware of the intentional structure of consciousness as the meeting of the internal and the external, and of the dynamic relatedness between thought and affectivity in intellectual activity as well as in the everyday life of action.

Not unlike the phenomenologist, as I have suggested above, Eulau defines the basic stuff of politics in terms of the conditions and consequences of individual action and the roles that the political actor plays in the social, cultural, and personal milieu. Most significantly, he has emphasized the importance of the meaning the actor attaches to his action. The presence of meaning, Eulau insists, makes the study of human behavior different from the study of natural phenomena. For this reason the distinct merit of the behavioral approach to the study of politics lies in its focus on the meaning of human behavior. Moreover, Eulau holds that the observation of political behavior must meet the test of an intersubjective agreement between observer and observed. There must be an agreement between the meaning given to behavior by the observer and that given by the actor himself. This, however, requires not that the observational language of political science should be the same as the language of the political actor, but rather that their meanings must be compatible with each other.

However, because of its physicalist view of human conduct (that which is only "public" or "observable"), political behavioralism, despite its claim to the contrary, is impervious to the intentional meaning-structure of human conduct. The intentional meaning-structure of human conduct is completely alien to political behavioralism in both theory and technique. The phenomenological criticism of political behavioralism is that it is inattentive to (1) the intentional meaning-structure of human conduct and (2) the body as lived rather than as a merely physical thing, an inert object.

By virtue of his action, man is called an active being, and his essence is his existence. Gabriel Marcel's idea of man as *homo viator* dramatizes the idea that man is active and, being active, that he is always in the making or becoming (that is, a being-

25. "Mechanism, Teleology, and Mind," p. 205.

on-the-way). To express it in a slightly different way, man is the only being who refuses to accept what he is [26] or, as Jean-Paul Sartre puts it, he is a "being which is what it is not, and which is not what it is." [27] By virtue of his action, man may be more or less an animal but he *is never* simply an animal.[28] This is not meant so much to deny the common characteristics shared by both man and other animals as to emphasize the uniqueness of man as man.

By action, man "extends" (in McLuhan's sense) himself, remolds his own image, and determines his own destiny. Unlike traditional natural law theory, the existentialist theory of man stresses that man is not an eternally fixed property like a thing— thus in no way is there a denial of his biological and social constants.[29] In existential philosophy man is described as a "project" or a "possibility." As a project his existence is neither in full possession of itself nor entirely estranged from itself, "because it is action or doing, and because action is, by definition, the violent transition from what I have to what I aim to have, from what I am to what I intend to be." [30] Because he is a possibility, man is open to the "invisible" future, that is, his future is in no sense predetermined. In his psychohistorical theory Robert Lifton, similarly, characterizes on a global scale twentieth-century man as protean.[31] Amitai Etzioni has recently proposed a sociological theory of "the active society," a theory of society based on the idea of man as a dynamic actor rather than a passive spectator.[32]

26. Albert Camus, *The Rebel,* trans. Anthony Bower (New York: Knopf, 1956), p. 11.
27. *Being and Nothingness,* p. 556 and *passim.*
28. Max Scheler, *Man's Place in Nature,* trans. Hans Meyerhoff (New York: Farrar, Straus, Noonday Press, 1963), p. 29.
29. For the very reason of the existentialist thesis that man is incomplete in an incomplete world, Simone de Beauvoir suggests that existentialism is "the only philosophy in which an ethics has its place." See *The Ethics of Ambiguity,* trans. Bernard Frechtman (New York: Philosophical Library, 1948), p. 34. For an existentialist critique of neoclassical natural law theory, see the author's paper "Leo Strauss's Conception of Political Philosophy: A Critique," *Review of Politics,* XXIX (October, 1967), 492– 517.
30. Merleau-Ponty, *Phenomenology of Perception,* p. 382.
31. *Boundaries: Psychological Man in Revolution* (New York: Random House, 1970), pp. 37–63.
32. *The Active Society* (New York: Free Press, 1968).

Phenomenology aims to describe the meaning-structure of human action from the standpoint of man as actor (that is, as attaching meaning to his action) rather than spectator. As an intentional analysis of meaningful action, phenomenology is not a psychology of introspection; it is not the opposite of behaviorism. For intentionality is neither entirely internal nor entirely external. By focusing on the essential structure of meaningful action, phenomenology attempts to avoid altogether a "psychologism" that reduces meaning (or everything) simply to psychological components. Only when the meaning of action is regarded as the simultaneous process of the internalization of the external and the externalization of the internal does one come to grips with the idea that man *is* his action.

In *The Structure of Behavior*, Merleau-Ponty repudiates the mechanical and causal explanation of human behavior (*comportement*). The human organism or the body (*organon*) cannot be understood in terms of physiology and/or biology alone, for the body is an active mode of Being-in-the-world. In order to avoid "mentalism" (subjectivism) on the one hand and "behaviorism" (objectivism) on the other, Merleau-Ponty describes the structure of behavior as meaning (*signification*), the idea of which is to integrate the "dialectics" of the physical (physiology), the vital (biology), and the mental (psychology). The human behavioral order is not reducible to any one of these "three orders of Being" alone. Insofar as behavior represents the human order, it is a field or a structure of meaning. Thus the human order as it is presented to a "normal man" exhibits no virtual distinction between the mental and the somatic. Rather, the body is a unified field, an alert, sentient "phenomenal field," not an inert, physical object. To characterize the human order as either a physical object or a mental faculty is to confuse the part with the whole. Rationalism is as false as mechanism, inasmuch as each depicts the image of man in a partial way. Man acts neither like a machine nor with mind alone, since the body (or the "flesh") is never solely a sum of "material" facts, or a substance, or a representation of the mind as idea. Through the body as a phenomenal field, as the root of an active mode of Being-in-the-world, the world also becomes a phenomenal field. For the player in action, for example, the football field is not just an object to gaze at but a reality which summons a certain mode of action. By the same token, perception, whose *subject* is the body, "opens on a reality which solicits our action rather than on a truth, an object of knowledge." [33]

Man can have a project because he is active. Insofar as action is a structure of meaning, it is an ongoing process based on a preconceived plan. Without analyzing in detail a complex network of unconscious drives, desires, motives, feelings, choices, efforts, decisions, and consents, it can summarily be stated that what characterizes the essence of meaningful action is the presence of a project. A resolution, the counterthrust of a hesitation, is the final decision to act out the project. The project is indeed an insight (in-sight), an "internal plan of operations." In the executing of a project, there is a fulfillment, the terminus of an action. By the very presence of a project, man's action is radically distinguished from the behavior of animals. For example, the chimpanzee can move, but only the human being is capable of moving with a preconceived plan. In short, the presence of a project makes human action "meaningful," "purposive," and "rational." Moreover, facts and values on the one hand and ends and means on the other enter into the planning of an action in a complex way. In the project, the importance of valuing can scarcely be overstressed. For Sartre, who defines the task of "existential psychoanalysis" as the conscious understanding of man as project, human reality is identified with and defined by the polyvalent *ends* man pursues.[34] As a matter of fact, valuing, according to Rollo May, is not only an act but *is* project itself: "It is in the act of valuing that consciousness and behavior become united." [35]

The project as a preconceived plan temporally precedes the actual performance or execution of action. Insofar as the actor has internal time-consciousness or inner flow of duration, action is not yet "meaningful." It is merely presignifying or prerational, for lived experience in the stream of consciousness acquires meaning only when it is grasped by the act of attention, that is, reflectively. Just as the project is the purposive basis of action, to have a project means to have a purpose or a goal. Thus Erwin Straus writes:

33. Merleau-Ponty, *Structure of Behavior*, p. 169.
34. *Being and Nothingness*, p. 557.
35. *Psychology and the Human Dilemma* (Princeton, N.J.: Van Nostrand, 1966), p. 220.

Purposive movements are directed toward a goal. A change is anticipated and realized through movements subserving a plan. In action, we reach beyond a given situation into the realm of possibilities; within a temporal horizon, open to the future, we busy ourselves producing a new situation. We do not simply react to things as they are, but we act on them—i.e., we move with the intention of modifying things from an actual to a desired condition.[36]

In the fulfillment of an action through a project, then, the possibility is realized. Fulfilled or achieved action through a project is a transcending act, that is, it transcends what is now in favor of possibility. Man is a "multitude of possibilities" which underscores the existential meaning of man as *homo viator*. Herein lies the convergence between phenomenology as a descriptive method and the existential ontology of man.

The upright posture of the human body, according to Straus, is a uniquely human mode of Being-in-the-world.[37] The uprightness of man has a moral as well as a factual connotation. It means to stand up perpendicularly to the ground, to be just, honest, and right. The moral quality of rectitude, standing up for one's own conviction or righteousness, is admired by others. Thus the upright posture of man is a truly human trait which no other animal species has. It is a specific placement of man's Being-in-the-world. As a spatial concept this upright posture determines one's place, factual and moral, in relation to one's natural, social, and cultural environment.

Like psychological behaviorism, political behavioralism may know a "physics" of the mind or the body but knows nothing of the human body as an active *subject* of perception, feeling, and cognition. Without the body as an active mode of his existence, man would be just an "absentee landlord" in the world. By means of his body as an instrument, man relates himself to the world and other people, and he "extends" himself to the making of cultural objects. It is not only as a rational animal but as a creature of flesh, blood, and bone that man distinguishes himself from other animals. The nonverbal forms of bodily expression, like laughing and crying,[38] are unique to humankind. The tools or

36. *Phenomenological Psychology*, pp. 197–98.
37. *Ibid.*, pp. 137–65.
38. For a phenomenological discussion of the nonverbal expressions of laughing and crying as uniquely human expressions, see Helmuth Plessner,

instruments man makes, for example, are referred to as *handi-works* or *handicrafts*. In a rudimentary sense the idea of *homo faber* indicates the ability of the human to tame, modify, and change his environment through the manipulation of his body. Through his body man also mediates between himself and the Other. The space defined by his body becomes a precondition for communication between himself and the social world as a whole. Only by recognizing that "I am *here*" am I able to determine that "he is *there*." By means of his spatial position, man has direct access to things and people. His body is an indispensable medium, not only for the self-interpretation of his own lived experience but also for his perception and understanding of others and thus ultimately for his political and social relationships. Ronald Laing shows that the self "is precluded from having a direct relationship with real things and real people" when there is a derangement of perception between the ego and the body in relation to the external world, that is, when the situation is "self ⇌ (body-other)" instead of "(self/body) ⇌ other." [39]

The human body is not just a physical object to be *had*. Man does not own his body as he owns an object or a thing. It is an organ, the vehicle of action or *praxis*. There is, according to Marcel, a radical difference between the body as a mode of "Being"- (*être*) in-the-world and "having" (*avoir*) it as a mere object. For man *is* his body. "I *am* my body," declares Marcel, "in so far as I succeed in recognizing that this body of mine *cannot*, in the last analysis, be brought down to the level of being this object, *an* object, a something or other. It is at this point that we have to bring in the idea of the body not as an object but as a subject." [40]

Man is a unique being who is able to reconcile the physical body (*Körper*), the impersonal and outside, with the lived body (*Leib*), the personal and inside. To distinguish between "being" and "having" in our discussion of the human body is not an idle

Laughing and Crying, trans. James S. Churchill and Marjorie Grene (Evanston, Ill.: Northwestern University Press, 1970).

39. *The Divided Self* (New York: Pantheon, 1969), p. 86.
40. *The Mystery of Being*, trans. G. S. Fraser (Chicago: Regnery, 1960), I, 124. See also "Existence and Objectivity," in *Metaphysical Journal*, trans. Bernard Wall (London: Rockliff, 1952), pp. 319–39; and Maurice Merleau-Ponty, "Husserl et la notion de Nature (Notes prises au cours de Maurice Merleau-Ponty)," *Revue de métaphysique et de morale*, LXX (July–September, 1965), 260–61.

exercise in abstract speculation; it has an import for the social sciences, whose basic area of investigation is human social action, which involves the mobility of a body that is simultaneously both a subject and an object. In sum, as John Wild stresses:

> Human behavior is neither a series of blind reactions to external "stimuli," nor the project of acts which are motivated by the pure ideas of disembodied, worldless mind. It is neither exclusively subjective nor exclusively objective, but a dialectical interchange between man and the world, which cannot be adequately expressed in traditional causal terms. It is a circular dialectic in which the independent beings of the life-field, already selected by the structure of the human body, exert a further selective operation on this body's acts. It is out of this dialectical interchange that human meanings emerge.[41]

The Meaning of Conceptual Rigor

PHENOMENOLOGY IS CONCERNED with a systematic analysis of meanings that are actively constituted by consciousness. As a meaning-endowing act, consciousness, whether naïve or theoretical, is always intentional: in thinking, imagining, feeling, perceiving, or willing. The intentionality of consciousness suggests that in every form or act of consciousness there is always a tripartite unity of the *subject* who is *conscious* of an *object* that may be ideal or real (*ego-cogito-cogitatum*). Meaning is then constituted in the encounter between the object and man who thinks, feels, imagines, perceives, and wills. In this sense, it is neither entirely subjective nor entirely objective. This meaning-endowing act is a uniquely human trait both in thinking and acting. The relevance of phenomenological thought to the empirical sciences of man or the human sciences (for example, psychology, sociology, political science, anthropology, history, and linguistics) lies in its explicit recognition and insistence on the radical *differentia* between what is merely natural (or physical) and what is genuinely human in terms of this meaning-creation. If this phenomenological view is correct, then a methodology of political science as an empirical science of man must be radically different from that of the natural sciences and thus

---

41. Foreword to Merleau-Ponty, *Structure of Behavior,* pp. xiv–xv.

must free itself from any preconceived, derivative conceptual boxes.

Since Galileo, as Husserl shows,[42] nature has been idealized or mathematized from the life-world (*Lebenswelt*). The idealized and mathematized nature in physics has gradually but decisively replaced the original nature accessible to sensibility (e.g., perception). This abstract, scientific attitude has now permeated the life-pattern of man and has gained significance for modern science, human as well as natural, philosophy and humanity. Now the ideal of *mathēsis universalis* has more than ever before become a reality for human thought—in the social sciences, and in the use of game theory, statistical techniques, cybernetics, and the "sciences of the artificial." Thus the idealized mode of thought embodied in physics has now become a model for all forms of knowledge. In this historical sedimentation of mathematized abstraction, the life-world, the source of all knowledge and action, has been forever reduced to oblivion and has become the hidden and forgotten background.

The garb of mathematized nature has replaced prescientific nature. Considered as a part of nature, man also partakes of the character of a mathematical manifold which, like nature, is subject to exact and precise measurement. Psychological data are being treated like natural or physical phenomena and reduced to the physical or, as Herbert Simon calls it, the artificial.[43] The philosophical justification for the behavioral approach in political science as a *predictive* science with an emphasis on artificial model building is embedded in the spirit and language of logical empiricism, naturalism, and operationalism. The concept of power, for example, has been central to political thought. However, "power is rapidly losing ground from the point of view of its operational, if not analytical, utility."[44] From the standpoint of exact measurement, power has become a concept difficult to define.

The methodological isomorphism of the human sciences and the natural sciences has been motivated by the phenomenal suc-

---

42. See *Crisis*, pp. 23 ff.
43. *The Sciences of the Artificial* (Cambridge, Mass.: M. I. T. Press, 1969). "Artificiality," according to Simon, "connotes perceptual similarity but essential difference, resemblance from without rather than within" (p. 13).
44. Eulau, "Political Behavior," p. 208.

cess of modern (or post-Galilean) physics in predicting. This has been accompanied by technological innovations and break-throughs as well as by mathematical precision and exactitude. Thus for Eulau, the possibility of further progress in behavioral research is simply a question of technology. However, because the human order is radically or qualitatively different from the natural order, it may not be isomorphically amenable to the techniques of the natural sciences. The *scientific* character of the human sciences should not be prejudged by the ready-made conceptual and methodological framework of the natural sciences. It must not be judged by how much physics, mathematics, and mechanics are found in it. To be sure, the scientific approach to human behavior is a recent event, in its infancy. The science of politics, however, is as old as the sciences of nature. Certainly, its slow or retarded development toward an exact, measurable, and predictive science, one begins to suspect, is due to something endemic to the nature of *human* behavior which, unlike natural phenomena, defies the ideal order of regularities and uniformities.[45]

Physicalism (the positivist doctrine that holds physics as paradigmatic to all sciences, natural and social) attempts to create "a self-consistent system of unified science capable of being utilized for successful prediction."[46] Sociology (or physicalistic sociology) is for Otto Neurath the way to discover sociological laws congruent with the laws of physics which can be utilized for prediction. For the positivist doctrine of science, theories and laws are formulated for the sake of prediction, which is the essence of scientific explanation. Brian Barry criticizes T. D. Weldon's *The Vocabulary of Politics* (1953) as being "an application of unreconstructed logical positivist criteria of meaning to traditional political thought rather than a detailed analysis of concepts"; and he defines "analytical politics" as "the attempt to simplify the complex reality of a situation by picking out certain aspects of it and then building a model relating to these aspects."[47] It seems that Barry is critical not so much of

45. Cf. Charles Taylor, *The Explanation of Behavior* (New York: Humanities Press, 1964), p. 272.

46. Otto Neurath, "Sociology and Physicalism," trans. Morton Magnus and Ralph Raico, in *Logical Positivism*, ed. A. J. Ayer (Glencoe, Ill.: Free Press, 1959), pp. 282–317.

47. *Political Argument* (New York: Humanities Press, 1965), p. 290.

Weldon's logical positivism as of the absence in his work of a constructive, detailed analysis of political concepts themselves.

For many practitioners of analytical politics, Anthony Downs and Herbert Simon, among others, theorizing is equated with abstract model building. In this sense, rigor becomes a declared trademark of political behavioralism as a scientific analysis.[48] For Downs, as for other analytical practitioners, rigor is a methodological principle for building theoretical models used ultimately for the sake of prediction or in order to increase the reliability of predictive knowledge. He postulates that, after the model of "economic man," man seeks to maximize his self-interest, and his behavior is "rational" insofar as it is directed primarily toward selfish ends.[49] Thus the model of "positive politics" as both a methodology and a theory of man is constructed from that of "positive economics." In the positivist model, theory is treated as "a body of substantive hypotheses" and is judged by "its predictive power for the class of phenomena which it is intended to 'explain.'"[50] For the exponent of positive economics Milton Friedman, the notion of prediction is limited not just to the forecasting of future events (that is, saying beforehand what will happen on the basis of theory and evidence); it is also extended to the causal explanation of "phenomena that have occurred but . . . on which [observations] have not yet been made or are

48. See Eulau, "Political Behavior," p. 203; Evron M. Kirkpatrick, "The Impact of the Behavioral Approach on Traditional Political Science," in *Essays on the Behavioral Study of Politics,* ed. Austin Ranney (Urbana, Ill.: University of Illinois Press, 1962), p. 4; Deutsch, *Nerves of Government,* p. 17; and Albert Somit and Joseph Tanenhaus, *The Development of American Political Science* (Boston: Allyn & Bacon, 1967), p. 177.

49. *An Economic Theory of Democracy* (New York: Harper & Row, 1957), pp. 3–20. The same methodological assumption ("methodological individualism") is made by James M. Buchanan in "An Individualistic Theory of Political Process," in *Varieties of Political Theory,* ed. David Easton (Englewood Cliffs, N.J.: Prentice-Hall, 1966), pp. 25–37.

50. Milton Friedman, *Essays in Positive Economics* (Chicago: University of Chicago Press, 1953), pp. 8–9. In order to avoid the confusion of telling what will happen in the future and explaining an event that has already taken place, it may be useful to distinguish prediction (pre-dict the future) and postdiction (retro-dict the past). See Stephen Toulmin, *Foresight and Understanding* (New York: Harper & Row, 1963), p. 27; and W. H. Walsh, *An Introduction to Philosophy of History* (London: Hutchinson, 1951), p. 41. Needless to say, so-called prediction in the social sciences has largely been of a postdictive rather than a predictive nature.

not known to the person making the prediction." [51] Like the methodology of positive economics, the model of positive politics, too, aims at accurate prediction, which, Downs himself insists, has very little to do with the *real* world of political man. Unlike the classical and conventional meaning of *theoria*, theory (or model) now is "a filing system" (Friedman's phrase) that facilitates prediction. Downs's model building is a methodolatry in the extreme, where conceptual clarity is likened to the rigid formulation of logical axioms and physical and mathematical theories. Analytical politics is eminently nomothetic in seeking the political knowledge that is completely impersonal, generalizing, uniform, and lawlike and discredits the factual description of unique and individual events, that is, the ideographic understanding of political things.

From a phenomenological point of view of thought and action, the idea of rigor in political behavioralism is exclusively a methodological principle, but it ignores another level of rigor that clarifies the nature of the knowing subject—the scientist as a knower. Science is a human activity which is founded upon the human life-world; there is no science without scientists and thus the scientist cannot ignore his rootedness in the life-world.

The rigor of phenomenology lies in its search for the presupposition or source of theoretical knowledge and activity, scientific or otherwise. It turns to the knowing subject as the locus of investigation and thus to science as a human project, *praxis*, and achievement, that is, to man as the subject of the human sciences. If "objectivity" entails an anonymous epistemological subject or a nameless thinker, then it is a scandal to science as well as to philosophy. Objectivity is "nothing but the expectation of a reality which was at once susceptible of appearing while affecting me in my receptivity and of letting itself be determined by articulate speech." [52] More importantly, however, all theoreti-

51. Toulmin challenges this predictivist thesis and denies the idea that prediction is "the kernel of science." Rather, prediction is a craft or technical application of science: "the predictive success of a theory is only one test of its explanatory power and neither a necessary nor a sufficient one" (*Foresight and Understanding*, pp. 35–36).

52. Ricoeur, *Fallible Man*, p. 109. Straus reminds us that "The logical form of a statement, the linkage with exact measurement, or the use of mathematical expressions are no guarantee of objectivity" (*Phenomenological Psychology*, p. 118).

cal knowledge and activity presupposes the ultimate and all-encompassing system of meanings called the pretheoretical or preconceptual life-world. "Straightforward experience, in which the life-world is given," writes Husserl, "is the ultimate foundation of all objective knowledge. Correlatively, this world itself, as existing prescientifically for us (originally) purely through experience, furnishes us in advance, through its invariant set of essential types, with all possible scientific topics." [53] The "phenomenological battle cry," in calling for a return "to the things themselves," is an urge to return to this everyday, preconceptual life-world as the world of "things" (*Sachen*) that is the genesis of all theoretical *praxis*. The life-world is the horizon of meanings grasped by our original, straightforward, immediate, and sensible experience. In this life-world, there are natural and cultural objects and human beings who are its subjects: all of which together constitute our environment or "surrounding world" (*Lebensumwelt*). In it we see, perceive, and know, for example, natural objects in terms of their color, shape, size, and weight. Husserl writes that "The contrast between the subjectivity of the life-world and the 'objective,' the 'true' world, lies in the fact that the latter is a theoretical-logical substruction, the substruction of something that is in principle not perceivable, in principle not experienceable in its own proper being, whereas the subjective, in the life-world, is distinguished in all respects precisely by its being actually experienceable." [54] Phenomenology, which is concerned with "things" experienced and experiential knowledge, is a radical empiricism; and Merleau-Ponty thus speaks of "phenomenological positivism." What is empirical or factual must not, therefore, be determined by any prior methodological commitment. When every fact is reduced to method and when science is judged merely on *how* it does rather than *what* it does, then there is methodolatry and the birth of technological rationality, where the medium becomes the message and what is important is not *what* is done or said but *how*.

Phenomenologically speaking, all objective knowledge—especially the objective knowledge of the human and social sciences —is the second-degree abstraction from the original experience in the life-world, just as geography presupposes the existence of

53. *Crisis*, p. 226.
54. *Ibid.*, p. 127.

the natural landscape. Such geometrical concepts as "straight line," "triangle," "circle," and "pentagon" have their "original" counterparts in nature itself. "The whole universe of science," as Merleau-Ponty puts it, "is built upon the world as directly experienced, and if we want to subject science itself to *rigorous scrutiny* and arrive at a precise assessment of its meaning and scope, we must begin by reawakening the basic experience of the world of which science is the second-order expression." [55] The natural scientists can abstract nature and discover the ideal order of regularities and uniformities and exclude on principle their personal and cultural concerns from their research. Unlike their colleagues in the natural sciences, however, the social scientists cannot exclude what Schutz calls "social reality," [56] the very reality which they are to investigate and whose subjects they are.

Phenomenology, then, seeks the radical root of theoretical knowledge in the pretheoretical understanding of the everyday life-world. To return to the life-world as "the locus of man's construction of reality and the point of access to his comprehension of all knowledge," [57] particularly in the sciences of man, is in no way a denial of the authenticity and objectivity of scientific knowledge. Such a return seeks its genetic source in the infra-scientific reality of the life-world upon which all sciences are founded.[58] In criticizing behaviorism (objectivist psychology) as

55. *Phenomenology of Perception*, p. viii (italics added).
56. By "social reality" Schutz means "the sum total of objects and occurrences within the social cultural world as experienced by the common-sense thinking of men living their daily lives among their fellow-men, connected with them in manifold relations of interaction" (*Collected Papers*, I, 53). For the latest view of Schutz's phenomenology of the life-world and its implications for the social sciences, see Peter L. Berger and Thomas Luckmann, *The Social Construction of Reality* (New York: Doubleday, 1966), pp. 19–46; and Alfred Schutz and Thomas Luckmann, *The Structures of the Life-World*, trans. Richard M. Zaner and H. Tristram Engelhardt, Jr. (Evanston, Ill.: Northwestern University Press, 1973).
57. Natanson, *Journeying Self*, p. 97.
58. Concerning objectification in philosophy and science, Merleau-Ponty points out that "Philosophical self-consciousness does not make science's effort at objectification futile; rather, philosophy pursues this effort at the human level, since all thought is inevitably objectification: only philosophy knows that on this level objectification cannot become carried away and makes us conquer the more fundamental relationship of co-existence. There can be no rivalry between scientific knowledge and the metaphysical knowing which continually confronts the former with its task. A science without philosophy would literally not know what it was talking about. A philosophy without methodical exploration of phenomena

practicing a "psychological Averroism," Erwin Straus comments that "objective psychology cannot exist without a black market furnished with contraband from the psychology of living experience. For by its observations, descriptions, and communications it belongs to the human world. The scholar acts and talks, he is pleased or he suffers, he is a man like all other men." [59] Thus phenomenology is critical of the methodological Averroism in which the construction of the "artificial puppet" has nothing to do with "real man." In the name of precision, exactness, and clarity, methodological Averroists treat the "operational language" of theory as if it were independent of the "natural language" of political man, instead of viewing the former as the theoretical construct of the pretheoretical construct of political man himself. Far more important than this is the phenomenological insistence that artificial constructionism or formalism cannot do away with the experiential knowledge of politics in the everyday life-world from which scientific constructs are abstracted.

The phenomenological posture implies more than a criticism of political behavioralism for inventing "a jargon that impedes communication and renders prose tortuous and dull" (that is, for an esoteric scholasticism), or for discounting "the utility and validity of impressionist accounts of political phenomena" [60]— although no doubt these criticisms are justified and, for that matter, might well include some thinkers of the phenomenological persuasion, too. All philosophical and scientific terminology is more or less esoteric jargon to the ordinary man on the street. Phenomenology is not demanding that the language of a theoretical enterprise ought to correspond to the language of ordinary man, a feat which has been mastered by only a few thinkers in the history of Western philosophy since Socrates.[61] It is not true

would end up with nothing but formal truths, which is to say, errors" (*Sense and Non-Sense*, trans. Hubert L. Dreyfus and Patricia Allen Dreyfus [Evanston, Ill.: Northwestern University Press, 1964], p. 97).

59. *Primary World of Senses*, pp. 111–12.

60. Michael Haas, "A Plea for Bridge Building in International Relations," in *Contending Approaches to International Politics*, ed. Klaus Knorr and James N. Rosenau (Princeton, N.J.: Princeton University Press, 1969), pp. 168, 163.

61. The idea that scientific understanding necessarily presupposes common-sense understanding is the essential thesis of Schutz's philosophy of the social sciences. See especially, "Common-Sense and Scientific Interpretation of Human Action," *Collected Papers*, I, 3–47, and cf. Harold Garfinkel, "The Rational Properties of Scientific and Common Sense Ac-

either that the investigation of how the everyday language of political man is used would dissolve all philosophical problems, or, for that matter, that a "journalistic style" is necessarily shallow, any more than a scientific style is *ipso facto* profound and elucidating.

The life-world is also a social reality, a network of interactions among human beings who are its subjects. Intersubjectivity is the "original datum" of the life-world itself. Value, that which we approve or disapprove, is the central and integral force of this social and cultural world of action. The "republic of science," or the community of scientists, also partakes of this characteristic of the everyday life of men as actors. As Husserl states, "If we cease being immersed in our scientific thinking, we become aware that we scientists are, after all, human beings and as such are among the components of the life-world which always exists for us, ever pregiven; and thus all of science is pulled, along with us, into the—merely 'subjective-relative'—life-world." [62] Like every other life-style, science itself is a human project and *praxis*. The life-world is relative in the sense that its "Heraclitean flow" is relative to the perspectives of individuals, societies, and cultures, which constitute a variety of its versions. In their respective ways, these different versions of the life-world have their own invariant structures, which are open to the theoretical formulation of the life-world as a universal system of meanings.

Thomas Kuhn, whose philosophy of science is being criticized as subjective and as relativizing science,[63] supports some of the phenomenological theses. Like Husserl's teleology of scientific history, Kuhn's analysis of science is historical and psychosociological, that is to say, the structure of scientific knowledge is sought from the historical development of science and in the context of an existing community of scientists.[64] In the first place,

tivities," in *Studies in Ethnomethodology* (Englewood Cliffs, N.J.: Prentice-Hall, 1967), pp. 262–83.

62. *Crisis*, pp. 130–31.

63. See *Criticism and the Growth of Knowledge*, ed. Imre Lakatos and Alan Musgrave (Cambridge: At the University Press, 1970); and Israel Scheffler, *Science and Subjectivity* (Indianapolis, Ind.: Bobbs-Merrill, 1967), pp. 1–19.

64. In asking questions concerning the nature of science and its growth, Kuhn comments that "Already it should be clear that the explanation must, in the final analysis, be psychological or sociological. It must, that is, be a description of a value system, an ideology, together with an

the change of a scientific paradigm is an alteration of perspective, a new *Weltanschauung,* as it were: "when paradigms change, the world itself changes with them" and "the scientist who embraces a new paradigm is like the man wearing inverting lenses." [65] To discover a new paradigm is, then, to turn on the switch of a new Gestalt, which influences or colors a scientist's own perception and experience. An example of this, among many, is the Aristotelian perspective of the "constrained fall" and the Galilean perspective of the "pendulum," which perceive the same phenomenon with equally true, though different, observations.

In the second place, for Kuhn, scientific theorizing involves "an inextricable mixture" of the descriptive and the normative, the thesis of which challenges the hard core of the behavioralist doctrine of value neutrality as the essence of scientific activity. A scientific paradigm on which the puzzle-solving of normal science depends requires the total commitment of a particular scientific community; likewise does the acceptance of a new paradigm rising out of an anomaly or the failure in puzzle-solving of an old paradigm. In recent years, the increasing challenge to the behavioralist "paradigm" is largely directed to and based on its unsatisfactory formulation of value or its relation of fact and value to the world of political action. A scientific revolution is brought about not merely by the objective evidence it presents but also by the normative judgment of a scientific community. [66] It is not accidental that for Kuhn a scientific revolution resembles a political revolution; and a fight for the ruling paradigm is a political fight. In conclusion, Kuhn writes that as there can be "no scientifically or empirically neutral system of language or concepts, . . . scientific knowledge, like language, is intrinsically the common property of a group or else nothing at all. To understand it we shall need to know the special characteristics of the groups that create and use it." [67]

---

analysis of the institutions through which that system is transmitted and enforced. Knowing what scientists value, we may hope to understand what problems they will undertake and what choices they will make in particular circumstances of conflict. I doubt that there is another sort of answer to be found" ("Logic of Discovery or Psychology of Research?," in *Criticism and the Growth of Knowledge,* p. 21).

65. *Structure of Scientific Revolutions,* p. 111, 122.

66. Cf. Michael Polanyi, *Knowing and Being,* ed. Marjorie Grene (Chicago: University of Chicago Press, 1969), pp. 65–66.

67. *Structure of Scientific Revolutions,* p. 146.

Political behavioralism, like logical empiricism, maintains the dualism of fact and value: in the name of "the norm of value judiciousness," they are kept apart and considered to be (logically) heterogeneous. According to Eulau, political science as "a behavioral science" has not attempted to make "the world a better place to live in. But it has given new hope that it might be a better place if political ignorance can someday yield to political knowledge." [68] So the aim of political science behavioralistically viewed is to increase the knowledge of political facts instead of creating political values, for values evince emotions which are irrational and therefore have no cognitive value. The emotive or noncognitivist view of value or ethics maintains that all meaningful statements are descriptive, that is, they report or describe the state of affairs (stating "conditions" rather than professing "preferences"), and that to be meaningful, all scientific statements must be descriptive. In contrast to value judgments that are "instrumental" or "extrinsic" and belong legitimately to the domain of scientific activity, value judgments that are "categorical" or "intrinsic" are not empirically verifiable. They cannot be validated as "true" or "false." [69]

The British analytical philosopher J. L. Austin, however, contends that this emotive theory of value commits what he calls "the descriptive fallacy"; that is, not all statements are necessarily reporting the state of affairs. There are statements which are "performative utterances." Performative utterances are "perfectly straightforward utterances, with ordinary verbs in the first person singular present indicative active, and yet we shall see at once that they couldn't possibly be true or false. Furthermore, if a person makes an utterance of this sort we should say that he is *doing* something rather than merely *saying* something" [70] ("I do,"

68. "Political Science," p. 210.
69. See Carl G. Hempel, "Science and Human Values," in *Aspects of Scientific Explanation* (New York: Free Press, 1965), pp. 81–96; and Felix E. Oppenheim, *Moral Principles in Political Philosophy* (New York: Random House, 1968), pp. 8 ff. The "policy sciences" belong to the domain of scientific activity as the value judgments they employ are purported to be "extrinsic" or "instrumental."
70. "Performative Utterances," in *Philosophical Papers*, ed. J. O. Urmson and G. J. Warnock (Oxford: Clarendon Press, 1961), pp. 220–39, esp. p. 222. See also "Performatif-Constatif," in *La Philosophie analytique*, Cahiers de Royaumont, Philosophie No. 4 (Paris: Minuit, 1962), pp. 271–81, and *How to Do Things with Words*, ed. J. O. Urmson (New York: Oxford University Press, 1965).

"I apologize," "I promise," etc.). For example, when I say "I promise that . . . ," I am performing an act; I am *doing* something rather than reporting something, or someone's act of promising, or his saying "I promise." I think political language, the language of political man, is largely of a "performative" nature. If Austin's view is right, then the noncognitivist theory of value based on the heterogeneity of value and fact is misleading. For there are indicative statements which are outside its "verifiability" criterion of truth or falsity, validity or invalidity, and the heterogeneous purity of fact and value is no longer the logical question, the logic of the "is" and the "ought," but is the question of an *attitude*. Not only evaluations but perhaps all statements, both descriptive and normative, are expressions of attitudes, and "attitudes are in general but tenuously connected with emotion, since thoughts, words and deeds are much more central manifestations of them." [71] All knowledge is more or less personal or, better, *inter*personal.[72] As political science as a theoretical activity is one of many human life-projects, its language cannot escape the ambiguous character of the language of political man in the life-world, in which thoughts, words, and deeds are all mixed with "emotion" as well as "reason." Thus, Austin's view refuses to accept the watertight containers of fact and value as something separable. Political science in pursuit of political knowledge, to paraphrase Alvin Gouldner, is a parcel of the political world as well as a conception of it.[73] The political scientist

71. J. O. Urmson, *The Emotive Theory of Ethics* (New York: Oxford University Press, 1968), p. 147.

72. The term "personal" is used by Michael Polanyi who rejects the idea of "scientific detachment" and considers scientific activity as the personal participation of the knower in the act of establishing contact with reality. Thus to be "personal" means to be neither subjective nor objective. See *Personal Knowledge: Towards a Post-Critical Philosophy* (Chicago: University of Chicago Press, 1958).

73. *The Coming Crisis of Western Sociology* (New York: Basic Books, 1970), p. 13. Cf. W. G. Runciman, *Social Science and Political Theory* (Cambridge: At the University Press, 1963), p. 174; E. H. Carr, *What Is History?* (New York: Knopf, 1962), p. 51; and Isaiah Berlin, *Four Essays on Liberty* (New York: Oxford University Press, 1969), p. 92. It is extremely important to note that in rejecting the traditional dualism of subject and object, inner world and outer world, and body and mind, the physicist Werner Heisenberg declares that "even in science *the object of research is no longer nature itself, but man's investigation of nature.*" What he says further on this matter is worthwhile quoting in some length: "When we speak of the picture of nature in the exact science of our age, we do not mean a picture of nature so much as a *picture of our relation-*

himself is a part of the common society and history from and in which he constructs his knowledge. We change the political world by changing our conception of it.

Thus theory and practice are two moments of man's Being-in-the-world. Man is both knower and actor. Every civilization is both a civilization of *theoria* and a civilization of *praxis*.[74] The world, however, cannot be reduced to the "I think," for one cannot theorize without first participating in the life-world that constitutes the background of theorizing activity. Theoretical knowing is a special, though important, way of existing in the world. T. D. Weldon's conception of political philosophy as a therapy of political words or linguistic confusions is ill-conceived, for it ignores the basic fact that language has no independent existence of its own apart from man who exists in the world. It should be remembered that words themselves do not lie; it is man as the user of words who lies: a lie without the liar is a scandalous abstraction.[75] Therefore, it seems more correct to say that words do not need therapy; it is the speaking man who needs it. By the same token, the function of the philosophy of political science cannot be conceived narrowly as a logical and linguistic analysis of theory construction and validation. For neither philosophy nor science can bypass the reality it purports to investigate directly or indirectly. From a phenomenological point of view, a philosophy of political science *is* also a philosophy of the political world.

In political behavioralism, as I have stated above, rigor is an

---

ships with nature. The old division of the world into objective processes in space and time and the mind in which these processes are mirrored—in other words, the Cartesian difference between *res cogitans* and *res extensa* —is no longer a suitable starting point for our understanding of modern science. Science, we find, is now focused on the network of relationships between man and nature, on the framework which makes us as living beings dependent parts of nature, and which we as human beings have simultaneously made the object of our thoughts and actions. Science no longer confronts nature as an objective observer, but sees itself as an actor in this interplay between man and nature" (*The Physicist's Conception of Nature*, trans. Arnold J. Pomerans [New York: Harcourt, Brace, 1958], pp. 24, 28–29; italics Heisenberg's).

74. Paul Ricoeur, *History and Truth*, trans. Charles A. Kelbley (Evanston, Ill.: Northwestern University Press, 1965), pp. 218–19.

75. Thus Merleau-Ponty declares that "To deal with given languages objectively is not enough. We must study the subject who is actually speaking. To the linguistic of language we must add the linguistic of the word" (*Primacy of Perception*, p. 84).

analytical and operational ideal that is identified largely with the procedures of model construction and exact quantitative measurement, which aim at prediction. I have also said, however, that there is another kind of rigor in describing and interpreting, as does phenomenology, the "sloppy data" of the human life-world without rigid conceptual castle-building. There is a kind of philosophical rigor that attempts to excavate, as it were, the existential foundation of theory as an activity. In order to seek a rigorous "archaeology" of the knowing subject, of the scientist as a knower, we need to introduce hermeneutics. Broadly speaking, hermeneutics is an existential analysis interpreting man's placement in the social and historical world. Thus it is applicable to all intellectual endeavors related to the sciences of man: political theory (especially the history of political thought as an "exegetical" exercise), literary criticism, history, art, and psychoanalysis, as well as theology. The applicability of hermeneutics to the sciences of man presupposes the idea that man is radically different from mere nature: both man and nature have a history, but only man knows that he has a history.[76] He is conscious of the past as the product of his own doing which in turn influences him (that is, of a present that has passed) and of a future which, as a possibility, will be of his own making. Hermeneutics is the way of integrating thoughts and actions, in particular a thinker's own thoughts and actions, in order to reveal through "a *creative interpretation*" the meaning of the human life-world as temporal and historical.[77]

In *Being and Time*, Heidegger singles out the importance of "historicity" (*Geschichtlichkeit*) in man's existence in the world.

76. Cf. C. F. von Weizsäcker, *The History of Nature* (Chicago: University of Chicago Press, 1949), p. 9. For the systematic treatment of knowing or thinking as a hermeneutical event, see particularly Hans-Georg Gadamer, *Wahrheit und Methode: Grundzüge einer philosophischen Hermeneutik* (Tübingen: Mohr, 1960); Paul Ricoeur, *Le Conflit des interprétations: Essais d'herméneutique* (Paris: Seuil, 1969), and *Freud and Philosophy*; Edmund Husserl, *Logical Investigations*, trans. J. N. Findlay, 2 vols. (New York: Humanities Press, 1970); Jürgen Habermas, *Knowledge and Human Interests*, trans. Jeremy J. Shapiro (Boston: Beacon, 1971); and Charles Taylor, "Interpretation and the Sciences of Man," *Review of Metaphysics*, XXV (September, 1971), 3–51. For an excellent historical survey of hermeneutics in this connection, see Richard E. Palmer, *Hermeneutics* (Evanston, Ill.: Northwestern University Press, 1969).

77. Ricoeur, *Fallible Man*, p. xxi.

For our present purpose, it is sufficient to note that historicity leads to the notion that knowing as a special way of existing in the world is not just "the observer's observation of the observed," as the behavioralist posture has it, where the knower's subjectivity becomes anonymous, the phenomenon which Heidegger calls "they" (*das Man*). Rather, it is a participating event or happening, the participation of the knower in the reality of things he observes: the knower is an observing *participant* in the ambient world.[78]

Take the simple example of so-called "fact." It is like "a sack —it won't stand up till you've put something in it." [79] A fact is not "something out there," independent of an observer, but the result of an interpretation or interpolation, a comprehension of a thing or an event by a conscious, knowing subject. Michael Oakeshott thus declares:

> Fact, whatever else it may be, is experience; without thought there can be no fact. Even a view which separates ideas from things must recognize that facts are ideas. Fact is what has been made or achieved; it is the product of judgment. And if there be an unalterable datum in experience, it certainly cannot consist of fact. Fact, then, is not what is given, it is what is achieved in experience. Facts are never merely observed, remembered or combined; they are always made. We cannot "take" facts, because there are none to take until we have constructed them. And until a fact is established, that is, until it has achieved a place in a coherent world, it is no more than an hypothesis or a fiction.[80]

Facts are no more to be taken as "givens" than are values. A *factum* is a thing done, made, or experienced, and as such it reveals the accomplished performance of one who experiences in relation to an event, i.e., an interpretative participation of the knowing subject. The criterion of relevance always and decisively enters into the determination of a fact. By stressing the interrelatedness of "facts," "observation," and "theory" in scientific

78. Merleau-Ponty echoes this spirit when he writes that "Because of the fact that the order of knowledge is not the only order, because it is not enclosed in itself, and because it contains at least the gaping chasm of the present, the whole of history is still action and action already history. History is the same whether we contemplate it as a spectacle or assume it as a responsibility" (*Primacy of Perception*, p. 194).
79. Carr, *What Is History?*, p. 9.
80. *Experience and Its Modes* (Cambridge: At the University Press, 1933), p. 42.

discovery, Norwood Hanson regards "facts" as not being "pictura-
ble, observable entities." [81] Facts in relation to theory, and in turn
theory in relation to facts, are really hermeneutical events. Kuhn
also shows that in scientific discovery, which is "a complex event"
that "involves recognizing both *that* something is and *what* it is,"
both theory and fact, both conceptualization and observation are
"inseparably linked." [82] For Merleau-Ponty, similarly, Husserl's
Wesensschau (intuition of essence) is the mental operation
which consists of a reading of the essential meaning structure of
a multiplicity of facts. In theorizing, the factual and the essential
are mutually related.[83] Therefore, there are no facts that are raw
and crude. Needless to say, moreover, the language of statistics
without interpolation is a disjointed, meaningless collection of
dots, numbers, lines, and graphs. I am inclined to agree with
Sheldon Wolin when he says that "facts are more multi-faceted
than a rigid conception of empirical theory would allow" and that
"noting . . . is more necessary as a condition for theorizing
than that facts not be univocal." [84]

Embodiment and Artificial Reasoning

Eulau uses the phrase "logic of science" as the key
device in separating the inner (subjective) from the outer (objective) and taking one side, the outer, as the only valid domain
of scientific discourse. As has been indicated in Lane's and
Deutsch's conceptions of consciousness, political behavioralism
takes for granted a complicity between outer expression and
inner thought, cognition and affectivity (or feeling), and mind
and body, as illustrated particularly in Lane's divisive conception
of "consciousness" and "intelligence."

It is in *The Principles of Psychology* (1890) that the radical
empiricist William James distinguishes between "knowledge-
about" (conceptual knowledge) and "knowledge by acquaintance" (preconceptual knowledge) and attempts to show their
mutual relatedness. As pure experience is feeling, knowledge by

81. *Patterns of Discovery* (Cambridge: At the University Press, 1969),
p. 31.
82. *Structure of Scientific Revolutions,* p. 55.
83. Merleau-Ponty, *Primacy of Perception,* pp. 54 ff.
84. "Political Theory as a Vocation," *American Political Science Review,* LXIII (December, 1969), 1073.

acquaintance is felt knowledge, whereas knowledge-about is thought knowledge: "Through feelings we become acquainted with things, but only by our thoughts do we know about them. Feelings are the germ and starting point of cognition, thoughts the developed tree." [85] Thus there is the mutual dependency between feeling and symbolization. As for feeling or felt meaning, it is "an inward sensing" that is definitely there inside us as "a concrete mass"; nevertheless, it is hard to specify what it *is*.[86] Like thinking or any other form of consciousness, feeling is intentional (that is, feeling is always feeling-of-something). But unlike thinking, which has a sharp cleavage between subject and object, feeling is "the manifestation of a relation to the world which constantly restores our complicity with it, our inherence and belonging in it, something more profound than all polarity and duality." [87] Feeling as some "non-mediatizable immediate," therefore, is an embodied mode of participation in the world.[88] To introduce feeling in our discussion, it is worth realizing, is not to slight conceptual knowledge but to insist stubbornly on the inseparability of the two and on the unity of mind and body.[89]

Felt meaning is a presymbolic, ongoing flow of experiencing. It has an important function in what we think, observe, and perceive and in how we behave. Although it is yet to be articulated fully in symbols, this felt, flowing mass of human experience is richer and broader than thought, observation, speech, and action. It makes sense to say that "we can know more than we can tell" and "we mean (or 'sense') more than we can say." [90]

85. 2 vols. (New York: Dover, 1950), I, 222.
86. Eugene T. Gendlin, *Experiencing and the Creation of Meaning* (New York: Free Press, 1962), p. 11.
87. Ricoeur, *Fallible Man*, p. 129.
88. Marcel, *Mystery of Being*, I, 127–53.
89. L. S. Vygotsky's genetic and developmental theory of thought and language is most poignant in making the idea of the inseparability between thought and affectivity clear. For him there is no sharp line of division between the inner and the outer since they are two moments of one process and every thought has an affective volitional basis. See his *Thought and Language*, ed. and trans. Eugenia Hanfmann and Gertrude Vakar (Cambridge, Mass.: M. I. T. Press, 1962). Vygotsky's distinction between "sense" and "meaning" parallels James's distinction between knowledge by acquaintance and knowledge-about on the one hand and Eugene Gendlin's distinction between felt meaning and symbolic meaning on the other.
90. Cf. Michael Polanyi, *The Tacit Dimension* (New York: Doubleday, 1966), p. 4.

Broadly speaking, meaning is not limited to what is symbolically expressive, that is, it is not concerned merely with the logical, syntactical, and semantic structures of symbols. If it were, human thought process would be like the working of pro-grammed computers and human speech would be like playing a record on a phonograph. As feeling and symbolizing go hand in hand, one is capable of symbolizing his felt meaning or ex-pressing it in words or speech. Our thought is the mediation be-tween felt meaning and symbols, and the latter have a direct and selective reference to the former.

Furthermore, the phenomenological notion of man as an em-bodied agent offers a tentative, negative answer to Eulau's claim that no segments of political behavior are "intrinsically immune to scientific analysis," [91] since there are no a priori or inherent limits to scientific techniques. As scientific creativity "knows of no predetermined limitations," all segments of political behavior can in principle, or potentially, be treated "behaviorally," for "the future is always contingent, and contingencies are difficult to foresee." [92] The scientific analysis of political behavior is then posed as potentially a technological question. It seems that the possible perfection of computer technology or artificial intelli-gence is what Eulau has in mind. He believes that the progress of science, like the "progressive" spirit of liberalism in which he has faith, has no a priori or inherent limitations. Eulau's scien-tific faith may be challenged by the phenomenological considera-tion that man is an embodied agent, an idea which seems to point to the absolute limit of simulation as applied to the understand-

91. Eulau, *Behavioral Persuasion in Politics,* p. 32.
92. "Behavioral Treatment of Politics," p. 149. Eulau often endorses Morris R. Cohen's views of science and liberalism as two complementary systems of undogmatic attitudes. See Cohen, *The Faith of a Liberal* (New York: Holt, 1946), pp. 437–69. Interestingly enough, Eulau assigns to psychoanalysis the task of curing resistance to behavioralist techniques (*Behavioral Persuasion in Politics,* p. 32). It might also be suggested that an equally interesting task for psychoanalysis is to determine *why* science and technology have become thaumaturgy for modern man, both the in-tellectual and the layman alike. In *The Psychology of Science* (Chicago: Regnery, 1966), Abraham Maslow remarks that "these 'good,' 'nice' scien-tific words—prediction, control, rigor, certainty, exactness, preciseness, neatness, orderliness, lawfulness, quantification, proof, explanation, vali-dation, reliability, rationality, organization, etc.—are all capable of being pathologized when pushed to the extreme. All of them may be pressed into the service of the safety needs, that is, they may become primarily anxiety-avoiding and anxiety-controlling mechanisms" (p. 30).

ing of human behavior. The obvious fact that computers are not human or man is not a machine because he is an embodied agent ought to be elaborated. The technological limitation or possible perfection Eulau speaks of here is ultimately the question whether the computer simulation of human intelligence is limited or possibly perfectible.

In recent years there have been attempts to justify the science of politics in terms of the models of artificial intelligence or cybernetics. Herbert Simon, for example, attempts to make psychology a science of the artificial and goes so far as to say that the proper study of mankind is not man but the science of the artificial design [93]—a claim which indeed exceeds the initial vision of Norbert Wiener for the possibilities of an exact science of man and society.[94]

Karl Deutsch's cybernetic model is one of the philosophically most sophisticated justifications in political behavioralism for the use of artificial intelligence or cybernetics in the investigation of the functions of a political system. For him the model is any "physical device" which, under a set of operating rules, can process a set of symbols: "the set of symbols and the set of operating rules form a *symbol system* or a *model*" (for example, a language, a system of geometry, a logical calculus, chess, or poker).[95] As an intellectual device for the understanding of reality, it is necessarily simplified, rather than a "complete replica." For Deutsch the shortcomings of both classical mechanism and organism are the following: that the quantitative approach of the former excludes the qualitative categories of change, growth, novelty, and purpose, and that the qualitative approach of the latter lacks details of quantitative measurement. The cybernetic

93. *Sciences of the Artificial*, p. 83. Cf. Gaston Bachelard, *La Formation de l'esprit scientifique: Contribution à une psychanalyse de la connaissance objective* (Paris: Vrin, 1947), pp. 250–51.
94. See *Cybernetics*, 2d ed. (Cambridge, Mass.: M.I.T. Press, 1961), p. 164: "[W]hether our investigations in the social sciences be statistical or dynamic—and they should participate in the nature of both—they can never be good to more than a very few decimal places, and, in short, can never furnish us with a quantity of verifiable, significant information which begins to compare with that which we have learned to expect in the natural sciences. We cannot afford to neglect them; neither should we build exaggerated expectations of their possibilities. There is much which we must leave, whether we like it or not, to the un-'scientific,' narrative method of the professional historian."
95. *Nerves of Government*, p. 10.

model he proposes, then, is supposed to be an alternative model
to accommodate the shortcomings of these two models, in that
it is "applicable to problems involving both quantity and quality
. . . [by] facilitating the recognition of patterns, together with
measurement and verifiable predictions." [96] In seeking an essential unity between the mental and the physical, Deutsch claims
that his model is strikingly different from the Cartesian mode of
thought, which makes "a sharp division between the process of
mind and the physical world accessible to science." [97] Although
Deutsch acknowledges the complexity of human information
processing, the present technological impossibility of building a
complex machine that can adequately perform the functions of
human thought processes, and the dynamic quality of human
mind (that is, mind as "a single run pattern of information
flow"), his cybernetic model nonetheless succumbs to physicalism as it paves the way to rigorous and quantitative measurement and prediction. Human mind, for example, is an analogue
to the information process of artificial intelligence. Information
is defined as "a patterned relationship between events" which is
physical, being "carried by matter-energy processes"; and because
it is different from "form" it is analyzable into *discrete units*"
that can be quantitatively measured. Subsequently, mind is "any
self-sustaining physical process which includes the seven operations of abstracting, communicating, storing, subdividing, re-
calling, recombining and reapplying [discrete] items of information." [98] As a symbol is "an order to recall from memory a
particular thing or event, or a particular set of things or events,"
meaning is by the same token a "physical position in a sequence
of events." [99]

The optimism expressed by researchers in cognitive simulation or artificial intelligence is now being challenged by the
findings of existential phenomenology.[100] According to the phe-

96. "Mechanism, Teleology, and Mind," p. 192.
97. *Ibid.*, p. 222.
98. *Ibid.*, p. 216.
99. *Nerves of Government*, p. 10, and "Mechanism, Teleology, and
Mind," p. 221.
100. See Hubert L. Dreyfus, *Alchemy and Artificial Intelligence*, RAND
Paper P-3244 (Santa Monica, Calif.: RAND, December, 1965); "Phenomenology and Artificial Intelligence," in *Phenomenology in America*,
ed. James M. Edie (Chicago: Quadrangle, 1967), pp. 31–47; and "Why
Computers Must Have Bodies in Order to Be Intelligent," *Review of Meta-*

nomenological tradition of Husserl, Heidegger, and Merleau-
Ponty, researchers in artificial reason are necessarily committed
to the following two assumptions:

1. An epistemological assumption that all intelligent behavior
   can be simulated by a device whose only mode of information
   processing is that of a detached, disembodied, objective observer.
2. The ontological assumption, related to logical atomism, that
   everything essential to intelligent behavior can in principle be
   understood in terms of a determinate set of independent elements.[101]

Proceeding from these two assumptions, researchers in artificial
intelligence believe that human intelligence can essentially be
simulated or formalized, or that psychology *is* a science of the
artificial. According to this thesis, the acquisition of knowledge
is viewed as the function peculiar to the disembodied mind as a
rational faculty or, in the cybernetic model of Deutsch, as the
function of an electronic network. "Machines," Hubert Dreyfus
declares, "are perfect Cartesians. They are able to deal only with
the determinate and *discrete bits of information* which Descartes
called 'clear and distinct ideas.' "[102]
   Although they may reject the "metaphysical cargo" of
Descartes, theorists of artificial intelligence rely on the Cartesian
idea of mind as a thinking substance or thing, a necessary
corollary of the psychophysical parallelism (mind and body both
as substances or *res cogitantes* and *res extensae*).[103] By replacing the *res cogitans* with artificial rationality and rationalism
with artificial-ism, they accept the idea of man as a disembodied
mind. Man and his behavior can be understood without under-

physics, XXI (September, 1967), 13–32. Dreyfus' most comprehensive
critique of artificial reason is found in *What Computers Can't Do* (New
York: Harper & Row, 1972).
   101. Dreyfus, "Why Computers Must Have Bodies," p. 14.
   102. *Alchemy and Artificial Intelligence*, p. 66 (italics added).
   103. It is extremely important to note that one of the most serious
dilemmas that confronts the Cartesian notion of man as a *substance*, and
thus the cybernetic model and the science of man as an artifact in relation
to the *social* sciences, is that these concepts are incapable of rendering a
philosophically consistent justification for intersubjectivity or sociality.
For, as Sartre rightly points out, once the self and the other are regarded
as substances, which is to say, two separate substances, solipsism is in-
escapable (see *Being and Nothingness*, p. 233).

standing his physiology or biology,[104] just as the computer can be understood without understanding the physical properties of its hardware. So human language itself is an artificial design, and the acquisition of language is regarded as a purely intellectual or cognitive operation. Speaking of the relation of language and thinking, Simon is willing to say that "only the thinkable is expressible"[105] and the signified is identified with the signifiable. But in fact the contrary is true: the acquisition of language involves

> a kind of *habituation*, a use of language as a tool or instrument. The employment of language, which is an effect and also one of the most active stimuli of intellectual development, does not appear to be founded on the exercise of pure intelligence but instead on a more obscure operation—namely, the child's assimilation of the linguistic system of his environment in a way that is comparable to the acquisition of any habit whatever; the learning of a structure of conduct.[106]

I see no reason why the same process may not be assumed for any human learning, for the adult and the child equally, unless one believes in two ontological orders of a different sort, one for the child and another for the adult.

Phenomenology has now shown conclusively, I think, the qualitative differences between the information-processing of a computer (which, by the way, must have a "body" in order to "think") and the intelligence of a fully embodied agent in (1) pattern recognition, (2) problem solving, and (3) bodily skills.[107] The existence of this difference does not overlook the fact that some *specific* intelligent performances of man can be simulated by a computer. But it does mean that "*fully* intelligent behavior would be impossible in principle for a digital machine."[108] Human behavior, individual or social, cannot be fully predicted by simulation. Because it is capable of handling only "unambiguous, completely structured information," the machine is in-

---

104. For an excellent criticism of cybernetics from a biological point of view, see Hans Jonas, "Cybernetics and Purpose: A Critique," in *The Phenomenon of Life* (New York: Dell, 1966), pp. 108–34.
105. *Sciences of the Artificial*, p. 52.
106. Merleau-Ponty, *Primacy of Perception*, p. 99.
107. See Dreyfus, "Why Computers Must Have Bodies," and *What Computers Can't Do*, esp. pp. 143 ff.
108. Dreyfus, "Why Computers Must Have Bodies," p. 31.

capable of handling the ambiguous and "ill-structured data" of the human daily life-world.[109]

It may be concluded, therefore, that the basic and radical difference between man and the machine is that man is a fully embodied agent, an agent with the living body necessary for both thinking and acting, whereas the machine is only a thing with an artificial body which, when not out of order, may be faster, more efficient, and more error-free than man. But at best it can be only a replica of man. It is not because of "human pride," as Simon suggests, that an objection is raised here against the identification of man and the artificial. It is indeed feasible to produce servomechanisms that will surpass the human intelligence in speed and accuracy. The objection raised here is based not on the human pride of superiority but on the way in which man in his embodiment thinks and behaves qualitatively *differently* from any other organism or any mechanism. By proposing to reduce human thought to a "program" or "information flow" and the human body to an information container or hardware, Deutsch's cybernetic model and particularly Simon's science of artificial intelligence both of which focus solely on the clear "thinking" or "intellective" component of man, help us to understand him as a "cyborg" but fail to understand him as a natural and embodied being. Herein lies, perhaps, an answer to Eulau's faith that all segments of political behavior are accessible in principle to behavioralist techniques and that the progress of scientific analysis is just a question of technology. The behavioralist philosophy of man and his behavior fails in the end to take into account the dialectic of thought and feeling (or of symbolic and felt meaning) on the one hand, and the body as an active mode of Being-in-the-world on the other. Above all, it suspends or leaves out the theorizer himself as the *subject* of his own thought and action in the everyday social and historical life-world.

CONCLUSION

THE PHENOMENOLOGICAL CRITIQUE of the epistemology of political behavioralism in this paper is based on the ideas,

109. Dreyfus, *Alchemy and Artificial Intelligence*, p. 66.

first, that the question of the nature of political knowledge cannot ignore the question of political science as a human project, *praxis*, and achievement; and, secondly, that the methodology of political science must be consonant with the nature of political things, the most basic component of which, as Eulau would agree, is the *behavior* of man, political man. Political behavioralism shows indifference to and intolerance of the living, and often ambiguous, dialectic of the "visible" ("outer") and the "invisible" ("inner") by bifurcating the objective and the subjective, science and the life-world, cognition and affectivity, value and fact, and finally action and thought. The behavioralist methodological ideal of rigor, scientific objectivity, operational exactitude, quantitative measurement, and finally prediction, in order to build the citadel of an exact science after the model of the natural and mathematical sciences, especially physics, points to its indifference to science as a human project and the scientist as a human being. Insofar as it touches on the visible or outer perimeter of man, behavioralist philosophy provides an incomplete image of man and science. If the incomparable gadfly of ancient civilization, Socrates, is forthright in professing that the life unexamined is not worth living, then the foremost duty of scientific life is to examine and reflect on itself as a human *praxis*, which is the first order of rigor and magnitude.

Conceptual parsimony, or rather operational stricture, short-circuits the profusion of human experience and is insensitive to the agility, elasticity, and ephemeral quality of human thought, ignoring the experiential knowledge of political things in the everyday life-world as the source of scientific knowledge. The political behavioralist who refuses to recognize himself as the knowing *subject* in the life-world or who thinks of himself as an anonymous epistemological subject may be likened to the philosophical solipsism Wittgenstein once professed: (to paraphrase Wittgenstein's passage) the behavioralist self is not the human being, not the human body or the human soul, but rather the scientific subject, the limit of the world—not a part of it.[110] A way to overcome this scientific solipsism is the phenomenological archaeology of the political scientist as a knowing subject in relation to the life-world. The historicity of the political theorizer

110. *Tractatus Logico-Philosophicus*, trans. D. F. Pears and B. F. McGuinness (London: Routledge & Kegan Paul, 1961), p. 119.

suggests the idea that political theory as a human activity is a hermeneutical event.

Political behavioralism as a scientific technique necessarily reduces the inner to the outer and takes the latter as the only legitimate domain of scientific enterprise. This physicalist view regards human consciousness as an epiphenomenon of the physical and is incapable of understanding the intentional structure of human behavior as a structure of meaning which is neither entirely subjective nor entirely objective in the traditional sense of these terms. Moreover, it ignores the notion of embodiment (*Subjektleib* or *sujet incarné*), the idea that the body is not a mere physical object but essentially is the *subject* of consciousness and behavior. Man may no longer be the physical center of the universe, just as the geocentrism of Ptolemy is replaced by the heliocentrism of Copernicus; but he is still the *meta*-physical center of the world.

Phenomenologically speaking, the philosophy of political science *is* at the same time the philosophy of the political world. Theoretical activity, scientific or philosophical, is a special way of existing in the world, and political knowledge is a part of the political world as well as a conception of it, for the world is an active synthesis of what is given and what is constructed. Like action, thought itself is an active mode of participation in the world. Theory thus conceived is no longer a formalistic enterprise, for example, a logical and linguistic analysis. A phenomenology of politics or, better, the hermeneutics of politics suggests a new perspective or "paradigm" in political theory that is capable of synthesizing philosophy and science, fact and value, and knowledge and action. In other words, it is capable of synthesizing *theoria* and *praxis* the tension of which has been the twilight zone of Western political theorizing since its inception in ancient Greece. If "the goal is man," in the final analysis this goal cannot merely be a methodological credo. It is ultimately an ethical one. The theorizer, the scientist as well as the philosopher, is the "servant of humanity," and it is this phrase that defines his true *vocation*. He can no longer remain as an ethical amnesiac.[111]

---

111. See further the author's article "An Introductory Essay: The Political Relevance of Existential Phenomenology," in *Existential Phenomenology and Political Theory: A Reader* (Chicago: Regnery, 1972), pp. xvii–lv.

Phenomenology and
Political Science

Carl J. Friedrich

IN ITS MAIN THRUST, phenomenology is at variance
with the goals of contemporary political science and its concern
with scientific method. In Husserl's own word, all sciences are
for phenomenology only *Wissenschaftsphänomene;* they are only
phenomena themselves. "Scientifically induced or deduced realities etc. derived from hypotheses, facts, axioms remain excluded.
Phenomenology is the research into essence. Its field is the a
priori within the absolute self givenness." [1] This means, if it
means anything, that those political scientists and jurists who
have pleaded for the adequate recognition of the role of philosophy in providing a grounding for scientific work, and especially
those who have objected to talking in terms of "essences," should
find themselves impelled to look elsewhere for the guidance they
are seeking.

Thus I wrote some years ago that an important part of theoretical work addresses itself to defining the political phenomena.
Adequate theorizing requires defining, because without reasonably precise definitions it is impossible to state coherently argu-
able, let alone demonstrable, propositions. But, I added, scientific
defining—we will say empirically valid defining—must start
from the phenomena rather than from the words. Therefore, one
should avoid asking "what democracy really is" or "really means"

1. Edmund Husserl, *Die Idee der Phänomenologie, Husserliana* II, ed.
Walter Biemel, 2d ed. (The Hague: Nijhoff, 1958), p. 9 (hereafter cited
as *Idee*); cf. English translation by William P. Alston and George Nakhnikian, *The Idea of Phenomenology* (The Hague: Nijhoff, 1964), p. 7.
Note: all translations in the text are my own.

(asking, in other words, for the essence of it) and ask instead what the general features, traits, or characteristics of a particular phenomenon are, describing it in general terms and then attaching to it the verbal symbol among the available terms that is most nearly suitable.

In short it is not a matter of discovering or determining what a term "really means," but rather a problem of describing a certain phenomenon in as general a form as the available data permit. With Locke, Dewey, and many others I should be inclined to say "so the thing be understood, I am indifferent as to the name." [2] But in the political perspective, one cannot, of course, be indifferent to the name. If democracy is meant to describe a political order roughly similar to those of the United States and Britain, characterized by the protection of human rights, an independent judiciary, and two or more parties between which a choice is exercised in reasonably free elections, then it does not describe a political order such as that of the Soviet Union, with a single party having a monopoly of mass communications, etc. The use of the term is here determined by political considerations and is not indifferent. It may also be worthwhile to search for the common ground of the two orders. All of this goes to demonstrate the importance of stressing the actual phenomena to which the words refer, the "referents," in Ogden's and Richards' phrase. In Husserl's perspective, these are all transcendencies with which philosophy is not concerned. And yet, his approach to knowledge and cognition (see below) frees the student of these political phenomena from a great deal of metaphysical ballast. For it leaves him free to identify a phenomenon of primary experience in the political field, including politics itself. Such theorizing in political science, i.e., such search for generalization based upon established matters of fact, should not be confused with political philosophy, that branch of philosophy and political science by which, as I see it, the two are linked. And when Husserl argued that value and valuing are subject to the same kind of analysis as appearing and that which

2. Cf. my *Man and His Government* (New York: McGraw-Hill, 1963), p. 3 (hereafter cited as *M & G*); John Locke, *An Essay Concerning Human Understanding* (1687), in *The Works of John Locke* (London: 1759), § 146; and John Dewey, *The Quest for Certainty* (New York: Balch, 1929), p. 357.

appears (the double meaning of *Erscheinung* in German), he touched one of the basic problems of political philosophy.

Husserl's stress on the view that science is based on philosophy, and not philosophy on science, runs counter to much work in politics. It would seem to have the implication that political science (and all other sciences) are plunged into the quagmire of highly, indeed hopelessly, controversial issues. For there are so many philosophies, past and present, that any attempt at reaching agreement among even a small group seems out of the question.[3] The fact that philosophers do not agree on what philosophy itself is, is part of this difficulty, and Husserl and his followers are certainly quite dogmatic on the subject, and mean only that science must be based upon *their* philosophy —the critical evaluation of knowledge and cognition. The Concise Oxford Dictionary does not agree with them and defines philosophy as "love of wisdom or knowledge, esp. that which deals with ultimate reality, or with the most general causes & principles of things." Much of this transcends philosophy in Husserl's view.

On the third stage of phenomenological inquiry, Husserl believes that it is the task, step by step,

> to explore the given in all its modifications [*den Gegenbenheiten in allen Modifikationen nachzugehen*] . . . the simple and the synthetic, those which constitute themselves with one stroke and those which according to their nature only build themselves step by step, those which are absolutely valid and those which acquire a given . . . in the process of cognition in a limitless escalation [*Steigerung*]. . . . Thus we come to understand how the object of experience constitutes itself in continuity and how this kind of constitution is prescribed for it.[4]

And Husserl goes on to claim that on this road we find "the methodic forms which are determining for all sciences and which are hence constitutive for all scientific givens." This process clarifies the theory of science and implicitly thereby clarifies

3. Cf., e.g., *The Age of Analysis*, ed. Morton White (New York: Mentor, 1954), or Arthur Huebscher, *Denker unserer Zeit* (Munich: Piper, 1956), *passim*.

4. Husserl, *Idee*, p. 13; cf. *Idea*, p. 10.

all the sciences. Only implicitly and only after this huge clarifying work has been accomplished will it be possible "to offer a critique of the several sciences, and hence . . . utilize them for metaphysics." [5]

Let me finally recall Husserl's own definition of a phenomenon. It has a double meaning (*ist doppelsinnig*), due to the essential correlation between *appearing* and *that which appears* (*Erscheinen und Erscheinendem*). The Greek word *phainomenon* means originally that which appears, but preferably it is employed for the appearing itself, the subjective phenomenon (if I may be permitted, Husserl adds, to use this expression which may easily be crudely misunderstood psychologically). In this connection, Husserl asserts that phenomenology also has to solve the parallel problems of *valuing* and *value*, a problem to which Max Scheler devoted himself in a famous contribution to the *Jahrbuch für Philosophie und phänomenologische Forschung* [6] to be discussed below. Husserl himself remained preoccupied with cognition; at a number of points he states that the critique of cognition is the very linchpin of phenomenology. [7]

"Phenomenology signifies a science, a correlation of scientific disciplines; phenomenology at the same time signifies a method and an attitude of mind: the specific philosophic attitude of mind, the specific philosophic method." [8] Philosophy cannot be based upon other sciences, as the thinkers of an earlier age (the seventeenth century) thought; it is located in a completely novel dimension. It needs new starting points and a new method. It may itself have significant implications for other sciences, but not they for it. Phenomenology is thus a radical extension of the Kantian problem: how is cognition, how is knowledge of any kind possible? From this preoccupation, Husserl arrived at his insistence upon *reduction:* all that transcends cognition in this general sense must be excluded, must be treated as indifferent, as nil for cognitional theory. This "index" says: the existence

5. *Ibid.*, pp. 13–14; cf. *Idea*, p. 11.
6. It was later published as a book under the same title, *Der Formalismus in der Ethik und die materiale Wertethik* (Bern: Francke, 1916; 2d ed., 1921; 3d ed., 1926), (hereafter cited as *Ethik*); English translation by Manfred Frings and Roger Funk, *Formalism in Ethics and Non-Formal Ethics of Values* (Evanston, Ill.: Northwestern University Press, 1973).
7. Husserl, *Idee*, p. 23; cf. *Idea*, p. 18.
8. *Ibid.;* cf. *Idea*, pp. 18–19.

of all these transcendencies, whether one believes them or not, does not concern the philosopher; it remains outside his task. In this connection, Husserl is particularly opposed to all kinds of psychologism and anthropologism. I myself have repeatedly criticized the prevailing tendency in American political science to transform political problems into psychological ones, and have urged that the psychological dimension be "bracketed out." [9] Such bracketing out was also a key concern of Husserl's; he never wearied of warning against the distortion and corruption of the philosophical theory of cognition by the introduction of the investigations of a special science, namely, psychology. For him the work of men like Bruner would have served no doubt as an *exemplum horribile*.[10] The process is further elaborated elsewhere in this volume.[11] I should like to stress here that for much contemporary political science, particularly its so-called "behavioral" branch, a tendency opposite to Husserl's view is characteristic. Every phenomenon is psychologized, and attitudinal studies are flooding the journals in the discipline. It is also characteristic of much political science that it is quite uncritical on the subject of scientific cognition.[12] Many methodological studies assume that scientific inquiry presupposes the adoption of the methods of natural science or some other closely related method. Such an assumption often reflects a curious kind of intellectual arrogance—just the opposite of Husserl's modesty, and indeed humility (which he shares with Kant).

The reemergence of values as a key problem of political science should have produced an appreciation of the work of Max Scheler.[13] But such is by no means the case. Besides the author, hardly anyone ever mentions this crucial thinker who

9. *M & G*, p. 382, and *passim*.
10. Jerome S. Bruner, Jacqueline J. Goodnow, and George A. Austin, *A Study of Thinking* (New York: Wiley, 1956).
11. Cf. Maurice Natanson's Introduction to this volume.
12. From the plethora of books on this subject, let me mention the following: Fred M. Frohock, *The Nature of Political Inquiry* (Homewood, Ill.: Dorsey, 1967); Robert T. Golembiewski, et al., *A Methodological Primer for Political Scientists* (Chicago: Rand McNally, 1969); Eugene J. Meehan, *The Theory and Method of Political Analysis* (Homewood, Ill.: Dorsey, 1965); Jean Meynaud, *Introduction à la science politique* (Paris: Armand Colin, 1959); but there are many others. Not one of these works even mentions Husserl or Scheler, let alone discusses either philosopher.
13. See Scheler, *Ethik*, and his lecture "Der Mensch im Weltalter des Ausgleichs," in *Ausgleich als Aufgabe und Schicksal* (Berlin: Rothschild, 1929).

has established a phenomenology of values. No political analysis has ever been undertaken without touching values, and the efforts made to work out a "value-free" approach in the name of science, objectivity, and so forth are, from a logical viewpoint, self-contradictory.[14] Scheler himself stated his purpose as that of a "strictly scientific and positive foundation of a philosophic ethics dealing with all essential basic problems." And he stressed that in general the limits of what is demonstrable have not been transcended, for they are strictly a priori essentialist ideas and essentialist interrelations (interrelations of essences?). In this connection, Scheler intended to criticize the ethical doctrines of Kant, but such a critique is not his main concern, and we shall leave it aside here. Scheler himself stresses his deep respect for Kant's achievement, and says that he merely wishes to demonstrate the limitations of what was, until his writings, the "most perfect of strictly scientific insight into philosophic ethics." [15] He stresses the "methodological awareness of the unity and meaning of the phenomenological approach" which he says he and others owe to Husserl. It has been pointed out repeatedly that Scheler eventually came very close to Schopenhauer's conception of will (as had Bergson),[16] but in his key work on ethics he is centrally a phenomenologist. The phenomena he wishes to analyze are the values—not abstracted from goods and not misunderstood as goods, as in so much contemporary American political science and philosophy. Among these values he distinguishes between *Selbstwerte* and *Konsekutivwerte*—a distinction which I stressed by speaking of inherent and instrumental values [17] and insisting that "both are there." They are not subjective artifacts, imputed to the entities which are said to be valuable or have value by subjects who apprehend them as devoid of such value. Scheler puts a related point thus: "No philosophical theory of values can presuppose goods or things.

14. See Arnold Brecht, *Political Theory* (Princeton, N.J.: Princeton University Press, 1959), esp. pp. 117 ff., 135 ff., 261 ff.
15. Scheler, *Ethik*, pp. v–vi.
16. *Ibid.*
17. Cf. Herrmann Boenke, "Woertliche Übereinstimmungen mit Schopenhauer bei Bergson," *Jahrbuch der Schopenhauer-Gesellschaft,* V (1916), 37–86; and Peter Knudsen, "Die Bergsonsche Philosophie in ihrem Verhältnis zu Schopenhauer," *Jahrbuch*, XVI (1929), 3–44. It has been noted that the concept of will in the late Scheler also bears a close relationship to Schopenhauer's.

But . . . it is quite possible to discover a material set of values and an order within it which is completely independent of the world of goods and its varying structures and which is a priori." Hence such a proposition as the oft-cited definition of a state as implying an "authoritative allocation of values" (Easton) is utterly meaningless in the Schelerian perspective. Values exist, are there, and hence cannot be allocated, as goods and things can be. All this, in my opinion, seems to be implied in Scheler's elaborate and complex discussion of "values," which cannot be reproduced here.

Nicolai Hartmann has elaborated this aspect of the matter in his *Ethics*. Central is the proposition that *Werte haben ein Ansichsein*,[18] that is to say, values have a being of their own. Hartmann rightly adds that "values exist independently of consciousness." It may grasp them or it may miss them; it cannot create them. Thus values present the same problems which in the theory of cognition are presented by all beings by themselves (*ansichseiend*). They are objects of a *Wertschau* (seeing of values) but are not created by this seeing, this *Schau*. They are neither thoughts, nor *Anschau-ungen*,[19] nor *Vorstellungen*. Be-

18. Nicolai Hartmann, *Ethik* (Berlin: De Gruyter, 1926), p. 134; English translation by Stanton Coit, *Ethics*, 3 vols. (New York: Macmillan, 1932), I, 218.

19. In my *The Philosophy of Kant* (New York: Random House, 1949), I commented in my introduction, p. xxx, on the difficulty of translating *Anschauung* and *Vorstellung*. There I said: "The German word *Anschauung* is commonly rendered as intuition. . . . There are occasionally places where this term may possibly be right. But most of the time it is not; for it refers to a mental act that is generated inside a human being . . . where *Anschauung* means the exact opposite. The verb *anschauen* means to look at, to visualize, and the noun derived therefrom means: (a) the act of looking at something, (b) the thing-looked-at, (c) the impression or image in the mind resulting from these acts. In view of this, one must use whatever term would seem to fit the context. . . . Even more perplexing is the term *Vorstellung*. The term is often translated as 'representation' or 'presentation.' This usage is often misleading as the verb *vorstellen* means primarily 'to imagine' and the derivative noun may mean (a) the act of imagining, (b) the thing imagined, and (c) the image in the mind. It is clear that (c) overlaps with the third meaning of *Anschauung* and the resulting confusion is considerable." It is even greater in dealing with Husserl's thought, since he employs *Intuition* in German, where the term is clearly distinct from *Anschauung*, but in translation, due to the above noted custom of translating *Anschauung* as intuition, it becomes confused with that. The *Intuitionismus* of Husserl must not be confused with what is often spoken of as the intuitionism of Kant, even though what Kant means by *intellektuale Anschauung* comes close, it seems to me, to Husserl's *Intuition*.

cause of this, the notion of a *Wertschau* acquires its gnosiological importance.

I commented some years ago: "The object-like existence of values, facing the value-experiencing self as a datum to be experienced, ought not to be claimed as the ground for asserting that values are absolute, never-changing, eternal." Yet precisely this claim was advanced by Hartmann, who says that although goods may be relative, values, especially ethical values, are "absolute." "The ethical value of the behavior of a person exists evidently—at least as such—not 'for a subject' but inheres in a person or an act as its quality." [20] My doubts concerning this argumentation are based on the view that relative and absolute are not mutually exclusive alternatives, as they seem to be for Hartmann. For everything that man experiences as existing he experiences as changing. "Unchanging," "everlasting," and "absolute" are qualities which are not given in the experience of man. They are logical negations of the actual experiences of changing, passing, dependent actuality.[21] Values change, and in changing they become objectified. Scheler recognizes this changing character of the values in considering the present epoch of radical change.[22] But because values are real, because they are there, facing the self, value experience is universal. The basic values are experienced by most persons. They parallel other basic givens, such as colors, forms, and sounds. They are called basic —red, green, blue—precisely because they are nearly universally experienced. The occurrence of color blindness is no argument against this statement, and neither is value blindness. I would even argue that the test of the genuineness of experience is that such experience may not occur. In my opinion, one of the key lessons of Husserl's phenomenological approach is his demonstration of the inescapability of relying upon intuition for the basic experience upon which all knowledge is built. Husserl himself was primarily interested in the basic experience of cognition, and hence he focused attention upon the basic operations which he called *cogitationes;* but he accepted valuing as another such basic experience. I myself would prefer to speak of choosing, and Scheler eventually stressed willing. But willing pre-

20. Hartmann, *Ethik*, pp. 128 ff.; cf. *Ethics*, I, 206.
21. See my *M & G*, pp. 55–56.
22. Scheler, *Ethik*, pp. 38 ff., esp. n. 12 on *Ausgleich*.

supposes choosing, and choosing presupposes valuing; hence valuing is the intuiting of that which recommends itself to the self in choosing. The attention bestowed upon decision-making in recent political science is linked to these notions (though not often explicitly), but the phenomena that are being considered under these headings are rarely capable of searching analysis, because only the external aspects of such processes are capable of being empirically investigated. Decision suggests that actions are the result of deliberate choice; but many actions result from value preferences that were preexistent and allowed no alternative.[23] In Husserl's view these phenomena are "transcendent" and should be "bracketed" for truly phenomenological inquiry.

The idea of transcendence, used in so unusual a way by Husserl for the things of this world, when usually it refers to the "other world" of religious belief,[24] became the basis of one of the few theories in contemporary political science which show the impact of phenomenology, namely, Ernst Nolte's *Der Faschismus in seiner Epoche* (*Three Faces of Fascism*), published in 1963. The author interprets fascism as "resistance to transcendence." And he suggests that the "common element" in European philosophy from Hegel to Parmenides is "the distinction between a *finite* and an *eternal existence*." [25] It is this tradition which fascism challenges. Having asserted that "philosophy implies a unique and immense alienation," the author then proceeds to the assertion that the head-on clash "finds its most particular expression in the rivalry between revolution and conservation," and that "revolution is only conceivable when in the sphere of practical politics transcendence becomes perceptible." [26] He adds that "on its higher level practical transcendence will take the place of theoretical transcendence," and that in any case "Kant laid the foundation" for binding "theoretical and practical transcendence together as one uniform occurrence: dialectic as a doctrine of realization." This weird and incorrect interpretation of Kant, for whom the term "transcendental ideal-

23. See my *M & G*, pp. 73 ff.
24. Cf. my *Transcendent Justice* (Durham, N.C.: Duke University Press, 1964), *passim*.
25. Cf. Ernst Nolte, *Three Faces of Fascism* (Holt, Rinehart & Winston, 1966), pt. V, pp. 429 ff. (Nolte's italics).
26. *Ibid.*, pp. 431 ff., also esp. pp. 450 ff.

184 / Phenomenology and Political Science

184 / *Phenomenology and Political Science*

ism" had a very specific critical meaning, has some resemblances, it would seem, to Max Scheler's views as sketched above. It leads Nolte to the assertion that a "transcendental" definition of fascism presupposes a transcendental definition of "bourgeois society"; he believes that such a definition emerges from the work of Marx, Nietzsche, and Max Weber. The consequent "transcendental sociology of bourgeois society" makes Sovietism fundamentally different from fascism, despite all structural similarities, Nolte thinks, since Soviet concern with industrial production is "the total process of practical transcendence." The reason is that "fascism is resistance to practical transcendence (industrial production) as well as struggle against theoretical transcendence." Thus an intrinsically quite patent set of facts— namely, that the ideology of Soviet communism is fundamentally different from fascist ideology—is made obscure by such "explanations." If such were the contribution of phenomenology to political science, one could only exclaim: *Dieu nous en préserve!*

Not much more encouraging is a paper by Edith Stein on the state which Husserl published in his *Jahrbuch* in 1925.[27] This article, entitled "A Study of the State," is essentially conventional in its approach. It insists that sovereignty is decisive, a *conditio sine qua non,* and defines sovereignty as "self-determination [*Selbstgestaltung*] of a community"; at the same time it asserts that sovereignty and freedom of the individual person belong indivisibly together and that in the structuring of a state sovereignty plays a role analogous to that of freedom for the individual person.[28] Later on, the same article asserts that all that exists may be the subject (*Träger*) of a value and that therefore nothing is fully discussed if its value is not considered.[29] All these are conventional issues which are treated in an apodictic verbal fashion without any reference to historical experience or previous writings. This is not political science in the modern sense. The article antedates, of course, the development of contemporary political science, but this does not seem to me to excuse its failure to concern itself with empirical issues. Intuitionism without regard to concrete experience may be philosophy. It is not science.

27. Edith Stein, "Eine Untersuchung über den Staat," *Jahrbuch für Philosophie und phänomenologische Forschung,* VII (1925), 1–123.
28. *Ibid.,* pp. 42 ff.
29. *Ibid.,* p. 96.

Husserl's own work contains some very serious issues.[30] Husserl assumes that the natural person intuits what he calls the *Lebenswelt*, the living world, and that all science is a formalization and abstraction from it; it consists of "ideal objectivities" which rest upon the fundamental hypothesis of mathematical natural science that the intuited world becomes by such idealization capable of mathematical treatment. At one point Husserl says that "we measure the living world for a well-fitting garment of ideas," [31] and "this cloak of ideas has the effect that we take a method to be true being." This view of science, in a way related to that of Polanyi,[32] leads to a sharp condemnation of what has been the most marked trend of contemporary political science, namely, that toward quantification. As one commentator has said: "To regard nature as something in itself alien to mind and then to found the cultural sciences on the natural sciences, and thus supposedly to make them exact, is an absurdity." [33] This argument, though based on Husserl's difficult theories of intersubjectivity and so forth, coincides with others that rest upon the near-impossibility of quantifying many political data, either because of the secrecy of the proceedings or because of their elusive indeterminateness. To propose to "bracket" all that is part of the living world with which the social sciences and humanities (both of which Husserl refers to as the "cultural sciences") are concerned seems to block any significant path leading from phenomenology thus understood to political science.

If this living world is first of all a world that is separate for each individual (though not to be misunderstood as solipsistic), then everything in it relates to my actual historical situation, to

30. See Alfred Schutz, "Phenomenology and the Social Sciences," in *Philosophical Essays in Memory of Edmund Husserl*, ed. Marvin Farber (Cambridge: Harvard University Press, 1940), pp. 164–86 (hereafter cited as "Schutz").

31. *Ibid.*, p. 176, where Husserl is cited.

32. Michael Polanyi, *Personal Knowledge: Towards a Post-Critical Philosophy* (Chicago: University of Chicago Press, 1958). Cf. also William T. Scott, "Polanyi's Theory of Personal Knowledge: A Gestalt Philosophy," in *Massachusetts Review*, III (Winter, 1962), 349–68, and my own review essay in *Natural Law Forum*, VII (1962), 132–48. To these should be added the volume edited by Thomas A. Langford and William H. Poteat, *Intellect and Hope: Essays in the Thought of Michael Polanyi* (Durham, N.C.: Duke University Press, 1968).

33. Schutz, p. 178.

which belong also my pragmatic interests. The others, spoken of as alter egos, possess similar worlds of their own. These alter egos constitute a person's *Umwelt,* the world around him consisting of his associates, his *Mitwelt,* which consists of his contemporaries, his *Vorwelt,* composed of his predecessors, and his *Folgewelt,* composed of his successors.[34] That everyone relates somehow to persons living around him, with him, before him, and after him is a banality which is not made original by the weird terminology employed. Nor is it likely that political scientists will consider it impressive to suggest that these worlds are exhibiting certain centers of interest which raise the kind of problems suggested by the categories of familiarity and strangeness, or by that of accessibility.[35] When it is then asserted that "everything which has meaning for me also has meaning for the others with whom I share this living world," the political scientists will make a question mark and comment: "maybe." When one hears that "all this is self-evident to me in my naive life," [36] he wonders what the value of such banalities is for the study of politics in its transcendency. Nor is he likely to feel encouraged by the further observation that "all that has been said so far is no more than chapter headings for an extensive exploration." [37]

At this point, Husserl's phenomenology touches a key point in the methodology of Max Weber. For here the problem of meaning arises. "All these phenomena of meaning which obtain quite simply for the naive person, might be in principle exactly described and analyzed *within the general thesis.*" And this, we are told, is "the task of the cultural sciences": to accomplish such exploration of meaning on the level of intersubjectivity. Thus it is "a part of constitutive phenomenology to clarify their specific methods." [38] To this writer, little in the way of such clarification does in fact occur.

34. *Ibid.,* p. 181. In n. 18 the author explains that he is following the translation of Alfred Stonier and Karl Bode, in *Economica,* IV (1937), 406–24.
35. One study on this issue is found in David Truman, *The Governmental Process* (New York: Knopf, 1951); another in Carl Schmitt, *Gespraech über die Macht und den Zugang zum Machthaber* (Pfullingen: Neske, 1954).
36. Schutz, p. 182.
37. *Ibid.,* p. 183.
38. *Ibid.* The "general thesis" is what is usually spoken of as a general hypothesis, namely, that of assuming that the world exists.

Another such banality appears in the statement that "all science presumes a special attitude of the person carrying on science; it is the attitude of the disinterested observer." Such a statement is, in view of recent discussions on the problems of "value-free" social science, and the work by Polanyi,[39] not very illuminating, to say it frankly. Reference to such outworn approaches as "economic man" suggest that the entire discussion is out of date and related to a past stage of methodological inquiry. Nor is it acceptable to state that "idealization and formalization have just the same role for the social sciences as the one Husserl has stated for the natural sciences, except that it is not a question of mathematizing the forms, but of developing a typology." [40] The extended controversies over the meaning and significance of Max Weber's notion of "ideal type" [41] are indicative of the wide gap between Husserl's phenomenology and the road which modern political and social science has taken. It seems more than doubtful that political science and sociology will "find a guide" in Husserl's investigations in the field of transcendental phenomenology. To be sure, there are points of contact. But the way of intuitionist proceedings is the diametrical opposite of empirical political science and its methodological problems. The link to philosophy must be found in other fields. Any methodology which advocates the substitution of intuition for careful observation and analysis is a step backward toward the kind of speculative political philosophy which constitutes a large part of the history of political thought from Plato to Marx, in which what was to be explained is posited and patent facts are then subjected to an explanation.

Perhaps the most striking instance of such theorizing is the collection of contractual theories developed for the purpose of explaining the origin of the state.[42] Having posited isolated indi-

39. Polanyi, *Personal Knowledge*, p. 132 ff.
40. Schutz, p. 185.
41. Cf. my *Man and His Government*, pp. 28–33, esp. n. 2. Talcott Parsons, *The Structure of Social Action* (Glencoe, Ill.: Free Press, 1937), pp. 601 ff., discusses Weber's notion with great care, but without arriving at a clear conclusion. He in turn cites von Scheltings' study "Die logische Theorie der historischen Kulturwissenschaften von Max Weber . . . ," *Archiv für Sozialwissenschaft und Sozialpolitik*, XLIX (1922) 623 ff. See also his *Max Weber's "Wissenschaftslehre"* (Tübingen: Mohr, 1934).
42. In my "Constitutionalism versus Absolutism," in *Synopsis*, ed. Edgar Salin (Heidelberg: Lambert Schneider, 1948), pp. 133 ff., I argued this point in context.

viduals, usually in some kind of state of nature for the existence of which no available evidence can be cited with any confidence, it then became necessary to "explain" what is known, namely, that men live in politically ordered communities. How these developed and more particularly how the modern state came to exist is the real problem of political science, and its solution calls for historical and comparative analysis. A view which relegates all this data into the limbo of a transcendent living world would seem to be akin to Plato's and about as far removed from modern political science as any logic can be. It is a matter not of abstracting from the phenomenal world by the process of reduction that such political science asks for from philosophy, but on the contrary of linking politics effectively with the other realms of this living world, thus staying with this living world and seeking ways of convincingly generalizing from it.

The problem of the reality of this living world and of its potentialities of becoming known through observation and experience is particularly striking in the case of values. For values are not "ideal" [43] in the sense of being "not real." This ideal quality has been more particularly asserted in terms of inherent values, that is to say transcendent (not in Husserl's sense) values.[44] Values, it has been said, are never "realized." Value is, however, a particular kind of being, namely, the "ought-to-be being." This "ought-to-be" may or may not be actualized; but this lack of actuality is not inherent in the value or norm. The norm "Thou shalt not kill" implies that "life is valuable," that "life ought to be there." There is no need to employ a "reduction" from a particular state of affairs to make such a statement. It is just as true, whether few or many or none are killed.

Because values are real, because they *are there*, facing the

---

43. As is alleged by Hartmann, *Ethik*, pp. 135–40; cf. *Ethics*, I, 219–26.

44. Concerning value and value experience, and the general problem of "basic" experience, cf. *M & G*, chap. I, "The Theory of Politics as Human Experience"; cf. also Martin Heidegger, "Hegels Begriff der Erfahrung," in *Holzwege* (Frankfurt a.M.: Klostermann, 1950), pp. 105–19. It is a commentary on Hegel's unusual but basically sound, because broad, concept of experience; Hegel's ten pages are difficult, but Heidegger's commentary no less so. Cf. for contrast the straightforward discussion in John Dewey's *Experience and Nature* (New York: Dover, 1958), esp. chap. I.

self, every self, value experience is universal.[45] Some values may be experienced only by some persons, but the basic values are experienced by most persons; they parallel other basic givens, such as colors, forms, and sounds. These givens are called basic on account of their universality. They are so in spite of color-blind men; correspondingly, the occasional occurrence of value-blind men does not disprove the reality of values, nor does it prove their pure subjectivity. For the very test of the basicness of experience is that such experience *may not occur.* Values demonstrate that the basic given is experience. That something is real means that it has been universally experienced. Hence there is a degree of reality; givens may be more or less real, depending on their range of being experienced.[46]

Such a statement implies a broad conception of experience. The so-called sensationalist empiricists, preoccupied with the problems of natural science, were in error when they would allow only sense experience to be valid experience. Feeling and willing, as well as innovation, are part of human experience.[47] The realm of experience in politics is not primarily sense experience. I feel compelled at this point to recall an observation John Dewey made upon the philosophic preoccupation with certainty. He called it *"the* philosophic fallacy" by which the stable is substituted for the unstable, the lasting for the changing, being for becoming, and so forth. It is a technique by which "thinkers have relegated the uncertain and unfinished to an invidious state of unreal being, while they have systematically exalted the assured and complete to the rank of true Being." [48] There is no more striking illustration for this tendency than phenomenology, and it is no accident that Husserl explicitly rejected "empiricism" as an

45. See *M & G,* chap. I; Heidegger, "Hegels Begriff der Erfahrung"; and Dewey, *Experience and Nature.*

46. The problem of the reality of values remains highly controversial; Hartmann seems to adopt the view I favor; cf. *Ethik, passim.* Cf. also Luis Recasens Siches, "Human Life, Society and Law: Fundamentals of the Philosophy of Law," in *Latin American Legal Philosophy* (Cambridge: Harvard University Press, 1948), pp. 1–341, and *Direcciones contemporaneos del pensamiento jurídico* (Barcelona: Editorial Labor, 1929). For the problem see also R. S. Hartman's careful review in "Value, Fact, and Science," *Philosophy of Science,* XXV (1958), 97–108.

47. The implications of this view have been elaborated by Michael Polanyi in *Personal Knowledge.*

48. Dewey, *Experience and Nature,* p. 52.

allowable philosophic position.[49] Phenomenology disagrees with Dewey, who defined an empirical philosophy as one which perceives that thinking is "a continuous process of temporal reorganization within one and the same world of experienced things, and not a jump from the latter world into one of objects constituted once for all by thought."[50] We might add that for Dewey (and for much contemporary political science), "philosophy is inherently criticism having its distinctive position among various modes of criticism in its generality; a criticism of criticisms, as it were."[51] Yet it is obvious that such a statement would include Husserl's phenomenology, in which the critical evaluation of "givens" is so central an undertaking. "The idea of phenomenology, namely the exclusion of all positing of being and the inquiry into the subjective givens . . . became a universal program of work which was to make comprehensible all objectivity, all the meaning of existence."[52]

Hence the stress on the thought processes as a form of experience which in turn is related to the anti-empiricist slant of phenomenological philosophizing. The stress laid on "essence" (*Wesen*) commented on earlier is far removed from the medieval essentialist position in its "reductionist" passion for intellectual certainty. Political scientists and theorists often speak of the "essence" of this and that. Thus there is an "essentialist" literature on totalitarianism. We read that "essentialist, or what some prefer to call 'real' definitions include not simply those that, like Arendt's, take the form of 'the essence of totalitarianism is . . .' but all formulations that emphasize ideological content, system goals, and other relatively abstract and nonmeasurable attributes of a regime."[53] Here, and in many similar discussions, essence is

49. Husserl's rejection of empiricism is well known and permeates his entire work; cf. Marvin Farber, *The Foundation of Phenomenology* (Cambridge: Harvard University Press, 1943), and Schutz, "Phenomenology and the Social Sciences."

50. Dewey, *Experience and Nature*, p. 68; for my view regarding basic experience, see *M & G*, pp. 15 ff.

51. *Ibid.*, p. 398. Cf. also my article "Political Philosophy and the Science of Politics," in *Approaches to the Study of Politics*, ed. Roland Young (Evanston, Ill.: Northwestern University Press, 1958), pp. 172 ff.

52. See Hans-Georg Gadamer, *Wahrheit und Methode*, 2d ed. (Tübingen: Mohr, 1965), p. 231; though there is no mention of Dewey's work in this rangy analysis.

53. Benjamin R. Barber, "Conceptual Foundations of Totalitarianism," in *Totalitarianism in Perspective: Three Views*, ed. Carl J. Friedrich, Michael Curtis, and Benjamin R. Barber (New York: Praeger, 1969).

simply asserted—though it is presumably not an accident that
Hannah Arendt is a pupil of Karl Jaspers, an existentialist with
links to the phenomenological outlook. It is worth noting, however, in this connection that the author of the above-cited
quotation speaks of a phenomenological, as contrasted with an
existentialist, definition of totalitarianism, not in the sense of
Husserl's use of the term, but quite on the contrary; phenomenological definitions, he writes, attempt to isolate a concept's
objective attributes; that is to say, they identify the concept with
a "syndrome or pattern of interrelated traits, or with certain
limited performance characteristics that describe the objective
and therefore measurable behavioral and institutional characteristics of a particular class of regimes.[54] Evidently, the term is
employed in a sense diametrically opposed to Husserl; for the
very data of the living world that Husserl proposes to bracket as
not part of the real *phainomenon* are central to such an approach.
Hence it is not surprising that the phenomenological definition
contrasts sharply with the "essentialist" definition of totalitarianism. They are both "empiricist" in Husserl's sense and hence
belong to that world of experience from which phenomenology
must abstract by bracketing out such data. Hence the strictures
of a recent study of contemporary political thought in which it is
said that Husserl's is "an attempt to analyze experience," which
the author sees as closely connected with existentialism and
vitalism (Bergson). He asserts that "they have in common the
denial of meaning to objective and observable reality and the
postulation of an essential inner meaning, knowable only through
the actual process of experiencing existence." [55] This surely is a
rather misleading statement, unless the point is reinforced by
making quite explicit that Husserl was primarily interested in
the basic experience of cognition. Even then, there is no "denial
of meaning" in Husserl's phenomenology; quite on the contrary,
there is an insistence upon the *Sinnzusammenhang*. There is
merely an insistence that this meaning cannot be ascertained by

54. *Ibid.,* pp. 10–11.
55. Eugene J. Meehan, *Contemporary Political Thought: A Critical
Study* (Homewood, Ill.: Dorsey, 1967), p. 65. Meehan goes on to claim
that "the external world is considered 'absurd' and meaningless; the inner
world is held to be beyond the reach of scientific analysis." This surely is
an untenable proposition, but it shows how remote phenomenology is from
contemporary political science.

an empirical study of the "phenomena"—phenomena taken in the usual understanding of this word as that which appears to human beings from the outside.

Actually, Husserl's belief that this "living world" cannot become the subject of scientific any more than of phenomenological inquiry, that as we stated above science consists of "ideal objectivities" which are linked to the hypothesis that the intuited world becomes by such idealization capable of mathematical treatment, is a crucial point for quantifying political science. For it assumes that political data may be equated or at least treated analogically with natural data of the physical world—a view that Husserl very sharply rejects, as we have seen earlier in this analysis. The living world of values is here involved. Human subjectivity is one of the givens of our living world and deserves to be as carefully explored as are any other givens, but the method must not be "psychological" but "phenomenological." [56]

The difficulty that obstructs the response of the American political scientist to such explorations of the mind and such methods of critical analysis, although quite in keeping with Dewey's above-cited notion of philosophy, is the lack of that sophistication about knowledge which would spring from a full grasp of Kant's criticism of "reason." A great deal of theorizing in American political science (and not only in political science!) is precritically "naïve" in its approach to cognition. The uncritical response to Max Weber's work is often traceable to a failure to realize his Neo-Kantian philosophical base, with its rigid distinction of *Sein* and *Sollen,* of the phenomenal and the noumenal world—to use the Kantian terms—and the consequent conceit about a "value-free" social science. Hence the philosophical concern of Husserl, his desire to get beyond the limitations of this methodology, has little meaning to these *Nachbeter* of an untenable position.

Before concluding this inconclusive discussion, a few words might be added concerning Heidegger. He may be taken as representing the existentialist branch of phenomenological philosophizing. Considering the central position of the concept of power in political science and theory, it is a striking fact that

56. Paul Arthur Schilpp, *Karl Jaspers* (Stuttgart: Kohlhammer, 1957); Julius Kraft, *Von Husserl zu Heidegger: Kritik der phänomenologischen Philosophie,* 2d ed. (Frankfurt a.M.: Verlag "Oeffentliches Leben," 1957), pp. 40 ff. Cf. also Farber, *Foundation of Phenomenology.*

existentialist philosophers since Kierkegaard have been much preoccupied with the problem of power. Karl Jaspers takes up power at length in several places, e.g., in his great treatise on truth.[57] Jean-Paul Sartre has recurrently dealt with the problem of power.[58] And Martin Heidegger, in *Sein und Zeit* as well as in later works, has shown a central concern with the same problem of power. More specifically, in an essay dealing with Nietzsche's saying that God is dead,[59] Heidegger cites a key passage from *Thus Spake Zarathustra* as offering the key to the issue of God's dying: "Where I found a thing alive, there I found the will to power; even in the will of the servant I found the will to be master." Heidegger explores a number of other passages of Nietzsche, taken from *The Will to Power, Die Fröhliche Wissenschaft*, and so on. We cannot here retrace the rich and variegated exposition of Heidegger, except to stress that it leads him into the problem of values. He cites Nietzsche as observing that "the question of values is more fundamental than the question of certainty. The latter becomes serious only on condition that the question of value has been settled." In becoming conscious that "God is dead" we become conscious of a radical revaluation of all values (*Umwertung aller Werte*), Heidegger cites Nietzsche as saying; and he shows how this leads to the conception of the

57. Karl Jaspers, *Von der Wahrheit* (Munich: Piper, 1947), pp. 366 ff., 581 ff., and 803 ff. Jaspers stresses the dual nature of power, as I do (cf. *M & G*, chap. 9). Other major works on power include Harold D. Lasswell and Abraham Kaplan, *Power and Society: A Framework for Political Inquiry* (New Haven, Conn.: Yale University Press, 1950); George E. Catlin, *Systematic Politics* (Toronto: University of Toronto Press, 1962), and earlier works; Charles E. Merriam, *Political Power* (New York: McGraw-Hill, 1934); Robert A. Dahl, "The Concept of Power," *Behavioral Science*, II (1957), 201 ff.; Karl Deutsch, *The Nerves of Government* (Glencoe, Ill.: Free Press, 1963), chap. 9.

58. It is closely linked to his decisionism; cf. *L'Etre et le néant* (Paris: Gallimard, 1943); English translation by H. Barnes, *Being and Nothingness* (New York: Philosophical Library, 1956). Sartre's decisionism extends to morals, and he flatly proclaims that man "chooses" his "morals" in *L'Existentialisme est un humanisme* (Paris: Nagel, 1946), p. 78; cf. English translation by Bernard Frechtman, "Existentialism," in *Existentialism and Human Emotions* (New York: Philosophical Library, 1957), p. 43. See F. J. Brecht, *Heidegger und Jaspers: Die beiden Grundformen der Existenzphilosophie* (Wuppertal: Marées Verlag, 1948).

59. Martin Heidegger, *Holzwege* (Frankfurt a.M.: Klostermann, 1950), pp. 193 ff. For a very sharp criticism of Heidegger's views, and more particularly his verbal acrobatics, which make it almost impossible to translate him (*andenkendes Denken, das Ding dingt, Selbststand*, vs. *Gegenstand*, etc.), see Julius Kraft, *Von Husserl zu Heidegger*, pp. 89 ff.

superman: "The name of the essence of man which transcends man until now is 'superman'. The superman is the kind of man who is shaped by the will to power and the reality which it forms." Heidegger remarks that it is easy to become indignant in facing the figure of the superman, but it is irresponsible. For future thought cannot evade the noble responsibility by which Nietzsche reflected upon the essence of the kind of man who is destined to achieve world dominion as a result of his will to power. And he adds: "The essence of the superman is not the freedom of arbitrary raging [*Tobsucht der Willkür*]." In these sentences the tragedy of Heidegger's involvement with the Nazi students at Freiburg in 1933 is manifest. What seemed a dawn of the superman became raging tyranny. Yet the essay concludes with the telling line: "Thinking only begins when we have learned that reason, glorified since centuries, is the greatest adversary of thinking." [60] In such irrationalist appeals, the phenomenological approach through its intuitionism demonstrates its clash with political science. For to think politically, that is to say, to think in terms of the necessities of politics, is the core of that science. Heidegger never grasped it.[61] Nor did Karl Jaspers, who once informed me that it was nonsense to ask Germans to vote on their constitution (of Baden-Württemberg, in 1947), because they did not understand the meaning of its provisions, and that hence his maid who had refused to vote was wiser than he who had.[62]

What do these rambling reflections add up to? Essentially they lead to concluding what we stated at the outset, namely, that phenomenology is at variance with the goals of contemporary political science in its concern with scientific method. Phenomenology also fails to respond to the political challenge, except in preconceived notions of power which reflect a particular political tradition of the West that has ended in the holocaust. Yet, neither of these conclusions is inherently compelling. Much of the con-

---

60. Heidegger, *Holzwege*, pp. 220–21, 232, 234, 247.
61. This harsh judgment is confirmed by a collection of tidbits, *Heidegger im Gespräch*, ed. Richard Wisser (Munich: Alber, 1970).
62. See Karl Jaspers, *Wohin treibt die Bundesrepublik* (Munich: Piper, 1966), in its moralizing approach to difficult political problems without adequate knowledge of the facts, as pointed out in many comments by practical politicians, notably the Social Democrat Erhard Eppler, "Wohin treibt Karl Jaspers?," *Die Zeit*, July 22, 1966. Fortunately, the dire predictions of Jaspers turned out to be quite wrong.

fused methodological discussion in political science could have gained perspective and clarity by a consideration of the sharp critical analyses of Husserl's *Logische Untersuchungen*. And the apolitical intuitions of Heidegger, Jaspers, and Sartre could have been avoided (and much damage in the bargain), even within the framework of Husserl's notions of the living world, with its contemporaries, its associates, its predecessors, and its successors. For have we not lived for many a generation with Burke's moving statement of the same view that "society is a partnership not only between those who are living, but between those who are living, those who are dead and those who are yet to be born." [63]

63. Burke, as quoted in *Burke's Politics*, ed. Ross J. S. Hoffman and Paul Levack (New York: Knopf, 1949), p. 318.

Political Inquiry and the Concept of Action: A Phenomenological Analysis

John G. Gunnell

WHETHER OR NOT contemporary social science may be understood as experiencing what, in terms of Thomas Kuhn's popular formulation, might be conceived as a paradigm conflict or a crisis of scientific identity, it is becoming increasingly evident that a significant challenge is being presented to the dominant epistemological assumptions that have informed most of the recent theoretical and empirical work in these disciplines. What is taking place is not a subtle evolutionary transformation with the absorption of new elements into a cumulative corpus of theory and research but rather, without suggesting any strict isomorphic relation between this situation and Kuhn's analysis of natural science, a development toward an incipient confrontation between the currently accepted vision of these sciences and their subject matter and a "competing articulation" which is demanding a "new basis for the practice of science."[1]

PHENOMENOLOGY AND THE CHALLENGE TO BEHAVIORALISM

THIS ASSESSMENT OF the current state of controversy within and over the so-called sciences of man is highly interpretative, and any attempt to tersely characterize or label the alleged challenge and the position that is being challenged will inevitably be inadequate and will tend to distort some aspects of

1. Thomas S. Kuhn, *The Structure of Scientific Revolutions* (Chicago: University of Chicago Press, 1962), pp. 90, 6.

[197]

this emerging *Methodstreit* and the particular arguments that are involved. But although the various facets of the competing perspectives may not be easily reducible to clearly defined and neatly dichotomized intellectual stances, such as the difference between " 'objective' and 'subjective' ways of seeing the world" or "objectivism" and "mentalism," [2] it is apparent that in most of the disciplines, as well as in the philosophical literature concerned with these disciplines, there is a trend toward some such conscious sorting out and consolidation. This is probably most evident in psychology and in the philosophical analysis of psychological inquiry, where behaviorism and phenomenology have appeared not only as descriptive categories for contesting approaches and divergent conceptions of human behavior but also as designations to which practitioners have repaired for self-identification, despite the considerable differences between particular viewpoints.[3] In the other social sciences, the positions are less clear, but even here an awareness of an increasingly articulate challenge to what has been variously characterized as the naturalistic, positivistic, or behavioristic conception of social-scientific inquiry that has dominated these disciplines has become evident and can no longer be dismissed as obscurantist and antiscientific. Whether, as Maurice Natanson has recently suggested, the social sciences are actually at a point of "choice" between competing perspectives which will be "decisive for the kind of social science that will emerge during the next century" is difficult to judge,[4] but it would seem that a stage has been reached where every conscientious social scientist must engage in a critical self-examination of his intellectual framework.

The position that is being called into question is in some ways more easily identified than that of its opponents—at least in terms of its general enunciated resolve to forward the development of a social science that is logically symmetrical with that of natural science—but in sociology, largely through the impact

2. Maurice Natanson, "Introduction," in *Philosophy of the Social Sciences*, ed. M. Natanson (New York: Random House, 1963), p. 15; May Brodbeck, "Meaning and Action," in *Readings in the Philosophy of the Social Sciences*, ed. M. Brodbeck (New York: Macmillan, 1968), pp. 59–60.

3. See, for example, T. W. Wann, ed., *Behaviorism and Phenomenology: Contrasting Bases for Modern Psychology* (Chicago: University of Chicago Press, 1964).

4. Natanson, *Philosophy of the Social Sciences*, p. 4.

of the work of Alfred Schutz, there has been a growing recognition of what has been characterized, without too much distortion, as a phenomenological perspective that disputes not only this broad goal but also the specific methodological course chosen to achieve it. In a generic sense, the "phenomenological approach" may be said "to designate a general style of social science which takes human consciousness and its intended meanings as the proper locus for the understanding of social action," and it may be understood as encompassing "all positions that stress the primacy of conscious and subjective meaning in the interpretation of social action . . . and which accordingly place[s] major emphasis on the meaning social acts have for the actors who perform them and who live in a reality built out of their subjective interpretation." [5] The link between phenomenology and sociology is not surprising, since traditionally, especially on the Continent, they have been intimately connected.[6] If the term is not too closely identified with the history of the "phenomenological movement" in philosophy,[7] the conceptual standpoint it represents also accommodates and complements the more indigenous schools of transactionalism and symbolic interactionism exemplified in the work of such individuals as Mead, Cooley, and Thomas.

The case of political science is somewhat different. Despite a continuing and growing dissatisfaction with the failure of behavioralism or the behavioral movement [8] (which during the past two decades has exercised intellectual dominance over the discipline) to furnish an adequate vision of political inquiry and the character and scope of political phenomena, there has been little evidence in the literature of political science of the development of a clearly articulated alternative philosophy of inquiry. Although one can point to specific instances of research that might be interpreted as employing a phenomenological approach or an occasional methodological piece that moves in this direction and

5. Natanson, "A Study in Philosophy and the Social Sciences," in *ibid.*, pp. 283, 273.
6. See Edward A. Tiryakian, "Existential Phenomenology and the Sociological Tradition," *American Sociological Review*, XXX (1965), 674–88.
7. See Herbert Spiegelberg, *The Phenomenological Movement*, 2 vols. (The Hague: Nijhoff, 1960).
8. See, for example, Charles A. McCoy and John Playford, *Apolitical Politics: A Critique of Behavioralism* (New York: Crowell, 1967).

draws upon the writings of Schutz, no extended theoretical work has appeared that could be viewed as representative of this position. Much of the criticism of behavioralism either has been conducted from a posture so hostile to the very enterprise of social science that at times it has approached an attack on the very legitimacy of an autonomous empirical science of politics, or it has consisted of what might be termed external criticism of inherent cultural biases of the discipline and its lack of relevance to substantive political problems and moral values and concerns.[9] Whatever their emphasis, recent critiques of behavioralism have become increasingly sophisticated and can no longer be interpreted as merely a rear-guard action of traditionalists and institutionalists or, as Heinz Eulau has recently suggested, as part of a "battle between the ancients versus the moderns" where "the real issue . . . is the issue of tradition and innovation in scientific development."[10] Yet even as late as 1963 it could be argued that "no genuine philosophical critique of the new persuasion has yet appeared,"[11] and, with the exception of a few isolated articles, that judgment remains substantially correct today. The absence of such a critique may be partially explained by the persistent notion that behavioralism is in the vanguard of the discipline and a "new persuasion." This view has been perpetuated by its champions and seldom challenged by its critics, despite the fact that, at least in terms of its most general tenets and goals, behavioralism has existed as a rather consistent set of doctrines at least since the 1930s.[12] However, the paucity of systematic, internally oriented criticism either by philosophers or political scientists remains a fact.

Eulau has suggested that in recent years the controversy sur-

9. See Herbert J. Storing, ed., *Essays on the Scientific Study of Politics* (New York: Holt, Rinehart & Winston, 1962); Christian Bay, "Politics and Pseudopolitics: A Critical Evaluation of Some Behavioral Literature," *American Political Science Review*, LIX (March, 1965), 39–51.

10. Heinz Eulau, "Tradition and Innovation: On the Tension between Ancient and Modern Ways in the Study of Politics," in *Behavioralism in Political Science*, ed. H. Eulau (New York: Atherton, 1969), p. 2.

11. John H. Schaar and Sheldon S. Wolin, "Essays on the Scientific Study of Politics: A Critique," *American Political Science Review*, LVII (March, 1963), 125.

12. See Bernard Crick, *The American Science of Politics* (Berkeley, Calif.: University of California Press, 1959); and Albert Somit and Joseph Tanenhaus, *The Development of American Political Science* (Boston: Allyn & Bacon, 1967).

rounding behavioralism has largely centered around, and has been limited to, the issues of the "possibility" of political science, political science versus political philosophy as modes of studying politics, the problem of the place of values in the study of politics, and questions about the basic units of analysis.[13] Unfortunately, it is probable that this assessment quite accurately reflects the trend in most of the professional literature, and, with regard to the most fundamental issues, it also may well be true "that many of the controversies over behavioralism in political science have been subterranean—fought out at professional conferences or within university departments rather than in printed communication media."[14] It is difficult to point to any serious and focal dialogue between the proponents and opponents of behavioralism where there has been a common concern with methodological problems and where the protagonists have not been essentially "talking past each other."[15] Even where critics of the prevailing persuasion have joined the behavioralists in a common concern with forwarding the development of an empirical science of politics, little has been offered in the way of substantive alternatives. Although it may seem outrageously impressionistic to argue in the face of this situation that a significant methodological confrontation with behavioralism from the standpoint of phenomenology or some such related perspective has begun to emerge, or is even imminent, there is evidence that an increasing number of political scientists deeply involved with problems of the philosophy of political science are committed to such a confrontation. Yet even where a commitment to a sustained questioning of the behavioral approach as a viable ground of inquiry has appeared, the spokesmen of behavioralism have tended to ignore such challenges or dismiss them as part of the "persisting bi-polar conflict in the field between humanists and behavioralists."[16] It is difficult to judge how long the discipline will be able to contain such challenges to the dominant vision by subsuming them in such obsolete dichotomies as traditionalism/behavioralism, but there has been a continuing attempt to keep alive the idea of behavioralism as a disciplinary revolution still fighting

13. Eulau, "Tradition and Innovation," p. 3.
14. *Ibid.*, pp. 3–4.
15. *Ibid.*, p. 3.
16. Gabriel Almond, "Political Theory and Political Science," *American Political Science Review*, LX (December, 1966), 878.

the specter of traditionalism and perilously existing as one distinct but embattled approach within the field.

THE BEHAVIORAL VISION

ROBERT DAHL wrote in 1961 that the "behavioral mood" was a "successful protest" and would in fact disappear as "a distinctive mood and outlook," because it would become "incorporated into the main body of the discipline." [17] It would seem that in most respects this has proven to be a sound estimate and that, as Eulau has recently noted, "the behavioral persuasion has come to be recognized as an integral part of the established political science rather than a new establishment." [18] Yet as late as 1966, Gabriel Almond's Presidential Address to the American Political Science Association focused on the theme of relating "contemporary general theory to the great tradition" of political study and argued that the growth of the behavioral movement was to be viewed as evidence that, in Kuhn's sense, "a new paradigm is surely developing in political science" which constitutes "a significant step in the modern world of science." [19] Without even raising the problem of what might be understood as the substantive theoretical content of this revolution as well as that of the *ancien régime,* it would seem to have required considerable imagination to conceive of behavioralism as merely an emerging or "developing" movement. By 1969, David Easton's Presidential Address, drawing once more upon the Kuhnian notion of paradigmatic scientific revolution, acknowledged not only the ascendency of behavioralism but the appearance of a "postbehavioral revolution" growing out of a "deep discontent with the direction of contemporary political research." [20] However, what is striking, and disturbing, about the description of this latest "revolution" is the absence of any recognition of a challenge to the viability of prevailing theoretical and epistemological assumptions. The stress was on questions of the public responsibilities of the discipline and its relevance to its social context.

17. Robert A. Dahl, "The Behavioral Approach in Political Science: Epitaph for a Monument to a Successful Protest," in *Behavioralism in Political Science,* ed. Eulau, p. 85.
18. Eulau, "Tradition and Innovation," p. 8.
19. Almond, "Political Theory and Political Science," pp. 875, 878.
20. David Easton, "The New Revolution in Political Science," *American Political Science Review,* LXIII (December, 1969), 1052.

Although this emphasis does reflect the major thrust of recent animadversions on the behavioral movement, it is also symptomatic of the continuing propensity of behavioralists to sublimate criticism and interpret it either as the obsolescent and dead hand of traditionalism or as primarily an external issue of the relationship between political science and society. Despite considerable fuss within the political science establishment about the issue of public relevance, criticism of behavioralism from this quarter has been almost eagerly embraced. Such criticism tends to slide by methodological issues and to allow a diversion from analyses that raise problems about the internal integrity of behavioralism's vision of inquiry. In the 1969 Presidential Address, there was no suggestion that the current revolution was a theoretical revolution, and the implication was clear that in theoretical matters behavioralism remained the seat of innovation.

The elusiveness of these pronouncements is due both to the problem inherent in the attempt to characterize behavioralism as a conceptual revolution or scientific paradigm, in Kuhn's sense, and to the question of the cash value of any such attempt. Apart from some very fundamental questions about the intelligibility of Kuhn's theory as a vehicle for explaining changes in natural science, as well as its application to social science, it is not at all clear that behavioralism, despite its dominance over the discipline, possesses any of the relevant criteria for qualification as a scientific paradigm. Gabriel Almond offered little more regarding the substance of this paradigm than an overview of such loosely connected characteristics as a stress on "statistics," the isolation of "variables," the ubiquity of the "system concept," and recent concern with a "multi-linear theory of political development." The notation of "trends toward rigor and scope, systematic exploration of the consequences for politics of social and psychological variables, and the formulation of general analytical frameworks" would scarcely seem to constitute the elaboration of a scientific paradigm.[21] On the whole, behavioralism has probably emerged as a relatively circumscribed body of thought largely in terms of negative distinctions; its identity has been carved out, for the most part, in terms of its rejection of what it conceives as traditional (institutional, normative, and historical) approaches.

21. Almond, "Political Theory and Political Science," p. 879.

Most political scientists of every persuasion would agree that during the past two decades "a major transformation has overtaken essentially every sector of political studies" and something which may be described as "the new political science has advanced without serious resistance from the older political sciences," [22] but precisely what constitutes this transformation neither the proponents nor the opponents have been able to articulate in any definitive manner. Neither the content of "behavioralism" nor that of the "older political sciences" has been the object of any very systematic analysis. Sheldon Wolin has argued that, although the behavioral movement "clearly has succeeded in transforming political science," the view that it constitutes, in Kuhn's terms, "the inauguration of a new theoretical paradigm . . . is mistaken," since it lacks any "initiating theory" and instead is sustained primarily by its dedication to certain techniques of research and a commitment to "methodism" and the *"vita methodica."* [23] Wolin points out that "to say that there has been no political theory which has inspired the revolution in political science is not to say either that there has been no revolution or that no intellectual patterns are being widely promoted throughout the discipline"; he finds that "the idea of method is the central fact of the behavioral revolution" and provides its "guiding assumptions or framework" and communal ethic.[24] There can be little doubt that the obsession with method has characterized the behavioral movement, but whether this constitutes its defining characteristic as an intellectual posture and governs and informs other general philosophical assumptions apparent in the movement, or whether it is a function of, or a complement to, these assumptions, is difficult to determine. The concern with method has been central in the historical development of American political science and the general American intellectual climate in which it has been nurtured. But this concern is also characteristic of the positivistic philosophy of science to which behavioralism has turned for guidance and self-identification.

Probably little is at stake in resolving the issue of whether

22. Schaar and Wolin, "Essays on the Scientific Study of Politics," p. 125.
23. Sheldon S. Wolin, "Political Theory as a Vocation," *American Political Science Review*, LXIII (December, 1969), 1062–65.
24. *Ibid.*, pp. 1063, 1064.

behavioralism has signaled a scientific revolution in Kuhn's terms, and little would be gained by drawing out an analysis of this issue. Behavioralism clearly has come to dominate the discipline, but equally apparent, as Wolin argues, is the absence of any unifying substantive theoretical foundation. Most political scientists would agree that "despite the decades of public controversy over the definition of 'political behavior,' there is still an astonishing amount of confusion about how to define it and how to distinguish the behavioral school from other approaches." [25] Again, this is not to suggest that within the behavioral literature one cannot find elements of a relatively consistent philosophy of inquiry and a common set of methodological assumptions, but no coherent exposition of these ideas has been offered by either the critics or defenders of behavioralism. Also, one cannot fail to see the proliferation within the discipline of what have become known as theoretical, conceptual, or analytical frameworks. But neither the presence of general philosophical and methodological assumptions nor the existence of numerous conceptual frameworks necessarily entails or constitutes a substantive theoretical base or epistemology of political phenomena. It is in part the very nature of this tacit philosophy of inquiry, and its conception of theory and the relation between theory and fact, which has served to foster both a neglect of epistemological issues or the problem of political reality and the multiplication, without criteria, of conceptual schemata.[26] Despite the arguments of many critics, as well as behavioralists themselves, behavioralism does present an analyzable perspective, and those who wish to picture it as merely a highly pluralistic fellowship of individuals with a scientific bent tend to be somewhat ingenuous. There are enough common assumptions discernible within the literature of behavioralism that demand, and are capable of, scrutiny to put it beyond the pale of being merely a "mood," [27] but, although it may seem paradoxical, as far as furnishing a substantive conception of political phenomena that could provide the basis of a viable conception of explanation, the program of behavioralism has been largely an empty vision.

25. Peter Merkl, " 'Behavioristic' Tendencies in American Political Science," in *Behavioralism in Political Science*, ed. Eulau, p. 142.
26. See John Gunnell, "The Idea of the Conceptual Framework: A Philosophical Critique," *Journal of Comparative Administration*, I (August, 1969), 140–76.
27. Dahl, "Behavioral Approach in Political Science," p. 76.

Although it would seem to be beyond question that the establishment of criteria for evaluating moves in scientific inquiry, such as description and explanation, requires a theoretical specification of the phenomena to which it addresses itself and an articulation of its epistemological assumptions, such specification has been singularly lacking in the behavioral movement. This does not mean that in all modes of science these criteria are, or even can be, explicitly stated in any compact manner or that one could expect a member of a scientific community to possess neat answers to these types of questions. Such an explication emerges principally from an analysis of the theory and practice of a science by either reflective scientists or professional philosophers. It is certainly true that there is "an important sense in which a science has to discover what it is about," for it is only in retrospect that the character of a science's subject matter can be articulated. "The conceptual mechanisms employed by science amount to an implicit specification of what it means for phenomena to be similar in theoretically relevant respects; they thereby determine what kinds of phenomena the science is responsible for explaining." [28] The problem in political science is that an examination of the "theoretical" literature in the discipline fails to yield a coherent specification of its phenomena or a substantive notion of social-scientific inquiry; it has not arrived at any clear judgment concerning "what it is about." The very absence of this sense of "aboutness" is one of the most salient characteristics of the behavioral perspective.

The contemporary focus on the term "behavior" is significant, but its meaning remains nebulous. It is significant because it obviously is intended to indicate a particular attitude or distribution of emphasis in political inquiry, such as a stress on scientific procedures and the continuity of social and natural science. But "behavior" is a generic concept that is used to encompass a wide range of events and contexts, both conventional and natural. To refer to political *behavior* is to be either simply redundant, adding nothing to the meaning of "political," or to beg the question of the kind of behavior to which politics belongs. The phrase tends to be redundant in the same manner as "teaching behavior" and "learning behavior," terms employed by be-

28. Jerry A. Fodor, *Psychological Explanation* (New York: Random House, 1968), p. 10.

havioristic psychologists; the term "behavior" adds nothing to the meaning of "teaching," "learning," and "political" or to the specification of what exhibits these attributes. It may be argued that the implication is a straightforward one—the term "political" functions as an adjective that qualifies or isolates the types of behavior in question—but the problem, then, is to indicate what sorts of phenomena are designated by "behavior." This is the crucial problem in formulating an adequate conception of political reality and developing the criteria of explanation in political science.

Political scientists are quick to point to the "ambiguity" of the terms "behavioralism," "behavioral approach," and "political behavior" and the lack of agreement about their meaning,[29] and, in fact, they take a certain pride in the intellectual pluralism that they see as inherent in this diversity. Apart from distinguishing the current phase in the historical development of American political science and its divorce from "institutionalism," there would seem to be little disciplinary consensus about the criteria for application of these terms. Although it would seem that they do not refer to any well-developed and clearly articulated epistemological position, one idea that does emerge consistently from the literature is the wish to "provide 'verified' principles of human behavior through the use of methods of inquiry similar to those of the natural sciences" or "pure sciences." [30] A desire to emulate what is conceived as the logical structure of natural science and the belief that "the advancement of our discipline lies in the acceptance of generalization as its primary objective and of empirically testable theory as its principal method" [31] appear to be central to the behavioral vision. But although nearly every significant discussion of behavioralism and its identity is replete with phrases such as "the commitment to discovering regularities," "empirically testable theory," and "theory of political be-

29. See, for example, Dahl, "Behavioral Approach in Political Science," p. 68; and Vernon Van Dyke, *Political Science: A Philosophical Analysis* (Stanford, Calif.: Stanford University Press, 1960), p. 158.

30. David B. Truman, "The Impact on Political Science of the Revolution in the Behavioral Sciences," in *Behavioralism in Political Science*, ed. Eulau, pp. 39, 65.

31. Evron M. Kirkpatrick, "The Impact of the Behavioral Approach on Traditional Political Science," in *Essays on the Behavioral Study of Politics*, ed. Austin Ranney (Urbana, Ill.: University of Illinois Press, 1962), p. 14.

havior," [32] they have not been explicated in any detailed way, and their essential emptiness can hardly go unnoticed. It must be assumed that, when it is argued that "the behavioral approach" is distinguished by its purpose and that that "purpose is scientific," [33] there is a serious concern with what it would mean to engage in a scientific enterprise in general, and particularly with regard to the study of politics. But the attempt to isolate the behavioral approach as a distinct "intellectual tendency and a concrete academic movement" on the basis of a commitment to "a science of politics modeled after the methodological assumptions of the natural sciences" requires considerable elaboration beyond such lists of ambiguous dictums as the "assumptions and objectives" contained in Easton's famous eight points: the search for *"regularities,"* the need for *"verification,"* the employment of rigorous *"techniques,"* the emphasis on *"quantification,"* the distinction between facts and *"values,"* the concern for *"systematization,"* the primacy of *"pure science,"* and the commitment to disciplinary *"integration."* [34] Such language means very little unless substantive criteria of acceptable explanation are introduced. It becomes very difficult to evaluate current research, and the "behavioral approach" in general, in terms of such abstract phrases as "the scientific outlook" and a program stated in terms of

> an attempt to improve our understanding of politics by seeking to explain the empirical aspects of political life by means of methods, theories, and criteria of proof that are acceptable according to the canons, conventions, and assumptions of modern empirical science.[35]

Such statements hardly provide a theoretical paradigm, yet a survey of what are usually accepted as authoritative and representative statements of the philosophy of the behavioral approach during the past fifteen or twenty years reveals no tendency toward greater explicitness. Just what does it mean when inquiry seeks to explain "political life" and "aspires to the status of

32. Truman, "The Impact on Political Science," pp. 52–58.
33. Van Dyke, *Political Science*, p. 159.
34. David Easton, *A Framework for Political Analysis* (Englewood Cliffs, N.J.: Prentice-Hall, 1965), pp. 4, 7, 8.
35. Dahl, "Behavioral Approach in Political Science," pp. 80, 77.

science" and the use of "scientific procedures"? [36] One leading
exponent of behavioral science states that such a science "must
satisfy two basic criteria"—"it must deal with human behavior"
and "it must study its subject matter in a 'scientific' manner"—
but instead of giving concrete meaning to such truisms, he
merely intones the standard ritualistic phrases regarding "generalizations," "empirical evidence," "objectivity," and "verification" that are taken as the hallmark of explanation and prediction
in natural science.[37] In political science as well as in the other
behavioral sciences, this failure to go beyond formal and un-
packed statements about "the canons of scientific method" [38] can
largely be explained by the extent to which behavioralism has
turned to the traditional literature of the philosophy of science—
that of logical positivism and logical empiricism—for its assumptions about what constitutes the logic of the scientific enterprise. A recent definition of behavioralism states that it is "an
orientation to the study of social phenomena characterized
mainly by empiricism, logical positivism . . . and the influence
of behaviorism in psychology," [39] and if one were to attempt to
explain the sources of the behavioral conception of science and
its notions of the relationship between social science and natural
science, it would be necessary to explore these intellectual connections. In this context, however, it is sufficient to note that an
examination of the behavioral conception of science yields little
more than a series of characteristic pledges of allegiance to
"quantification," "systematic empirical theory," "interdiscipli-
nary" activity, "disciplined observation," "giving operational
meaning to political concepts," and discovering "laws of human
behavior," [40] all of which signal tenets of the positivistic school in
the philosophy of science.

36. Heinz Eulau, *The Behavioral Persuasion in Politics* (New York:
Random House, 1963), p. 35.
37. Bernard Berelson, ed., *The Behavioral Sciences Today* (New York:
Basic Books, 1963), pp. 2–3.
38. Eulau, "Tradition and Innovation," p. 15.
39. Joseph Dunner, ed., *Dictionary of Political Science* (Totowa, N.J.:
Littlefield, Adams, 1970), p. 46.
40. Kirkpatrick, "Impact of the Behavioral Approach," p. 12; Ithiel de
Sola Pool, ed., *Contemporary Political Science* (New York: McGraw-Hill,
1967), Introduction; Harold D. Lasswell, *The Future of Political Science*
(New York: Atherton, 1963), p. 235; Dahl, "Behavioral Approach in Political Science," p. 81; S. Sidney Ulmer, ed., *Introductory Readings in Political Behavior* (New York: Rand McNally, 1961), p. 2.

POLITICAL SCIENCE AND PHILOSOPHY

To SUGGEST that the notion of social-scientific inquiry embraced by behavioralists has been largely derived, either directly or indirectly, from the philosophy of positivism and logical empiricism and that this has inhibited the development of an autonomous conception of political science, its subject matter, and the criteria of explanation, inevitably raises the general problem of the relationship between philosophy and social science and the large number of delicately entwined issues that attend it. Although this is not the place for an extended analysis of this problem, certain points require some comment and clarification.

Despite the influence of literature in the philosophy of science on the conception of inquiry generally accepted within the discipline, it is also true that "during the past few years, work in political science has proceeded without much guidance from philosophy" and that the current controversy over behavioralism will not be resolved "until the basic issues have been squarely confronted on the basic and general plane of philosophy." [41] However, some careful distinctions must be entered regarding the referent of "philosophy." In one sense, "philosophy" may be understood as referring to that realm of assumptions and their rational support which informs a conception of science and its methodology, a realm that, within the discipline of political science, has been insulated from critical analysis and discussion. If by "philosophy," one refers to the literature of formal or academic philosophy, then it has been there that the kinds of epistemological problems that are inevitably raised by a methodology of empirical inquiry in social science have received detailed consideration; and although political scientists, for the most part, have not been exposed to, or influenced by, this literature in recent years, the influence of formal philosophy on the discipline at various points must not be underestimated. The relationship between political science and the philosophy of science has been an odd one if judged by the relationship between academic philosophy and natural science, where the former has had little impact on the latter. Behavioralism, in its

41. Schaar and Wolin, "Essays on the Scientific Study of Politics," p. 125.

aspiration toward "hard" or "pure" science, found in positivism's philosophical reconstruction of the logic of scientific explanation a convenient set of rules and definitions concerning the scope and character of science, but it failed to examine the validity of these reconstructions, their relevance for social science, and, possibly most important, the appropriateness of the turn of an empirical science to formal philosophy for an authoritative statement of the character and rules of scientific inquiry. In addition, although contemporary work in the philosophy of science has significantly challenged most of the suppositions of early positivism, this challenge has had little impact on the language and assumptions of political science.

The problems revolving around the question of the relationship between academic philosophical analysis in the philosophy of science and the various empirical scientific disciplines are complicated, but just as the philosopher must necessarily have considerable knowledge of the subject matter and the procedures of the specific disciplines which comprise the object of his analysis, as well as the relationship between these disciplines, so must the political scientist, for example, sometimes reflect not only on politics itself but also on what it means to think like a political scientist, what constitutes social-scientific inquiry in general, and what characterizes political phenomena. In doing so he perforce engages in a metascientific activity or, logically, what is characteristically a philosophical activity, and, in a sense, speaks a logically different language. It is interesting that social scientists have traditionally, for one reason or another, engaged in such activity far more frequently than natural scientists and, in fact, many aspects of the theoretical literature in social science, as is evident in many discussions of behavioralism, belong, at least in terms of gross logical dimensions, to this realm of metascientific reflection. In one respect, this has meant that historically social science has been closely tied to philosophy, but it is necessary to carefully differentiate between adopting this "philosophical" or metascientific posture and seeking and accepting methodological guidance from academic philosophy. Sometimes the two attitudes naturally tend to fuse together, since it is not surprising that when the scientist becomes self-conscious about his activity, either because of a theoretical crisis or an initial search for identity, he will turn to the formal disciplines whose business it is to analyze the logical and epistemological structure of such activities. It was such a search for scientific identity that brought behavioral science to the philosophy of science and the doctrines of logical positivism. The mistake was to assume, first, that the putative notions of scientific explanation found in this literature were indefeasible and authoritative, either as a representation of the structure of natural science or as a statement of the logical and epistemological requirements of social science, and, secondly and most importantly, that formal philosophy could provide adequate theoretical grounds for the practice of social science or any substantive empirical science. There may be no reason why a science should not draw upon or be guided by formal philosophy, but a critical awareness of what is involved in such a move must be maintained.

In general, it may be said that "the philosophical dimension of social science theory is located in its *Weltanschauung*," [42] or the paradigmatic assumptions and categoricals that govern its conception of the phenomena which it studies and its conception of explanation. In the case of behavioralism, this *Weltanschauung*, as unarticulated as it may be in many respects, has been profoundly influenced by contact with the philosophy of science and consequently it has appeared essentially as a set of abstract precepts (concerning laws, deductive theory, generalizations, operational concepts, testable hypotheses, immediate observation, and other ideas representative of a residual positivism) in search of concrete application. Whatever other particular problems may be related to this association with positivism, it is clear that behavioralism has not developed any substantive "philosophical" dimension of its own that could serve to specify the character of political phenomena in a way that would yield an intelligible set of criteria for the evaluation of explanations. At the same time, its ties with postpositivistic academic philosophy have been severely attenuated. This situation is unfortunate because it is in the contemporary philosophy of science, the expanding material in the philosophy of the social sciences, existential phenomenology, and recent analytic philosophy dealing with the concepts of behavior and action, that the greatest challenge to the assumptions that underlie the behavioral persuasion have emerged. Although disputes within formal philosophy may sel-

42. Natanson, *Philosophy of the Social Sciences*, p. 14.

dom have any significant impact on natural science, the convergence of issues in recent philosophical literature relevant to social science and its subject matter will be highly significant for the evolution of visions of social-scientific inquiry, if the past history of these disciplines provides any indication of their future development.

Most of the sorting out regarding competing explanatory perspectives in social science has taken place in academic philosophy, and appropriately so, since this is "after all, the philosopher's business"; strictly speaking, "a philosophy of the social sciences is beyond the province of the social sciences," [43] just as providing the methodological categoricals and theories of empirical science belongs to science and essentially stands outside the authority and competence of formal philosophy. But it must be stressed that the possibility of drawing such distinctions between these activities is not a basis for an isolationist argument; functional differentiation, either analytical or empirical, neither implies nor requires the absence of various forms of significant relationships. It would seem that at the point at which a number of logical and epistemological issues have become pressing in regard to the practice of social science and the integrity of its theoretical vision and where, at the same time, these issues have been the object of searching analyses in the literature of philosophy, there is sufficient reason to recommend that social science once again turn its attention to the literature of philosophy. This does not mean that it should seek from philosophy the procedural rules of inquiry or the definition of science (this unfortunate intellectual adventure should not be repeated). But it does mean that when questions such as those relating to the logic of social-scientific inquiry, its relationship to natural science, and the explication of concepts such as behavior and action become the focus of extended discussions in both social science and philosophy, the failure of the social scientist to consider the work of philosophers on these problems, and its implications for operative conceptions of inquiry, at a time of manifest theoretical tensions within these sciences, is as inexcusable as a philosopher not knowing his way around in the disciplines he analyzes, criticizes, and makes the object of his study.

43. *Ibid.*

BEHAVIOR AND POLITICAL REALITY

THE GENERAL PROBLEMS of the logic of social-scientific inquiry and the character of explanation on the one hand and the nature of social (or political) reality or social phenomena on the other are only analytically separable, since judgments about sociological method are ultimately tied to the conceptions of social reality, and since presuppositions about methodology may well determine in large measure what will count as social phenomena. Although the elusiveness of the behavioralist conception of science, apart from the general theses appropriated from positivist philosophy, must be attributed to the absence of any clear conception of the character of social phenomena, certain behavioralist assumptions about the demands of science have in turn precluded the development of a satisfactory specification of this datum.

In spite of the fact that there is probably little likelihood of unequivocally establishing the precise origins of the emphasis on the concept of behavior in political science, there can be no doubt that it can in part be attributed to the influence of behaviorism and positivism and their characteristic stress on objective, publicly observable, overt behavior, as distinguished from mentalistic or subjective phenomena, as the only data "amenable to empirical research." [44] Although it might be argued that any such genetic explanations may have little to do with the current meaning of the concept, no lucid exposition has appeared in the contemporary literature of behavioralism. It is clear, however, that any attempt to probe the vision of behavioralism and its conception of political phenomena must confront the ambiguity of the notion of behavior as indicating the subject matter of political science and the implications of this ambiguity for circumscribing the criteria of adequate explanation. It is necessary to note the extent to which certain philosophical assumptions about "the givenness" of observable phenomena have led to a neglect of a consideration of the problem of social reality, but even if one should grant the dubious assumption (that dogma of early philosophical empiricism which it appears most behavioralists

44. Merkl, " 'Behavioristic' Tendencies in American Political Science," p. 143.

entertain) that the data or "facts" of politics are adequately represented in our everyday observation language and that theories are instrumental constructs imposed on these facts in order to explain relationships between them, it is still necessary to inquire into what constitutes the units and boundaries of political analysis. It simply will no longer do to speak as if the object of political inquiry is largely unproblematical and can be adequately characterized by such vague phrases as "empirical reality," and "phenomenal reality," or "the range of actions," "mass of actions," and "interactions" that constitute the "empirical behavior which we observe and characterize as political life." [45] It may be salubrious for the discipline to aim toward the development of "empirical propositions and theories of a systematic sort, tested by closer, more direct, and more rigorously controlled observation of political events," [46] but it is precisely the scope and attributes of such events that require explication.

Political scientists today are usually emphatic in pointing out that behavioralism is not to be equated with the "antiquated" and "outmoded" theories associated with the "stimulus-response psychology of behaviorism." [47] Given the traditional intellectual affinities between philosophical positivism (which few would deny has exercised a formative influence on the behavioral vision) and behaviorism in psychology, as well as the acknowledged impact of behaviorism on the early stages of the development of American political science, these disclaimers are somewhat difficult to accept. This is especially the case in view of the lack of any account of what constitutes the differences between these perspectives and the behavioralist's repeated emphasis, so characteristic of behaviorism and positivism, on the "observed and observable behavior of men" and the unacceptability of data that do not meet the criterion of being open to "direct observation," [48] despite the endemic ambiguity and question-

45. Eulau, "Tradition and Innovation," p. 18; Easton, *Framework for Political Analysis*, p. 26.
46. Dahl, "Behavioral Approach in Political Science," p. 76.
47. David Easton, *The Political System* (New York: Knopf, 1953), pp. 151, 202; Eulau, "Segments of Political Science Most Susceptible to Behavioristic Treatment," in *Contemporary Political Analysis*, ed. James C. Charlesworth (New York: Free Press, 1967), p. 35.
48. Dahl, "Behavioral Approach in Political Science," p. 78; H. D. Lasswell and A. Kaplan, *Power and Society* (New Haven, Conn.: Yale University Press, 1950), p. 14.

begging character of such phrases. But there is little point in pursuing an issue for which there can be no satisfactory resolution, except to note that at least superficially there would appear to be considerable correspondence between behaviorism and behavioralism, both historically and conceptually, at least with respect to basic assumptions regarding the philosophy of empirical inquiry.

It has often been suggested that what distinguishes the behavioral approach is its focus on "individuals" and "individual behavior" or "its choice of individuals as the empirical unit of analysis," but this "molecular" approach, which professes to concentrate on "individual human beings" and "elevate the actual human being to the center of attention," only further exacerbates the need to elaborate the concept of behavior.[49] If "the political behavior of the individual person is the central and crucial data of the behavioral approaches to politics," [50] if this is what lies at the heart of the "behavioral persuasion," then it would seem that an explication of such concepts as person, individual, and behavior indeed becomes pressing. Although on occasion tentative distinctions between "behavior" and "purposive action" or behaving and acting have been suggested as representing ways of approaching political phenomena,[51] such distinctions have gained little attention in political science, and, for the most part, "behavior" and "action" have not been conceptually distinguished in the literature of social science in general. Whether this is a problem of "confounding" or "confusing" the concepts [52] or the result of a philosophical stance that obliterates the conceptual distinctions that these terms sometimes suggest is often difficult to assess. In the single most extensive treatment of action as the object of social-scientific inquiry in the literature of social science, *Toward a General Theory of Action*, edited by Parsons and Shils,[53] the distinctions are blurred, but this is the result not so much of a confusion about the relationship between these

49. Eulau, "Tradition and Innovation," pp. 14, 17; Ranney, *Behavioral Study of Politics*, p. 12; Easton, *The Political System*, p. 201, 202, 205; Kirkpatrick, "Impact of the Behavioral Approach," p. 12.
50. Eulau, *The Behavioral Persuasion*, p. 14.
51. Merkl, " 'Behavioristic' Tendencies in American Political Science," p. 143.
52. Robert Pranger, *Action, Symbolism, and Order* (Nashville, Tenn.: Vanderbilt University Press, 1968), p. 101.
53. Talcott Parsons and Edward Shils, eds., *Toward a General Theory of Action* (Cambridge: Harvard University Press, 1951).

concepts or a failure to recognize differences in the phenomena they represent as of the philosophical perspective from which the work was undertaken. The psychological premises are essentially those formulated in the somewhat "soft" or methodological behaviorism of E. C. Tolman, and the project represents one of the most thoroughgoing attempts to state the requirements of social-scientific theory in terms of instrumentalism, operationalism, the deductive model of explanation, sense-data phenomenalism, and other traditional doctrines of logical positivism and logical empiricism.

In this work, the generic category is the behavior of living organisms and more particularly the "activity of human beings." The task of social science is to deal with that aspect of behavior or activity which is "related in some manner to things outside the organism" and to discover the "principles of relationship." [54] The concept of action is chosen as the dominant focus, because it is viewed as "a more neutral term" than "behavior," which "generally connotes observable bodily movements and does not include thoughts." [55] Action refers primarily to normatively governed behavior or situations in which energy is expended in realizing various goals where the environment includes both objects and other actors. Although the principal concern is with "the goal-seeking actor" or how "the actor strives to achieve goals," the data are conceived as strictly "observational." The problem of thought and the "ultimate epistemological problem of the nature of our knowledge of other minds" is bracketed, and it is argued that "what the actor thinks or feels can be treated as a system of *intervening variables*" or instrumental theoretical entities and hypothetical constructs defined in terms of a language of observation or sense data referring to molar behavior.[56] In this view, then, "action" and "behavior" are to be "used interchangeably" in describing, explaining, and predicting modes of relationship between actors (individuals or collectives) and their environment, as distinguished from "mere movement or

54. Richard C. Sheldon, "Some Observations on Theory in the Social Sciences," in *Toward a General Theory of Action*, ed. Parsons and Shils, pp. 30–31; Parsons and Shils, "Values, Motives, and Systems of Action," in *ibid.*, p. 53.

55. Parsons and Shils, "Values, Motives, and Systems of Action," pp. 50–51.

56. Sheldon, "Theory in the Social Sciences," p. 42; Parsons and Shils, "Values, Motives, and Systems of Action," p. 64.

responses" that are rendered and explained intraorganically in physiological terms.[57] Action or behavior features in this scheme as a "dependent variable" which is "to be identified and defined . . . in terms of the ways in which it tends to manipulate or rearrange physical, social, or cultural objects relative to a given actor," and which is to be causally explained by such independent variables as environmental stimuli and physiological states mediated by pragmatically or experimentally authenticated intervening variables or analytical constructs such as drives, needs, and desires, which, as mental predicates, must be operationally defined or otherwise specified in terms of overt observable behavior.[58]

Whatever criticisms there may be of the Parsons and Shils volume, it does represent a relatively coherent and consistent treatment, grounded in identifiable psychological and philosophical theories, which can be confronted and analyzed and become part of an intelligible dialogue. This is in sharp contrast to discussions of these issues in most of the literature of social science, and especially that of behavioralism in political science, where terms such as "behavior" and "action" tend to be used rather indiscriminately and with only the vaguest signals about what sorts of assumptions might inform such discussions. Although a great deal of theorizing in political science, especially that revolving around such concepts as role and political culture, would appear to draw heavily on a perspective closely related to or derived from that developed by Parsons and Shils, there has been little in the way of a systematic analysis or defense of such an approach, or of the viability of such problematical notions as that of the "intervening variable," which has gained so much attention in psychology.

David Easton has stressed the "application of psychological categories" in explanations of "political phenomena," and in 1953 he stated that "it is now customary in political science to call this the study of political behavior." [59] But despite the frequent use of psychological categories in political studies, their reference and the precise character of their relation to other factors have received little systematic examination. Easton has repeatedly

57. Edward C. Tolman, "A Psychological Model," in *Toward a General Theory of Action*, ed. Parsons and Shils, p. 279.
58. *Ibid.*, p. 281.
59. Easton, *The Political System*, pp. 202, 203, 205.

pointed to the central place of the "feelings and motivations of the individual" in the behavioral approach and the concern with how individuals "act and react in any set of political circumstances" and has argued that for behavioral political science "the task is to determine the relation of human feelings, attitudes and motivations to each set of political circumstances." [60] It should scarcely be necessary to emphasize the problems raised by such statements, but for the most part these problems receive neither discussion nor recognition in Easton's work. To suggest that political science focus on explaining "why people act in the way that they do in political situations" [61] requires some preliminary explication of the several key concepts contained in such a phrase. Although one may take exception to particular aspects of the behavioral conception of science and its object, the difficulty is not so much that the answers of political scientists to these problems are "wrong" as that there is a lack of any sustained treatment of these problems that would make sense out of the tangle of concepts which are employed.

Probably more than most political scientists of the behavioral persuasion, Eulau has attempted to address himself to some of the issues attending the use of terms such as "behavior" and "action." He states that "because human action is purposive and goal oriented, the possibility of an altogether positive behavioral political science is indeed questionable" and that " 'behavior' in political behavior, then, refers not simply to directly or indirectly observable political action but also to those perceptual, motivational, and attitudinal components of behavior which make up man's political identifications, demands, and expectations, and his system of political beliefs, values, and goals." [62] What Eulau would conceive as the requirements of a "positive" science of politics is not entirely clear, but in a negative sense it appears that this position would seek either "to exorcise from social science what were considered 'merely mental' phenomena—drives, motivations, attitudes, defenses, and so on" or to define mentalistic concepts in terms of overt behavior. Eulau sees such restrictions as untenable, since "modern behavioral science is eminently concerned not only with the acts of man but also his cognitive, affective, and evaluative processes," and he argues, in a manner

60. *Ibid.*, pp. 202, 203.
61. Easton, *Framework for Political Analysis*, p. 33.
62. Eulau, "Tradition and Innovation," p. 16, and "Segments," p. 35.

that appears closely allied to Schutz's position, that social-scientific phenomena, unlike the "raw materials of the natural sciences" or "natural facts," are "already fashioned by human intervention even before the social scientist comes to deal with them" and "are invariably artifacts of human endeavor." [63] Eulau employs the terms "human action" and "human behavior" without explicit differentiation, but he stresses the idea that "the meanings people give to their political behavior are critical data for scientific observation," since in politics "there is no 'behavior as such' in a purely physical or mechanistic sense" but rather "acts" performed by an individual when he "rules and obeys, persuades and compromises, promises and bargains, coerces and represents, fights and fears." [64] Eulau stresses the concern of the "behavioral persuasion" with explaining what a "man does politically" in terms of "the meanings he attaches to his behavior" and maintains that any definition of politics "must itself be 'meaningful' in terms of the meanings that men give to their political behavior." [65]

To claim that "the study of political behavior is concerned with the acts, attitudes, preferences, and expectations of man in political contexts" can be taken as quite vague, but to specify that "the meanings that political actors, consciously or unconsciously, attribute to their own behavior are of interest to the political scientist because they provide a partial explanation of the motives for that behavior" [66] would seem, if compared with many of what are apparently representative doctrines of behavioralism, to carry with it some startling implications regarding the nature of explanation and concept formation in social science. It would also appear that these statements rest rather uneasily beside many of Eulau's own views about the requirements of science with regard to such matters as the search for "uniformities and regularities," the establishment of "universal validity for its propositions," and the necessity for "casual" rather than "teleological" hypotheses. [67] If such notions do find compatibility, it would seem incumbent on Eulau to demonstrate the manner in which such compatibil-

63. Eulau, "Segments," p. 35; "Changing Views of Representation," in de Sola Poole, ed., *Contemporary Political Science*, p. 59.
64. Eulau, *The Behavioral Persuasion*, pp. 114, 4–5.
65. *Ibid.*, pp. 5–6.
66. *Ibid.*, pp. 21, 6.
67. Eulau, "Tradition and Innovation," pp. 15, 17.

ity is manifest. Despite Eulau's relatively pointed comments on such issues as the acceptability of mentalistic terms and concepts in behavioral explanation, the same difficulties that have plagued most of the behavioralist literature are present in his work. Most evident is the sharp disjunction and the lack of ostensive conceptual links between the rhetoric about the enterprise of science and empiricism on the one hand and common-sense notions of social and political reality on the other. Equally important is Eulau's failure to engage in any extended analysis of the concepts of behavior and action and such related problems as the status of mental terms and their relation to descriptions and explanations of overt action. It is these shortcomings which make the development of a theory of action so pressing and which make the current challenge to behavioralism not so much a question of the substitution of one theoretical structure for another as the elaboration *de novo* of an intelligible and defensible vision of social-scientific inquiry and its subject matter.

PHENOMENOLOGY AND THE IDEA OF SECOND-ORDER ANALYSIS

IN URGING A PHENOMENOLOGICAL PERSPECTIVE as an alternative to behavioralism, no crucial historical importance should be attached to the use of the term "phenomenology." In this context, it is employed primarily as a generic category encompassing a cluster of related views about social phenomena and social-scientific explanation that stand in opposition to a number of assumptions usually associated with positivism and behaviorism, and where these views most directly challenge behavioralism in political science is precisely on those fronts where the doctrines of positivism and behaviorism have influenced this discipline. Although it may be charged that it is an oversimplification, and even a misrepresentation, to suggest that the major theoretical controversies in the social sciences can be reduced to "two distinctly opposed philosophic attitudes . . . taken as polar positions," such a reduction can be useful for focusing issues, especially when the poles are representative not of "narrowly conceived ideas or systems of ideas that might be readily associated with the name of a particular thinker or school of thought, but rather of quite broad ways of seeing the social world, of fundamental conceptions of the social itself." [68] From this standpoint, the phenomenological perspective may be understood as embracing commitments to the logical and methodological asymmetry of explanation and concept formation in the natural and social sciences, the second-order character of social-scientific inquiry and its epistemological symmetry with other second-order studies such as philosophy, the need for the elucidation of the concept of action, and the thesis that the phenomena of social science are primarily symbolic in character and that for the most part, despite the existence of objectified and institutionalized structures, what is to be taken as "social reality is made up of the meanings which actors on the social scene give to their actions and to their situations." [69] Together these views constitute the basis of a concrete and coherent vision of social-scientific inquiry which may be offered as a substantive alternative to behavioralism when the latter decries criticism that is negative and nonconstructive.

It is a mistake, sometimes logical and sometimes empirical, to assume that beyond the issue of the conflict between phenomenological and behavioral perspectives there lies a further question about "what is science," as if there were some given criteria of scientism which stood apart from the history and current practice of particular sciences, their theories, and visions of reality, or as if there were some metascientific realm such as philosophy to which one could reliably turn in order to elicit such criteria, or as if, among the empirical sciences themselves, there were some paradigmatic science such as natural science or one of its branches. The mistake is conceptual, a category mistake not unlike Gilbert Ryle's parable about the foreign visitor and his search for the university,[70] if one assumes that the term "science" refers to something that stands above, beside, or otherwise separate from the activities of the various sciences, and that what constitutes the criteria of application of the term, as far as distinguishing sciences from nonsciences, is anything more than a set of abstractions derived from noting family resemblances among a group of socially differentiated activities. The mistake is empirical if one assumes that among the general community

68. Natanson, *Philosophy of the Social Sciences*, p. viii.
69. *Ibid.*, p. 186.
70. Gilbert Ryle, *The Concept of Mind* (New York: Barnes & Noble, 1949), p. 16.

of practicing scientists there is understood to be a given hierarchy of sciences which provides a measure of proper scientific practice, or that there is some metascientific realm such as philosophy which possesses the authority and responsibility for establishing the norms of scientific logic. But, unfortunately, on both sides of the current controversy there has been a tendency to reinforce the notion that "science" is defined by either some external or by some internal hierarchical and universalistic criteria.

This mistake has been most common among those social and political scientists, such as the behavioralists, who have turned, directly or indirectly, to the philosophy of science for authoritative statements about the character of science, but the problem has also been accentuated by the willingness of those who, in an attempt to distinguish their position from the dominant vision, have awarded their opponents the title of "scientist" and have been content to accept the idea that their approach is "not 'scientific'—as we understand the nature of the empirical sciences." [71] In this way they have unnecessarily and prematurely surrendered the province of science to natural science, or even worse, to some philosopher's reconstruction of that enterprise; but this is too easy a capitulation to the philosophic dogma of the unity of science. There is no reason for a social scientist to voluntarily place himself outside the realm of empirical science simply because he may argue for an epistemological position that is different from that characteristic of natural science (or what certain schools in the philosophy of science have represented as the logical structure of natural science). Following such a course only creates conceptual confusion, for it is difficult to imagine an alternative realm of activity in society with which the social scientist could identify. To pose the problem of whether social science is really a science is about as significant as asking whether nontheistic Unitarianism can qualify as a religion. It is often suggested that such a relativistic conception of science opens the door to any group claiming the status of science, but whether, for example, Christian Scientists are to be understood as belonging to the community of science is much more a sociological question, or a "political" problem to be solved among

71. Peter L. Berger and Thomas Luckmann, *The Social Construction of Reality* (Garden City, N.Y.: Doubleday, 1967), p. 20.

those who wish to press such issues, than a genuine philosophical problem.

In developing a phenomenological position with regard to social-scientific inquiry, no attempt will be made here to build directly on either the work of Husserl and his concept of the *Lebenswelt* or the various aspects of existential phenomenology. Although much remains to be accomplished in this area, especially with regard to specific research problems in social science, the theoretical task of constructing an epistemology of social science on this basis has been carried forward to a significant degree in the work of Schutz and others, such as Maurice Natanson, who have further elaborated the themes associated with Schutz as well as providing significant emendations. An important case in point is the recent volume by Berger and Luckmann,[72] which draws upon the work of Schutz, Weber, Simmel, and Mead and applies their ideas in a detailed and original manner to the problems of the sociology of knowledge. The primary concern in this essay will be to investigate certain areas of contemporary analytic and linguistic philosophy, especially that literature focusing on the philosophy of action influenced by the later Wittgenstein and J. L. Austin, with a view toward elaborating the rudiments of a theory of action relevant to problems of explanation in social science and the specification of political phenomena. Although much of the phenomenological literature that is strictly conceived from the perspective of the problems of social science has only recently become available, it nevertheless has received considerably more attention than that of other schools of contemporary philosophy bearing on similar issues. However, a basic assumption will be that the analyses of action and social-scientific explanation deriving from work usually closely associated with individuals such as Schutz not only complement but also share many fundamental presuppositions with analyses developed in recent analytic philosophy and in what Austin termed "linguistic phenomenology." [73] Despite the fact that these approaches are often assumed to be quite disparate, the conceptual resemblances should be apparent.

An essential aspect of the argument presented here is the

72. *Ibid.*
73. J. L. Austin, "A Plea for Excuses," in *Philosophical Papers,* ed. J. O. Urmson and G. J. Warnock (Oxford: Oxford University Press, 1961), p. 130.

thesis that many of the most intransigent theoretical problems in political science derive from an attempt to conceive of the discipline, epistemologically, as concerned with first-order investigations, although the phenomena to which political science addresses itself, even as often conceptualized by those who view the enterprise as a first-order activity, essentially demand a second-order analysis. Social scientists have turned to an inappropriate model by seeking to employ natural science, let alone the philosopher's reconstruction of natural science, as a bench mark for concept formation and theory construction. This is in part what accounts for the great disjunction between what passes as "theory" in much of social science and a large portion of fruitful empirical work. Substantive social science research will often have the characteristics of second-order analysis despite its first-order pretensions and goals. These goals have, in most instances, been appropriated externally from the philosophy of science, rather than deriving from the intrinsic demands of social-scientific inquiry.

The distinction between first- and second-order studies cannot be easily elucidated, and no simple characterization is possible. Although as a starting point it may be suggested that the distinction turns on the difference between studies dealing with brute facts and those based on conventional or institutional facts, this is far from an adequate answer, and the only satisfactory course is to work through the numerous problems connected with this distinction. Contemporary Anglo-American philosophy is one area in which this distinction has gained prominence. It conceives of itself as an enterprise devoted not to system-building and primary speculation about the world but to the clarification and therapeutic analysis of the logic, language, and conceptual structure of first-order activities and their respective universes of discourse, ranging from the many aspects of the pervasive realm of what may be understood as ordinary life to such specialized disciplines as science and law. Yet, to recognize that a distinctive characteristic of recent philosophy is its second-order character and to defend the validity of the general distinction between first- and second-order activities is not to imply acceptance of all the intellectual baggage that some formulations of this distinction occasionally carry with them. Above all, what must be guarded against is the pitfall of allowing an epistemological distinction between first- and second-order inquiries to be equated with a distinction between a priori and empirical inquiries or between philosophy and science.

Peter Winch, while agreeing with contemporary philosophy's rejection of the notion of the philosopher as a "master-scientist," has criticized the "underlabourer" conception of philosophy, as embraced by such individuals as T. D. Weldon, which presses the legitimate distinction between linguistic or conceptual questions and empirical questions to the point of severing the intimate connection between language and the world or between concepts and perceptions of reality. With regard to social science, Winch argues that since it must specify "what is involved in the concept of a social phenomenon" and is concerned with "giving an account of the nature of social phenomena in general," [74] it includes conceptual questions which are not reducible to matters of empirical research. In addition, he maintains that since "a man's social relations with his fellows are permeated with ideas about reality" or even "are expressions of ideas about reality," [75] explanations of social phenomena entail an illumination of these ideas, concepts, rules, and language which comprise the actor's vision of his world, inform social activity, and constitute the criteria of meaningful behavior. Thus conceptual problems enter into social-scientific analysis not only at the level of social-scientific theory and its vision of reality, as with any science, but also at the level of its subject matter and data. Winch's principal thesis is rather straightforward, despite his somewhat awkward statement of it. It is that social-scientific inquiry is principally a second-order mode of inquiry in the sense that it is concerned with illuminating the conceptual structure of which social relations are an expression, and thus, epistemologically, parallels the concern of philosophy with conceptual analysis. Social-scientific explanation requires an understanding of the ideas of the social participants and the reasons, intentions, motives, etc., which govern their behavior, and these, he contends, are in turn intelligible only in terms of the context of the rules, conventions, and general *Weltanschauung* that constitute, in Wittgenstein's words, "a form of life" or form of social relations. But since a form of life and a language are interdependent and mutually informing, the inseparability of the

74. Peter Winch, *The Idea of a Social Science* (New York: Humanities Press, 1958), pp. 15–18.
75. *Ibid.*, p. 23.

conceptual and empirical aspects of social-scientific analysis once again presents itself. Above all, Winch wishes to demonstrate that there is a fundamental difference between the subject matter of the natural sciences and that of the social sciences and that, consequently, explanations in social science are "logically incompatible with the kinds of explanation offered in the natural sciences" [76] or the search for causal predictive laws.

However, Winch's actual development of this thesis tends to be confusing, because he allows his argument regarding the conceptual elements in the theoretical dimension of social science, and the epistemological parallels between social science and philosophy deriving from a common concern with conceptual data and forms of life, to slide over into an argument which comes close to blurring the lines between social science and philosophy as distinct and socially differentiated activities and to equating such notions as conceptual, philosophical, and a priori on the one hand and factual, scientific, and empirical on the other. With regard to social science, he states "that many of the more important theoretical issues which have been raised in those studies belong to philosophy rather than to science and are, therefore, to be settled by *a priori* conceptual analysis rather than by empirical research." [77] Similarly, he argues that just as "epistemology will try to elucidate what is involved in the notion of a form of life as such," social science cannot avoid "a discussion of the nature of social phenomena in general"; thus "this part of sociology is really misbegotten epistemology." [78] He also argues that since philosophy, or at least epistemology, is concerned with "an inquiry into the nature of man's knowledge of reality," it "may be expected to illuminate the nature of human interrelations in society." [79] However, the fact that philosophy and social science are epistemologically parallel and share a second-order orientation (the theoretical dimension of social science involves such conceptual questions as those relating to the nature of social reality and both philosophy and social science are concerned with a subject matter in which concepts are an important datum) does not warrant Winch's suggestion that social science and philosophy are actually the same activity

76. *Ibid.*, p. 72.
77. *Ibid.*, p. 17.
78. *Ibid.*, pp. 41, 43.
79. *Ibid.*, pp. 24, 40.

or that social science is in some way a species of philosophy. This suggestion, though, is in no way essential to Winch's thesis and has only tended to lead to misunderstandings and such exaggerated interpretations and criticisms of his position as A. R. Louch's assertion that he holds "that social analysis is conceptual or *a priori*" and that "the social analyst is really the social philosopher and social inquiry an examination of the tools of communication by which we initiate and describe action." [80] Winch's actual position is hardly so extreme. Nowhere does he argue that the practice of social science should be conceived as nonempirical and a priori or that it involves merely a conceptual analysis of a society's principles, rules, and linguistic conventions.

There is much in Winch's short treatment, such as his notion of rules, that is far from adequately explicated, and he tends to move from a conception of human action to a notion of what social science must be that takes little account of what social scientists actually do or what kinds of problems they set for themselves. But the basic thesis offered by Winch remains sound. Part of the problem of stating such a position appears in the search for analogies to illustrate the argument. Winch's appeal to the parallels between social science and philosophy is illuminating, but his difficulties, as well as those of his critics, emerge when arguments about epistemological parallelism are not carefully distinguished from arguments about identity. There are various ways in which the point about social science as a second-order activity can be made, but many of Winch's analogies are either misleading or are carried too far. Louch is critical of what he believes are unfortunate implications in Winch's work: his belief that social science is really philosophy or merely a kind of a priori conceptual analysis and his focus on the dichotomy between conceptual and empirical studies. But Louch, whose attack on current positivistic/behavioristic conceptions of social science and its search for general laws similar to those of natural science and whose thesis about the explanation of social phenomena largely coincide with Winch's arguments, is equally quick to jump to misleading dichotomies and analogies. He argues that explanations of human action, since they refer to and describe reasons, motives, principles, and other elements

80. A. R. Louch, *Explanation and Human Action* (Berkeley, Calif.: University of California Press, 1966), p. 174.

often associated with justification and appraisal, are in fact a species of "moral explanation," and that therefore "the idea of a science of man or society is untenable." [81]

Although many social scientists have mistakenly assumed that the investigation of social phenomena must be epistemologically symmetrical with natural science in order to qualify as science, opponents of this view such as Winch and Louch have been equally wrong in accepting this restrictive definition of science and empiricism and in suggesting that the subject matter of such investigations renders them nonempirical or unscientific. Viewed "sociologically," social science and natural science are coordinate enterprises, but when logical and epistemological analogies are sought, the second-order character of much of the contemporary philosophy that is oriented toward conceptual analysis may present a more illuminating parallel. There is no reason to assume that if an activity is to qualify as an empirical science it must be epistemologically of a first-order character. Epistemologically, social science is primarily a second-order enterprise, because its object is principally the language, thought, and action of various social communities. In this sense it is what might be termed a metadiscipline. But caution must be exercised, since it is necessary to guard against allowing epistemological analogies to slip into arguments suggesting some sort of wider criteria of identity. Although as formal disciplines viewed in terms of aims, methods, and various other conventional characteristics, philosophy and social science are strongly dissimilar, in this sense social science and natural science will present numerous parallels, such as the empirical attitude, a concern for the development of empirically testable systematic knowledge about their objects of study, and other general characteristics which might be understood as attributes of the scientific mood. As Schutz has pointed out, it is necessary not to leap "to the erroneous conclusion that the social sciences are *toto coelo* different from the natural sciences, a view which disregards the fact that certain procedural rules relating to correct thought organization are common to all empirical scientists." [82] Social science and philosophy are no more the "same" than

81. *Ibid.*, chap. 4, and p. viii.
82. Alfred Schutz, "Common-Sense and Scientific Interpretation of Human Action," in *Collected Papers*, ed. Maurice Natanson (The Hague: Nijhoff, 1962), I, 6.

natural science and the various aspects of everyday life, the paradigm cases of first-order activities, are the "same." The latter are first-order activities only because they provide primary interpretations of the world, and therefore show certain epistemological similarities, and because, as realms of thought and action, they feature as the object of such disciplines as philosophy and social science. They may be understood as "primary" interpretations, because there is no going beyond the theories of natural science and the *Weltanschauungen* of everyday life, or what Wilfrid Sellars has termed the "scientific image" and the "manifest image," [83] to more fundamental conceptions of the way the world is. The world is opaque apart from the collective representations of the manifest image and the theories of the scientific image. These images may peacefully coexist, compete, or evidence numerous other connections and relationships, just as the existential relations between second-order activities such as philosophy and social science may be infinitely variable and problematical.

There are numerous problems revolving around the relationship between first- and second-order activities, such as the troublesome question of the proper relationship between natural science and the philosophy of science (or social science and the philosophy of social science), and although these problems may vary at different times and in different contexts, certain aspects of this relationship are, in a certain sense, logically "given." First-order activities constitute the object or subject matter of second-order analyses, and the language and concepts of the two realms, despite some inevitable overlap, are logically distinct. The membranes separating these realms may be, existentially, quite permeable, since, for example, the language of everyday life may be influenced by social science and philosophy, and since the latter disciplines must refer to the language of everyday life in the course of their analyses. But, strictly conceived, the language of everyday life cannot be the language of the social sciences and philosophy any more than the language of chess playing can be utilized for describing and explaining the rules and moves of chess. The languages of philosophy and social science are necessarily metalanguages, and their mode of analysis is meta-

83. Wilfrid Sellars, *Science, Perception and Reality* (New York: Humanities Press, 1963), chap. I.

analysis. Yet the very fact that these languages and activities are metalanguages and meta-activities means that they are, in a fundamental sense, derivative in a way that natural science is not.

While in natural science it ultimately makes no sense to ask about the nature of the physical world apart from the scientist's theoretical construction of that world, the language and conceptual configurations of social science (although logically autonomous in the sense that in any science peculiarly scientific constructs replace those of everyday life and a science necessarily determines its own problems of investigation, distribution of emphasis, criteria of explanation, and mode of description) refer to an ontologically independent realm of thought and action. While in natural science facts and observational data are not only theory-dependent but, in a significant sense, functions of the theories which give structure and meaning to the natural world, "the facts, events, and data before the social scientist are," as Schutz has argued, "of an entirely different structure."

> His observational field, the social world, is not essentially structureless. It has a particular meaning and relevance structure for the human beings living, thinking, and acting therein. They have preselected and preinterpreted this world by a series of common-sense constructs of the reality of daily life, and it is these thought objects which determine their behavior, define the goal of their action, the means available for attaining them—in brief, which help them to find their bearings within their natural and socio-cultural environment and to come to terms with it. The thought objects constructed by the social scientist refer to and are founded upon the thought objects constructed by the common-sense thought of man living his everyday life among his fellow-men. Thus, the constructs used by the social scientist are, so to speak, constructs of the second degree, namely constructs of the constructs made by the actors on the social scene, whose behavior the scientist observes and tries to explain in accordance with the procedural rules of his science.[84]

It is the conception of social science as a second-order enterprise which most significantly ties together the approaches of Schutz and individuals such as Winch. When Winch argues that the

84. Schutz, "Common-Sense and Scientific Interpretation of Human Action," pp. 5–6.

subject matter of social science, unlike natural science, is principally rule-governed activity, and that it is these rules, in addition to those which govern the social scientist's activity, which
must be taken into account in describing, for example, what
phenomena are to count as the "same" or what acts belong to
the "same" activity, this is not an argument "for the impossibility
of a science of man," as some have charged, but rather a recognition of the demands of a science which epistemologically
functions essentially as a second-order form of inquiry.[85]

To further clarify the general character of second-order investigations, it may be helpful to refer to another second-order
activity, such as the philosophy of natural science. The way in
which the actor, in this case the scientist, conceptualizes his
behavior and the world he confronts constitutes the basic subject
matter of the philosophy of science, and although, in explaining
the logical structure of science, the philosopher will order his
field of study according to the language and concepts generated
by his discipline, what constitutes his "facts" and the units and
boundaries of analysis is not simply a function of the philosopher's conceptual framework or categories of description and
classification. It is also clear that making the activity of natural
science intelligible at any time or place, whether it is the logical
structure studied by the philosopher or the more specific representations of scientific practice developed by the sociologist or
historian of science, is not a matter of developing general theories and laws concerning scientific thought and behavior that in
any significant sense parallel those associated with the first-order
enterprise of natural science itself. The generalizations of the
philosopher of science are principally representations of the
general rules, logic, and norms of practice, either conscious or
unconscious, that govern scientific activity. In a second-order
discipline, the distinction between "theory" and "fact" is pronounced in a manner in which it never is in a first-order discipline. In natural science, theories do not merely govern the
conceptualization of facts but essentially carry with them their
own facts—or at least distinctions between theory and fact are
more pragmatic than ontological. A possible exception may be
those instances in which one might speak of explaining the

85. Winch, *Idea of a Social Science*, p. 87; Brodbeck, "Explanation,
Prediction, and 'Imperfect' Knowledge," in *Readings in the Philosophy of
the Social Sciences*, p. 398.

"facts" of everyday life in terms of scientific theories, but even this really means either the substitution of the scientific for the manifest image or the translation or reduction of the latter to the former. However, the subject matter or facts that are observed and studied in a second-order activity and the criteria of their existence belong to a dimension that in a significant sense is independent of any second-order conceptualization. Care must be exercised in pressing this point, since critics are quick to suggest that it implies the "reproductive fallacy" [86] or the belief that the aim, for example, of social science is to conceptually reproduce the world it encounters, that the language of social science must be the language of its object, and that the criteria of viable concepts and their authentication is their recognition or understanding by the actors to whose activity they refer. But none of these implications follows, since the claim is merely that the object of second-order studies exists apart from any second-order conceptualization of it, and in a sense that is significantly different from the manner in which the natural world can be said to exist apart from the conceptual constructions of natural science. A second-order activity possesses its own terms, problem orientations, and categories of classification and description—in short, its own language and conceptual structure—and it will inevitably differ substantially from the language and conceptual structure of the activity which constitutes its object. It would be a mistake to suggest that the social-scientific representation of the social world can or should be a conceptual reduplication of that world, but an explanation of the forms of activity to which second-order inquiries address themselves demands reference to the structure and content of this preconceptualized first-order universe.

In political science, specifically, attempts at concept formation and theory building have yielded little more than intricate systems of classification and definition and a language for expressing descriptive generalizations. Although political and social scientists often attempt to appropriate the modes of expression, including quantification, that are typical of natural science, there is substantially little or no theoretical correspondence. There are many problems that attend the proliferation of conceptual frame-

86. Richard Rudner, *Philosophy of Social Science* (Englewood Cliffs, N.J.: Prentice-Hall, 1966), p. 70.

works in political science, but one of the most salient, and one that points most strikingly to the difficulties of assuming that the discipline can operate as a first-order activity, is that which revolves around the attempt to define and circumscribe the character of political phenomena. A survey of the literature of political science would soon suggest that the specification of political activity, institutions, and events is merely either arbitrary or at best the product of traditional disciplinary foci or intuitive common-sense understanding. It is quite clear that most political scientists proceed on the assumption that for the most part political relations may be analytically defined and specified a priori, but if political phenomena are second-order phenomena, political science is no more free to analytically designate the boundaries and content of politics than the philosopher of science is to arbitrarily designate what constitutes natural science. It is the task of the political scientist to ascertain the scope and character of political phenomena, but this is a matter for empirical investigation, not merely conceptual fiat. It must be emphasized again that this does not mean that the social scientist does not, or should not, have a language and conceptual repertoire of his own or that he is not free to develop the conceptual tools necessary for the conduct of his research. A second-order enterprise must, by definition, have its own realm of discourse, which may not even be intelligible to the actors whom it studies. It would be a distortion of the theory of second-order analysis to insist "on the adoption of the principle of concept formation" that would require "that classifications of social action" and "the concepts of the political scientist must be meaningful to the actor as well as the observer." [87] The language of political science is not, and logically cannot be, the language of politics, but the specification of politics is an empirical problem and not merely a matter of arbitrary conceptual choice as it so often has been treated in the discipline.

Although one problem related to the issue of distinguishing between the subject matter of first- and second-order disciplines is manifest in one way or another in a number of areas of social science, there may be particular reasons for the aggravated form in which it appears in the literature of political science. It is

87. Arthur S. Kalleberg, "Concept Formation in Normative and Empirical Studies: Toward Reconciliation in Political Theory," *American Political Science Review*, LXIII (March, 1969), 33.

not easy to characterize this problem, but it may be tentatively and generally described as a confusion about the logical use or function of certain terms and concepts. More specifically, it involves a conflation of what may be understood as the stipulative, or explicative, and the lexical, or ordinary functions of terms such as "politics" and "political." When employed by social scientists, terms such as "politics" characteristically perform at least two logically different functions that are often inadequately differentiated. The political scientist is in one sense free to use the term "politics" in any manner he finds convenient, and he may find it useful to employ it in a stipulative manner to designate any particular phenomena, class of phenomena, or functionally equivalent activities or structures. In other words, a stipulative definition may be given to the term, and it may be employed as a special item in the disciplinary vocabulary. But there is another use of the term "politics," both in the language of political science and in ordinary language, which often is not sufficiently distinguished from the stipulative use. "Politics" is also used to refer to a concrete and spatiotemporally circumscribed realm of activity which has been preinterpreted and defined by social actors and which does not necessarily coincide with the various senses assigned to the term by social scientists. Because of this, there is a danger of confusion if the political scientist merely applies the concept of "politics" according to his own predilections or the conventions of his discipline. He cannot use the term "politics" in the same way that the specialized terms of natural science and natural history are employed, any more than the philosopher of science may arbitrarily stipulate the referent of "science." It is this preinterpreted realm of politics that is the object of political science and cannot be ignored in explanations of political action. Although it is sometimes argued that "politics" may be employed as a theoretical term in much the same way that a term such as "motion" is used in natural science, despite the fact that its meaning may be quite different in the language of everyday life, it should be apparent that in natural science the use of "motion" and the place of this concept in the structure of the manifest image are in no sense the object of natural-scientific investigation and have no place in the conceptual structure of scientific investigation, while the everyday conceptualization of politics must be an essential concern of the political scientist and the term, as used in the everyday sense, must inevitably be part of the vocabulary of the political scientist.

This point can be clarified by comparing "politics" with a term such as "religion," which does not characteristically function on two different logical levels. On one level, these terms may be employed in a similar manner. "Politics" can be used as a generic term or classificatory label to designate, for example, any system of power relationships in society, just as "religion" might be utilized to designate any belief in the supernatural. However, the term "politics" also functions on a further logical level on which "religion" does not: that is, in its reference to a particular and sociohistorically differentiated mode of activity. The equivalent term in the area of "religion" would be a species of religion, such as Christianity or Buddhism. Although the political scientist may use "politics" in both the generic and specific sense, explanations and descriptions of political phenomena ultimately require reference to, and illumination of, the modes of activity represented by the specific and ordinary function of this term.

One of the most prevalent notions in social science is that the development of any science moves from systematic description and classification to theoretical explanation, or from natural history to science. But this is incorrect—both logically and historically. Although such systems of classification as those provided by the various conceptual frameworks in political science may be of some heuristic value, they do not fulfill the role for which they are generally conceived, that is, as the elementary step in the development of general theoretical explanations. The description and explanation of social phenomena are not merely functions of the application of analytical constructs. The obvious objection to this line of argument, and one that has become a persistent refrain in the literature of social science, is that one cannot approach the social world free from presuppositions, and that it is best for the concepts that inevitably order encountered phenomena to be made explicit, defined operationally, and shared intersubjectively. There is a certain truth and appeal to this argument, but it tends to slip past and distort the issue at stake. The proffered choice between approaching the phenomena in terms of preconceived analytical categories and approaching the social world in an unstructured manner is a false one. The social scientist will necessarily bring to his enterprise preconceptions and categories for discriminating between phenomena, but these need not be exclusively, or even primarily, of the same logical character as the preconceptions which are usually associated with either the natural historian or the natural scientist. In a second-order discipline, how one divides and orders the encountered world, no matter what specific terms he wishes to utilize as a part of his disciplinary vocabulary, is not merely a function of a scheme of classification such as that utilized by the natural historian but a function of the manner in which the world has been conceptually ordered by the actors in it. Thus there is a significant sense in which theory in social science cannot be logically comparable to theory in the natural sciences.

It is a mistake to simply assume that there must be a theoretical dimension of social science that approximates the logical structure of theory in natural science or the representation of that structure by positivistic philosophers of science. The "theoretical" dimension of social science may be difficult to isolate, but it does not consist of general theories and laws. It may best be understood as consisting primarily of assumptions about social reality and the epistemological demands that flow from them. There is also such a dimension to natural science, but it is precisely the content of this dimension which dictates that laws and general theories are the appropriate modes of explanation. In a second-order discipline such as social science, the epistemological requirements entail a different logic of explanation. There are no second-order theories and laws of politics in the same sense that there are first-order theories and laws of motion, light, and subatomic particles; and this is a function not merely of the immaturity of social science, but of the very character of the enterprise. In almost every instance, the major difficulties in concept formation and theory construction in social science can be related to attempts to follow what are taken to be the procedures of explanation and concept formation characteristic of natural science, without first considering the epistemological demands of the phenomena to which the discipline addresses itself. But to suggest that social science is, and must be, a second-order enterprise requires the development of a substantive conception of social reality. More specifically, it requires a view of social reality as a realm of action that is to be described and explained principally by an illumination of the rules and conceptual structure which inform it.

BEHAVIOR AND ACTION

THE PROBLEMS of political science are not necessarily the problems of psychology and philosophy, and it would be a mistake to engage in a detailed recapitulation of the theoretical history of psychology and recent philosophical critiques and defenses of behaviorism [88] in the belief that these apply in any direct way. Unlike psychology, political science, for the most part, has not developed any coherent epistemological position regarding the application of mental predicates such as "purpose" and "intention" and their relation to overt behavior, despite the central place of such problems in most political science research. But a great many assumptions that political scientists make about social and political phenomena would indicate a certain continuity between theoretical problems in these two disciplines. This is apparent in such issues as that revolving around the rather indeterminate meaning of the concept of "behavior." Behaviorism has never been a unitary doctrine, either in psychology or philosophy, and it has varied from Watson's early S-R theory and rejection of mental data to the intricate formulations of such individuals as Tolman, B. F. Skinner, and C. L. Hull. There is a wide range of opinion as well as to whether what should be taken as the subject matter or proper level of analysis are gross actions or the discrete physiological events that constitute such actions (molar and molecular behavior) and whether references to consciousness and the attribution of mental predicates are to be excluded completely or merely translated into statements in an observation language (radical and methodological behaviorism). This variety of formulations has contributed to the elusive meaning of the term "behavior," yet there is a more significant aspect to the explanation of this ambiguity. In psychology as well as other social sciences, the use of this term, which is broad enough in its usual application to refer to both conventional human activity and events in the natural world, has served to deemphasize the distinctions between these realms and to reinforce the philosophical thesis of the unity of science

88. See Theodore Mischel, "Scientific and Philosophical Psychology: A Historical Introduction," in *Human Action*, ed. T. Mischel, (New York: Academic Press, 1969), pp. 1–40.

and other doctrines of positivism, such as the verificationist theory of meaning and the requirement of specifying the meaning of concepts by correlation with observable data.

The conceptual links between behaviorism in psychology and positivism in the philosophy of science have not only been historical—in the sense that psychologists such as Tolman have clearly accepted positivism's doctrines about the character of scientific theories and the criteria of scientific data—but logical. Such tenets of positivism as operationalism (which holds that theoretical concepts and references to theoretical entities are merely abbreviated descriptions of, and abstractions from, observable phenomena describable in everyday terms) and instrumentalism (which holds that theoretical statements are properly not even statements at all with any real empirical reference but only analytical constructs featuring as calculational devices and predictive tools) implicitly either rule out explanations that make reference to mental episodes or require that they be reducible to patterns of overt behavior or dispositions to behave in particular ways. As one observer writes: "Anyone who seriously accepts these assumptions is also committed to defend some form of philosophical behaviorism." [89] Although the problem of the status of theoretical terms has not been as great a focus of controversy in political science as it has in psychology, the same assumptions have tacitly informed most theorizing in the discipline. The views of operationalism and instrumentalism were central to early positivism, but today they find few defenders among philosophers of science as adequate conceptions of the status of theoretical terms and entities in natural science. In psychology, too, the crude physicalist versions of early behaviorism to which instrumentalism and operationalism gave support have either been severely challenged as an adequate epistemological posture or have given way to a more extreme yet methodologically sophisticated centralist theory of behaviorism which stresses an identification of mental states or mental events, and references to mental processes with the physiological states of the brain and the description of brain states. But just as in psychology, where, despite growing reservations about traditional behavioristic programs, "the methodological rhetoric

89. Bruce Aune, *Knowledge, Mind, and Nature* (New York: Random House, 1967), p. 15.

of behaviorism lingers on because a more adequate conceptual
framework for the empirical study of human behavior has, so
far, failed to emerge," [90] the language of behaviorism and positivism continues to provide the framework for most discussions
of explanation in political science, even though ostensive links
between these areas may not always be particularly apparent.

Although in psychology the use of the term "behavior" has
gained a certain specificity of meaning from its application
within the context of fairly well-defined theories (despite the
ambiguities arising within these theories and resulting from
competition between them), political scientists have developed
few, if any, such theoretical contexts that would endow the term
with a significance that goes beyond the general wish of the
discipline to stress its "continuity, in spirit and method, with
physical and biological science." [91] There has been no satisfactory
refining of the meaning of the concept of behavior that would
provide any adequate specification of the scope of social-scientific inquiry, the criteria of explanation, or what kinds of phenomena are included and excluded. Even the critics of the idea
of the "continuity" of natural and social science have often reinforced the tendency to leave the term "behavior" unexplicated
by allowing the vague equation of "behavior" and "scientific" to
stand unchallenged and by distinguishing behavioral (and even
empirical) explanations as inappropriate to human activity. Inevitably, mediating positions have been developed such as that
of David Braybrooke, who suggests that social science encompasses two modes of inquiry and explanation revolving around
a distinction between "questions about human *behavior* and
questions about human *action*," or between applying the "same
methods as the natural sciences" and "discovering the *meaning*
of actions." [92] Yet such conciliatory efforts tend to beg the question that is at issue. The problem is not one of looking at the
"same phenomena" from different or "complementary" perspectives [93] or of seeing and interpreting them as different things, for

90. Mischel, *Human Action*, p. 3.
91. Abraham Kaplan, *The Conduct of Inquiry* (San Francisco: Chan-
dler, 1964), p. 407.
92. David Braybrooke, "Introduction," in *Philosophical Problems of the
Social Sciences*, ed. D. Braybrooke (New York: Macmillan, 1965), p. 13.
93. *Ibid.*, p. 8.

then the problem remains of specifying what the things are that are so seen or interpreted; that is, the conceptual problem of the nature of social reality and the scope of social-scientific inquiry is still left unresolved.

Braybrooke argues that *"the elementary subject matter of the social sciences"* consists of "the actions and behavior of individual persons"; thus he seems to suggest that it is "persons" that constitute "the same phenomena" about which "both action and behavioral questions can be raised." [94] He implies that a behavior question can be asked about a person's action or that an action can be seen as a piece of behavior which is not "essentially different" from that associated with animal stimulus-response conditioning.[95] If an action explanation is conceived as one in which what persons "do" is seen in terms of action, a behavioral explanation is supposedly one that involves "treating persons as organisms" and is concerned "with counting or measuring reinforcements and responses." [96] But the idea of treating persons as organisms and actions as behavior is certainly conceptually problematical. Braybrooke's purpose is to utilize the behavior/action nexus as a "philosophical principle of sorting" [97] that discriminates between complementary modes of explanation in social science; but it is misleading to characterize "behavior" and "action" as logically equivalent attributes that may be ascribed to the same phenomena. It may be possible to argue that social science can, does, or should accommodate different forms of explanation and include in its subject matter more than one kind of phenomena, and it may make sense to specify these different forms of approach in terms of behavior and action, but it is quite another thing to suggest that these two theories, languages, and sets of epistemological assumptions can be compatibly applied to the same phenomena, or that, for example, explanations in terms of human agency and stimulus reinforcement can be equally valid with regard to the "same" events.

It would seem that unless otherwise cogently stipulated, the relationship between such pairs of concepts as behavior and

94. *Ibid.*, p. 3 (italics Braybrooke's).
95. *Ibid.*, p. 6.
96. *Ibid.*, pp. 3, 4.
97. *Ibid.*, pp. 1, 4.

action or organism and person is best understood in terms of the relation between a genus and species in which the "ultimate genus is *animal movement*"; thus behavior may be viewed as a kind of animal movement generally distinguished in terms of "what animals do, in contrast with what they suffer," and human action may be considered as a species of behavior characterized by such predicates as "direction and directiveness, purpose, aim, intent" and attributed to, or brought about by, that kind of organism understood as a person who is the agent or actor.[98] Since behavior is a generic term, it is necessary to specify a species of behavior in order to isolate a particular form of explanation or designate a subject matter for investigation. The concept of action is normally employed to particularize the more generic notion of behavior. Although, strictly speaking, maybe not everything that one can be said to "do" (or every instance in which a form of this verb is employed) is an action, actions may be generally understood as something people do, cause to happen, or otherwise bring about, as distinguished, for example, from what happens to them—and this is why the idea of agency is central to the theory of action. "Act" and "action" may, in many instances, be used interchangeably, but while "act" usually functions as a further particularization or to designate an episode of action, it would be a mistake to assume that acts are a species of action. Often, "action" implies some sort of overt physical movement, as contrasted with, for example, not only passiveness but thought and speech, but care must be exercised that the significance of such gestures as refraining from overt action and such items as mental acts and speech acts not be disqualified out of hand. "Activity" carries a number of senses, but it usually refers primarily to the background or context of particular acts or forms of action. However, it cannot be assumed that actions and acts merely receive their identity by association with a mode of activity, since often an activity is largely circumscribed in terms of the kinds of actions characteristically associated with it. The purpose here is not to provide a complete analysis of the concept of action, but only to make some elementary conceptual distinctions before entering into a discussion of action as the focus of social-scientific inquiry.

98. D. S. Schwayder, *The Stratification of Behavior* (New York: Humanities Press, 1965), pp. 202, 24, 33.

LANGUAGE AND THE CONCEPT OF ACTION

THE ARGUMENT TO BE DEVELOPED HERE is that a number of current issues in the philosophy of action and the philosophy of the social sciences, as well as certain related theoretical problems in social science connected with the conceptualization of social phenomena and the explanation of social action, can be clarified by viewing them in light of recent work in the philosophy of language and the analysis of linguistic meaning. Although it is customary to conceive of speech (both oral and written) as a species, kind, or form of action, it may well be that at the present time it is possible to produce a more definitive notion of what it is to say something (or of the meanings of words or expressions) than of what it is to do something (or of the meaning or significance of actions in general). In addition, it is common to conceive of action (both linguistic and nonlinguistic) as intimately tied to the idea of thought and what it means to acquire, possess, and utilize concepts, that is, to conceive of action as a manifestation or expression of the general capacity for symbolization and the ability to use particular concepts. But, again, these notions are on the whole more problematical than the very things they are assumed to subsume; or at least current theories of thought and action are as replete with conflicts and anomalies as the idea of what it is to use a language.

The form of argument to be employed is one that may be loosely described as retroductive: it is a process of moving from a theory of linguistic meaning to an elaboration of the essential characteristics of any form of action, that is, a process of attempting to extend the scope or range of application of the theory as far as possible. The argument is based on the idea that speech and nonlinguistic action are analogous and homologous; but although they share a number of family resemblances, analogy does not entail identity. Yet despite the possibility of conceptual and empirical differentiation, it is difficult to posit definite boundaries between speech and nonlinguistic action. For example, although there may be, strictly speaking, no dictionaries of standard nonlinguistic actions as there are dictionaries of the standard uses of words, many actions in a social context are highly conventionalized, and it would be going too far to suggest that "with non-linguistic action . . . the distinc-

tion between actual and standardized uses has no application." [99]
This is not to say that it is useless to specify or recognize distinctions between linguistic and nonlinguistic action (hereafter sometimes referred to as speech and action) but only that they are "cognate notions." [100] Despite the fact that in many contexts, including ordinary language and the collective representations of everyday life, as well as in the conceptual repertoire of specialized disciplines and realms of discourse, they may be, and have been, differentiated and/or related in numerous ways and to varying degrees and for various descriptive, normative, explanatory, and definitional purposes, it is impossible to establish any universal and fixed criteria of differentiation. The intention is not to blur or compress useful distinctions between these concepts or the phenomena to which they are ascribed, but only to suggest that they share a number of common features and that, at the boundaries, they tend to merge.

Recent work in the philosophy of language, most notably and specifically that of the late J. L. Austin, suggests a framework of analysis that with some emendations may be effectively extended to the construction of the basic elements of a general theory of action and to the solution of a number of conceptual problems revolving around the explanation of action. It was a central aspect of Austin's argument that an adequate understanding of the meaning of speech was related to the fact that speech involved not merely saying something but doing something, that is, that speech is a mode of action. Austin did not develop any systematic treatment of "doing something" or action in general,[101] but his analysis of what he took to be speech acts may provide a number of insights into the concept of action. It may well be that Austin's dictum can be turned around or broadened to encompass the idea that, in an important sense, action is not merely doing something but saying something, or, more properly, that saying something and the various modes of doing something must manifest a number of common characteristics if they are

---

99. Stephen Toulmin, "Concepts and the Explanation of Human Behavior," in *Human Action*, ed. Mischel, p. 85.
100. *Ibid.*
101. "It would be claiming too much to claim that Austin set forth, or even held at all, anything like a general *theory* of action . . ." (L. W. Forguson, "Austin's Philosophy of Action," in *Symposium on J. L. Austin*, ed. K. T. Fann [New York: Humanities Press, 1969], p. 128).

both forms of action. The core of Austin's thesis is the proposition that to say something normally involves doing, simultaneously, a number of analytically distinguishable things, including the act of uttering certain noises (phonetic act), the act of uttering certain words belonging to a certain vocabulary and conforming to certain rules of grammatical construction, conventional forms of intonation, etc. (phatic act), and the act of using words in accordance with rules of sense and reference that constitute what is often construed as meaning (rhetic act). The totality of these acts or "the act of 'saying something' in this full normal sense" is what Austin christened "the performance of a locutionary act." [102] In developing a subsequent, and in many ways similar, theory of speech acts, John Searle has compressed Austin's three distinctions into "utterance acts" (uttering words) and "propositional acts" (reference and predication),[103] but the difference is not crucial for this discussion. For both Austin and Searle, the point is to stress that a necessary condition of fully intelligible speech is to use words in accordance with rules and conventions that provide the utterances with recognizable propositional content. But although the performance of a locutionary act or the expression of an utterance with propositional content is a necessary condition of meaningful speech, it is not a sufficient condition.

For Austin, the making of the sounds (or marks) that constitute a phonetic act is necessary for the performance of a phatic act; thus, in doing the latter, one is necessarily doing the former, and the former is the means of doing the latter. The phonetic and phatic act together (or, in Searle's terms, the utterance act) are necessary for the performance of a rhetic (Austin) or propositional (Searle) act, but not every sound or mark (for example, the imitative calls of a mynah bird) qualifies as a phatic act or utterance act, and not every utterance act succeeds as a propositional or rhetic act. But even the rules and conventions covering the performance of a full locutionary act are still not adequate for understanding an expression or the performance of a successful or fully meaningful speech act, for "to perform a locutionary act is in general, we may say, also or

102. J. L. Austin, *How to Do Things with Words* (Cambridge: Harvard University Press, 1962), pp. 92–94.
103. John R. Searle, *Speech Acts* (Cambridge: At the University Press, 1969), p. 24.

eo ipso to perform an *illocutionary* act," and "to determine what illocutionary act is so performed we must determine in what way we are using the locution." [104] The performance of a locution is to an illocution, Searle has suggested, something like marking an X is to the act of voting or like buying a ticket is to taking a train trip; [105] it is a collateral act necessary for the performance of the full speech act. (Not only is this analogy illuminating in itself, but it is interesting that for both Austin and Searle analogies with nonlinguistic action appear essential in illustrating the character of meaningful speech, although neither presents a general theory of action which would tie together linguistic and nonlinguistic action.) The "doctrine of 'illocutionary' forces," [106] then, centers on the notion that the identity and meaning of speech acts derive ultimately and most essentially from the linguistic uses to which they are put, and these uses, although almost infinitely variable, are intelligible only in view of the rules and conventions to which they conform. Austin attempted an initial categorization in terms of "general families of related and overlapping speech acts," but the basic point is that to say something is either explicitly or implicitly to state, ask, command, warn, promise, evaluate, describe, commend, advise, etc., and although one can analytically distinguish between locutions (and their various components) and illocutions, "every genuine speech act is both." [107]

Whether illocutionary (or performative) force is to be taken as a part of a meaning or a coordinate of meaning can be a troublesome problem, but there would seem to be no reason why it should cause difficulty as long as relevant distinctions are maintained. Austin does on occasion distinguish between "*force and meaning*," but this seems to be primarily for the purpose of distinguishing performative force from linguistic meaning in the "traditional sense" that has been equated with sense and reference.[108] He does not appear to believe that this distinction is in itself a critical one and suggests that it is useful only because there is a "sense in which meaning is equivalent to sense and reference," and that it is essential only in the same way that "it

---

104. Austin, *How to Do Things with Words*, p. 98 (italics Austin's).
105. Searle, *Speech Acts*, p. 24.
106. Austin, *How to Do Things with Words*, p. 99.
107. *Ibid.*, pp. 146, 149.
108. *Ibid.*, p. 109 (italics Austin's).

has become essential to distinguish between sense and reference within meaning" (as traditionally understood, not because there is any significant break between force and meaning).[109] It would seem that Austin can best be interpreted as saying that illocutionary force and sense and reference are both aspects of meaning or the meaningful use of words. Whether one distinguishes between meaning and performative force or between dimensions of meaning seems to make little difference, as long as it is recognized that there can be no sharp separation between the rules governing locutions and the wider conventional context in which speech acts take place. Meaning is intelligible only in terms of "the issuing of an utterance in a speech act situation," and the concern is with the "total speech act in the total speech act situation." [110] What must be understood is that linguistic meaning derives from an expanding series of semantic and social contexts beginning with the sentence and extending to the general activity and realm of discourse in which a speech act features. In Searle's terms, "speaking a language is engaging in a rule-governed form of behavior," [111] and these rules that constitute the meaning of language extend from the rules of grammar and syntax to the rules and conventions that make the utterance of certain words in a certain conventional context the act of promising, evaluating, describing, commanding, etc., and render them capable of being understood as such. Although an agent may not always be conscious of these rules and their various dimensions (for example, the rules of grammar), there is nevertheless an intentional as well as conventional dimension to following them. Not only do the rules give meaning to utterances but people also mean or intend something by these utterances. In other words, as Searle suggests, in principle "there is a series of analytic connections between the notion of speech acts, what the speaker means, what the sentence (or other linguistic elements) uttered means, what the speaker intends, what the hearer understands, and what the rules governing the linguistic elements are." [112] At least in principle, "whatever can be meant can be said," [113] and whatever is said has meaning, although in

109. *Ibid.*, p. 100.
110. *Ibid.*, pp. 138, 147.
111. Searle, *Speech Acts*, p. 16.
112. *Ibid.*, p. 21.
113. *Ibid.*, p. 17.

practice much can go wrong, and it may well be that one does not always say what he means or mean what he says.

It is this ever-present possibility of language "going-wrong" that Austin attempts to explain by "the doctrine of Infelicities." [114] Speech presupposes "an accepted conventional procedure having a certain conventional effect, the procedure to include the uttering of certain words by certain persons in certain circumstances." [115] Thus it is always possible that an utterance may be "unhappy" in the sense that it may be performed by the wrong person, uttered insincerely or in inappropriate circumstances, incorrectly executed, incomplete, etc. The result will be various forms of unhappiness such as "misfires," "abuses," "misapplications," "misexecutions," and "hitches." [116] In addition, ambiguity, vagueness, and misunderstanding are inevitable sources of difficulty. Since performative utterances or illocutionary acts may be, and often are, "implicit" or otherwise oblique as well as "explicit," [117] even the most well-defined context will not always make it clear what sort of speech act has been performed. On the whole, this picture of meaning may appear to have conservative or static overtones, since neither Austin nor Searle deals at any length with the problems of change and innovation in linguistic rules and conventions, but this is more a matter of distribution of emphasis than an endemic defect of the theory, and Austin recognizes that one can reject, challenge, or otherwise question operative rules of procedure and/or institute new ones.[118] It also may seem that his theory is restricted to ordinary language or the standard modes of discursive speech that form the basis for most of his examples. But although Austin does explicitly exclude from discussion what he considers "parasitic" uses of language and makes distinctions between "normal use" and such "nonliteral" and "non-serious" uses as poetry, he suggests that "they might be brought into a more general account." There would appear to be no reason why Austin's theory cannot be easily extended to various specialized realms of language use.[119]

Finally, in addition to the locutionary and illocutionary uses

114. Austin, *How to Do Things with Words*, p. 14.
115. *Ibid.*, p. 26.
116. *Ibid.*, pp. 16, 34–36.
117. *Ibid.*, p. 32.
118. *Ibid.*, p. 29.
119. *Ibid.*, pp. 22, 121.

of speech, a third sense of use, function, or purpose must be distinguished that is neither strictly an aspect of linguistic meaning nor primarily governed by linguistic conventions. This is related to the performance of what Austin terms a *"perlocutionary act or a perlocution"* [120] and involves the semantically external uses to which language can be put. In this sense language may be employed for such purposes as causing certain things to happen, evoking certain responses, and producing certain effects on the emotions, thoughts, and actions of others. Things one may do with language, such as convincing, persuading, frightening, etc., are not speech acts, although in certain contexts various kinds of speech acts may be used for these purposes and may produce or result in other intended and unintended consequences. Just as it is necessary to distinguish between speech acts and their use in the pursuance of numerous existential activities such as giving lectures, writing fiction, composing poetry, as well as more vague and marginal "doings" such as implying, insinuating, and suggesting, it is necessary to distinguish between an illocution and its consequence (or goal). A line can be, and often must be, drawn between the successful performance of an illocutionary act and its consequences and effects in the world. Although a successful illocutionary act implies certain effects or consequences (for example, being understood), these "conventional" effects and consequences must be distinguished from the numerous, and in some sense causal, effects and consequences that may attend the performance of a speech act and constitute a perlocutionary act. Although there may be conventions which characteristically relate certain speech acts to the obtaining of certain ends, these are not strictly linguistic conventions. The point is that the relationship between illocutions and perlocutions is largely a contingent relationship and may vary considerably between different contexts.

This is a sketchy rendering of an approach to the philosophy of language that in its theoretical implications extends beyond the specific arguments contained in the work of Austin and Searle, and there has been no attempt to explore all of the subtleties and the full scope of the arguments. But enough has been presented to begin an exploration of the relevance of these ideas to an analysis of some problems in the explanation of nonlinguis-

120. *Ibid.*, p. 101.

tic action. However, before turning to that task, it is necessary to recall the substance of the thesis to be developed here. Although the basic character of this thesis is hardly original and is in some respects common to the work of a number of individuals, such as Peter Winch and Stephen Toulmin, several aspects of this general argument require further explication with regard to its relation to specific issues revolving around the explanation of action. In broad terms, this thesis embodies, in Toulmin's words, the notion "that the 'meaning' of linguistic expressions and the 'significance' of human actions derive from a common source," and that consequently "no hard-and-fast line can be drawn separating the (analytical) meaning or significance of *speech-acts*, or linguistic behavior, from the (explanatory) meaning or significance we place on the associated *nonlinguistic* actions and behavior patterns."[121] Both Winch and Toulmin build upon Wittgenstein's theory of language and the notions that linguistic and social conventions are inextricably entwined and that the meaning of linguistic expressions derives from their standard or rule-conforming use in a "language-game" which is in turn intelligible only in terms of a wider context of paradigmatic behavior or "form of life." They argue that both the explanation of nonlinguistic action and the explication of linguistic meaning involve the discerning of "the overall constellations (the forms of life) within which the actions or expressions are to be interpreted, and then [the locating of] the specific action or utterance, by 'placing' it in a particular context (behavioral and conceptual) within that wider pattern." But beyond this explanatory parallel lies the fact that "in development, as in actual use, the linguistic and nonlinguistic elements in our forms of life are complementary and interdependent."[122] Just as the meaning of linguistic expressions is bound up with conventions of various social contexts and activities, the structure of the social context is in part constituted by the structure and content of language. The argument, *in fine*, then, is that speech and action are both logically analogous and empirically interdependent. But as persuasive as this view may be in general, it leaves many unanswered questions when presented in such broad terms. It is

---

121. Toulmin, "Concepts and the Explanation of Human Behavior," pp. 72–73 (italics Toulmin's).
122. Winch, *Idea of a Social Science*, p. 14; Toulmin, *ibid.*, p. 85.

precisely Austin's theory of speech acts and linguistic meaning that provides a purchase for delving deeper into the character of the relationship between speech and action.

ACTIONS AND THEIR ANALYSIS

FEW QUESTIONS in the philosophy of action and psychological/social-scientific theory have been more critical and problematical than those turning on the issue of the relation of physical or bodily movements to action, and this issue provides a convenient point of entry into the general problem of the conceptualization of action. Although it would seem that the idea of action is closely tied to the idea of physical movement and that in most normal circumstances actions somehow involve bodily movements, it should be clear, despite the claims and assumptions of some behaviorists, that actions and bodily movements are not simply numerically identical. It is easy to conceive of examples where the performance of an action can be accomplished by various kinds or sequences of bodily movements and where the same bodily movements may be associated with very diverse kinds of action. Nevertheless, it might still be maintained that in any particular instance there is an identity between an action and some physical movement or movements. Given the apparent inseparability of action and bodily movements, individuals such as A. I. Melden have argued that although actions are not *merely* bodily movements, in certain contexts or under certain circumstances bodily movements will *count* as actions. In this view the same basic physical event is describable in two different languages (physical and action). Thus it is possible to impose upon gross physical movements another conceptual framework besides the physically descriptive and to "see a bodily movement as an action" or see an action as something more than a mere physical movement.[123] However, the whole notion of "seeing bodily movements as actions" is misleading, for it usually implies that such movements are either components of action or logical preconditions of action. But either assumption tends to lead to some version of the mistaken "reduction of such per-

123. A. I. Melden, *Free Action* (New York: Humanities Press, 1961), p. 187.

ception of human beings in action to observations of physical movements." [124] Although bodily movements might in some sense be criteria or even conditions of action or might constitute an aspect of an action, they are no more elements of actions than vocal noises are elements of words or words are merely a way of "hearing" such noises. A complex action may be understood as composed of more basic or atomic actions, and although an atomic action may have distinguishable parts analyzable into bodily movements, these movements cannot be conceived as parts of the action or things that are "done." A basic or atomic action, say swimming, may be "seen as" the more complex action of engaging in an aerobics program, but it is a mistake to suggest that one perceives or sees a series of basic bodily movements and then further interprets, conceptualizes, or "sees" them as, for example, swimming. Although actions may be normally related in some way to bodily movements (while not all bodily movements constitute actions), it is difficult to understand why bodily movements need be considered either perceptually or logically more primitive than actions. Many of the difficulties surrounding this issue have been generated by the undemonstrated and unwarranted assumption that it is bodily movements that are most fundamentally given, what one most basically "sees," and that an inferential move or act of interpretation is required if one is to conceive of an event as an action and describe it as such. Actually, no such conceptual jump is involved. On the contrary, it would seem that there is nothing to bar the conception of actions as perceptually primitive—and in fact they are so perceived. It is actions that are interpreted, and bodily movements feature as necessary aspects or conditions of actions that can be abstracted by analysis in the process of their interpretation.

The first step out of this dilemma is to realize that actions are ascribed to persons, not to physical movements, since actions are things that persons do. To neglect this fundamental point leads to the type of difficulty present in the argument offered by Donald Davidson:

> I flip the switch, turn on the light, and illuminate the room. Unbeknownst to me I also alert a prowler to the fact that I am home.

124. Virgil C. Aldrich, "On Seeing Bodily Movements as Action," *American Philosophical Quarterly,* IV (July, 1967), 230.

Here I do not do four things, but only one, of which four descriptions have been given.[125]

The immediate and inevitable question raised by this example and its analysis is that if four descriptions of the same thing have been given, what is the one thing which has been done? What has been described by these four descriptions? Is there an unarticulated basic action hidden under these descriptions? It might be suggested that it is actually a bodily movement which supports these descriptions, but clearly a bodily movement is not something that is done, and one would search in vain for the bodily movement that was numerically identical with the four descriptions. To avoid this kind of impasse, it is best, first of all, to drop the idea, despite its common-sense persuasiveness, that actions are particulars (which appears to be assumed by Davidson in this case) and instead conceive of actions as well as speech acts (although Austin does not explicitly make this point) as universal predicates ascribed to persons. From this perspective, it is neither "logically or definitionally impossible" for different persons, or one person on different occasions, "to perform the same action." [126] In ascribing and describing an action, any amount of particular data may be appended (time, place, etc.); but this does not change or modify the action, although it does particularize or specify the act, act-event, or act-episode which manifests the action, that is, the fact that it is performed or instantiated by a person in specific circumstances. It is the person, however, who instantiates the action or literally constitutes an instance of the action.[127] Turning again to Davidson's example, the one "thing" which underlies the "descriptions" is not a particular action (or bodily movement) but the person or "I," and the question is how many actions are to be attributed to the person. One might suggest on this basis that what are presented by Davidson are not four descriptions of one particular action but rather "four actions performed at the same time by the same person." [128] But although under some circumstances it may be

125. Donald Davidson, "Actions, Reasons, and Causes," in *Readings in the Theory of Action*, ed. Norman S. Care and Charles Landesman (Bloomington, Ind.: Indiana University Press, 1968), pp. 180–81.

126. Charles Landesman, "Action as Universals: An Inquiry into the Metaphysics of Action," *American Philosophical Quarterly*, VI (July, 1969), 248.

127. *Ibid.*, p. 250.

128. *Ibid.*, p. 252.

possible to conceive of four actions being performed simultaneously, it is difficult to see how this interpretation can be intelligibly applied in this case without the addition of considerable hypothetical data. Both the idea of four descriptions of one particular action and the idea of four actions performed at the same time seem to be unsatisfactory interpretations of what took place. It is at this point that Austin's theory becomes pertinent.

Without a more definitive specification of the context, it is difficult to ascertain from the data supplied by Davidson precisely what has happened. It is clearly problematical, at best, to suggest that in this case four actions have been performed literally at once, since a person can no more usually perform four logically discrete actions simultaneously than he can make four statements at once or perform four different kinds of speech acts at once in the course of uttering one sentence. It is possible to imagine cases in which a person could perform four logically discrete actions simultaneously, for example, smoke a cigarette, drive a car, talk to a passenger in the car, and turn on the radio, but this is not easily analogized to the case at hand. There also may be instances of ambiguity about what has been done or said or different interpretations of what has been done or said, but the resolution of such problems would not be in terms of positing either multiple actions or equally valid descriptions of one action. There are certainly cases of doing things simultaneously which could be understood as a relation between simple and hybrid or complex actions (such as swimming and aerobics), or cases of relating actions to activities (such as checkmating and playing chess), but neither of these interpretations would seem to be relevant to the example suggested by Davidson.

One way to make sense of Davidson's example is to interpret what he offers as four descriptions as analytically separable subacts or dimensions of one action and its consequences, in the manner that Austin divides a speech act into its constituent parts and perlocutionary effect. From this perspective, it could be argued that what is presented here is one action, that is, *turning on the light*. This entails or involves making certain *bodily movements* (here unspecified) analogous to Austin's phonetic act and *flipping the switch*, which is a collateral act of manipulating certain things in a conventionally intelligible manner or performing certain conventionally significant acts corresponding to Austin's phatic and rhetic acts. Together these constitute the performance of an act that is analogous to a locutionary act. However, this gains complete meaning and becomes intelligible only in terms of the purpose of turning on the light, which corresponds to Austin's illocutionary force and identifies and specifies the action and the conventions which allow the expression of that purpose. Although in some context illuminating the room or alerting the prowler might be construed as self-sufficient actions, it would seem that here they are not fundamentally autonomous actions at all. Rather, they are the intended (illuminating the room) and unintended (alerting the prowler) consequences (effects or results) of the action, which are only contingently (rather than conventionally) related to it, and which correspond to Austin's perlocutionary act. This is one way in which the problem presented by Davidson could be resolved, but the solution ultimately remains hypothetical outside a more definitive context. The point is that a completely explicated and intelligible, meaningful, or significant action will yield elements comparable to those found in Austin's and Searle's treatments of speech acts.

A necessary condition and aspect of significant action is normally some kind of bodily movement or the performance of what may be termed a *somatic act,* but not every bodily movement qualifies as an element or aspect of an action, any more than every vocal sound qualifies as a word or aspect of a speech act. Only if it conforms to some conventionally specifiable and constituted or rule-related act, such as flipping the switch (which belongs to a repertoire of conventional acts) does a somatic act succeed or become intelligible as an aspect of an action, although the somatic act is necessary for the performance of a *repertory act.* Similarly, the repertory act of flipping the switch, although necessary for the performance of what may be termed an *overt act,* does not succeed as such in a context where it has no conventional significance and intelligibility, or where, for example, there is no switch to flip, any more than "the King of New York" succeeds as a locution with complete sense and reference or propositional content. However, these three acts, or the dimensions, levels, or aspects of the intelligible *discrete act* of flipping the switch, would not in most circumstances constitute the performance of a fully significant action. To flip the switch normally would be at the same time to perform a *purposive act* (such as turning on the light) which provides the determining dimension of significance and identifies the action. The difference between the purposive act and the discrete act is in part the difference between what action was done and how it was done. To identify an action and understand its significance, it is necessary to determine its use or function, that is, its purpose, or what the person performing it was meaning to do, and the place of that purpose in a social or conventional context. The discrete act of marking an X on a ballot, for example, becomes significant in relation to the purposive act of voting, and together these acts constitute an action intelligible in terms of a complex of social and political rules and conventions. As with the problem of the meaning of speech acts, it would seem that although it is possible to speak of significance as related to the discrete act and its component subacts, it is preferable to view significance as applying primarily to the complete action which is governed most basically by the purposive act and its place in the complete action situation.

Related to, but logically and empirically separable from, the significance of an action are the results, effects, and consequences, both intended and unintended, which the action may cause or otherwise produce. Like speech acts, actions may be performed for various purposes or may result in various events that are distinct from the identification and significance of the action. Thus to perform an action may also be to engage in a *causal* act analogous to Austin's perlocutionary act, such as illuminating the room or alerting the prowler, but these are not actions as such, at least as they appear to feature in Davidson's example. Although certain actions, such as turning on the light, may characteristically, or even necessarily, result in the illumination of the room or be used causally for that purpose, the relationship is in principle a contingent one. Although it may be said that an action sometimes gains meaning or significance through its association with particular effects that it may produce, this aspect of significance must be distinguished from the significance an action possesses in terms of its ascription to a person acting purposively in the context of certain rules and conventions that serve to define and explain it.

ACTION AND RULES

IN BOTH the philosophy of action and the philosophy of the social sciences few issues have created as much controversy

as that revolving around the concept of *"following a rule"* or the
phenomena of "rule-conforming behavior." [129] Although the proposition that *"man is a rule-following animal"* [130] has been assumed
to be closely tied to the specification, description, and explanation of action, the manner in which it is exemplified and its
implications for determining the criteria for adequate explanations of action have not been satisfactorily treated. It would seem
to be impossible to explicate the concept of action and the conditions of understanding action apart from the idea of rules, yet
the questions of precisely what is meant by a rule and what relation obtains between rules and action have remained obscure.
Although it would require a tour de force to postulate a perfectly
isomorphic relation between the way in which rules and conventions function with regard to language and speech and the
manner in which they are manifest in various forms of nonlinguistic action (to suggest, for example, that there is, strictly
speaking, a grammar and syntax of action), the difference, as
with the distinction between speech and action in general, is
more pragmatic than logical. What must be stressed is the fact
that both speech and action are impossible (both logically and
empirically) outside a context of rules and conventions and that
an understanding of the meaning of language and the significance of action is predicated on an illumination of these rules
and conventions.[131] The difficulty with most of the recent treatments of the relationship between rules and action, such as those
offered by Winch, Melden, R. S. Peters, and Dorothy Emmet, is
that they fail to yield any generally applicable theory that would
account for the diverse kinds of relations that appear to obtain.
They generally fail to explore this relationship systematically,
neglect to make crucial distinctions between various kinds of
rules, and often tend to base their arguments on examples drawn
from some restricted form of rule-conforming activity, such as
chess, which is not easily generalized to cover other modes of
action and neither explains how action is rule-conforming nor

129. Winch, *Idea of a Social Science,* p. 23 (italics Winch's); Toulmin, "Concepts and the Explanation of Human Behavior," p. 87.
130. R. S. Peters, *The Concept of Motivation* (New York: Humanities Press, 1958), p. 5 (italics Peters').
131. Although there would seem to be little general agreement on the relationship between rules and conventions, conventions will usually be treated in this discussion as a species of rules.

demonstrates that in general it is in fact rule-conforming. One reason for these deficiencies is that the thrust of most of the arguments usually is directed primarily toward distinguishing explanations of human behavior from those of natural science or understanding conventional or social action as opposed to behavior and physical movements that are merely conditioned. But if the distinction between the *"rule-conforming* character" of human action and the *"law-governed* character of natural phenomena" is a significant one, it becomes all the more necessary to reach a more adequate and principled view of the former than has yet been presented in general statements to the effect that "to study human society is . . . to take account of conduct which is partly at least rule-directed." [132]

Peters' discussion of rules and action yields little more than the almost unexceptionable idea that, since men develop and conform to social standards, conventions, normative laws, traditions, and other types of rules, explanations of action require reference to such phenomena if we are to understand the reasons for, and purposes of, their actions. Winch attempts to develop in more detail what is involved in the concept of following a rule. He stresses that it entails "that somebody else could in principle discover the rule"; that the idea of following a rule is "inseparable from the notion of *making a mistake"*; that the criteria of deciding questions of "sameness" in any context are connected with the idea of applying a rule; that although an individual could "adhere to a *private* rule of conduct" or act in accordance with a standard not articulated as a rule, it must be in principle something that can be publicly grasped and assessed as a rule; that no one could develop private rules who had had no experience with society and social activity at all; and that rule-following need not be strictly conscious activity, although there must in principle be a *"possibility"* of reflection on such conduct.[133] However, these points, despite the extent to which they may throw some light on the concept of a rule, hardly add up to a comprehensive theory of the place of rules in action explanations, and although Winch constantly moves back and forth between discussions of rules in

---

132. Toulmin, "Concepts and the Explanation of Human Behavior," p. 86 (italics Toulmin's). Dorothy Emmet, *Rules, Roles and Relations* (New York: St. Martin's Press, 1966), p. 11 (italics Emmet's).

133. Winch, *Idea of a Social Science*, pp. 30–33, 58–59 (italics Winch's).

relation to action and the place of rules in language, he does not pursue the connection much beyond establishing the general analogy.

Melden argues that social action is "logically connected with the concept of rules" and that "central to the concept of a rule is the idea of obeying or following it" (and that "the notion of disobeying is dependent upon the more fundamental idea of obeying," just as the notion of formulating a new rule is intelligible only in terms of previously having followed or obeyed rules). He does not distinguish between "obeying" and "following" and "observing" a rule (nor does he demonstrate their similarity), but he does differentiate cases where behavior merely "*accords*" with or accidentally conforms to a rule and where neither the rule has been learned nor proficiency gained in the practice or form of action to which the rule belongs. Learning a rule is to acquire a "specific way of thinking and doing," that is, "a habit, practice, custom—that way of thinking and doing that characterizes the man who knows his way about in situations by following the relevant rules." Melden's aim is primarily to distinguish between action and bodily movements, for "without this practice of obeying the rules, what we see is merely bodily movement." When viewed in the context of rules, a description of "the physical movement that occurs takes on a wholly new aspect." Melden often uses an analogy with chess moves to illustrate his argument about action and rules, and although he notes, for example, "the enormous differences between the permissive rules of chess and the prescriptive and justifying rules of morality," as well as "all the misunderstandings" to which the analogy "between chess moves and other actions may give rise," he nevertheless maintains that an analysis of the game of chess suggests what is common "in the case of other types of action, namely, the crucial importance of the practical context of common or shared practices involved in following rules, applying criteria, observing principles, acting on policies, and so on." Thus, although Melden recognizes that the differences between such things as games, morals, and traffic laws make it "misleading to speak of the term 'rule' as univocal," he argues "that just as in the case of the concept of a chess move, so in the case of the concept of any action the context of practices in which rules are obeyed, criteria employed, policies observed—a way of thinking and doing—is essential to the understanding of the difference between . . . bodily movements and action." [134] Melden in some ways provides a more systematic and comprehensive account of the concept of following a rule than either Peters or Winch, but his treatment suffers from the limited perspective of focusing on the differences between actions and bodily movements. Winch, Peters, and Melden all provide insights into the place of rules in describing and explaining action, but in each case the concern is more with broad distinctions between causal or natural-scientific explanations and explanations of action in a social context than with an analysis of precisely how rules function in explanations of action and the types of rules that must be taken into consideration.

Some indication of what would constitute adequate answers to these questions can be gained from a consideration of the place of rules in language or speech, but such an approach to the problem entails the recognition that philosophers of language have also failed to provide anything approaching a completely satisfactory account of the concept of a rule or the relation between rules and the use of language. It has already been noted that Austin, although he wishes to demonstrate that speech may be understood as a species of doing or action, provides no general treatment of action. Consequently, his insistence on the importance of conventions in understanding the various kinds of speech acts and their component dimensions is to some extent vitiated by a lack of any coherent discussion of the general relation between conventions and action (as well as conventions and rules) and a failure to make explicit whether those conventions applicable to, and necessary for, understanding illocutionary acts and the "total speech act in the total speech act situation" are merely linguistic conventions or a more general order of social conventions and rules. Similarly, Searle's argument concerning language as rule-governed behavior is not supported by any general analysis of the scope and content of such behavior. He maintains that linguistic facts or speech acts must be understood not as "brute facts" but as a species of "institutional facts" that derive their meaning from, and are defined by, systems of constitutive rules (as distinguished from regulative rules), and he argues that the particular conventions involved in speaking various lan-

134. Melden, "Action," in *Readings in the Theory of Action,* ed. Care and Landesman, pp. 37–44.

guages are a realization of such underlying rules.[135] But he pro-vides neither an elaboration of these constitutive rules of language nor, apart from some examples confined to such games as football and chess, any general discussion of how conventions, regulative rules, and constitutive rules relate to rule-informed and rule-conforming behavior. Nevertheless, it would seem, even in view of such shortcomings and lacunae, that the concept of a speech act, and especially the notion of illocutionary force, offers the best starting point for gaining an adequate view of the relation between rules and action.

Whatever one considers to be Austin's and Searle's precise position on the question, it would seem that the understanding (or explaining) of a speech act involves more than an under-standing of (or reference to) strictly linguistic rules and con-ventions. Whether illocutionary force is to be taken as an aspect of linguistic meaning or something additional to and coordinate with linguistic meaning, illocutionary or performative force depends on and derives from a conventional dimension that ex-tends beyond the linguistic rules and conventions that identify and constitute a speech act (and its component acts) as a certain type by virtue of the semantic meaning of the words uttered. To understand and/or explain a speech act requires an understand-ing and/or illumination of its purpose (or intention), and that is necessarily a conventional purpose which may or may not be overtly and explicitly expressed in linguistic conventions. But illocutionary acts which are nonconventional in this sense (that is, which do not seem to conform to any specifiable speech-act convention) must nevertheless manifest a dimension of conven-tionality which makes it possible for the author to express an intention and for that intention to be understood. Such a context of social conventions must always be present in addition to more formal linguistic rules, and in cases where there is a lack of any specifiable linguistic convention governing an illocutionary act it is the only means for communicating an intention. "The point is that any intention capable of being correctly understood . . . must always be a socially conventional intention."[136] Even if it is

135. Searle, *Speech Acts*, pp. 50–53, 33–42.
136. Quentin Skinner, "Conventions and the Understanding of Speech Acts," *Philosophical Quarterly*, XX (April, 1970), 133. For further discus-sion of meaning, illocutionary force, and conventions see K. T. Fann, ed., *Symposium on Austin*, pt. IV.

possible in principle to conceive of an intention that is not conventional or rule-conforming, such as cases of "social and linguistic innovation," intelligibility requires that "the act must necessarily, for that reason, take the form of an extension or criticism of some existing attitude or project which is also convention-governed and understood." [137] Although it is sometimes charged that a theory of action tied to the notion of conventional behavior is necessarily deficient as far as accounting for change, this is because there is a tendency to construe conventional behavior as behavior which is accepted or normal. As employed here, the concepts of rule and convention are viewed as encompassing rule-contravention and unconventionality. The determinative contrast in this context is not between what is conventional and unconventional but between what is conventional and nonconventional or between natural facts and conventional facts. The very notion of conformative and conventional behavior presupposes not only violation as well as conformance but criticism and replacement.

In moving from speech acts to action writ large, the same general arguments apply. An analysis of any action will in most cases yield a number of dimensions analogous to those of a speech act, and although in the case of most nonlinguistic actions there may be nothing precisely comparable to, for example, the rules of grammar and syntax, these dimensions will have conventional import. But the determinative dimension for establishing the identity and significance of an action is that which corresponds to illocutionary force, and it is on this dimension that any theory attempting to solve the problem of the relation between action and rules must focus. In seeking to demonstrate the rule-related character of social action, theorists such as Melden and Winch have for the most part tended to confine their discussions either to rather commonplace and simple actions or to actions performed within highly structured social contexts and activities encompassed by a system of formal constitutive rules. Consequently, they may open themselves to the charge that they "do not allow for the variety of relationships in which an agent may stand to a rule to which his behavior conforms." [138] However,

137. Skinner, "Conventions and the Understanding of Speech Acts," p. 135.
138. Alasdair MacIntyre, "The Idea of a Social Science," *Aristotelian Society*, Supplementary Volume XLI (1967), 104.

this does not falsify their general thesis that all action is intelligible only in terms of the purposes of the actor and various dimensions of rules, any more than Austin's and Searle's analyses of illocutionary acts in terms of explicit linguistic performatives and relatively circumscribed discursive language games need obscure the fact that the intelligibility of *any* speech act and its specification depend on an illumination of what the agent means to say or his intention and the conventional meaning of the utterance. Although some actions may conform to systems of explicitly statable or avowable constitutive rules, or rules that not only impose regulations but also are definitive of a practice or activity (or create a form of behavior or activity) in which conformance to the rules is required (the rules of English, chess, football, for example), while others are bounded and governed by restrictive or regulative rules that do not constitute the activity which is regulated (morality, law, etiquette), many actions do not clearly fall under either category. Such actions are intelligible only in terms of some kind of rules and conventions that indicate their illocutionary or intentional force. It would be a formidable task to adequately specify and conceptually differentiate all members belonging to the family of rules, their relations to one another, and their relations to various kinds of action and dimensions of action,[139] but despite the problems created by the conceptual complexities involved in distinguishing between kinds of rules and the empirical questions revolving around the actual relationship of rules to specific actions and forms of actions, a theory of the explanation of action cannot be divorced from the concept of conforming to a rule.

Clearly, there is a problem of how wide a scope should be allotted to the concept of rule and how it is possible to definitively differentiate between kinds of rules, between rules and conventions, and between such things as moral and political principles, maxims, regulations, and customs, as well as between rules and the practices and activities to which they are related. It may seem to strain the idea of a rule to suggest, as Winch does, "that all behavior which is meaningful (therefore all specifically human behavior) is *ipso facto* rule-governed" and that all action

139. See, however, Shwayder, *Stratification of Behavior*, pt. 4. Also Max Black, "The Analysis of Rules," in *Models and Metaphors* (Ithaca, N.Y.: Cornell University Press, 1962).

264 / *Phenomenology and Political Science*

involves the *"application* of a rule."[140] Winch realizes the difficulty with this broad idea of a rule and notes that "we must exercise care in the use we make of the notion of a rule";[141] but rather than making close distinctions between kinds of rules, or even explicitly using "rules" as a generic category, rather than specifying various species of rules and how they relate to one another and to action in general, he tends to simply make rules synonymous with social behavior. But if Winch's equation of rules with the entire corpus of social behavior somehow seems to go beyond the ordinary sense of "rule," making the concept so broad that it becomes devoid of meaning, it nevertheless must be remembered that neither philosophers nor social scientists have succeeded in establishing any wide agreement as to either the ordinary or technical use of the term. It is difficult to see where a line can be drawn between actions that exemplify rules and those that do not. In view of this, it would seem that Winch's general thesis that action cannot be specified, understood, and explained apart from linguistic and nonlinguistic rules and conventions and the context of practices and activities in which they feature is not invalidated by his failure to consider in any systematic manner the way in which distinctions can be made between kinds of rules and the way in which these specific kinds of rules function with regard to various kinds of actions.

At the theoretical level, the relation of rules to action may be expressed by extending Searle's argument regarding speech acts to action in general. That is, there is in principle a series of analytical connections between the notion of an action, what the actor means to do or the purpose of the act, the significance or meaning of the action, what the actor intends or his reason for acting, how the action is understood or explained by others, the rules, conventions, and forms of life informing the action and to which the action conforms (or violates), and the practices and activities constituted and/or regulated by these rules and conventions. But once this is said, there remains, in any particular instance, the empirical problem of substantively specifying these elements and the connections between them, and it must be noted that nonlinguistic actions, like speech acts, always face the existential dangers of "unhappiness" and the "infelicities"

140. Winch, *Idea of a Social Science*, pp. 50, 52 (italics Winch's).
141. *Ibid.*, p. 52.

which may occasionally break down these connections or render them wholly or partially unintelligible. There are also the many problems which surround the relationship between actions and their intended and unintended consequences, results, and effects. Despite the obvious dangers inherent in insufficiently explicated general arguments about the requirements of locating actions in a context of rules, there remains no alternative avenue for identifying and explaining actions. The explanation of actions requires relating them to the conventions and rules of "wider constellations of behavior," paradigms, or forms of life, and "showing the 'significance' of an action provides an 'explanation' of that action in a way strictly analogous to explaining the meaning of a linguistic utterance." [142]

THE PROBLEM OF POLITICAL REALITY

AT THIS POINT it is necessary to return to the specific problem which occasioned this exploration of the character of speech and action, that is, the development of a conception of social reality and a substantive notion of political phenomena. Although the focus of this paper has been on extending a theory of speech acts to the analysis of nonlinguistic action, it is now appropriate to emphasize the extent to which social phenomena are linguistic phenomena and the extent to which many explanations in social science involve the relationship between linguistic and nonlinguistic action. The discussion of speech acts, then, is not merely instrumental. The purpose was not simply to gain a conceptual grasp of nonlinguistic action, for in many instances the data of social science are linguistic. This is true not only with regard to explanations directed toward events belonging to some dimension of the past where the data are principally written records, recorded statements of actors, reports of events, and other primary and secondary linguistic artifacts, but also with regard to those cases, which may well constitute the greater portion of social-scientific research, where data are generated either from oral or written responses to structured questionnaires and interviews or from an analysis of unsolicited linguistic mate-

142. Toulmin, "Concepts and the Explanation of Human Behavior," pp. 85–86.

rial. Thus, in many instances, the principal events to which social scientists address themselves are essentially linguistic events, and, what is more, most explanations of what may be considered basically nonlinguistic phenomena are accessible only through the medium of some form of linguistic evidence. In view of this, it is remarkable that social scientists have paid so little attention to the conceptualization of linguistic action and the criteria of its description and explanation, but this is no more remarkable than the failure to attend to the development of a general theory of action that goes beyond the obsolescent ideas associated with logical positivism and behaviorism.

Although in some sense it is possible to differentiate, both analytically and empirically, between the data of social science in terms of the categories of linguistic and nonlinguistic action, it must be emphasized that the phenomena subsumed by these categories are complementary and interdependent. Social reality presents itself as a realm of symbolically informed and expressed behavior, that is, action, where the meaning and significance of particular phenomena ultimately derive from, and are only intelligible in terms of, a context involving a complex configuration of linguistic and nonlinguistic elements. It should be apparent that speech and nonlinguistic action are not merely conceptually analogous as species of action, but inevitably are also related empirically. If the context of rules, conventions, and activities that ultimately makes a speech act intelligible (the significance-bestowing context) extends beyond what can be defined as linguistic rules and conventions, and if even an entire language game, in Wittgenstein's sense, becomes intelligible only in terms of a wider context or form of life which includes nonlinguistic action, then it becomes important to understand the relationship between linguistic and nonlinguistic action and the rules and conventions that inform them. As Toulmin has noted, not only is the form and content of language in part determined by the wider activities to which it belongs, but also participating in, and learning to participate in, these activities usually presupposes certain linguistic skills and the ability to understand and conform to linguistic rules and conventions. In most cases, "some linguistic grasp is indispensable, even in learning non-linguistic behavior," [143] and it would be difficult to point to any significant

143. *Ibid.*, p. 89.

dimension of action in which a linguistic capacity does not possess an essential place.

In turning to the particular question of political reality or specifying the character of political phenomena, little substantive information can be, or need be, supplied in this context, but this very fact bears considerable significance and flows naturally, even if not obviously, from the preceding arguments—especially those regarding the distinction between first- and second-order studies. Unlike the problem of analyzing the concept of action or specifying the nature of social reality, the identification of political action and the delimitation of politics as a particular activity or realm of speech and action are essentially empirical problems rather than conceptual ones. Although in most instances "the question of what constitutes social behavior is a demand for an elucidation of the *concept* of social behavior" [144] (just as the question of what constitutes language would usually be a demand for an elucidation of the concept of language or linguistic phenomena), the question of what constitutes politics is normally a demand for empirical propositions about the form and content of a certain sphere of social behavior (just as the question of what constitutes scientific language is a demand for a description of a certain concrete realm of language use). The point is not to establish some arbitrary distinction between conceptual (or theoretical) and empirical questions or to invoke closure with regard to the criteria of what constitutes such questions, since what will be taken as a conceptual as opposed to an empirical question is largely a matter of the context in which it is asked and who is asking it. Least of all is the intention to suggest that such distinctions indicate or presuppose the absence of significant relationships between conceptual and empirical questions. Yet it is necessary to emphasize the importance of these distinctions at certain junctures. At a certain logical level one might designate the problem of circumscribing and defining politics as a conceptual issue, but this would be, in effect, to conceive of it as identical with the problem of specifying the character of social reality or human behavior in general, as opposed to, for example, biological or physical phenomena. To pose the problem at this level, either as a philosopher or a social scientist, is to pose it at the level of the epistemology of social science or in terms of

144. Winch, *Idea of a Social Science*, p. 18.

the criteria of adequate social-scientific knowledge. Here, it would be of little significance to distinguish between what is political and what is nonpolitical (or what is political as opposed to, for example, what is religious), any more than it would be significant to distinguish between kinds of speech acts in terms of illocutionary force when a problem arises about what the nature of a speech act is as such, despite the fact that the problem may arise from some substantive empirical context. At the conceptual or theoretical level, the question of what constitutes politics is either a request for an elaboration of the concept of social phenomena in general or it is empty.

Nevertheless, political scientists, as well as social scientists in general, have, almost without exception, insisted on treating substantive and empirical issues, such as those relating to the boundaries and content of politics and other aspects of social life, as conceptual problems to be settled by the imposition of various a priori conceptual schemata, models, taxonomies, and definitions that are presumed to possess some sort of universal applicability. As noted earlier, this procedure, and even the inevitable and admitted element of arbitrariness inherent in it, usually is justified on the basis of the requirements of orderly empirical analysis and an intersubjective language for the practice of social science; the presumed historical and logical progression from rigorous description and classification to nomothetic explanations; and the persistent specter represented by the idea that since all perception ultimately involves presuppositions, paradigms, and conceptual screens of various sorts, it is in the best interests of systematic empirical inquiry to make them explicit. But behind these avowed reasons lies an even more determinative yet subtle, and maybe in some sense unconscious, assumption which, because of its unarticulated character, must be brought to the surface for critical discussion. This is the assumption that politics (as well as other forms of social phenomena), despite historical variations in form and content and differences between contemporary manifestations, possesses a certain quality of givenness. This notion of givenness has two distinct but related aspects.

The first aspect is exemplified in the blinks of incredulity which meet assertions to the effect that politics is not a necessary or even a ubiquitous phenomena, outside of Western culture and those societies significantly touched by it. Surely, it is maintained, "politics, rightly considered, is an inevitable aspect not merely of governmental and institutional life, but of social life in general," [145] and every society must by definition as well as empirical necessity possess political processes and structures. Of course they must, if all that is meant by "politics" is, for example, a range of functionally analogous phenomena such as power relations. There is a failure to distinguish between the two logically different levels on which the term "politics" may be used, which were discussed earlier. Part of the reason for the incredulity and the failure to make these distinctions is that, in both their everyday and disciplinary lives, individuals approach the world in terms of categories derived from their own cultural collective representations. Thus it is assumed that social science concepts such as politics, while operating as an abstract descriptive category for classifying phenomena related by one set of criteria or another, nevertheless designate some universal mode of social relations. But the persistence of this whole syndrome, which is associated with one aspect of the assumption of givenness, is rooted in a second and still more fundamental aspect. The belief that it is possible to extract categories of description and explanation from one context and apply them universally, or simply to delineate a priori the boundaries and units of a political analysis in terms of various conceptual frameworks, entails more than the mere notion that politics is in some sense a universal form of life. The rather simple ethnocentrism and bias apparent and inherent in most of the conceptual frameworks of political science and their failure to describe non-Western societies as well as to capture significant aspects of domestic politics has been notorious and almost monotonously criticized for a number of years, and the same is true of the more esoteric models such as those based on cybernetic systems and other mechanistic theories. The question that presents itself is why these constant criticisms have made such little impact, and part of the answer is that there is operating a more fundamental notion of givenness which goes beyond the mere assumption of some substantive universality of politics.

This second aspect is manifest in the idea that politics as well as social phenomena in general presents itself to the social scien-

145. Frederick M. Watkins, in *A Design for Political Science,* ed. James C. Charlesworth (Philadelphia: American Academy of Political and Social Science, 1966), p. 33.

270 / Phenomenology and Political Science

tist primarily as a realm of observed facts which provide the foundations of empirical knowledge and which can be grasped and illuminated by the conceptual schemes and analytical constructs of social science. The conceptual apparatus of social science, in this view, does not itself constitute or reflect our knowledge of these facts, but rather provides the theoretical instruments, calculational devices, and methods for discerning, organizing, and relating the factual data, and, in general, for attaining knowledge of them. When these conceptual systems and the descriptions and hypotheses formulated in terms of them fail to coincide with this independent order of factual reality and do not yield an adequate guide for finding our way around in this realm, then they are, as with any deficient tool, cast aside in favor of better devices. Such assumptions derive from an attempt to emulate what is believed to be the logic of theory in natural science and the acceptance of the idea that all empirical knowledge rests on an epistemological bedrock of factual propositions couched in an observational language which is independent of any theoretical formulation and which provides a test of such formulations. But apart from the many questions that are begged by this attempt at emulation, including the most obvious and general question as to whether there is symmetry between the logical and the epistemological requirements of natural and social science and between social and physical reality, it demonstrates a failure to come to grips with the fact that these assumptions about natural science have been appropriated from an outmoded theory of empiricism in the philosophy of science rather than from an examination of natural science itself. They reflect the doctrine of theoretical instrumentalism which is based on an ontological distinction between theory and fact and a view of the status of theories and theoretical entities as fictional constructs for ordering and explaining slices of brute reality presented in an observational language. On the contrary, however, there are sound reasons for believing that, in natural science, theories function in such a way that they are basically constitutive of facts and physical reality and that distinctions between theory and fact are more pragmatic than ontological. If the notion of brute facts is operative at all, it is within the area of testing hypotheses, where both the formulation of the hypotheses and the designation of factual criteria occur within a wider and common theoretical context. This is not the place to pursue the implications of this issue, but it is necessary to note that assumptions about the givenness and brute-fact character of social phenomena have tended not only to support the proliferation of conceptual schemes but, more significantly, to preclude social and political science from entering into a consideration of the conceptual problem of the character of social reality and the substantive epistemological criteria of adequate explanation.

Paradoxically, these ideas have also obscured the extent to which social phenomena, unlike natural phenomena, do possess a certain dimension of givenness, but this sense of givenness must be carefully distinguished from the assumptions discussed above. The givenness of social phenomena resides in their character as conventional or institutional facts, that is, facts that are not constituted by the rules of another conventional order. Their identity and the criteria of their existence, unlike the theoretically constituted facts of natural science, are not merely functions of the theories, concepts, and metalanguage of the social scientist, any more than the meanings of words, the rules of games, and the conventions of etiquette are merely functions of the formulations of Noah Webster, Edmond Hoyle, and Amy Vanderbilt, although the latter may have considerable impact on the former. There are two essential characteristics of conventional facts that must be especially recognized and stressed. Such facts are not given either in the sense of being universal or necessary (that is, they could have been different or not at all), or in the sense of having an existence apart from the rules, concepts, and ideas that are constitutive of various forms of social action and modes of social relations. On the other hand, they are given in the sense that they are not constituted by the conceptual scheme of social science, philosophy, or any other second-order activity. In view of this, any attempt to treat the question of the form and content of politics as a conceptual question or a question to be decided within the realm of discourse and meta-activity of social science is as impossible, or misdirected, as the attempt of a philosopher of language to specify, a priori, the constitution of any particular and substantive language game. However, a philosopher of language must face the conceptual problem (within the context of his activity) of the nature of language or speech acts in general, just as the political scientist must face the theoretical problem of elucidating the concept of social reality. The most natural objections to this argument are, first, that it suggests a false dichotomy between conceptual and empirical issues, and, second, that locating the theoretical dimension of social-scientific inquiry in concepts of social reality does not obviate the fact that any approach to the investigation of social phenomena entails other presuppositions about the substantive character of social phenomena which influence the manner in which they are conceived.

In response to the first objection, it must once again be emphasized that distinctions do not entail the absence of significant relationships, that distinctions (such as those between conceptual and empirical problems, the conceptual and empirical aspects of inquiry, or the theoretical construction of social reality and the substantive specification of forms of social life) neither entail the absence of important, and even necessary, relations between them, nor prejudge, in any definitive manner, the character of these relations, any more, for example, than a theory of speech acts employed by the philosopher of language is unrelated to the analysis of substantive speech acts and distinctions between kinds of speech acts. The point is merely that such a theory does not prejudge the empirical issue of the existence and character of particular kinds of speech acts, or, in the case of a theory of social reality, the givenness of politics and the form and content of political action. However, it should be noted that, although such a theory provides the basis for deciding between conflicting empirical descriptions and explanations posed within it, the conceptual or theoretical problem of choosing between an approach to social-scientific inquiry based, for example, on a theory of conventional action as opposed to behaviorism belongs to the theoretical realm and cannot be solved by reference to some theoretically independent realm of given observational "facts."

With regard to the second objection, it may be useful to distinguish between what might be termed "conceptual levels" in social-scientific inquiry. Since social science, like natural science, presupposes a realm of paradigmatic or regulative ontological, epistemological, and logical assumptions and ideals that are pretheoretical, premethodological, and prefactual and which govern the context of investigation, it is tempting to suggest that the specification of substantive social phenomena such as politics cannot be relegated to the realm of empirical questions. Such phenomena, it might be argued, cannot be assumed to be self-constituting and self-identifying, any more than can the elements, and distinctions between elements, in the natural world. Therefore they must be theoretically or conceptually mediated— if not (at least at the present stage in the development of social science) by theories and laws comparable to those of natural science, then by a system of explicit constructs and categories that will replace the tacit, unexamined, and somewhat chaotic presuppositions through which every individual's view of the world is inevitably filtered. What makes this objection difficult to deal with is that its claims are partially valid. The social scientist must necessarily possess a language for description and explanation independent of the activities to which he addresses himself and which constitute his subject matter. Since social science itself constitutes a practice or activity, it is a conventional form of life with its own rules and realm of discourse that are as logically and empirically independent of the various forms of social life which constitute its object as, for example, the philosophy of language is independent of the modes of linguistic use toward which it directs its analysis. The social scientist formulates and defines his problems of research, and in addition to the fact that the specification of these problems will be governed by his epistemological assumptions and by other paradigmatic principles related to his conception of social reality, the particular choice of problems will involve a number of other considerations, including both personal propensities and the conventional constraints of his profession and the community of scholars to which he belongs. Furthermore, he will inevitably bring to his research a number of other assumptions, including models, ideal types, and presuppositions about what he will find that are based on past research experience and various other factors. In other words, there does appear to be a significant level of concepts and assumptions that in some way stand between theoretical questions regarding the character of social reality and empirical propositions regarding substantive social phenomena.

Nevertheless, it must be insisted that the congeries of factors which may influence the orientation toward a subject matter and the distribution of emphasis within research should not be viewed as conceptually constitutive of substantive social phenomena such as politics, in the manner that either the theories of natural science are constitutive of natural phenomena or conceptions of social reality are constitutive of the criteria of what will count as the data of social science. Although political science must possess a language for talking about politics in order to perform the task of describing and explaining political phenomena, the task of political science is not to answer the question "what is politics" at the theoretical or definitional level. The conceptual constitution of politics occurs at the level of political action and presents itself as part of the empirical data of political science. However, there still may remain a lingering doubt about whether the elucidation of the concept of politics and the description and explanation of political action can be distinguished as an empirical problem, since the very acts of description and explanation would seem to be acts of conceptualization performed in terms of the observer's categories. The answer, once again, is that surely in some sense this is correct, but yet as stated the assertion does not allow for what is peculiar about social phenomena. It is true that when the object of empirical investigation consists of conventional facts the categories of description and explanation belong to the language of social science. But it is also true that what is described and explained is an ontologically autonomous and conceptually self-constituted realm, whose existence and mode of existence cannot be presupposed and about which no assertion can be considered empirically incorrigible.

CONCLUSION

IN AN ESSAY OF THIS SORT, it may be more important, and it is certainly easier, to summarize what has not been said than what has been said. Despite the fact that the issue of the distinction between natural and social science is closely linked to most of the arguments that have been presented, the principal focus has not been, in any systematic way, on this distinction, although some points of differentiation have emerged explicitly in the discussion and others follow by implication from the thesis developed here. General arguments on both sides of the controversy over the logical and epistemological symmetry of natural and social science have too often taken place in an abstract and slightly distorted context, where those pressing the demand for symmetry have carved their image of natural science from a highly questionable representation of that enterprise in the literature of the philosophy of science and where the antisymmetrists have failed to produce an adequately concrete vision of social phenomena that would lend substance to their protestations. The goal of this essay has been to take a modest step forward with regard to the latter task. But in addition to recognizing the abbreviated and tentative character of the treatment of linguistic and nonlinguistic action presented above, as well as the absence of adequate conceptual bridges between this treatment and the manifold specific problems arising in the course of substantive social-scientific inquiry, it must also be recognized that this discussion, as it stands, remains severely truncated and has only begun to come to terms with two dimensions of what is essentially a three-dimensional problem.

It was mentioned earlier that both linguistic and nonlinguistic action are normally conceived as "intimately tied to the idea of thought and what it means to acquire, possess, and utilize concepts," and throughout the preceding discussion, the notions of intention and purpose have occupied a central place. However, the problems relating to mental acts or episodes and the connection between thought and action, despite their importance for both the philosophy of social science and empirical social-scientific disciplines, were not directly confronted. Yet a view of the status of mentalistic concepts and mental predicates in the specification, description, and explanation of action must be an essential aspect of any theory of action and a principal concern of the epistemology of social science. More specifically, the philosophical problems of the knowledge of other minds and the place of reasons and causes in explanations of social action must be viewed in relation to the methodology of social science.[146]

146. For a preliminary discussion, see Gunnell, "Social Science and Political Reality: The Problem of Explanation," *Social Research*, XXXV (Spring, 1968), 187–201.

PART VII

Phenomenology
and Economics

The Responsibility of Reason and the Critique of Political Economy

John O'Neill

My INTENTION IN THIS ESSAY is to examine the crisis of Western knowledge, as formulated by Husserl,[1] in the context of political economy, and thus to present the problem as one which affects rational social science knowledge in general. In attempting to show these connections, I hope to point the way to a synthesis of phenomenology and critical theory, which I conceive to be a necessary task in the light of contemporary discussion.[2] My argument will be concerned with economic knowledge as a species of rational knowledge, which must be critically related to its institutional and value assumptions. The analysis will move from the works of Husserl and Heidegger into Marcuse, Weber, Hegel, and Marx. My study of this constellation represents an

1. Husserl speaks of the crisis of European knowledge, but the intentionally broader notion of a crisis in Western knowledge and civilization is endorsed by Aron Gurwitsch in "The Last Work of Edmund Husserl," in his collected *Studies in Phenomenology and Psychology* (Evanston, Ill.: Northwestern University Press, 1966), and it is also supported by Husserl's remarks on "spiritual Europe," in *The Crisis of European Sciences and Transcendental Phenomenology: An Introduction to Phenomenological Philosophy,* trans. David Carr (Evanston, Ill.: Northwestern University Press, 1970), pp. 273–76 (hereafter cited as *Crisis*).
2. Jürgen Habermas, *Knowledge and Human Interests,* trans. Jeremy J. Shapiro (Boston: Beacon Press, 1971); Herbert Marcuse, *Negations: Essays in Critical Theory,* with translations by Jeremy J. Shapiro (Boston: Beacon Press, 1968); *Critical Interruptions: New Left Perspectives on Herbert Marcuse,* ed. Paul Breines (New York: Herder and Herder, 1970); Louis Althusser, *For Marx,* trans. Ben Brewster (New York: Random House, Vintage Books, 1970). For a detailed response to this literature, see John O'Neill, "On Theory and Criticism in Marx," in *Situating Marx: Evaluations and Departures,* ed. Paul A. Walton (London: Chaucer Press, 1972).

[279]

effort to integrate the grounds of rational knowledge and freedom in an "originary" matrix of the human praxis which sustains Western knowledge and its regional sciences of nature and society. In particular, it responds to Husserl's call for a new kind of philosophical method, which I have called "documentary work"; [3] this method has already borne fruit in the historical and social sciences, where it is suited to the hermeneutic problem which arises from the essentially reflexive nature of human knowledge and praxis. Finally, I shall develop the notion of documentary work in connection with Merleau-Ponty's concept of "institution," [4] in order to relate the reflexive features of knowledge to the dialectic of institutional order and individual freedom, which is the ground of critical theory as I understand it.

Husserl's description of the crisis of Western knowledge is clearly not a prophecy of its impending failure. Western knowledge is methodically successful. Indeed, we can so take for granted the expansion of the physical and social sciences that what is at stake is not their phenomenal success, but our residual capacity to raise any questions about their nature. This is the transcendental question which Husserl sees can no longer be raised outside history and still be efficacious, or, as he would say, "responsible." The successes of the physical and social sciences accumulate by means of a method of objectifying, specializing, and technifying, which makes it possible for the practitioners, working in teams, bureaucracies, and planning agencies, to proceed without raising any radical questions about the foundations of their knowledge. It is important to understand that to raise such fundamental questions by no means implies any need to take the house of science apart brick by brick. Nor does it mean the desire to leave it to rot and decay. Such interpretations merit the impatience and anger of scientists of all kinds, who are concerned to get on with the job and able to appeal to a generalized philosophy of the improvement of mankind through science. Perpetual philosophical beginnings are no better than the dark night of primitive man.

---

3. Husserl, *Crisis*, pp. 389–95. This notion is kin to Harold Garfinkel's "documentary method of interpretation," developed in his *Studies in Ethnomethodology* (Englewood Cliffs, N.J.: Prentice-Hall, 1967).

4. John O'Neill, *Perception, Expression and History: The Social Phenomenology of Maurice Merleau-Ponty* (Evanston, Ill.: Northwestern University Press, 1970), pp. 46–64.

In speaking of a crisis of Western knowledge Husserl is quite aware that he is engaged in a paradoxical exercise. The increasing rigor of the sciences appears indeed to leave philosophy itself in a backwater. But Husserl's logic is to raise a question, not about the success of the physical and human sciences, but about their meaning for human existence. In other words, Husserl is questioning the fact-value separation which has been integral to the pursuit of science. This is the same question with which Max Weber struggled in his essays on the respective vocations of science and politics, and, of course, in his historical studies of capitalist and noncapitalist social orders. Moreover, Husserl states explicitly that his question of the meaning of the sciences is a historical question, since scientists themselves have not always made a rule of the irrelevance of social and political values to science, as witness the Renaissance and Enlightenment conceptions of science. "Thus the positivistic concept of science in our time is, historically speaking, a *residual* concept."[5] The dominance of the positivist concept of science is, therefore, the problem of a cultural order whose self-aspiration is something less than the traditional aspiration toward a rational civilization. Rationality is reduced to the microprocesses of scientific and technical rationality, and is unconcerned to raise any questions about its consequences for civilized reason and humanity.

We have also become aware in the most general way . . . that human philosophizing and its results in the whole of man's existence mean anything but merely private or otherwise limited cultural goals. In *our* philosophizing, then—how can we avoid it?—we are *functionaries of mankind*. The quite personal responsibility of our own true being as philosophers, our inner personal vocation, bears within itself at the same time the responsibility for the true being of mankind; the latter is, necessarily, being toward a *telos* and can only come to realization, *if at all*, through philosophy—through *us*, if we are philosophers in all seriousness. Is there, in this existential "if," a way out? If not, what should we, who *believe*, do in order to *be able* to believe? We cannot seriously continue our previous philosophizing; it lets us hope only for philosophies, never for philosophy.[6]

It is easy to misunderstand Husserl's reflections here as another attempt to raise philosophy, if not phenomenology, by its

5. Husserl, *Crisis*, p. 9.
6. *Ibid.*, p. 17.

bootstraps. Such an exercise leads to understandable irritation but will in any case leave all but the philosophical virtuosos behind. However, I do not think this is the underlying method of Husserl's reflections. Rather, I think that Husserl here understands philosophy, in its seriousness *pro nobis*, as a collective enterprise in which social scientists must do their part to reflect on the *telos* of civilized humanity. Given this, moreover, I think *we* can find a tradition of reflection on social science knowledge which is complementary to Husserl's intentional history of the scientific method, if we take as our topic rationality in its socioeconomic and political contexts. Like Hegel, we shall then be able to avoid a metaphysical alienation of reason by preserving "the labor of the notion" of rationality within the dialectic of historically specific social structures.[7]

THE CONCEPT OF MODERN KNOWLEDGE AND THE UTOPIAN METHOD OF MARXIST ECONOMICS

AN ESSENTIAL FEATURE of modern knowledge is its *infinitude.* It has been the central theme of Goethe's *Faust,* Hegel's *Phenomenology of Mind,* Marx's *Capital,* as well as the motive of the reflections of Husserl and Weber. "But with the appearance of Greek philosophy," remarks Husserl,

> and its first formulation, through consistent idealization, of the new sense of infinity, there is accomplished in this respect a thoroughgoing transformation which finally draws all finite ideas and with them all spiritual culture and its [concept of] mankind into its sphere. Hence there are, for us Europeans, many infinite ideas (if we may use this expression) which lie outside the philo-

7. Here I would like to draw attention to a series of studies by Benjamin Nelson on the fusion of the "rationales of conscience" underlying the Protestant Reformation and the scientific and philosophical revolutions of the sixteenth and seventeenth centuries. Professor Nelson's patient studies, together with the literature cited in them, are absolutely essential to the full understanding of the complex history that forms the background to the question of the meaning (*Selbstbesinnung*) of social science rationality. See Benjamin Nelson, "Scholastic Rationales of 'Conscience,' Early Modern Crises of Credibility, and the Scientific-Technocultural Revolutions of the 17th and 20th Centuries," *Journal for the Scientific Study of Religion,* VII (Fall, 1968), 157–77.

sophical-scientific sphere (infinite tasks, goals, confirmations, truths, "true values," "genuine goods," "absolutely" valid norms), but they owe their analogous character of infinity to the transformation of mankind through philosophy and its idealities. Scientific culture under the guidance of ideas of infinity means, then, a revolutionization [*Revolutionierung*] of the whole culture, a revolutionization of the whole manner in which mankind creates culture. It also means a revolutionization of [its] historicity, which is now the history of the cutting-off of finite mankind's development [*Geschichte des Entwerdens des endlichen Menschentums*] as it becomes mankind with infinite tasks.[8]

The infinitude of modern knowledge constitutes a problem for social science knowledge, which I shall focus as the Hobbesian problem of order. First, however, I shall follow Husserl in presenting a schematic outline of the shift between the ancient and modern conceptions of knowledge and the essence of being, with attention to the consequences for human praxis.

The post-Renaissance scientific approach to nature and its laws of motion no longer ascribes permanence through change to the work of the Platonic demiurge. The rationality of form in motion no longer requires that nature be pervaded by intelligence or a hierarchy of being. In part, this is the legacy of the Judaeo-Christian conception of a mindless nature, subject only to the rationality of God and the human being made in his image, the latter for that reason being in but not of the world. Transcendental monotheism abolished the "souls" or spirits of nature, paving the way for the strictly quantitative dynamics of nature unleashed in the seventeenth century. The Cartesian dualism of *res cogitans* and *res extensa* reduces a cosmological principle to a methodological subjectivity which is the source of the alternatives of materialism and idealism that have struggled for philosophical and scientific dominance to this day. However, the price which the Cartesian ego pays for certainty is to remain an enigma to itself, without intelligible principle, since all life-forms fall outside the study of inertial motion, unless reduced to the behaviorist study of the animal and human "machine."

The notions of "mathematics," "creation," and "universe" belong together, but, as Hans Jonas has observed, they do not refer to the same constellation of meaning and purpose in Greek

8. Husserl, *Crisis*, p. 279.

philosophy and in modern physics.[9] "Thus it is wonderfully made
known to us how in the very origination of things a certain Divine
mathematics or metaphysical mechanics is employed and the
determination of the greatest quantity takes place."[10] What
appears to be a return in the seventeenth century to the Py-
thagorean-Platonic tradition of mathematics is in fact a radical
change in the conceptions of mathematics and ontology, as a
result of the idealization of knowledge as an algebraic calculus of
functions or processes. The ancient hierarchy of forms is replaced
by an inverted order of complex and simple functions. The
idealization of knowledge proceeds, therefore, in terms of an
ontological reduction of nature to its simplest and least rational
(in terms of classical ontology) parts.

> It was the paramount interest in *motion*, as against the satisfac-
> tion with pattern, which prompted the ascendance of algebraic
> method in physics: motion instead of fixed spatial proportions
> became the main object of measurement. This marks a radically
> novel attitude. In the early stages of modern science, analysis of
> becoming supplants contemplation of being. The role of "*t*" in
> physical formulae indicates the new attitude. The "forms" here
> envisaged are no longer those of the terminal products, but those
> of the continuous processes of nature. Process, as such, is defined
> solely by its own form, the law of the series, and in no way by its
> end (of which there is none) or any temporary formations en
> route. Greek geometry had considered the relations of unchanging
> figures and bodies—intuitive ultimates: the abstract algebra of
> analytical geometry and of the infinitesimal calculus made it
> possible to represent the geometrical form itself as a function of
> variables, that is, as a phase in their continuous growth, and so
> to formulate the laws of its "generation." These generative, de-
> termining laws became the true objects of mathematical cognition,
> instead of the descriptive, determinate forms, which had lost
> their independent status for that of transitional limits.[11]

Marcuse has commented on the contrast between the results
of the ancient and medieval approaches to the "essence" of being

9. Hans Jonas, "Is God a Mathematician? The Meaning of Metabolism," in his *The Phenomenon of Life: Toward a Philosophical Biology*
(New York: Dell, 1968).
10. Gottfried Wilhelm von Leibniz, "On the Ultimate Origin of Things"
(1697), in *The Monadology and Other Philosophical Writings*, trans.
Robert Latta (Oxford: Clarendon Press, 1898), p. 342.
11. Hans Jonas, *Phenomenon of Life*, pp. 67–68.

and the consequences of the modern reduction of being to the object of authentic and certain knowledge.[12] The medieval and Platonic conceptions of essence, of the unity and universality of being, were not purely epistemological, but included critical and ethical elements. The premodern conceptions of being were concerned with the tension between essence and existence, in which *eidos* was a dynamic constituent of things moving toward their "true being" and "good," and subject to the moral critique of their unrealized potential, or bad facticity. In modern philosophy, the problem of essence is reduced to a problem of logic and epistemology. The authentic potentiality of being is now the exercise of subjective thought seeking absolutely certain knowledge in a nature subject to mathematical calculation and the domination of applied science. Henceforth the method of philosophy is the transcendental organization of experience and nature in the "concept of the unconditioned." The transcendental reduction in its various stages from Descartes and Kant to Husserl represents, in Marcuse's judgment, a progressive abandonment of the critical task of philosophy.[13] In this respect phenomenology and positivism, however differently they view themselves and one another, are surpassed by materialist theory, which restores the real dynamics of essence and appearance, thus continuing the legacy of Hegel.

In the materialist dialectic the tension between essence and appearance becomes a historical theory of the development of man through specific forms of social and economic organization. The Hegelian-Marxist conception of essence does not refer to an immutable ontological difference, but to a historical relationship between men, which is the motive for knowledge and for the transformation of praxis. The mode of materialist knowledge is to relate particulars to wholes, which are masked in inessential relations that determine immediate practice, but which can be seen historically to be disproportions (*Missverhaltnis*) of the true development of man.

In truth, an *a priori* element is at work here, but one confirming the historicity of the concept of essence. It leads back into history

12. Herbert Marcuse, "The Concept of Essence," in his *Negations*, pp. 43–87.
13. Marcuse's judgment here would seem to overlook the *Crisis*, where, as I shall show, Husserl is concerned precisely with the historical responsibility of phenomenological philosophy as a communal aspiration.

rather than out of it. The immemorially acquired image of essence was formed in mankind's historical experience, which is preserved in the present form of reality, so that it can be "remembered" and "refined" to the status of essence. All historical struggles for a better organization of the impoverished conditions of existence, as well as all of suffering mankind's religious and ethical ideal conceptions of a more just order of things, are preserved in the dialectical concept of the essence of man, where they have become elements of the historical practice linked to dialectical theory.[14]

It is important to understand the materialist theory of essence if we are to have any adequate grasp of Marx's economic analysis. For Marx did more than flirt with the Hegelian method in *Capital*. The determination of man's essence has traditionally governed idealist philosophy through historical contingencies external to its own formal interests. However, once reality is conceived as the totality of the relations of production—material, social, political, and ideological—then the interests of domination and recognition provide a structural organization in which form and content, essence and appearance, are separate only within particular historical patterns of community and class interests. The result of this materialist conception is that its theory functions at two levels: at one level concepts deal with the relations between reified phenomena, and, at another, they deal with the real or essential relations between reified phenomena whose subjective constitution has been revealed as a historically specific praxis. Marxian economics therefore employs a first set of concepts, such as profits, wages, entrepreneur, and labor, in order to present the real but "phenomenal" forms of the processes of production and reproduction. At the next level, the processes of production and reproduction are regarded as an antagonistic unity aimed at the realization of capital, which then requires concepts such as surplus value to bring out the essential relations of class exploitation and to reveal the true content of the formal analytic categories employed at the first level.

The two levels of analysis, however, are dialectically related through the intentional structure of the first level, which is to "produce" man. The historical alienation of this first-level intentional structure can only be grasped through a second-level

14. Marcuse, *Negations*, p. 75.

analysis in which the materialist dialectic furnishes a critical theory of economic reification.

> The dialectical concepts transcend the given social reality in the direction of another historical structure which is present as a tendency in the given reality. The positive concept of essence, culminating in the concept of the essence of man, which sustains all critical and polemical distinctions between essence and appearance as their guiding principle and model, is rooted in this potential structure. In terms of the positive concept of essence, all categories that describe the given form of existence as historically mutable become "ironic": they contain their own negation. In economic theory this irony finds its expression in the relationship of the two sets of concepts. If, for instance, it is said that concepts such as wages, the value of labor, and entrepreneurial profit are only categories of manifestations behind which are hidden the "essential relations" of the second set of concepts, it is also true that these essential relations represent the truth of the manifestations only insofar as the concepts which comprehend them already contain—their own negation and transcendence— the image of a social organization without surplus value. All materialist concepts contain an accusation and an imperative.[15]

What Marcuse adds to our understanding of the concept of essence and the subjectivity of modern knowledge is the Hegelian unity of reason and freedom which is demanded by the concept of the essence of man. This concept is therefore as much an ethical as a rational one; it is critical as well as descriptive, and in this respect its historical and political dimensions are effectively utopian. This utopian conception of the essence of man is opposed to the idealization of freedom and reason outside the real world in which the palace of ideas sits next to the hovels of the poor and hungry. Nor is it a simple materialism, although it rests on economic foundations insofar as these are transcendentally oriented to the "production" of a human world. It rests on science and technology; but its utopian nature asks questions about science that are beyond the pale of idealist and positivist reason. Its concern with the future *as human future* lies beyond the predictive controls of science in general, and, needless to say, of economics in particular.

I have appealed to Marcuse's critical analysis of the concept

15. *Ibid.*, p. 86.

of essence because what I have called its *utopian* feature emphasizes an element in the teleology of reason which otherwise appears to be purely cognitive. By stressing the utopian nature of knowledge and rationality, we may be reminded that the crisis of reason is not just a matter of philosophical ennui or failure of nerve. It is a crisis in the utopia of social-scientific knowledge, which is the form philosophical reason assumes in order to mediate human praxis. Moreover, it is through its utopian dimensions that the concept of the essence of man can be adequate to its intentional universality and to the present need to hold in theory what in the future will be an everyday reality.[16]

RATIONALITY, ORDER, AND THE CRITIQUE OF POLITICAL ECONOMY [17]

THE CHANGE IN THE ENDS OF KNOWLEDGE between the ancient and modern world, that is, the shift from speculative to practical knowledge, pushes theory toward practice and away from contemplative wisdom. Modern knowledge is knowledge of "works," through the knowledge of the laws of nature's motion. Such knowledge is intrinsically tied to technology. Its values are utilitarian, aimed at the reduction of human misery, if not the production of happiness. Aristotelian knowledge produced happiness in the soul of its possessor by reason of the nobility of the objects of its contemplation; it lifted the individual soul into the cosmic order. The uses of Aristotelian knowledge are intrinsic to

16. "In the history of revolution, deep faith in man and deep faith in the world have long gone hand in hand, unmoved by mechanistics and opposition to purpose. But militant optimism, as the subjective side of real progress, also implies searching for the where-to and what-for on the objective side—of forwardmoving being without which there is no progressive consciousness. And the *humanum* is so *inclusive* in the *real possibility* of the *content of its goal, that it allows all movements and forms of human culture location in the togetherness of different epochs. The humanum is so strong that it does not collapse in face of a wholly mechanistically conceived cyclic time*" (Ernst Bloch, *A Philosophy of the Future*, trans. John Cumming [New York: Herder and Herder, 1970], p. 140; italics Bloch's).

17. In this section I have drawn on my argument in "The Hobbesian Problem in Marx and Parsons," in *Explorations in General Theory in the Social Sciences*, ed. Jan Loubser, et al. (New York: Free Press, forthcoming).

its possession and its effects upon the soul. But the pursuit of wisdom leaves unsolved the problem of freedom as freedom from necessity; indeed, it presupposes the slavery of the household economy and the idiocy of its inhabitants, who are excluded from the *polis* and thus from philosophical and political life.[18] Baconian knowledge puts nature to the sovereign use of man, but without any other wisdom than the necessity of man's mastery of nature, which is otherwise the source of his miseries. The calling of modern science entails unremitting toil on the part of the scientist to relieve the misery of his fellow men. In short, far from presupposing leisure, modern knowledge becomes essentially a work which is, moreover, never finished and which never produces harmony in the soul of the scientist, except as a wager on progress and posterity.

We need to understand how the metaphysics of modern knowledge shapes and is in turn shaped by the modern world, its economy, its political and moral structures of the self, and its institutional orders. There are various ways of presenting the constellation of knowledge, technique, and social order which constitutes the dynamics of the modern world. Our effort must be to tie together the transcendental understanding of knowledge with the life-worlds of economics and politics—to grasp the meaning of the accumulation of knowledge, values, and power.

The problem of knowledge and values involved in the methodological success of modern rationality is sometimes expressed as the problem of value-free knowledge. The Platonic philosopher's return to the cave is a necessity because of the cosmological ties between the orders of knowledge, the soul, and the world. The philosopher's knowledge is intrinsically responsible: it requires no felicific calculus to justify its action on society. Moreover, as wisdom, it works on souls and not on an empty nature. The dualism of man and nature is, however, essential to the practice of modern knowledge. The result of this dualism is the conquest of nature, which as a praxis treats its own transcendental presuppositions as an enigma. Utilitarianism is both a metaphysics and a method for the resolution of the implications for the moral and political orders of the dominance of technical rationality. What is usually referred to as the Hobbesian problem of order derives from the reduction of substantive ra-

18. Aristotle, *Politics* 1252 a. 2.

tionality to a deterministic theory of the conditions of rational conduct based on the model of mechanical physics. It is assumed that the ends of action are random, and that under these conditions rationality consists in the most efficient pursuit of whatever ends man proposes to himself. Hobbes's so-called "state of nature" is indeed a historical fiction, in the sense that it reveals the sociological preconceptions of modern civil society.[19] In Hobbes's view, the basic problem of rational egoism is to command the services and recognition of other men, so equal in nature and "equality of hope" that there is nothing to restrain them from fraud and violence in the pursuit of their own ends.

The fiction of a social contract fails to solve the question raised by Hobbes, since, as Marx later pointed out, the costs of keeping promises can be shifted onto a class which lacks the freedom to contract, and thus Hobbes's "state of war" becomes "class war." The problem of order is, therefore, ultimately a problem of power, which could not be solved within the liberal utilitarian tradition. But theoretical difficulties are often patched in practice, and in this case Locke's postulate of the natural identity of interests matched the early experience of liberal individualism better perhaps than Hobbes's more consistent fears. Thus the problem of order came to rest in the doctrine of the natural identity of interests, until Marx demonstrated that the capitalist system of social exchange and division of labor produces a class which recognizes itself only in the conditions of its own dehumanization.

The Hobbesian problem must be considered in the context of the challenge to modern knowledge raised by the collapse of the feudal community. The loss of a natural basis for community raised the question of whether it was possible to construct a community out of the principles of individualism and rational egoism. It had always appeared, from the medieval standpoint, that only chaos could result from slipping the divine anchor and allowing the passions free play. This was the fearful prospect of Renaissance and Reformation freedom, especially once it had found in the market an infinite field for the expansion of desire and the accumulation of power. At the same time, this sudden and terrible expansion of moral and political freedom was being

19. C. B. Macpherson, *The Political Theory of Possessive Individualism: Hobbes to Locke* (Oxford: Clarendon Press, 1962).

transformed into an orderly system of economic exchanges which in turn rested on the growth of mathematical and physical knowledge and its applications to technology and commerce. But there is a subtle yet profound change between the ancient and medieval conceptions of order and the Hobbesian conception. It is a change which stems from the shifts in the definitions of truth and knowledge which occur between ancient, medieval, and modern philosophy.[20]

Modern rationality and its institutional organization rests on the axiom of man's domination of nature, which radicalizes the subject-object split and propels knowledge toward quantification and the creation of a moral and political arithmetic. Socrates, it will be remembered, turned away from the study of physical nature in favor of the study of human nature. In this manner Socrates raised the question of the unity of human knowledge as a praxis whose values are revealed in the effects on the soul of the kinds of knowledge pursued in a given social order. With the Renaissance discovery of the experimental method, the dramatic affinity of Western knowledge for power was revealed, unfettered by the moral universals of the ancient and medieval world. Yet to Erasmus the Baconian equation of knowledge and power appeared to be a pagan reversal rather than the intensification of the inherent logic and axiology of Western knowledge. "Never forget," he remarked, "that 'dominion,' 'imperial authority,' 'kingdom,' 'majesty,' 'power,' are all pagan terms, not Christian. The ruling power of a Christian state consists only of administration, kindness and protection." [21] Erasmus' comment is a reflection of the crisis of community fought out in the political and religious controversies of the late sixteenth and early seventeenth centuries. In the face of the collapse of church unity and the rise of individual conscience, the normative grounds of community could no longer be presumed upon; and yet it became clear that any particular covenant or contract was nothing more than, in Milton's words, "the forced and outward union of cold, and neutral, and inwardly divided minds." Hobbes's concept of philosophy as the pursuit of clear and precise discourse on the

20. Michael Oakeshott, Introduction to *Leviathan*, by Thomas Hobbes (Oxford: Blackwell, 1946).
21. Quoted by Erich Hula in his Comment on Hans Jonas, "The Practical Uses of Theory," in *Philosophy of the Social Sciences: A Reader*, ed. Maurice Natanson (New York: Random House, 1963), p. 151.

model of geometry dictates his aim of bringing peace and order into civil life by a set of political definitions founded on sovereign authority which would put an end to the anarchy of values and opinions.

> For I doubt not, but if it had been a thing contrary to any man's right of dominion, or to the interest of men that have dominion, *that the three angles of a triangle, should be equal to two angles of a square;* that doctrine should have been, if not disputed, yet by the burning of all books of geometry, suppressed, as far as he whom it concerned was able.[22]

Henceforth, rationality is never a substantive concept based on the "nature of things"; the task of reason is confined to providing conclusions "about the names of things." The standard of rationality furnished by Hobbes's science of politics is totally divorced from the traditional sentiments and usages of reason.

> This dilemma faced by Hobbes was partly owing to a failure to realize what other apostles of "scientific" politics have not yet seen, that one of the basic reasons for the unsurpassed progress of science was that scientific discourse, unlike political discourse, had rejected not only the common vocabulary of everyday life, but also the modes of thought familiar to the common understanding.[23]

In the end Hobbes failed to solve the problem of order in any but an external fashion. Hobbes's citizens live in a common, mutual fear which corrodes their private lives and leaves society dependent on the sovereign whose power can never be anything but the exercise of fiat because the civil order lacks any sense of community or constituency.

The Hobbesian problem prefigures the crisis of reason of which Husserl spoke and illuminates his rejection of Enlightenment rationalism. However, in order to appreciate the weight of Husserl's arguments for social science rationality, we need to be aware of the Hegelian and Marxist critique of the utilitarian and Enlightenment conceptions of reason and social order. Hegel and Marx made it explicit that the metaphysics of reason determine the methodology of the social sciences, and thus the preconceptions of utilitarian economics and politics.

22. Hobbes, *Leviathan,* p. 68 (italics Hobbes's).
23. Sheldon S. Wolin, *Politics and Vision: Continuity and Innovation in Western Political Thought* (Boston: Little, Brown, 1960), p. 261.

Hegel regarded history as a process which unfolds through living ideologies, such as the Enlightenment, utilitarianism, and the Absolute Liberty of the French Revolution. Each of these ideologies is related to a definite cultural and social reality, through which the nature of human rationality and freedom is progressively revealed. Once the Enlightenment had won its struggle with religious superstition, the question arose as to the nature of the philosophical truth which the Enlightenment was to set in its place. The truth of the Enlightenment is utilitarianism, which judges everything by its usefulness to man; but utilitarianism is unable to solve the dilemma of man's utility to other men, which raises the problem of exploitation, insoluble within the utilitarian tradition.

As everything is useful for man, man is likewise useful too, and his characteristic function consists in making himself a member of the human herd, of use for the common good, and serviceable to all. The extent to which he looks after his own interests is the measure with which he must also serve the purposes of others, and so far as he serves their turn, he is taking care of himself: the one hand washes the other. But wherever he finds himself there he is in his right place; he makes use of others and is himself made use of.[24]

Marx seizes upon this dilemma in utilitarianism in a passage characteristic of his own development of Hegelian insights:

Hegel has already proved in his *Phänomenologie* how this theory of mutual exploitation, which Bentham expounded *ad nauseam*, could already at the beginning of the present century have been considered a phase of the previous one. Look at his chapter on "The Struggle of Enlightenment with Superstition," where the theory of usefulness is depicted as the final result of enlightenment. The apparent stupidity of merging all the manifold relationships of people in the *one* relation of usefulness, this apparently metaphysical abstraction arises from the fact that, in modern bourgeois society, all relations are subordinated in practice to the one abstract monetary-commercial relation. This theory came to the fore with Hobbes and Locke, at the same time as the

24. G. W. F. Hegel, *The Phenomenology of Mind*, trans. with an Introduction and notes by Sir James Baillie (London: Allen and Unwin, 1910), pp. 579–80.

first and second revolutions, those first battles by which the bourgeoisie won political power.[25]

Once the physiocrats had demonstrated the nature of the economic process as a circular flow, all that remained to complete classical political economy was to give an account of individual attitudes and motivations within that economic framework. This was Bentham's contribution, although, as Marx observes, the theory of utility could not have the generality it claimed because it ignored its own institutional assumptions. For a time, the utilitarian theory of the natural identity of interests had some empirical basis in the facts of the social division of labor and exchange. It was not until Marx adapted Locke's labor theory of value to demonstrate that it contained the working principles for the exploitation of formally free labor that the sociological framework of classical economics was shattered. For utility is subject to appropriation in the form of capital, which is then able to command the services of others to their disadvantage, whatever the circumstances of a formally free contract. Hence the attempt to base the social and political order on the postulate of the natural identity of interests fails once and for all.

Between them, Hegel and Marx developed a thorough critique of the social and political foundations of utilitarian economics. Classical liberalism depended on the protection of a sphere in which the values of personal integrity, property, and contract could be realized as the expression of market society. But, as Hegel showed in the *Philosophy of Right,* in a society conceived solely as a field for market behavior, economics cannot provide the only framework for law, if personality, property, and contract are to be preserved as anything more than instruments of civil society. The political principles of liberal utilitarianism can only be preserved by a system of state laws based on Reason, which differentiates them from the laws of the market.[26] In other words, Hegel argues that the utilitarian conception of economic society based on economic laws grounds civil society (*bürgerliche Gesellschaft*) in positive but not substantively rational law. The laws of economic society and civil society are in turn distinct

25. Karl Marx and Friedrich Engels, *The German Ideology,* trans. Ryazanskaya (Moscow: Progress Publishers, 1964), pp. 448–49.
26. G. W. F. Hegel, *Philosophy of Right,* trans. with notes by T. M. Knox (Oxford: Clarendon Press, 1942), pt. 3, subsec. 2, "Civil Society," pp. 122–55.

from the state, which is the highest stage of the realization of Reason and the ethical will.

Marx's critique of the liberal bourgeois concept of the state, society, and individual rights is substantially the same as Hegel's. The difference is that Marx's argument also contains a destructive critique of Hegel's own concept of the state and its bureaucratic rationality. Marx's critique in many ways anticipates Max Weber.[27]

> If power is taken as the basis of right, as Hobbes, etc. do, then right, law, etc. are merely the symptom, the expression of *other* relations upon which State power rests. The material life of individuals which by no means depends merely on their "will," their mode of production and form of intercourse, which mutually determine each other—this is the real basis of the State and remains so at all stages at which division of labor and private property are still necessary, quite independently of the *will* of individuals. These actual relations are in no way created by the State power; on the contrary they are the power creating it. The individuals who rule in these conditions, besides having to constitute their power in the form of the *State,* have to give their will, which is determined by these definite conditions, a universal expression as the will of the State, as law—an expression whose content is always determined by the relations of this class, as the civil and criminal law demonstrates in the clearest way.[28]

The utilitarian conception of society, i.e., of civil society, is characterized by the separation of state and society which reduces the enforcement of law to the preservation of property and those personal rights necessary for its acquisition and alienation.[29] Thus the utilitarian conception of society enforces a radical dualism between private and public man which is the basis for all other forms of individual and social alienation.

THE SUBJECTIVE MEANING OF THE ECONOMIC WORLD

THE OBJECTIVE AND METHODOLOGICAL NATURE of modern knowledge is an essentially subjective praxis, with specific

27. Henri Lefebvre, *The Sociology of Marx,* trans. Norbert Guterman (New York: Random House, Pantheon Books, 1968), chap. 5, "Political Sociology: Theory of the State," pp. 123–85.
28. Marx, *German Ideology,* p. 357.
29. Mitchell Franklin, "On Hegel's Theory of Alienation and Its Historic Force," *Tulane Studies in Philosophy,* IX (1960), 50–100.

historical and institutional bases. This is especially true of knowledge in the social sciences; I shall return to this point as part of the discussion of the views of Marx and Weber on the process of rationalization. I shall first, however, deal with the question of the subjective grounds of the modern economic world as developed in Hannah Arendt's argument concerning the hybridization of the realms of politics and economics, and then turn to the discussion of these phenomena in Marx and Weber.[30]

In the Graeco-Roman world the boundary between the public and private realms was clear, and men were conscious of the threshold that separated the two. Although the ancient city-state grew at the expense of the family household and kinship group, the boundary between these realms was never erased. Indeed, the definition of the public realm as an area of freedom and equality presupposed the recognition of "necessity" in the household economy. The needs of maintenance and reproduction defined the social nature of man and the family and the sexual and social division of labor between man and woman, master and slave. In the modern period this ancient boundary between public and private realms was dissolved with the emergence of "society" and the liberal concept of mini-government. A whole new world —the social universe—emerged, confounding public and private life.

The public aspect of the social universe has its roots in the subjectivization of private property and the limitation of government to the minimal agenda of social equilibration of individual and public interests. Seventeenth-century politics originated the narrow limits of "government" in order to exploit the boundless domain of possessive individualism, which C. B. Macpherson has described as the central impediment of modern liberal-democratic ideology.

> Its possessive quality is found in its conception of the individual as essentially the proprietor of his own person or capacities, owing nothing to society for them. The individual was seen neither as a moral whole, nor as a part of a larger social whole, but as an owner of himself. The relation of ownership, having become for

30. I shall not give any detailed refutation of Arendt's interpretation of Marx's conceptions of labor and the human world, since she mistakes Marx's analysis of these concepts under capitalist conditions for his own views. See W. A. Suchting, "Marx and Hannah Arendt's *The Human Condition*," *Ethics*, LXIII (October, 1962), 47 55.

more and more men the critically important relation determining their actual freedom and actual prospect of realizing full potentialities, was read back into the nature of the individual. . . . Society becomes a lot of free individuals related to each other as proprietors of their own capacities and of what they have acquired by their exercise. Society consists of relations of exchange between proprietors. Political society becomes a calculated device for the protection of this property and for the maintenance of an orderly relation of exchange.[31]

Liberal practicality shied away from any utopian conception of the public domain and was content with an order that seemed to emerge through nonintervention in the natural processes, or rather the metabolism, of society. As Hannah Arendt argues, the extraordinary identification of the notions of society and economy may be traced in part to the liberal devaluation of politics.

What concerns us in this context is the extraordinary difficulty with which we, because of this development, understand the decisive division between the public and private realms, between the sphere of the polis and the sphere of household and family, and finally, between activities related to a common world and those related to the maintenance of life, a division upon which all ancient political thought rested as self-evident and axiomatic.[32]

The separation of public and private experience which characterizes modern society derives from the essential nature of its processes of work and intellectual activity. Ancient knowledge possessed intrinsic ties to action and purpose, that is, to human initiative and the realm of politics and history. By contrast, modern knowledge is without such limits; it consists only of the self-infinitizing labor of the man of culture, as well as of the man of property. But we cannot speak of knowledge outside the context of human action and purpose, or apart from human initiative and the bonds of promise and forgiveness. The accumulation of modern knowledge, the self-infinitizing labor of the man of

31. C. B. Macpherson, *Political Theory of Possessive Individualism,* p. 3. The liberal concept of "society" provoked the counterconcept of "organic society" in conservative and Marxian thought, which have more in common with each other than either has with liberalism. See Karl Mannheim, *Essays on Sociology and Social Psychology* (New York: Oxford University Press, 1953), chap. 2, "Conservative Thought."

32. Hannah Arendt, *The Human Condition* (Chicago: University of Chicago Press, 1958), p. 28.

culture and the man of property, is the labor of modern self and its alienation from the world. As Kafka put it, modern man "found the Archimedean point, but he used it against himself; it seems that he was permitted to find it only under this condition." The modern age is built upon the paradox that its expansion of technological, economic, and social activity has produced a massive alienation and domination of the world, coupled with universal migration, which are motivated by what Weber called "innerworldly asceticism." The release of these forces was preceded, as we have shown, by the collapse of the ancient and feudal conceptions of the world as a political realm of public deeds and public speech resting on the citizen's or the lord's control of his own household and its private economy. So long as the household economy was embedded in the political order, labor served to produce objects whose value was subordinate to the social values created by the thoughts, deeds, and speech of political man. The modern world, however, is built on an inordinate expansion of individual utilities, which subordinates labor and production to a cycle of consumption and destruction divorced from the political order. This is the source of the modern conception of "society" as solely a field of individual interests, which inspired Hobbes's nasty vision, and whose essentially contradictory features were later analyzed, as we have seen, by Hegel and Marx.

The question which underlies the "crisis" of the social sciences is the question of the meaningfulness of the subjectivization of the bases of need and utility, once these are broken off from their political matrix. It is this issue which focuses the sociological tradition through Marx, Durkheim, and Weber. The relevance of these classical theorists for our problem is that they were concerned with the historical process whereby legal and economic rationality undermines the traditional, sentimental bonds of association in favor of market freedoms or property rights. Both Marx and Durkheim elaborated critiques of the utilitarian theory of conduct in order to raise the transcendental question of the meaningfulness of individual behavior in different orders of society. In other words, they raised the question of the substantive basis of the legitimacy of social and political orders *as a problem of economic knowledge.*

Classical utilitarian thought from the time of Hobbes through Locke, Marx, and Durkheim, must be understood in the light of the constitutional, class, and industrial crises in which the doctrine of the natural identity of interests, however logically objectionable, provided a metaphysical prop for the drama of modern individualism and market rationality. As the framework of market society, class, and property gradually evolved, the shift from the sentimental ties of kinship to the rational social division of labor can be seen as the articulation of modern self-consciousness. The problem of order is historical as well as sociological. It is the problem of the origins and teleology of civilization, and was seen in this light by Marx, Durkheim, Weber, and, of course, Freud. Another aspect of the same question comes into modern consciousness through Nietzsche, Dilthey, Burckhardt, and Husserl;[33] for them, the problem of order is the riddle of history, that is, the problem of man's estrangement through civilization, the need to set restraints on the infinitude of wants. Durkheim attempted to draw a distinction between individuality and personality in order to cope with the ways in which society at once provokes and ennobles individual aspirations. Moreover, Durkheim was aware that these problems were wider than the limits of law and the bonds of solidarity. He sensed their origins in the ambivalence of modern knowledge, including sociology, despite his hopes for the latter as a social remedy.[34] Marx argued that the forces which divide man against himself derive from the division of property on the basis of class, which is prior to the problems of specialization and division of labor. But the deeper question is, what is the meaning of the "surplus repression" (Marcuse), or the value set on value accumulation, which provides the driving force, the glory, and the misery of modern civilization?

The understanding of Western rationality demands a structural analysis as well as a phenomenological description of the dialectic of man's fundamental historical and social nature and its alternations between freedom and determinism. It is necessary to start from the institutional matrix in which specific norms of action shaped, and were in turn shaped by, a particular conception of human nature. With the rise of capitalism, man's rational

33. Reinhard Bendix, "Max Weber and Jacob Burckhardt," *American Sociological Review*, XXX (April, 1965), 176–84.
34. Reinhard Bendix, "The Age of Ideology: Persistent and Changing," *Ideology and Discontent*, ed. David E. Apter (New York: Free Press, 1966), chap. 8, pp. 294–327.

nature was increasingly understood in terms of an instrumental orientation toward the domination of physical nature. At the same time, this orientation toward nature involved an expressive as well as cognitive reorientation of perception of self, society, and the elements of nature. The essence of this shift was grasped by Hegel and Marx in their conception of human freedom as "man making himself." Between Hegel's *Phenomenology of Mind* and Marx's *Communist Manifesto* the "world" has become the immanent term of human thought and activity which sustains the alternation of freedom and determinism. The significance of Marx's critique of the relationship between ideologies and philosophical thought is that it brings human ideas into a permanently efficacious present, shaped by and giving shape to the processes through which a society endures and changes. Thus the weight of the past, articulated in the social division of labor and the ideological superstructure of past religions and philosophies, is not just the residue of historicism or relativism. It is the phenomenological reality of truth as the product of social life and the creation of *homo faber*.[35]

Benefitting from Hegel, Marx grasped the internal logic of knowledge and action in modern society. Furthermore, with the advantage of a more detailed knowledge of the nature of capitalist institutions, Marx was able to show that the logical connection between man's technological domination of nature and the complete integration of man's individual and social experiences lay outside the utilitarian conception of rationality. Marx's analysis of capitalist society is directed primarily to the connections between social norms and economic systems. Marx, no less than Weber, makes very clear the ascetic basis of capitalist rationality and its motivation toward the accumulation of value.

In a remarkable passage from the *Economic and Philosophical Manuscripts*, Marx explains how political economy develops against the background of the breaking away of labor and property from their anchorages in use values. The emancipation of labor makes possible the substitution of exchange values for use values, which leads to the subordination of all forms of life and property to the accumulation and expansion of wealth. In their endlessly reproducible forms, as the prices of capital and the

35. Kurt H. Wolff, "On the Significance of Hannah Arendt's *The Human Condition* for Sociology," *Inquiry*, IV (Summer, 1951), 67–106.

power of labor, private property and labor alienate human needs in favor of market wants. Marx concludes that the impulse to modern individualism is the subjectivization of the bases of feudal community, which simultaneously supplies the orientation toward market behavior. The physiocrats identified all wealth with land and cultivation, which, while leaving feudal property intact, shifted the definition of land to its economic function and thereby exposed feudal property to the later attacks on ground rent. The objective nature of wealth was also in part shifted to its subjective basis in labor, inasmuch as agriculture was regarded as the source of the productivity of land. Finally, industrial labor emerged as the most general principle of productivity; the factors of production, land, labor, and capital, became nothing but moments in the dialectic of labor's self-alienation.

Thus, from the viewpoint of this enlightened political economy which has discovered the *subjective* essence of wealth within the framework of private property, the partisans of the monetary system and the mercantilist system, who consider private property as a *purely objective* being for man, are *fetishists* and *Catholics*. Engels is right, therefore, in calling Adam Smith the *Luther of political economy*. Just as Luther recognized *religion* and *faith* as the essence of the real *world*, and for that reason took up a position against Catholic paganism; just as he annulled *external* religiosity while making religiosity the *inner* essence of man; just as he negated the distinction between priest and layman because he transferred the priest into the heart of the layman; so wealth external to man and independent of him (and thus only to be acquired and conserved from outside) is annulled. That is to say, its *external* and *mindless* objectivity is annulled by the fact that private property is incorporated in man himself, and man himself is recognized as its essence. But as a result, man himself is brought into the sphere of private property, just as, with Luther, he is brought into the sphere of religion. Under the guise of recognizing man, political economy, whose principle is labor, carries to its logical conclusion the denial of man. Man himself is no longer in a condition of external tension with the external substance of private property; he has himself become the tension-ridden being of private property. What was previously a phenomenon of *being external to oneself*, a real external manifestation of man, has now become the act of objectification, of alienation. This political economy seems at first, therefore, to recognize man with his independence, his personal activity, etc. It incorporates private property in the very essence of man, and it is no longer, therefore, conditioned by the local or national *characteristics of private property* regarded as existing outside itself. It manifests a cosmopolitan, universal activity which is destructive of every limit and every bond, and substitutes itself as the *only* policy, the *only* universality, the *only* limit and the *only* bond.[36]

Marx and Weber raised a common question: what is the human value of the mode of social organization called capitalism; what is its *raison d'être;* what is the sense in its universality? Admittedly, Weber may have gone further in the comparative study of the conditions under which the normative and institutional bases of capitalism emerged. But each took the same view with regard to the major task of understanding the historically unique role played by the rational domination of nature and the accumulation of values in determining human action in capitalist society.

We need to understand the "vocation" of Western science and rationality. Modern science is chained to progress through invention and discovery. Every scientific finding asks to be surpassed in the light of accumulated knowledge. Each scientist resigns himself to making only a partial and fleeting contribution to a task that is conceived as limitless. "And with this we come to inquire into the meaning of science. For, after all, it is not self-evident that something subordinate to such a law is sensible and meaningful in itself. Why does one engage in doing something that in reality never comes, and never can come to an end?" [37] Weber compares his own question of the meaning of science to Tolstoy's question about the meaning of death in modern civilization.[38] Civilized man has broken with nature. Cultural values have replaced use values, and the cycle of life familiar to the peasant and the feudal lord has exploded into a self-infinitizing progression of the accumulation of cultural values. The peasant could encounter the totality of meaning ordained for him in the feudal order and die at peace with his station in life because his daily life was congruent with the whole of his life. But modern man,

36. Karl Marx, "Economic and Philosophical Manuscripts," *Early Writings,* trans. and ed. T. B. Bottomore (London: Watts, 1963), pp. 147–48.
37. Max Weber, "Science as a Vocation," in *From Max Weber: Essays in Sociology,* trans., ed., and with an Introduction by H. Gerth and C. Wright Mills (New York: Oxford University Press, 1958), p. 138.
38. Leo Tolstoy, *The Death of Ivan Ilych,* trans. Aylmer Maude (New York: New American Library, 1964).

pitted against an ever expanding universe of ideas, problems, and values, though he can be weary of life, always encounters death as meaningless, for death robs him of infinity. "And because death is meaningless, civilized life as such is meaningless; by its very 'progressiveness' it gives death the imprint of meaningless-ness." [39]

For want of a science of ends which might illuminate the ideal of Western rationality and its affinity for power and accumulation, Weber turned to the notions of "calling" and the "ethic of responsibility." It is implicit in Weber's "ideal type" method that the growth of rationality in science, politics, and economics is a meaningful way of representing Western experience only so long as we choose to understand it *in its own terms* (*verstehen*). But as soon as we consider Western rationality from the standpoint of comparative history it loses its self-evidence. In other words, the increasing rationality of modern science and technology becomes an enigma.

HISTORICAL RESPONSIBILITY AND THE VOCATION OF REASON

MODERN CONSCIOUSNESS is greatly affected by the standpoints of anthropology and historicism, which reveal that all knowledge about man and nature presupposes some metaphysical stand on the relation between human facticity, knowledge, and values. Thus we need, as Husserl observes, "a new method of philosophical work," which will explore the reflexive ties between rational subjectivity and the regional ontologies of science, economics, politics, and everyday life.[40] Instead of pursuing the ideal of an objective *mathēsis universalis,* a complete mathematical formalization of biological, linguistic, and economic values, which still lures modern structuralists, we need a philosophical method which we may call, borrowing from Husserl, "documentary work." This work would be profoundly anthropological and archaeological, provided we recover the historico-intentional origin of these modes of work. At the same time it will be necessary to translate the transcendental question of the possibility of rational knowledge and freedom into a

39. "Science as a Vocation," p. 140.
40. Husserl, *Crisis,* p. 351.

question about the *institution* of science and the social sciences as a human praxis, a collective endeavor, which develops a tradition while still remaining open to rebellion and change. We must turn the transcendental question of the possibility of knowledge and freedom into a question of the "origins" (*Ursprünge*) of critical thought. In this way we shall be true to the ultimately ethical responsibilities of phenomenological and social-scientific knowledge. To Weber's reflections on the vocations of science and politics, insofar as these vocations are stoically responsible and not plunged into nihilistic despair, may be joined the notion of "tradition" in Husserl and Heidegger, which integrates the question of the origins of reason with the nature of human authenticity. Such a conception is worthy of attention as a propaedeutic to the discussion of institutional alienation, which I shall not otherwise treat, though it provides an obvious gloss on the problem we are about to consider.

I have argued that the alienation of the world inherent in capitalism, as well as its innerworldly asceticism, is due to the classical utilitarian reduction of the world to a calculus of utilities, from which man himself could not be saved as an ultimate standard of value. Kant's categorical imperative raised a standard of action and personal conduct which had no foundations in the context of class inequality and exploitation that reduced most men to the status of means and not ends. Marx drew from Hegel the essence of modern subjectivity, the notion that man produces himself. But, as Hegel pointed out in *The Phenomenology of Mind,* modern subjectivity consumes itself in an unstable utilitarianism, which destroys the substantive rationality of things and the orders of nature and society, at the same time that it represents the greatest release of subjective rights and freedoms. More recently, Hannah Arendt has described the processes of destruction of the world, the cycle of meaningless labor, and the activity of "science" which designs the landscape and invents the scenarios of modern violence.[41] The disenchantment of the world and the devaluation of nature are the results of a consistent utilitarianism, driven by the rational asceticism of modern subjectivity guessing at a hidden God. Once man no longer has an end beyond himself, nothing stops him in the relentless exploita-

41. Arendt, *Human Condition,* chap. 6, *"The Vita Activa* and the Modern Age," pp. 225–97.

tion of the world and himself. In this project the vocabularies of liberal individualism and progress provide motivational supports for the private appropriation of world resources and the unthinking pollution of alternative human environments. It is no longer possible within this ideological framework to separate the processes of production and destruction. For modern labor is the inspiration of a divine madness, working upon a promised land, where abundance feeds rapacity and denies conservation.

We need to generate a countermyth to the ideology of world domination. To this end it is necessary to separate the notion of work from the self-infinitizing logic of utilitarianism. The human world is an artifice built upon everyday passions, but also against time and eternity. Much of human life is spent in incessant labor aimed at the simple reproduction of life and the satisfaction of bodily needs; these labors consume a good part of the mental energies of men, so that it is necessary to distinguish, Arendt argues, that "science" which serves wants from "thought," whose aim is nonutilitarian. *Thought* serves no obvious purpose; it is the riddle of human activity, the source of religion, magic, myth, and art. Thought produces objects for their own sake; preeminently in art it draws from time and destruction a world of essence, an immortal home for mortal men. Of itself thought produces nothing without human hands, eyes, ears, and tongues; these materialize thought and embody its creations, which would otherwise lose man in reflection, dream, and imagination. Thought transcends science, logic, and intelligence; it can never be expropriated by computerized homunculi, who merely aid mental labor in the service of wants. The prevalence of thought demands the reversal of modern utilitarianism and the subordination of economics to politics. Upon this reversal hangs the question of the humanization and conservation of the world, not as an emporium, but as a public space in which men's words might be memorable and their deeds glorious. Without such a space history and politics are polluted, and the human story reduced to an insane series of commercials.

If the *animal laborans* needs the help of *homo faber* to ease his labor and remove his pain, and if mortals need his help to erect a home on earth, acting and speaking men [*political men*] need the help of *homo faber* in his highest capacity, that is, the help of the artist, of poets and historiographers, of monument-builders or writers, because without them the only product of their activity, the story they enact and tell, would not survive at all. In order to be what the world is always meant to be, a home for men during their life on earth, the human artifice must be a place fit for action and speech, for activities not only entirely useless for the necessities of life, but of an entirely different nature from the manifold activities of fabrication, by which the world itself and all things in it are produced. We need not choose here between Plato and Protagoras, or decide whether man or a god should be the measure of all things; what is certain, is that the measure can be neither the driving necessity of biological life and labor, nor the utilitarian instrumentalism of fabrication and usage.[42]

The radical and monumental features of thought, as Hannah Arendt speaks of it, require as its world-historical medium a viable conception of tradition and criticism distinctly different from the liberal antitradition of change and criticism.

The ill repute of speculative philosophies of history has generally caused the social sciences to neglect the temporal and historical features of individual conduct and institutional life. Husserl's concern with the structures of the life-world brought his attention to the temporal dimensions of interpersonal conduct and the continuity of tradition. The horizon-structure of experience requires that its temporal organization, as a field of retrospective and prospective concerns, is its own intrinsic historicity. The problem presented by Husserl's transcendental ego is to relate its own inner time-consciousness to the communal structures of human history, within which there is no such transcendental standpoint. But even to put the problem this way is to misrepresent it with respect to Husserl's task in the *Crisis*.[43] For the *Crisis* requires that the consciousness of the historicity of human knowledge and specific scientific praxes be grasped as an existential structure, always open to forgetfulness and recovery. However, Husserl and especially Heidegger offer the bridging notion of an intersubjectively open horizon of "things," interests, and activities, which through their capacity for repetition (*Wiederholung*) become a living tradition of recollection and projection of future work, values, and meaning.[44] Our communal life,

42. *Ibid.*, p. 153.
43. Paul Ricoeur, "Husserl et le sens de l'histoire," *Revue de metaphysique et de morale*, LIV (July–October, 1949), 280–316.
44. Husserl, *Crisis*, pp. 358–60.

its beliefs and practices, is "world-historical" through and through, that is, it involves the integration of the realms of predecessors, contemporaries, and successors as temporalized regions of our collective life. The integration of these domains of our communal being is achieved by means of an explicit repetition or recovery of the Dasein that "has been," in the sense of "having been there" (*dagewesen*). The past of a living communal tradition is thus not a determinate weight so much as a legacy, a "handing down" (*Überlieferung*) of the authentic possibilities of Dasein that has been. Moreover, the authentic repetition of the past is critical to the present inasmuch as it is grounded in an anticipatory resoluteness, which is the recovery of Dasein from its circumscriptive, falling concern with everydayness.

Understood in this way, Husserl and Heidegger present a concept of tradition as a structure of "monumental, antiquarian and critical" concerns.

As historical, Dasein is possible only by reason of its temporality, and temporality temporalizes itself in the ecstatico-horizonal unity of its raptures. Dasein exists authentically as futural in resolutely disclosing a possibility which it has chosen. Coming back resolutely to itself, it is, by repetition, open for the "monumental" possibilities of human existence. The historiology which arises from such historicality is "monumental." As in the process of having been, Dasein has been delivered over to its thrownness. When the possible is made one's own by repetition, there is adumbrated at the same time the possibility of reverently preserving the existence that has-been-there, in which the possibility seized upon has become manifest. Thus authentic historiology, as monumental, is "antiquarian" too. Dasein temporalizes itself in the way the future and having been are united in the Present. The Present discloses the "today" authentically, and of course as the moment of vision. But in so far as this "today" has been interpreted in terms of understanding a possibility of existence which has been seized upon—an understanding which is repetitive in a futural manner—authentic historiology becomes a way in which the "today" gets deprived of its character as present; in other words, it becomes a way of painfully detaching oneself from the falling publicness of the "today." *As authentic, the historiology which is both monumental and antiquarian is necessarily a critique of the "Present."* Authentic historicality is the foundation for the possibility of uniting these three ways of historiology. But the *ground* on which authentic historiology is founded is *temporality* as the existential meaning of the Being of care.[45]

Reflecting upon the sources of the crisis of Western rationality, Husserl called for a method of philosophical and scientific thought which would be monumental, world-building, and at the same time "poetic" in the exchanges between itself and the world. The consequence of history is that the universality and truth pursued by thought are not an intrinsic property of the idea, but an acquisition which must be constantly established with a community of knowledge, which calls for and depends on the free response of its members. Merleau-Ponty has remarked how well Husserl's notion of *Stiftung*, foundation or institution, captures the fecundity of cultural works, through which they endure into the present where they open new relevances and options on the future.

> It is thus that the world as soon as he has seen it, his first attempts at painting, and the whole past of painting all deliver up a *tradition* to the painter—*that is*, Husserl remarks, *the power to forget origins* and to give to the past not a survival, which is the hypocritical form of forgetfulness, but a new life, which is the noble form of memory.[46]

It is important for us to retrieve the notion of the fecundity of tradition, craft, and thought, if we are to avoid the Weberian alternation between cultural pessimism and charismatic fatality, the alternatives of ineffectual alienation and unfulfilled utopianism. These are considerations which bear on economic and sociological knowledge, inasmuch as these must be grounded in an adequate conception of human institutions. Human experience, its labors and visions, accumulates only in the circle of institutions which enlarge and deepen the meaning of our sentiments, our deeds, and our work. This is the circle of alienation, but also of freedom, provided we do not lose our sense of the collectivity, whose history knows of tradition and of a future. In this sense, human institutions are never wholly reified; they are

45. Martin Heidegger, *Being and Time,* trans. John Macquarrie and Edward Robinson (New York: Harper & Row, 1962), pp. 448–49 (italics Heidegger's).
46. Maurice Merleau-Ponty, *Signs,* trans. Richard C. McCleary (Evanston, Ill.: Northwestern University Press, 1964), p. 59; and Ricoeur, "Husserl et le sens de l'histoire," pp. 293–95.

made and unmade in each of us according to his grain. As I understand it, then, the consequence of this conception of institution is that it grounds criticism itself in tradition and membership. The critic labors in the same fashion as anyone else in the community of work, language, and politics. This is not to say that the critic is not rebellious; it is merely to draw the consequences of solidarity and of the responsibility of reason under which Hegel and Marx, as well as Husserl and Weber, lived, worked, and which they left for us as a legacy.

Praxeology as the Method
of Economics

Murray N. Rothbard

THE PRAXEOLOGICAL METHOD

DURING THE PAST GENERATION, a veritable revolution has taken place in the discipline of economics. I am referring not so much to the well-known Keynesian Revolution, but to the quieter but more profound revolution in the methodology of the discipline. This change has not simply occurred in the formal writings of the handful of conscious methodologists; it has spread, largely unnoticed, until it now permeates research and study in all parts of the field. Some effects of this methodological revolution are all too apparent: let the nonspecialist in economics pick up a journal article or monograph today and contrast it with one of a generation ago, and the first thing that will strike him is the incomprehensibility of the modern product. The older work was written in ordinary language, and was comprehensible to the layman with moderate effort; the current work is virtually all mathematics, algebraic or geometric. As one distinguished economist has lamented, "economics nowadays often seems like a third-rate sub-branch of mathematics," and one, he added, that the mathematician himself does not esteem very highly.

Of course, economics shares this accelerated mathematization with virtually every other field of knowledge, including history and literature. But, laboring under the common notion that it is a science with a special focus on *quantities*, economics has

[311]

312 / *Phenomenology and Economics*

proceeded farther and faster than any of its sister disciplines down the mathematical and statistical road.

The emphasis on mathematics is a symptom of a deeper change in the discipline: the rapid adoption of what we may broadly call "positivism" as the guide for research and the criterion for the successful construction of economic theory. The growing influence of positivism has its source in the attempt of all social sciences to mimic the (allegedly) supremely successful science, physics. For social scientists, as for almost all intellectuals, physics has unfortunately all but replaced philosophy as the "queen of the sciences." In the hands of the positivists, philosophy has almost come to seem an elaborate running commentary on and explication of physics, too often serving as the handmaiden of that prestigious science. What positivists see as the methodology of physics has been elevated, at their hands, to be *the* scientific method, and any deviant approach has been barred from the status of science because it does not meet the rigorous positivist test.

At the risk of oversimplification, the positivist model of the scientific method may be summarized as follows:

Step 1. The scientist observes empirical regularities, or "laws," between variables.

Step 2. Hypothetical explanatory generalizations are constructed, from which the empirically observed laws can be deduced and thus "explained."

Step 3. Since competing hypotheses can be framed, each explaining the body of empirical laws, such "coherence" or consistent explanation is not enough; to validate the hypotheses *other* deductions must be made from them, which must be "testable" by empirical observation.

Step 4. From the construction and testing of hypotheses a wider and wider body of generalizations is developed, which can be discarded if empirical tests invalidate them, or be replaced by new explanations covering a still wider range of phenomena.

Since the number of variables is virtually infinite, the testing in Step 3, as well as much of the observation in Step 1, can only be done in "controlled experiments," in which all variables but the ones under study are held constant. Replicating the experimental conditions should then replicate the results.

Note that, in this methodology, we proceed from that which is known with *certainty*—the empirical regularities—up through ever wider and more tentative hypotheses. It is this fact that leads the layman to believe erroneously, that Newton "overthrew" his predecessors and was in his turn "overthrown" by Einstein. In fact, what happens is not so much substitution as the addition of more general explanations for a wider range of phenomena; the generalizations of a Newton or an Einstein *are* far more tentative than the fact that two molecules of hydrogen combine with one molecule of oxygen to produce water.

Now, I am not expert enough in the philosophy of science to challenge this positivist model of the methodology of physics, although my reading in the philosophy of nature leads me to suspect that it is highly inadequate.[1] My contention is rather that the wholesale and uncritical application of this model to economics in recent decades has led the entire discipline badly astray.

There is, however, unbeknownst to most present-day economists, a competing methodological tradition. This tradition, the method of most of the older classical economists, has been called "praxeology" by Ludwig von Mises, its most eminent contemporary theorist and practitioner. Praxeology holds that, in the social sciences where human beings and human choices are involved, Step 3 is impossible, since, even in the most ambitious totalitarian society, it is impossible to hold *all* the variables constant. There *cannot* be controlled experiments when we confront the real world of human activity.

Let us take a recent example of a generally unwelcome economic phenomenon: the accelerated price inflation in the United States in the last few years. There are all manner of competing theoretical explanations for this, ranging from increases in the money supply to a sudden increase in greed on the part of the public or various segments thereof. There is no positivist-empirical way of deciding between these various theories; there is no way of confirming or disproving them by keeping all but one supposedly explanatory variable constant, and then changing that variable to see what happens to prices. In addition, there is the well-known social science analogue of the Heisenberg un-

1. On this, see Andrew G. Van Melsen, *The Philosophy of Nature* (Pittsburgh, Pa.: Duquesne University Press, 1953).

certainty principle: positivist science contains predictions, but how can predictions be tested when the very act of prediction itself changes the forces at work? Thus, economist A predicts a severe recession in six months; acting on this, the government takes measures to combat the supposedly imminent recession, the public and the stock market react, and so on. The recession then never takes place. Does that mean that the economist was basing his prediction on erroneous theories, or that the theories were correct but inappropriate to the actual data, *or* that he was "really" right but that prompt action forestalled the dreaded event? There is no way to decide.

One further example: Keynesian economists hold that depressions can be cured by massive doses of deficit spending by the government. The United States government engaged in large-scale deficit-spending to combat the depression in the late 1930s, but to no avail. The anti-Keynesians charge that this failure proves the incorrectness of Keynesian theory; the Keynesians reply that the doses were simply not massive enough, and that far greater deficits would have turned the tide. Again, there is no positivist-empirical way to decide between these competing claims.

Praxeologists share the contention of the impossibility of empirical testing with other critics of positivism, such as the institutionalists, who for this reason abandon economic theory altogether and confine themselves to purely empirical or institutional economic reportage. But the praxeologist does not despair; he turns instead to another methodology which *can* yield a correct body of economic theory. This methodology begins with the conviction that, while the economist cannot, like the physicist, test his hypotheses in controlled experiments, he is, in another sense, in a *better* position than the physicist. For while the physicist is certain of his empirical laws but tentative and uncertain of his explanatory generalizations, the economist is in the opposite position. He begins, not with detailed, quantitative, empirical regularities, but with broad explanatory generalizations. These fundamental premises he knows with certainty; they have the status of apodictic axioms, on which he can build deductively with confidence. Beginning with the certain knowledge of the basic explanatory axiom, A, he deduces the implications of A—B, C, and D; from these he deduces further implications, and so on. If he knows that A is true, and if A implies B, C, and D, then he knows with certainty that B, C, and D are true as well. The positivist, looking through the blinders imposed by his notion of physics, finds it impossible to understand how a science can possibly begin with the explanatory axioms and work downward to the more concrete empirical laws. He therefore dismisses the praxeological approach as "mythical" and "apriorist."

What are these axioms with which the economist can so confidently begin? They are the existence, the nature, and the implications of human action. Individual human beings exist. Moreover, they do not simply "move," as do unmotivated atoms or molecules; they *act*, i.e., they have goals and they make choices of means to attain their goals. They order their values or ends in a hierarchy according to whether they attribute greater or lesser importance to them; and they have what they believe is technological knowledge to achieve their goals. All of this action must also take place through time and in a certain space. It is on this basic and evident axiom of human action that the entire structure of praxeological economic theory is built. We do not know, and may never know with certainty, the ultimate equation that will explain all electromagnetic and gravitational phenomena; but we *do* know that people act to achieve goals. And this knowledge is enough to elaborate the body of economic theory.[2]

There is considerable controversy over the empirical status of the praxeological axiom. Professor Mises, working within a Kantian philosophical framework, has maintained that, like the "laws of thought," the axiom is a priori to human experience and hence apodictically certain. This analysis has given rise to the designation of praxeology as "extreme apriorism." Most praxeologists, however, hold that the axiom is based squarely in empirical reality, which makes it no less certain than it is in Mises's formulation. If the axiom is empirically true, then the logical

2. Thus, the fact that people must act to achieve their goals implies that there is a scarcity of means to attain them; otherwise the goals would already have been attained. Scarcity implies costs, which, in a monetary system (developed much later in the logical elaboration) are reflected in prices, and so forth. For a consciously praxeological development of economic theory, see Ludwig von Mises, *Human Action* (New Haven, Conn.: Yale University Press, 1949); and Murray N. Rothbard, *Man, Economy, and State*, 2 vols. (Princeton, N.J.: Van Nostrand, 1962).

consequences built upon it must be empirically true as well. But this is not the sort of empiricism welcomed by the positivist, for it is based on universal reflective or inner experience, as well as on external physical experience. Thus, the knowledge that human beings have goals and act purposively to attain them rests, not simply on observing that human beings exist, but also on the introspective knowledge of what it means to be human possessed by each man, who then assents to this knowledge. While this sort of empiricism rests on broad knowledge of human action, it is also prior to the complex historical events that economists attempt to explain.

Alfred Schutz pointed out and elaborated the complexity of the interaction between the individual and other persons, the "interpretive understanding" or *Verstehen,* upon which this universal, prescientific knowledge rests. The common-sense knowledge of the universality of motivated, intentional human action, ignored by positivists as "unscientific," actually provides the indispensable groundwork on which science itself must develop.[3] For Schutz this knowledge is empirical, "provided that we do not restrict this term to sensory perceptions of objects and events in the outer world but include the experiential form, by which common-sense thinking in everyday life understands human actions and their outcome in terms of their underlying motives and goals."[4]

The nature of the evidence on which the praxeological axiom rests is, moreover, fundamentally similar to that accepted by the self-proclaimed empiricists. To them, the laboratory experiment is evidence because the sensory experience involved in it is avail-

3. "It is . . . not understandable that the same authors who are convinced that no verification is possible for the intelligence of other human beings have such confidence in the principle of verifiability itself, which can be realized only through cooperation with others by mutual control" (Alfred Schutz, *Collected Papers,* Vol. II: *Studies in Social Theory,* ed. A. Brodersen [The Hague: Nijhoff, 1964], p. 4).
4. Alfred Schutz, *Collected Papers,* Vol. I: *The Problem of Social Reality,* ed. Maurice Natanson (The Hague: Nijhoff, 1962), p. 65; see also pp. 1–66, as well as Peter Winch, "Philosophical Bearings," and Maurice Natanson, "A Study in Philosophy and the Social Sciences," in *Philosophy of the Social Sciences: A Reader,* ed. Maurice Natanson (New York: Random House, 1963). On the importance of the common-sense, prescientific presuppositions of science from a slightly different philosophical perspective, see Van Melsen, *Philosophy of Nature,* pp. 6–29.

able to each observer; the experience becomes "evident" to all. Logical proof is in this sense similar; for the knowledge that B follows from A becomes evident to all who care to follow the demonstration. In the same way, the fact of human action and of purposive choice also becomes evident to each person who bothers to contemplate it; it is just as evident as the direct sense experience of the laboratory.

From this philosophical perspective, then, all disciplines dealing with human beings, from philosophy to history, psychology, and the social sciences, must take as their starting point the fact that humans engage in motivated, purposive action and are thus different from the unmotivated atoms and stones that are the objects of the physical sciences. But where, then, does praxeology or economics differ from the other disciplines that treat human beings? The difference is that, to the praxeologist, economic *theory* (as distinct from applied economics, which will be treated below) deals, not with the content of human valuations, motivations, and choices, but with the formal fact *that* people engage in such motivated action. Other disciplines focus on the content of these values and actions. Thus, psychology asks how and why people adopt values and make choices; ethics deals with the problem of what values and choices they *should* adopt; technology explains how they should act in order to arrive at chosen ends; and history tries to explain the content of human motives and choices through recorded time. Of these disciplines, history is perhaps the most purely *verstehende*, for the historian is constantly attempting to describe, understand, and explain the motivations and choices of individual actors. Economic theory, on the other hand, is the least *verstehende*, for while it too begins with the axiom of purposive and intentional human action, the remainder of its elaborated structure consists of the deduced logical—and therefore true—implications of that primordial fact.

An example of the formal structure of economic theory is the well-known economic law, built up from the axiom of the existence of motivated human action, that if the demand for any product increases, given the existing supply, the price of that product will rise. This law holds regardless of the ethical or aesthetic status of the product, just as the law of gravity applies to objects regardless of their particular identity. The economic theorist is not interested in the content of what is being demanded, or in its ethical meaning: it may be guns or butter or even textbooks on philosophy. It is this universal, formal nature of economic law that has earned it among laymen the reputation of being cold, heartless, and excessively logical.

Having discussed the nature of the axiom on which the praxeological view of economics is grounded, we may now turn to examine the deductive process itself, the way in which the structure of economic laws is developed, the nature of those laws, and, finally, the ways in which the praxeological economist applies these economic laws to the social world.

One of the basic tools for the deduction of the logical implications of the axiom of human action is the use of the *Gedankenexperiment,* or "mental experiment." The *Gedankenexperiment* is the economic theorist's substitute for the natural scientist's controlled laboratory experiment. Since the relevant variables of the social world cannot actually be held constant, the economist holds them constant in his imagination. Using the tool of verbal logic, he mentally investigates the causal influence of one variable on another. The economist finds, for example, that the price of a product is determined by two variables, the demand for it and its supply at any given time. He then mentally holds the supply constant, and finds that an increase in demand—brought about by higher rankings of the product on the value scales of the public—will bring about an increase in price. Similarly, he finds, again using verbal deductive logic, that if these value scales, and therefore public demand, are mentally held constant, and the supply of the product increases, its price will fall. In short, economics arrives at *ceteris paribus* laws: *given* the supply, the price will change in the same direction as demand; *given* the demand, price will change in the opposite direction from supply.

One important aspect of these economic laws must be pointed out: they are necessarily *qualitative.* The fact that human beings have goals and preferences, that they make choices to attain their goals, that all action must take place over time, all these are qualitative axioms. And since only the qualitative enters into the logical process from the real world, only the qualitative can emerge. One can only say, for example, that an increase in demand, given the supply, will raise the price; one *cannot* say that a twenty per cent increase in demand will bring about a twenty-five per cent increase in price. The praxeologist must reject all attempts, no matter how fashionable, to erect a theory consisting of alleged quantitative laws. In an age that tries desperately to imitate prestigious physics, with its emphasis on mathematics and its quantitative laws, many social scientists, including many economists, have ignored this methodology because of this very insistence on the qualitative bounds of the discipline.

There is a basic reason for the quantity-quality dichotomy between the physical and the social sciences. The objects of physical science do not act; they do not choose, change their minds, and choose again. Their natures may therefore be investigated, and the investigations replicated indefinitely, with quantitative precision. But people do change their minds, and their actions, all the time; their behavior cannot be predicted with exact and therefore scientific precision. Among the many factors helping to determine the demand and the supply of butter, for example, are: the valuations placed by each consumer on butter relative to all other products available, the availability of substitutes, the climate in the butter-producing areas, technological methods of producing butter (and margarine), the price of cattle feed, the supply of money in the country, the existence of prosperity or recession in the economy, and the public's expectations of the trend of general prices. Every one of these factors is subject to continuing and unpredictable change. Even if one mammoth equation could be discovered to "explain" all recorded prices of butter for the past fifty years, there is no guarantee, and not even the likelihood, that the equation would have anything to do with *next* month's price.

In fact, if empirical success is the test, it is surely noteworthy that all the determined efforts of quantitative economists, econometricians, and social scientists have not been able to find one single quantitative constant in human affairs. The mathematical laws in the physical sciences contain numerous constants; but the imitative method in the social sciences is proven vain by the fact that not a single constant has ever emerged. Moreover, despite the use of sophisticated econometric models and high-speed computers, the success rate of forecasting economic quantities has been dismal, even for the simplest of aggregates, such as the Gross National Product, let alone for more difficult quantities; the record of GNP forecasting by economists has been poorer than a simple layman's extrapolation of recent trends.[5] In fact, the federal government has had notably poor success even in forecasting the one variable under its own absolute control: its *own* expenditure in the near future. Perhaps we will revise our critical opinion of econometric science if and when the econometricians prove themselves able to make flawless predictions of activity on the stock market—and make themselves vast fortunes in the process.

Except for the fact that they are not quantitative, however, the predictions of the praxeologist are precisely the same kind as those of the natural scientist. The latter, after all, is not a prophet or soothsayer; his successful prediction is not what *will* happen in the world, but what *would* happen if such and such should occur. The scientist can predict successfully that if hydrogen and oxygen are combined in proportions of two to one, the result will be water; but he has no way of predicting scientifically how many scientists in how many laboratories will perform this process at any given period in the future. In the same way, the praxeologist can say, with absolute certainty, that if the demand for butter increases, and the supply remains the same, the price of butter will rise; but he does not know whether the public's demand for butter will in fact rise or fall, let alone by how much it will change. Like the physical scientist, the economist is not a prophet, and it is unfortunate that the econometricians and quantitative economists should have so eagerly assumed this social role.[6]

The English economist John Jewkes suggests the properly

5. See Victor Zarnowitz, *An Appraisal of Short-Term Economic Forecasts* (New York: National Bureau of Economic Research, 1967). For the record of recent forecasting, see "Bad Year for Econometrics," *Business Week* (December 20, 1969), pp. 36–40.

6. The English economist P. T. Bauer properly distinguishes between scientific prediction and forecasting: "prediction, in the sense of the assessment of the results of specified occurrences or conditions, must be distinguished from the forecasting of future events. Even if the prediction that the producers of a particular crop respond to a higher price by producing more is correct, this prediction does not enable us to forecast accurately next year's output (still less the harvest in the more distant future), which in the event will be affected by many factors besides changes in price" (Peter T. Bauer, *Economic Analysis and Policy in Underdeveloped Countries* [Durham, N.C.: Duke University Press, 1957], pp. 10–11; see also pp. 28–32).

limited role for economic forecasting, as well as for applied economics generally:

> I submit that economists cannot, without stepping outside their discipline, predict in the sense of telling us what will happen in the future. . . .
>
> In the most general sense, there is, indeed, no such thing as the *economic* future. There is only *the* future in which economic factors are bound together, inextricably and quite without hope of separate identification, with the whole universe of forces determining the course of events. . . . Anyone who proposes to look at it [the future] before the event must take as his province the whole of experience and knowledge. He must cease to behave as a specialist, which means that he must cease to behave as an economist. . . .
>
> The economist's claim to predictive authority must be false in that it leads to a palpable absurdity. If the economic future can, indeed, be described, why not also the scientific future, the political future, the social future, the future in each and every sense? Why should we not be able to plumb all the mysteries of future time? [7]

What, then, is the praxeological view of the function of applied economics? The praxeologist contrasts, on the one hand, the body of qualitative, nomothetic laws developed by economic theory, and on the other, a myriad of unique, complex historical facts of both the past and the future. It is ironic that while the praxeologist is generally denounced by the positivist as an "extreme apriorist," he actually has a far more empirical attitude toward the facts of history. For the positivist is always attempting to compress complex historical facts into artificial molds, regarding them as homogeneous and therefore manipulable and predictable by mechanical, statistical, and quantitative operations in the attempt to find leads, lags, correlations, econometric relations, and "laws of history." This procrustean distortion is undertaken in the belief that the events of human history can be treated in the same mechanistic way as the movements of atoms or molecules—simple, unmotivated, homogeneous elements. The positivist thereby ignores the fact that while atoms and stones have no history, man, by virtue of his acts of conscious choice,

7. John Jewkes, "The Economist and Economic Change," in *Economics and Public Policy* (Washington, D.C.: Brookings Institution, 1955), pp. 82–83.

creates a history. The praxeologist, in contrast, holds that each historical event is the highly complex result of a large number of causal forces, and, further, that it is unique, and cannot be considered homogeneous to any other event. Obviously, there are similarities between events, but there is no perfect homogeneity, and therefore no room for historical "laws" similar to the exact laws of physical science.

While accepting that there are no mechanical laws of history, however, the praxeologist holds that he can and must use his knowledge of other nomothetic sciences as part of his *verstehende* attempt to understand and explain the idiographic events of history. Let us suppose that the economic historian, or the student of applied economics, is attempting to explain a rapid rise in the price of wheat in a certain country during a certain period. He may bring many nomothetic sciences to bear: the sciences of agronomy and entomology may help reveal that an insect mentioned in the historical record was responsible for a drastic fall in wheat production; meteorological records may show that rainfall was insufficient; he may discover that during the period people's taste for bread increased, perhaps imitating a similar preference by the king; he may discover that the money supply was increasing, and learn from economic theory that an increase in the supply of money tends to raise prices in general, including therefore the price of wheat. And, finally, economic theory states that the price of wheat moves inversely with the supply, and directly with the demand. The economic historian combines all of his scientific knowledge with his understanding of motives and choices to attempt to explain the complex historical phenomenon of the price of bread.

A similar procedure is followed in the study of such infinitely more complex historical problems as the causes of the French Revolution, where, again, the historian must blend his knowledge of causal theories in economics, military strategy, psychology, technology, and so on, with his understanding of the motives and choices of individual actors. While historians may well agree on the enumeration of all the relevant causal factors in the problem, they will differ on the weight to be attached to each factor. The evaluation of the relative importance of historical factors is an art, not a science, a matter of personal judgment, experience, and *verstehende* insight which will differ from one historian to another. In this sense, economic historians, like economists (and indeed other historians), can come to qualitative but not quantitative agreement.

For the praxeologist, forecasting is a task very similar to the work of the historian. The latter attempts to "predict" the events of the past by explaining their antecedent causes; similarly, the forecaster attempts to predict the events of the future on the basis of present and past events already known. He uses all his nomothetic knowledge, economic, political, military, psychological, and technological; but at best his work is an art rather than an exact science. Thus, some forecasters will inevitably be better than others, and the superior forecasters will make the more successful entrepreneurs, speculators, generals, and bettors on elections or football games.

The economic forecaster, as Professor Jewkes pointed out, is only looking at part of a tangled and complex social whole. To return to our original example, when he attempts to forecast the price of butter, he must take into consideration the qualitative economic law that price depends directly on demand and inversely on supply; it is then up to him, using knowledge and insight into general economic conditions as well as the specific economic, technological, political, and climatological conditions of the butter market, as well as the values people are likely to place on butter, to try to forecast the movements of the supply and demand of butter, and therefore its price, as accurately as possible. At best, he will have nothing like a perfect score, for he will run aground on the fact of free will altering values and choices, and the consequent impossibility of making exact predictions of the future.[8]

THE PRAXEOLOGICAL TRADITION

THE PRAXEOLOGICAL TRADITION has a long history in economic thought. We will indicate briefly the outstanding figures in the development of that tradition, especially since these

---

8. We may mention here the well-known refutation of the notion of predicting the future by Karl Popper: that, in order to predict the future we would have to predict what knowledge we will possess in the future. But we cannot do so, for if we knew what our future knowledge would be, we would *already* be in possession of that knowledge at the present time. See Karl R. Popper, *The Poverty of Historicism* (Boston: Beacon Press, 1957), pp. ix–xi.

economic methodologists and their views have been recently neglected by economists steeped in the positivist world view.

One of the first self-conscious methodologists in the history of economics was the early-nineteenth-century French economist, Jean-Baptiste Say. In the lengthy introduction to his magnum opus, *A Treatise on Political Economy,* Say laments that people

> are too apt to suppose that absolute truth is confined to the mathematics and to the results of careful observation and experiment in the physical sciences; imagining that the moral and political sciences contain no invariable facts of indisputable truth, and therefore cannot be considered as genuine sciences, but merely hypothetical systems. . . .

Say could easily have been referring to the positivists of our day, whose methodology prevents them from recognizing that absolute truths can be arrived at in the social sciences, when grounded, as they are in praxeology, on broadly evident axioms. Say insists that the "general facts" underlying what he calls the "moral sciences" are undisputed, and grounded on universal observation.

> Hence the advantage enjoyed by every one who, from distinct and accurate observation, can establish the existence of these general facts, demonstrate their connexion, and deduce their consequences. They as certainly proceed from the nature of things as the laws of the material world. We do not imagine them; they are results disclosed to us by judicious observation and analysis. . . . That can be admitted by every reflecting mind.

These general facts, according to Say, are "principles," and the science of

> political economy, in the same manner as the exact sciences, is composed of a few fundamental principles, and of a great number of corollaries or conclusions drawn from these principles. It is essential, therefore, for the advancement of this science that these principles should be strictly deduced from observation; the number of conclusions to be drawn from them may afterwards be either multiplied or diminished at the discretion of the inquirer, according to the object he proposes.[9]

9. Jean-Baptiste Say, *A Treatise on Political Economy,* trans. C. C. Biddle (New York: Kelley, 1964), pp. xxiv, xxv, xlv, xxvi.

Here Say has set forth another important point of the praxeo-logical method: that the paths in which the economist works out the implications of the axioms and the elaborated system which results will be decided by his own interests and by the kind of historical facts he is examining. Thus, it is theoretically possible to deduce the theory of money even in an economy of primitive barter, where no money exists; but it is doubtful whether a primitive praxeologist would have bothered to do so.

Interestingly enough, Say at that early date saw the rise of the statistical and mathematical methods, and rebutted them from what can be described as a praxeological point of view. The difference between political economy and statistics is precisely the difference between political economy (or economic theory) and history. The former is based with certainty on universally observed and acknowledged general principles; therefore, "a perfect knowledge of the principles of political economy may be obtained, inasmuch as all the general facts which compose this science may be discovered." Upon these "undeniable general facts," "rigorous deductions" are built, and to that extent political economy "rests upon an immovable foundation." Statistics, on the other hand, only records the ever-changing pattern of par-ticular facts, statistics, "like history, being a recital of facts, more or less uncertain and necessarily incomplete." Furthermore, Say anticipated the praxeologist's view of historical and statistical data as themselves complex facts needing to be explained. "The study of statistics may gratify curiosity, but it can never be productive of advantage when it does not indicate the origin and consequences of the facts it has collected; and by indicating their origin and consequences, it at once becomes the science of political economy." Elsewhere in the essay, Say scoffs at the gullibility of the public toward statistics: "Sometimes, moreover, a display of figures and calculations imposes upon them; as if numerical calculations alone could prove any thing, and as if any rule could be laid down, from which an inference could be drawn without the aid of sound reasoning." [10]

Say goes on to question sharply the value of mathematics in the construction of economic theory, once again referring back to the structure of the basic axioms, or general principles, for his argument. For political economy is concerned with men's

10. *Ibid.*, pp. xix–xx, li.

values, and these values being "subject to the influence of the faculties, the wants and the desires of mankind, they are not susceptible of any rigorous appreciation, and cannot, therefore furnish any data for absolute calculations. In political science, all that is essential is a knowledge of the connexion between causes and their consequences." Delving deeper into the then only embryonic use of the mathematical method in economics, Say points out that the laws of economics are strictly qualitative: "we may, for example, know that for any given year the price of wine will infallibly depend upon the quantity to be sold, compared with the extent of the demand." But "if we are desirous of submitting these two data to mathematical calculation," then it becomes impossible to arrive at precise quantitative forecasts of the innumerable, ever-changing forces at work: the climate, the quantity of the harvest, the quality of the product, the stock of wine held over from the previous vintage, the amount of capital, the possibilities of export, the supply of substitute beverages, and the changeable tastes and values of the consumers.[11]

Say offers a highly perceptive insight into the nature and probable consequences of the application of mathematics to economics. He argues that the mathematical method, with its seeming exactitude, can only gravely distort the analysis of qualitative human action by stretching and oversimplifying the legitimate insights of economic principles:

> Such persons as have pretended to do it, have not been able to enunciate these questions into analytical language, without divesting them of their natural complication, by means of simplifications, and arbitrary suppressions, of which the consequences, not properly estimated, always essentially change the condition of the problem, and pervert all its results; so that no other inference can be deduced from such calculations than from formula arbitrarily assumed.[12]

In contrast to the physical sciences where the explanatory laws or general principles are always in the realm of the hypothetical, in praxeology it is fatal to introduce oversimplification and falsehood into the premises, for then the conclusions deduced from them will be irredeemably faulty as well.[13]

11. *Ibid.*, pp. xxvi, xxvi *n.*
12. *Ibid.*, p. xxvi *n.*
13. One of the most pernicious aspects of the current dominance of positivist methodology in economics has been precisely this injection of

If mathematics and statistics do not provide the proper method for the political economist, what method is appropriate? The same course that he would pursue in his daily life. "He will examine the immediate elements of the proposed problem, and after having ascertained them with certainty . . . will approximately value their mutual influences with the intuitive quickness of an enlightened understanding. . . ." [14] In short, the laws of the political economist are certain, but their blending and application to any given historical event is accomplished, not by pseudo-quantitative or mathematical methods, which distort and oversimplify, but only by the use of *Verstehen*, "the intuitive quickness of an enlightened understanding."

The first economists to devote their attention specifically to methodology were three leading economists of mid-nineteenth-century Britain: John E. Cairnes, Nassau W. Senior, and John Stuart Mill. Cairnes and Senior, at least, may be considered as protopraxeologists. Cairnes, after agreeing with Mill that there can be no controlled experiments in the social sciences, adds that the latter have, however, a crucial advantage over the physical sciences. For, in the latter,

> *mankind have no direct knowledge of ultimate physical principles.* The law of gravitation and the laws of motion are among the best established and most certain of such principles; but what is the evidence on which they rest? We do not find them in our consciousness, by reflecting on what passes in our minds; nor can they be made apparent to our sense . . . the proof of all such laws ultimately resolving itself into this, that, assuming them to exist, they account for the phenomena.

In contrast, however,

---

false premises into economic theory. The leading extreme positivist in economics, Milton Friedman, goes so far as to extol the use of admittedly false premises in the theory, since, according to Friedman, the *only* test of a theory is whether it predicts successfully. See Milton Friedman, "The Methodology of Positive Economics," in *Essays in Positive Economics* (Chicago: University of Chicago Press, 1953), pp. 3–46. Of the numerous critiques and discussions of the Friedman thesis, see in particular Eugene Rotwein, "On 'The Methodology of Positive Economics,'" *Quarterly Journal of Economics*, LXXIII (November, 1959), 554–75; Paul A. Samuelson, "Discussion," *American Economic Review, Papers and Proceedings*, LIII (May, 1963), 231–36; Jack Melitz, "Friedman and Machlup on the Significance of Testing Economic Assumptions," *Journal of Political Economy*, LXXIII (February, 1965), 37–60.

14. Say, *Treatise on Political Economy*, p. xxvi *n.*

The economist starts with a knowledge of ultimate causes. He is already, at the outset of his enterprise, in the position which the physicist only attains after ages of laborious research. If any one doubt this, he has only to consider what the ultimate principles governing economic phenomena are . . . : certain mental feelings and certain animal propensities in human beings; [and] the physical conditions under which production takes place. . . . For the discovery of such premises no elaborate process of induction is needed . . . for this reason, that we have, or may have if we choose to turn our attention to the subject, direct knowledge of these causes in our consciousness of what passes in our own minds, and in the information which our senses convey . . . to us of external facts. Every one who embarks in any industrial pursuit is conscious of the motives which actuate him in doing so. He knows that he does so from a desire, for whatever purpose, to possess himself of wealth; he knows that, according to his lights, he will proceed toward his end in the shortest way open to him. . . .[15]

Cairnes goes on to point out that the economist uses the mental experiment as a replacement for the laboratory experiment of the physical scientist.

Cairnes demonstrates that deduced economic laws are "tendency," or "if-then," laws, and, moreover, that they are necessarily qualitative, and cannot admit of mathematical or quantitative expression. Thus, he too makes the point that it is impossible to determine precisely how much the price of wheat will rise in response to a drop in supply; for one thing, "it is evident that the disposition of people to sacrifice one kind of gratification to another—to sacrifice vanity to comfort, or decency to hunger—is not susceptible of precise measurement. . . ."[16] In the preface to his second edition, two decades later in 1875, Cairnes reiterated his opposition to the growing application of the mathematical method to economics, which, in con-

---

15. J. E. Cairnes, *The Character and Logical Method of Political Economy* (1857; 2d ed., London: Macmillan, 1875, repr. 1888), pp. 83, 87–88 (italics Cairnes's). The emphasis of Cairnes and other classical economists on wealth as the goal of economic action has been modified by later praxeological economists to include all manner of psychic satisfactions, of which those stemming from material wealth are only a subset. A discussion similar to that of Cairnes can be found in F. A. Hayek, "The Nature and History of the Problem," in Hayek, ed., *Collectivist Economic Planning* (London: Routledge, 1935), pp. 10–11.

16. Cairnes, *Character and Logical Method*, p. 127.

trast to its use in the physical sciences, cannot produce new truths; "and unless it can be shown either that mental feelings admit of being expressed in precise quantitative forms, or, on the other hand, that economic phenomena do not depend upon mental feelings, I am unable to see how this conclusion can be avoided." [17]

Cairnes's older contemporary, Nassau Senior, was the most important praxeologist of that era. Before Senior, classical economists such as John Stuart Mill had placed the fundamental premises of economics on the shaky ground of being *hypotheses;* the major hypothesis was that all men act to obtain the maximum of material wealth. Since this is clearly not always true, Mill had to concede that economics was only a hypothetical and approximate science. Senior broadened the fundamental premise to include immaterial wealth or satisfaction, a complete, apodictic, and universally true principle based on insight into the goal-seeking nature of human action.

> In stating that every man desires to obtain additional wealth with as little sacrifice as possible, we must not be supposed to mean that everybody . . . wishes for an indefinite quantity of everything. . . . What we mean to state is that no person feels his whole wants to be adequately supplied; that every person has some unsatisfied desires which he believes that additional wealth would gratify. The nature and urgency of each individual's wants are as various as the differences in individual character.[18]

In contrast to the physical sciences, Senior pointed out, economics and the other "mental sciences" draw their premises from the universal facts of human consciousness:

> The physical sciences, being only secondarily conversant with mind, draw their premises almost exclusively from observation or hypothesis. Those which treat only of magnitude or number, . . . the pure sciences, draw them altogether from hypothesis. . . . They disregard almost entirely the phenomenon of consciousness. . . .
>   On the other hand, the mental sciences and the mental arts draw their premises principally from consciousness. The subjects

17. *Ibid.*, p. v.
18. Nassau William Senior, *An Outline of the Science of Political Economy* (1836; reprinted. New York: Kelley, n.d.), p. 27.

with which they are chiefly conversant are the workings of the human mind.[19]

These latter premises are "a very few general propositions, which are the result of observation, or consciousness, and which almost every man, as soon as he hears them, admits, as familiar to his thought, or at least, as included in his previous knowledge." [20]

During the 1870s and 1880s, classical economics was supplanted by the neoclassical school: in this period the praxeological method was carried on and further developed by the Austrian School, founded by Carl Menger of the University of Vienna and continued by his two most eminent disciples, Eugen von Böhm-Bawerk and Friedrich von Wieser. It was on the basis of their work that Böhm-Bawerk's student Ludwig von Mises later founded praxeology as a self-conscious and articulated methodology.[21] As it was outside the increasingly popular intellectual fashion of positivism and mathematics, however, the Austrian School has been greatly neglected in recent years, and dismissed as an unsound approximation of the positivist-mathematical theory of the Lausanne School, founded by Léon Walras of Lausanne and continued by the Italian economist and sociologist Vilfredo Pareto.

A few followers or sympathetic observers, however, have carried on investigations into the methodology of the early Austrian School. Leland B. Yeager notes what we now see as the typically praxeological view of the unique advantage of economic theory over the physical sciences: "While the basic elements of theoretical interpretation in the natural sciences, such, he [Menger] says, as forces and atoms, cannot be observed directly, the elements of explanation in economics—human individuals

19. Marian Bowley, *Nassau Senior and Classical Economics* (New York: Kelley, 1949), p. 56.
20. *Ibid.*, p. 43. See also p. 64, where Miss Bowley points out the similarity between Senior's methodological views and the praxeology of Ludwig von Mises.
21. The outstanding example is Mises, *Human Action*. See also his *Theory and History* (New Haven, Conn.: Yale University Press, 1957); *The Ultimate Foundation of Economic Science* (Princeton, N.J.: Van Nostrand, 1962); and *Epistemological Problems of Economics* (Princeton, N.J.: Van Nostrand, 1960). Also see F. A. Hayek, *The Counter-Revolution of Science* (Glencoe, Ill.: Free Press, 1952); Lionel Robbins, *An Essay on the Nature and Significance of Economic Science*, 2d ed. (London: Macmillan, 1949); and Israel M. Kirzner, *The Economic Point of View* (Princeton, N.J.: Van Nostrand, 1960).

and their strivings—are of a direct empirical nature." Furthermore, "the facts that economists induce from the behavior of
themselves and other people serve as axioms from which a useful
body of economic theory can be logically deduced, much as in
geometry an impressive body of theorems can be deduced from
a few axioms." In short, "Menger conceived of economic theory
as a body of deductions from basic principles having a strong
empirical foundation." Referring to the dominant positivist
economists of our own day, Yeager adds perceptively,

> Not sharing . . . Menger's understanding of how empirical con-
> tent gets into so-called "armchair theory," many economists of our
> own day apparently regard theoretical and empirical work as two
> distinct fields. Manipulation of arbitrarily-assumed functional re-
> lationships is justified in the minds of such economists by the idea
> that empirical testing of theories against the real world comes
> afterward.[22]

Other writers have discovered links between the Austrian
method and various strands of the *philosophia perennis*. Thus,
Emil Kauder finds a close relationship between this method and
Aristotelian philosophy, which was still influential in Austria
at the end of the nineteenth century. Kauder points out that all
the Austrians were "social ontologists," and that as such they believed in a structure of reality "both as a logical starting point
and as a criterion of validity." He notes Mises's statement that
economic laws are "ontological facts," and he characterizes the
concern of Menger and his followers to uncover the "essences"
of phenomena, rather than to treat superficial and complex economic quantities, as both ontological and Aristotelian. Kauder
also points out that for Menger and the Austrians, economic
theory deals with types and typical relations, which provide
knowledge that transcends the immediate, concrete case and is
valid for all times and places. Concrete historical cases are thus
the Aristotelian "matter" which contains potentialities, while the
laws and types are the Aristotelian "forms" which actualize the
potential. For the Austrians, and especially for Böhm-Bawerk,
furthermore, causality and teleology were identical. In contrast
to the functional–mutual determination approach of Walras and

22. Leland B. Yeager, "The Methodology of Henry George and Carl
Menger," *American Journal of Economics and Sociology*, XIII (April,
1954), 235, 238.

of contemporary economists, the Austrians traced the causes of economic phenomena back to the wants and choices of consumers. Wieser especially stressed the grounding of economic theory on the inner experience of the mind.[23]

Furthermore, Ludwig M. Lachmann, in contrasting the Austrian and Lausanne Schools, shows that the Austrians were endeavoring to construct a *"verstehende* social science," the same ideal that Max Weber was later to uphold. Lachmann points out that the older Ricardian economists adopted the "objective" method of the natural sciences insofar as their major focus was upon the quantitative problem of income distribution. In their analysis, factors of production (land, labor, and capital goods) react mechanically to external economic changes. But, in contrast, "Austrian Theory is 'subjective' also in the sense that individuals . . . perform acts and lend the imprint of their individuality to the events on the market." As for the contrast between Austria and Lausanne,

> it is the contrast between those [Lausanne] who confine themselves to determining the appropriate magnitudes of the elements of a system (the conditions of equilibrium) and those [the Austrians] who try to explain events in terms of the mental acts of the individuals who fashion them. Most Austrian thinkers were dimly aware of this contrast, but before Hans Mayer, Mises and Hayek were unable to express it concisely. The validity of the Lausanne model is limited to a stationary world. The background of the Austrian theory, by contrast, is a world of continuous change in which plans have to be conceived and continually revised.[24]

We may conclude this sketch of the history of the praxeological tradition in economics by treating an important but

23. Emil Kauder, "Intellectual and Political Roots of the Older Austrian School," *Zeitschrift für Nationalökonomie,* XVII, no. 4 (1958), 411–25.

24. English abstract of Ludwig M. Lachmann, "Die geistesgeschichtliche Bedeutung der österreichischen Schule in der Volkswirtschaftslehre," *Zeitschrift für Nationalökonomie,* XXVI, nos. 1–3 (1966), 152–67, in *Journal of Economic Abstracts,* V (September, 1967), 553–54. Also see Lachmann, "Methodological Individualism and the Market Economy," in *Roads to Freedom: Essays in Honour of Friedrich A. Von Hayek,* ed. E. Streissler (New York: Kelley, 1969), pp. 89–103; and Israel M. Kirzner, "Methodological Individualism, Market Equilibrium, and Market Process," *Il Politico,* XXXII, no. 4 (December, 1967), 787–99.

much neglected debate on economic methodology which occurred at the turn of the twentieth century between Pareto and the philosopher Benedetto Croce. Croce, from his own highly developed praxeological position, opened the debate by chiding Pareto for having written that economic theory was a species of mechanics. Vigorously rejecting this view, Croce points out that a fact in mechanics is a mere fact, which requires no positive or negative comment; whereas words of approval or disapproval can appropriately be applied to an *economic* fact. The reason is that the true data of economics are not "physical things and objects, but actions. The physical object is merely the brute matter of an economic act. . . ." [25] Economic data, then, are acts of man, and these acts are the results of conscious choice.

In his lengthy reply, Pareto reiterates the similarity between economics and mechanics, and, like the positivists of today, defends unrealistic mechanistic assumptions as simple abstractions from reality, in the supposed manner of the natural sciences. Professing, in a typical positivist gambit, not to "understand" the concept of value, Pareto writes: "I see . . . that you employ the term *value.* . . . I no longer use it as I do not know what it would convey to other people. . . ." The concept of value is vague and complex and not subject to measurement; therefore, "the equations of pure economics establish relations between quantities of things, hence objective relations, and not relations between more or less precise concepts of our minds." [26] Criticizing Croce's evident concentration on the essences of economic action, as exemplified in his insistence that "one ought to study not the things which are the result of actions but the actions

25. Benedetto Croce, "On the Economic Principle: I" (1900), *International Economic Papers*, no. 3 (1953), pp. 173, 175. On Croce's views on economics, see Giorgio Tagliacozzo, "Croce and the Nature of Economic Science," *Quarterly Journal of Economics*, LIX (May, 1945), 307–29. On the Croce-Pareto debate, see Kirzner, *Economic Point of View*, pp. 155–57.

It is of interest that the Walrasian economist Joseph Schumpeter, in his only untranslated work, *Das Wesen und der Hauptinhalt der theoretischen Nationalökonomie* (Leipzig: Duncker and Humblot, 1908), specifically declared that the economist must only treat changes in "economic quantities" as if they were caused automatically, without reference to the human beings who may have been involved in such changes. In that way, causality and purpose would be replaced in economic theory by functional, mathematical relationships. See Kirzner, *Economic Point of View*, pp. 68–70.

26. Vilfredo Pareto, "On the Economic Phenomenon" (1900), *International Economic Papers*, no. 3, p. 187.

themselves," Pareto complains that this method is an ancient scientific fallacy. "The ancients conjured up cosmogonies instead of studying astronomy, wondered about the principles of the elements water and fire . . . , instead of studying chemistry. Ancient science wanted to proceed from the origin to the facts. Modern science starts from the facts and proceeds towards the origin at an extremely slow pace." Typically, Pareto sets forth the objectivist, positivist position by arguing from the analogy of the method of the natural sciences, thus completely begging the question of whether the methodologies of the natural and the social sciences should or should not be similar. Thus he concludes that "science proceeds by replacing the relationships between human concepts (which relationships are the first to occur to us) by relationships between things." [27]

Croce replies by criticizing Pareto's restriction of economics to measureable quantities as arbitrary; for what of those economic situations where the objects of action or exchange are not measurable? Croce suggests that it is Pareto who is really being metaphysical, while Croce is the true empiricist. For "your implied metaphysical postulate is . . . this: that the facts of man's activity are of the same nature as physical facts; that in the one case as in the other we can only observe regularity and deduce consequences therefrom, without ever penetrating into the inner nature of the facts. . . . How would you defend this postulate of yours except by a metaphysical monism. . . ?" In contrast, writes Croce, "I hold to experience. This testifies to me of the fundamental distinction between external and internal, between physical and mental, between mechanics and teleology, between passivity and activity. . . ." As for value, it is really a simple term wrapped up in human activity: "Value is observed immediately in ourselves, in our consciousness." [28]

In his rejoinder, Pareto begins with a typical example of metaphysical obtuseness: he does *not* believe that "the facts of man's activity are of the same nature as physical facts" because he doesn't know what "nature" may be. He goes on to reiterate various examples from physical science to demonstrate the proper methodology for all disciplines. He wishes to follow the "masters of positive science" rather than mere philosophers.

27. *Ibid.*, pp. 190, 196.
28. Croce, "On the Economic Principle: II" (1901), *International Economic Papers*, no. 3, pp. 198–99.

Pareto concludes with a concise summation of the differences between the two men and the two methodologies:

> We experimentalists . . . accept hypotheses not for any intrinsic value they may have but only in so far as they yield deductions which are in harmony with the facts. You, considering the nature of things independently from the rest, establish a certain proposition A, and from it come down to the concrete facts B. We may accept proposition A, but only as a hypothesis, therefore making not the slightest attempt to prove it. . . . Then we see what can be deduced from it. If those deductions agree with the facts we accept the hypothesis, for the time being of course, because we hold nothing as final or absolute.[29]

METHODOLOGICAL INDIVIDUALISM

ONLY AN INDIVIDUAL has a mind; only an individual can feel, see, sense, and perceive; only an individual can adopt values or make choices; only an individual can *act*. This primordial principle of "methodological individualism," central to Max Weber's social thought, must underlie praxeology as well as the other sciences of human action. It implies that such collective concepts as groups, nations, and states do not actually exist or act; they are only metaphorical constructs for describing the similar or concerted actions of individuals. There are, in short, no "governments" as such; there are only individuals acting in concert in a "governmental" manner. Max Weber puts it clearly:

> These collectivities must be treated as solely the resultants and modes of organization of the particular acts of individual persons, since these alone can be treated as agents in a course of subjectively understandable action. . . . For sociological purposes . . . there is no such thing as a collective personality which "acts." When reference is made in a sociological context to . . . collectivities, what is meant is . . . *only* a certain kind of development of actual or possible social actions of the individual persons.[30]

29. Pareto, "On the Economic Principle" (1901), *International Economic Papers*, no. 3, p. 206.
30. *The Theory of Social and Economic Organization* (Glencoe, Ill.: Free Press, 1957), quoted in Alfred Schutz, *The Phenomenology of the Social World* (Evanston, Ill.: Northwestern University Press, 1967), p. 199. For an application of methodological individualism to foreign policy, see Parker T. Moon, *Imperialism and World Politics* (New York: Mac-

Ludwig von Mises points out that what differentiates purely individual action from that of individuals acting as members of a collective is the different *meaning* attached by the people involved.

> It is the meaning which the acting individuals and all those who are touched by their action attribute to an action, that determines its character. It is the meaning that marks one action as the action of the state or of the municipality. The hangman, not the state, executes a criminal. It is the meaning of those concerned that discerns in the hangman's action an action of the state. A group of armed men occupies a place. It is the meaning of those concerned which imputes this occupation not to the officers and soldiers on the spot, but to their nation.[31]

In his important methodological work, Mises's disciple F. A. Hayek has demonstrated that the fallacy of treating collective constructs as directly perceived "social wholes" ("capitalism," "the nation," "the class") about which laws can be discovered stems from the objectivist-behaviorist insistence on treating men from the outside, as if they were stones, rather than attempting to understand their subjectively determined actions.

> It [the objectivist view] treats social phenomena not as something of which the human mind is a part and the principles of whose organization we can construct from the familiar parts, but as if they were objects directly perceived by us as wholes. . . .
> There is the rather vague idea that since "social phenomena" are to be the object of study, the obvious procedure is to start from the direct observation of these "social phenomena," where the existence in popular usage of such terms as "society" or "economy" is naively taken as evidence that there must be definite "objects" corresponding to them.[32]

Hayek adds that emphasis on the meaning of the individual act "brings out that what of social complexes is directly known to us are only the parts and that the whole is never directly perceived but always reconstructed by an effort of our imagination." [33]

---

millan, 1930), p. 58. For a more general political application, see Frank Chodorov, "Society Are People," in *The Rise and Fall of Society* (New York: Devin-Adair, 1959), pp. 29–37.

31. Mises, *Human Action*, p. 42.
32. Hayek, *Counter-Revolution of Science*, pp. 53–54.
33. *Ibid.*, p. 214.

Alfred Schutz, the outstanding developer of the phenomenological method in the social sciences, has reminded us of the
importance of going back "to the 'forgotten man' of the social
sciences, to the actor in the social world whose doing and feeling lies at the bottom of the whole system. We, then, try to
understand him in that doing and feeling and the state of mind
which induced him to adopt specific attitudes towards his social
environment." Schutz adds that "for a theory of action the subjective point of view must be retained in its fullest strength, in
default of which such a theory loses its basic foundations,
namely its reference to the social world of everyday life and experience." Lacking such a foundation, social science is likely to
replace the "world of social reality" by a fictional nonexisting
world constructed by the scientific observer. Or, as Schutz puts
it succinctly: "I cannot understand a social thing without reducing it to human activity which has created it, and beyond it,
without referring this human activity to the motives out of
which it springs." [34]

Arnold W. Green has recently demonstrated how the use of
invalid collective concepts has damaged the discipline of
sociology. He notes the increasing use of "society" as an entity
which thinks, feels, and acts, and, in recent years, has func-
tioned as the perpetrator of all social ills. "Society," for example,
and not the criminal, is often held to be responsible for all
crime. In many quarters "society" is considered almost demonic,
a "reified villain" which "may be attacked at will, blamed at
random, derided and mocked with self-righteous fury, [and]
may even be overturned by fiat or utopian yearning—and somehow, in some way, buses will still run on time." Green adds that,
"if on the other hand, society is viewed as people whose insecure
social relationships are preserved only by the fealty paid their
common store of moral rules, then the area of free choice available in which with impunity to demand, undermine, and wreck,
is sharply restricted." Moreover, if we realize that "society" does
not itself exist, but is made up only of individual people, then to
say that "society is responsible for crime, and criminals are not
responsible for crime, is to say that only those members of society who do not commit crime can be held responsible for crime.
Nonsense this obvious can be circumvented only by conjuring up

34. Schutz, *Collected Papers*, II, 7, 8, 10.

society as devil, as evil being apart from people and what they do." [35]

Economics has been rife with fallacies which arise when collective social metaphors are treated as if they were existent objects. Thus, during the era of the gold standard there was occasionally great alarm that "England" or "France" was in mortal danger because "it" was losing gold. What actually happened was that English*men* and French*men* were voluntarily shipping gold overseas and thus threatening the people who ran the banks of those countries with the necessity of meeting obligations to pay in gold which they could not possibly fulfill. But the use of the collective metaphor converted a grave problem of banking into a vague national crisis for which every citizen was somehow responsible.

Similarly, during the 1930s and 1940s many economists proclaimed that, in contrast to debts owed overseas, the size of the domestic public debt was unimportant because "we only owe it to ourselves." The implication was that the collective national person owed "himself" money from one pocket to another. This explanation obscured the fact that it makes a substantial difference for every person whether he is a member of the "we" or the "ourselves." [36]

Sometimes the collective concept is treated unabashedly as a biological organism. Thus, the popular concept of economic growth implies that every economy is somehow destined, in the manner of a living organism, to "grow" in some predetermined manner. The use of such analogical terms is an attempt to overlook or even negate individual will and consciousness in social and economic affairs. As Edith Penrose has written in a critique of the use of the "growth" concept in the study of business firms:

> where explicit biological analogies crop up in economics they are drawn exclusively from that aspect of biology which deals with the unmotivated behavior of organisms. . . . We have no reason whatever for thinking that the growth pattern of a biological organism is *willed* by the organism itself. On the other hand, we

35. Arnold W. Green, "The Reified Villain," *Social Research*, XXXV (Winter, 1968), 656, 664. On the concept of "society," see also Mises, *Theory and History*, pp. 250 ff.

36. See Murray N. Rothbard, "The Mantle of Science," in *Scientism and Values*, ed. H. Schoeck and J. W. Wiggins (Princeton, N.J.: Van Nostrand, 1960), pp. 168–70.

have every reason for thinking that the growth of a firm is willed by those who make the decisions of the firm . . . and the proof of this lies in the fact that no one can describe the development of any given firm . . . except in terms of decisions taken by individual men.[37]

There is no better summary of the nature of praxeology and the role of economic theory in relation to concrete historical events than in Alfred Schutz's discussion of the economic methodology of Ludwig von Mises:

No economic act is conceivable without some reference to an economic actor, but the latter is absolutely anonymous; it is not you, nor I, nor an entrepreneur, nor even an "economic man" as such, but a pure universal "one." This is the reason why the propositions of theoretical economics have just that "universal validity" which gives them the ideality of the "and so forth" and "I can do it again." However, one can study the economic actor as such and try to find out what is going on in his mind; of course, one is not then engaged in theoretical economics but in economic history or economic sociology. . . . However, the statements of these sciences can claim no universal validity, for they deal either with the economic sentiments of particular historical individuals or with types of economic activity for which the economic acts in question are evidence. . . .

In our view, pure economics is a perfect example of an objective meaning-complex about subjective meaning-complexes, in other words, of an objective meaning-configuration stipulating the typical and invariant subjective experiences of anyone who acts within an economic framework. . . . Excluded from such a scheme would have to be any consideration of the uses to which the "goods" are to be put after they are acquired. But once we do turn our attention to the subjective meaning of a real individual person, leaving the anonymous "anyone" behind, then of course it makes sense to speak of behavior that is atypical. . . . To be sure, such behavior is irrelevant from the point of view of economics, and it is in this sense that economic principles are, in Mises' words, "not a statement of what usually happens, but of what necessarily must happen." [38]

37. Edith T. Penrose, "Biological Analogies in the Theory of the Firm," *American Economic Review*, XLII (December, 1952), 808.
38. Schutz, *Phenomenology of the Social World*, pp. 137, 245.

PART VIII

Phenomenology
and Legal Theory

Phenomenology and
Legal Science

Wolfgang Friedmann

IT WILL BE the object of this essay to survey and assess the significance of the phenomenological movement in philosophy for the contemporary science of law. It is not necessary, nor is it within the competence of this writer, to define the many-sided philosophical aspects of phenomenology—and of existentialism, which, especially in the work of Jean-Paul Sartre, has links with phenomenology. However, as a background for the following survey, it is essential to establish a link between the general aspects of phenomenological inquiry and the contemporary movements in legal thought characterized in these terms.

A recent authoritative analysis of the phenomenological movement enumerates the following seven steps of the phenomenological method: [1]

1. investigating particular phenomena;
2. investigating general essences;
3. apprehending essential relationships among essences;
4. watching modes of appearing;
5. watching the construction of phenomena in consciousness;
6. suspending belief in the existence of the phenomena;
7. interpreting the meaning of phenomena.

Spiegelberg observes that only the first three steps "have been accepted, at least implicitly, and practiced by all those who have

1. Herbert Spiegelberg, *The Phenomenological Movement: A Historical Introduction,* 2d ed. (The Hague: Nijhoff, 1965), II, 659.

aligned themselves with the Phenomenological Movement; the later ones only by a smaller group." It would probably be a fair generalization to say that the phenomenological jurists have been concerned with the first three, as well as the seventh, of the approaches indicated by Spiegelberg. The basic aspiration of the legal phenomenologists—as of phenomenologists in general—has been the overcoming of the Kantian antinomy between the individual and the world, between the categories of thinking and the objects which the individual seeks to understand, through the apprehension of the "immediately given" in the world of consciousness, the concrete experience of the phenomena, as they confront man in their undivided fullness and immediacy. This means, for the jurist, the investigation of the particular (legal) phenomena, the distillation of the general essences of legal institutions and of the relations among them. And since all legal processes involve the interpretation of legal principles, the application of general norms to specific and concrete situations, we may add the interpretation of the meaning of legal phenomena as part of the phenomenological approach to law.

PHENOMENOLOGY AND EXISTENTIALISM

EXISTENTIALISM—a word as fashionable in contemporary philosophy as it is difficult to define—cannot, by itself, contribute much to a philosophy of law. All the main exponents of existentialism—such as Heidegger, Jaspers, and Sartre—have been concerned with the loneliness of man's existence, the relation between being and nothingness.[2] The concern of all these philosophers with the ways in which the individual can overcome his loneliness by realizing himself in a hostile world are basically antithetic to the concept of legal order, which is concerned with regulating the principles and procedures in society with mutual respect for each other's existence and self-realization. Of the leading existentialists, Karl Jaspers comes nearest to the bridging of the gap between individual loneliness and legal order. In his *Philosophie* he sees the legal order not merely as an external

2. See especially Jean-Paul Sartre's principal philosophical work, *Being and Nothingness,* **trans.** Hazel Barnes (New York: Philosophical Library, 1956).

compulsion imposed by a hostile world upon the individual, but as part of his self-realization:

> [Man] cannot deny nature without destroying himself, . . . and neither can he, without blurring, reject society, marriage, family, his trade, his state. Only by entering into all those can he find himself.[3]

This acknowledges that existence can only realize itself in communication; and the law, by giving man a minimum of security through protecting him from the fear of the "invasion of the uncertain," exercises a necessary protective function for his existence.

This thought—which is of course the basis of all legal philosophy and has been expressed in different ways by legal philosophers of every age, from Aristotle to Kant, Fichte, Bentham, and Stammler—has been developed further by a contemporary German legal philosopher.[4] Maihofer seeks to overcome the essentially isolationist individualism of existentialist philosophy by conceiving man as a being that does not live by and for himself but as "subject-object, world-man . . . particular man in this particular world which is his." This is a development of Sartre's observation that man exists "in the sum of relations in which he lives." In other words, man exists not only as an isolated being; he is part of a wider universe in a double sense. Man has an individual vocation as judge, as physician, as husband, as buyer or seller of goods. He is also "man in general," with a universal vocation. In Maihofer's analysis, the dereliction of man—which is a basic theme of existentialist philosophy—does not derive from his own antisocial nature but from the "antagonistic, antinomic, paradoxical structure of the world." He gives as an illustration of such conflicts the choice—so often referred to in various encyclicals and directives of the popes—between the certain death of the mother by refusal of an abortion and the killing

3. Jaspers, *Philosophie*, 2d ed. (Berlin: Springer, 1948), p. 838, English translation by E. B. Ashton, *Philosophy*, 3 vols. (Chicago: University of Chicago Press, 1969–71), III, 166.
4. Werner Maihofer, "Le Droit naturel comme dépassement du droit positif," *Archives de philosophie du droit*, VIII, trans. Poulantzas and Mavrakis (Paris: Sirey, 1963), 177. See also the same author's "Ideologie und Naturrecht," in *Ideologie und Recht*, ed. W. Maihofer (Frankfurt am Main: Klostermann, 1969). pp. 121 ff.

of the embryo by performance of the abortion, in cases where the mother would not survive the birth of the infant.

This development of existentialism, which we might call the "socializing" of existentialist philosophy, leads Maihofer and some other contemporary existentialist jurists to a kind of modernized natural law philosophy:

> The law is no longer rationalized and justified abstractly and speculatively by a known or presumed nature of man, as the older doctrine of natural law asserted, by invoking a natural or divine order of things and nature of man. Rather it is based on a postulated nature of man, which becomes apparent only by the manner in which man behaves in this world.
>
> This means always simultaneously a concrete analysis of the factual situation—the existing conditions of the world and the dominant consciousness of man—and the concrete anticipation of productive concepts—more humane conditions in a more perfect world, in orientation toward which the existing conditions and dominant consciousness are to be interpreted theoretically and modified in practice. In our modern age this is basically brought out in the two great liberal and social utopias: the legal utopia of a cosmopolitan society [*weltbürgerliche Gesellschaft*] and the social utopia of the classless society [*klassenlose Gesellschaft*]. . . .
>
> From all this results an absolute NO to natural law as ideology but at the same time an unconditional YES to natural law as utopia, without which all legal order would be in danger of being lost and exhausting itself in the conservation of that which exists. Just as positive law is necessarily the expression of that which has been and has become, so natural law is in our sense the outline of what is future and becoming.[5]

A similar conception, developed by Poulantzas, a French jurist, will be discussed in more detail later in this essay, as it is essentially based on phenomenological premises.[6]

PHENOMENOLOGICAL THEORIES OF LAW

WITHIN THE more specifically phenomenological orientation of contemporary jurists, we may perhaps distinguish be-

5. Maihofer, "Ideologie und Naturrecht," pp. 145–46 (my translation).
6. For a critique of the value assumptions imported into this evolution of existentialist legal philosophy, see the concluding observations in this essay, below.

tween three basic approaches: (*a*) the deduction, from the essence (*Wesenheit*) of legal concepts and institutions, of certain structural qualities, believed by the proponents of this approach to be a priori, immanent, and therefore immutable; (*b*) a somewhat related, but more elastic, approach to the legal order, whose key concept is the *Natur der Sache* (*nature des choses, "nature of the thing"*); and (c) an essentially Latin American trend in contemporary legal philosophy, which is derived from the phenomenological value philosophies (*Wertphilosophie*) of two German thinkers, Max Scheler and Nicolai Hartmann.

a. Essential structures of law

By way of illustration of this approach—which is not meant to be exhaustive—we may take the theories of a German and a French jurist, separated by half a century.

In 1913 Adolf Reinach published a thesis entitled *Die apriorischen Grundlagen des bürgerlichen Rechts*, which attempted to establish a priori foundations of civil law on a phenomenological basis. Its basic thesis is given in the following introductory section:

> We will show that the structures which are generally described as specifically legal have an existence, as much as numbers, trees, or houses; that this existence [*sein*] is independent of whether it is perceived by men or not and that it is in particular independent of any positive law. It is not only wrong but ultimately senseless to describe legal structures as creations of positive law, as senseless as it would be to call the establishment of the German Empire or any other historical event a creation of the history of science. Positive law finds the legal concepts which enter into it; it does not produce them.[7]

Reinach goes on to show that legal structures such as claims, liabilities, and properties have their independent existence, and that "for the legal structures they are a priori maxims. This a priori character is not dark and mystical; it is oriented in the simple facts."

7. Reinach, *Die apriorischen Grundlagen des bürgerlichen Rechts* (Halle: Niemeyer, 1913), p. 4 (my translation).

Reinach's thesis is best illustrated in his discussion of the concept of property (*Eigentum*). He says that what is described as property is "a relation between person and object, described as a relation of belonging or property, which is ultimate, irreducible, and cannot be dissolved into any elements. It can be constituted even when there is no positive law. If Robinson Crusoe on his island makes all sorts of things for himself, these things belong to him." In Reinach's analysis, property is a particularly close and powerful link between person and object. "It is based on the essence of belonging, and it means that he to whom the object belongs has the absolute right to deal with the object of his ownership in any way he chooses." Although Reinach concedes that the owner can incur liabilities concerning his property, or agree not to make use of certain rights inherent in it, or grant derivative rights to others, he specifically rejects the conception that property is the *sum* or *unity* of all rights in things. He also rejects the concept of divided property, as distinct from the partition or distribution of objects in which there is property.

Reinach explicitly distinguishes this a priori doctrine of law from natural law doctrine. While he approves the search of natural law philosophy for a sphere that is uninfluenced by the manifold formations of positive laws and retains its eternal verity, he rejects the use of "nature" as a basis of natural law doctrine, since it is based on the nature of man. "It is necessary . . . to find access to the realm of purely juristic legalities, which in every sense are independent of nature, independent of human perception, independent of human organization, and independent above all of the factual development of the world."

The main link between this German thesis, published in 1913, and a French thesis published in 1964 is that the latter also seeks to establish the objective nature of the *Phénomén Juridique*.[8] According to Amselek, the *Phénomén Juridique* is the application of a norm to an object. The Ought (*devoir-être, Sollen*) is nothing but a way to express the structure of the norm model.[9] The science of law rests on the hypothesis that there exist objectively observable juridical norms. These formulated

8. Paul Amselek, *Perspectives critiques d'une réflexion épistémologique sur la théorie du droit: Essai de phénoménologie juridique* (Paris: Librairie générale de droit et de jurisprudence, 1964).
9. The affinity of this formulation to the "pure theory" model of Kelsen is obvious.

norms are "syntactic propositions constituting models."[10] They are instruments of judgments, obligatory in the sense that they are assigned the vocation of having to be compulsorily (*obligatoirement*) respected and executed.

The lawyer must accordingly conceive law not only as an object of cognition and deductive reflection (*homo sapiens*) but as artisan (*homo faber*) who engages in technical activities [*politique juridique*], i.e., the forging of legal instruments and institutions, and technological activities [*art juridique*], i.e., an effort to make the technical instruments more relevant, more systematic, more rational.[11]

Amselek's conclusion is that legal science must seek to observe objectively the "intersubjectivity" of juridical norms. He contrasts this with what he describes as the classical theory, which is concerned with "prediction" or "uncertainty." Phenomenological positivism must study the reasons for a particular legal institution, and accordingly develop a psychological and sociological theory of law. It must, in Amselek's words, have *historicité, mondanité, facticité, temporalité*. He contrasts this with what he regards as the classical view, according to which the subject that perceives is simply a receptacle of the outer world.[12]

The most elaborate application of this approach to legal institutions, in Amselek's study, is the nature of corporate personality, which he describes as one of phenomenological relativity. This is contrasted with what, according to Amselek, is the traditional approach to corporate legal personality as an absolute.[13]

b. The Natur der Sache

A much more important and sophisticated attempt to develop a phenomenological approach to the "essence of legal principles

10. Amselek, *Perspectives critiques*, p. 144 (my translation).
11. *Ibid.*, p. 275.
12. *Ibid.*, p. 447.
13. Amselek appears to be unaware that the relativity of the corporate legal personality has, for at least half a century, been discussed by a large number of both Anglo-American and Continental legal philosophers and sociologists, and applied in hundreds of decisions. See Wolfgang Friedmann, *Legal Theory*, 5th ed. (New York: Columbia University Press, 1967), pp. 206 ff.

and institutions"—which is neither positivistic, i.e., confined to the ordering and interpretation of the various elements of a legal order "posited" by either legal authority or empirical data—nor a natural law philosophy in the sense that legal principles and precepts are derived from an immutable order of things posited by God or reason—is that described by the term *Natur der Sache*. The concept itself is much older than the specific version of the phenomenological legal theory which now uses it. As long ago as 1883 the German jurist Puchta said:

> If the judge finds himself deserted by the outer forces, he must derive the proper legal norm from the principles of the existing law (not from the so-called natural law); basing himself on the nature of the thing [*Natur der Sache*] he obtains the principle by way of juristic deduction and analogy.[14]

In modern times, and especially in postwar German and French jurisprudence, the *Natur der Sache* has become the key concept for the many attempts to steer between the Scylla of positivism and the Charybdis of natural law philosophy. And just as the phenomenological movement in philosophy has been almost entirely a preserve of German and French thinkers, so the representatives of this particular type of juristic thinking have also been German and French. In the following pages a brief analysis of the most important representatives of this school of thought will be given.

It is only in the present century that contemporary jurists have sought to link the concept of the *Natur der Sache* with the phenomenological concept of *Wesenheit* and the psychological-philosophical concept of *Gestalt*. What is common to the manifold contemporary juristic philosophies of the *Natur der Sache* is the belief that legal concepts and institutions have certain immanent properties, just as phenomenological philosophy has discovered such properties in the phenomena of the world apprehended by the individual and Gestalt psychology has applied its theory to the interpretation of behavior. We may also compare the attempts of these jurists to isolate certain typical structures and qualities of legal institutions with the concern of modern sociologists and philosophers for "types" of social institutions and human behavior. Thus, Max Weber, in his classic study, bases his

14. Georg Friedrich Puchta, *Pandekten* (Leipzig: Barth, 1883), p. 22.

categorization of sociological concepts on "types" of social behavior, of economic and technical distribution, of dominion, of
associations, and of legal thought.[15] The German philosopher
Eduard Spranger, in a widely read work entitled *Lebensformen*,
has isolated six "basic types of individuality": theoretical man;
economic man; aesthetic man; social man; power man (*Macht-
mensch*); and religious man.[16]

In all these various approaches, there is a desire to establish
order in the infinite variety and complexity of human and social
phenomena, and to build a bridge between stability and evolution.
But, as the following selective survey will show, the concept of
the *Natur der Sache*—not surprisingly—covers a great variety of
approaches which articulate rather than overcome the inevitable
conflicts of values and ideas that characterize the life of man.

We may begin with Gustav Radbruch, a leading philosopher
of the present century, one of whose last contributions was an
essay on "the nature of the thing as form of juristic thought." [17]
Except for a tentative and fragmentary conversion to a kind
of natural law philosophy after World War II, and under the
impact of the brutalities of the Nazi regime, Radbruch, through
his main work, is the most important representative of the legal
philosophy of relativism. This means, following Max Weber's
celebrated essay on the value neutrality of science, that there are
no absolutely and scientifically binding legal values.[18] It is the
task of legal philosophy as *Kulturwissenschaft* to realize values.
It is a matter of practical, not pure, reason. Legal philosophy is
concerned with three essential tasks:

1. The clarification of the means appropriate to reach a given
   legal object.

15. *Grundriss der Sozialökonomik*, pt. 3, *Wirtschaft und Gesellschaft*,
2d ed. (Tübingen: Mohr, 1925), English translation by Edward Shils and
Max Rheinstein, *Max Weber on Law in Economy and Society*, 20th Century Legal Philosophy Series, Vol. VI (Cambridge: Harvard University
Press, 1954).
16. Eduard Spranger, *Lebensformen*, 6th ed. (Halle: Niemeyer, 1927),
English translation from 5th ed. by Paul J. W. Pigors, *Types of Man*
(Halle: Niemeyer, 1928).
17. Gustav Radbruch, "Die Natur der Sache als juristische Denkform,"
in *Festschrift zu Ehren von Rudolf Laun*, ed. Gustaf Hernmarck (Hamburg: Toth, 1948), p. 157.
18. Max Weber, "Der Sinn der Wertfreiheit der soziologischen und
ökonomischen Wissenschaften," in *Gesammelte Aufsätze zur Wissenschaftslehre* (Tübingen: Mohr, 1922).

2. The clarification of legal values and postulates to their ultimate philosophical foundations.
3. The analysis of possible legal systems in their affinities and antinomies.

The choice between conflicting values is a matter of personal decision; it is a question not of science but of conscience. Law must be directed toward the realization of justice, but—as Aristotle said two and a half thousand years ago—justice as a general idea can say no more than that equals shall be treated equally. The filling out with concrete content of this idea of equality between equals varies according to conflicting philosophies of life and values.

How does the concept of the *Natur der Sache* fit into this philosophy? For Radbruch, it is the moving force and the transformation of legal institutions in response to social change. It is thus a dynamic concept. As an illustration, Radbruch cites the relatively new discipline of labor law. Whereas the civil law as embodied in the German civil code and other civil legal codifications only knows legal subjects who conclude contracts with each other by free resolutions, labor law represents the development of combinations and associations of employers and employees. This leads to a new type of legal institution, the collective agreement, which expresses this new type of social relationship. It is the *Natur der Sache*, the nature of this new type of social relationship between interest groups, that creates new legal forms, institutions, and procedures. The *Natur der Sache* is thus an agent of legal progress. In Germany, for example, special courts deal with all types of disputes between employers and employees, as well as with the interpretation of collective agreements. Generally, the discipline of *Arbeitsrecht* has established itself as a new branch of law which cannot be allocated to the traditional categories of public and private law but contains elements of both. But what Radbruch describes as *Natur der Sache* appears to be essentially a paraphrase of the continuing need of the law to adapt itself to new social developments, and to create legal concepts, principles, and institutions which reflect such social developments.

A more static concept of the *Natur der Sache*, which seeks to derive certain "highest principles of law" from the essence of legal institutions, is stressed by a contemporary German legal philosopher, Helmut Coing.[19] For Coing, unlike Radbruch, the *Natur der Sache* contains elements of natural law. There are certain basic values, such as the elementary feeling of justice which is expressed by the familiar principles of the Roman jurists: *Honeste vivere, neminem laedere, suum cuique tribuere.* The basic principles of justice are determined by certain basic moral values as well as by changing social data. Among the basic values, derived from the nature of the corresponding institutions, are the autonomous dignity of personality, the function of the state as a protector of material existence, the values of utility represented by economic institutions, and the values of truth and free inquiry represented by universities and other institutions of research. Among specific legal institutions, contract is based on the principle of reciprocity, whereas marriage implies at least a minimum of permanence and community between the spouses.

Similarly, another contemporary German jurist has spoken of

institutional principles, . . . insofar as the perspectives of the nature of the thing and of the function of the institution in a given legal system makes certain principles appear as necessary. "Necessary" in this sense is, for example, the *par conditio creditorum* as a principle of bankruptcy. . . . An institutional principle implies, because of its function, a number of consequences attached to the nature of the thing. Tutelage demands a certain delimited circle of functions of the guardian, the dominion implicit in *iura in rem* demands a certain publicity, freedom of contract demands a definition of legal transactions which the law does not recognize.[20]

What is stable and what is variable in the nature of legal institutions and principles was pointed out a generation earlier by François Gény, a French jurist, who did not use the concept of the "nature of things." His legal philosophy was strongly influenced by Henri Bergson, whose philosophy of metaphysical intuition and creative evolution has definite links with the philosophy of one of the leading phenomenologists, Gabriel Marcel.[21] In his great work, *Science et technique en droit privé*

19. Coing, *Die obersten Grundsätze des Rechts* (Heidelberg: Schneider, 1947); *Grundzüge der Rechtsphilosophie* (Berlin: de Gruyter, 1950).
20. Josef Esser, *Grundsatz und Norm in der richterlichen Fortbildung des Privatrechts* (Tübingen: Mohr, 1956), p. 104.
21. See Spiegelberg, *Phenomenological Movement*, II, 430 ff.

positif, Gény applied to the law the classical distinction between thought and will, knowledge and action.[22] Corresponding to this, in legal science, is the distinction between science and technique. The latter supplies the element of creative intuition (Bergson), the ability to see the phenomena of life in their living unity instead of dissecting them into categories. By means of juristic technique—which Gény calls *Le Construit*—the lawyer molds the given material to make it correspond to the needs of social life. Accordingly, Gény divides legal materials, which form the basis of legal interpretation and action, into four categories, called *donnés:*

1. *Le donné réel*, which consists of the physical and psychological realities, such as the facts of sex or climate, religious traditions, and social habits of people.
2. *Le donné historique*, which consists of all the facts, traditions, and circumstances of environment which mold those physical and psychological facts in a particular manner.
3. *Le donné rationnel*, which consists of those principles which derive from the reasonable consideration of human relations. It embodies most of the principles of the classical natural law, the fundamental postulates of justice such as the sanctity of human life, the development of human faculties, and more specifically such strongholds of liberal creed as freedom of thought and inviolability of the person.
4. *Le donné idéal*, which provides a dynamic element, as it embodies the moral aspirations of a particular period and civilization. It is a result of intuition rather than of reason and, for this last of the four principal social data, Gény admits that it overlaps to a considerable extent with the sphere of technique.

Clearly, at least the first three of Gény's four *donnés* comprise much of what later jurists have described as the *Natur de Sache* or the *nature des choses*. As a contemporary German jurist has pointed out, a large element in the *Natur der Sache* consists of

22. Gény, *Science et technique en droit privé positif*, 4 vols. (Paris: Tenin, 1914–24).

the physical factors which determine, for example, the legal rules on the period of gestation or on paternity.[23] Whereas jurists such as Reinach or Coing are essentially concerned with the distillation of certain essential and immutable characteristics of legal institutions, two contemporary jurists, one German and one French, give a far more ambitious place to the *Natur der Sache*. In their analysis it becomes nothing less than the directive factor in the evolution of the legal order in its continuing struggle for the liberation of man. For Werner Maihofer, the *Natur der Sache* is a superpositive yardstick of rights and justice, an extrastatutory source of law, which brings the abstract imperatives of the law into a court with the norms of conduct prescribed by the social situation of a concrete legal condition.[24] A typical way of doing this is the use of certain general legal clauses, such as "good faith" (*Treu und Glauben*) in modern codifications, e.g., the German Civil Code. The provision in Article 242 of the German Civil Code that all obligations must be performed in good faith has enabled the courts to develop and modify the law in accordance with changing social needs and concepts of justice. Thus, during the height of the inflation that prevailed in Germany in the 1920s and led to a catastrophic slump in the value of the currency, the equilibrium of contracts, and of the mutual obligations between creditor and debtor, was profoundly disturbed by the inflation which enabled debtors to discharge huge obligations at purely nominal cost. The courts used the general clause of Article 242 to effect a general adjustment of obligations in favor of the creditors, which was subsequently consolidated by statute. It may be said that in doing so the courts looked to the true nature of the contract, and the reciprocity of obligations implicit in it, as against a purely formalistic and nominalistic interpretation.

As we have seen above, Maihofer links his philosophy of the *Natur der Sache* with the phenomenological-existentialist approach. For him, natural law becomes an existential law and an instrument for the implementation of a human order *digne*

23. Erich Fechner, *Rechtsphilosophie* (Tübingen: Mohr, 1956), pp. 146 ff.
24. Maihofer, "Die Natur der Sache," *Archiv für Rechts- und Sozialphilosophie*, no. 44 (1958), pp. 145–74; see also the same author's "Le Droit naturel comme dépassement du droit positif."

d'être vécu, an order that is directed toward the greatest satisfaction of human needs and development of human faculties.

Probably the most ambitious and comprehensive attempt to make the concept of the *nature des choses* the link between phenomenological and existentialist approaches to life and law is that of a French-Greek jurist published a few years ago.[25] In the Introduction, the author defines as his objective the overcoming of the Kantian dualism between fact and value by "an immanent sense of the real," conceived as a totality of fact and value.[26] In Poulantzas' wide-ranging and searching essay, the most important intellectual godfathers are Hegel, Husserl, Scheler, Hartmann, and, among jurists, Maihofer. From Husserl, the author derives the insight that "the values—the ideal beings —have themselves an essence, they 'are.' " To Scheler and Hartmann, he owes the analysis of the *être de valeur*, the reality of values. But it is Hegel's phenomenology which more than any other system of thought inspires Poulantzas. The most characteristic aspect of Hegel's philosophy, in all its manifold manifestations, has been the overcoming of opposites, both in a logical and in a historical sense. In his *Phenomenology of the Spirit*, Hegel proposed the ontological principle of objectivization or exteriorization (*Entäusserung*). Man, according to Hegel, cannot become conscious of himself except by a dialectical process, expressed in the triad of thesis, antithesis, and synthesis. In developing Hegel's thesis that man exists only in relation to others,[27] Poulantzas states:

> Man is only by his projects, his acts in the world; the project is creator of an ideal, of a value which itself incites toward action and the realization of the project that constitutes human existence. Human existence is by its ontological structure, value. Man cannot exist, cannot act, except by virtue of values, and these values are created because man must exist, because man is ek-sistence, i.e., a project directed toward the future, which transcends the given toward the future.[28]

25. Nicos Poulantzas, *Nature des choses et droit: Essai sur la dialectique du fait et de la valeur* (Paris: Librairie général de droit et de jurisprudence, 1965).
26. *Ibid.*, pp. 8–9.
27. We might mention here that reciprocity, the awareness of others as part of the knowledge of oneself, is also brought out in Fichte's philosophy.
28. Poulantzas, *Nature des choses*, pp. 82–83.

However, whereas Hegel is Poulantzas' intellectual godfather, Marx is his political prophet. The market economy is seen as an alienation, and therefore a destruction, of the true human individual. A true realization of man is through work, which leads to the social and economic foundations of a society that realizes human liberty. In this context, Poulantzas introduces the qualification that values (*valeurs*) must be "valables" in order to be recognized:

> An economic and social system requires a positive axiological significance for the establishment of legal values, to the extent that it historically constitutes a step of the human struggle against the circumstances [*donnés*] which alienate man and turn him into an object, toward the creation of a "human" universe, where man can create his proper dignity and realize his generic being.[29]

Like Maihofer, Poulantzas interprets the *nature des choses* as leading the legal order toward an increasing realization of human liberty, but with a definite emphasis on "work" as a predominant value in the Marxist sense.

c. The "value" phenomenology of Scheler and Hartmann and Latin American legal philosophy

The main contribution of Max Scheler and Nicolai Hartmann to phenomenology has been their demonstration that values are real, objective, and autonomous essences (*Wesenheiten*), which can be intuitively experienced and apprehended by man.[30] Using Aristotle's "scale of virtues" as a base, Scheler established five criteria to determine rank in the hierarchy of values. Hartmann developed this approach further by establishing a hierarchy of values, which does not mean the acceptance of an invariable and absolutely valid "good." In Hartmann's philosophy, there is a clear differentiation of the ethic of values from natural law philosophy, insofar as the latter establishes an

29. *Ibid.*, p. 342.
30. Max Scheler, *Der Formalismus in der Ethik und die materiale Wertethik* (1913; 5th ed. rev., Bern: Francke Verlag, 1966), English translation by Manfred Frings and Roger Funk, *Formalism in Ethics and Non-Formal Ethics of Values* (Evanston, Ill.: Northwestern University Press, 1973). Nicolai Hartmann, *Ethik* (1925; 3d ed. unrev., Berlin: de Gruyter, 1949), English translation by Stanton Coit, *Ethics* (New York: Macmillan, 1932).

absolute and immutable hierarchy of values. The "good" for Hartmann is the realization, for each individual, of the utmost of which he is capable, the attainment of the highest value in his scale. This gives an existentialist aspect to Hartmann's value philosophy.

Building on the theories of Scheler and Hartmann, the Spanish-Mexican jurist Luis Recaséns Siches has sought to reconcile the objectivity of juridical values with the historicity of juridical ideals.[31] Luis Recaséns Siches distinguishes five sources of historicity: (1) the fact that social reality is diverse and changing; (2) the diversity of obstacles which in each situation must be overcome in order to materialize the requirements of value in such a situation; (3) the lessons drawn from practical experience as to the adequacy of the means of materializing a value in a concrete situation; (4) the priorities raised by the gradations of urgency of the social needs which historical events bring up; and (5) a multiplicity of values, some of which refer to universal human qualities and needs, whereas others are attached to specific historical conditions, which engender particular norms for each community and each situation. As to the hierarchy of values, Recaséns Siches seeks to demonstrate that humanism or personalism, which regards the state and the law as means in the service of the individual, is superior to transpersonalism, which regards the individual human person as a mere means in the service of the state, because individual consciousness is the center and proof of all other realities, and because human life, in its relation to the world, is a first point of departure for all philosophy.

Another Mexican jurist, Eduardo García Máynez, while accepting the objective validity of juridical values, declares that they have various forms of relativity, which he classifies into three groups: (1) relativity to persons; (2) relativity to concrete situations; and (3) relativity to space and time.

Probably the most influential of the Latin-American legal philosophers who have sought to combine the Neo-Kantian

---

31. The principal work of Luis Recaséns Siches has been translated under the title "Human Life, Society and Law," by Gordon Ireland, in *Latin-American Legal Philosophy*, 20th Century Legal Philosophy Series, Vol. III (Cambridge: Harvard University Press, 1948), pp. 1–341. See also his own account of his legal philosophy in *Natural Law Forum*, III, no. 1 (1958), 148.

thought of Kelsen with existentialist and phenomenological thinking is the Argentianian Carlos Cossio. Law is an "egological object," i.e., it is human conduct in its intersubjective perspective. Cossio is mainly concerned with the analysis of the judicial decision, which he divides into three elements: the logical structure given by a basic framework, such as a constitution; the contingent elements of a situation, which are supplied by the circumstances of the case; and the juridical evaluation which the judge imposes on these two elements in a given situation. Having quoted some Argentinian decisions, in which the court pointed out the need to make decisions in accordance with principles of justice and public utility, Cossio observes that "in the absence of any norm, they are obliged to endeavour by following the principles of the legislation in force, or basic norms of what may be considered just, to arrive at a decision founded on a conception of justice." He calls this process the "phenomenology of the decision." [32]

Some Critical Observations on Phenomenological Theories of Law and Justice

THE SURVEY of representative phenomenological approaches to law and justice which has been attempted in the preceding pages reveals three major elements—even though not all of the aforementioned theories stress all three of them:

1. The bridging of the antinomy between fact and value, by demonstrating that values are objective realities, immanent in the appreciation of the world of facts.
2. The application of the phenomenological concepts of *Wesenheit* and *Wesensschau* to the world of law, leading to the distillation of essential and "immanent" properties of legal concepts and institutions.
3. The dynamic use of the fusion of fact and value, particularly in the concept of the *Natur der Sache,* for a theory of social change and human progress, i.e., as a way to attain certain ideals of law.

32. See Cossio, "Phenomenology of the Decision," trans. Gordon Ireland, in *Latin-American Legal Philosophy,* pp. 343–400.

Now we must inquire to what extent these attempts have succeeded, and in particular whether they have opened up new avenues to the solution of the perennial tension between law and justice, between the law as it is and the law as it ought to be.

Among the legal phenomenologists, Poulantzas has made the most elaborate attempt to bridge the philosophical gap between fact and value.[33] "Human existence is, by its very ontological structure, a value. Man cannot exist, cannot act, except by virtue of values." [34] "The act constitutes the first substrata of human existence: it is through the act conceived as the 'practical activity' of man at a given place and at a given moment of history that we must perceive the process of comprehension of juridical values." [35]

It is, as we have seen, essentially Hegel's philosophy of the phenomenology of the spirit that has inspired Poulantzas. Hegel "was the first to state the basic ontological problem for the philosophy of law, of the ontological 'reciprocity' of human beings which, according to him, consists in the 'reconnaissance' (*Erkenntnis*) of the self in that of another." [36] But Poulantzas—who, in his own ideology of law, adopts the Marxist concept of "work" (*travail*) as the true realization of the human spirit, i.e., an essentially socialist conception—entirely omits to tell us to what conclusions Hegel's philosophy of the realization of the self through his relationship with others has led him. For Hegel, the true "liberty" of man—which unfolds in an enormous edifice of dialectical triads, from elementary being to the state—is only realized in the state. And as anybody can read in Hegel's *Philosophy of Right,* the final realization of the human individual, the fulfillment of the *Weltgeist,* both in its logical and its historical unfolding, is the hereditary Prussian monarchy of Frederick William IV, the monarchy under which Hegel held his chair at Berlin. In substituting the Marxist value of "work" for the Hegelian value of the nationalist monarchic state as the perfection of the world spirit, Poulantzas adopts, in fact, one ideology in substitution for another. The fusion of fact and value proves to be an illusion. Poulantzas shares with Maihofer the belief in

33. See, in particular, Poulantzas, *Nature des choses,* sec. 2, "La Relation entre fait et le valeur," pp. 82–103.
34. *Ibid.,* p. 83.
35. *Ibid.,* p. 90.
36. *Ibid.,* pp. 114–15.

the development of human freedom and human faculties as an existential role. In his most recent essay, Maihofer has described the progress toward human freedom and the classless society as two of the essential realities of our time.[37] All this means disguising the perennial conflicts of values under pretended objective realizations of values in the factual activity of man.

In a more specific field, the illusion that facts constitute legal values per se is demonstrated in Poulantzas' discussion of "la situation de fait dans le droit." [38]

The so-called *Faktische Vertragsverhältnisse* has been the subject of a number of recent analyses by German jurists.[39] The term is applied to a number of relationships in the fields of associations, employment, rent, and provision of activities where the relationship is outside the forms prescribed by the relevant statutes, as condition of the legal validity of the relationship. In various ways, the courts have come to attribute certain legal consequences to these de facto relationships. For Poulantzas, this means the "direct and immediate transposition of the practical situation, of the infra-structure, into the juridical universe." [40] But as the author of the leading treatise on the subject has observed:

> It is improper to appeal to the nature of the "Faktische Vertragsverhältnisse" as *a priori* data, in order to exclude the prevailing statutory regulation as contrary to such nature. . . . The "Faktische Vertragsverhältnisse" must be subjected to the same treatment as any other contractual relationship which is deficient from the standpoint of the legislator. In other words, these factual situations are simply one of many ways in which the constantly continuing evolution of social facts and relationships challenges the existing legal order and demands some legal adjustment to bring the law into conformity with social realities.[41]

The interrelationship between law and social change has been the subject of a number of analyses,[42] but this is a very different

37. Maihofer, "Ideologie und Naturrecht."
38. Poulantzas, *Nature des choses*, pp. 290 ff.
39. See, notably, Spiros Simitis, *Die faktische Vertragsverhältnisse als Ausdruck der gewandelten sozialen Funktion der Rechtsinstitute des Privatrechts* (Frankfurt am Main: Klostermann, 1957).
40. Poulantzas, *Nature des choses*, p. 292.
41. Simitis, *Die faktische Vertragsverhältnisse*, p. 104.
42. See, for example, Wolfgang Friedmann, *Law and Social Change in Contemporary Britain* (London: Stevens, 1951), and *Law in a Changing Society* (Baltimore, Md.: Penguin, 1964).

proposition from the identification of fact and value, from the assertion that certain factual relationships as such have "immanent" legal value. It is only to the extent that legislators and courts respond to the new relationships—which they do with much discrimination—that legal values are adjusted to new social facts. As one of many examples, we might cite the way in which the law takes note of the cohabitation of a man and a woman who are not legally married. For certain purposes, but not for others, this relationship may be recognized as legally relevant. Thus, during World War II, the military authorities in Britain regarded a de facto wife as entitled to a dependent's allowances to the same extent as a properly married wife. But for most other purposes, e.g., rights of succession, legitimacy of children, etc., the legal distinction between marriage and de facto relationships remained unchanged. The legal order, i.e., the system of legal values, responds—sometimes quickly, sometimes haltingly, and sometimes not at all—to new phenomena of society, but this does not mean the fusion of fact and value.

The concept of *Natur der Sache*, which plays so considerable a part in postwar German legal philosophy, is undoubtedly a valuable one. It has been of great help in distilling the essence, the inherent characteristics, of legal institutions from their more transient and variable aspects. But the *Natur der Sache* cannot by-pass the conflict of values and ideologies. Writing shortly before the outbreak of the World War I—when the interferences of public law with private property were insignificant compared with what they are today—Reinach described indivisibility and transferability by consent between assignor and assignee as immanent qualities of *Eigentum*. But this is not only an entirely civilian concept of property—quite different from the common law concept of property, which through the institutions of trust, estate, and in other ways accepts both the divisibility of the rights inherent in property and degrees of property (in land law)—it also assumes an essentially individualistic order, which is based on the sanctity of private property. Today, property is a composite of private law powers and public law restrictions (e.g., with regard to the tenure of land) which is a response to, and will continue to be modified by, continuing changes in the relation of private and public interests.

While it may be possible to isolate certain essential and "immanent" characteristics of property contract, marriage, and other legal institutions, this tells us little about such important questions as whether a breach of contract or liability for a tort shall be based on fault or the act as such, i.e., the interference with the protected interest of the other side—the contract partner as the victim of an accident, the employee injured in the course of his employment, and so on. Even if we accept monogamy as the essence of marriage—a Western but by no means a universal conception—this does not tell us anything as to the permissibility of divorce or, granting such permissibility, the proper grounds for divorce. In all these domains there have been profound changes within the last generation.

A telling illustration of the pitfalls of disguising a particular social ideology under the objective-sounding name of *Natur der Sache* is a 1953 decision of the West German Supreme Court, interpreting the legal status of the married woman in the light of the Bonn Constitution of 1949.[43] The Court declared it to be in the *Natur der Sache* that the husband, as head of the family, represents it toward the "outer world" (*nach aussen*), while the wife devotes herself to the "internal order" (*innere Ordnung*). This interpretation—which has been sharply criticized by one of the leading philosophers of the *Natur der Sache* [44]—is, of course, simply an infusion of the Court's own very conservative view of the respective social functions of husband and wife into the Constitution, a by no means uncommon phenomenon. It is totally at variance with the increasing equality and independence of the married woman in matters of child education, business and professional responsibilities, and administration of assets. Like the related, though not identical, natural law philosophy, the *Natur der Sache* thus can easily serve to give to specific political and social ideologies the halo of "immanence" or "a natural order of things."

Finally, to what extent can a phenomenological approach to law—in the different forms discussed earlier, i.e., through the alleged fusion of fact and value or through the apprehension of certain essential characteristics of legal institutions—point the way toward a specific social goal? The answer to this question follows from what has been said with respect to the first two basic elements of phenomenological jurisprudence. Maihofer and

43. B.G.Z. 11, App. 34 (1953).
44. Maihofer, "Ideologie und Naturrecht," pp. 121 ff.

Poulantzas assert that the progress toward human liberty and the realization of human faculties is in the "nature of things," an inevitable phenomenon of history. Any observer of the contemporary scene, with its increasing encroachment of giant slum cities, mass media, governmental and commercial data controls, and the gradual destruction of the environment of a life *digne d'être vécue*, cannot but express some surprise at the naïveté of such assertions. But is it tenable even as a matter of theoretical analysis? Is it not another case of the wish being father to the thought? Poulantzas himself seems to give the case away by speaking of "valeurs valables," i.e., by distinguishing between acceptable and unacceptable values. In his Preface to Poulantzas' book, a noted French legal philosopher has observed:

> Can we subscribe to this axiom, that the only "valeurs valables" consist in the exhortation of universal liberty and of the power of man? If this were so, I ask myself what profit we should derive from it for what matters, the finding of legal solutions. The task of the judge is to decide between conflicting interests, to give to each what is due, to divide assets between different people none of whom can be accorded absolute liberty. The beautiful utopia of liberty and the infinite power of man is of no help for it gives us no criterion with regard to such allocations. . . . And in practice, from where do we derive the law? Is Mr. Poulantzas not compelled to rely on the facts of the "infrastructure" whatever they may be, to the blind march of history whether or not it serves the unfolding of universal liberty? No doubt, inspired by the Marxist dogma of progress, it will be answered: History marches inevitably toward liberty. But nothing is less sure. Do we then have to conclude that, in terms of his own enterprise, Mr. Poulantzas has relapsed into a flat positivism, having failed in his effort to overcome the dualism and to construe a synthesis between fact and value? [45]

One is reminded of the great illusion of an earlier French jurist, Léon Duguit, who, inspired by Durkheim, proclaimed that social solidarity was a fact, and, from that fact, deduced limitations on the sovereignty of the state, class cooperation, and the rejection of any individual right, concluding with Auguste Comte that "the only right which any man can possess is the right always to do his duty." [46] In all these formulations, neither the

45. M. Villey, Preface to Poulantzas, *Nature des choses*, pp. x–xi.
46. Comte, *Système politique positive*, 5th ed. (Paris: Au Siège de la société positiviste, 1929), I, 361.

conflict of ideologies nor the dichotomy of fact and value is abolished; they are disguised by being proclaimed as if they were facts of human existence, of social life, or of history. What Carlos Cossio described as "phenomenology of the decision" is simply an analysis of the public policy and lawmaking factors in the judicial decision, as they have been formulated, without the language of phenomenology, by such jurists as Gény, Pound, Cardozo, and Radbruch, or in the language of Article I of the Swiss Civil Code.[47]

The conflict of values is an ineradicable part of human life. Phenomenological interpretations of law have helped in methodology and in the elimination of such conflicts, but they have not abolished them.

47. This celebrated article directs the judge to decide as he would if he were a legislator where he finds a gap in the law that he cannot fill by ordinary means of judicial interpretation.

The Phenomenological Description of Law

Paul Amselek

IT IS STRIKING TO NOTE how well the dictum of "the return to things themselves" (*zu den Sachen selbst*), formulated almost three-quarters of a century ago by Edmund Husserl, coincides with the prevailing spirit of our own civilization. The distrust of abstractions and of the distortions inherent in systems, the will to grasp things directly, in their sober, frank, and phenomenal purity—these are the attitudes which typify the mind of today and which permeate most types of intellectual activity. One has only to think of modern artistic expression, which is completely permeated by the desire to perceive and to represent reality as it is, as it appears to the direct gaze. This drive "toward the concrete"[1] is probably bound up with the particular conditions of the industrial society, such as the development of the audiovisual mass media, which condition us to direct contact with things themselves, and to that acceleration of history and of the rhythms of life which tends to exclude all the digressions which were the delight of the speculation of former times. In addition, there exists, perhaps, a kind of slow pendulum movement in the history of civilization, as if at certain times the human mind tended to become unharnessed from the real, and from direct contact with things, only to react by attempting to return to the source. Such a pendulum movement is suggested, at least in Western thought, by the unfolding of the centuries: first the sixteenth, with the Renaissance (whose themes are so

Translated from the French by Raoul Mortley.

1. To quote the striking title of Jean Wahl's book, *Vers le concret* (Paris: Vrin, 1932)

[367]

close to those of Husserl); [2] then the seventeenth, dominated by abstract metaphysico-theological speculation; then the eighteenth, swinging back to the sixteenth; then the nineteenth, with the renewal of abstract metaphysico-scientific speculation; and finally the twentieth, with its phenomenological reaction.

In any case, it should be noticed that the movement toward the concrete, which is basic to the twentieth century and which phenomenology attempts to handle in a systematic way, has not developed uniformly in all fields. Certain areas present particular difficulties for the program of the "return to things themselves," and that of "Law" constitutes a typical example. There are probably few fields in which the consciousness of what is discussed and dealt with, or of the types of activity engaged in, is more tangled and confused. In daily experience, and this applies equally to the lawyer and to the man in the street, our picture of the object Law is furnished by a few vague clichés which are rather uninformative as to the real structure of the thing in question. If an author ventures to go beyond these everyday clichés, he encounters considerable difficulties: "Tracking down a definition of law is an undertaking which drives one to despair," notes Virally. [3]

What is the explanation of this curious situation? One must, of course, take certain data into consideration—in the first place, the basic fact that law is a "human thing." It is a fact that one naturally tends to pay more attention to that which is outside and

2. See Jean-François Revel, *Histoire de la philosophie occidentale*, 2 vols. (Paris: Stock, 1968–70), II, 45 ff. The author shows clearly that the Renaissance was characterized by a reaction against the "hearsay culture" of the Middle Ages: "After a thousand years of theories which were too easily produced, too easily refuted, too numerous, and too ingenious for what they set out to explain, after so many centuries of mushrooming philosophies, the catch-cry became the search for the authentic."
3. Michel Virally, *La Pensée juridique* (Paris: Librairie générale de droit et de jurisprudence, 1960), p. 1. Cf. Giorgio del Vecchio, *Philosophy of Law*, trans. Thomas O. Martin (Washington, D.C.: Catholic University Press, 1953), p. 244: "Each of us knows approximately what Law is. The precise definition of the concept, however, presents notable difficulties"; Jacques Leclerc, *Du droit naturel à la sociologie* (Paris: Spes, 1960), I, 53: "Law is one of the most important social realities. Everyone talks about it, and everyone has the impression that he is well acquainted with what he is talking about. The Civil Code is law, and the constitution. But when it comes to defining it exactly, and defining its object, its field, and the characteristics which make law a reality different from all other social realities, agreement ceases, and each jurist functions with his own definition."

foreign to oneself, rather than to one's own behavior, or to one's way of life and its component parts, which is probably why those disciplines which deal with natural phenomena are in advance of those which deal with man and human phenomena. It must be added that within our cultural universe law constitutes a very ancient structure with which man has entertained a kind of longstanding tacit complicity, which prevents him from seeing it in a naïve way. One perceives law and legal phenomena only through certain crystallized stereotypes, which often go back to periods very distant in time, and whose power of suggestion, or "signifying" power, has long since disappeared. Law is part of the obscurity which swathes the general environment of things which are familiar. It should also be pointed out that one is constantly involved in the legal experience—which is comparable (as we shall see) to that of a craftsman—and this proximity eliminates the possibility of an objective approach. As Bergson has pointed out, "The workman's tool is an extension of his arm"; [4] it is, so to speak, part of himself, like "an artificial limb which is an extension of the human organism." [5] It follows that such a workman ceases to be conscious of the presence of the tool used by him; it merges into his own subjectivity. A phenomenon of this kind manifests itself in our relationship with law and legal tools; our contact with them is normally more lived out than thought out.

Two further factors should be added with a view to explaining the confused awareness of law which obtains even in specialized legal circles. On the one hand, it must be recognized that the mechanics of law are not readily grasped. What might be called the outer frame of law, that which is immediately visible (i.e., in practice, principally legal pronouncements or "statements of the law" by public authorities), is far from exhausting the total reality of law; it represents nothing more than a superficial covering. To obtain a complete perspective one has to penetrate into the interior of the mental circuits which underlie this superficial covering and form the very substrate of the law. What must be explored is the particular intention more or less explicitly

---

4. Henri Bergson, *The Two Sources of Morality and Religion*, trans. R. Ashley Audra and Cloudesley Brereton, with W. Horsfall Carter (New York: Holt, 1935), p. 298 (translation slightly modified).

5. Bergson, *Creative Evolution*, trans. Arthur Mitchell (New York: Holt, 1911), p. 141.

ascribed to legal proposals by the men-actors participating in the legal experience; those more or less subtle intellectual processes implied by such instrumental purposiveness must be subjected to examination. Such an investigation is, of course, highly difficult. The exploration of that which takes place within the human mind, that "kingdom of dissimulation" in the words of Paul Valéry, is always problematic; one constantly comes up against the unformulated, the unconscious, the allusive, the obscure, and the uncertain. On the other hand, it should be noted that those who deal with the philosophy of law and jurisprudence have often failed to operate from a disinterested point of view, working with presuppositions (conscious or unconscious) of a religious, metaphysical, ethical, or political nature. Thus the image proper of law has tended to become increasingly obscure and confused, with the syncretistic infusion of foreign elements. It could be said that legal thought as we have it from theoretical jurists, particularly within the university milieu, is distorted to a large extent by the somewhat insidious influence of our heritage of legal philosophies, which form an obstacle to the naïve approach.

It is true that the absence of a clear consciousness of the object Law does not in practice prevent one from talking about it, using it, or making it the basis of theoretical constructions.[6] This is an example of a more general fact which one meets in many other areas, namely, the remarkable success of the *approximate* in ordinary human experience; one manages to live with the approximate without too much difficulty. But it must be noted that this fundamental failing is at the root of many nebulous or even absurd forms of reasoning, as well as of numerous valueless discussions and false perspectives, which vitiate many of the opinions expressed about the law and contaminate the ideas of some of the most scholarly books, even those of a purely technical or dogmatic character.[7] The fact that it is possible to adapt

6. "The idea of law, and particularly that of positive law, would seem to be of necessity absolutely familiar to the thinking of jurists. Is not law their only goal, and could they reasonably hope to attain it if they had not first grasped and were at all times in possession of its essence? However, this is far from being the case" (François Gény, *Science et technique en droit privé positif* [Paris: Sirey, 1914], I, 42–43).

7. See, on this, Paul Amselek, *Méthode phénoménologique et théorie du droit* (Paris: Librairie générale de droit et de jurisprudence, 1964), pp. 86 ff.

oneself to the approximate in daily experience should not serve to conceal its inevitably negative implications. In this respect, the use of the phenomenological method of returning to things themselves, and of entering once more into full possession of the law itself, seems to be salutary.

THE EXPRESSION "phenomenological *method*" indicates a step which should be emphasized. As I have shown elsewhere,[8] there exists within phenomenological thought a certain method, on the one hand, which is that outlined by Husserl in his writings, and, on the other, certain doctrinal themes, which are debatable and more or less metaphysical, developed by different phenomenologists, including Husserl.[9] This distinction would seem to be fundamental; the theory of law, if it is to see its subject matter in a fresh light, can only gain from contact with the phenomenological method, but purely doctrinal borrowings would lead to greater confusion rather than to genuine elucidation of the ideas involved.

One may agree with Roger Caillois that "phenomenology represents a method of describing things themselves, namely, the world as it appears to direct vision, apart from any conceptual system. . . . This method is neutral and has no realist or idealist metaphysics behind it, any more than the term 'phenomenon' implies a reference to things in themselves; it simply designates the positiveness of the datum as it appears." [10] The principal elements of the method are as follows.

To enable the consciousness to grasp things once more in

8. *Ibid.*, pp. 9, 30 ff.
9. See, on this, Hermann Pos, *Problèmes actuels de la phénoménologie,* Actes du colloque international de phénoménologie (Brussels: Van Breda, 1951), p. 33. The author distinguishes clearly between the methodological aspects of the phenomenological movement and the "ontological, metaphysical, and anthropological consequences" drawn by the different phenomenologists. Cf. Emile Bréhier, *Histoire de la philosophie allemande,* 3d ed. (Paris: Vrin, 1954), pp. 182 ff.
10. Roger Caillois, *Panorama des idées contemporaines,* comp. Gaëtan Picon (Paris: Gallimard, 1957), p. 55. Cf. K. H. Volkmann-Schluck, "La Doctrine de Husserl au sujet de l'idéalité de la signification en tant que problème métaphysique," in *Husserl et la pensée moderne, Phaenomenologica* II (The Hague: Nijhoff, 1959), p. 246: "The term 'phenomenology' designates the concept of a philosophical method which consists in describing and grasping things as they are given and within the limits in which they are given."

their phenomenal or "objectal" (to use a current expression) purity, Husserl suggests that a series of reductions should be performed. This notion has a specific value in phenomenology; as Gaston Berger notes, "The term should not suggest the idea of impoverishment, but that of purification. Phenomenology thus becomes a series of successive purifications." [11] These purifications, by eliminating all impurities which may impair one's communication with things, serve as a progressive unveiling of them in their authentic modality—in their *selbstgegeben*. Three kinds of reduction are involved.

a. *Philosophical reduction* first consists in "diverting one's attention from theories about things to the things themselves." [12] As Ludwig Landgrebe observes,

> Reduction begins with a process of systematic bracketing, by ruling out as invalid any interpretation of being which has its source in philosophical and scientific theories, in order that being may be brought under scrutiny, exactly as primarily and immediately given in experience. Even the horizons within which the daily world makes its appearance are always jointly predetermined by a presupposed scientific and philosophical interpretation of the world. To bracket them in this way means by-passing all explanatory concepts provided by ordinary language, and reexamining the intuition which primarily endowed them with meaning. . . . Here reduction signifies the process of returning through and beyond the world as interpreted immediately or mediately by science, to the world as already lived and given in immediate experience prior to all science.[13]

The task is, then, in Husserl's famous words, "to start again at the beginning," to return deliberately to an originary experience of things.

b. Second, *eidetic reduction* consists in the systematic elimination of the "factual" elements of the object under contemplation, of the accessories of its contingency, with a view to laying bare its fundamental structure, its essence or *eidos*.

When one looks at an object in a way which precludes all

11. Gaston Berger, "La Phénoménologie transcendantale," in *L'Encyclopédie française*, Vol. XIX (1957).

12. *Ibid.*

13. Ludwig Landgrebe, "La Signification de la phénoménologie de Husserl pour la réflexion de notre époque," in *Husserl et la pensée moderne*, *Phaenomenologica* II, p. 226.

empirical investigation of the conditions of its occurrence in the world (Husserl's idea of "factuality," see infra, note 92), one can discern in it, beyond that which is perceived to be variable and contingent, a certain typical structure, which is irreducible in the sense that when it is not present as such and when one causes it to vary in fact or even in the imagination, one is conscious of having another kind of object before one's eyes.[14] It is this typical structure which is to be apprehended and described in its pure state; in fact, it is precisely in virtue of the technique of variation, particularly on the level of the imagination, that it is possible to sort out that which is essential from the different appearances emitted by the object. The *eidos* of the object is constituted by the elements which remain invariable throughout all the variations undergone by the object in one's imagination, that is, the elements without whose presence one is no longer conscious of the same type of object.[15]

These notions of *eidetic reduction* and *typical structure* have been the object of many misunderstandings and of many hasty interpretations. By proposing this experience of eidetic reduction and the seeing of essences (*Wesensschau*), Husserl invites us to do nothing other than undergo once more the already experienced conceptualization of objects. At the basis of one's conceptualizations there is a certain experience, a certain apperception in things of what constitutes their essential properties, their categorial constitution. One's concepts are not developed arbitrarily; they correspond to a certain datum perceived in things by one's

14. "If one keeps no matter what object fixed in its form or category and maintains continuous evidence of its identity throughout the change in modes of consciousness of it, one sees that, no matter how fluid these may be, and no matter how inapprehensible as having ultimate elements, still they are by no means variable without restriction. They are always restricted to a set of *structural types*, which is 'invariable,' inviolably the same: as long as the objectivity remains intended as *this* one and as of this kind, and as long as, throughout the change in modes of consciousness, evidence of objective identity can persist" (Husserl, *Cartesian Meditations: An Introduction to Phenomenology*, trans. Dorion Cairns [The Hague: Nijhoff, 1960], p. 51).

15. It will be noticed that the method of variation developed by Husserl is already present in embryonic form in Hegel, who remarks in his *Théorie de la mesure* (trans. André Doz [Paris: Presses Universitaires de France, 1970], p. 82) that "in the usual manner of representing things to oneself, one considers that one has succeeded in conceiving of how things come to be or cease to be when one sees them as *gradually* (*allmählich*) arising or disappearing."

consciousness. It is this originary experience that Husserl invites us to undertake and to relive systematically, in order to reactivate our conceptual apparatus, to "fill" it with clear intuitions from contact with things themselves; by returning to them in this way, to the essential structures in which they confront our vision, the concepts which we use frequently in our discourse about things cease to be empty shells or purely formal frameworks devoid of any real power of suggestion.

Eidetic investigation represents in this context, from a methodological point of view, the indispensable procedure basic to the exercise of any discipline: "Before working in physics, one must examine what the physical fact actually is, and what its essence is; and the same is true of other disciplines. From the definition of the *eidos* as apprehended by originary intuition, one may draw methodological conclusions for the guidance of empirical research." [16] This observation is obviously valid for the legal disciplines. If one wishes to study to some effect an aspect of law, one must begin by sensing clearly what law is in its typical structure, or run the risk of drifting into syncretism. [17]

c. Finally, *transcendental reduction* constitutes the ultimate stage of phenomenological inquiry. Its aim is to reveal the transcendental subject to itself, to disclose to it the thing "consciousness" by virtue of which it may accede to other things. The method suggested is again that of "bracketing." The subject will try to "bracket off" the world which occupies his consciousness so as to prove itself, through "transparency" as it were, to be pure transcendental ego, pure "consciousness of," directed toward the world.

Thus, in the thought of Husserl, transcendental reduction is a psychological experience of a very special kind, an introspective experiment carried out by the subject on itself which enables his consciousness to perceive itself as such, through reflection on

16. Jean-François Lyotard, *La Phénoménologie* (Paris: Presses Universitaires de France, 1959), pp. 15 ff.
17. "History also shows us a number of juridical systems. But according to Husserl the investigation of relevant historical facts in which just law is manifested remains 'confused,' unless one has determined what just law is, in principle, by a reflection that is not the empirical order" (Maurice Merleau-Ponty, "Phenomenology and the Sciences of Man," in *The Primacy of Perception*, ed. James M. Edie [Evanston, Ill.: Northwestern University Press, 1964], p. 86; reprinted *supra*, Vol. I, pt. 1).

itself in the very act of focusing on the world. Thus the essential structure of the thing consciousness is revealed to the subject, i.e., *intentionality*, the drive toward that which transcends it.

But, as has been shown elsewhere, the invitation for the subject to turn his gaze away from the things with which he is dealing, onto himself, could constitute an epistemological directive of a much wider range of usefulness.[18] For it could be enormously useful, on the threshold of any intellectual discipline, to be fully aware not only of the type of object to be considered but also of the type of operation to be engaged in with regard to this object. Thus it would seem indispensable that jurists, those who "practice law," should be constantly and clearly aware not only of the authentic structure of the object Law but also of the kind of intellectual activity they exercise upon this object. On what basis do they do so; in what transcendental conditions do they approach the subject and study it? It is indispensable that this point should be elucidated. All jurists do not engage in the same type of activity all the time; failure to appreciate this is also a source of syncretism.

Such a broad interpretation of transcendental reduction of course takes us away from that of Husserl; it seems nevertheless to constitute the necessary complement to eidetic reduction in any phenomenological inquiry prior to the exercise of an intellectual discipline.

THE IDEA OF EMPLOYING phenomenology in the field of law is not new; it was developed by Husserl himself. The first systematic applications of it go back to the beginning of the century, with the works of Adolphe Reinach,[19] Fritz Schreier,[20] Felix Kaufmann,[21] Julius Kraft,[22] Karl Reisdorf,[23] and Gerhard

18. See Amselek, *Méthode phénoménologique*, pp. 23, 361 ff.
19. *Die apriorischen Grundlagen des bürgerlichen Rechts* (Halle: Niemeyer, 1913), reedited in 1953 under the title *Zur Phänomenologie des Rechts*.
20. *Grundbegriffe und Grundformen des Rechts*, 1924; *Reine Rechtslehre und Privatrecht, Gesellschaft, Staat und Recht, Untersuchungen zu reinen Rechtslehre, Kelsen-Festschrift*, 1931.
21. *Logik und Rechtswissenschaft* (Tübingen: Mohr, 1922); *Kriterien des Rechts* (Tübingen: Mohr, 1924).
22. *Die wissenschaftliche Bedeutung des phänomenologischen Rechtsphilosophie*, Kantstudien, Vol. XXXI (Hamburg/Leipzig/Berlin, 1926).
23. *Die Grundlegung der Rechtswissenschaft*, 1930.

Husserl,[24] the son of the founder of the phenomenological movement. Since then there have been numerous attempts, to the
extent that an exhaustive bibliography of all books and articles
on law and phenomenology published to date in Germany,
France, Italy, Spain, Latin America (particularly in Argentina),
and elsewhere would probably require a complete volume of its
own.[25]

It must, however, be recognized that the results of all these
efforts have hitherto been extremely disappointing. The application of phenomenology to the field of law has often resulted in
nothing more than hollow and limited verbiage; thus the label of
phenomenology has fallen largely into discredit in legal circles.
"It could not be said from a scientific point of view that phenomenology has contributed to the clarification of problems;
rather, the opposite is the case." [26] "Phenomenology reverts to the
pre-critical period. . . . The phenomenological idea involves a
renewal of the old ontology; it results in a metaphysic long since
out of date, unless it be . . . the counterpart of artistic im-
pressionism." [27] "Heidegger remarked one day: 'The word, when
it is meaningless, is by nature *saying*.' One wonders once again
whether the legal eidetic is not an admirable illustration of
Heidegger's idea." [28]

The causes of this failure are basically the result of the fact
that phenomenology has tended to constitute, in the field of law,
a kind of flag of convenience for different doctrines instead of
seeking to apply a neutral method of observation and description.
Jean-François Revel has described, not without humor, "the
fashion in which the philosopher of today seizes on an aspect of
linguistics, genetics, or psychoanalysis and absconds with it in

24. *Rechtskraft und Rechtsgeltung* (Berlin, 1925); *Recht und Welt*
(1929; reedited, Frankfurt am Main: Klostermann, 1964); *Der Rechtsgegenstand* (Berlin: Springer, 1933); *Recht und Zeit* (Frankfurt am Main:
Klostermann, 1955).

25. Toward a bibliography, see Amselek, *Méthode phénoménologique,*
pp. 30 ff., 453 ff.; Albert Brimo, *Les Grands Courants de la philosophie du
droit et de l'état* (Paris: Pedone, 1967), pp. 424 ff.; and Simone Goyard,
"Essai de critique phénoménologique du droit" (thesis, Sorbonne, 1970),
pp. 462 ff.

26. Jaromir Sedlacek, "L'Oeuvre de François Gény et la science du
droit pure," in *Recueil d'études en l'honneur de François Gény* (Paris:
Sirey, 1935), I, 279.

27. J. Haesaert, *Théorie générale du droit* (Brussels: Bruylant, 1948),
p. 276.

28. Brimo, *Les Grands Courants,* p. 380.

order to digest it and to incorporate it into a metaphysic whose themes are thus updated, but whose essence remains archaic." [29] In the same way, phenomenology has largely been a kind of screen behind which legal philosophers have endeavored to endow old metaphysical theses with a modern flavor.

It should further be noted that other philosophers, tackling law from the outside, are also responsible. They have approached it in a highly superficial way, with the pretext of developing a phenomenology of law, motivated not by the desire to elucidate carefully all aspects of law, but with the intention of seeking out a simple illustration for more or less nebulous theories. Instead of contributing something to law, they have tended more often to use or manipulate it. Such philosophers have thus undertaken to associate phenomenology in the legal context with a certain line of thought, but not with a method of clarifying thought.

These doctrinal versions of the phenomenology of law have developed in two diametrically opposed directions, with variations from one author to another. The first could be termed *axiological* and the second *existentialist* phenomenology.

a. From the point of view of *axiological phenomenology* (which stems from Husserl himself, as well as from Max Scheler and Nicolai Hartmann), "values" have a natural existence as such, although these authors sedulously avoid investigating them or telling us what they are in concrete terms. They are said to be realities which may be apprehended by intuition; faced with an object, the subject senses its "value" more or less to perfection, and on this basis norms are set up. These norms can only be constatations which describe something *seen* by the subject.[30] It may be noted that this approach tends to assimilate the status of the *essences* (*eidos*) of things and that of their *values*. This is particularly clear in authors like Reinach, who are inclined, somewhat oddly, to reduce legal norms to concepts and to treat

29. Revel, *Histoire*, II, 146.
30. "Husserl and the phenomenological school have clearly demonstrated that a norm is in no sense a mystical being, but simply a judgment expressed in a particular grammatical form. That which is expressed in a normative form may be expressed even more forcefully and logically in theoretical truths. The norm, 'love thy neighbor,' thus means in the last analysis, 'it is good to love your neighbor,' 'loving one's neighbor is a positive value'" (N. Alexiev, "L'Acte juridique créateur comme source primaire du droit," in *Le Problème des sources du droit positif*, Annuaire de l'Institut international de philosophie du droit et de sociologie juridique, 1934, p. 194).

them as such. In this way the basic sense of Husserl's *eidos* is lost, meaning as it does the typical structure of objects as given to one's vision. In any case, within this perspective the role of phenomenology is to assist in obtaining a clearer and purer view of the values contained in things. Husserl's principle of "the return to things themselves" would make it possible to rediscover the authentic values of things, of which one's ordinary experience permits only a confused or tangled intuition, through direct observation and through ridding them of their factuality and contingency by the method of eidetic reduction.

On the basis of these a priori positions, the following conclusions are drawn with regard to law. The legal norms set up by public authorities, which apparently constitute in practice the object Law, are simply theoretical statements on the legal values contained in the nature of things, but we are still not told what these "legal values" really are. In order to apply the phenomenological directives, the jurist who wishes to apprehend law correctly must turn his attention away from the legal norms promulgated by those in authority and focus it on things themselves, in order to rediscover an originary intuition of the values they contain. From there the jurist-phenomenologist will formulate authentic legal norms, describing exactly (and far more so than the public authorities) the objectively apprehended legal values. The phenomenological theory of law is thus described as a discipline which "procures norms." [31]

In other words, instead of seriously seeking to elucidate that which in reality is given as the object Law, that is, the legal norms set up in different societies by the public authorities, legal phenomenologists invite us to pay no attention to it! Instead of working on law itself, attempting to restore its original structure, such authors, on the basis of an indefensible prejudgment, claim to be dealing with a so-called legal datum present in things, in other words, with illusions. Such activity has rightly been designated "a vain game of the imagination." [32]

Nevertheless it is not difficult to explain the success that this approach has had in some quarters; its relationship with the traditional metaphysics of the natural law school is clear. The fact that the positive law formulated by public authorities is

31. See, for example, Carlos Cossio, "La Norme et l'impératif chez Husserl," in *Mélanges Roubier* (Paris: Dalloz, 1961), I, 153.
32. Haesaert, *Théorie générale du droit*, p. 65.

imperfect and that adjacent to positive law one can rediscover an authentic law which is independent of the will of men are old and well-known refrains. And this "phenomenology of values" has of course been hailed as a return to natural law.[33]

b. The approach which I have suggested calling *existentialist phenomenology* takes an entirely different direction. Its tenets imply that man possesses complete freedom and responsibility within his existence and that this expresses itself particularly in the establishment of law, although one is not clearly told what law actually is. Man is the only being who creates himself and through whom all values make their appearance, in particular legal values, though we are still not told what they actually are.

> So, in the bright realm of values, we have no excuse behind us, nor justification before us. We are alone, with no excuses. That is the idea I shall try to convey when I say that man is condemned to be free. Condemned, because he did not create himself, yet, in other respects is free; because, once thrown into the world, he is responsible for everything he does. The existentialist does not believe in the power of passion. He will never agree that a sweeping passion is a ravaging torrent which fatally leads a man to certain acts and is therefore an excuse. He thinks that man is responsible for his passion. The existentialist does not think that man is going to help himself by finding in the world some omen by which to orient himself. Because he thinks that man will interpret the omen to suit himself. Therefore, he thinks that man, with no support and no aid, is condemned every moment to invent man.[34]

Such complete freedom in the realm of values, and especially in the realm of legal values, gives rise to a certain giddiness and anguish which take us far from the tranquil intellectual comfort afforded by the idea that law is given "to be discovered":

> In making a decision he can not help having a certain anguish. All leaders know this anguish. That doesn't keep them from acting; on the contrary, it is the very condition of their action. For it

33. See Albert Brimo, *La Doctrine du droit naturel dans la science juridique française contemporaine*, Annales de la Faculté de droit de Toulouse, VI, fasc. 2, 1959, 216 ff.; Brimo, *Les Grands Courants*, pp. 394 ff.; Michel Villey, *Leçons d'histoire de la philosophie du droit* (Paris: Dalloz, 1962), p. 100; and Nicos Poulantzas, "La Renaissance du droit naturel en Allemagne après la seconde guerre mondiale" (diss., Faculté de droit de Paris, 1961).

34. Jean-Paul Sartre, "Existentialism Is a Humanism," trans. Bernard Frechtman, in Sartre, *Existentialism and Human Emotions* (New York: Philosophical Library, 1957), p. 23.

implies that they envisage a number of possibilities, and when they choose one, they realize that it has value only because it is chosen.[35]

As has been seen, this approach leads to a certain conception of man's legal experience: law is a free and arbitrary creation of men in the historical context of their existence. One should be suspicious of any comforting theory which tends to relieve man of this total responsibility by appealing to transcendent entities, situated beyond man himself. Law is entirely the work of man and participates in the absurdity of the human condition.[36] These themes in themselves are not without interest; they even provide, if only through the use of a new vocabulary, some light on the historical experience of men in the legal field. But the problem of the elucidation of the object Law remains intact, i.e., that of the naïve description of its typical structure and of its original and irreplaceable mode of being present (*Gegebenheitsweisen*).[37]

Here again the success which existentialist phenomenology has enjoyed with certain philosophers of law may be explained above all by the close relationship between this approach and the classical themes of legal voluntarism and secular humanism (springing in particular from the French Revolution), which also deny the existence of a natural law, more or less religious in essence, intended to serve as a model for positive law, which is in practice formulated by the public authorities.

Hence it can be seen that, for the most part, phenomenology in the area of law has simply provided an opportunity for ancient legal metaphysical systems to deck themselves out in new finery, thus taking on a new lease of life; both the supporters and the opponents of natural law have tried to obtain their arguments from it. In other words, phenomenology has been nothing but a pretext for transporting old hostilities into a new arena. "But what has law to do with all this?" rightly inquires Albert Brimo.[38]

35. *Ibid.*, pp. 20–21.
36. It has been said that "with Jaspers and Sartre, we are witnessing an inroad of the absurd into the field of legal science" (Albert Brimo, "L'Existentialisme et le fondement du droit," in *Mélanges Gidel* [Paris: Sirey, 1961], p. 87).
37. See *ibid.*, pp. 87 ff.: "Existentialism constitutes a magnificent effort to renew the essential concepts of legal science. . . . It has formulated the problem of the foundations of law in a new way, but provides no new response to the eternal problem: what are legal prescriptions? What is law?"
38. Brimo, *Les Grands Courants*, p. 390.

It seems to me that the real program of a phenomenology of law should be, first, to describe, with the aid of the method of phenomenological elucidation, and of that only, the *eidos* of the thing Law, i.e., that which constitutes the typical elements of its own identity and without which law is no longer itself, and, second, to describe the different kinds of relationships that obtain between man and law, the different kinds of activities relating to law in which men engage. Phenomenological inquiry in the area of law should properly be limited to this description.

It is precisely this task that I propose to undertake. Within the limited context of this paper it will, however, be necessary to restrict our efforts to the first point of the program outlined; [39] an attempt will be made to cast some light on the thing Law, in a somewhat summary way but with the sole aim of indicating the value of the phenomenological method for the legal disciplines, as well as for the social sciences in general. It will be seen that the thing Law puts us into direct contact with some fundamental data of the human condition.

IN ORDER TO RETURN to law itself, and to learn to see it again in its "objectal" purity, the phenomenological approach consists, as has been noted, in the systematic implementation of the method of reduction in both its philosophical and its eidetic senses.

In this respect, one author seems to me to be the precursor of an authentic legal phenomenology, although his work does not formally come under this heading: Hans Kelsen. There has been a general tendency to contrast—radically—Kelsenism with phenomenology.[40] However, what is really at stake here is Kelsen's doctrinal positions in relation to those of phenomenologists of law. From a strictly methodological point of view, it should be

---

39. For an attempt at "transcendental reduction" of the activities of "legal theorists," see Amselek, *Méthode phénoménologique*, pp. 361 ff.

40. See, for example, Georges Gurvitch, *L'Idée de droit social* (Paris: Sirey, 1932), pp. 122 ff.; Carlos Cossio, "Egologische Theorie und reine Rechtslehre," *Osterreichische Zeitschrift für öffentliches Recht*, V (1952), 15 ff., and "La Norme et l'impératif chez Husserl," in *Mélanges Roubier*, pp. 145 ff.; Charles Donius, "L'Analyse existentiale du droit" (diss., Faculty of Law, Strasbourg, 1955), pp. 4 ff.; and Nicos Poulantzas, "Notes sur la phénoménologie et l'existentialisme juridiques," *Archives de philosophie du droit*, VIII (1963), 218. Various other authors who claim, somewhat significantly, an affinity with both Husserl and Kelsen could be quoted, such as Felix Kaufmann, Karl Reisdorf, or Fritz Schreier.

noted that Kelsen has adopted methodological principles which bear a fundamental relationship to those defined by Edmund Husserl. Given that the phenomenological method comes down to an operation of *purification,* is not Kelsen's primary concern the elaboration of a *pure* theory of law (*reine Rechtslehre*), or an eidetic theory of law which restores its own typical structure, its essential meaning, beyond the factual and contingent accoutrements through which it is perceived in daily experience? "The pure theory of law is a theory of positive law, of positive law in general and not of particular law. It is a general theory of law and not an interpretation of a particular national or international legal order." [41] With this profoundly anti-ideological reaction, Kelsen is speaking the real language of phenomenology:

> A pure theory of law, by which I understand a theory exempt from any political ideology and from any element associated with the natural sciences, but which is conscious of having an object regulated by its own laws. From the beginning my aim has been to elevate the theory of law, which consisted essentially in more or less disguised statements of legal policy, to the status of an authentic science which could take its place beside other ethical sciences. The task undertaken was the detailed examination of research carried out in order to determine the nature of law, putting aside its various aspects, and to strive as far as possible toward objectivity and accuracy, the ideal of all science. [42]

Doing battle with the same syncretism which Husserl had sought to combat within the social sciences, the Pure Theory

> seeks to remain a theory, confining itself to grasping its object to the exclusion of all others. It endeavors to determine what law is and how it is formed, without asking what it should be or how it should be formed. It is not a legal policy, but a science of law. By calling itself a *pure* theory, it suggests that it intends to constitute a science with law as its only object, passing over all that does not strictly respond to its definition. The fundamental principle of its method is thus to eliminate from the science of law all elements which are foreign to it. [43]

In principle, Kelsen's method seems to bear a fundamental relationship to the phenomenological movement, but in the

41. Kelsen, *Théorie pure du droit,* 1st ed., French trans. by Henri Thévenaz (Neuchâtel: La Baconnière, 1953), p. 17.
42. *Ibid.,* p. 11.
43. *Ibid.,* p. 17.

search for the pure and typical structure of law it has provided results of unequal value. It should be pointed out in passing that the *eidos*, or the typical structure of a given object, comes before our consciousness in the form of a number of essentially irreducible elements which set themselves out in a mental pattern which moves from the general to the particular. Certain elements appear as generic; they represent the genus of which the object in question forms a part. Others are given as specific; they represent the species of object of which the object in question forms a part. Lastly, other elements appear as the ultimate difference which gives a special character to the type of object in question and which distinguishes it from the other types of object which together with itself belong to the species immediately above.[44] In respect to the object Law, Kelsen has given an excellent explanation of its eidetic generic elements; while his approach could certainly be improved upon, it nonetheless remains true that his work has made an important contribution. On the other hand, Kelsen's work on the other eidetic elements, those which are specific and particular to law, has been much less successful, and it would seem that the direct vision of the thing Law has been rendered obscure by certain doctrinal considerations, in particular by a fairly marked Kantian influence.

I have attempted to develop and reactivate the positive side of Kelsen's contribution (see Husserl's idea of the "development of an already present"), endeavoring to take it further by a more rigorous application of the principles of the phenomenological method. The inquiry has led us to see three series of elements in the *eidos* or the typical structure of the object Law, elements which are irreducible in the sense that if one applies the method of imaginary variation, eliminating one of these elements in one's consciousness of law, the latter disappears from one's field

44. Husserl remarks apropos of this elementary datum: "Every essence . . . has its proper place in a graded series of essences, in a graded series of *generality* and *specificity*. The series necessarily possesses two limits that never coalesce. Moving downward we reach the *lowest specific differences* or, as we also say, the *eidetic singularities;* and we move upwards through the essences of genus and species to a *highest genus.* Eidetic singularities are essences, which indeed have necessarily 'more general' essences as their genera, but no further specifications in relation to which they themselves might be genera (proximate or mediate, higher genera)" (*Ideas: General Introduction to Pure Phenomenology*, trans. W. R. Boyce Gibson [New York: Humanities Press, 1931], p. 71; paperback [New York: Collier, 1962], pp. 63–64).

of vision: it is no longer law itself which is given, but something else. Thus it is clear that it is the eidetic elements of the thing Law which are involved. These elements set themselves out in the following manner, in accordance with what has already been said:

1. Generic eidetic elements: law presents itself in its most essential state as a set of *norms;* it belongs to the eidetic genus of the normative.
2. Specific eidetic elements: the norms which constitute law present themselves more precisely as *ethical* norms; and, even more precisely, as *ethical norms with the function of commands.*
3. Particular eidetic elements: these commands which constitute law *are part of the function of the public direction of human behavior.* Herein may be found the eidetic particularity of the object Law.

The following pages will attempt to describe successively the three series of elements which make up the *eidos* of law.[45]

[1] GENERIC EIDETIC ELEMENTS OF THE OBJECT LAW: LAW AS A BODY OF NORMS

IF ONE ATTEMPTS, through the method of reduction, to examine the way in which law presents itself to one's consciousness beyond the factuality and the contingency of its historical manifestations, the immediate and primary datum is that of the *rule,* or *norm.*[46] In the first place, law appears to us as being constituted of rules and norms, and that is the most essential,

45. In the following passage I shall reexamine a number of viewpoints which have already been treated in my *Méthode phénoménologique et théorie du droit,* published in 1964. However, I now feel compelled to modify or go beyond the standpoint taken at that stage, thus illustrating the following observation of Maurice Merleau-Ponty: "The philosopher . . . is a perpetual beginner, which means that he takes for granted nothing that men, learned or otherwise, believe they know. It means also that philosophy itself must not take itself for granted, in so far as it may have managed to say something true; that it is an ever-renewed experiment in making its own beginning; that it consists wholly in the description of this beginning" (*Phenomenology of Perception,* trans. Colin Smith [New York: Humanities Press, 1962], p. xiv).

46. I understand the terms "rule" and "norm" as being entirely synonymous, in accordance with current terminology.

most irreducible, and most clear-cut profile of its structure. It is significant to note here that no distinction is made in practice between the expressions "law," "legal rules or norms," and "juridical rules or norms." Etymological data tend to confirm these immediate findings of the consciousness: [47] "In the word *droit* (law, right) is implied the idea of a rule (*directum*), and this image is present in all modern languages." [48] "The word derived from the low Latin *directum* and found in an identical form in several Indo-European languages (*diritto, derecho, recht,* right . . .) suggests the idea of rectitude. The lawful, or right, is that which is correct, or fitting, adapted or adjusted to the rule, not only in physics and mathematics (straight line, right angle, the right or straight way: *ligne droite, angle droit, voie droite* . . .) but also in ethics and psychology (right action, upright character, right intentions: *action droite, caractère droit, intention droite* . . .)." [49]

How has it come about that certain authors have been able to dispute this obvious reduction of law to a set of norms? [50] There is certainly a misunderstanding at the root of this; such authors maintain that within the province of law there are two primary and irreducible phenomena, namely, legal rules and judgments. It is held that law appears in its most essential aspects in the form of both rules and judgments. Furthermore, historically, in ancient society, judgments were the first to manifest themselves, so that they would thus constitute the originary typical element

47. It should be emphasized here that the phenomenological method of Husserl rightly attaches considerable importance to current usage; often, frequently used words and expressions contain, over and above that which they suggest to the consciousness in ordinary experience, illuminating images which correspond to more primary intuitions and which are buried as it were under the deposits of successive meanings. This is an extremely valuable means for refinding or reactivating the clarity of the things themselves. Thus Husserl, as Hermann Pos remarks, "wishes to retain all the metaphors through which a person's direct intuition expresses itself; similarly he attaches great importance to the impressions, feelings, and linguistic insights thrown up by the natural consciousness in immediate living" (*Problèmes actuels de la phénoménologie*, p. 50). Frequent use will be made of this technique in the following pages.
48. Paul Roubier, *Théorie générale du droit* (Paris: Sirey, 1951), p. 5.
49. Jean Dabin, *Théorie générale du droit* (Brussels: Bruylant, 1953), p. 13.
50. See, in particular, Jean Carbonnier, "Sur le caractère primitif de la règle de droit," in *Mélanges Roubier*, I, 109 ff., and "Théorie sociologique des sources du droit," duplicated lectures on juridical sociology (Paris, 1960–61), pp. 74 ff.

in the history of law. This analysis thus attributes, somewhat curiously, two different generic structures to the same object. It is, however, based on a confusion. In reality, law is never given otherwise than in the form of norms laid down by the authorities (if not, one would be in the presence of a something which is not the something currently designated "law," a something which would have another nature, another structure). Those called "pronouncers of law" (*juridici*) in early Roman law, whose responsibility was to "pronounce the law," not only undertook judgments (of the kind: "the conduct of X is valid or invalid"), but were more essentially concerned with pronouncing legal norms—norms which, it must be admitted, were very concrete, very circumscribed: "X ought to do this," "X may do this," "X ought to refrain from doing this," etc. This "pronouncing of the law" (*jurisdiction*) simply represented a certain form of regulation with a particular content, of a more or less *blow-for-blow type*.[51] All legal experience in antiquity in which law is expressed, at least partially, through "pronouncers of law," who claimed moreover to be interpreting the divine will, can be reduced to the statement of legal norms. For example, "in primitive Greece, in the time of Homer and later, arbitrators (the elders of the tribe) are to be found and law-givers, later to become magistrates or *thesmothetai*, who were originally 'pronouncers of law' or kinds of soothsayers whose decisions, *thesmoi*, were dictated by the gods in each particular case."[52] But in fact these *thesmothetai* were nothing other than a variety of legislator, as the etymology of the word indicates: *thesmos* means "law" and *tithêmi* means "I lay down." Thus the Old Testament example given by the author, in which one has Moses "pronouncing" the law to the people,[53] should be analyzed in an identical way.

It should also be noted that there exists no fundamental difference between the "pronouncers of law" (*juridici*) of ancient

51. The concrete form of legislation is involved with the primitive human mentality, which is resistant toward the abstract and consequently toward the general. See Haesaert, *Théorie générale du droit*, p. 411, who demonstrates how "in ancient times, as is shown by certain rules of the XII Tables, law was strongly resistant to generalization." Cf. André Maurois, *Petite Histoire de l'espèce humaine* (Paris: Cahiers de Paris, 1927), pp. 27 ff.

52. Etienne Antonelli, "Le Droit institution sociale," in *Mélanges Roubier*, I, 23.

53. *Ibid.*, p. 25.

society and today's courts,[54] contrary to what is often thought to be the case. "Judges" in modern society remain public authorities whose essential role is to set forth concrete, particular, and individual legal norms. Their role is not limited to that of *judging*, as one might conclude from their designation, or of evaluating the positive or negative value of the human conduct involved in the cases which are submitted to them. Their basic function is to take steps, or to "make orders" with a view to putting an end to the litigation, i.e., to lay down rules which prescribe that which the parties in question may or ought to do.[55] From this point of view there is no difference between judges and other normative authorities.[56] There *is* a difference in that the judicial office in modern society functions within the context of legal norms laid down by other public authorities which judges are responsible for applying through their own decisions, whereas the ancient "pronouncers of law" had much more latitude—an originary power of creating norms; [57] furthermore, the distinction must be made between our "statute-based" legal systems and "judicial" legal systems of the Anglo-Saxon type, which of course provide judges with much wider rule-making powers.

While this misapprehension has been clarified, it is impossible to overemphasize the methodological necessity for treating the

54. The French word *juridiction,* derived from the Latin *jurisdictio* (pronouncement of law), is normally used to designate the courts—Trans.

55. The "judgments" of the courts are really normative provisions (the operative part of the judgment) based on certain assessments of fact and certain judgments in the strict sense of the word (i.e., the grounds of the judgment).

56. Moreover, it is significant that one should encounter practical difficulties in distinguishing judicial acts from the other normative actions of public authorities and that sometimes even the courts, after imputing a judicial quality to a category of acts, retreat, seeing therein actions of a purely administrative nature. (See, as regards France, A. de Laubadère, *Traité élémentaire de droit administratif* [Paris: Librairie générale de droit et de jurisprudence, 1970], I, 200 ff.)

57. Indeed, it is this difference which appears clearly in the work of Gioffredi: "Gioffredi's position is founded on an etymological analysis of the Roman Law formula, *jus dicere,* which is at the root of our notion of jurisdiction, and he shows that in early Roman Law, *jus dicere* is not the declaration of a preexistent rule of law. *Jus dicere* is the pronouncement of the law, of a formula which will create law, create a legal situation: *ita jus esto,* let that which is lawful be thus, let the rightful situation be thus, in accordance not with a preexistent rule of law, but with an innate, intuitive feeling of justice" (Carbonnier, duplicated lectures on juridical sociology cited above, p. 79). Carbonnier thus interprets the ancient *jus dicere* as an instantaneous originary creation of law.

object Law in its proper generic structure, as a set of regulations. At the risk of lapsing into syncretism, the legal disciplines must never lose the consciousness of revolving around this original material, whether they be devoted to the dogmatic study of law, in a purely technical perspective, or to the sociological study of human legal experience.[58] The aim is always the systematization of *rules,* and rules only, or the study of phenomena of human activities which relate to *rules* (such as activities involving the creation, consciousness, or utilization of rules), and rules only.

I have stressed elsewhere the necessity of apprehending law in its given state (*Gegebenheitsweisen*), attacking certain of the verbal excesses to which a failure to respect this postulate will lead. The main aim of this study is the examination of the normative datum itself in law, with a view to giving a phenomenological description of it, elucidating it fully by going beyond the obscure clichés which are usually deemed satisfactory in ordinary experience. Law is reduced to a certain variety of norms, but before going any further in the specification of law, we must ask how the thing Norm confronts one's consciousness, this genus under which law is subsumed.

Beyond all its contingent manifestations, the most essential datum in the structure of the thing Norm is immediately noticeable: one is confronted with an *instrument.* Thus it has been observed that a "legal rule manifests itself to one's primary experience as something which can be used: it is thus an instrument."[59] This clear datum of being an instrument which one perceives in law is of course related to its normative structure; it is immanent in all norms. To conceive a norm is to conceive of a certain instrument available to man. Here again etymology is a valuable guide: *norma* in Latin means an instrument of a material or physical nature, in fact a square comprising two perpendicular elements for checking or drawing right angles or rectilinear perpendicular lines (whence the adjective *normatus,* signifying "upright," "vertical").[60] The word "rule" also originally referred to a certain type of instrument, and this has moreover entered common usage, "made of an elongated piece of wood or

---

58. On this fundamental distinction, see Amselek, *Méthode phénoménologique,* pp. 364 ff.
59. Donius, "L'Analyse existentiale du droit," p. 10.
60. See André Lalande, *Vocabulaire technique et critique de la philosophie* (Paris: Presses Universitaires de France, 1960), p. 691.

of a shaft with right-angled cross pieces, helpful in guiding the pencil or pen when drawing a line or making a measurement, etc." [61] The fact that the words "norm" and "rule" have since been used to designate something other than these instruments indicates that the "other" involved was also thought to be an instrument.

Any tool presents itself as a something endowed with a purpose, that is, matter to which underlying human intention has assigned a certain instrumental function, and its instrumental function constitutes the most basic datum of the tool. As Heidegger observes, a tool is a *tool for;* it is this "being for" which constitutes the essential in its reality as an instrument. What then is the function or instrumental purpose of the norm, of norms in general? A little reflection shows that the role of a norm is to provide a *measure,* or *standard.* Thus it is significant that law (a group of norms) should be symbolized by the scales; [62] it is also significant that in current usage no distinction is made between pronouncing norms, in particular legal norms, and *taking measures.* Again, when different norms are applied to similar cases it is said that "deux poids et deux mesures" [63] have been used. The syllogism itself, which is, as we shall see, the act by which an object is mentally subsumed under a norm, evokes the idea of measure or of calculation in its originary sense.[64]

But norms and rules clearly constitute a particular variety of measures or standards. That which serves as the standard or measuring instrument is abstract, impalpable; it does not have physical reality, since its existence is situated within the intelligible rather than the sensible. It is a *thing present to the mind,* a thought content, an intellectual representation—a meaning, or a suggestion immanent in the mind. Such a suggestion

61. Paul Robert, *Dictionnaire alphabétique et analogique de la langue française* (Paris: Société du nouveau littré, 1964), VI, 35.
62. See the following remarks of Bergson: "Justice has always evoked ideas of equality, of proportion, of compensation. *Pensare,* from which we derive 'compensation' and 'recompense,' means *to weigh.* Justice is represented as holding the scales. Equity signifies equality. Rules and regulation, right and righteousness, are words which suggest a straight line. These references to arithmetic and geometry are characteristic of justice throughout its history" (*Two Sources of Morality and Religion,* p. 60).
63. An idiomatic expression meaning that different norms or "measures" are applied to a problem which would normally merit consistent norms.—Trans.
64. See Revel, *Histoire,* I, 167.

may be transmitted by sensible signs; however, as will be seen, it is not these signs which constitute the normative standard, but the meaning which they transmit or the thing which they endeavor to present to the mind.

However, this specification is not in fact sufficient to identify the thing Norm, to distinguish it from other mental standards such as concepts or conceptual patterns. The particular eidetic aspect of the thing Norm or of the thing Rule is that of constituting a mental representation of *an unfolding of the course of things,* an "evental" development. We shall see how this datum becomes clear in the light of etymological analysis and of the method of imaginary variation.

In sum, the eidetic structure of the thing Norm may be described as follows: A norm is a mental representation of a certain unfolding in the course of things, which is then used as a standard or as a measuring instrument. These different eidetic elements will be studied in greater detail below.

The thing Norm as having an instrumental measuring function

The first task will be the disclosure of the instrumental purpose in question, prior to developing several highly important implications.

The disclosure of this instrumental measuring function. What in fact is a standard, or measure? The datum which comes to mind immediately is that of a *referential object,* a *model,* or a *canon;* to take something as a standard is to imply that this thing is to function as a point of reference, or as a model in regard to an object or to a series of given objects, that it is to function as the incarnation of that to which an object or a series of given objects is supposed to conform. The notions of "model" and of "measure" coincide exactly. To use something as model for other objects comes down to deciding that this thing is to represent the measure of these objects, i.e., the how-they-ought-to-be, that which testifies to their conformation, to their mode of being, or to their modality. Thus tailors' models are simply instrument-standards which give the measure to be used in cutting cloth. It is significant, furthermore, that the Latin for measure is *modus.*[65]

---

65. Hegel clearly grasped the identity of the notions of *measure* and *model* (*Théorie de la mesure,* pp. 22 ff.). But this intuition remained to

To measure or assess an object is to confront it with the object-standard in order to bring out the proportion between the two. The value of an object, its "measure" (this time in the sense not of a measuring instrument but of the result of the implementation of the instrument; the two things should not be confused even though the same term is used), is nothing other than its relationship with the object-standard. In other words, the value or measure of an object is the determination of what it is in relation to. . . .[66] Thus Bergson observes that "in general, measuring is an entirely human operation, which implies that one superimposes in reality or mentally one object onto another a certain number of times." [67]

On reflection it may be perceived that there are two principal kinds of standard and evaluation. In the case of things which may be numbered, or divided into homogeneous fractions and counted out (things such as lengths, surfaces, volumes, weights, etc.), one may use a basic unit-standard for measuring, that is, a term of reference constituted by a certain fraction of the thing in question, which is divided up in a conventional way. This basic unit-standard (for example, the meter) is conceived so that multiplication or division may be carried out to form infinitely larger units (decameter, hectometer, kilometer, etc.) or infinitely

---

some extent an inspiration within an obscure and opaque body of thought. When Hegel deals with the themes, familiar from Greek philosophy, which assimilate the idea of *measure* to that of *limit* or *finitude* (and, inversely, the idea of *absence of measure* to that of the *infinite*, or *limitlessness*), he has only a most confused grasp of the question (*ibid.*, pp. 23, 84 ff.; see also *Geschichte der Philosophie, Aesthetik; Jubiläums-Ausgabe* [Stuttgart: Glockner, 1965], sec. 18, p. 239). One has only to observe that by stipulating that an object A ought to conform to a certain object B (taken as a standard), one implies in a certain sense that a restriction, a subjection, or a servitude is applied to A; thus its possibilities of being are reduced because it ought to be thus and not otherwise. The intellectual procedure thus implied by the instrumental logic of the measure or the standard suggests the idea of limit; for this reason this notion is frequently associated with that of measure. In the same way, the idea of an object which is in no way tied to a model, is without measure, and thus is free of any restriction naturally suggests the idea of the infinite, the unlimited, and the undetermined.

66. Through a still highly confused apperception of this datum, Hegel is led to observe that "there is in the measure the idea of the essence" (*Théorie de la mesure*, p. 23).

67. Bergson, *Creative Evolution*, p. 218 (translation slightly modified). Cf. Robert, *Dictionnaire*, IV, 541: "*Measure:* the act of determining the value of certain quantity by comparison with a constant quantity of the same type, used as a term of reference."

smaller units (decimeter, centimeter, millimeter, etc.). Evaluation consists in staking out the object in question, that is, determining to which multiple of this unit (or derivative units) the object to be evaluated is equal, or equals.[68] One is confronted here by a quantitative form of evaluation or measurement, and this form is by definition limited to quantifiable things only—to quanta. Thus Heidegger observes: "The size of a room is given in so many meters of length, breadth, and height. But its size is only possible because the room as such is spatial; it has a top, bottom, back, front, and sides—in short, it is a quantum. . . . Quantity always presupposes the quantum; size as measure, as such and such a number, is always the measure of a thing endowed with size." [69]

In other cases, as a measuring instrument one uses a standard which represents in an absolute, indivisible, innumerable way how the object to be measured ought to be. In this case its value will result uniquely from its conformity (positive value) or its lack of conformity (negative value) to the object-model. Here, then, is a nonquantitative form of evaluation or measure.[70] Rules

68. *To equal* designates nothing else here than being in accordance with a certain quantity of measuring units, unit-models. Thus quantity is defined as "the number of units or measures which serve to determine a collection, a group of things considered to be homogeneous or a portion of matter" (Robert, *Dictionnaire*, V, 705).

69. Martin Heidegger, *What Is a Thing?*, trans. W. B. Barton, Jr., and Vera Deutsch (Chicago: Regnery, 1967), pp. 195 ff. (translation slightly modified).

70. It will be observed that in this context the object to be evaluated may be more or less different from the object-standard used. Of course the latter does not permit of itself measurement of this difference. But it is possible to evaluate this nonconformity, or gap, between an object and a nonquantitative standard by referring to other appropriate standards which may be themselves, depending on the situation, either instruments of quantitative measure or nonquantitative instruments. Quantitative instruments will be used when the object originally compared with the nonquantitative standard is numerable or quantifiable—a quantum. Thus the gap between a stick and another taken as absolute standard of length may be measured quantitatively by reference to a unit-model of length—the meter, for example. On the other hand, the gap between a certain form of behavior and a certain model of behavior cannot be measured quantitatively, as it is not quantifiable. One cannot here determine a quantity but only a degree of nonconformity by referring to a plurality of nonquantitative measuring instruments, arranged in a scale, each measuring a different level of difference. (On the difference between quantitative measuring instruments and "gradual" measuring instruments, see the useful observations of Heidegger on "extensive size" and "intensive size," *ibid.*, pp. 222 ff.)

or norms come in with this second variety of standard; they make it possible to attribute the quality of "normality" or of "correctness" to objects which are in accordance with them, and the quality of "abnormality" or of "incorrectness" to objects which are not in conformity with them.

This having been said, it should be noted that in both cases the mental process implemented in order to determine the value of objects remains fundamentally the same. The problem is always to establish a relationship of conformity or nonconformity between the object to be measured and an object-standard or an object-model. It is always this relationship of conformity or of nonconformity which constitutes the value or measure of an object. In simple terms, either it involves a quantified value, expressing the conformity or equivalence of the object to a certain quantity or fractions of it, taken as unit-standards, as measuring units; or it involves a nonquantified value, expressing in a more abrupt way the conformity or nonconformity of the object to some other object taken as complete standard, or as ultimate indicator of its modality.

The great value of Kelsen's work, in my opinion, is that he has clearly perceived that norms, and in particular legal norms, are to be considered under the category of measures or instrument-standards, and this involves placing normative disciplines under the banner of *metrology,* that is, the theory of measure. Kelsen has thus perfectly dismantled the instrumental mechanics of norms and has brought out very clearly the connections between the notions of "norm," "value," and "judgment" or "evaluation," notions which had hitherto been extremely vague both in law and in the other normative disciplines.

When a norm prescribes a certain conduct, actual conduct may either correspond to the norm or contradict it. It corresponds to the norm, or conforms to it, when it is such as it ought to be according to this norm; it contradicts the norm when it is not such as it ought to be according to this norm, that is, when it is the contrary of conduct conforming to this norm. The assertion that actual conduct is such as it ought to be according to a norm . . . is a value judgment, or more precisely a positive value judgment. It means that the actual conduct is *good.* The assertion that actual conduct is not such as it ought to be according to a norm . . . —being the opposite of a conduct in accordance with the norm—is a negative value judgment. It means that the actual conduct is bad.

A norm . . . which stipulates that certain conduct ought to take place lays down a positive value and a negative one. Conduct which conforms to the norm has a positive value; the conduct which contradicts it has a negative value. The norm . . . plays the role of value-standard for actual conduct.[71]

Of course, certain faults could be found with this approach to the normative. For Kelsen, only "actual conduct" can be measured by a norm:

The object of judgment or evaluation is actual conduct. Only actual conduct can, when confronted by a norm, be judged as having a value or as being foreign to all values; it alone can have a positive or negative value. It should not be forgotten that what is evaluated, that which may or may not have value, positive or negative, is reality.[72]

This view is rather curious. In fact, any object, "any thing whatever" in the words of Husserl,[73] can be evaluated by reference to a norm, even if it has no actual reality (*reale Wirklichkeit*), no existence in space and time. Thus, for example, purely imaginary conduct or even simply anticipated conduct can be equally well confronted with a norm and evaluated as "actual conduct." [74] But it must be admitted that Kelsen has been able to perceive and reconstitute the essential.

It should not be surprising, moreover, that it was a jurist who thus disclosed the essence of the normative. It is within legal phenomena that the idea of the normative emerges the most

71. Hans Kelsen, *Théorie pure du droit*, 2d ed., French trans. by Charles Eisenmann (Paris: Dalloz, 1962), p. 23.
72. Kelsen, "Justice et droit naturel," in *Le Droit naturel*, Vol. III, Annales de philosophie politique (Paris: Presses Universitaires de France, 1959).
73. Husserl, *Ideas*, pp. 123–24; paperback, p. 111.
74. In the same context Kelsen quite wrongly claims that a norm cannot itself be evaluated: "How could a norm which constitutes a value . . . be evaluated? How could a value have a value, or indeed a negative value? How could a norm, or duty, be such as it ought to be? Only a reality can be such as it should be or not be such as it ought to be. . . . A value endowed with value, a norm in accordance with the norm is a pleonasm; a value foreign to all values, a norm contrary to the norm represents an internal contradiction" (*Justice et droit naturel*, pp. 4–5). As a cautious jurist, Kelsen should have taken care that the dogmatic theory of law pronounce on the legal norms with which it deals, picking out gaps, contradictions, socially dangerous aspects, etc.

clearly; here "the normative is fully obvious." [75] The illuminating nature of the symbol of the scales, which has already been pointed out, clearly places law under the label "weights and measures." It could be added that the mythological data concerning law are also very enlightening. "It is remarkable [it has been noted] that from the union of Jupiter and Themis, Diké was born, the goddess of judgment (sister of Truth, also a daughter of Jupiter), with the function of settling or resolving litigation." [76] Such mythical data do seem to suggest a link between norms and the resultant judgments. The very terminology used in the legal field is particularly indicative. Mention has already been made of the instrumental aspect of the term *droit* ("law") itself, and through it of the term *règle* ("rule"); similarly the term *tort* (derived from the verb *tordre*, "to twist," and its participle *tordu*, "twisted") expresses perfectly the idea of nonconformity to law, to the rule of law, which underlies the notions of fault, offense, and infringement. Current legal language also speaks of *manquement* ("lack," or "noncompliance") in relation to a norm, or of *dépassement* ("excess"), which also indicates the "weights and measures" aspect of norms. Mention should be made, too, of the *exteriority* of historical legal phenomena, the objective formulation by public authorities of legal norms and, at least to a certain extent, of judgments based on them, which allows greater awareness of the mental mechanisms involved. Thus legal theory seems to be in the best position of all normative disciplines to elucidate the most fundamental things dealt with by them. [77]

The perspectives provided by this disclosure. The reduction of norms to "measures" just outlined opens up certain particularly important perspectives.

In the first place, it makes it possible to effect a clean break with the obscure verbalism which weighs so heavily on the normative disciplines (whether law, ethics, or logic) and to rediscover the primary intuitions which are inherent in such language. One example suffices: that of concepts involving "is" (*sein*) and "ought" (*sollen*). These are, of course, notions which

75. André Lalande, *La Raison et les normes* (Paris: Hachette, 1948), p. 148.

76. Giorgio del Vecchio, *La Justice, la vérité* (Paris: Dalloz, 1955), p. 10.

77. See, on this, Léon Husson, *Les Transformations de la responsabilité: Etudes sur la pensée juridique* (Paris: Presses Universitaires de France, 1947), p. 6.

are basic to the normative disciplines, particularly as espoused by legal philosophy, and which are entirely nebulous, giving rise to rather curious discussions. According to received opinion, two worlds are in existence, two mysterious and irreducible universes: that of "is" and that of "ought," with law belonging to the latter.[78]

In fact, by means of these concepts of *sein* and *sollen,* an attempt is being made to reinstate the function of measures or models which norms, and particularly legal and moral norms, fulfill in respect to the objects to which they apply. When one makes of something a standard or model, one presupposes logically (and it is in this sense that there is a standard or model) that an object or a series of given objects "ought" to be in conformity with this something; to take object *A* as the model of object *B* is to imply that *B* ought to be identical to *A*. All notions of standard or model are contained in this notion and it is, so to speak, gathered up into the elliptical term "ought," which, considered by itself and independently of the reality which it endeavors to epitomize, seems more than obscure. The idea of a radical separation between the spheres of *sein* and *sollen* expresses sometimes the simple fact that there is obviously a difference in nature between an object pure and simple and an object to which the instrumental function of measure or model has been ascribed. An object which is employed as model cannot be reduced, even by hypothesis, to a mere object (or to its purely objective appearances), because of the transcendent human intention of which it is the recipient. Further, an object can never be given as model of itself, independently of transcendent human intention. This is what is really meant by the famous assertion of Protagoras that "man is the measure of all things," i.e., that all measures (and, more generally, all tools) are human, marked with man's seal. Thus the gulf between the universe of the *sein* and that of the *sollen* expresses this other very elementary datum that an object pure and simple is not an evaluated object; between the two there stands that irreducible difference constituted by the transcendent, external intervention of man armed with a standard, in virtue of which the object is assigned its value. The

---

78. See, for example, Virally, *La Pensée juridique,* p. xvii; Pierre Pescatore, *Introduction à la science du droit* (Luxembourg: Office des imprimes de l'état, 1960), p. 418.

clear apperception of the normative essence thus makes it possible to move out of the obscurity of pure verbalism.

Above all, the reduction of norms to the category of measures reveals and enables one to touch on two given elements of the human condition which are of crucial importance. The first, briefly, is the environment of measures, models, or standards which characterizes man's artificial universe. Bergson rightly defines that which is specific to man by the idea of *homo faber*.[79] But of all the types of instruments which stake out human space, measures clearly take an important position; it may be said that the intensive use of measures is specifically human, and that it corresponds in all probability to the fundamental needs dictated by man's finitude. In one way or another man is always using measures or standards, sometimes concrete and sometimes purely mental, such as rules or concepts. It is worth noting that the most salient social phenomena, to which attention has long been drawn by philosophers and sociologists, are in the last analysis metrological experiences. Those areas so well documented by Gabriel Tarde and by Bergson may be cited as examples—phenomena of social conformism, fashion, or the exemplarism of the Father and the Hero.

The second datum is worth close attention. The reduction of one's judgmental experiences to metrological experiences gives a clear insight into their relativity. All judgments, evaluations, or measures have some particular slant, intervening on any level, which implies on the part of the subject the use of a measuring instrument, model, or standard, the value attributed to the object being by hypothesis a function of the instrument employed. Thus ethical judgments within the general category of human action necessarily imply the conscious or unconscious application of ethical norms. Man needs standards and norms in order to judge and to make evaluations, since the latter consist precisely in confronting an object with an object-model or an object-standard. Even when an individual speaks of measuring himself against another, in the field of sport for example, the standard is there, incarnated in this case by his adversary.

This means, in other terms and in opposition to the school of

79. See Bergson, *The Creative Mind,* trans. Mabelle L. Andison (New York: Greenwood, 1968), p. 99: "It is of man's essence to create materially and morally, to fabricate things and to fabricate himself. *Homo faber* is the definition I propose."

axiological phenomenology described above, that the value of an object is not immanent; it does not constitute an intrinsic property of the object which is simply observed by the subject. As Kelsen remarks in respect of ethical judgments, "Value is not inherent in the object judged, but attributed to it by a norm. It represents the relation between the object and the norm. The analysis of an object or of human behavior does not make it possible to discover its value, since the latter is not immanent in empirical reality and cannot be deduced from it." [80] How could an object reveal of itself its conformity to, or its lack of conformity to, other than by the transcendent intervention of a term of reference whose function it would be to determine such a characteristic? The idea that value is immanent in an object is not false, but absurd, like that of a round square.

It is true that the naïve vision of the relativism of values within human facts clashes with the desire for an absolute and arouses a certain feeling of anxiety or uncertainty. This no doubt explains why many thinkers have found such a solution unpalatable. Such is the case with Max Scheler, in spite of his phenomenological pretensions: "Neither the notion of *duty* nor that of *norm*," he observes, "can constitute the basis of ethics or pass for the standard which alone makes it possible to distinguish between the good and the bad." [81] Then, significantly, he remarks: "The disciples of this theory are incapable of showing, even in the most approximate way, where this *standard, idea,* or *aim* comes from, or why their adoption of it is not purely arbitrary, as in conventional measures such as the meter." [82]

Before concluding, it seems indispensable to mention two

80. Kelsen, *Théorie pure du droit*, 1st ed., p. 88. See, by the same author, *Justice et droit naturel*, pp. 68 ff.: "No 'ought' can be immanent in an 'is,' no norm in an act, no value in empirical reality. Only by applying from the outside an 'ought' (*sollen*) to an 'is' (*sein*), or norms to acts, can [acts] be considered as in accordance with the norm, that is, good or just, or contrary to the norm, that is, bad or unjust; only thus may reality be evaluated, that is, described as being endowed with, or devoid of, value. To imagine that norms can be discovered or recognized in acts, or values in reality, is an illusion. For this to be the case it would be necessary, in order to be able to deduce them, to project even unconsciously into the realm of facts those norms which are presupposed and which constitute values."

81. Max Scheler, *Formalism in Ethics and Non-Formal Ethics of Values*, trans. Manfred Frings and Roger Funk (Evanston, Ill.: Northwestern University Press, 1973), pt. 2, chap. 4, sec. 1.

82. *Ibid.*

hypotheses which at first sight could seem to imply the possibility of judging independently of any standard or norm.

The first hypothesis concerns judgments made on the basis of norms which are entirely interiorized and integrated, as it were, into the judging subject. First, it should be noted that the standards used in judgments, like judgments themselves, are not necessarily revealed to the exterior, or exteriorized; they may remain entirely immanent in the mind. I may judge, for example, within myself, without manifesting anything, that the conduct of X is not in accordance with such and such a norm which I have in mind—also without revealing it. Judgment and standard used will remain, in this hypothesis, completely hidden from the outside, without this changing anything of the process of evaluation, which is experienced purely internally. One can go further. There are norms which one applies unconsciously, without having a clear objective vision of them, norms which we make our own, integrating them into our own subjectivity in accordance with the psychological process described by Sigmund Freud (the theme of the superego and of interior auto-repression on the part of the individual) and taken up more recently by Herbert Marcuse.[83] Such norms are received from the outside, or established by oneself, attaching to one's subjectivity, and are not perceived as such in our judgmental experiences—which may suggest the idea that judgments are made without the intermediate norms. This is a mere illusion, as Freud's works clearly show. The norm is indeed present in the person even if that person is not clearly conscious of it, or if his experience of it is lived rather than thought out. This norm dictates his judgments, creating feelings of guilt or a guilty conscience.[84]

The second hypothesis to be examined is that of emotional judgments. These are in fact experiences of a very particular nature, hitherto very inadequately explained, to which many authors such as Max Scheler have curiously thought it possible

83. See, for example, *Eros and Civilization* (Boston: Beacon Press, 1955), pp. 31–32, 44 ff.
84. Max Scheler has well observed this phenomenon, which one is tempted to describe as a merging of the cultural into the natural: "There exists a *practical* obedience (and disobedience) in respect of laws (in the sense in which we should perceive their legality, or that we should *know* of it), which are rather *lived*, in the very unfolding of conduct, as observed or violated and are given only in these lived experiences" (*Formalism in Ethics*, pt. 1, chap. 3; translation modified).

to reduce the totality of one's nonquantitative evaluation experiences. At first sight, emotional judgments would seem not to need the intermediary of standards. Thus, when aroused by a natural landscape I judge it to be "beautiful" or "ugly," it seems scarcely feasible that in doing so I should at some point or in some way be in the process of confronting it with another, selected for comparison; the very idea seems absurd. The problem is clarified, however, if one endeavors to unveil completely the specifically lived experience behind the judgment made on such an occasion. This specific experience involves essentially the ideas of *receptivity* and *sensitivity*. The emotional experience is one in which the subject experiences a feeling of attraction or openness, or in other cases a feeling of repulsion or blindness, in respect to certain things. How can this imply a judgment, or the attribution of a positive or negative value to the things in question? When confronted by a landscape for which one feels some attraction, one should, in order to express the emotional state thus registered, be content with saying "I like this countryside." How can one attribute a positive value to the countryside by asserting that *it is beautiful?*

Indeed, a quite complex mental process takes place within the subject. It must be seen that the affective reactions of attraction and repulsion spring from the predispositions of the subject, of his tendencies (one also speaks of *aspirations, penchants, tastes,* etc.), or the receptivity by which he is able to accept certain things and not others, exactly as a radio can receive certain broadcasts and not others. It is by living out this affective experience, by feeling attracted or repelled by such and such a thing, that the subject becomes aware in practice of his own state of receptivity, of these latent tendencies which dwell in him and which are in a sense immanent in the structure of his person.[85] In feeling attracted by a certain landscape I become aware of my receptivity, of the existence of tendencies within myself, and I sense that these tendencies are satisfied, that I am confronted by a thing which coincides with those to which I am predisposed. At this point I may pronounce a judgment. When I deduce from my feeling of attraction (or, conversely, of repulsion) that I am confronted by a thing which is in accordance (or, conversely, not in accordance) with the type of thing to which I

85. See Lachelier's remark (quoted in André Lalande, *Vocabulaire,* p. 30): "The tendency comes to us only through emotion."

am inclined to respond favorably, such a deduction is expressed in the statement that this thing is "beautiful" or "good" (or, conversely, "ugly" or "bad"). Thus there is indeed in the mind of the subject the idea of a reference object which provides formal support for the making of a judgment, or attributing a value; this reference object is the object immanent in the tendency, the that-toward-which-I-tend.

Such an affective judgment takes place in very special conditions. It is not a case of the pure and simple confrontation of one thing with another which serves as model; it involves deduction made on the basis of a datum which is in this case a certain affective state, that such and such a thing is in accordance with another referent. The same kind of judgment may be found outside the area of emotions, in all other analogous experiences of receptivity, that is, every time one observes the suitability or adequation (or, conversely, nonsuitability or nonadequation) of an object A to another object B, and one deduces the conformity (or lack of conformity) of A with the type of object to which B, given his structure, is predisposed to respond favorably. Such is the situation, for example, when after inserting a key into a lock and observing that it turns, I conclude that it is "good" (i.e., in accordance with the kind of key which may be used in this lock, to which it will "respond").

One may go even further in observing that this kind of evaluation judgment belongs to a more general form of metrological experience, which could be labeled indirect or indicative evaluation, or judgment by indicator or by assumption. There are in practice two main procedures of evaluation to be distinguished: direct evaluation, which consists in confronting directly an object with a model and in deducing its conformity or lack of conformity to this model; and indirect evaluation or indicative evaluation, which consists in deducing by presumption this conformity or lack of conformity from a certain indicator or from a certain criterion. Thus, instead of constituting an "honest man" model which would enable me to judge whether X or Y is honest, I can define a criterion, an indicator, or an inductive "sign" of the honest man (an open face, for example), thus implying that honest men have open faces. When confronted by an individual with an open face, I conclude that he is honest, that he conforms to the image of the honest man. This image is not itself defined; it remains purely implicit. By making such a judgment, as can be seen, I do not register the conformity of an object to a model on the basis of direct confrontation; I simply deduce this conformity from the constatation of an indicator. Similarly, the attraction or repulsion felt for an object is the indicator as to whether or not it is in accordance with my tendencies, or with the type of thing to which I am inclined to respond favorably. Of course, it remains true that if I make a judgment or formulate an evaluation, it is because (and only because) I refer mentally (even indirectly and in a purely formal way) to a model. If I say that such and such a thing is good, it is because (and only because) I deduce from my feeling of attraction a state of conformity to a referent, though this may remain implicit if its consistency is not explicitly given to my consciousness.

Many authors make the error of reducing all nonquantitative evaluation experiences to this very special and finally marginal kind of evaluation represented by the affective judgment, and of believing that the value which we attribute to things springs always and necessarily from one's attraction toward them, that "nothing has value, even truth, except in relation to the will." [86] In fact, not all one's judgments belong to this specific affective context. Legal judgments do not, based as they are on norms laid down by those in authority, whether or not these norms are liked by the public or for that matter by those in authority themselves.[87] Thus the ideas of "value" and "norm" are associated only through an indefensible form of syncretism, both in legal and ethical theory, with the idea of "will" and affective data.[88]

86. Louis Lavelle, *Traité des valeurs* (Paris: Presses Universitaires de France, 1951), I, p. 192.

87. It is true that one can always begin by making an affective judgment on an object which is subject to legal norms, and then endeavor to make the legal judgment performed on the basis of legal norms correspond to it, if one forces somewhat the consistency of the latter; but this is another problem (see Joseph C. Hutcheson, Jr., "Le Jugement intuitif; la fonction du "hunch" dans la décision judiciaire," in *Recueil d'études en l'honneur de François Gény*, I, 531 ff.).

88. On syncretism in legal theory, see Amselek, *Méthode phénoménologique*, pp. 76, 103 ff. It should, however, be observed that very often legal theorists use the word "will" in the sense of "command," or "authoritarian decision," leaving aside any affective element or element of "desire" or "aspiration." In this way legal acts are currently defined, along with acts of pronouncing law, as "manifestations of will." In fact, this is simply a way of showing that one is dealing with the formulation of legal commands. But, precisely, the use of the word "will" here is both a reminiscence and a perpetuation of the confusion of normative with affective phenomena.

The mental nature of normative measures

I shall not dwell on this point. It suffices to observe that the function of measure or standard can be attributed to anything, to an "anything whatever," to use the previously quoted formula of Husserl. One can thus take as measure or standard a physical or material thing, "of flesh and blood," which belongs to the realm of the senses and of the perceptible—for example, such and such a chair, house, piece of lead, stick, etc. As has been shown, the words "norm" and "rule" originally designated precisely such physical standards used as referents for straight lines or right angles. But in later usage there was a broadening of meaning, from the concrete to the abstract; the words "norm" and "rule" were used to designate nonmaterial standards, thereby forming pure thought content. Indeed, things may be made to function as standards or models—things which are not present externally but only in one's mind—and may be analyzed as thought data or as mental perspectives, lacking material consistency. This is the category to which rules and norms belong. They constitute, in this respect, standards of a special sort. The texture and the material of the referent in this context is purely mental or "ideal"; it is thought content, something which one imagines intellectually and which is purely immanent in one's mind—the object embraced in thought (whether in intuitive or discursive thought). It is this something, present in one's mind, which serves as model for an object or a series of given objects.

Whence the special mental mechanism necessitated by the use of this sort of standard, that which is designated by the term "syllogism"? On the intellectual level, the syllogism is the equivalent of the physical operation involved in placing a pattern on a piece of cloth which is to be, or has already been, shaped, thus showing the outlines which the cloth should take in order to be a true copy of the model in question. This operation then guides the hand of the tailor, or else provides a means of passing judgment on the finished garment. When it is a question of mental standards, the operation of superimposing the standard on the object (or of subsuming the object under the standard, which is the same thing) will be carried out in a purely ideal, or purely intellectual, manner. By the process of thought, the standard is applied to an object which is seen as a simple project, hypothesis or reality, thus tracing out the form which it should have. The subject will then be able to reproduce this model or else to pass judgment if need be.[89]

The mental texture of the standard-norm has another important consequence: namely, the mediate character of the communication of norms or rules in interpersonal relationships. The things which belong to the category of the sensible are in effect things which can be immediately and personally perceived by means of the senses. On the other hand, mental things or thought contents cannot be perceived in person from the outside, by another person. I may try, of course, to communicate with someone, to exteriorize my thoughts, by means of sensible signs, which can be perceived, such as spoken or written words, gestures, diagrams. But the only function of these signs is to suggest to the mind of another person the thought content immanent in my own mind; the signs are not themselves this thought content. The perception of these signs cannot therefore reveal immediately and personally my thought contents to another person. If this thought content is to pass into the thought of another person, the latter must engage, on the basis of the perceived signs, in a specific mental process—a process of comprehension and understanding which consists in leaping from the signifier to the signified, or in finding that which I intended to express, in deciphering the message of which the symbols are simply vehicles. This operation, of course, involves various risks of equivocation, ambiguity, and misunderstanding.

It is in this sense that the mediacy of the interpersonal communication of norms is to be understood. Another person may express to me the norm-standard present in his mind, by means of perceptible signs. But these signs, by virtue of which a norm present in another person is communicated to me, are not identical with the norm itself; they are merely its vehicle. The norm or normative measure is the *meaning* with which these symbols

---

89. It should be noted in passing that judgment is not to be confused with the syllogism, as is sometimes the case. The syllogism is the simple operation of superimposing a mental standard on an object: for example, the application of the norm "Anyone causing damage to another ought to compensate for it" to a concrete case implying that X has caused damage would seem to indicate obliquely that "X ought to compensate for this damage." The act of passing judgment consists in verifying whether the case in question conforms to the model thus applied to it, that is, in the example given above, whether X has or has not made amends for the damage he has caused.

are charged, that is, "that which a word, a sentence, or any other symbol of a similar kind *endeavors to express* or to communicate to the mind." [90] I can take possession of this meaning only by a mental operation of comprehension through and beyond the simple perception of the signs themselves. Let us take, for example, the case of a rule formulated as follows: "Thou shalt not kill." Clearly, it is not this group of words which effectively constitutes the rule or normative measure, but the meaning of which this verbal sequence is the vehicle, the that-which-it-suggests-to-my-mind, in this case the nonpossibility of behaving as a murderer. Thus whenever symbols transmitting a rule are perceived, they must be deciphered and interpreted so as to have present in the mind, and to be able to use if need be, the normative measure of which these symbols are simply the vehicles. This interpretation, with all the problems it implies, is basic in apprehending a rule, because depending on whether an individual gives one meaning or another to the same symbols, one rule or another will be present in the mind. The importance of interpretation and of theories of interpretation in the field of legal rules is well known in this respect.

This said, it is, of course, possible to take a group of written or spoken words as a standard as such, or a model as such, that is, as an object of reference with relation to other sequences of written or spoken words. This is true, for example, of certain collections of formulas or formularies used by attorneys and others engaged in the practice of law, in drawing up certain acts for which they are responsible. Indeed, these formulas function as models for such practitioners. However, rules and norms (especially legal norms) are not models or measures of this concrete, physical sort. The normative model or measure is a mental content, something which is the object of thought, and which it is as impossible to reduce to the signs which endeavor to express it as it is generally to reduce the signifier to the signified.

Moreover, before concluding, it is essential that we go further in formulating carefully an important reservation on the way in which we understand this characterization of normative measures as thought contents, as things-grasped-in-thought, taken as models or referents. In effect, I can think of something not directly, but indirectly, through the intermediary of words, state-

90. Lalande, *Vocabulaire*, p. 973.

ments, which suggest in a decomposed fashion this something to my mind. This discursive mode of thought—this kind of second-degree thought—should not give rise to misconceptions. The words and statements along which discursive thought travels internally are nothing but instruments at the service of one particular thought procedure. They do not constitute the content of my thoughts, the something which I conceive or which I embrace in thought. In this respect, norms (in particular, legal norms), as thought content and as things occupying the mind, cannot be reduced to the internal discourse along which my consideration of the things in question develops. Any move which endeavors to reduce rules to discourse, or to treat normative phenomena and in particular legal phenomena as a mere matter of language and syntax, is bound to fail since such a procedure will involve bypassing that which constitutes the real structure of the norm, namely, the message of such normative discourse and the function of model assigned to this message.

A fortiori, as previously suggested, rules (and particularly legal rules) are not to be confused with "external" sensible signs, by which they are communicated to another person—written or pronounced words, gestures, etc. This lack of coincidence between rules and their "position," that is, their exteriorization, is very evident moreover in the current legal use of the expression "positive law," understood in its originary sense as "law given position" (*droit posé*). In referring to the possibility of law which is nonpositive, i.e., purely "ideal," and purely immanent in the mind of the public authorities, this expression indicates clearly that the "position" of the legal rule is not part of its essential constitution.

The evental content of normative measures

It is not sufficient to characterize norms as being things thought, or intellectual representations to which the role of measure or standard is assigned. Moreover, it is to be emphasized that this representation-standard constitutive of norms has a specific content. We are dealing here with *the representation of a certain unfolding of the course of things, of a certain evental development*. I shall attempt to give a general elucidation of this evental aspect of norms, endeavoring to cast light on the relation of this idea to legal norms.

The evental perspective of norms. If one thinks of any sort of rule (game rules, scientific rules, moral rules, aesthetic rules, methodological rules, etc.) one quickly encounters a common denominator which is part of the very essence of any norm or any rule. In each case it is the thought or the mental representation of a certain evental unfolding or pattern which constitutes the standard or model. In general, the rule constitutes the measure or model of the occurrence of events in the course of things, and these model evental patterns can be schematically reduced to four general categories:

1. The representation of an evental pattern according to which something can occur or come to pass; thus a pattern implying the possibility of a certain event, or the possibility of something taking place in the course of things;
2. The representation of an evental pattern in which something may not occur or take place; thus a pattern implying the possibility of something not occurring in the course of things;
3. The representation of an evental pattern in which something cannot occur and must necessarily not happen; thus a pattern implying the obligation or necessity of something not occurring in the course of things;
4. The representation of an evental pattern in which something may not fail to occur, must necessarily occur; thus a pattern implying the obligation or necessity of something appearing in the course of things.

Thus all rules constitute (in conditions or in a mental context which of course may be very different, but we shall leave aside these differences for the moment) models of evental patterns; referring to the previous example, game rules measure the unfolding of the match, and its vicissitudes; they represent model patterns according to which certain things may or ought to happen or not happen in the course of the game, and according to which the players may or ought to behave or not behave in this way or that. In the same way, scientific rules reveal the unfolding of natural or human facts; they constitute the model patterns which have been worked out on the basis of experience and according to which certain facts, certain natural and human events, may or ought to occur or not occur in reality. And this is the case for all varieties of rules.

Indeed, the evental perspective of norms appears clearly in the etymology of the word itself. The latin word *regula,* in its most originary sense, designated a movement or passage in a straight line; it has been shown elsewhere that the words *norma* and *regula,* inasmuch as they refer to tools, first served to designate material instruments used for drawing or checking rectilinear or perpendicular lines. The idea of course or distance covered, of a trip or trajectory, of movement or of development, is thus implicit in the originary meanings of these words. It is precisely this idea which was behind the broadening of the meaning which later came about. Norms or rules, while designating standards of a mental kind, have retained traces of their earliest symbol. The standards in question constitute a way of measuring the course of things, the unfolding of facts—of evental development. This meaning comes out, moreover, in the French term *régime,* which designates the that-which-the-rules-intended-to-establish. The word *régime* contains the image of a course, a passage, a flow; thus one speaks of the *régime* ("course") of a river or the *régime* ("cycle") of a mobile machine.

Being models of occurrence or of the emergence of events in the course of things, norms or rules can be described as *models with existential content,* if the idea of existence is taken in its originary sense (*ex-sistere* in Latin means "to go beyond," "to emerge," "to occur," "to happen").[91] Norms are thus in opposition to concepts, which are mental models of constitutional or structural content. In point of fact, a concept does indeed constitute a model which is present in the mind in the same way as a rule; but it is a model of the essence or categorial structure of a thing, or the representation of the essential traits of its appearance, or of its *constitution.* This enables us to judge whether other things

---

91. Other similar expressions may be used, for example, "models of natural content," "models of the nature of things," taking the word "nature" in its originary sense (coming from the latin verb *nasci,* "to be born")—the existence, the production, the development of things (see Jean Ehrard, *L'Idée de nature en France dans la première moitié du XVIIIe siècle* [Paris: Editions de l'Ecole Pratique des Hautes Etudes, 1963]). But this term, because of its connotations, could be highly ambiguous. A more neutral expression which would be just as capable of suggesting that which I am trying to express might be "models of coming about," or "measures of the coming about of things."

do or do not conform to this model and do or do not belong to the same category of things. On the one hand, a rule is the representation of existence and of the manifestation of things in the evental flow; it is on this basis that judgments can be made as to whether the occurrence of a certain thing—and not the thing in itself—does or does not conform to the normative model of reference. On the other hand, the objects to which norms can be applied are not constitutive structures, but more exactly "cases" (*cas*) or "occasions" (from the latin *casus*, "event"; *cadere*, "to fall or to happen").

Furthermore, the conceptual models constitute measures of the categorial physiognomy of things, whereas normative models serve to measure the emergence of things in the world (Dasein); the latter have to do with the succession of things and the former with their profile.[92]

This development reveals, incidentally, the futility of the so-called phenomenological procedures of authors such as Reinach. It is absurd to treat law as a group of concepts or conceptual models which may be reactivated by Husserl's method of eidetic reduction. This would be to lapse into a regressive syncretism, since law is in fact given as a group of norms or normative models and as a result is situated on an existential rather than a structural plane. It is useful at this point to clear up once and for all two sources of ambiguity.

1. First, it is obvious that legal rules (like all other rules) implement concepts in their very formulation; how could it be otherwise? More precisely, it happens that certain legal rules provide for the possibility or the necessity of the occurrence or the nonoccurrence of something which they define at the same time, and of which they themselves formulate the concept. This should not be misunderstood. In such cases one is not purely and

---

92. This distinction elucidates the one Husserl observes between the a priori research of the eidetic disciplines (whose aim is the study of the profile of things, apart from the conditions of their occurrence in the world) and the empirical research of the scientific disciplines (whose aim is to study the progression of things, the conditions in which they occur in the world). Contrary to certain hasty interpretations, Husserl in no wise means that eidetic research (as opposed to scientific research) is not experimental, or that it is not based on the experience of the things which it embraces, but merely that by the very object of its procedure it implies the epoché, that is, the bracketing of the existential or factual aspects of things, and the desire not to confuse these existential elements with properly essential elements.

simply confronted by concepts which the legislator would limit himself to formulating and which would therefore be identifiable as such with an aspect of law. In reality, what one encounters here is a set of rules, that is, a measure of the occurrence of things—a set of rules which simply develops one of the concepts which it sets forth in function of its own requirements; this concept is never anything more than an element of the rule and not an autonomous datum. In other words, law, which presents itself as a group of rules, must not be confused with certain elements which form the partial content of certain of these rules; the part should not be confused with the whole. The fact that the legislator sometimes defines the structure of the thing of which he regulates the occurrence does not make it possible to reject the very principle of his procedures or to see therein anything other than the formulation of rules, or measures of evental unfolding —in this case, a mere formulation of concepts and conceptual models.

2. Second, it is to be noted that it is possible to take as the object of conceptualization the content, and in particular the contingent content, of a given rule or of a given group of legal rules constituting a system—whether it is the content of legal rules actually laid down by public authorities or whether it is the content of purely imaginary rules. It is thus possible to pick out concepts which provide models for certain categories of possible contents of legal regulations, that is, concepts representing the typical structure of certain evental patterns which could form the content of legal rules (such as the concepts of "statutory limitation," "installment plan," "limited company," "Supreme Court," "separation of property in marriage," "parliamentary system," etc.); moreover, this is a process frequently used by legal theory when systematizing its study of legal regulations. Here again we must not be misled. Obviously, legal rules (models of the occurrence of things enabling judgment by confrontation on the conformity or nonconformity of the occurrence of this thing or that) cannot be reduced to the concepts of certain possible categorial contents of legal regulations which merely permit the recognition of the conformity or nonconformity of the structure of the contents of a given legal regulation in relation to the categorial content which they represent. The notions of "statutory limitation" or "parliamentary system," for example, will permit us, when confronted with legal regulations of a certain content,

to recognize or not to recognize the typical system of "limitation" or the typical system of "parliament." If we claim that certain conceptual models of possible regulation content, that is, certain types of evental structures, represent "true" law and that they enable us to distinguish among the rules made by public authorities those which are authentically legal from those which are not, this is a process of a purely metaphysical nature, which under the would-be mantle of the concept law conceals ideological positions on legal policy and the contingent content of legal rules.

The extrication of the evental perspective in legal norms. If close examination is made of a body of legal norms reproduced in any textbook, and if an attempt is made to discover the most essential structure of the content of these norms, this evental or existential perspective which has just been mentioned, and which is the very nature of any rule, will quickly be perceived. Legal norms appear to constitute *models of the unfolding of facts of human activity* [93] *in the course of things, models of the occurrence of human things in the evental flux;* they provide a measure for the emergence in the world of human events, or, to put it another way, they represent models of the unfolding of human history. They can be reduced to this general schema: "In certain circumstances, at a certain moment, a certain person or category of persons may (or may not) accomplish this or that," or, in an impersonal form, "in certain circumstances, at a certain moment, certain human events, certain facts of human activity, may (or may not) occur."

This structure clearly appears in most legal norms, namely, those of which the verbal formulation turns on the words "may" and "ought" or their synonyms. It is of little importance in this respect whether the norms in question have to do with the regulation of the occurrence of multiple human events conceived as capable of recurring and of repeating themselves (they are frequently called "general" norms; for example, "any person causing damage to another ought to compensate for it"), or whether they are norms regulating the occurrence of unique human events, seen as occurring once and once only (these are frequently called "particular" or "individual" norms, of the type:

---

93. This striking expression is borrowed from Georges Hostelet, *L'Investigation scientifique des faits d'activité humaine* (Paris: Rivière, 1960).

"X may or ought to do such and such a thing on such and such a date").

However, although in certain cases this evental structure is less evident in the formulation of legal regulations, it is nonetheless present. This is the case for legal norms formulated according to the following models: "A certain body has been created"; "X has been appointed to such and such a post or has been relieved of his duties"; "such and such an assembly is dissolved"; "martial law is declared"; "such and such a legal act is rescinded or annulled"; "such and such a word or formula set forth in such and such a legal instrument means this"; "certain persons are deprived of certain rights"; etc. In general, it would be possible to quote here all the legal measures which suggest, by their formulation, the idea that public authorities "pronounce" something (an appointment, a dismissal, an establishment, etc.). But misunderstanding should be avoided. Behind such formulations there are indeed norms which regulate the occurrence of human events. In simple terms, the verbal fabric used is elliptical. The formula "A certain body has been created" is a shortened statement of the measure according to which this body ought to come into being or ought to take place in the course of things; in the same way, the formula "X is appointed to a certain position, or is relieved of his duties" expresses in short form the idea that X ought to occupy (and ought to be considered as occupying) certain functions or that he ought to cease (and be considered as having ceased) to occupy them; "such and such an assembly is dissolved" means similarly that the assembly in question ought to cease to exist or to meet. The proclamation of martial law is simply a formulation of the rule by which a special legal state of affairs shall apply from a certain date; the rescinding or annulment of a legal act means simply that this act ought to cease to be applied or even ought to be considered as never having been in force. Again, when the legislator stipulates that a certain word or sentence appearing in previous legislation has such and such a meaning, he thereby intends to make a norm, an interpretative norm, by virtue of which a certain meaning ought to be given to a certain legislative provision.

The above-mentioned examples simply show (contrary to what is often thought) [94] that the verbal formulation of a norm

94. See, in this respect, Amselek, *Méthode phénoménologique*, pp. 72 ff.

is not necessarily modeled on a uniform syntactical outline, in this case an outline which expresses explicitly the notions of "may" or "ought." Our linguistic apparatus finds room for varying formulations, and in particular for elliptical formulations. Again, the essential is the normative message of which these verbal formulas constitute the vehicle.

It is this perspective of evental unfolding in legal norms which is more or less confusedly expressed in the current notion that these norms are intended to regulate "human behavior." The idea of "behavior" should be understood here in its existential aspects, as when one speaks of the *behavior of nature,* that is, the occurrence of events in the context of natural facts. The behavior of a thing in this sense is the series of its manifestations, of its movements and the pattern of emergences revealing its presence in the world. Thus legal norms constitute the measure of human behavior in the course of things, the measure of human "products" [95] in the sense in which one may speak of the "products" of nature (that is, the occurrence of things in the context of natural facts). Human behavior understood in this way can of course include physical behavior as well as purely mental behavior, as was seen previously in the case of interpretative legal norms.

When the study of legal norms is broached (and, more generally, the study of ethical norms), it should not be forgotten that these norms always evaluate human "behavior" in the sense just given. It is only by a linguistic short cut that it is said of an individual that he is subject to legal norms. This in no way means that the individual is measured as such by legal regulations, or that he is capable as such of being in conformity or nonconformity with these regulations, but that his behavior (i.e., the emergence of the manifestations of his being-in-the-world, the occurrence of the events of his history) is measured by legal standards.[96]

Now it is striking that in both legal and ethical theory authors generally have no clear awareness of the evental perspective of

95. This expression is based on the French *se produire,* to occur or happen.—Trans.
96. This is what Kelsen is trying to say when he asserts: "It is not men as individuals who form the content of legal norms, but their actions and their abstentions as individuals, i.e., a certain form of human conduct" (*Théorie pure du droit,* 2d ed., p. 220).

the norms which they study and discuss; frequently they have only a confused notion of what is meant by the very ideas of "right" and "obligation." When somebody says that *he has the right* to do or to refrain from doing something, this means that he refers more or less consciously to a model evental pattern implying the possibility for him to behave in a certain way in the course of things. If he is prevented for one reason or another from behaving in this way, he will speak of *an infringement of his rights,* which expression simply means that he finds himself unable to behave in the manner indicated by this permissive norm. In the same way, when somebody considers that *he is obliged* to do or not to do something, this means that he refers to a normative measure which implies the necessity for him to behave in a certain way within the evental flux. To be *at fault,* or to *fail to comply* is to render this normative measure ineffective by not carrying out the necessary behavior implied by it, so that the situation will reveal a *failure* in relation to the model evental pattern, or on the other hand by behaving in a way prohibited by the norm, so that the situation will reveal a *going beyond* or *excess* in relation to the model evental pattern. Very often the analyses of legal or ethical theorists conceive of "rights" and "obligations" (and, by corollary, infringements of rights, and faults) as autonomous data, completely leaving aside the normative context in which they are situated. Thus rights and obligations are frequently treated as sorts of "properties" or "attributes" of the individuals concerned, which only serves to cloud the issue.[97] Such an odd approach completely obscures the fact that "rights" and "obligations" are simply the expression of the evental unfolding aspect of norms, which occupy in a more or less confused way the field of consciousness of such authors. It is because legal and ethical norms as such measure the modality of the occurrence of things that they express the notions of "right" or "power," of "obligation" or "necessity"; a "possible" thing is simply a thing *whose occurrence is possible,* and an "obligatory" thing is one *whose occurrence is obligatory.* It will be noted, moreover, that this curious way of looking at things is ill-suited to an entire series of legal or ethical norms—those which are expressed in impersonal form, disregarding the individuals or categories of individuals concerned. Such is the case with norms of

97. On this, see Amselek, *Méthode phénoménologique,* pp. 97 ff.

the following type: "such and such a train must arrive at such and such a time"; "such and such a building must contain certain safety appliances"; "such and such an establishment must remain open on Sundays"; etc. In all these cases, regulations constitute models of the unfolding of human events, but non-personalized models. The human facts whose emergence is thus regulated are not attached to particular persons or categories of persons, but are mentioned in a purely objective fashion. Such norms are not rare in positive law. With them one encounters powers or duties of emergence of human things which do not permit themselves to be reduced as such to the idea of personal attributes, proper to such and such a person.

Another equally unsatisfactory conception current in legal theory is that legal rights and obligations necessarily form binomials, or express themselves in complementary couples, every "right" belonging to X implying a corresponding "obligation" on the part of Y, and vice versa. I have already made some criticisms of this curious conception.[98] What should be said here is that this mode of thought manifests an ignorance of the evental aspects of norms, which the notions of rights and obligations simply express.

All such theoretical conceptions are the more tangled in that a certain confusion exists in the minds of some scholars between the obligatory content of imperative norms and their structure as measures or models. All norms, by the very fact that they constitute models or standards, imply that the object to which they could be applied *ought to be* in conformity with them; this "ought" expresses the instrumental logic of the norm as measure. Rather strangely, in the context of legal, and more generally of ethical, norms there is a tendency to confuse this generic instrumental datum with the content of normative measures and to imagine that all legal norms, and more generally all ethical norms, possess an imperative content, expressing obligations or duties. In this respect both legal and ethical theory are essentially based on legal or ethical obligation, as if this represented the specific and exclusive characteristic of ethical norms. There is thus a tendency to ignore the existence of permissive legal (or, more generally, ethical) norms expressing powers or rights, that is, possibilities of the occurrence of human things. This con-

98. *Ibid.*, pp. 195 ff., 265 ff.

fusion should be completely cleared up. The metrological logic of ethical norms is one thing, and their contents another. The obligation of occurrence or of nonoccurrence expressed by an imperative norm should not be confused with its nature as model with which measurable objects ought to be in conformity; further, it should also be recognized that beyond the "may" content of the permissive norm, there is the "ought" of its metrological structure. A permissive norm in fact implies that something *ought to be able* to happen or not to happen.

[2] Specific Eidetic Elements of the Object Law: Law as a Body of Norms with an Ethical Function, and More Exactly with the Function of Commands

If the thing Law is given in its generic essence as a body of normative measures, it appears that the normative measures involved manifest, at a second level, certain specific characteristics. Legal norms in effect belong to the category of *ethical norms* and, more particularly, that of *commands*. Some attention should be given to these two specifications.

The ethical essence of legal norms

Legal norms are currently defined as *ethical* norms, but to what typical structure found in the thing Law does this term refer? Here again it seems indispensable to return to things themselves, to endeavor to elucidate clearly the ethical *eidos* of legal norms, since the current concepts are so "empty of meaning" and precise significance for the consciousness. Thus many theorists tend to assimilate, somewhat syncretistically, this ethical structure to a certain type of content of normative measures. For them, it would seem, an ethical norm is a norm which deals with human behavior, which regulates the occurrence of human things, and it is thus that legal norms are considered to constitute ethical norms. This is a highly imperfect view of the reality of things. Ethical norms of course have the human content referred to, as I have already mentioned in respect to legal norms; but this is a contingent datum in relation to the *eidos* of ethical norms. One has only to think of rules formulated in the different social sciences (for example, psychological and sociological laws), whose content also consists in the unfolding of human events, the occurrence of human things, without their being given to our consciousness as ethical norms.

In fact, this association with the norms or laws of the social sciences shows clearly that the ethical structure of norms relates to their function, their instrumental role, and not directly to their content. The link between the ethical aspect and a certain specific instrumental role emerges moreover in the terminology employed: ethics, in its most fundamental sense, is defined as *the art of directing conduct*. Thus ethical norms represent the ideal technique for this art: they are norms which have the special instrumental function of guiding or directing human conduct. This specific instrumental role implies, consequently, a certain type of content in ethical norms—a human content—but this is not itself, as such, the essential element of the ethical norm.

Indeed, it is in order to express the ethical function of legal norms that legal theorists frequently define the latter as "rules governing human conduct." [99]

99. See, for example, Kelsen, *Théorie pure du droit*, 2d ed., pp. 44 ff. It should be noted here that authors often mention the hypothesis that in antiquity certain laws directing human conduct had as a sort of secondary function the control of animals, plants, or inanimate things. In fact this hypothesis is far from being proved, since the examples given by these authors always involve law regulating human conduct. For example, Kelsen notes: "It is said in the Bible that the ox which has killed a man should be put to death, and this clearly represents a punishment. In antiquity, a special court existed at Athens for proceedings directed against the stone or the spear, or any other object by which a man had been killed, probably unintentionally. Again, in the Middle Ages it was possible to take proceedings against an animal, for example a bull which had caused the death of a man, or locusts which destroyed the harvests. The accused animal was thus convicted in accordance with legal procedure, and executed, in exactly the same way as a human criminal" (pp. 43 ff.). The legal norms here mentioned in no way regulate the behavior of animals, plants, or inanimate things but they do regulate the behavior of men in respect of them (the human behavior consisting in destroying a certain animal or a certain thing which proved harmful, or undertaking an entire ritual and pronouncing sacramental formulas in respect of this animal or thing). Such human behavior obviously seems curious and it is quite clear that such regulations were inspired by metaphysical and animist conceptions; but on the other hand it does not seem that these metaphysical conceptions ever resulted, in antiquity, in the public authorities being given the absurd and inane function of directing anything other than human behavior, and therefore of checking anything other than human behavior (just as certain present-day legal systems, strongly influenced by religious beliefs—for example, in Muslim countries—do not cease to be legal systems governing human behavior).

I shall attempt to restore this specific instrumental function of ethical norms; after that I shall endeavor to demonstrate the distinction between ethical norms and scientific norms, even when the latter have the same type of content, that is, patterns of human events.

The specific instrumental function of ethical norms. When one speaks of the directive function or the function of direction of human conduct belonging to ethical norms, one means that these norms are instruments for the creative, "constructive" activity of man, in exactly the same way as tailors' models. Their role is to constitute measures of that which ought to happen in the context of the facts of human activity, measures of the unfolding of human history, for the use of the makers and also the actors in this history, so that they will be able to cut out their work (that is, their own behavior, the development of their emergences in the world), to fashion it, and to adjust it to these models. In other words, they are drawn up and set forth as measures which are to be "fulfilled," reproduced, and followed. This is their specific instrumental function—to serve, in the context of the facts of human activity, as tools of reference guiding the action of men in the creation of themselves, in the constructing of their own behavior.

One notices here that the existence of ethical norms (and particularly of legal norms) in our cultural universe is based on a fundamental datum of the human condition, namely, that man is at least partly the master of his behavior, of the sum of his activity, and of the events which reveal his presence in the world; he is able at least partly to fashion or model them as he wishes. Within the limits of his finitude, in the context of the mechanisms which form the pattern of his constitution, there is room for some movement or liberty—a sort of *marginal liberty* (which is different from the "total liberty" invoked by Sartre and which is

---

In any case it is of small consequence whether this very marginal hypothesis, of purely antiquarian interest, of an authentic law allegedly relating to animals, plants, and inanimate things is historically true or false. Even assuming it is true, the hypothesis would not have any great effect on the reduction of the law to a body of ethical norms intended to govern human conduct. In fact, such a hypothesis would necessarily be based on an anthropomorphic assimilation of the structure of animals, plants, and inanimate things to the structure of man, and on a projection of human "conduct" into such nonhuman beings. In this way the legal norms in question would continue to appear as ethical norms for the guidance of human conduct.

in effect meaningless since it implies the nonfinitude of man).
The very fact that ethical norms exist is the clearest sign that
man is not governed by a total mechanical or instinctive determination of his emergences in the world. The fact that men draw
up and use measures in respect to their own history, that they
endeavor to "make it to measure," indicates clearly that in reality
human history is not ready made, at least not in its totality. It is
against this background that the existence of ethical norms in
our environment assumes its full significance. "It is difficult to
admit," observes Bergson, "that nature, which instituted society
at the end of the two major lines of evolution which produced the
hymenoptera and man, has settled in advance all the details of
the activity of each ant in its anthill and neglected to provide
man with general directives at least, for the coordination of his
conduct with that of his fellows. Human societies no doubt differ
from insect societies in that they leave the action of the individual and indeed that of the community undetermined." [100]
But as Bergson also notes, "It [nature] endowed man with a
creative intelligence. Instead of providing him with instruments,
as with many animal species, it preferred him to construct them
himself." [101]

Thus ethical norms are the type of instrument invented by
the human intelligence in reply to the challenge of nature, which
left man at least partially to be the master of his "fate."

It will be noticed here again how much current language can
suggest to the attentive mind. Thus the image behind the expression "rules of *human conduct*," used to define ethical norms,
reveals particularly clearly the specific instrumental function of
these norms. This idea of *human conduct* [102] suggests the human

100. Bergson, *Two Sources of Morality and Religion*, pp. 96–97 (translation slightly modified). See also *Creative Evolution*, p. 126, where Bergson
clearly demonstrates that the evolution process of living forms directed
itself toward structures involving an ever greater margin of free movement: "From the most humble moneron to the most gifted insects, and
the most intelligent vertebrates, the progress involved was above all that
of the nervous system with, at each step, all the creations and com-
plications that this progress required. . . . A nervous system, with neu-
rons placed end to end in such a way that the extremity of each one of
them contains multiple routes (in each of which a question is put) is a
real *reservoir of indetermination*" (translation slightly modified).
101. Bergson, *Two Sources of Morality and Religion*, p. 273 (translation slightly modified).
102. The French word *conduite* can also suggest the action of driving
a car.—Trans.

datum in terms of *spatial locomotion,* which probably corresponds to the most originary and most direct vision of man's being-in-the-world, of the human phenomenon. Men in the evental flux are given first as animated machines, which move, which go from place to place, which come and go. But behind these "animations," behind the behavior of the machine, behind the "mask" (*persona*) by which men give an external manifestation of their presence in the world, there is a more intimate and more essential reality. The "animator," the driver of the machine, who directs it and who holds the controls or the "rudder,"[103] is also present. Within this fresco representing the man-driver of the vehicle of his own person, ethical norms take on the aspects of *rules of conduct,* with the function of guiding men-drivers (*conducteurs*) in their movements and in their goings to and fro; they trace for their guidance *lines of conduct* to be followed and they act as guidelines. Thus, in the perspective of this imagery, ethical norms appear as a kind of *human highway code.*

Modern thought, particularly in its existentialist aspects, has tended to substitute for this locomotive picture of reality (which is deeply rooted in our modes of expression) the image of the craftsman, which has become much more familiar to our minds. Here man is depicted as a being who at least partially makes himself, produces himself, and constructs his existence, his acts, and his gestures; behind human events, behind that which occurs in the context of human actions, there is man—craftsman, master craftsman, and producer. But this slightly different imagery seeks to express basically the same originary intuitions. Whether ethical norms are represented as models of conduct for the purpose of guiding the direction of men as drivers of themselves, or as models of construction of human history for the purpose of guiding men considered as craftsmen of themselves, the same datum of consciousness is being described.

Another revealing aspect of the terminology is the current description of ethical norms (and particularly of legal norms) as *precepts* or *prescripts;* it is often said that law or ethics prescribes human behavior. These terms also explain the specific instrumental function of such norms. As measures for guiding

103. *Gouvernail,* with obvious connotations. See also "direction" (*gouverne*).—Trans.

the creative action of men in the construction of their manifestations in the world, ethical norms thus imply (within the logic of
this *archetypal* purposive instrumentality) that they must be at
the service of the man-craftsman prior to the completion of his
work. They must be grasped by him beforehand (*prae-capio,
prae-ceptum*) and thus, where appropriate, be communicated
and formulated verbally for him in advance by another person
(*prae-scriptio*).[104]

*The different instrumental functions of ethical and scientific
norms.* The function of science is to set forth and to formulate
norms which are currently called *scientific laws* or *principles,*
or else *laws of nature.*

Very frequently ethical theorists, and particularly legal theorists, categorically deny that these scientific formulations possess
a normative character—rather curiously, scientific rules are not
considered to be real rules! This assertion is clearly based on a
misunderstanding. There is no doubt that a scientist sets forth
(and that his professional function is to set forth) normative

104. This explanation allows us to clear up in passing the obscurity
which currently surrounds legal theory on the question of the retroactive
character of certain rules of law. Authors readily assume that anomalies
sometimes exist in legal experience, anomalies which on the part of the
legislator, for example, might consist in deliberately enacting in 1973 a
rule regulating human behavior which should have occurred in 1972. This
notion attributes to the legislator methods which are somewhat absurd.
In fact, the rather diverse hypotheses usually placed under the heading of
"retroactivity" cannot be reduced to this outline. To take some typical
examples: rules which require X to pay a tax or to be sentenced for past
acts are said to be retroactive. These are clearly intended to constitute
archetypes not of acts already accomplished but of acts to be accomplished
(the payment of a tax by X, the infliction of a penalty on X by the com-
petent authorities). Similarly, rules which annul or regularize *ab initio*
previous legal instruments, i.e., earlier formulations of legal rules, are
described as retroactive. Here again norms of this kind aim in fact at
constituting archetypes of behavior "to be followed," and they mean that
"in the future" a certain legal instrument must be considered as never
having existed or that a certain legal instrument irregularly formulated
must be considered as having always been regularly formulated. Such considerations imply certain consequences under the legal system in force.
Finally, another example: a public authority (and particularly a judge)
may take a legal step, e.g., a court "sentence," basing this measure on a
retroactive application of another legal measure. Thus a judge may sentence X to compensate for damages because X's behavior in 1972 was incorrect in relation to such and such a legal norm formulated in 1973. Here
again we in no way encounter an absurd statement of such a legal norm
ruling on already accomplished acts; only the motivation of the making
of a legal norm (i.e., of the judgment) is in question.

measures, that is, measures of the unfolding of the course of things, models of the emergence of natural or human things. When science states, for example, that "heated metal must expand," this is indeed a norm; and, moreover, it is by more or less conscious reference to this norm, or to this normative measure, that one usually concludes, when confronted by the expansion of metal due to heat, that "it is normal." [105] The social sciences in particular, such as sociology and psychology, formulate normative measures which have exactly the same kind of content as ethical norms, that is, they deal with the occurrence of human things. Thus when one reads a legal code or a collection of legal texts, if one brackets off the ethical nature of the norms in question, one has the impression of dealing with, or of the possibility of dealing with, scientific norms; inversely, the same experiment can be made with scientific laws.

If scholars in the ethical disciplines generally refuse to recognize the normative character of scientific laws, it is in fact because they assimilate syncretistically *norms* and *ethical norms*. It is of course true that scientific laws, although they constitute authentic norms, certainly do not constitute ethical norms, even when they have a human content. They have an entirely different specific instrumental function. Whereas ethical norms have a directive function, scientific norms have a function which could be labeled *recognitive*. The aim of science, in effect, is not that of drawing up and formulating models to be reproduced or realized, models of construction for guiding the creative action of men. In fact, the objective of the scientist is to construct models which represent reality itself, the how-it-ought-to-be of what is actually realized in the world. More exactly, the function of scientific norms is to constitute models of the unfolding of

---

105. In this respect, when it is said that there are no "value judgments" in the context of science, it is simply meant that it is not part of the function of a scientist to set forth emotional or metaphysical assessments of the thing he studies. On the other hand, he does set forth, in conditions which will be stated, instruments of judgment making it possible to give a measure or a value to things which occur in reality. There is a tendency to speak here of "reality judgments," which are considered to be radically different from "value judgments," but these expressions are very defective. All judgments are in their very principle attributions of value. The fact that scientific norms on the basis of which judgments are capable of being made are of a particular type and that reality is their object does not allow one to give an incomplete picture of the judgmental operation itself, which remains fundamentally the same.

things in reality, instruments of reference indicating the modality of the emergence of things in the course of the real, or, in other words, instruments giving the measure of the course of events which actually happen and not the measure of the course of events which are to happen, or to be realized. Their purposive instrumentality is to provide, for the benefit of men, *tools of recognition* to enable them to recognize and to identify the course of things which actually occur before their eyes and thus to recognize themselves and to find themselves in the evental flux which reality unravels before their consciousness. Thus science is currently associated with the idea of "forecasting"; scientific norms, as models of the unfolding of reality, enable men to *measure in advance*, by syllogistic application, the evental developments of reality and consequently to adapt their behavior to them.

The existence of such scientific norms in our cultural universe goes back, like that of ethical norms, to a fundamental hypothesis: namely, that reality repeats itself partially, or is capable of repeating itself and does in fact repeat itself at least in part according to a determined mode. This double condition makes it reasonable for men to endeavor to establish efficient tools for the recognition of the evental pattern of reality. If reality never repeated itself, if identical things never recurred in the course of reality, if reality emerged in entirely different series of events, it would obviously be absurd to attempt to construct tools for the recognition of the occurrence of things in reality. This is the real meaning of the famous formula of Aristotle that "science can only apply to the general." If reality simply consisted of unique events, science would have no *raison d'être;* scientific norms aim, by their very function as tools of recognition, to provide models for the occurrence of multiple events, conceived of as being capable of repeating themselves and of recurring. But apart from this condition of the repetitiveness of reality, scientific norms presuppose, in order to constitute efficient tools, another condition. To be able to set forth measures of the occurrence of things in reality (to be able to assert, for example, that in reality "A occurs or may occur when B and C have themselves occurred"), and for these measures to enable men in practice to locate themselves in the course of reality, the existence of a certain regularity and of a certain determined order in the completion of things, and in the unfolding of things which become, must be presupposed. In order to draw up as a kind of compass a model of the manifestation of things in reality, it must be presupposed that in reality things appear according to a certain determined mode, in a constantly uniform fashion, so that it is possible to postulate usefully that the course of reality *ought to be* thus and not otherwise. Or, in other words, in order that the emergence of real things correspond effectively to models or rules set forth by men and that these models or rules may provide authentic tools of recognition, it must be presupposed that there is in reality a certain determined mode of emergence and a certain regularity in the manifestation of things.[106] It is something of a miracle that this hypothesis is verified at least partially in practice, and that consequently science is possible.[107] Thus the existence of ethical norms goes back to the hypothesis of man's freedom, of a certain lack of determination in his behavior; the existence of scientific norms goes back to the hypothesis of a certain order in reality and of determination in the unfolding of things which are realized.

In any case, one can see the difference which separates ethics and science: whereas ethical norms are instruments for the *direction* of men, tracing out their itineraries and marking out a route, scientific norms are instruments for a kind of human *lantern*, that is, topographical indicators enabling man to set his bearings on the terrain.[108]

Thus there is, of course, a difference in the modes of setting forth the two kinds of norms. Scientific laws, in order to efficiently fulfill their function, must be based on the observation

---

106. See note 65 on the link between the idea of measure and the idea of determination and of limit, which implies a link between the idea of a thing supposed to correspond to a measure and the idea of a thing supposed to be determined, or limited, in its modes of being.

107. See the observations of Bergson in *Creative Evolution*, p. 231: "The main problem of the theory of knowledge is to know how science is possible, that is to say, in effect, why there is order and not disorder in things." Bergson also recognizes that the existence of order in the evental flux of reality constitutes a "mystery," which is only a way of expressing its contingency.

108. It may be noted in passing that this difference in instrumental function throws light on a point which has caused a great deal of discussion. Since they are supposed to be "photographs" of reality, scientific norms may be *true* or *false* according to whether things appear objectively to be realized as they indicate or otherwise. Whereas in the case of ethical norms, which have the function of guiding the achievements of men-craftsmen, their productions may only be *effective* (i.e., followed by an effect or by effectualization or achievement by men-craftsmen) or *ineffective*.

of the reality of which they aim to constitute a copy and of which they aim to reproduce the eventual regularities. More exactly, they must be set out as far as possible on the basis of the observation of a series of becomings of the same things, in order to perceive more surely the modality of the occurrence of the things appearing in these series. Just by varying experimentally certain elements of observed eventual patterns, one perceives more clearly the concatenation of reality. By observing that in the course of reality a certain phenomenon A apparently always occurs (or, on the contrary, never occurs) under certain conditions, the scientist is able to set forth the norm: "In certain conditions A ought to occur, or not occur." Similarly, after patiently observing that in the course of reality phenomenon B sometimes occurs, or sometimes fails to occur, in certain given conditions, the scientist sets forth the rule: "In certain given conditions B may, or may not, occur." Scientific models are of practical use only in that they faithfully reproduce the modes of emergence observed in the real course of things, the perceived processes of the realization of things in the world. Ethical norms (and particularly legal norms) obviously cannot be made in this way; their establishment calls for essentially inventive procedures on the part of man. In this respect the words of Jean Giraudoux in *La Guerre de Troie n'aura pas lieu* may be interpreted literally: "Law is the most powerful of the schools of the imagination."

If our consciousness of this specific instrumental function of scientific norms is usually confused, it is because we are still heir to former metaphysical conceptions which render our perspectives very obscure. In fact, man has a primary tendency to reduce everything to his own image and in particular to project his ethical experience (and especially his legal experience) onto the rest of the universe. Hence the anthropomorphic conception by which nonhuman things are thought to be regulated in their behavior, like men themselves, by ethical norms which they ought to "obey," by decrees, or by "laws" deriving from a supreme Legislator of a divine nature. These "laws" of nature are thought to be "behind" the regularity observed in the real course of things. And the specific role of science would be to "discover them," to find them out as such. The norms formulated by science were thus originally conceived of as ethical norms, or as essentially legal archetypes "discovered" by the scientist. This pan-legal vision of the universe has for a long time interfered with scientific work, with the result that only relative attention was paid to the data of experience, since the laws of nature could by hypothesis be "disobeyed," giving rise to effects not in conformity with their prescriptions.[109] Even today, after the admittedly somewhat ambiguous triumph of positivist ideas and the acceptance of the experimental in the sciences, conceptions of science remain strongly influenced by reminiscences of past thinking. There is a continuing tendency to conceive, more or less confusedly, of the norms established by the scientist as "laws," that is, as ethical norms of the same kind as legal norms, as "commands" addressed to nature:

> In the eyes of most men physical law, social or moral law—indeed any law—is a command. There is a certain order in nature which expresses itself in laws; the facts are considered to *obey* these laws in order to conform to this order. The scientist himself can scarcely refrain from believing that the law *presides* over the facts and consequently precedes them, like the Platonic Idea with which reality had to conform. The greater the degree of generalization, the more he tends, for better or for worse, to endow laws with this imperative characteristic. One has to struggle against oneself in order to conceive of the principles of mechanics otherwise than as inscribed for all eternity on transcendent tablets, which modern science has retrieved from another Sinai.[110]

It is remarkable that this projection of the legal into the scientific has involved, by a sort of reverse action, a distortion of the conceptions of the law itself which has proved equally

109. See the remark of Emile Meyerson concerning scientific laws: "The conviction that these laws are subject to no exceptions, to no disobedience similar to that represented by felonies or the infringement of civil laws, is a recent idea which would not be entirely accepted by certain thinkers" (quoted in Lalande, *Vocabulaire*, p. 585).

110. Bergson, *Two Sources of Morality and Religion*, p. 4 (translation slightly modified). For a topical example of the resurgence of these animistic ideas, see Jacques Rueff, *The Gods and the Kings* (New York: Macmillan, 1971). Even the most careful scientists use highly ambiguous metaphysical language. Thus, in his *Chance and Necessity* (New York: Knopf, 1971), Jacques Monod, having vigorously denounced animist temptations in contemporary scientific thought (see pp. 29–44, 170–80), refers like other biologists to the anthropomorphic image of a genetic "code," of "messages" or "information" which are considered to be communicated and deciphered within the cell tissue (see pp. 104–17, 193–96) in order to describe the mechanisms of corpuscular interaction which preside over hereditary phenomena, and more precisely over the natural fabrication of protein. This involves projecting the human psychic datum beyond the human structure and onto the micromolecular system.

tenacious. The vision of a supreme Legislator formulating laws and precepts for all things has in fact created the impression that such transcendent laws—the laws of nature, or "natural law"— were also formulated for man himself; this natural law of divine origin is thus considered to be the only *real* law. Law formulated by human public authorities (human positive law) can only be authentic if it reproduces exactly the prescriptions of this natural law. This metaphysical conception of law was to be associated with the new approaches in the conception of science. When science became "positivist" in the nineteenth century, that is, when it was decided to consider only laws which had been rigorously verified by experience as seriously established (those laws verified in accordance with the reality of the facts), legal theory also claimed to have become "positivist," although it must be admitted that this really represented nothing more than an intellectual pretension, without practical significance. For some, this label implied the reduction of the study of law to the experimental study of social reality and to the restitution of laws which set out its exact outline, these sociological laws being assimilated to legal norms themselves (cf. the theses of "sociological positivism," used under the cloak of phenomenology by the Argentinian "egological" school of Carlos Cossio); for others, the label "positivist" implied at bottom that the study of legal norms formulated by public authorities (which alone were held to be law) had henceforth to be limited to effective legal norms, effectively obeyed, effectively realized, and thus in conformity with reality. Only effective law was considered to be authentic, or at least worthy of interest (cf. the theses of "legal positivism").[111] All these strange conceptions, which are still very much alive in current legal thought, are simply the pervasive result of the initial confusion between scientific and legal norms.

Apart from these general conceptions, one can pick out in legal thought many other more fragmentary consequences of this confusion of the legal and the scientific. Thus, for example, jurists still tend to think that legal norms can only be "general"; as with science, law can only apply *to the general*.[112] There is

111. On all these points, and particularly on the evolution from the nineteenth century onward of the meaning of the expression "positive law" (no longer simply law "given position" but also "effective" law), see Amselek, *Méthode phénoménologique*, pp. 150 ff., 287 ff., 312 ff.
112. See *Ibid.*, pp. 297 ff.

even a tendency to assimilate purely and simply the idea of *rule* and that of *rule of the general* (see, for example, these remarks of Jean Carbonnier: "A rule is an abstract provision that is general in space, permanent in time, and which presupposes the repetition of cases and potential applicability to an indefinite number of future hypotheses").[113] Such authors are not aware that they are subscribing to a subtle confusion between the ethical norms of law and scientific norms. It is true that often they have only a somewhat nebulous and syncretistic consciousness of what is meant by this notion of the "general" to which they refer. In practice it is easy to move from the ideas of the "multiple" or "repeatable" and the "unique" or "nonrepeatable" to those of the "collective" and of the "individual" (this is, moreover, the case in the above quotation from Carbonnier). "General" legal norms are thus conceived not only as norms dealing with repeatable events but also and particularly as norms with a non-individualized content, regulating the occurrence of collective events, or the behavior of categories of individuals. They are contrasted with "individual" or "particular" norms conceived as norms regulating the occurrence of individual events, the behavior of individuals designated by name. Thus, basically, the statement that legal norms must be general, like scientific norms (or like all other norms), depends on an ideological point of view (which in France goes back to the Revolution) which favors "class" law, that is, giving identical treatment to all those who are in the same situation and who belong to the same category, without discriminating between individuals.

In any case the confusion which thus developed must be dealt with.[114] Norms regulating the occurrence of *collective events*, which concern a class of individuals or a category of human things, are one thing, and norms regulating the occurrence of *multiple or repeatable events*, conceived as being capable of recurring, are another—the latter endeavor to provide a representation of the mode of occurrence of such multiple

---

113. Carbonnier, *Droit civil* (Paris: Presses Universitaires de France, 1969), I, 15.

114. This confusion has some significance for legal practice itself; it gives an uneven character to the distinction made in administrative law, and particularly in French administrative law, between "statutory administrative acts" and "individual administrative acts" (see, for example, Michel Stassinopoulos, *Traité des actes administratifs* [Paris: Sirey, 1954], pp. 65 ff.).

events in the complete series of their products. Similarly, norms which measure the occurrence of *individual events,* concerning one or several individuals designated by name, are one thing, and norms which regulate the occurrence of *unique events,* considered to be capable of occurring once and once only, are another. A norm can regulate perfectly well the occurrence of a unique event while referring to a category of individuals (norms of the type: "Everyone born in 1953 will be drafted on January 1, 1973"); and, inversely, a norm can regulate perfectly well the occurrence of a multiple event considered as capable of recurring, although referring to one individual only (norms of the kind: "Under such and such conditions, X may or ought to do such and such a thing").

Legal ethical norms as having the essence of commands

Legal norms belong to a subclass of ethical norms: the subclass of *commands* (or, in other words, *orders, instructions, injunctions,* or *decisions* in the strong sense). This is what is meant by the famous Latin aphorism, *jus est quod jussum est.* This is also what is meant by legal theorists when they invoke in relation to legal norms the ideas of *constraint, necessity, coercion* or *coercibility, the obligatory,* and other similar concepts. But, here again, to what specific structure recognized in legal rules does this refer? It may be noted once more the extent to which the conceptions on the basis of which we live in ordinary experience are nebulous, confused, and distant from the things themselves to which they refer. I have already mentioned the tendency of authors in the normative disciplines to confuse *norm* and *ethical norm,* to bring into the generic *eidos* of the normative, elements of the specific *eidos* of ethical norms; but there is an equal amount of confusion in practice between *norm* or *ethical norm* and *command,* probably because there is a tendency to assimilate the simple metrological structure of norms (the "ought" implied in their logic as measures) to the specific structure of commands.[115] This is a regrettable form of syncretism. As

115. This confusion is particularly obvious in the following remark of L. Boisse (cited in Lalande, *Vocabulaire,* p. 690): "It is difficult to imagine that an ideal does not imply in some way the obligation to attain it. The notion of the ideal is always more or less the negation of a defec-

André Lalande remarks, "A norm is not necessarily a law or command; it may be an ideal without any characteristic of obligation." [116]

But even authors who distinguish between norms or ethical norms and commands have only a very confused view of what constitutes the typical structure of the latter; this is particularly the case with legal theorists. In this respect a kind of double level of consciousness is evident in the way in which jurists currently depict the command *eidos* of rules of law. There is first a kind of primary, spontaneous, and unconsidered vision, which is at the same time vague, obscure, and ambiguous—the immediate basic datum of the command *eidos* of law, as given to the ordinary consciousness of jurists. The latter conceive of law at first sight as a *system or technique of constraint,* as a *technique of compulsion or coercion.*[117] Thus there is a tendency to attribute more or less obscurely to legal norms the character of instruments of compulsion or pressure, making it possible to break the will, to force men to act in a certain way; legal norms are considered to be mysteriously endowed with a kind of *power* or *force* (the expressions "legal force" and "power of the law" are frequent; it is also said that legal rules are "in force"), and are thought of as fetters weighing on the individuals concerned, compelling them to submit to the prescriptions which they contain. This curious vision is clearly evident in numerous obscure essays on legal theory: "In contrast to laws of a physical kind which cannot be ignored, and to moral or intellectual laws for the benefit of the conscience or the intelligence and which may be transgressed without any other sanction than that arising from the internal responsibility of the culprit, the essence of social laws is that they impose *not only duties which command, but obligations which bind. They brook neither resistance nor insubordination.*" [118] "Law is not simply a body of intellectual

---

tive or insufficient reality and an affirmation of a better and fuller reality. How then can one refrain from deriving an imperative from the normative?"

116. *Ibid.,* p. 691.

117. This type of expression is constantly found in the writings of jurists; see, for example, Kelsen, *Théorie pure du droit,* 2d ed., pp. 46 ff.; Jean Dabin, *Théorie générale du droit,* new ed. (Paris: Dalloz, 1969), pp. 45 ff.; Virally, *La Pensée juridique,* pp. xxv ff.; Haesaert, *Théorie générale du droit,* pp. 121 ff.; and del Vecchio, *Philosophy of Law,* pp. 297 ff.

118. Georges Burdeau, *Traité de science politique* (Paris: Librairie générale de droit et de jurisprudence, 1949), I, 153.

propositions. It deserves its name only because it imposes respect, because it *actually* authorizes, forbids, or directs human
behavior."[119] Numerous quotations could be given along these
lines.[120]

At a more reflective and developed level of consciousness,
theorists who wish to go beyond this sort of vague primary impression of the command *eidos* perceived in law are often led
to develop the conception that there is in law a specific essential
datum. For some, this consists in the fact that infringements
against the prescriptions of legal norms automatically involve
(or could involve) a penalty imposed by the public authorities on
the lawbreaker.[121] For others, this specific datum consists more
precisely in the fact that legal norms themselves endow their
prescriptions with sanctions, of the type "X ought to do this or
that under penalty of such and such a punishment."[122]

119. Virally, *La Pensée juridique*, pp. 80 ff.; see also p. 8.
120. It is, moreover, this same obscure vision of the command structure
of legal norms which has caused certain errors concerning the etymology
of the latin words *lex* and *jus*. Some have claimed that the word *lex* is
derived from the verb *legare,* which means "to bind" (see, for example,
Léo Pelland, *Introduction aux sciences juridiques* [Montreal: Bellarmin,
1960], p. 71); in reality it is soundly established that *lex* comes from
legere ("to read"), which refers to a certain mode of communication of
legal rules and not to a claimed assimilation of law to "bonds" or to
"chains." Similarly, for a long time it was thought possible to derive the
term *jus* from a root implying the idea of "yoke," but the most recent
philological research reveals that this term in fact comes from another
root (which is also thought to be the origin of the verb "to swear": *jurer*),
which simply involves the idea of measure, model, or rule, and goes back
to the most essential legal datum. "Etymologically, there is a very widespread impression that the words *jus, justum, justitia* come from the
Sanscrit root *ju* (*yu*), which means 'bond' (see *jugum, jungere,* etc.).
More recently, however, another point of view has found favor among
philologists, put forward for the first time by Kuhn (in "Zeitschrift ver-
gleichende Sprachforschung," IV [1855], 374), who asserts that *jus* (for-
merly *jous*) is rather connected with the Vedic *yos* and the Avestic *yaôs.*
These terms are rather ill-defined, but are certainly of religious significance: safeguard, defense against evil, propitiation, or, in the opinion of
other scholars, purifications—but always in reference to the divine will"
(del Vecchio, *La Justice, la vérité,* pp. 8 ff.).
121. See, for example, Roubier, *Théorie générale du droit,* pp. 32 ff.;
Dabin, *Théorie générale du droit,* new ed., pp. 45 ff.; del Vecchio, *Philosophy of Law,* pp. 297 ff.; Gény, *Science et technique en droit privé,* I,
47; and R. Bonnard, "L'Origine de l'ordonnancement juridique," in *Mélanges Hauriou,* p. 68.
122. See particularly Kelsen, *Théorie pure du droit,* 2d ed., pp. 48 ff.;
cf. Claude du Pasquier, *Introduction à la théorie générale et à la philosophie du droit* (Neuchâtel-Paris: Delachaux et Niestlé, 1967), pp. 112 ff.

It is not my intention to linger on these conceptions and the blind alleys into which they lead.[123] I should simply like to elucidate the still very unclear datum of the consciousness which is at the basis of such conceptual representations, that is, the typical command structure of which the thing Law partakes.

If one attempts to observe carefully the difference in one's consciousness between a norm conceived simply as an ethical norm and a norm conceived as a command (particularly in the form of a legal norm), it will quickly be seen that the difference consists in the *more developed specification of the instrumental function of the command.* Ethical norms, as has been seen already, are norms whose function is to provide models for manufacturing, measures to be followed, to be reproduced, and to be used as supports or guides for human realizations. Commands are given as ethical norms with the function of constituting measures to be *compulsorily* followed and reproduced, to be *compulsorily* used as supports or guides for the realizations of the individuals concerned. It is inherent in the instrumental purposiveness of the command that it constitutes not simply the measure of something which is to be realized, but the measure of something which must be realized, of something which it is necessary to do. It should be said more precisely that a command is a model of a human eventual pattern, a model of the occurrence of human events in the course of things, with the specific purpose of having to be compulsorily realized by those whose behavior is directly or indirectly affected (this last hypothesis concerns norms having an impersonal form).

In other words, commands constitute a particular technique of ethics, or of the art of directing human conduct,[124] that which could be labeled the technique of authoritarian or imposed direction, which consists in tracing out rigid model-lines of conduct from which the men-drivers (*hommes-conducteurs*) concerned should not in principle depart and which consequently implies a limitation on their initiative. This technique is different from the technique of flexible direction, or of proposed direction, in the

---

123. See, on this, Amselek, *Méthode phénoménologique,* pp. 219 ff., 251 ff.

124. The French word involved (*conduite*) means both "conduct" or "behavior" and "driving." This association is behind the following passage. Thus the expression *homme-conducteur* used by the author suggests both the idea of "man-driver" and that of "man-behaver."—Trans.

form of *recommendations*. These may be analyzed as ethical norms whose realization is considered desirable but not compulsory and are thus left to the discretionary appreciation of the men-drivers concerned; they involve model-lines of conduct considered to be advisable, but which are not binding on men-drivers. Thus it is inherent in their very function that they may be departed from.[125] In a sense, with commands one is confronted with what might be called automatic-pilot instruments for conduct; their instrumental purposiveness implies that the man-driver has only to fix his rudder and to follow the already-traced line represented by a number of compulsory checkpoints— whereas in the case of recommendations the traced line does not have the function of securing the rudder of the driver. It involves only a recommended itinerary, which does not exclude, but on the contrary implies, the possibility of assessment and of freedom of movement on the part of the driver-behaver. Or, in other words, men use *hard* model-lines and *soft* model-lines to construct their own history; commands and recommendations correspond respectively to these two varieties of tool.[126]

It is perhaps useful to observe that the technique of commands, like that of recommendations, does not necessarily imply (contrary to what might be thought) a context of relations be-

125. Hence André Lalande observes that "the normative is a genus which contains two principal species: the imperative and the estimative" (*Vocabulaire*, p. 691). It is this difference between commands and recommendations which jurists seek particularly to express when they contrast in the traditional way law (a body of compulsory norms) and morals (a body of noncompulsory norms). The term "morals" is here understood as a synonym pure and simple of "recommendations," as when one speaks of somebody "moralizing" (*faire la morale à quelqu'un*), which means that he wishes to recommend a line of conduct to a person; the "moralist," understood in the sense of the person who "moralizes," does not command —he recommends.

126. It will be noted that this distinction between commands and recommendations does not exactly coincide with the Kantian distinction between "categorical imperatives" and "hypothetical imperatives." The latter endeavors to classify ethical norms in virtue of the expression of their content (either conditional or hypothetical content, of the type "X ought to do such and such to be able to do this or that," or unconditional or categorical content—"X ought to do such and such a thing"), whereas the distinction developed here endeavors to classify ethical measures according to the compulsory or noncompulsory character of their realization as implied in their function. With this reservation, commands may be characterized as measures of "categorical" realization, and recommendations as measures of "hypothetical" realization, since it is subject to the consent of those concerned.

tween two or more individuals, some being in the position of superiors with the function of giving commands or recommendations for the benefit of the others, and others being in the position of subordinates. One can create for oneself ethical norms with the function of commands or of simple recommendations; or, again, commands and recommendations can be set up on the basis of joint agreement between two or more individuals concerned (e.g., legal contracts). In other terms, a man can be not only the craftsman or the builder of himself, but also his own legislator, his own architect—the leader determining his self-guidance. Man is in the unique situation of being able to cumulate several roles: that of the machine, which is driven; that of the driver, pilot, or operator who holds the rudder; and that of the director of conduct or captain laying down in the form of commands or recommendations certain model-lines of conduct or ethical measures which the operator needs for his guidance. The fact that an individual commands others, that is, exercises under certain conditions a function of authoritarian direction of their conduct, is a purely contingent datum in relation to the basic technique of the command. The latter does not necessarily imply an interpersonal phenomenon of "alienation" from such guidance, but simply a plurality of roles to whomever these belong.

Thus it may be said in summary that the normative measures constituted by commands are specific tools for the authoritarian direction of human conduct, and this does not necessarily imply either heteronomy (the authoritarian direction of the conduct of X by Y) or unilaterality (the unilateral direction of the conduct of X by X alone or of X by Y alone).

This rapid survey of the *eidos* of the commands throws some light on one's consciousness of law. As commands of the public authorities, legal norms imply by their specific instrumental function that the measures constituted by them are compulsorily to be carried out. This element of instrumental purposiveness is glimpsed confusedly in language which speaks of *force* or *compulsion* in law, when legal norms are associated with instruments of coercion. These expressions are obviously defective, since the instrumental function of commands must not be confused with pressure which could be brought on the individuals concerned and which could compel them inexorably to realize the prescribed behavior. It is true that in fact the command technique presupposes, in order to be reasonably put into practice, a certain disposition on the part of individuals for realizing effectively the required precepts. The factors which may underlie this attitude of subordination and submission are of little relevance here, particularly in a heteronomical context: fear, reverence, habit, etc. It would be absurd to issue commands to drivers who were determined not to comply with them or to obstruct their function. But this is an existential, "factual," and empirical datum which is foreign to the *eidos* of commands. It does, however, tend to cause ambiguity in the area of legal experience. When the legislator makes a legal command, his doing so reasonably assumes a certain human context of receptivity and thus a certain probability that the command will be carried out. This means that the legislator has thereby and to this extent come to grips directly with reality. Thus there is the abbreviated notion according to which the word of the legislator is creative, begetting directly the acts with which it deals, and the idea that the law formulated by public authorities "acts" or "retroacts" on reality (or, conversely, becomes a dead letter, like a dud cartridge). Hence there are also the elliptical formulations of legal norms by which the public authority "pronounces" a certain establishment, abolition, dissolution, appointment, etc., that is, expresses a norm to be put into effect compulsorily as if it were already thus.[127] These short cuts in thought and language are a source of confusion and ambiguity in the way in which law is currently depicted. They are also behind the tendency to assimilate scientific norms to a variety of law or of legal commands, and are responsible for the multitude of fatalist images which accompany this pan-legal vision of the universe (the idea that events in reality cannot fail to occur as they do since "it is written"; the Word of the supreme Legislator of the universe, the *Logos*, is considered to be the creator at the origin of things in reality, like the word of the human legislator).

Whereas legal theorists are not basically "very far" from the command structure of legal norms when they sense confusedly that there is a compelling element in law, they depart completely from this structure when they endeavor to place (very artificially) a well-cut conceptual garment on this vaguely perceived datum. At this developed and considered level of con-

127. The very expression "public authorities," by which one currently designates the bodies responsible for making legal norms, suggests both the idea of *commanding* and that of *begetting* or *creating*.

sciousness, they really lose connection with things themselves. It is evident that the command *eidos* does not imply of itself any determined ethical norm content; the specific character of the command is not located on this level but on that of the instru- mental function of normative tools. The fact that legal com- mands in practice often prescribe such and such a form of behavior for such and such an individual or category of individ- ual, under penalty of such and such a punishment (and in par- ticular under penalty of police action) is a purely contingent datum.[128] It is sufficient, moreover, to note that in any case this type of content can only be found in one type of norm-commands —those which express "obligations" on human events to occur or not to occur in the course of things; only failures to come up to positive duties or lack of compliance with prohibitions may be punished. Now, ethical norms with a permissive content can of course be framed as commands, and particularly as legal com- mands. In this case one would be confronted by a human evental pattern model to be compulsorily observed, a pattern implying the possibility of the occurrence or the nonoccurrence of such and such a thing.[129] Moreover, when a command stipulates that if

128. Kelsen himself recognizes in certain passages the contingency of the sentencing content of legal norms: "The assertion that law is a tech- nique of compulsion is based on a comparative study of so-called legal systems which exist at present or have existed in the course of history. It is the result of empirical research on the content of positive social or- ders" (*Théorie pure du droit*, 1st ed., p. 62). But this does not prevent Kelsen from integrating this contingent element into the very concept of law. It seems, moreover, that Kelsen has yielded here to the tendency of the man in the street by taking his image of the law from one branch of it, i.e., criminal law, which, as its name indicates, is a form of law con- cerned with penalties. It is clear that in practice this branch of the law does not embrace the whole, and also that it is an out-of-date image linked to the bygone age of the "police state."

129. It should be noted here that some authors tend to assimilate commands and ethical norms with imperative content (the term "impera- tives" is currently used, moreover, to designate both of these), which gives the impression that law is made up of norms with imperative contents only (see, for example, du Pasquier, *Introduction à la théorie générale* pp. 93 ff.; del Vecchio, *Philosophy of Law*, pp. 286 ff.; Dabin, *Théorie générale du droit*, new ed., pp. 82 ff.), as if a permissive measure could not form the content of a command in the way that an imperative meas ure may form the content of a recommendation. Hence there is confusion between the command structure and both the metrological structure of norms in general (with the "ought" thus implied) and the structure of the content of imperative norms (with the "obligation" of the occurrence or nonoccurrence of something in the course of things thus implied). In

X does not behave in a certain way he will be liable to such and such a penalty imposed by such and such a public authority, it does not regulate the behavior of *X*, but that of the public authority in question. Clearly it is not possible at the same time to enforce by threat of penalty the latter's duty to impose a penalty without involving a *regressio in infinitum*. The vision of a law with purely imperative contents attaching a penalty to all human behavior regulated by it would thus be absurd.

Before concluding, it could be useful to formulate two further series of observations.

The first concerns a problem which is generally dealt with by philosophers of law, usually under the heading of "the foundation—or the foundations—of law," a problem which can be thus expressed: "Why is law compulsory?" "Why must legal rules be obeyed?" This is a particularly ambiguous question. In this connection, some theorists endeavor to make an objective investigation of the causes of the state of receptivity (or, as is more readily said today, the causes of the *consensus*) of men in regard to legal commands: Under what conditions is the technique of legal commands efficient and practicable? This involves research of a purely empirical nature in the field of the social sciences.

---

addition, there is confusion in the assimilation of the metrological "ought" structure of norms to an imperative content. It may be said in this respect that the concept of "duty" or "obligation" in the normative disciplines (and particularly in the legal disciplines) is one which lends itself the most to syncretism.

It is true, on the one hand, that a certain effort is necessary to be able to conceive clearly a permissive command and how it is distinguished from a recommendation; one tends to get lost here in a kind of subtle game of mirrors, in a maze of "duties" and "powers" which seem in one's mind to fit into each other like Russian dolls. On the other hand, it is true that one could be tempted to think that at first sight there is scarcely any noticeable practical difference to the individual between receiving a command granting him the power to do a certain thing and receiving a recommendation expressing the obligation or the power to do the same thing. But these purely factual considerations must of course yield before the methodological necessity of eliminating any syncretism which could ultimately falsify one's over-all vision of things. Ethical measures conceived as commands are one thing, whatever their contingent content, and ethical measures conceived as recommendations, whatever their contingent content, are another. This difference is not without practical repercussions; contrary to what one might be tempted to suppose in the first place, there is indeed a difference in psychological context between the person who receives even a permissive command (which exercises control over him even in the latitude it allows him) and the person who receives a mere recommendation (which leaves him, by definition, the freedom to take his own direction).

Others attempt to provide men with reasons for effectively obeying legal commands, demonstrating at the same time that their obedience must limit itself to the cases in which the public authorities follow a certain specific legal policy. Here one moves from the scientific context to a moral and ideological context. This is the meaning of the classical statements on "Justice," the "Common Good," and any other "values" which legal rules should endeavor to promote and which are alone considered as imposing the observance of these rules. Thus the corollary of a "right" or even of a "duty" to disobey an unjust law, the "right" or the "duty" to resist oppression, etc.

Finally, still others tend to engage in a purely gratuitous intellectual exercise devoid of meaning and springing from a simple intellectual confusion. I should like to pay some attention to this rather widespread tendency. It consists in detaching, so to speak, the obligation to obey implied in legal commands from their specific instrumental function, from the very structure of law, and to treat this obligation as an autonomous datum, external to law, which one attempts to grasp "objectively" with no moralizing or ideological presuppositions.[130] In other words, there is thought to be a certain datum accompanying the legal phenomenon, constituting an obligation to obey legal norms, which is related to but external to them and to their structure. What does this obligation consist of? What is its nature? From what does it derive? How can it be explained? Kelsen, in order to reply to these unlikely questions, endeavored to develop his famous but obscure theory of the "hypothetical fundamental norm." There is supposedly at the basis of the "positive" legal norms (see the earlier discussion of the meaning of "legal positivism") made by the public authorities a fundamental ethical norm, which is not expressly formulated by them but whose existence must be "assumed" and which "the science of law" must admit as "a hypothesis"—a norm according to which one ought to obey the constitutional legal norms from which other norms in a given legal system usually derive.[131] This fundamental norm would thus

---

130. This intellectual deviation is basically, in Kantian terminology, the result of treating the analytic statement "legal norms are compulsory" as a synthetic statement. (On this distinction, see Kant, *Critique of Pure Reason*, trans. Norman Kemp Smith [New York: St. Martin's Press, 1965], pp. 48–51; and Heidegger, *What Is a Thing?*, pp. 160–65.)

131. See, in particular, Kelsen, *Théorie pure du droit*, 2d ed., pp. 286 ff.

be the foundation of the duty of obedience to legal norms in general, since if one ought to conform to constitutional legal measures, one ought consequently to conform to other legal measures made on the basis of these constitutional measures. It is not our concern to analyze all the weaknesses in this theory or in the reasoning involved.[132] It is sufficient here to point to the initial fallacy on which this is based. The "obligation to obey" implied by legal norms is an element of their structure and constitution; it is not the content of a mysterious ethical norm external to law. It is an element of the instrumental command function of legal norms, an element of the *being for* of the tool command. To conceive a command or to communicate one to another person is to conceive or express to another person a measure to be compulsorily realized.[133] Or, in other words, the "obligation to obey" suggested by the consciousness of a command is simply the expression of the function proper to the authoritarian direction of conduct which all commands, by definition, are intended to promote. The problems here are in no way limited to law or to legal norms.

The second series of observations is of another kind, dealing with another source of possible ambiguity. One might be tempted to think that law cannot be completely reduced to a body of commands, particularly in view of those legislative or other legal acts which obviously do not express commands. The following

132. In this respect, see Amselek, *Méthode phénoménologique*, pp. 346 ff. The ultimate contradiction involved in all this laborious demonstration should be pointed out; in fact, the obligation to obey the provisions of the constitution (provisions conceived by Kelsen as noncompulsory in themselves and therefore as something other than real commands) does not in any way logically imply the obligation to obey other legal norms, as claimed by Kelsen. As Kelsen well knows (see *Théorie pure du droit*, 2d ed., pp. 258 ff.), a legal system does not appear in practice as an axiomatic system with particular propositions which are derived from general propositions; essentially a constitution contains provisions for the benefit of the public authorities themselves and for regulating the machinery by which they make legal norms. To suppose that these public authorities are obliged to observe such constitutional provisions (conceived, again, as noncompulsory in themselves and in their essential function) does not necessarily imply that other men are themselves obliged to obey the legal norms made by these authorities (also conceived by Kelsen as noncompulsory in themselves).

133. Thus, just as one must refrain from considering the constitutional elements expressed in the context of a norm as autonomous data, or concepts pure and simple, similarly one cannot consider the existential elements expressed in the context of a concept (in this case the obligation to obey involved in the concept of command) as autonomous data or ethical norms pure and simple.

point should be made: in practice, law regulates among other things the conditions of the making of legal norms by such and such a public authority. Thus legal regulations organize the procedures of syntactical formulation which allow such authorities to make legal norms in the various ways. Formulations thus regulated by law are called "legal acts," as are legislative acts, decrees, and other administrative decisions, court judgments, etc. One cannot, however (and in practice one is careful not to), assimilate every effective "legal act" to a legal rule-making act. Sometimes the public authority involved formulates (under the procedural conditions provided for by legal regulations) acts which are not commands (e.g., legislative acts or resolutions of local authorities expressing simple recommendations, wishes, opinions, advice, etc.), or which are not even norms or ethical norms (e.g., the satisfaction or dissatisfaction expressed by the members of a local authority in respect to some initiative of the central authority). In neither case are we confronted by a formulation of "law" or legal measures, but by a syntactical formulation carried out in accordance with the forms organized by law for the making of legal norms, a formulation regulated by law, subject to the legal regulations on the making of legal measures, but which is not itself the making of law or of legal norms.[134] In other words, and it will be necessary to return to this, care must be taken not to assimilate all speech and all statements of the public authorities to the making of legal norms, even when such a statement occurs in conditions provided for legal statements or for the making of legal measures. Moreover, even in a

---

134. It will be seen that such enactments are not always incorrect in respect of the applicable legal regulations. In fact, it can happen that the regulations provide for one and the same procedure for the making of legal commands and simple recommendations by the same body (or, again, they organize a procedure of syntactical formulation without placing express limits on its function). The situation is such in France, for example, in the case of the resolutions of local authorities which are intended to formulate both legal commands and recommendations; numerous other examples could be quoted of bodies exercising at the same time and in the same form a consultative and a decision-making (i.e., command) function. Even if the procedure provided for making such instruments is identical, even if the regulations (including those relating to contentious proceedings) governing the instruments so made are similar, and even if there is thus a tendency in practice to include them under the label "legal acts," it remains true that recommendations thus formulated cannot be confused with commands (i.e., with the legal norms proper) formulated in the same way.

legal act giving effective formulation to legal commands, it should not be thought that all the statements it comprises constitute law—the title, the date, the "objects and reasons," or the signature are all elements of the act which are regulated by law but do not themselves constitute law.

[3] PARTICULAR EIDETIC ELEMENTS OF THE OBJECT LAW: LAW AS A BODY OF COMMANDS WITH THE FUNCTION OF THE PUBLIC DIRECTION OF HUMAN CONDUCT

CONTRARY TO THE SYNCRETISTIC THEORIES of scholars who reduce the idea of law to that of "compulsion," it is clear that not all commands are legal commands or norms. If I formulate a command, I am nevertheless not conscious of formulating law. What then distinguishes legal norms from other commands, thus constituting the eidetic particularity of the thing Law, the ultimate difference which makes the structure Law an original one among all other possible structures?

Many authors have thought it possible to discover the basis of this originality by which law represents itself, or "takes its origin" in one's consciousness, in a certain typical content which should necessarily be found in all legal norms. This typical content is considered by some, as has already been seen, to be a punitive content. This is the thesis of Kelsen in particular, for whom the characteristic element of rules of law is that of prescribing human behavior under penalty of sanctions.[135] For others, the typical content which characterizes law is constituted by the "external conscience" of men; in contrast to moral norms, legal norms are thought to be norms for regulating the "external" conduct of men, to the exclusion of their internal life.[136] Others

135. See, for example, *Théorie pure du droit*, 2d ed., pp. 46 ff., 85 ff., where Kelsen thus distinguishes law from that which is not law, and especially from morals: "Law can be essentially distinguished from morality only if it is conceived as a system of compulsion, that is, as a normative system which seeks to bring about human conduct by attaching socially organized acts of compulsion to the opposite conduct, whereas morality is a social order which does not establish sanctions of this kind, but whose sanctions may be found uniquely in approval of conduct which is in conformity with the norms and in disapproval of conduct contrary to the norms; the use of force does not come in at all."

136. See, for example, Roubier, *Théorie générale du droit*, pp. 42 ff.

have thought it possible to discern the mark of the legal not in the content but in the formal structure of the rules of law. Such is the thesis developed by Michel Virally, for example, for whom the distinctive trait of legal rules in relation to other ethical rules lies in their dualist structure. Legal norms are thought of as conferring rights on certain individuals and at the same time (as a corollary) imposing obligations on others. This dualistic structure makes it possible to distinguish law and morals, the latter consisting of monolithic rules imposing pure obligations only.[137]

I do not intend to dwell on these different ideas,[138] except to point out simply that they each share a common fault—that of looking for law where it cannot be found. The acid test again is found in the fact that I may endeavor to formulate commands with the alleged typical content or formal structure, without being conscious of formulating law. The content and the formal structure of legal commands are thus contingent data in relation to the *eidos* itself of law.[139]

In fact, the eidetic particularity of law is to be found elsewhere; it corresponds, like the previous eidetic elements, to a more detailed specialization of the instrumental command function which constitutes the thing Law. We shall endeavor to throw some light on this eidetic particularity of law.

137. Virally, *La Pensée juridique*, pp. 39 ff., 76 ff.
138. See, on this, Amselek, *Méthode phénoménologique*, pp. 245 ff.
139. It should be noted in respect of the conceptions described above that, while they are sometimes based on unexpressed ideological intentions or considerations of legal policy (the desire to ascribe to law, to the "true" law, a certain content favored by oneself), they are also frequently based on a logical error. There are two very different ways of "characterizing" something: either one describes the constitutional elements of this thing—its properties—or else one simply describes indicators or criteria which do not coincide (or which only partially coincide) with the constitution of this thing, but which are presumed to show in practice the presence of the thing in question (e.g., a flower in the buttonhole signifies X, without being part of his identity; the color green signifies my car, green cars being rare in my town, but the color is nevertheless only a partial element of the identity of my car). In one case there is a direct identification of the thing, while in the other the identification is indirect or indicative, by an interposed indicator (see earlier the distinction between direct and indicative evaluation). These two procedures are obviously very different and should not be confused; but, precisely, there is an ambiguity in this respect in the way in which legal theorists currently "characterize" legal rules. The fact that one can in practice recognize a norm to be legal from the fact that it expresses a sanction imposed by a public authority or by other indicative signs is one thing; and the fact that these signs embody the identity proper of legal norms is another.

If one considers them carefully, legal commands appear at first to be given to our consciousness as commands *emanating from public powers or authorities*. In fact, one cannot conceive of law without having, at least implicitly, the notion of public power or authority present to the mind. And conversely, moreover, if I myself formulate commands, imagining myself to be a public authority or leader, I am indeed conscious of formulating law, on a purely imaginative basis, "as a joke," but it is nevertheless law. What does this mean? What do the notions of "public power" and "public authority" cover exactly? The term "public" suggests essentially the idea of a collection of individuals; that which is "public" is that which is relative to an entire human population, which concerns all the members of a people or of a human community. Thus one speaks of the "public," or "public places," "public security," "the public good," "the *res publica*," or "public affairs," etc. Public powers, public leaders or governing authorities, are bodies which direct the conduct or behavior of all members of a human population. More especially, as public "authorities," the public powers are defined as bodies which command all individuals living together as a population, bodies which direct in an authoritarian fashion the conduct (that is, which control the "rudder") of all individuals living together as a people. It is essentially in order to designate this power of command in regard to all that one speaks of "public power." Law and legal norms are given to our consciousness as commands by public authorities thus defined, that is, the commands of the public authorities acting in an authoritarian fashion.

But this datum of the consciousness should be examined further. When one thinks of law (a body of commands emanating from the public authorities), strictly speaking one does not imply that any command given by a person with the title of public authority is a legal command. It is also necessary that such a command be given by this person in his official capacity and in the exercise of his function of public direction—the direction of the over-all behavior of a population. Commands formulated by him outside his public function, in his "private life," do not appear as such to constitute legal norms by the simple fact that they emanate from the person in question. This means that the legal nature of law is not bound up with the person of a public authority but with the function of public direction of which he is the instrument. This means, in turn, that this legal nature corresponds in the final analysis to a certain particular instrumental function of legal norms. Law is constituted by commands which are part of the exercise of public power, commands intended to effect "public direction," i.e., the direction of the conduct of all men living together. In other words, the commands of which law is composed are given as tools of the authoritarian public direction of human conduct. Law is nothing other than a technique of the public direction of conduct.

The existence of law and of legal norms in our cultural universe refers of itself to two fundamental data of the human condition, which scarcely merit lengthy discussion in view of their obvious truth. The first is what may be called the human social fact. In reality men do not live isolated from one another, but in peoples and societies.[140] If this condition were not fulfilled and if this phenomenon of human population did not exist, the legal technique would lose its *raison d'être* and would scarcely be able to emerge to existence. The other datum is what may be called the human political fact, using the term "political" not in its originary sense (which suggests simply the idea of men living in population—see, for example, the expression "political economy") but in its current sense (which suggests the idea of public power). Man is not only a social animal, living among people; he is also a political animal, capable of receiving or accepting public authoritarian direction which applies to the behavior of his fellow men as a whole. If receptivity or "consensus" did not exist, the legal technique would scarcely be practicable; anarchy or nonlaw would be the order of the day. Public command is in practice possible only where there exists among men living together as a people a certain inclination to accept over-all authoritarian government and to accept at least a partial abdication from controlling their own direction. The factors which underlie or stimulate this inclination are of little importance; it is on this basis that the exercise of public authority is in fact possible, that this differentiation between public governors and the governed which typifies human society can in fact develop.[141]

140. Sociologists speak of "over-all societies" to refer to those groups of men living together in populations. They wish thus to distinguish between peoples proper, which are given as such to our consciousness, and groups of men which form within such peoples as secondary, nonautonomous parts of a whole.

141. It is perhaps important to note that law does not necessarily imply heteronomy, in contrast to an idea often put forward since Kant, and

More profoundly, the existence of this public direction, and particularly of this authoritarian public direction in human populations, clearly suggests the existence of a human need. I have already discussed the specific nature of the structure of man, of the human being, in that it provides for a certain amount of play, that is, a certain marginal liberty of self-determination. Hence the need historically felt by man (at least since the time when he emerged from the state of being a purely biological or instinctual mechanism) for regulation of his behavior, for ethical norms, for conduct-models to follow, enabling him to give himself a direction and to create his own movements. Legal norms respond to a human need which is not only individual but collective. Since men live together as peoples, endowed with a marginal liberty of self-determination, it becomes clear that it is indispensable to coordinate, to harmonize, and to synchronize at least partially the conduct of the different persons. It is indispensable that there should be an over-all government and particularly a public authority to promote collective discipline—"police" in the originary sense of the term. Here is the meaning of the famous Latin aphorism, *ubi societas ibi jus.*

The fact that law is thus composed of commands emanating from public powers, which participate in a function of the public direction of human conduct, is confirmed in many ways. The etymology itself is again revealing as it shows the relationship between the words "law" (*droit, directum*) and "king" (*roi, rex,* from *regere:* "to rule"; *regnum:* "reign"). The links between law and the governing authorities are also evident in many other names historically given to the latter and which reveal the essence of their function: "regents," "rulers," "governors," "dukes," etc.

But it is also this instrumental aspect of public direction which is behind the expressions used by certain authors in reference to legal rules when they speak of "social" rules or when they state that law regulates relationships between men living in

---

in contrast also to what at first sight could be considered to be the significance of the idea (also widespread since Duguit) of the differentiation between the governors and the governed. The existence of law as a technique of the public direction of human behavior presupposes the existence of a human population, but does not imply that within this population the public command is exercised by only some persons over the rest, which would exclude all forms of the democratic use of public power. When, for example, the people acting together as a whole establish a constitution, they do exercise on a given occasion (but with no element of heteronomy) the power of public command, they formulate law—constitutional law.

society. These expressions are, however, rather obscure and can wrongly give the impression that legal rules have a certain type of content or that they always regulate relationships between two or more individuals, in accordance with the following outline: "X may or ought to behave in a certain way with respect to Y." Hence the easily developed conceptions on the dualist structure of legal norms, on the right-obligation pair which they are invariably supposed to contain. In fact, legal norms do not, strictly speaking, in their general principle aim at regulating relationships or the interaction between the members of human societies (thus, norms forbidding motorists to use a certain lane or compelling certain establishments to equip themselves with safety devices express no relational content). It is more exact to say that they derive from the desire to command in a synchronized fashion the conduct of the different individuals living together. Or, in other words, the role of the public authorities is that of regulating harmoniously the behavior of all members of the group, envisaging the behavior of each as a part of the whole; they do not simply endeavor to regulate the conduct of the members of the community in relation to one another. The instrumental function of law in the interpersonal context should not be confused with its own content.

In addition, it is to express this instrumental aspect of the public direction of conduct that the idea of law is currently associated with the idea of the "common good." In this link, and throughout all the ideological and moral developments that have been ascribed to it, there is an originary intuition. Law thus belongs, in its very essence, to the notion of the common direction of the conduct of men living together as a people; the norms which constitute it thus represent, in a certain sense, standards of the "common good."

Another highly revealing datum is the very hesitation scholars feel in ascribing precise limits to the area of the existing law. There is some uncertainty on the problem of knowing whether or not commands emanating from persons who have not the official capacity of public authorities may be considered as law, when they act on the basis of legal norms made by legitimate public authorities, ascribing this competence to them. The differences of viewpoint on the subject indicate in fact a deep unity of opinion regarding what constitutes the essence of law. What varies from author to author is the analysis of the situation in question—

which is, it must be confessed, a rather ambiguous one—in respect of a basic and shared intuition of what constitutes law. On the one hand, these commands are made by simple "private persons," that is, persons who are not officially invested with the function of the public direction of conduct; thus one is tempted not to consider them as law even if they are made in accordance with law. But, on the other hand, it could be considered that the right to command conferred by legal norms, by the commands of legitimate public authorities, is equivalent to a dismembering of the power of public command itself. When a public authority accords, by legal command, to private persons the right to command, the situation may be analyzed as a kind of passing on or partial delegation of the power of public command or as a kind of decentralization of this power. Is not commanding on the order of public "commanders" in fact participation in the power of public command? [142]

In fact, the situation is not as simple as it might seem. Thus Claude du Pasquier writes, "It is the law which establishes the principle that a child should obey his father; does this mean that any order given by a father to his child creates a legal duty?" [143] It is not obvious that the answer is in the affirmative. In fact, it is necessary to determine in each case whether the legal norm empowering a certain private person or category of persons to command aims at making these individuals participate occasionally in the exercise of public power (like the delegations of the power of accredited public authorities to other accredited public authorities), or if it involves a simple regulation on "private" conduct (regulations by the public authorities of the command behavior of certain members of the population, this command behavior being conceived exactly as any other behavior of governed persons). Although not only legislative acts, decrees, judgments, and other legal commands issued by the accredited public authorities, but also contracts, testaments, and any other commands (or, as they are imperfectly called, "manifestations of

142. Such is the position of Kelsen in particular. His vision of the "dynamic hierarchy" of legal norms, from constitutional norms down to the commands of private persons, corresponds to the intuition of a dividing up of legal power, in the form of a cascade of normative competences, with each authority deriving from its superior authority the power of command up to a supreme authority, i.e., the constituent authority (see *Théorie pure du droit*, 2d ed., pp. 255 ff.).
143. Du Pasquier, *Introduction à la théorie générale*, p. 16.

will") issued by private persons are often classified as "legal acts," the majority of scholars see in this second category only the formulation of simple "private" commands regulated by law (by that branch of law which is for this reason called "private law"). But such fluctuations in the handling of the concept of law are finally of little importance; what is important, from my point of view, is that they bear witness to an identity in the intimate originary consciousness of the legal *eidos* itself.

ALL PHILOSOPHICAL UNDERTAKINGS are in principle somewhat pretentious. The merit of the phenomenological enterprise is that it has limited pretensions: it does not endeavor to reveal that which is beyond the world in which we live, but the world itself, beyond our usual confused ideas of it. Phenomenology simply aims at bringing us to see more lucidly that which has already been seen; thus it has been said that with phenomenology "we have embarked on a voyage to bring ourselves to a point at which we have already arrived without knowing it." [144] It is true that a rediscovery of ancient lands with a new gaze can cause the same sensations of astonishment and wonder as the discovery of mysterious distant lands hitherto unexplored.

Our phenomenological inquiry on the eidetic constitution of law has thus led us to approach those shores on which we have lived from time immemorial with the result that we are no longer able to see them. The findings of our inquiry can be summed up in the following way. Law appears to our consciousness as a technique of the public direction of human conduct; it is composed of norms or normative measures with a particular function, that of directing in an authoritarian fashion the conduct of all men living together as a population. On our way we have been able to rediscover the concrete consistency of this instrumental nature (*being for*) of legal norms which paradoxically tends to escape us in our ordinary craftsman's experience of the law, at the very time when it is, so to speak, "in our hands." Like the originary *norma*, rectilinear model-line or model plumb line, the psychic norm constitutes a model course of events represented in thought, a model-pattern of the unfolding of the course of things which is present to the mind. In contrast to the conceptual model, normative models in fact measure not the image but the "régime"

144. Berger, "Phénoménologie transcendentale."

of things, the modality of their passing or their occurrence in the evental flux; they regulate the manifestations of things, which are expressed by "may" and "ought."

In the case of legal norms, as for all other ethical norms, what is involved is a thread of human events to be reproduced, to be realized, constituted as models for manufacturing. Ethical norms are presented in this respect as models of *conduct,* model-behavior lines for the direction of men analogous to Ariadne's thread—more precisely as models of *self-behavior* for the benefit of men-behavers themselves, which goes back to the extraordinary dichotomy in the structure of the human being, a being which partially makes itself, embodying at one and the same time the creator and the creature. In contrast to scientific norms, ethical norms thus measure not the course of things which pass in the evental flow, but the course of things which should be made to pass there; they regulate the human "to-be-done" (*des "à-faire humaines"*).

More exactly, legal norms constitute models of conduct which are to be compulsorily realized and which emanate from public authorities, from bodies of public direction or of the direction of peoples—which goes back to the extraordinary way in which men live, in collectively governed and policed populations. In other words, legal norms regulate the public "to-be-done" (*des "à-faire publiques"*).

It is scarcely surprising that the task of defining law at first appears disheartening. We have been able to observe the extent to which syncretism is operative within this problem. It influences practically all levels of the *eidos* of law: the generic elements, the specific elements, and the particular elements of the latter are mingled and confused with each other; this can only lead to a confused vision of the thing Law. Such a state of affairs should be eliminated and law should at last be treated with respect in its identity proper, in its "ipseity" or "ecceity." [145]

But this rediscovered countryside will scarcely have become familiar to us when it will begin again to escape us. As in the myth of Sisyphus, the phenomenological enterprise is thus condemned, in the words of Husserl, to an "infinite meditation."

145. From the scholastic Latin *ipseitas* and *ecceitas.*—Trans.

The Mandarinism of Phenomenological Philosophy of Law

Mitchell Franklin

INFLUENCE AND CRITICISM OF PHENOMENOLOGICAL PHILOSOPHY OF LAW

IN HIS PRESENTATION of contemporary legal and social philosophy in the USSR, Hubert Rodingen (Mainz) writes that of particular countries West Germany enjoys the greatest attention. He says that "Bogomolov classifies currents in West Germany and in Austria into those that are scientific in form (Neo-Kantianism, empirio-criticism, logical positivism, critical ontology) and those that are irrational (philosophy of life, Neo-Hegelianism, existentialism). Phenomenology in conformity with Husserl forms the connecting link." [1]

Amselek writes that today the phenomenological "attitude" and analytical school dominate French philosophy of law.[2] In 1965, Villey published a paper entitled "Phénoménologie et existentiale-marxisme à la Faculté de droit de Paris." [3] This, in part, stimulated Peshka's response in 1967, entitled "La Phénoménologie dans la philosophie du droit moderne." [4] In the

---

1. Hubert Rodingen, "Die gegenwärtige rechts- und sozialphilosophische Diskussion in der Sowjetunion," *Archiv für Rechts- und Sozialphilosophie*, LVI, no. 2 (1970), 231–32.
2. Paul Amselek is the author of *Méthode phénoménologique et théorie du droit* (Paris: Librairie générale de droit et de jurisprudence, 1964).
3. Michel Villey, "Phénoménologie et existentiale-marxisme à la Faculté de droit de Paris," *Archives de philosophie du droit*, X (1965), 157, discusses Amselek and Poulantzas.
4. Vilmos Peschka, "La Phénoménologie dans la philosophie du droit moderne," *Archives de philosophie du droit*, XII (1967), 259.

[451]

same volume Szabo published "Marx et la théorie marxiste 'moderne' du droit." [5] Villey is professor of law at Paris. Peschka is a member of the Institute of Juridical Sciences at Budapest. Szabo is a member of the Hungarian Institute of Sciences and professor of the faculty of law of Budapest.

Latin-American philosophy of law, too, has been dominated by the phenomenological attitude. This influence was traced by Kunz in a book published several years ago.[6] Kunz's conception of phenomenology could be founded on his own Austrian background and, as he himself expressly says, on the thought of Farber.

Perhaps this is sufficient to show the widespread influence of phenomenology in contemporary philosophy of law. But it is not a description of the contemporary influence of phenomenology in American philosophy of law. It is true that as early as 1926 Ralph Barton Perry had directed attention to Husserl.[7] In the same volume, Perry, without reference to Husserl, describes the philosophical situation which produced him:

> The revival of Kant in Germany in the 1860's was followed by a revival of those very post-Kantian tendencies against which the Kantian revival had itself protested. Although neo-Kantianism sprang from a desire to purge Kantianism of the alien elements introduced by Hegel, Fichte, and Romanticism, it was promptly followed by neo-Hegelianism, neo-Fichteanism, and neo-Romanticism. There appears, in other words, to be an inevitable and recurrent cycle through which the thought of Kant passes, inspired by the intellectualistic Kant of the *Critique of Pure Reason*, the voluntaristic and moralistic Kant of the *Critique of Practical Reason*, and the aesthetic and intuitionistic Kant of the *Critique of Judgment*. Reject the conception of the thing-in-itself, as all later Kantians proceed promptly to do, and mind and its creations are left in possession of the field. There then arises a rivalry of emphasis among the several modes of the mind's activity, thought, will, and feeling. Each, after absorbing the other two, may claim to be the original and generative principle of experience and reality.[8]

5. Imre Szabo, "Marx et la théorie marxiste 'moderne' du droit," *Archives de philosophie du droit*, XII (1967), 163.
6. Josef L. Kunz, *Latin-American Philosophy of Law in the Twentieth Century* (Dobbs Ferry, N.Y.: Oceana, 1950).
7. Ralph Barton Perry, *Philosophy of the Recent Past* (New York: Scribner, 1926), p. 208.
8. *Ibid.*, p. 145.

At the end of the volume, Perry, again without any reference to Husserl, nevertheless wrote: "It is possible that philosophy is now nearing the close of a great phase that began with Descartes." [9]

Before 1926, when Perry wrote, Marvin Farber, on his own initiative, studied phenomenology under Husserl, and then introduced this movement as philosophy into the United States. Farber founded and edited *Philosophy and Phenomenological Research* in 1940. Roscoe Pound, at Harvard, discussed Husserl as a philosopher of law at least as early as 1927–28, as this writer's student notes show. In the fifth edition of his *Outlines of Lectures on Jurisprudence*, published in 1943, Pound classified phenomenology as the fifth of six "social philosophical schools" of philosophy of law.[10] Here Pound mentions Husserl himself, Reinach, Schapp, Kaufmann, Schreier, and G. Husserl. He calls attention to Spiegelberg, and "for application" Pound mentions G. Husserl and Engisch. It may be mentioned that the fourth current of social philosophy of law named by Pound in his *Outlines* was described by him as a neo-idealist social philosophical school which "seems to be arising—a logical-psychological relativist idealism." Here Pound refers to Tourtoulon, Binder, and Recaséns Siches. Gurvitch is indicated because of his critique of Radbruch. The sixth social philosophical current is described by Pound thus: "In France the same movement took the form of a revival of natural law." The above details are important because Recaséns Siches became identified with the history of phenomenological philosophy of law and because legal phenomenology has stimulated the so-called revival of natural law.

In 1959 Pound published his most important work, *Jurisprudence*. However, here the treatment of phenomenology of law is terse. Pound says that phenomenology is not of importance in the United States because what it seeks to accomplish is done in America by legal realism.[11] This means Pound perceived that in the United States legal subjectivity could be realized without recourse to legal phenomenology, which purports to overcome legal subjectivity. The hidden thought here is that Pound conceived that the objectivity of legal phenomenology masked and

9. *Ibid.,* p. 221.

10. Roscoe Pound, *Outlines of Lectures on Jurisprudence,* 5th ed. (Cambridge: Harvard University Press, 1943), p. 20.

11. Roscoe Pound, *Jurisprudence* (St. Paul, Minn.: West, 1959), I, 282.

justified legal subjectivity. Peschka has realized the importance
of Pound's thinking, though for a moment he presents the
matter as it seems to be to the phenomenological jurists. Peschka
writes:

> In the conception of the phenomenological philosophy of law, the
> science of law must abandon all nominalism, voluntarism, tra-
> ditional positivism; it must, in summary, abandon all manner of
> seeing which reduces the object of the science of law to juridical
> phenomena alone and sees its task in simple description, in in-
> terpretation, and in the rationalization of the phenomena in ques-
> tion. One must not attribute to chance that Roscoe Pound puts
> juridical phenomenology in relation to American legal realism,
> precisely because of the position occupied by the former relative to
> the theory of science: ". . . juristic phenomenology styles itself a
> theory of actuality as its American analogue calls itself realism."
> The a priori phenomenological theory of law considers as object of
> the science of law not direct juridical phenomena, but juridical
> formations which have an existence (*"Sein"*) independent of
> positive law and of human knowledge. The science of law does not
> have as its task the description of juridical norms.[12]

Quoting Amselek, Peschka says:

> It is necessary to refrain from confounding the "description" of
> juridical norms with the activity of cognition properly called, as is
> often done. . . . Moreover, it is not merely the description and
> interpretation of juridical norms which can be considered as the
> science of law, but also juridical practice, the activity of the
> creation and of the application of law, which Amselek designates
> by the term "technology," and at the interior of which he dis-
> tinguishes legislative policy, dogmatics, and cases forming the
> technology of the creation and the application of law. The science
> of law—according to the phenomenological philosophy of law—
> must grasp juridical phenomena in their essence and scientific
> research must be a return to the things themselves (*Rückkehr zu
> den Sachen selbst*); it must discover the eidetic connections of
> juridical formations, existing a priori, independently of our com-
> prehension, and being eternally valid.[13]

However, as Peschka continues his presentation, he writes:

The gnoseological roots of the semblance of objectivity of phenomenological philosophy of law, of the creation of a "new objectivity"

12. Peschka, "La Phénoménologie," p. 262.
13. *Ibid.*, p. 263.

and of a new *organon* of knowledge of the latter, consists in the separation of phenomenon and essence, notably in the fact that all connection between phenomenon and essence is suppressed by detaching them. . . . [T]he phenomenological philosophy of law absolutizes in an inadmissible fashion the relativity of the stability, the perpetuity, and the duration of the essence, in declaring for that reason the essence illuminated in the phenomenological vision of essences as atemporal and unhistorical. . . . This semblance of objectivity and of atemporality of essence to uncover by the science of law, as well as the subjective foundations, the arbitrariness and irrationalism of the latter, are equally reflected in the concrete phenomenological definition of the object and of the task of science. . . . [C]onnection with concrete historical reality is negative and the vision of the essence is subjective and intuitive.[14]

It is a consequence of the vague and arbitrary character of the phenomenological method, notably of the intuitional vision of essence, Peschka writes, that explains the divergent solutions given by the epigones of phenomenology of law. Peschka insists on the "irrational arbitrariness" of phenomenological intuition.[15]

Peschka perceives that phenomenological philosophy of law develops into existentialist philosophy of law. He writes that "a rapprochement of the existentialist philosophy of law is manifested in the effort toward the concretization and relativization of natural law as well as in the dissolution of positive law in law created by the judge in the sphere of the application of law (*judge-made law*), which can be observed . . . above all with G. Husserl. . . . Husserl prepares the way for the central problem of existentialist theory of law, that is to say, for the appreciation of concrete cases in the form of existential judicial decisions." [16] These remarks explain why Pound has said that phenomenological philosophy of law has no place in the United States because the mission of legal phenomenology is already accomplished by American legal realism. However, as American law, save in Louisiana and Puerto Rico, has historically been committed to juridical mandarinism, the task of phenomenology of law, which developed largely in modern Roman law or civilian national states, where the positive law usually has been codified or formulated since the French Revolution, has been more diffi-

14. *Ibid.*, p. 268.
15. *Ibid.*, p. 269.
16. *Ibid.*, p. 284.

cult than the task of American legal realism, which does not confront codification, though it does face the formulated constitution and recent important legal formulations, such as the Uniform Commercial Code, which was prepared at least in part by American legal realists. The American legal realists know that their own formulated law is subordinated to their philosophy of law. Because Peschka realizes that phenomenological philosophy of law is dominant in legal regimes based on codification of law, he says that phenomenological philosophy of law has the "decentrating" [17] task of justifying judge-made law, or what the Abbé de Mably in the eighteenth century condemned as the mandarinism of the theory of legal despotism of the French physiocratic jurists, who may be the ancestors of Husserl and phenomenological philosophy of law. Within the realm of uncodified Anglo-American common law, phenomenological philosophy of law and its derivatives probably have had most notice in Australia.

Tasks of Phenomenological Philosophy of Law

There are several contradictory tasks that bourgeois legal idealism, including legal phenomenology, must accomplish. In the first place, it must justify the bourgeois legal order. This is a necessity because bourgeois law emerges as a negation of the negation of religious ideas of law (though the negated religious ideas themselves may be a negation of older legal ideas). The constitution and the civil code overcome and surpass religious ideas, which means that the *Rechtsstaat* must be established. This suggests that there may be a tendency toward an objective idealist theory of law, though in truth the negation of the negation of religious ideas through the French and American revolutions established the *Rechtsstaat* or rule of law on the ground of mechanical materialism. But such mechanical materialism dominated only the earlier stages of bourgeois legal thought, when such thought was historically progressive.

In the second place, bourgeois legal idealism must justify

17. *Ibid.*

legal activism and may thus contradict the posited legal order, either by developing or by overcoming its legal superstructure, as the historical contradictions of the infrastructure may require. This activism suggests that there may be a tendency toward a subjective idealist theory of law. Insofar as objective idealistic conceptions prevail, the legal order, as a bourgeois superstructure, reflecting a bourgeois infrastructure, has the semblance of freedom from the arbitrariness of feudal law which the earlier bourgeois jurists condemned through conceptions of rationalist, mechanical natural law, and seems designed to suppress what Bracton even in the thirteenth century and Hegel in the nineteenth century called legal "agility." But insofar as the bourgeois superstructure reflects the development of and later the crises of the bourgeois infrastructure, legal agility or activism emerges and seeks to be justified. This crisis appears in Kant, although the problem there is a rivalry between German bourgeois and German feudal forces. Hence Hegel attacked Kant's activism as fraudulent because it justified the oscillation or activism between antinomies, which reciprocally overcame or subordinated each other. Hegel perceived that Kant's social and legal theory was hypocritical in that it dominated the antinomies by the activist *Verstellung* of the holy moral legislator, an external mediator who (which) appropriated or alienated the antinomies. Such Kantian methodology was, however, older than Kant, though with him it was both activist and yet justified postponability. The Kantian conceptualism which may be presented today is that of an abstract rivalry of antinomies, between *Sein* and *Sollen,* that is, between "is" and "ought," between positive law and natural law, during the present period of the legal crisis of the recent bourgeoisie. However, this does not mean that Husserlian phenomenology of law is unanimously understood to justify natural law theory as such. This problem is reserved for later consideration in this essay. It is sufficient to say now that there is a conflict between natural law theory which sees nature as the foundation of the social world (for instance, the materialistic natural law theory of the Enlightenment) and idealistic natural law theory which is teleological, or which (adapting the thought of Pound) is expressive of the ideals, received or otherwise, of the legal order, and which (adapting the thought of certain phenomenology and existentialism) is expressive of the intentionality and of the activist or *projet* aspect of the *Verstehen* theory which anticipated intentionality theory. Moreover, it is sufficient to say that the abstract rivalry between *Sein* and *Sollen* is dialectically vulnerable because, as Hegel shows, "is" and "ought" are a unity of opposites, separated by a barrier which is negated.

The above discussion, in which both subjective and objective idealism seem present in bourgeois legal thought, brings forth the crisis of recent bourgeois philosophy of law. There are thus multiple subjects and multiple objects, each of which may be veered into its opposite, and which require hidden, external, or unhistorical mediation, ultimately justifying new faith or fideism.

Husserl perceived that there is a crisis, but stated it only superstructurally, that is, as a philosophic crisis. This is apparent in the *Crisis*, which shows no appreciation of the threat of German fascism. Moreover, he did not state even the superstructural crisis correctly, and falls away from the intellectual level which Kant had reached. Husserl perceived a rivalry between the rationalism of Descartes and the empiricism of Locke. He did not accept the thought that both were required by the mechanical materialism of the bourgeois revolution. In his discussion of the struggle of enlightenment with superstition, Hegel writes:

> Enlightenment illuminates that world of heaven with ideas drawn from the world of sense, pointing out there this element of finitude which belief cannot deny or repudiate, because it is self-consciousness, and in being so is the unity to which both kinds of ideas belong, and in which they do not fall apart from one another; for they belong to the same indivisible simple self into which belief has passed, and which constitutes its life. . . . Belief has by this means lost the content which furnished its filling, and collapses into an inarticulate state where the spirit works and weaves within itself. Belief is banished from its own kingdom; this kingdom is sacked and plundered, since the waking consciousness has forcibly taken to itself every distinction and expansion of it and claimed every one of its parts for earth, and returned them to the earth that owns them. Yet belief is not on that account satisfied, for this illumination has everywhere brought to light only what is individual.[18]

18. G. W. F. Hegel, *The Phenomenology of Mind*, 2d ed., trans. J. B. Baillie (New York: Macmillan, 1931), p. 588.

Elsewhere in the same discussion, Hegel says that

> on the view enlightenment takes of the action of belief, the rejection of enjoyment and possessions is looked upon as wrong and purposeless. As to the wrong thus done, enlightenment preserves its harmony with the believing mind in this:—that belief itself acknowledges the actual reality of possessing property. . . . In insisting on its property, it behaves with all the more stubborn independence and exclusiveness.[19]

As has been said, both empiricism and rationalism were required by the mechanical materialism of the bourgeois revolution. In the natural sciences the bourgeoisie ultimately justified empiricism as materialism, and in the social sciences they justified rationalistic materialism or materialistic natural law. The crypto-infrastructuralism of Hegel is very important here. He perceived that both sides of mechanical materialism were justified by the bourgeois situation. Indeed, Descartes, Locke, and Diderot were theorists of both empiricism and rationalism. Thus, Locke condemned innate ideas in his scientific theory and justified innate ideas of materialistic natural social law. Diderot approved Locke's attack on innate ideas, but he also praised the materialistic natural law engraved in our hearts, a standard formula of the history of natural law.

In emphasizing the rationalism of Descartes, Husserl slighted his materialistic side, from which mechanical materialistic natural social law developed, and which ultimately leads to the problems considered by Berkeley, Locke, Hume, Holbach, and Kant. Husserl's idealism leads him to a rationalistic idealist conception of the natural world. He is preoccupied by the history of geometry, which obviously was important in the theory of mechanical materialism, and he seeks to idealize it. However, the undialectical Abbé de Mably, responding to the rationalism of the legal despotism of the French physiocrat theorists of law of the eighteenth century, said that geometry, unlike legal science, dealt merely with "simple objects."[20] The problem of the relationship between Husserl and physiocratic natural law will be discussed next.

19. *Ibid.*, p. 585.
20. Gabriel Bonnot de Mably, *Doutes proposés aux philosophes économistes sur l'ordre naturel et essentiel des sociétés politiques*, in *Oeuvres complètes de l'abbé de Mably*, XI (London, 1789), 45.

CERTAIN HISTORICAL ANTECEDENTS
OF PHENOMENOLOGICAL PHILOSOPHY OF LAW

CARTESIAN RATIONALISM developed on one side into
mechanical materialistic natural law. This seems confusing if
phenomenological legal philosophy is related to present-day idealistic natural law. However, as Husserl is an idealist, the question is whether Cartesian rationalism also justified idealist
natural law. This it did through Malebranche and issued as the
natural law theory of the French physiocrats. The physiocrats
are known as the founders of economic theory. Though their aim
seemed feudal, their thought was firmly veered by Adam Smith
into bourgeois economic theory. The physiocrats were also concerned with social theory which reflected their economic theory;
and, indeed, their social theory, especially that of Le Mercier de
la Rivière, was praised by Smith in the *Wealth of Nations.*
Because of their common Cartesianism it would not be wise to
consider Husserlian phenomenology of law without study of the
natural law of the physiocrats, especially that of Le Mercier de la
Rivière and Quesnay, the founder of the physiocratic movement.
 Knittermeyer writes that Husserl regarded Malebranche as
one of the greatest thinkers of all time.[21] Lukács says that the
present-day attack on causality, "the distinction of objectivity
and of the conformity to law of an external world existing independently of our consciousness," began with the influence of
Malebranche on Schopenhauer and passed into the ideology of
contemporary imperialism. Lukács especially mentions Simmel,
whose *Verstehen* influence on Heidegger will be indicated later
in this essay.[22] Ricoeur believes that Husserl's analysis in *Ideas*
"joins that of St. Thomas, Descartes, and Malebranche." [23] Ricoeur holds that there is a difference between Thomistic and
phenomenological intuition.

21. Heinrich Knittermeyer, "Philosophie der Neuzeit: Von Cusanus
bis Nietzsche," in Fritz Heinemann, *Die Philosophie im XX. Jahrhundert*
(Stuttgart: Klett, 1959), p. 207.
 22. Georg Lukács, *Die Zerstörung der Vernunft* (Berlin: Aufbau,
1954), p. 190.
 23. Paul Ricoeur, *Freedom and Nature: The Voluntary and the Involuntary,* trans. Erazim V. Kohák (Evanston, Ill.: Northwestern University Press, 1966), p. 149, n. 3. See also Stephen Strasser, *Phénoménologie
et sciences de l'homme,* trans. Kelkel (Louvain: Publications Universitaires
de Louvain, 1967), p. 238.

In the *Crisis* Husserl both states and misstates the development which begins with Descartes and includes Malebranche. He writes:

> If we now follow the lines of development which proceeded from Descartes, one, the "rationalistic," leads through Malebranche, Spinoza, Leibniz, and the Wolff school to Kant, the turning point. Here the spirit of the new kind of rationalism, as implanted by Descartes, thrusts forward enthusiastically. . . . Here the conviction reigns, then, that through the method of *mos geometricus* an absolutely grounded, universal knowledge of the world, thought of as a transcendent "in-itself," can be realized. Precisely against this conviction, against the new science as having such scope as to extend to something "transcendent," indeed finally against this "transcendence" itself, English empiricism reacts—even though it is likewise strongly influenced by Descartes. . . . Of greater interest for us, however, because of its immense effect on psychology and the theory of knowledge, is Locke's critique of the understanding. . . . This line of development is especially significant in that it is an essential segment of the historical path on which the psychologically adulterated transcendentalism of Descartes (if we may already so call his original turn to the ego) seeks, through unfolding its consequences, to work its way through to the realization of its untenability. . . . The primary and historically most important thing here was the self-revelation of empirical psychologism (of the sensationalistic, naturalistic cast) as an intolerable absurdity.[24]

There are several mistakes in this presentation of the eruption of Cartesianism into two lines of thought. That which Husserl regards as a separation of Cartesianism into rationalism and empiricism, or into rationalism and "psychologism," was a rivalry between idealism and mechanical materialism, not a rivalry between rationalism and positivism, as Husserl's distinction between "rationalism" and "psychologism" may suggest.

In *The Holy Family*, Marx and Engels wrote:

> *Descartes* in his *physics* endowed matter with self-creative power and conceived *mechanical* motion as the act of its life. He completely separated his *physics* from his *metaphysics*. *Within* his physics *matter* is the only *substance*, the only basis of being and

24. Edmund Husserl, *The Crisis of European Sciences and Transcendental Phenomenology*, trans. David Carr (Evanston, Ill.: Northwestern University Press, 1970), pp. 83–84.

of knowledge. . . . *Metaphysics* of the seventeenth century, represented in France by *Descartes* had *materialism* as its *antagonist* from its very birth. . . . In the seventeenth century metaphysics (cf. Descartes, Leibnitz, and others) still had an element of *positive*, profane content. . . . This appearance was done away with as early as the beginning of the eighteenth century. . . . Metaphysics had gone stale. In the year in which Malebranche and Arnauld, the last great French metaphysicians of the seventeenth century died, *Helvetius* and *Condillac* were born.[25]

In his essay on Malebrancheanism in the *Encyclopédie*, Diderot says, "A page of Locke contains more truths than all the volumes of *Malebranche*, but a line of the latter shows more subtlety, imagination, fineness of genius perhaps than all the coarse work of Locke." [26]

In his considerations concerning the fundamental rivalry between materialism and idealism, Hegel, too, opposes Husserl's distancing between rationalism and empiricist psychologism. Writing of the eighteenth century, Hegel said that

the French proceeded to materialism or naturalism. . . . Hence they accept sensation and matter as the only truth to which must be reduced all thought, all morality, as a mere modification of sensation. . . . To this one-sidedness belongs the opposition between *sentir* and *penser* . . . making the latter only the result of the former; there is not, however, any speculative reconciliation of this opposition in God, such as we find in Spinoza and Malebranche. This reduction of all thought to sensation . . . took place with Locke. . . . [E]ven psychology passed into materialism, as for instance, we may find in La Mettrie's work *L'homme Machine*. . . . [M]atter alone exists.[27]

Though Husserl seeks to absolutize the separation or estrangement between rationalism and empiricism, Hegel shows that the opposition collapses into bourgeois ground which explains both. Or putting the matter somewhat differently, because Descartes distances or ruptures rationalism and empiricism, such estrange-

25. Karl Marx and Friedrich Engels, *The Holy Family*, trans. R. Dixon (Moscow: Progress Publishers, 1956), p. 169.
26. Denis Diderot, *Dictionnaire encyclopédique*, Vol. V, in *Oeuvres*, XVII (Paris, 1821), 315.
27. G. W. F. Hegel, *Lectures on the History of Philosophy*, trans. E. S. Haldane and Frances H. Simson (London: Routledge & Kegan Paul, 1894), III, 398.

ment or alienation is undialectical and necessitates external or unhistorical mediation. Hegel writes:

> Descartes . . . established the intellectual sphere in contradistinction to matter, and on it based the independent subsistence of mind; for in his *cogito* "I" is at first only certain of itself, since I can abstract from all. Now we find the necessity of a mediator to bring about a union of the abstract and the external and individual. Descartes settles this by placing between the two what constitutes the metaphysical ground of their mutual changes, God. He is the intermediate bond of union, in as far as He affords assistance to the soul in what it cannot through its own freedom accomplish, so that the changes in the body and soul may correspond with one another. If I have desires, an intention, these receive corporeal realization; this association of soul and body is, according to Descartes, effected through God.[28]

Because Descartes was undialectical, Hegel wrote: "The Philosophy of modern times made its first independent appearance after the Thirty Years' War with Bacon, Jacob Böhme and Descartes; it begins with the distinction contained in: *cogito ergo sum*."[29]

The relation between Husserl and Descartes and between Husserl and Malebranche, the latter of which stimulates the problem of the relation between phenomenological philosophy of law and physiocratic philosophy of law, appears in Husserl's undialectical distancing or "bracketing" of the material world. The surface impression of his "bracketing" is that Husserl has thus overcome or subordinated empiricist psychologism, understood as Kantian agnosticism, brought about by the unknowability of the thing-in-itself. Hence Husserl's attack on materialism, like Kant's, is indirect. However, Husserl's "bracketing," considered more closely, is a development of the idealistic occasionalism of Malebranche. Because Cartesianism separated mind from matter, there was thus also a separation or "bracketing," a rupture or distancing, which Husserl continues. Knittermeyer writes that Husserl's phenomenological reduction "was to him important only as a passage, as an 'act of deactualization (*Entwirklichung*).'"[30] Malebranche, in the language of phenom-

---

28. *Ibid.*, p. 251.
29. *Ibid.*, I, 110.
30. Heinrich Knittermeyer, *Die Philosophie der Existenz von der Renaissance bis zur Gegenwart* (Vienna: Humboldt, 1952), p. 203.

464 / Phenomenology and Legal Theory

enology and existentialism, "radicalized" Descartes's separation
or distancing of mind and matter, preparing the way for physiocratic idealistic natural law, because, as Marx and Engels said
in the passage quoted earlier, Descartes "in his *physics* endowed
matter with self-creative power" and because "*Within* his physics
matter is the only *substance.*" Malebranche's "radicalism" consists in his overcoming the "self-creative" power of matter or in
idealizing matter through a god. Malebranche "radicalizes" Cartesian external mediation.

Merleau-Ponty secularizes the discussion. He veers Malebranche's objective idealism toward subjective idealism, writing
that "The problem which Malebranche tried to resolve by occasionalism or Leibniz by pre-established harmony is carried over
into human consciousness." [31] Sartre also perceives the relation
between Heidegger and Malebranche and the problem of subjectivity in both. "The 'being-with,' conceived as a structure of my
being, isolates me as surely as the arguments for solipsism,"
Sartre writes.

> The reason for this is that Heidegger's *transcendence* is a
> concept in bad faith: it aims, to be sure, at surpassing idealism,
> and it succeeds in so far as idealism presents us with a subjectivity
> at rest in itself and contemplating its own images. But the idealism
> thus surpassed is only a bastard form of idealism, a sort of
> empirical-critical psychologism. Undoubtedly Heidegger's human-
> reality "exists outside itself." But this existence outside itself is
> precisely Heidegger's definition of the *self.* It resembles neither the
> Platonic (Neo-Platonic?) ekstasis where existence is really aliena-
> tion, existence in an Other, nor Malebranche's vision in God, our
> own conception of the ekstasis and of the internal negation. . . .
> [T]he flight outside the self is a flight toward the self, and the
> world appears as the pure distance between the self and the self.[32]

What Sartre does not say in this presentation is that Heidegger's
subjective "distancing," like Malebranche's "vision in God," masks
social alienation in that it is appropriative and dominates social
relations.

This, too, may be said of Husserl's phenomenological "brack-

---

31. Maurice Merleau-Ponty, *The Structure of Behavior*, trans. Alden L.
Fisher (Boston: Beacon Press, 1963), p. 220.
32. Jean-Paul Sartre, *Being and Nothingness*, trans. Hazel E. Barnes
(New York: Philosophical Library, 1956), p. 249.

eting," which is also a form of distancing or of appropriative alienation. This alienation passes into the legal theory of phenomenology, which is concerned with property and contract (more exactly, with the *acte juridique* or *Rechtsgeschäft*).

The role of "bracketing" in phenomenology must be considered more closely. It must be shown just how bracketing leads, as Knittermeyer says, to "deactualization," and what "deactualization" means.

Because Descartes created two worlds, mind and matter, the outcome of such distancing, separation, *coupure*, or *Trennung* was that each was a thing-in-itself and not both a thing-in-itself and a thing-for-other, in a dialectical unity of opposites. The truth of each was not in its other. Since there was no dialectical totality or wholeness because there was no interpenetration, the being of Husserl's naïve natural world and of the world of essences collapses into nothingness through bracketing. As the being of both mind and matter lacked the truth of determination through the other, each was nothing or deactualized. Through his bracketing, Husserl, who said that he was hostile to nineteenth-century positivism, accepted positivism's destruction of the naïve material world and intensified this crypto-idealistic "victory" by destruction of the materialism of essence, which dialectically is essence as history. However, Husserl's intensification of the work of Mach, so that both appearance and reality collapsed into nothingness, was, in accordance with the late history of idealism, masked as being, though such empty or relationless being is always nothingness or deactualization because it has been deprived of motion or of becomingness.

In *The Phenomenology of Mind*, Hegel writes:

> The thing is set up as having a being of its own, as existing for itself or as an absolute negation of all otherness; hence it is absolute, negation merely relating itself to itself. But this kind of negation is the cancelling and superseding of *itself*, or means that it has its essential reality in an other. . . . The object is really in one and the same respect the opposite of itself—for itself "so far as" it is for another, and for another "so far as" it is for itself. It is for itself, reflected into self, one; but all this is asserted along with its opposite, with its being for another, and for that reason is asserted merely to be superseded.[33]

33. Hegel, *Phenomenology of Mind*, p. 174.

This should explain Peschka's more directly presented criticism of Husserl.

> The eidetic juridical connections reveal themselves in the phenomenological vision of essences, which has for a condition the putting between parentheses of the intentional object, that is to say, the abstraction from its reality and from its existence; it is only after the eidetic regularities of the intentional object put between parentheses—in our case the essence of law and its eidetic regularities—have become clear in a phenomenological intention that the opening of the parentheses, that verification of the objective reality of the object, can take place. Fundamentally the question here is of a false identification of the essence, grasped in the phenomenological intuition, therefore of an object irrationally thought, with a real object; it affirms that it has here certain objective and a priori regularities of law which exist independently of human consciousness, but whose structure and substance are nevertheless determined by the individual consciousness which accomplished the cognition.[34]

In the *Logic,* Hegel describes the dialectical negation in being-in-self and being-for-other. He writes:

> Primarily Being-in-Self and Being-for-Other are distinct; but, further, Something also has in itself that which it is in itself, and conversely it is in itself what it is as Being-for-Other, and this fact constitutes the identity of Being-in-Self and Being-for-Other. . . . We may remark that the meaning of the Thing-in-itself here becomes plain: it is a very simple abstraction, though for some time it was considered a most important and, as it were, high class determination, just as the proposition that we do not know what Things-in-themselves are, was a piece of wisdom held in high esteem.—Things are called "in themselves," in so far as we abstract from all Being-for-Other, which means that they are thought of quite without determination, as Nothings.[35]

Because Husserl's essence is the deactualization, the separation, the "bracketing," the distancing, the appropriative alienation of Husserl's natural world, each collapses into nothingness. Because Husserl's essences have only the semblance or dis-

---

34. Peschka, "La Phénoménologie," p. 267.
35. G. W. F. Hegel, *Science of Logic,* trans. W. H. Johnston and L. G. Struthers, 2 vols. (New York: Humanities Press, 1929), I, 133.

simulation of determined juridical essences, they are in truth nothings or anythings, as unhistoric bourgeois legal science may require. Perhaps Diderot would have perceived this. Husserl's distanced essences cannot be historically determined essences and therefore are nothings, masked as being. "He who says *rien*," Diderot writes, "declares by his language that he distances [*éloigné*] all reality." [36] But indetermination, or *rien*, means nothing or anything. In "The Indiscreet Toys," he writes, "Our flight had been long when I saw a building suspended in the void of space, as by enchantment. It was huge. I shall not say that it had no foundation, because it rested on nothing." [37]

The above, which is partially based on Hegel and on Diderot, may be thus developed:

a. Husserl's bracketing, *coupure*, distancing, *Trennung* establishes the nothingness or deactualization of both "sides" of the "bracket" or separation, because the two sides of the separation do not interpenetrate through their own self-motion. Because of his rupture or destruction, Husserl only consecrates being-in-itself. But because being-in-itself is not a unity-in-opposition with its other, being-in-itself is untruth because the truth of being-in-itself is in its other. Despite his condemnation of Neo-Kantianism, Husserl's thought repeats the crisis of the Kantian antinomies in which there also is abstraction of the unity of the opposites, thus seemingly justifying the external mediator. Before Kant, the external mediator juridically had been the unhistoric prince of the Enlightenment and later of Bentham. With Kant, the holy moral legislator had emerged. Reference may be made to the role of the god-assistant of Descartes, the role of God with Malebranche, and the role of the holy watchmaker of Leibniz.

b. In the philosophy of law the deactualization means that the "facts" of legal contentiousness and of normative legal formulation and determination cease to be related to the material social base. In the phenomenology of law a return to "empiricism," subsequent to the bracketing and to the abstract, essentialist methodology of the phenomenological jurist, is not a return to the contradictions of a materialistic conception of bourgeois law.

36. Diderot, *Dictionnaire encyclopédique*, V, in *Oeuvres*, XVII, 471.
37. Diderot, "The Indiscreet Toys," in *Diderot: Interpreter of Nature*, trans. Jean Stewart and Jonathan Kemp (London: Lawrence and Wishart, 1937), p. 39.

Phenomenology of law has historically emerged because of the contradictions in material social structure.

c. As Husserl's distancing or separation or deactualization means that both sides of the "bracketing" have collapsed into nothingness because of their reciprocal lack of self-motion, phenomenology in general (and phenomenological philosophy of law, as an aspect of such phenomenology) requires the masking or misuse of the nothingness. However, this is not a novelty of phenomenology of law. The most succinct summary of Hegel's *Phenomenology* is that it is an account of the historical masks of juridical nothingness which have developed in response to the infrastructures of different historical systems of property relations, expressing appropriative alienation. Hegel condemned the role of the mask or *persona* in stoic Roman law, which veered the so-called subject of law or "person" into the object of law. He also condemned Kantian semblance and romantic irony and hypocrisy in his considerations relating to law. Nietzsche required and justified the mask. Bloch directs attention to the mask. Lukács considers the incognito. Ricoeur is the theorist of guile.

d. The nothingness of Husserlian ideas of essence is masked by putative being. The mask reifies, corporealizes, the nothingness of essence. In truth, the phenomenology of law becomes a study of ideal types—largely of contract, property, crime—with which Hegel begins his own *Philosophy of Law* and which he himself called "abstract," though in reality its formalism was bourgeois and antifeudal. If Husserlian phenomenology of law is concerned with phenomenological types, it is in part designed to overcome the weakness of Max Weber's theory of ideal types. Weber's *Verstehen* theory of ideal types, which was therefore anticausal, made certain concessions to the natural world and to causal principle. The essence or type which emerges from Husserl's "bracketing" is designed to develop and to strengthen the anticausal individuating Neo-Kantian *Verstehen* or comprehension or "understanding" theory without necessity of the causality, dialectical or otherwise, of the natural or empirical world, and without collapse into individuation or particularism by justifying only the universal or essential. *Verstehen* theory in all its historical manifestations seeks to have as its outcome anticausally justified typology, the meaning or hermeneutics of typology, and, it must be added, the activism of the *projet, Entwurf,* or formal possibility of the typology. Thus Alfred Rosenberg, the leading

Nazi philosopher, conceived that to be a type-German was a *projet* which required activist racial purification.

e. The "bracketing" of the object required the phenomenological bracketing or distancing of the subject. This drove Husserl to the transcendental subject. The nothingness of the transcendental subject is the consequence of Husserl's rupture or deactualization of the natural world in which historic mediation is overcome by separation of that which is dialectically total or whole and in which the rupture is not dialectical negation. This was exploited, against Husserl, by Sartre in *The Transcendence of the Ego*,[38] whose subject became the liberty of nothingness in consequence of Husserl's deactualization or distancing of the natural world.

The problem of the reality of the other in phenomenology is too well known to be restated here. It leads to the monadic subject of Husserl and to the *Mitsein* of Heidegger, both of whom are condemned by Sartre. Heidegger's theory of *Mitsein* is overcome by Hegel's theory of recognition and by his dialectical theory of social being through the other and yet the negation of such negation. The reality of the subject is based on Hegel's theory of recognition in historical domination and historical suppression. Each gets his being through the other, but, through struggle, has his historical independence of the other. There is a negation of the negation through historical activism. Hegel's theory of recognition through struggle is, it must be repeated, dialectical, unlike usual juridical theory of recognition and usual juridical theory of social relations, which are not necessarily based on struggle to negate oppression. Here Sartre must be mentioned once again. Having condemned Husserl's monadic subject and Heidegger's *Mitsein*, Sartre acknowledges the reality of the other, not as subject but as object. In *Being and Nothingness* he condemns the subjectivity and states the failure of both Husserl and Heidegger, while acknowledging the superiority of Hegel. Nevertheless, Sartre concludes that each *pour-soi* is the object of the other. This is a very important presentation, because the bourgeois theorists of law, including Kant, conceive that the subject of law is not the object of law. This ought to be true even in criminal law. The writer held during World War II that the Nazi war

38. Jean-Paul Sartre, *The Transcendence of the Ego*, trans. Forrest Williams and Robert Kirkpatrick (New York: Farrar, Straus, Noonday Press, 1957), p. 93.

criminals were not objects of law but passive subjects of law, that is, that such persons could only be defendants and never plaintiffs in legal process. Probably without so intending, Sartre's theory of the reality of the other only as object, not as subject, threatens bourgeois ideas of the rule of law or *Rechtsstaat,* which is founded on the idea that the "persons" of the legal order are subjects, not objects. It will be recalled that in the *Phenomenology* Hegel said that the stoic Roman law idea of the "person" was pejorative, and that in the *Philosophy of Law* he described the persons involved in judicial contentiousness as the "bondsmen" of judicial process. This is correct, insofar as the infrastructure of the legal order is founded in appropriative alienation.

In overcoming feudalism the bourgeoisie replaced religion with law. Law is the god of the bourgeoisie. The legal theory of the rule of law or *Rechtsstaat* is a theory of the supremacy of law in social life and of the coequality of the subjects of law "before" the law. But Husserl and Heidegger seem to threaten the reality of social life and Sartre perceives the subject as an object, or the legal subject of law as a legal object of law. This means, to repeat, that phenomenological philosophy of law is based on alienation in the correct sense of the word. Alienation means seizure, appropriation, *occupatio* by the other subject of law with the semblance of consent of the appropriated subject of law. The outcome of this criticism of phenomenological philosophy of law is that the bourgeois rule of law is the rule of bourgeois appropriation or alienation. It may be readily perceived that phenomenological philosophy of law may have enjoyed a role in making possible an impending structuralist philosophy of law.

f. If Husserl's "bracketing" ruptures, severs, or deactualizes the unity of opposites, the material, empirical world and its essence as history, the unity cannot be restored internally. As has been said, an external or unhistoric mediating force is then dissembled and introduced to dominate or to rule the antinomy. This is the permanent problem and solution of undialectical thought, of thought which does not acknowledge interpenetration of self-moving opposition. In the third thesis on Feuerbach, Marx discusses the unhistoric prince or external mediator. "The materialist doctrine concerning the changing of circumstances and upbringing forgets that circumstances are changed by men and that it is essential to educate the educator himself. This doctrine must, therefore, divide society into two parts, one of which is superior to the other." [39] This states the problem of the jurist as mandarin.

Fink discusses the problem presented here concerning the role of Husserl's rupture of the natural and the essential through which phenomenology seeks to justify an undialectical, antinomical structured Neo-Kantian–Neo-Hegelian pyramid or *Stufenbau* crowned by the transcendental subject. Writing at the request of Husserl, as late as 1933, Fink says:

> The *epoché* still remains thoroughly misconceived when it is explicated as a mere *abstinence-modification* of the universal world thematic, of all acts belonging to natural life in the world. It then acquires the character of being a casting off and a distancing from the thematic which exists *before* the *epoché*. It then means: instead of living in the belief in the world we bracket it. . . . The reduction is not understood in its transcendental-phenomenological meaning as long as one directly identifies the ego living within the belief in the world with the ego exercising the *epoché*.

He states the problem thus:

> Phenomenology does not disconnect the world in order to withdraw from it and occupy itself with some other philosophical thematic, but rather, as philosophy, does it stand within the question as to what the world is: phenomenology disconnects the belief (as the universal world apperception) in the world in order ultimately to know the world. Yet how, when the world is recognized by the *epoché* as a being-meaning (*Seinsinn*), as a correlate of the belief in the world which has already given and which continues to give the world, can we prevent robbing ourselves, by disconnecting that belief within which the world is and continually "holds" for us, of the possibility of knowing what it is? This apparent *aporia* disappears when we make the "identity" of the ego which disconnects the belief in the world itself a problem. This identity is not the self-sameness of the simply active ego, which "until now" lived within the naive performance of its positings and which "from now on" will suspend such performances and hold them in abeyance, but it is rather the unique *identity* of the phenomenological reduction's *three egos*.[40]

39. Marx, "Theses on Feuerbach," in Karl Marx and Friedrich Engels, *The German Ideology*, trans. Ryazanskaya (Moscow: Progress Publishers, 1968), p. 660.

40. Eugen Fink, "The Phenomenological Philosophy of Edmund Husserl and Contemporary Criticism," in *The Phenomenology of Husserl*, ed. R. O. Elveton (Chicago: Quadrangle, 1970), pp. 114–15.

Farber is reserved in his thought relating to Fink as a phenomenologist. But as Husserl himself approved of the presentation
given here by Fink, it is appropriate to follow Fink's discussion
of the "three egos":

> In truth, the *epoché* is not a "direct" refraining from belief par-
> alleling the believing life of the thematic experience of the world
> which directly enacts its beliefs, but—and this cannot be over-
> emphasized—is a structural moment of *transcendental reflection*.
> The *epoché* is a reflexive *epoché*, that is, it is a refraining from
> belief on the part of the reflecting "observer" who looks on the
> belief in the world in the actuality of its live performance *without
> taking part in it*. Transcendental reflection, however, is essentially
> different from every natural reflective attitude. . . . The tran-
> scendental bracketing of the world, and here this implicity means
> the disconnection of self-acceptances (the "human ego"), renders
> possible for the first time the establishing of a reflecting-self which
> does not from the start stand within the human self-apperception,
> but which is rather *"outside"* of it. . . . The disconnection of the
> world, however, not only makes possible the formation of a non-
> worldly reflecting-self, but, as we have already mentioned, also
> makes possible the discovery of the true "subject" of the belief in
> the world: the "transcendental subjectivity" which accepts the
> world.[41]

Somewhat later, Fink says: "Our glance finally reveals that the
phenomenological reduction is at bottom a transformation of
the 'self'; it transcends the pure and 'indissoluble' unity of the
human ego, divides it, and brings it together within a higher
unity." [42]

Fink does not pass over the matter of opposition-in-unity between the "thing in itself" and "the thing as it for us," but merely
says that this contradiction is "essential to the natural attitude."
He goes on to say that phenomenology "does not dissolve the
world into mere being-for-us, but by suspending the natural attitude, it primarily inquires into the transcendental belief from
which this difference (and accordingly the antithesis of world
and our representation of the world) itself springs." [43] Fink seeks
to surpass Hegel's unity-in-opposition through negation of being-
in-itself and being-for-other (which is not exclusively a subject-

41. *Ibid.*, p. 115.
42. *Ibid.*, p. 117.
43. *Ibid.*, p. 119.

object problem, precluding dialectic of nature) by justifying an undialectical passage from being-for-us of being in the world to the world's being-for-transcendental-subjectivity. Fink's Malebrancheanism rests on Neo-Kantian–Neo-Hegelianism, which overcame Hegel's dialectic of negation and negation of the negation by subordinating dialectic to objective idealism without dialectic. "The radical difficulty of expounding phenomenology's basic thought," Fink holds, "which is present as the paradox of leading out of the natural attitude by starting within it, consists of transforming the intramundane departure from the intramundane belief in the world into the discovery of the *transcendental* belief in the world, and is therefore the transition from the being-for-us of beings to the world's being-for-transcendental-subjectivity." [44]

Fink describes this passage as "distancing," as "tension," and as "pathos." "Distancing" will be considered more generally later in this essay. "Tension" is a Kantian antinomical rejection of the negating dialectic of contradiction. It thus justifies external mediation because of the insolubility or impossibility of internal mediation. "Pathos," as will be seen later, is a Nietzschean and *Lebensphilosophie* justification for appropriative alienation by the "distancing" dominant force of the dominated force. Fink writes: "These indications of the reduction's formal performance-structure, no matter how vague and indeterminate they might be, point to a tension existing between the 'egos' which can be distinguished within the framework of an all-encompassing unity, a tension which essentially belongs to the carrying out of the phenomenological reduction and which defines phenomenology's *pathos*." [45] To sum up the criticism which has been made: The reductions, which begin as nothingness because of the original reduction, are not justified dialectically as negation and negation of the negation. The "tensions," which justify the hegemony or "distancing" of phenomenology, connote both its grounding and its Malebranchean hierarchical supremacy in the undialectical antinomies of Kant, *Lebensphilosophie*, Neo-Kantian–Neo-Hegelianism, that is, in antinomies which lack internal mediation and which therefore justify absurdity, including the absurd external mediation of the unhistoric prince. Fink's thought

44. *Ibid.*, p. 121.
45. *Ibid.*, p. 116.

culminates in a structured pyramid or *Stufenbau*, crowned by the transcendental subject or observer, which is an unknowable-thing-in-itself, veiling an objective idealism or a god. Phenomenology, which begins as a subjective idealism, becomes a double idealism, which creates new problems for phenomenology. Fink's thought, which has been pursued here as that of Husserl's, perhaps justifies the statement of Merleau-Ponty made earlier in this essay, that phenomenology represents the interiorization of the god of Malebranche. This is the mission of intentionality, which is both subject and object. In the words of Hegel, this is impure intentionality, because of the concealment of the social infrastructure.

However, there is a distinction between phenomenology and Malebranchean natural law. The third ego, or the hierarchically supreme ego, is an objective idealism, which is an unknowable thing-in-itself. It is the external mediator of Kantian "tensions" by which juridical elitism or mandarinism is privileged and justified. But in Malebranchean thinking, natural law is knowable not only by the prince but also by his subjects. The outcome with Malebranche is that the prince must recognize the conceptions of natural law made known by his subjects. The result appears, it seems to this writer, in the First Amendment of the Constitution, which guarantees the right of petition. The physiocratic natural law jurists, who derive from Malebranche, do not in this maintain Malebranche's level of development, though they justified public education.

There seems to be a resemblance between Fink's *Stufenbau* theory of egos and Kelsen's legal theory, which is a Neo-Kantian, positivist *Stufenbau* theory in which the basic norm is the constitution. However, Kelsen is not himself a phenomenological jurist, and he has attacked the subjectivity of existentialist philosophy of law, both in German and in English. However, certain phenomenological jurists have turned to Kelsen despite his positivism and his hostility to natural law. Felix Kaufmann discussed the relation between Kelsen and phenomenology as early as 1922 in *Logik und Rechtswissenschaft*.[46] Of course, Kelsen's positivism conceals idealism, as is usual with positivism. The relation of legal positivism and natural law with phenomenology will be discussed later.

46. (Tübingen: Mohr, 1922), p. v.

However, it is important here to focus on phenomenology it-self. Husserl's mediator, which dominates the rupture or the bracketing, is an external transcendentalism. In effect, Fink describes the transcendental Malebranchean objective idealist mediator as the unhistoric "transcendental observer" or "on-looker." [47] He says that transcendental bracketing disconnects "the human ego" and makes possible "a reflecting-self . . . which is rather '*outside*' " of "human self-apperception." [48] "Tran-scendental life," Fink holds, "stands 'outside of ' the world." [49] For him, and presumably for Husserl, the *epochē* "acquires the char-acter of being a casting off and a distancing from the thematic which exists *before* the *epochē*." [50] As has been said, the theory of distancing as appropriative alienation or of *Entfernung* as *Entfremdung* will be discussed generally later in this paper. Fink says that phenomenology has indicated "a task: the keeping of all mundane representations belonging to any sort of knowl-edge-thematic at a distance." [51] Phenomenological idealism, he writes, maintains that "It is important first of all to keep all representations which would relate to the world as the 'one' back to a transcendental subject as the 'other' at a distance." [52]

It may be said that phenomenological transcendentalism, of which phenomenology of law is a derivative, reflects the decay of recent bourgeois thought, and justifies such decay through bracketing or deactualization. If Kant's bourgeois transcenden-talism is reversed and set on its feet, that is to say, materialized, it may connote an aspect of certain historically and socially created elements of human knowledge as a self-making of hu-manity. "For not only the five senses, but also the so-called mental senses—the human nature of the senses—comes to be by virtue of its object, by virtue of *humanized* nature," Marx wrote in *The Economic and Philosophic Manuscripts of 1844*. "The forming of the five senses is a labor of the entire history of the world down to the present." [53] But phenomenological tran-

---

47. Fink, "Phenomenological Philosophy of Husserl," pp. 116, 142.
48. *Ibid.*, p. 115.
49. *Ibid.*, p. 113.
50. *Ibid.*, p. 114.
51. *Ibid.*, p. 127.
52. *Ibid.*, p. 139.
53. Karl Marx, *Economic and Philosophic Manuscripts of 1844*, ed. Dirk J. Struik, trans. Martin Milligan (New York: International Publish-ers, 1964), p. 141.

scendentalism excludes a historical a priori. Hegel also laid the foundation for an activist historical theory of knowledge, based on the dialectic of the abstract-concrete. By its bracketing, phenomenological transcendentalism excludes such dialectic. Peschka in effect says this, because its bracketing justifies arbitrariness, which infects the subsequent development.[54] Such irrationalism has been intensified, especially since Freud has been invoked by Ricoeur, among many others, to relate the "tensions" among the egos of phenomenology. Husserl himself justifies fideism, religious or otherwise. The distanced phenomenological "onlooker" is a god "where the thematic field is the transcendental intending of the world. . . . [H]e observes this belief without taking part in or becoming involved with it." [55] There is a "tension" among the phenomenological egos which essentially belongs to the carrying out of the phenomenological reduction and which defines phenomenology's *"pathos."* [56] Contrary to this, Marx wrote in 1844: "[A]theism and communism are no flight, no abstraction; no loss of the objective world created by man." [57] And before Marx, Hegel wrote: "[W]e must become acquainted with empirical nature, both with the physical and with the human. The merit of modern times is to have accomplished or furthered these ends. . . . Without the working out of the empirical sciences on their own account, Philosophy could not have reached further than with the ancients." [58]

In *Phénoménologie et vérité*, de Waelhens discusses some of the problems which have been indicated here.[59] He suggests that Husserl's intentionality of the transcendental subject does not assure the necessity of the object. However, if the necessity of the object is threatened, it seems that the necessity of the transcendental subject is also jeopardized by Husserl's intentionality. De Waelhens suggests the problem whether Husserl's intentionality does not seem to be a futile effort to strengthen subjective Neo-Kantian ideas of *Erlebnis* or reliving of the putative object. If

54. Peschka, "La Phénoménologie," p. 285.
55. Fink, "Phenomenological Philosophy of Husserl," p. 116.
56. *Ibid.*
57. Marx, *Economic and Philosophic Manuscripts*, p. 187.
58. Hegel, *Lectures on the History of Philosophy*, III, 176; see also pp. 219, 361.
59. Alphonse de Waelhens, *Phénoménologie et vérité* (Paris: Presses Universitaires de France, 1953), see esp. pp. 39, 41, 161, and also pp. 10, 11, 36.

both subject and object are not necessitated, it seems that both are replaced by intentionality, which is both subject and object. Such intentionality may veer between subjective and objective idealism, as bourgeois ambiguity requires. De Waelhens raises doubt whether Husserl's object is univocal. But Kantian *Verstellung*, equivocation, or hypocrisy is required because of the crisis of recent bourgeois philosophy of law. Later in this paper attention will be directed to Husserl's *Logical Investigations*, from which the problem of the role of juridical method in phenomenological intentionalist philosophy of law will be extracted. If legal methodology becomes a phenomenological a priori of law, what may seem to be intentionalist univocality may conceal ambiguity, if the social infrastructure so requires. These questions of phenomenology of law are inevitable because the bourgeoisie is not a universal class and requires ambiguity.

From the point of view of philosophy of law, the above questions cannot be evaded. Hegel's *Philosophy of Law* is concerned with them. The physiocratic natural law jurists of the eighteenth century raised the question whether legislation which violated natural law did not have as sanction the infamy of the wrongdoer. Infamy is a most important instrument of criminal law, because, like death itself, it ruptures the social relations of the criminal, turning him dialectically into nothingness. This sanction, democratized, appears generally in the text of the Fifth Amendment of the Constitution. Infamy appears in the *Phenomenology*, in which Hegel discusses the struggle between the noble consciousness and the infamed or base consciousness in feudalism. Although the physiocrats mention the infamy of the legislator in mistaking the natural law, this sanction does not touch the infamy of the magistrature or the jurists, who are privileged because of the mandarinism of physiocratic natural law. After the French Revolution, the *code civil* provided in substance that the judge who refuses to decide a case on the ground of the insufficiency, obscurity, or silence of the law is guilty of the crime of denial of justice.

PHYSIOCRATIC LEGAL THEORY AND PHENOMENOLOGY

MOVED BY MALEBRANCHE, Emil Lask advanced toward a conception of phenomenological philosophy of law in 1905. He may be regarded as a transitional force. He wrote:

The teleological tinge of all legal concepts may best be studied in the alterations and introjections, unjustified from a mere naturalistic and psychological standpoint, to which mental realities are necessarily subject in the legal order. In the juridical view, mental existence, just like the corporeal world, serves as mere material to be worked upon for projection into the practical world of action. Jurisprudence thus serves especially well to prove that the disciplines which are misleadingly called "spiritual sciences" by no means consist of an analysis of mental phenomena. . . . Indeed, there is hardly a single juridical problem where the methodological approach has not labored under an insufficient distinction between the purely psychological concept and the very variable concept of the will. . . . Here, a wide field is open to the methodology of the future. There has been as yet no attempt at separating the truly psychological-naturalistic and the teleological elements in the juridical elaboration of psychological concepts. . . . Perhaps such a distinction between psychological and teleological elements may aid both sciences to gain a fuller methodological knowledge of themselves. For the practical element which is fused with the psychical concepts and which naturalistic psychology has to disregard, attains its highest possible degree of precision in jurisprudence.[60]

Lask continues:

It may be suggested in passing that the controversy between the doctrines of will and of purpose can be settled only by close attention to the teleological function of concepts, which is equally relevant here. This controversy, made famous by Jhering, has become immeasurably worse confounded because a clear answer has never yet been given, despite all attempts, to this question: whether purpose lies "beyond" the dogmatic legal concepts and therefore belongs only in the field of social theory . . . or whether it involves metajuridical social factors overlapping into the general formation of concepts.[61]

As he is writing in 1905, it is not surprising that Lask does not mention Husserl, but he obviously refers to Malebranche. He

60. Emil Lask, "Legal Philosophy," in *The Legal Philosophies of Lask, Radbruch, and Dabin*, trans. Kurt Wilk (Cambridge: Harvard University Press, 1950), p. 34.

61. *Ibid.* For general background, see Karl Larenz, *Metodologia de la ciencia del derecho*, trans. Enrique G. Ordeig (Barcelona: Ariel, 1966), chap. 4, which discusses Stammler, Rickert, Lask, Radbruch, Sauer, Binder, Schönfeld, Reinach, Welzel, and G. Husserl.

MITCHELL FRANKLIN / 479

mentions that certain jurists "have noticed this peculiar com-
mingling of the worlds of the Is and the Ought and their interplay, which very nearly recalls the metaphysics of occasionalism;
and they have endeavored to grasp the conceptual forms of origination, disappearance, involution, in short, of connection in the
'legal world.' " [62]

If the development pursued has been correct, attention now
should be directed to the history of the legal theory of the French
physiocrats of the eighteenth century, insofar as they emerged
from the "bracketed," objective idealist aspect of Cartesianism,
especially that of Malebranche.

If Husserl's turn toward the idealistic moment in Descartes
in recent bourgeois philosophy of the twentieth century has had
consequences in philosophy of law, the problem necessarily exists
whether Descartes also influenced early bourgeois legal theory,
which in general is related to the rationalistic, mechanistic,
materialist natural law of the bourgeois revolutions. But the
philosophical idealism of Husserl does not derive from the materialist aspect of Descartes. The connection between Husserl and
early bourgeois Cartesian legal ideas must be sought in natural
law theory as it developed from the idealist aspect of Descartes.
This points to the importance of Malebranche. And, as has been
said, it is the merit of Merleau-Ponty that he perceives the
importance of Malebranche in Husserl's thought. Of course, Merleau-Ponty was not qualified to consider the import of Malebranche on natural law thinking, and did not attempt to pursue
the relation.

The influence of Malebranche appears in the history of
French physiocratism. This movement virtually begins the history of economic theory. It passed into the economic theory of
Adam Smith, who veered it firmly toward early bourgeois
thought. Physiocratic economic theory influenced Marx, perhaps
becoming an element in his dialectic of infrastructure and superstructure. Its influence on French philosophic *structuralisme,*
which has arisen in response to both twentieth-century phenomenology and twentieth-century existentialism, cannot yet be assessed.

It is the superstructural history, that is, the social or ideological theory, which is important here in considering physiocratic

62. Lask, "Legal Philosophy," p. 33.

natural law ideas, based on *évidence*. This history seems to have been lost sight of, although Adam Smith in the *Wealth of Nations* directed favorable attention to physiocratic social theory. The American theory of judicial supremacy, embodied in *Marbury* v. *Madison*, is explained by the history of physiocratic legal theory. This statement is designed to contradict attempts to justify such judicial hegemony in the United States on the foundation of English feudal and bourgeois history.

The most important theorists of the French physiocrats were Quesnay, the founder of the movement, and Le Mercier de la Rivière. Quesnay justified the theory of *évidence*. Le Mercier de la Rivière was the leading physiocratic theorist of natural law known through *évidence*. As such *évidence* of natural law was known to the magistrature by virtue of office, the judicial supremacy of the magistrates over certain other organs of the state machinery was justified. This thought was condemned by the Abbé de Mably, the theorist of French utopian communism. Certain problems of present-day phenomenology were overcome or ignored by the physiocratic jurists because knowledge of *évidence* was corporealized, incarnated, fetishized, or reified in the magistrature. As the magistrature was thus elitist or mandarinist, Le Mercier de la Rivière justified, through such reification, what was called legal despotism. It was the idea of the physiocratic jurists that arbitrary or feudal despotism could be replaced only by legal despotism. Diderot, who was not a physiocrat, justified the natural law of the magistrature on the ground of Newtonian physics. The physiocrats were contributors to Diderot's *Encyclopédie*. However, Diderot condemned Malebranche, who influenced physiocratic theory of natural law. The problem of the truth of *évidence* seems to have been solved by the physiocrats through the reification or corporealization of natural law in the magistrature. Several aspects of the theory of *évidence* of physiocratism may be mentioned because of their relation to the infrastructural problems of contemporary legal phenomenology.

Quesnay, in the *Encyclopédie*, begins his essay on *évidence* which certainly is one of the longest in this eighteenth-century scholarly enterprise, as follows:

[T]he term *évidence* signifies a certitude so clear and so manifest by itself that spirit cannot resist it. There are two sorts of certitude: faith and *évidence*. Faith tells us of truths which cannot be known by the light of reason. *Évidence* is limited to natural knowledge. Nevertheless faith is always united to *évidence;* for in *évidence* we cannot know any motive for credence, and consequently we cannot be instructed in super-natural truths. . . . *Évidence* is not in faith; but the truths that faith teaches us are inseparable from *évident* knowledge. Thus faith cannot contradict the certitude of *évidence;* and *évidence,* limited to natural knowledge, cannot contradict faith.[63]

These statements as to the relation between faith and *évidence* raise the problem whether Husserl's bracketing in phenomenology, like Quesnay's, is also fideistic. In the *Crisis,* Husserl rejects positive religion, the idea of alliance between religion and science, and the traditional faith of "revealed" religion.[64] In speaking of "God's ontic validity," [65] Husserl realizes that religion as such cannot solve the problems of internal mediation or negation. Nevertheless, he writes that "the total phenomenological attitude and the epochē belonging to it are destined in essence to effect, at first, a complete personal transformation, comparable in the beginning to a religious conversion." [66] What Husserl perhaps has missed is that in the twentieth century fideism has been secularized, though he himself assisted in effectuating such development. This indicates the blindness of his *Crisis,* which was formulated during the period of Nazi fascism and which shows no hostility toward its secular fideism. Instead, Husserl seems to justify European (today restated as "Western") "man" superstructurally or ideologically. Husserl does not join Kolnai, whose influential book, *The War Against the West,* shows something of the relation of nazism to the fideism of philosophical idealism. It may be mentioned that Kaufmann, at this late date, has recently attacked Kolnai.[67]

As Quesnay and Husserl both justify limited or bracketed knowledge, they open the door to secularized fideism. Although Husserl attacks positivism, he does not condemn its agnosticism, which justifies fideism. His own bracketing or separation not only leaves the agnosticism of positivism intact, but the bracketing is

63. *Encyclopédie, ou dictionnaire raisonné des sciences, des arts, et des métiers,* Pellet ed. (Bern, 1779), XIII, 397.
64. Husserl, *Crisis,* p. 390.
65. *Ibid.,* p. 288.
66. *Ibid.,* p. 137.
67. Walter Kaufmann, ed., *Hegel's Political Philosophy* (Chicago: Aldine, 1970), p. 143.

itself a limit which would have veered materialism, if it had been acknowledged as actual on the further side of the bracketing, into idealism and thence to fideism, secular or otherwise. Hegel's condemnation of Kant's theory of limited knowledge (including the perpetually unknowable-thing-in-itself) makes Quesnay a predecessor and Husserl a successor of Kantian theory of fideism. It must be repeated that, because of his bracketing, Husserl does not really overcome Kantian distancing through limit. "In that Husserl separates the logical from mankind, opposes the logical as ideal being to real, empirical, perceivable being, and also to the psychical life of mankind (in so far as it is united with real being)," Heise, Zweiling, and Oiserman write, "he seeks to establish that the study of the actuality surrounding us and knowledge of the spiritual life of mankind presupposes 'the scientific knowledge of the essence of consciousness.'"[68] Separation or distancing is the problem, too, in the latter-day Heidegger's preoccupation with the Diltheyan "thinker," to whom knowledge may emerge from the chiaro-oscuro, light-dark, distanced-near, limitation of Being and beings.

It is not necessary to reconsider fully here the problem of the actuality of the other or of the other as class or national state which haunts Husserl's thinking. Perhaps it is sufficient to recall Sartre's discussion of the failure of Husserl's other as subject; the other is object. In effect, Schutz counters Sartre's discussion of Husserl's other. Whether the other is being or nothing, subject or object, it cannot be evaded by the bourgeois theorist of the rule of law. Hegel perceived this weakness of the history of law in societies based on private property, beginning as he does with stoic Roman law and concluding with the legal theory of the romanticism of his own period. Hegel begins his own *Philosophy of Law* with the abstract bourgeois "person," although he had described with contempt the "person" of stoic slaveholding Roman law. Hegel perceived, throughout legal history, the relation of jurist and "subject" of law (the "parties" or "persons" of the legal order) as objects of law, founding himself on his famous discussion of domination and servitude in the *Phenomenology*. Similar ideas explain Kafka's *Prozess* and possibly certain writings by Brecht and Musil. The physiocrats accept the ac-

---

68. M. A. Dynnik et al., *Geschichte der Philosophie*, 6 vols. (Berlin: VEB Deutscher Verlag der Wissenschaften, 1963), V, 465.

tuality of the other. Their position, founded on the rivalry of the bourgeoisie and the feudal forces on the eve of the French Revolution, as well as on inner bourgeois relations, required this. The physiocratic jurists begin with the truth of such rivalries, which they explain in terms of interest theory, as inspired by Helvétius and Holbach. Marx and Engels write:

> The content of the theory of exploitation that was neglected by Helvétius and Holbach was developed and systematized by the physiocrats who worked at the same time as Holbach; but as they took as their basis the undeveloped economic relations of France where feudalism, under which landownership plays the chief role, was still not broken, they remained in thrall to the feudal outlook in so far as they declared landownership and land cultivation to be that [productive force] which determines the whole structure of society. . . . Thanks to the Physiocrats, political economy for the first time was raised to the rank of a special science and has been treated so ever since. As a special branch of science it absorbed the other relations—political, juridical, etc.—to such an extent that it reduced them to economic relations. But it considered this subordination of all relations to itself only one aspect of these relations, and thereby allowed them for the rest an independent significance also outside political economy.[69]

Physiocratic theory overcame the acknowledged rivalries within French society through natural law theory based on *évidence*. Le Mercier de la Rivière, Husserl-like, said that "our spirits have a natural tendency toward *évidence*." [70] He continues: "This natural tendency of our spirit toward *évidence* is tied with the two *mobiles* which are in us." [71] It should be noticed at this point that Le Mercier de la Rivière writes here of *mobiles* and not of *motifs*. This distinction between *mobiles* and *motifs*, which, except for Pfänder, Ricoeur, Aron, Schutz, and Sartre, seems largely to have escaped American discussion of phenomenology and existentialism, raises the problem of the relation of these latter-day movements to attempts to unite subjective and objective idealism. This problem necessarily arises because Husserl emerged during a period in which subjective Neo-Kantianism sought to strengthen itself by unification with Dilthey's anti-

69. Marx and Engels, *German Ideology*, p. 463.
70. Le Mercier de la Rivière, *L'Ordre naturel et essentiel des sociétés politiques* [1767] (Paris: Depitre, 1910), p. 47.
71. *Ibid.*

dialectical objective idealist Neo-Hegelianism. Le Mercier de la Rivière goes on to say that the *mobiles* in us, "the appetite of pleasures and the aversion of pain have the great interest of not being deceived in the choice of means of satisfying them; that is why we can be tranquil only after we have acquired a certitude which can only result from *évidence:* it is by this same reason again that the liberty of employing all the means which lead to *évidence* makes an essential part of the liberty of enjoyment without which the law of property would cease to exist." [72] It may be mentioned that contemporary phenomenology of law has been, to a very great degree, devoted to phenomenology of property and of contract (or, to be more accurate, to the *acte juridique* or *Rechtsgeschäft*). Le Mercier de la Rivière continues, "*Évidence* of geometrical truths passes to *évidence* of social truths, to *évidence* of this natural and essential order which procures to humanity its best possible state." [73] Quesnay overcomes acknowledged social rivalry through natural law theory based on *évidence*. To him a "decisive" as distinguished from an "indecisive . . . human will which expresses sensations more or less agreeable . . . excludes another decisive will, for two decisive wills cannot exist at the same time; they annihilate each other . . . there are not two decisive wills; thus the soul does not have the divided moral power [*double pouvoir*] of acquiescing or of not acquiescing decisively in the same thing: therefore it is not free in this regard . . . this decision is a simple and definitive act, which absolutely excludes any other decision. The soul therefore does not have the divided moral power of deciding or of not deciding for the same thing." [74]

The meaning of this is that Quesnay has established a materialistic social contradiction which cannot be resolved dialectically, that is, which cannot be resolved or mediated within the materialistic contradiction itself, and which, because such conception of interest is mechanistic, justifies the unhistoric or external mediation of the rival *mobiles* by God or, in law, by the magistrature who (which) corporealizes or incarnates God. This is an anticipation of the external mediation of Kant's antinomies and of Husserl's intentionality by means of which the antinomies as objects are hidden and justify what Hegel called irony,

72. *Ibid.*
73. *Ibid.*, p. 48.
74. *Encylopédie* (1779), XIII, 414.

Verstellung, or shifting. The remarks of de Waelhens concerning Husserl's inability to justify or to necessitate intentionality as object may here be recalled, if such remarks are developed into intentionality as ambiguous subject-object.

The external mediator who (which) is thus "necessitated" by Quesnay is God, known to the corporealized magistrature through the *évidence* "toward" which, as has been said, spirit has a "natural tendency." The crisis of *mobiles* is mediated by the God of Malebranche. In section 56 of his essay on *évidence* in the *Encyclopédie,* Quesnay wrote:

> Man is not a simple being, he is composed of body and soul; but this perishable union does not exist by itself; these two substances cannot act on each other. It is the action of God which vivifies animated bodies, which continually produces every active form, sensitive and intellectual. Man receives his sensations by the mediation of the organs of the body, but the sensations themselves and his reason are the immediate effect of God on the soul; thus it is in this action on the soul in which the essential form of the reasonable animal consists: the organization of the body is the conditional or instrumental cause of the sensations; and the sensations are the *motifs* or the determining causes of reason and of the decisive will. Free will, considered simply in itself, consists in this state of intelligence and in the force of intention. . . . Natural liberty is related to two states equally opposed to liberty itself: these two states are the *invincibility* of *motifs* and *deprivation* of *motifs.* When the affective sensations are very pressing and very live, relative to instructive sensations and to other actual *motifs,* the soul cannot conquer by itself without supernatural aid. . . . In the tranquil exercise of liberty the soul determines itself nearly always without examination and without deliberation. . . . Natural law presents itself to all men, but they interpret it diversely; positive and determined rules are necessary in order to fix and to assure their conduct.[75]

Having deepened the crisis, Quesnay continues:

> Thus rule which guides usages suffices in the moral order to determine them without hesitation and without deliberation; whereas the contrariety of interest which affects others, resists rule; whence arises the exercise of animal liberty, which is always a disorder in man, combat intended [*intenté*] by strong passions which result

75. *Ibid.*

from a bad organization of the body. . . . This animal liberty or the conflict of affective sensations which limit the attention of the soul to illicit passions . . . I say must be distinguished from moral liberty or intelligence, which is not obsessed by deranged feeling; which recalls to each his duties toward God, toward himself, toward others. . . . It is in the idea of such liberty, to which man is elevated by his union with divine intelligence, that we perceive we are really free. . . . These primary *évidentes* truths are the base of supernatural knowledge.[76]

Thus the contradictions among material interests or passions, that is, within the materialist "side" of Descartes, justify the appropriative mediation of the idealistic or Malebranchean side of Descartes. Such mediation, founded on limit, monadization, distance, "bracketing" of forces which are not a unity-in-opposition, must be external or idealistic. The Malebranchean or external mediator thus required is the physiocratic magistrature. This is somewhat the same as Pound's American theory of balance of interest through legal method. This is the methodology today of the Supreme Court and of certain American idealist legal "realists" who conceive of law as "policy." This is also somewhat the same as Kant's external mediator who mediates antinomies.

Ricoeur's considerations suggest that Husserl "radicalizes" idealism, so that such "radical" idealism, even "bracketed," may not be set on its feet, that is, reversed, so as to justify materialism once more through such reversal or veering of the "radicalized" idealism. Ricoeur writes:

> The first radical reflection on the priority of consciousness over its objects must be attributed to Descartes. By virtue of this, he is the originator of the transcendental motif, which alone is capable of destroying the dogmatic naïveté of naturalism. . . . Going almost to the end of the universal "suspension" of being, he made the "apodictic foundation" emerge: *ego cogito cogitata.* This fully elaborated formula indicates that the world, lost as the disclosure of an in-itself, can only be reaffirmed as "that which I think"; the cogitatum of the cogito is the sole indubitable being of the world. In enlarging the sphere of the cogito, which is impervious to doubt, to the cogitata, which he called ideas, Descartes implicitly posited the important principle of intentionality . . . and by this means undertook to bring all objective evidence back to the primordial evidence of the cogito.

76. *Ibid.,* p. 416.

Then he continues:

> Descartes, however, was the first to betray himself. . . . He remained a prisoner of the evidences of Galileo; likewise, as he saw it, the truth of the physical is mathematical, and the whole enterprise of doubt and the cogito served only to reinforce objectivism. Thereafter, the I of the I-think is understood as the psychological reality, the *res cogitans* or the real psyche, which remains when one subtracts the mathematical nature. But on the other hand, it is necessary to prove that this soul has an "outside," that God is the cause of the idea of God, that the material "thing" is the cause of the idea of this world. Descartes did not see that the ego "de-mundanized" by the *epoché* is no longer soul, that soul "appears" just as the body does, for "he did not discover that all distinctions of the type I and thou, internal and external, are 'constituted' only in the absolute ego." [77]

However, though he is focusing immediately on Descartes, Ricoeur also questions whether the external mediation of Malebranche can escape materialist reversal through external mediation of the first degree; that is, the external mediation of God must be surpassed by the more profound external mediation of the absolute ego or of the second degree. This, too, is futile. Such absolute ego became, in Sartre's *Transcendence of the Ego,* nothingness, and, in his later *Being and Nothingness,* "profound" intentionality. What Ricoeur makes it possible to suggest, in the light of Quesnay's clash of *mobiles* or material passions, is that the external mediation of the first degree is founded on subjective idealism and that the external mediation of the second degree is an objective idealism masked as transcendental subjectivity; and that the unity of the two undialectically related idealisms is established by intentionality, which is the ironic subject-object, in that it can veer arbitrarily between two idealisms. Ricoeur himself writes of Galileo that

> the founder of mathematical physics is the ambiguous genius who, in uncovering the world as applied mathematics, covers it over again as a work of consciousness. Here we can grasp the actual style of Husserl's historical explication, for it is clear that this inspection of Galileo's motives can only be a retrospection.

77. Paul Ricoeur, *Husserl: An Analysis of His Phenomenology,* trans. Edward G. Ballard and Lester E. Embree (Evanston, Ill.: Northwestern University Press, 1967), pp. 164–65.

. . . [T]he only important thing is the sense of the whole which proceeds from his work and which was decided in the history that issues from that work. One could call the analysis of motivation a rational psychoanalysis much as Sartre speaks of an existential psychoanalysis, history being the special revealer of the project.[78]

What Ricoeur should have said here is that because Sartre's existentialist freedom approaches the reef of the dialectic of *mobiles-motifs* Sartre escapes catastrophe, that is, a reversal of existential idealism into materialism, by putting his idealist freedom under the protection of Freud. This is because Sartre's intentionality acknowledges both intentionality and profound intentionality. It may be, too, that Ricoeur and Sartre both turn to Freud because they must conceal the double idealism of Neo-Kantian–Neo-Hegelianism out of which Husserl emerged. What has been considered here is inspired by Marx's theory of ideology and by his third and fourth theses on Feuerbach, which mean that the external mediator is really a historical materialistic mediator whose intention is appropriative alienation. The question of the dialectic of *mobiles-motifs* is reserved for more general consideration in this essay, but it is important to reiterate now the pervasive influence of Freud on phenomenology and existentialism, including their philosophies of law. Relying on several Anglo-American thinkers, Ricoeur writes:

This way of approaching the epistemological status of psychoanalytic propositions assumes that an explanation through motives is irreducible to an explanation through causes, that a motive and a cause are completely different. I agree with this analysis: the statements of psychoanalysis are located neither within the causal discourse of the natural sciences nor within the motive discourse of phenomenology. Since it deals with a psychical reality, psychoanalysis speaks not of causes but of motives; but because the topographic field does not coincide with any conscious process of awareness, its explanations resemble causal explanations, without, however, being identically the same, for then psychoanalysis would reify all its notions and mystify interpretation itself. It is possible to speak of stated or reported motivations, provided that this motivation is "displaced" into a field analogous to that of physical reality. This is what the Freudian topography does.[79]

78. *Ibid.*, pp. 163–64.
79. Paul Ricoeur, *Freud and Philosophy*, trans. Denis Savage (New Haven, Conn.: Yale University Press, 1970), p. 360.

What Ricoeur does not say here is that the dialectic of *mobiles-motifs* became, with Neo-Kantianism and its successors, the distinction between individuating *Verstehen,* comprehension or "understanding," and *Erklärung,* the latter of which signifies the causality of the natural as distinguished from the social sciences, and that the turn of idealism toward Freud is designed to strengthen *Verstehen* theory from collapse because of its subjectivity by screening or sheltering it behind psychoanalysis and its irony. What is valuable here in Ricoeur is that he relates his thought to interpretation, a basic problem in law.

As far as Quesnay and Le Mercier de la Rivière are concerned, the Malebranchean theory of external mediation or appropriative alienation was achieved through the reification or fetishization or incarnation of the mandarinist magistrature. It is not necessary to discuss here Pound's theory of interest and American legal "policy" theory, which begin idealistically for various reasons, including rejection of the dialectic of infrastructure and superstructure, and then subordinate the idealistic foundation to the further idealism of the jurist, who is described as "neutral" but whose neutrality masks a historic intentionality and a historic juridical irony. Kant, too, really begins with already idealized, limited antinomies because time and space are withdrawn from the object and deposited with the Kantian subject. Physiocratic legal theory is, as has been said, an anticipation of Kantian methodology, of antinomical methodology in general. As with Kant, the limited antinomies are posited as limited, bracketed being-in-themselves or relationless nothings; the external, limited, bracketed idealist appropriating mediator, also a relationless nothing, is introduced as the profound lord of the contradictions or possibilities and chooses among them. In his *Critique of Judgment,* Kant said, "We see that the removal of the antinomy of the aesthetical judgment takes a course similar to that pursued by the critique in the solution of the antinomies of pure theoretical reason. And thus here, as also in the *Critique of Practical Reason,* the antinomies force us against our will to look beyond the sensible and to seek in the supersensible the point of union for all our *a priori* faculties, because no other expedient is left to make our reason harmonious with itself." [80]

80. Immanuel Kant, *Critique of Judgment,* trans. J. H. Bernard (New York: Hafner, 1951), pp. 186–87.

Kant here justifies not only the physiocratic, "unhistoric" jurist, but also Descartes's god-assistant, Kant's own holy moral legislator, and Leibniz' holy watchmaker. Marx's third thesis on Feuerbach considers the unhistoric prince of the French Enlightenment, to which Engels added Benthamism (Robert Owen), which (who) dominates, appropriates, occupies, or alienates the already limited, idealized antinomy. Such external mediation or lordship justifies the irony, ambiguity, equivocation, *Verstellung*, or hypocrisy for which Hegel repeatedly condemns Kant, certain aspects of Fichte, and German romanticism in general. Moreover, the Kantian "ought" and the Fichtean "yearning" justified the principle of postponement, for which Hegel also condemned them.

Although it is not the purpose of this essay to discuss Hegel's theory of religion, it may be suggested that his religious thought be considered in relation to the connection of physiocratic juridical theory with phenomenology and existentialist legal thought, despite the seeming disparity of questions presented. Because of the theory of *évidence* of physiocratic natural law and of the corporealization or incarnation of the magistrature, there should be study of the relation between Hegel and this juridical movement because of Malebranche's influence on the latter. Le Mercier de la Rivière invokes Malebranche and religious texts to justify physiocratic theory of natural law.[81] Hegel's discussion of revealed religion and religion as a spiritual work of art, both in the *Phenomenology* and in the *Lectures on the History of Philosophy*, is especially valuable.

Certain aspects of such connection may be briefly suggested here. Husserl's own considerations on religion, including revealed religion, as presented by him in the *Crisis* have already been mentioned. Insofar as Husserl therein rejects religion it has been suggested that he has not thereby rejected secular or political fideism, and that he even referred to the phenomenological attitude (perhaps focusing would be a better word, because Husserl emerged during the great period in the scientific history of photographic and microscopic optics) as "comparable in the beginning to a religious conversion," adding, "which then, however, over and above this, bears within itself the significance of the greatest existential transformation which is assigned as a task to

81. Le Mercier de la Rivière, *L'Ordre naturel,* pp. 333–34.

mankind as such." [82] This may justify reference to a relation between Hegel's conception of revealed religion (and religion as a spiritual work of art) and phenomenology, and to its outcome in philosophy of law.

Hegel relates the theory of revealed religion to the history of the rule of law, especially to the stoicism of Roman law. The so-called subjects of law, the "parties" in Anglo-American legal usage, become subordinated to the jurist, who is the so-called neutral judge of the rule of law. Hegel's is an alienation theory in the sense that these subjects are in truth objects because they have been seized or appropriated by the neutral jurist. Though in the *Philosophy of Law* Hegel describes the nineteenth-century jurist as enjoying the domination that the owner has in the alienation relation of master and slave, in his discussion of religion he relates such dominion to the alienation in the ambiguous or shifting unhappy religious consciousness described by him in the *Phenomenology*. However, in all his discussions of law Hegel perceives the rule of law as an untrue appearance which masks the truth of arbitrariness and the truth that arbitrariness is directed against historical necessity through the power of the jurist, himself alienated, over the contradiction or Kantian antinomy. This possibility of choice is the jurist's historic intention or historic *projet*. Post-Hegelian Neo-Kantian–Neo-Hegelianism developed the active or *Entwurf* aspect of *Verstehen* theory, that is, of comprehension or of "understanding." As has been suggested, the physiocrats state the materialistic activism or passions of the subjects of law and declare that the magistrature, through idealist *évidence*, reveals the immutability of the natural law known through *évidence*. Thus, Le Mercier de la Rivière says that it is the legislative authority which has the power to "make arbitrarily" [83] all sorts of positive laws, which the magistrature through *évidence* of immutable natural law must overcome.

This means that the idealist Malebranchean theory of *évidence* has reversed the dialectical relation between appearance and reality, so that the truth of the *évidence* is not natural law as a seeming thing-in-itself, but the arbitrariness of the magistrature as a seeming thing-in-itself. This idealist reversal of

82. Husserl, *Crisis*, p. 137.
83. Le Mercier de la Rivière, *L'Ordre naturel*, p. 82.

Cartesian materialism is concealed in the reification, corporealization, fetishization, or incarnation of the Malebranchean jurist.
It may be ventured that Malebranchean or physiocratic natural law is suggestive of an attempt to unify the two aspects of
Hegel's dialectic of religion—religion as a spiritual work of art
and religion as revealed religion—an inversion which in turn
is partially founded on Hegel's dialectic of the stoicism of Roman
law. It is beyond the scope of this essay to develop this thought
fully, save to repeat that Husserl's transcendental idealism, including his theory of *évidence,* may be a reworking of physiocratism, the two above-mentioned elements becoming a force
through his discussion of technique or methodology in the *Logical Investigations.*

Husserl's methodological thought will be considered later in
this essay. For the time being it will be sufficient to perceive the
outcome of existentialist theory of methodology as it appears in
Heidegger. Lingis writes:

> This then is the meaning of Heidegger's tactic of seeking to
> retrieve, in understanding, the original indistinction of *technē*
> and *poiēsis.* "The essential reflection on technique, and the
> decisive explication with it, must take place in a domain which,
> on the one hand, would be akin to the essence of technique,
> and, on the other hand, would nonetheless be fundamentally dif-
> ferent from it. Art is such a domain." Heidegger's endeavor re-
> quires this appeal not exactly to the domain of art, whose essence
> is poetry, but to the still more primordial ground where *technē*
> and *poiēsis* were yet one, in the production of truth in splendor.
> This return to the source, to this origin, is necessary in order for
> us to find a ground upon which technique can be *understood.* (If
> Heidegger's meditation on technique gravitates toward this origin,
> it is by no means because Heidegger intends to awaken a poetic
> or aesthetic *alternative* to technique.) This return to an origin, in
> historical experience, before *technē* became technique and *poiēsis*
> became art, this historical return to an originating or primordial
> disclosure, is the form that the cultural *epochē* always takes in
> Heidegger.[84]

84. Alphonso Lingis, "On the Essence of Technique," in *Heidegger
and the Quest for Truth,* ed. Manfred S. Frings (Chicago: Quadrangle,
1968), p. 133. "Art is the great means of making life possible, the great
seducer to life, the great stimulus to life" (Nietzsche, *The Will to Power,*
trans. A. M. Ludovici [London: Allen and Unwin, 1924], II, 290).

The outcome of the hegemony of legal methodology as art—indeed, as religious art secularized, hence as an aspect of the aesthetics of legal history—must be pursued from the Malebranchean physiocratic jurists into its ground, *mobiles, Beweggrund*, that is, into appropriative alienation disguised as existential distance and as existential nearness.

Hegel's dialectic of the relation between religion as a work of art and revealed religion does not consider as such physiocratic natural law of the magistrature. This relation may not be readily granted, because legal method as art or otherwise is not presented as such by the physiocratic jurists. The scholarly history of Romanist legal method does not comprehensively emerge until after the French Revolution. During the nineteenth century the objective idealist Savigny brought forward legal technique or method as a weapon of the feudal German historical school of law against the bourgeois content of the French Civil Code. With Savigny, Romanist legal method (or, more exactly, historical legal methods) became the Kantian a priori which legislated for the Kantian content or a posteriori of law. Savigny's great successor, Windscheid, said legal method was an "art," and not science.[85] Legal method is an elitist art. Hence, it usually is not formulated in the newer Romanist codes, unless an aspect of legal method is deliberately forged into a textual legal sword. As such it appeared even in the United States, in the new Uniform Commercial Code, which justified the development of the formulated law by analogy to determine unprovided-for problems. As such, it appears in the Ninth Amendment of the Constitution of the United States, so that the particularism of the text of the Bill of Rights formulated in the first eight amendments may explode into more general force as new historical situations may require. Such American material relating to legal method is remarkable, because Anglo-American law is hostile to formulated or codified law and does not justify the dialectic eruption of the unity-in-opposition of general-particular (the meaning of legal analogy) on the ground of formulated law. However, the methodological mission of the Ninth Amendment is justified by the history of Romanist legal method. But the warning must be given that the role of legal method may sometimes be that of the destruction

85. B. Windscheid, *Lehrbuch des Pandektenrechts*, 9th ed. (Frankfurt am Main: Literarische Anstalt Rütten & Loening, 1906), I, 98.

of positive law. Aristotle perceived this. Perhaps Kohler, the Neo-Hegelian philosopher of law, may be mentioned in this connection. He writes:

> A special law of equity (*Billigkeitsrecht*) may be established, which, however, becomes in turn logically formalized law, and, therefore, is inadequate to fit all cases: for, as soon as it envelops itself in the form of logical law, it too suffers the fate of being insufficient, in the ramifications of its ideas, to the demands of justice. Or the expedient may be adopted of framing legal judgments so elastically that they are able to meet the demands of the individual case. The former method was represented in earlier legal systems (Roman law, English law); the latter is what our modern legal structure is striving towards.[86]

The role of *évidence* in mandarin physiocratic legal theory was a masked justification for the hegemony of legal method, which of course in any legal system is activist and because of its opaqueness justifies legal irony, ambiguity, *Verstellung*, hypocrisy. Although Savigny was later to be the founder of comprehensive juridical self-consciousness or *prise de conscience* of the force of legal method, the Abbé de Mably, the last great figure of the French Enlightenment, the friend of Jefferson and of John Adams, and the most important opponent of the legal theory of the physiocrats, knew and mentioned legal method, especially as an American problem at the very conclusion of the American Revolution. During the English revolution of the seventeenth century there was a struggle between Hobbes and Coke over the esoteric role of English legal method or *"Artificiall perfection of Reason"* as it was called.[87]

The theory of legal method reappears today in phenomenology and existentialism as the problem of hermeneutics or interpretation. Philosophers tend to make the mistake of conceiving of interpretation as a problem of religion, forgetting or not knowing its role in the history of legal method in twenty-six centuries of Roman law. However, it is the merit of Hegel that, contrary to usual ideas, he perceived religion, at least in large measure, as reflecting Romanist legal ideas.

Marx has much to say here: "Property, etc., in short, the

86. Josef Kohler, *Philosophy of Law*, trans. A. Albrecht (Boston: A. M. Kelley, 1914), p. 86.
87. Thomas Hobbes, *Leviathan*, Cambridge ed. (1904), p. 193.

entire content of law and state is the same in North America and in Prussia, with few modifications. In North America the *republic* is thus a mere *form* of the state as monarchy is here. The content of the state remains outside these constitutions. Hegel is right therefore, when he says: the political state is the constitution, that is, the material state is not political. There is only an external identity here; a mutual determination takes place." [88] This does not mean that there is no internal mediation between the form and the content of law. It seems to mean that the state represents the general interest of a universal class, such as the bourgeoisie claimed to be, although in civil society the particularism of ownership of private property created crisis and the conflict of private passions of Quesnay. Such appearance of universal externality also characterizes revealed religion. However, dialectically, form (that is, state and law) and content (that is, private property) constitute an internal unity of opposites. The content precipitates its own form historically, and such historic form may dominate and may determine the historic content out of which it erupts. Legal method is the form which dominates the legal content. The great weakness of Kant was that, because of his theory of limit, he did not acknowledge that form and content were a unity-of-opposites, in which material content creates its own form and then may be dominated by it until new historical crises emerge. As Marx continues, he shows that the apparent externality of religion became the apparent externality of the state, though in truth such appearance or phenomenon of externality masked appropriative alienation as essence. He writes:

Of the various phases in a people's life the most difficult was the formation of the political state, the constitution. It emerged as universal reason in contrast to other spheres, and as the aspect most removed from these spheres. The historical problem then was their revindication, but the particular spheres are not aware that their private nature coincides with the distant nature of the constitution or political state, and the far removed existence of the political state is nothing but the affirmation of their own alienation. Up to now the *political constitution* has been the *religious sphere*, the *religion* of the people's life, the heaven of their universality in contrast to the particular *mundane existence* of their actuality. The

88. Karl Marx, "Critique of Hegel's Philosophy of the State," in *Writings of the Young Marx on Philosophy and Society,* trans. and ed. Lloyd D. Easton and Kurt H. Guddat (Garden City, N.Y.: Doubleday, 1967), p. 175.

political sphere was the state's only sphere within the state in which both content and form were a generic content and the genuinely universal, but in such a way that its content became formal and particular because these spheres stood in contrast to each other. *Political* life in the modern sense of the word is the *scholasticism* of a people's life. *Monarchy* is the completed expression of this alienation. The *republic* is the negation of alienation within alienation. It is obvious that a political constitution as such is formed only where the private spheres have achieved independent existence.[89]

If it is agreed that the *évidence* theory of physiocratic jurists masked the equivocation or the possibilities of legal form or legal method or legal art, it will be recalled also that Le Mercier de la Rivière said that the physiocratic jurist "inclined" toward *évidence*. This may mean that such intentionality is an activist appropriative alienation or domination of contradictions through legal method.

Intentio, too, is a concept of Roman law and hence is older than the scholastic meaning of the thought. In the formulary procedure of Roman law the protagonist made his claim through the *intentio*. The *intentio* stated the aggressive *projet* of the protagonist. In the words of Savigny, the *intentio* stated "the ground (*Grund*)" of the contestation.[90] The *intentio* is the activist formulation of a social eruption; it announces a fissure or contradiction in social relations.

The corporealization of the physiocratic magistrature suggests the corporealization which appears in Hegel's dialectical considerations of the alienation and inversion in revealed religion. This is valuable because the intentionality-alienation of bracketed, distanced, revealed religion and that of bracketed, distanced, secular phenomenology of law may be historically related. Hegel writes:

Spirit, here, has in it two sides, which are above represented as the two converse propositions: one is this, that substance empties itself of itself, and becomes self-consciousness; the other is the converse, that self-consciousness empties itself of itself and makes itself into the form of "thing," or makes itself universal self. Both sides

89. *Ibid.*, p. 176.
90. Friedrich Carl von Savigny, *System des heutigen römischen Rechts* (Berlin, 1841), V, 69.

have in this way met each other, and, in consequence, their true union has arisen. The relinquishment or "kenosis" on the part of the substance, its becoming self-consciousness, expresses the transition into the opposite, the unconscious transition of necessity, in other words, that it is *implicitly* self-consciousness. Conversely, this emptying of self-consciousness expresses this, that implicitly it is Universal Being, or—because the self is pure self-existence, which is at home with itself in its opposite—that the substance is self-consciousness explicitly *for the self,* and, just on that account, is spirit.[91]

Marx discussed this as alienation. Wahl, who perceived the activism in Hegel's discussion of religion, goes no further than to write: "The conception at which he arrives is of an incessant action where God and we make each other. . . . I am finite, God is infinite. These determinations, finite, infinite, are only certain moments of process. God exists also as finite and the *moi* as infinite; God is this movement in itself, and it is for this that he is living God." [92] This is double idealism. In his introduction to the *Critique of Hegel's "Philosophy of Law"* Marx sees religion as appropriation, and in so doing he is addressing himself to Hegel: "The foundation of irreligious criticism is this: man makes religion, religion does not make man. Religion is, in fact, the self-consciousness and self-esteem of man who has either not yet gained himself or has lost himself again. But man is no abstract being squatting outside the world. Man is the world of man, the state, society. This state, this society, produce religion, which is an inverted world-consciousness because they are an inverted world." [93] In the "Theses on Feuerbach," Marx writes of the "self-alienation" which explains religion. "Feuerbach," he says, "starts from the fact of religious self-alienation, of the duplication of the world into a religious world and a secular world. His work consists in resolving the religious world into its secular basis. But that the secular basis detaches itself from itself and establishes itself as an independent realm in the clouds can only

91. Hegel, *Phenomenology of Mind,* p. 755.
92. Jean Wahl, *La Malheur de la conscience dans la philosophie de Hegel,* 2d ed. (Paris: Presses Universitaires de France, 1951), p. 133.
93. Karl Marx, Introduction, *Critique of Hegel's "Philosophy of Right"* [Law], trans. Annette Jolin and Joseph O'Malley (Cambridge: At the University Press, 1970), p. 131. Throughout the text I cite this title as *Philosophy of Law,* which is a more accurate translation than *Philosophy of Right.*

be explained by the cleavages and self-contradictions within this secular basis." [94] Because this "self-alienation" is appropriative alienation, Hegel relates religion to the stoicism of Roman law, the intentionality of which rests on the appropriation of the "subjects of law" by the jurist. With Hegel, such "subjects of law" are objects of the jurist, who is subject or substance. Hegel says that the words "legal person" are pejorative. Moreover, Hegel relates his discussion of religion in the *Phenomenology* particularly to his discussion of the doubled, "unhappy," dissatisfied consciousness, which, because it vacillates between the distance of heaven and the nearness of earth, is appropriated by the power of religion or by the rival secular power of the state, the latter legitimating itself by religious ideas. In his discussion of religion Hegel often introduces the concept of the "thing." With the physiocratic jurists the "thing" is truly the corporealized or reified magistrature of Roman or French law. The physiocrats secure the *évidence* of natural law through such corporealization, but the theory of *évidence* and the theory of reification are masks for appropriative infrastructural intentionality-alienation. The *évidence* suggests the distancing which alienation as social appropriation connotes. The corporealization does not negate the remoteness which expresses the power of the dominating force over the dominated. For Nietzsche, this was the pathos of distance. However, as will be noted later, Heidegger grasped the role of social appropriative alienation as a theory both of distancing (*Entfernung*) and of nearness (*Ent-fernung*).

Of course, Hegel realizes that the externality or imperfect internality of mediation, or of distancing and of nearness, is a great problem in religious theory. He writes, in *Lectures on the History of Philosophy*, "The assertion of Religion is that the manifestation of Truth which is revealed to us through it, is one which is given to man from outside. . . . The assertion of positive Religion is that its truths exist without having their source known, so that the content as given, is one which is above and beyond reason." [95] In the *Phenomenology* he writes, of revealed religion, "The alienation of the Divine Nature is thus set up in its double-sided form: the self of Spirit, and its simple thought, are the two moments whose absolute unity is Spirit itself. Its aliena-

94. Marx, "Theses on Feuerbach," p. 660.
95. Hegel, *Lectures on the History of Philosophy*, I, 71.

tion with itself consists in the two falling apart from each other. . . . Their mediating, though still empty, ground is existence in general, the bare community of their two moments. The dissolution of this opposition does not take effect through the struggle between the two elements, which are pictured as separate and independent Beings." [96] Marx discussed this, too, as alienation. The physiocratic social theorists sought to present this, in part, through the reification of the magistrature—a thought which should be considered in contemporary struggles relating to bourgeois law. But corporealization of law in the external mediator-jurist is only a moment in physiocratic theory of alienation. Distance, social distance, ontological distance, and anthropological distance are synonyms not only for religion but for bourgeois social science, including law, in general. However, Heidegger's theory of appropriation is a theory of *Entfernung–Ent-fernung*, that is, of distance-nearness. *Entfernung*, or distance, suggests the power of the dominant force, as owner, over the subjugated force; *Ent-fernung*, or nearness, suggests the power of the dominant force, as possessor, over the subjugated force. This reciprocity of *Entfernung–Ent-fernung* is summed up juridically in the legal concept of property, both ownership and possession, the classic expression of which is in French civil law. But the leading theorist of existentialist juridical alienation theory is not Heidegger, but Carl Schmitt, the most prominent Nazi jurist. Schmitt created an existential rivalry between friend and foe, which was indicated by their distance, first geopolitically and ultimately anthropologically. Theory of social appropriation or alienation also appears in Hegel's discussion of revealed religion. "The conditions 'past' and 'distance' are, however, merely the imperfect form," he writes, "in which the immediateness gets mediate or made universal; this is merely dipped superficially in the element of thought." [97] Insofar as the alienating or appropriating condition is "past," Hegel may be condemning his feudal rivals—Schelling, the German romantics, Savigny, and the German historical school of law with its theory of law as a system of rights based on long-continued use or on temporal distance. Insofar as the alienating or appropriating force is "distance," Hegel perhaps may be condemning bourgeois alienation theory

96. Hegel, *Phenomenology of Mind*, p. 773; see also pp. 763, 780.
97. *Ibid.*, p. 763.

as presented in Kant's distancing postponability idea of the holy moral legislator.

Before terminating the discussion of the features of physiocratic legal theory of *évidence,* it is necessary to present very briefly the condemnation of *évidence* by the Abbé de Mably, because it suggests a basis of criticism of contemporary phenomenological philosophy of law. Moreover, Mably's opposition to the physiocrats was noticed during the nineteenth century by Windelband, who presents the physiocratic Quesnay as in collision not with the Enlightenment, but with the utopian communists Morelly and Mably.[98] This antagonism, Windelband believes, led to nineteenth-century Neo-Kantian philosophy of culture. Mably opposed the theory of legal despotism of the physiocrats with a theory of legislative supremacy over the magistrates and the general partition of the executive power (traces of which appear in the text of the Constitution of the United States).

Mably confronted the legal theory of Le Mercier de la Rivière in his *Doutes proposés aux philosophes économistes sur l'ordre naturel et essentiel des sociétés politiques,* published in 1768.[99] The Abbé condemns the physiocratic jurist because his legal despotism divides citizens into unequal classes, depending on the relation to immovable property. This legal despotism, says Mably, is directed against "every species of democracy." It develops from the "natural order" of Le Mercier de la Rivière that some are "susceptible of *évidence* and consequently can do only good." The others, who suffer from "ignorance," have, "in place of *évidence,* a certain faith, a *certitude established on* évidence *which is found in the class of the instructed group."* The latter are the magistrates. *"Évidence,"* Mably tells Le Mercier de la Rivière, ". . . is a magic talisman for your magistrates." Mably thus condemned the fideism founded in the theory of *évidence.* "Your legal despotism," Mably continues, "necessarily becomes arbitrary." It is arbitrary because the magistrates, despite the theory

98. Wilhelm Windelband, *A History of Philosophy,* trans. James A. Tufts, 2 vols. (New York: Harper, 1901, 1958), II, 523.

99. *Oeuvres complètes de l'abbé de Mably,* Vol. XI. On the materials mentioned in this discussion, see Mitchell Franklin, "Influence of the Abbé de Mably and of Le Mercier de la Rivière on American Constitutional Ideas Concerning the Republic and Judicial Review," in *Perspectives of Law: Essays for Austin Wakeman Scott,* ed. Roscoe Pound, Erwin Griswold, and Arthur E. Sutherland (Boston: Little, Brown, 1964), pp. 96, 112–13.

of *évidence*, are subject "to the superior force of the passions." Through the legislative power, the people must put themselves "on guard against the passions of the magistrates." But Mably failed to consider whether the power of the magistrates would be overcome if as judges they were permanently dominated by their own legal method. Yet in his observations on the United States addressed to John Adams many years later, Mably justified the Continental Congress of the United States because it was to be governed by juridical method, even though the congress was not necessarily one of judges.

STRUVE'S CALL TO HUSSERL

HERE IT WOULD BE CORRECT to examine more closely the methodology of Husserl, especially as this developed in the *Logical Investigations,* which has had great influence on phenomenological philosophy of law. However, at this point attention will be directed to the political import of Husserl, which gives the profound meaning or which indicates the *mobile* of Husserl's work in law and in social science. Although Husserl lived through the horror of the rise to power of nazism, which threatened him physically, there is an impression that he remained in academic isolation and ignored the catastrophe. Nevertheless, the Nazis on their part reluctantly acknowledged the importance of Husserl, if this writer's recollection of the content of G. Lehmann's work, *Deutsche Philosophie,* published in 1943, is correct. This volume is described in the German edition of I. M. Bocheński's *Europäische Philosophie der Gegenwart,* published in 1947, as *"tendenziöses, nationalsozialistisches Werk."* [100] In the 1935 Vienna Lecture, published in the *Crisis,* Husserl said:

> There are only two escapes from the crisis of European existence: the downfall of Europe in its estrangement from its own rational sense of life, its fall into hostility toward the spirit and into barbarity; or the rebirth of Europe from the spirit of philosophy through a heroism of reason that overcomes naturalism once and for all. Europe's greatest danger is weariness. If we struggle against this greatest of all dangers as "good Europeans"

100. (Bern: A. Franke, 1947), p. 259.

with the sort of courage that does not fear even an infinite struggle, then out of the destructive blaze of lack of faith, the smoldering fire of despair over the West's mission for humanity, the ashes of great weariness, will rise up the phoenix of a new life-inwardness and spiritualization as the pledge of a great and distant future for man: for the spirit alone is immortal.[101]

Indeed, Husserl's entire career seems to be a struggle against "naturalism," that is, materialism. Husserl's essay, "Philosophy as Rigorous Science," which included his dialogue with Dilthey, appeared in the first volume of *Logos* (1910–11) as an international journal, based on the cooperation of Eucken, Gierke, Husserl, Meinecke, Rickert, Simmel, Troeltsch, Max Weber, Windelband, and Wölfflin—all famous in the history of Neo-Kantian idealism. It was announced that an international commission, which included Kroner, had been established. It was also stated that a Russian edition, with the cooperation of P. Struve, among others, had been created, and there is no doubt that such a Russian version was published. It was also announced that scholars from other countries would contribute, among them Bergson and Boutroux for France, Croce and Varisco for Italy, and Münsterberg and Royce for America. In the issue of *Logos* in which Husserl published "Philosophy as Rigorous Science," "Peter von Struve," of St. Petersburg, published an essay which discussed Marx, Savigny, Brentano, St. Thomas, socialism, and Quesnay. Struve wrote, "The opposition of the universal and singular conception has its analogous area in the antithesis—realism and nominalism. There are forms of universal conception, which rest consciously or unconsciously on a type of conceptual realism. In our time, where the idealist-positivist nominalism in philosophy going back to Berkeley and Hume is displaced (Husserl!), it is doubly indicated to refer to perils of universal tendency in the particular sciences." [102] Struve continues: "The critical resurrection of logical realism should not serve to the entrenchment of uncritical, universal construction in the particular sciences, since the rejection of the nominalist view in logic does not mean forthwith the universalization of particular sciences." [103]

101. Husserl, *Crisis*, p. 299.
102. Struve, "Ueber einige grundlegende Motive im national-ökonomischen Denken," *Logos*, I (1910–11), 349.
103. *Ibid.*

This essay indicated, in general, that as early as 1910–11 Struve raised the question whether Husserl's phenomenological method absorbed Marxism.

Struve, as the leading personality in the movement known as legal Marxism, drew the name of Husserl into a struggle between himself and Lenin which covered a period of decades and which had been preceded by a struggle between himself and Plekhanov. Jowtschick writes that "Plekhanov moved against the 'legal Marxism' of Struve, Bulgakow, and others first in the period of 1901–1902; according to his own statement he expected next that the 'Elements of Marxism' would vanquish step by step the bourgeois constituent elements (Brentano theory) in Struve's views." [104] Iovchuk, Oiserman, and Shchipanov state a relation between Struve and Berdiaev.[105] Scholars in the USSR describe this period of struggle between Lenin and Struve as a struggle between dialectical materialism and Neo-Kantianism, organized internationally by Neo-Kantianism. In his essay in *Logos*, Struve predicted "the Russian revolution." [106]

It is important to mention that Lenin emphasizes that legal Marxists proceed from an "undialectical opposition of the abstract and the concrete, of the general and individual." [107] Husserl's bracketing or distancing of actuality is in effect thus condemned. The early struggle between legal Marxism and dialectical materialism shows that Lenin's knowledge of dialectic did not begin only after he had published *Materialism and Empirio-criticism* in 1908. Moreover, because Struve was an economist and a jurist who knew the thought of Quesnay, and perhaps the natural law theory of the physiocrats, the phrase "legal Marxists" may have a juridical as well as a political meaning. If this is justified, the contemporary interest in phenomenological philosophy of law may be the second coming which a religious figure such as Struve would have welcomed.

104. In Dynnik et al., *Geschichte der Philosophie* (1962), IV, 151.
105. M. T. Iovchuk, T. I. Oiserman, and I. Ia. Shchipanov, eds., *Compendio de historia de la filosofia*, trans. Jose Lain Entralgo, 2 vols. (Montevideo: Pueblos unidos, 1969), II, 561.
106. Struve, "Ueber einige grundlegende Motive," p. 360.
107. In Dynnik, *Geschichte der Philosophie*, V, 45.

HEGEL'S ATTACK ON THE INSIGHT AND IMPURE INTENTIONALITY OF THE ENLIGHTENMENT

THE BRACKETING BY PHENOMENOLOGY has as its outcome the deactualization or nothingness both of the natural world and of the reduced world. Such Cartesian nothingness is equally Cartesian being, because motionless being is motionless nothingness. As has been suggested, Diderot's *rien* is both being and nothingness. Hegel's two *Logics* are anti-Cartesian because the first categories of the *Logics* state the identity or unity in opposition of being and nothingness. Being is nothingness because it is not becoming or motion. Nothingness is being because it is not becoming. But becoming or motion cannot become unless there is negation or mediation of being and nothingness as a unity of opposites. The phenomenological bracketing or *coupure* excludes negation of being and nothingness and therefore immobilizes becoming. Thus materialist being is condemned to its nothingness, and nothingness is condemned to its being.

Both Hegel and Husserl accept intentionality. In the *Phenomenology*, Hegel says:

> The I does not contain or imply a manifold of ideas, the I here does not *think;* nor does the thing mean what has a multiplicity of qualities. Rather, the thing, the fact, *is;* and it *is* merely because it *is*. It *is*—that is the essential point for sense-knowledge, and that bare fact of *being*, that simple immediacy, constitutes its truth. In the same way the certainty *qua relation*, the certainty "of" something, is an immediate pure relation.[108]

But Hegel's intentionality cannot become knowledge unless there is sense-certainty and mediation. He says:

> But, when we look closely, there is a good deal more implied in that bare pure being, which constitutes the kernel of this form of certainty, and is given out by it as its truth. A concrete actual certainty of sense is not merely this pure immediacy, but an example, an instance, of that immediacy. Amongst the innumerable distinctions that here come to light, we find in all cases the fundamental difference—viz. that in sense-experience pure being at once breaks up into the two "thises," as we have called them, one this

108. Hegel, *Phenomenology of Mind*, p. 150.

as I, and one as object. When *we* reflect on this distinction, it is seen that neither the one nor the other is merely immediate, merely *is* in sense-certainty, but is at the same time *mediated:* I have the certainty through the other, viz. through the actual fact; and this, again, exists in that certainty through an other, viz. through the I. . . . The object, however, is the real truth, is the essential reality; it *is*, quite indifferent to whether it is known or not; it remains and stands even though it is not known, while the knowledge does not exist if the object is not there.[109]

Because of the distancing or separation or bracketing of the natural world, this presentation cannot be justified by phenomenology, though it could be understood as an aspect of a crypto-dialectical materialism. But the distancing or bracketing of the natural world makes possible what Hegel called the "bad" or feudal intention of the clergy, which justifies appropriative alienation; or the "impure" intention of the bourgeois Enlightenment, which, too, justifies appropriative alienation.[110] "This action consists," Hegel writes in the *Phenomenology*, "in cancelling the particularity of the individual, or the natural form of its self-existence." [111] As Hegel's discussions not only of revealed religion and of religion as a spiritual work of art, but also of the struggle of the Enlightenment with superstition, are keys to Husserl, the discussion of "impure" intention may be closely followed. Hegel continues:

Since in this action purposiveness and end are distinguished, and pure insight likewise takes up negative attitude toward this action, and denies itself just as it did in the other moments, it must as regards purposiveness present the appearance of being stupid and unintelligent, since insight united with intention, accordance of end with means, appears to it as an other, as really the opposite of what insight is. As regards the end, however, it has to make badness, enjoyment and possession, its purpose, and prove itself in consequence to be the impurist kind of intention, since pure intention, *qua* external, an *other*, is similarly impure intention. . . . Enlightenment finds it foolish for consciousness to absolve itself of its characteristic of . . . possessing property of its own, by its demitting its own property, for thereby it shows in reality that this isolation is not really serious. . . . Pure insight finds . . . [i]t

109. *Ibid.*
110. *Ibid.*, pp. 562, 574.
111. *Ibid.*, p. 574.

is purposeless to renounce a pleasure and give away a possession, in order to show oneself independent of pleasure and possession. . . . Insight . . . in fact declares itself to be a very *impure* intention which ascribes essential value to enjoyment and possessions of this kind. . . . In other words this pure intention is in reality a deception, which pretends to and demands an inner elevation, but declares that it is superfluous, foolish, and even wrong to be in earnest in the matter, to put this uplifting into concrete expression, into actual shape and form, and demonstrate its truth. Pure insight thus denies itself both as pure insight—for it denies directly purposive action, and as pure intention—for it denies the intention of proving its independence of the ends of individual existence.[112]

In the *Phenomenology*, Hegel condemns intentionality if it cannot truly represent the real possibility involved in a social contradiction which has erupted historically. He criticizes the Enlightenment in its struggle with superstition because it so fettered, bracketed, and monadized itself that its intentionality preserved the intentionality of the other in itself, that is, the thought of the Enlightenment was infected with the generalized alienation ideas of feudalism. This includes revealed religion.

We have, therefore, to see how pure insight and pure intention manifests its negative attitude towards that other which it finds standing opposed to it. Pure insight and intention, operating negatively, can only be—since its very principle is all essentiality and there is nothing outside it—the negative of itself. As insight, therefore, it passes into the negative of pure insight, it becomes untruth and unreason; and as intention it passes into the negative of pure intention, becomes a lie and sordid impurity of purpose. It involves itself in this contradiction by the fact that it engages in a strife and thinks to do battle with some alien external other. It merely imagines this, for its nature as absolute negativity lies in having that otherness within its own self. The absolute notion is the category; it is the principle that knowledge and the object of knowledge are the same. In consequence, what pure insight expresses as its other, what it pronounces to be an error or a lie, can be nothing else than its own self; it can only condemn what itself is. . . . When reason thus speaks of some other than itself is, it in fact speaks merely of itself; it does not therein go beyond itself. This struggle with the opposite, therefore, combines in its mean-

112. *Ibid.*

ing the significance of being insight's own actualization. This consists just in the process of unfolding its moments and taking them back into itself. . . . *Qua* pure insight it is without any content; the process of its realization consists in itself becoming content to itself; for no other can be made its content.[113]

Here Hegel has been showing that bracketed bourgeois intentionality remains infected with the actuality of appropriative property conceptions or appropriative alienation. Moreover, because his discussion of exchange of commodities penetrates to the heart of Anglo-American law of consideration in contract, which does not justify will as phenomenological volition, save as "bargain," that is, only insofar as the requirements of theory of infrastructural surplus-value justify enforcement of the volition, Hegel's theory of bourgeois impure intention or alienation-intention emerges. In the civil law, insofar as *causa* theory is legally required in order to justify recognition and enforcement of phenomenological volition, Hegel's conception of impure bourgeois intention also should be regarded. Insofar as the civil law of contract does not require *causa* in order to legitimate recognition of phenomenological volition, the problem of infrastructural-superstructural bourgeois *mobiles-motifs* should be considered in assessing the truth or purity of the intention and of the *projet*. In general, for Hegel intentionality is impure if it separates theory from social praxis, and if it has a hidden, alienating content.

Hegel's conception of impure intention seems to derive from his attack on bourgeois social contract theory. This was a theory of appropriative alienation of consciousness. In discussing Beccaria's theory of criminal law in the *Philosophy of Law*, Hegel held that the criminal wills his own punishment and in so doing he seems to have recast social contract theory as intentionality theory:

The injury [the penalty] which falls on the criminal is not merely *implicity* just—as just, it is *eo ipso* his implicit will, an embodiment of his freedom, his right; on the contrary, it is also a right *established* within the criminal himself, i.e. in his objectively embodied will, in his action.[114]

113. *Ibid.*, p. 565 f.
114. G. W. F. Hegel, *Philosophy of Right* [Law], trans. T. M. Knox (Oxford, 1942), p. 70.

508 / *Phenomenology and Legal Theory*

Before proceeding, it may be mentioned that in the *Phenomenology* Hegel emphasizes intention as activity: "The actual crime, however, finds its inversion, and its inherent nature *qua* possibility, in the intention as such, but not in a good intention: for the truth of intention is simply the deed itself." [115] Hegel continues in the *Philosophy of Law* thus:

> Beccaria denied to the state the right of inflicting capital punishment. His reason was that it could not be presumed that the readiness of individuals to allow themselves to be executed was included in the social contract. . . . [W]hat is involved . . . is . . . the abstract rationality of the individual's *volition*. Since that is so, punishment is regarded as containing the criminal's right and hence by being punished he is honoured as a rational being.[116]

This signifies that Hegel justified the theory of self-determined responsibility of the criminal not on the ground of social contract, but on a theory of intentionality in which the particular volition expressed or exteriorized in an act was understood also as in unity with the universal, social volition of the accused, and in accordance with the dialectic of which the criminal is condemned. Hegel's social theory of intentionality, in general, was essentially a historic theory of intentionality based on appropriative alienation. Hegel himself discussed bourgeois intentionality as bourgeois cultural negation of feudal culture:

> Pure insight . . . has to begin with the *intention* of making pure insight universal, i.e. of making everything that is actual into a notion, and one and the same notion for every self-consciousness. The intention is pure, for its content is pure insight; and this insight is similarly pure, for its content is solely the absolute notion, which finds no opposition in an object, and is not restricted in itself. In the unrestricted notion there are found at once both the aspects—that everything objective is to signify only the self-existent, self-consciousness, and that this is to signify something universal, that pure insight is to be the property of all self-consciousnesses. This second feature of the intention is so far a result of culture, in that in culture both the distinctions of objective spirit, the parts and express determinations of its world, have come to naught. . . . Genius, talent, special capacities one and

115. Hegel, *Phenomenology of Mind*, p. 206.
116. Hegel, *Philosophy of Right* [Law], p. 70.

all, belong in the world of actuality, in so far as this world contains still the aspect of being a herd of self-conscious individuals, where, in confusion and mutual violence, individuals cheat and struggle with one another over the contents of the real world.[117]

Hyppolite has pointed out that Hegel's theory of culture is essentially a theory of alienation. Bourgeois theory of intentionality is impure insofar as the infrastructural material ground is separated or distanced, thus justifying seizure or alienation-intention. Phenomenological theory of law thus is subject to reproach insofar as its theory of intentionality is impure because the *Grund* is idealistic, and has a hidden content, as it has with Husserl and Kelsen. Such conclusion, in part, is further strengthened by Hegel's general ideas relating to Kant and to revealed religion, and by his presentation of "historic *mobiles*" in *Reason in History*.[118] Although these are readily veered into materialistic, infrastructural *mobiles*, Husserl in the *Logical Investigations* seeks to regard the *Grundnorm* as idealistic and superstructural, as an abstraction from "valuational interest." [119] Even as late as the *Crisis*, Husserl "brackets" the infrastructure of fascism. Desanti relates a permanent weakness of Husserl to section 15 of the *Crisis*.[120] Here Husserl wrote:

> The type of investigation that we must carry out, and which has already determined the style of our preparatory suggestions, is not that of a historical investigation in the usual sense. Our task is to make comprehensible the *teleology* in the historical becoming of philosophy, especially modern philosophy. . . . We are attempting to elicit and understand the *unity* running through all the [philosophical] projects of history that oppose one another and work together in their changing forms. . . . We are attempting ultimately to discern the historical task which we can acknowledge as the only one which is personally our own. This we seek to

117. Hegel, *Phenomenology of Mind*, p. 557.
118. G. W. F. Hegel, *La Raison dans l'histoire*, trans. Kostas Papaioannou (Paris: Plon, 1965), p. 101.
119. See Edmund Husserl, *Logical Investigations*, trans. J. N. Findlay, 2 vols. (New York: Humanities Press, 1970), I, 84. Cf. Husserl's discussion of the "good soldier" with Kelsen's response in "Zum Begriff der Norm," reprinted in H. Klecatsky, R. Marić, and H. Schambeck, *Die wiener rechtstheoretische Schule* (Vienna: Europa, 1968), II, 1455, 1461, n. 9.
120. Jean T. Desanti, *Phénoménologie et praxis* (Paris: Editions sociales, 1963), p. 111.

discern not from the outside, from facts, as if the temporal becoming in which we ourselves have evolved were merely an external causal series. Rather, we seek to discern it from the *inside*.
Only in this way can we, who not only have a spiritual heritage
but have become what we are thoroughly and exclusively in a his-
torical-spiritual manner, have a task which is truly our own. We
obtain it not through the critique of some present or handed-down
system, of some scientific or prescientific *"Weltanschauung"*
(which might as well be Chinese, in the end), but only through a
critical understanding of the total unity of history—*our* history.
For it has spiritual unity through the unity and driving force of
the task which, in the historical process—in the thinking of those
who philosophize for one another and with one another across
time—seeks to move through the various stages of obscurity
toward satisfying clarity until it finally works its way through to
perfect insight. . . . For we are what we are as functionaries of
modern philosophical humanity; we are heirs and cobearers of
the direction of the will which pervades this humanity; we have
become this through a primal establishment which is at once a re-
establishment [*Nachstiftung*] and a modification of the Greek
primal establishment. In the latter lies the *teleological beginning*,
the true birth of the European spirit as such.[121]

If Husserl's deactualization of social infrastructure, of philosophy, and, eventually in philosophy of law, of the *Grundnorm* is
veerable into materialistic actualization, his idealism is vulnerable. This may explain why Heidegger, unlike Husserl, seems to
suggest that ground is groundless. Landgrebe adverts to this
development.[122] He does so with the aim not of justifying materialism but of strengthening idealism, though he shows that
Heidegger's idealism is a theory of threatened idealism. It may
be said in passing that contemporary theory of Roman law and
twentieth-century theory of comparative law remain confined
within Husserlian or similar outlooks which ignore historical infrastructures.

As phenomenology maintains separation, fissure, and distancing, it can veer between motionless being, which is motionless nothing, and motionless nothing, which is motionless being.
But this does not mean that distancing is motionless. In the first

121. Husserl, *Crisis*, pp. 70–71 (brackets in translation).
122. Ludwig Landgrebe, *Major Problems in Contemporary European
Philosophy: From Dilthey to Heidegger*, trans. Kurt F. Reinhardt (New
York: Frederick Ungar, 1966), p. 75.

of the "Theses on Feuerbach," Marx mentioned the importance of the active side of idealism. Because of the phenomenological rupture, the external mediator or the unhistoric prince of the Enlightenment or the god-assistant may emerge as the active, ironic external mediator of the Kantianized, seemingly immobilized, contradictory forces. This means several things. In the first place, it means that the activism of the external mediator is, in law, the jurist, the methodology of the jurist, and the intentionality by which these are related and directed. Ricoeur totally obscures this, though he realizes that the dialectic of negation must be acknowledged: "Husserl's concept of intentionality takes on a new look after this bath in [Hegelian] negativity. It becomes the original distance, the stepping away of the self from itself, the nothing which separates existence from its having-been." [123] But in truth the primary or profound mediator, whose intention is both "impure" and concealed, is the distanced, dominating, particularistic, historic force, supposedly external to the universality of the state, which appropriates or alienates social antinomy or social rivalry. Law becomes the intention or the instrument of such a contradiction-ridden dominant social force (unless such hegemony is weakened or is weakening) masked as the rule of law. In the second place, the distanced intentionality may be ironical, that is, it may be free to choose arbitrarily among possibilities. This is its *projet* or *Entwurf,* which may reverse its own posited civil code or constitution so that at most each remains *projet* or *Entwurf* or *schema,* subject to such "impure" intentionality and to legal method as the appropriative artistry or aesthetics of "impure" intentionality. The hidden or profound intentionality is such because of the bracketing or distancing of the natural and social world, including the contradictions of the social infrastructure. The intentionality seems incarnated in the jurist; or, to be more exact, legal method is alienated or seized by hidden or "impure" intentionality. The jurist, again, through appropriation (which begins in the law faculties), seems to incarnate the legal methodology. These appropriations are negations. "*The occupation assumes an independent existence owing to division of labour,*" Marx wrote. "The very nature of their craft causes them to succumb the more easily to illusions regarding the connection between their craft

123. Ricoeur, *Husserl,* p. 211.

and reality. In their consciousness, in jurisprudence, politics, etc., relationships become concepts: since they do not go beyond these relationships, the concepts of the relationships also become fixed concepts in their mind. The judge, for example, applies the code, he therefore regards legislation as the real, driving force." [124]

These problems must now be considered more closely in relation to Husserl.

The external mediator in the phenomenology of law, the see-er, is the jurist, monadized or enslaved or alienated by legal methodology. Without specific reference to philosophy of law itself, Husserl discusses the hegemony of methodology. In his *Logical Investigations,* he makes the following very important presentation as part of the text entitled "Theoretical disciplines as the foundation of normative disciplines":

> It is now easy to see that each normative, and, *a fortiori*, each practical discipline, presupposes one or more theoretical disciplines as its foundations, in the sense, namely, that it must have a theoretical content free from all normativity, which as such has its natural location in certain theoretical sciences. . . .
>
> The basic norm (or basic value, or ultimate end) determines, we saw, the unity of the discipline: it also is what imports the thought of normativity into all its normative propositions.[125]

At this point it is appropriate to mention the role of Kelsen's *Grundnorm* or constitution, and, earlier, Ihering's theory of the role of purpose or *Zweck* in the legal order, which Pound accepted. Husserl continues:

> But alongside of this general thought of measurement in terms of a basic norm, these propositions have their own theoretical content, which differs from one case to another. Each expresses the

---

124. Marx, "From the Manuscript 'I. Feuerbach,' " in Marx and Engels, *German Ideology,* p. 672. But cf. Nicos Poulantzas, *Nature des choses et droit* (Paris: Librairie générale de droit et de jurisprudence, 1965), p. 231; Louis Althusser, *For Marx,* trans. Ben Brewster (London: Penguin Press, 1969), p. 111. See letter, Engels to Schmidt, London, October 27, 1890, in Karl Marx and Friedrich Engels, *Correspondence 1846–1895* (New York: International Publishers, 1935), pp. 477, 481.

125. Husserl, *Logical Investigations,* I, 87. See J. Kalinowski, "La Logique des normes d'Edmund Husserl," *Archives de philosophie du droit,* X (1965), 107.

thought of a measuring relation between norm and what it is a norm for, but this relation is itself objectively characterized—if we abstract from valuational interest—as a relation between condition and conditioned, which relation is set down as existent or non-existent in the relevant normative propositions. . . . The new proposition is purely theoretical: it contains no trace of the thought of normativity. . . .

It is now clear that the theoretical relations which our discussion has shown to lie hidden in the propositions of normative sciences, must have their logical place in certain theoretical sciences. If the normative science is to deserve its name, if it is to do scientific work on the relations of the facts to be normatively considered to their basic norms, it must study the content of the theoretical nucleus of these relations, and this means entering the spheres of the relevant theoretical sciences. In other words: Every normative discipline demands that we know certain non-normative truths: these it takes from certain theoretical sciences, or gets by applying propositions so taken to the constellation of cases determined by its normative interest. This naturally holds, likewise, in the more special case of a technology, and plainly to a greater extent. The theoretical knowledge is there added which will provide a basis for fruitful realization of ends and means.[126]

Without focusing on phenomenology of law, Husserl sees that "every normative discipline demands that we know certain non-normative truths . . . in the special case of a technology, and plainly to a greater extent." This states the hegemony of legal method as art over the norm or content of law, or over its structure. This hegemony is stated as activist. But the legal method also has a certain relationship to the basic norm: its activism is stimulated by the basic norm so that it discovers the extranormative possibilities of the norm or structure. What Husserl has here accomplished juridically is in part a phenomenological-ization of an aspect of Ihering, who before Husserl justified both legal method and *Zweck* or teleology. Through Pound and apart from Husserl, Ihering's thinking passed into American legal philosophy. One consequence appears in Nazi and American legislation, each of which, after Ihering, exploited the teleological role of the preamble, and weakened the force of the content of the text as content. In part, Husserl also relates to Kelsen's

126. Husserl, *Logical Investigations*, pp. 87–88.

514 / *Phenomenology and Legal Theory*

theory of the basic norm or constitutional law. However, what has just been said does not explain the plenitude of Husserl's position. This can only be grasped by relating Husserl to aspects of the thought of Kant. Kant's forward-reaching categorical intention or categorical imperative, which Hegel condemned because of its formalism and its nothingness, reappears in Husserl's thought as the basic norm. Kant's holy moral legislator and his artist-genius choose their possibilities arbitrarily or ironically through the legal method of the jurist, insofar as the basic norm masks or comes to mask a thing-in-itself which becomes knowable to the mandarinist jurist. This Hegel condemned in the *Philosophy of Law* and elsewhere; and this Kafka, who was a jurist, attacked in his writing. The irony of juridical method is masked because Husserl does not relinquish the relation of the jurist to the norm or structure. This reveals itself to the jurist. But it may reveal the nothingness of abstract being to him.[127] This is true of what Pound called legal "standards" and of what Kohler, the Neo-Hegelian jurist, called legal "flexibility" (as distinguished from the "mechanization" of the older Roman and Anglo-American distinction between law and equity). American legal realism condemns Pound's theory of "standards" because it is not "radical" enough; that is, it asks whether the entire system or structure of norms, whether "standards" or firmly determined "rules," may not be totally reconsidered as a system of flexible conceptions. Pound's "standards" may also be called abstract or stoic universals, which are void of content, as Hegel once said. Thus, the civil code may impose responsibility for "fault," or the Anglo-American law may impose responsibility for lack of "due care under the circumstances" or may guarantee "due process" of law. The jurist recognizes, in Hegel's sense of the concept of recognition as a struggle between contradictory social forces, the text or the "law" by pouring his content as subject into the bracketed nothingness of the text or of the "law." Such stoic nothingness of the content explains the terseness of the Constitution of the United States and of the French and German bourgeois civil codes. However, the norm may have determined or determinable content, and phenomenologically this may be said to reveal itself to the jurist. But, because of the mediation of legal method, the juridical

127. For an important discussion, published in the German crisis year of 1933, see Justus Wilhelm Hedemann, *Die Flucht in die Generalklauseln: Eine Gefahr für Recht und Staat* (Tübingen: Mohr, 1933).

problem is whether the revelation possesses the strength to be recognized.

Here again recognition must be understood in Hegel's sense. The prototype is Hegel's discussion in the *Phenomenology* of recognition in the struggle between the oppressor and the oppressed, and his discussion in the *Philosophy of Law* of recognition among national states in international law. Because of the hegemony of the methodology of the jurist over the self-revelation of the text or of the norm or of the content (called in vulgar legal work the "intention of the lawmaker"), the jurist may or may not recognize the revelation, or may distort or restate it. Because of his hegemony relative to the norm, supposedly justified by the basic norm, the irony of juridical method emerges. The agility of the jurist was condemned over seven centuries ago by the English Romanist jurist, Bracton. Hegel perceived that the freedom of Kant's holy moral legislator and of the jurist of German romanticism justified irony, hypocrisy, equivocation, *Verstellung*, ambiguity. Kierkegaard's dissertation at Copenhagen was directed against Hegel's discussion of irony, including Socratic irony. Hegel justified Socratic irony because it was the objective irony of history. Kierkegaard, in effect, held that his own irony required the appearance or semblance of positivity in order to realize his destructive negation, which because the positive itself was masked nothingness could not realize the new positivity of negation of the negation. This, too, Husserl does when he brackets or deactualizes or separates the structure, the norm, the jurist, and the *Grundnorm* from the natural world. Although the Neo-Kantian, Kelsen, is not a phenomenological jurist, he has influenced phenomenological philosophy of law. Kelsen says that the constitution makes the people, and not vice versa. The Constitution of the United States, formulated under mechanical materialist influence, says that the people make the constitution. If the idealist, distanced *Grundnorm* is related to the natural world, it is reversed and materialized, and together with the normative order and legal method becomes an aspect of the process or of the dialectic of infrastructure-superstructure. If Husserl's bracketing did not deactualize both sides of the bracket, the becomingness of Husserl's activist juridical methodology would unfetter or overcome the possibilities of the norm and the infrastructural *Grundnorm* of the superstructural *Grundnorm*. These superstructural norms would be negated through legal methodology, either to close the gap in the system of norms consistent with the intention of the infrastructural *Grundnorm* or *mobile*, or to destroy the force of the norm consistent with the changing intention of the infrastructural *Grundnorm* and the contradictions therein.

The role of legal method as art is justified by impure or alienation-intentionality. The *Grundnorm* seems to be the *Grundnorm* of the positive law. But this *Grundnorm* is superstructural and separated from the infrastructure by bracketing. Such bracketing, which connotes the abstractness or nothingness of the superstructure masked as being, conceals the distanced but actual alienating or appropriating *Grundnorm* of the infrastructure. The intentional relation between the infrastructure and the superstructure is realized through legal method. The alienation-intentionality of the infrastructure is masked as ideology and appears in the superstructure as the reciprocity of impure intention of legal method and superstructural *Grundnorm*. Though Husserl discusses method as technique, it is technique as art. Windscheid spoke of this in his masterwork on Roman law. Kant suggested this in his *Critique of Judgment,* where he relates genius and aesthetic theory to social life. As has been shown, Heidegger, too, desires this. Savigny, like Husserl, conceived of legal method as science, but as such method was subordinated to the objective idealism of theory of *Volksgeist,* the hegemony of the silent intention of the *Volksgeist* established an irrationalism over Savigny's rationalistic methodology of Roman law. With little difficulty Dufrenne could attain the same hegemony through theory of imagination, which Heidegger had made prominent, especially since language and law are related by Savigny.

Some light may be thrown on the ontology of the transcendental imagination by the psychology of the empirical imagination: the imagination is that which is least human in man. As in a Pythic delirium, it wrenches man away from himself and plunges him into ecstasy; it puts him into secret communion with the powers of nature: "Who speaks to me, with my own voice?" The genius yielding to inspiration no longer belongs to himself; he is a force of nature; his "I" is an other. Thus the imagination is an origin (*est originaire*) because it alienates man to join him to that which he is not. But the imagination conceived ontologically is not this faculty of losing oneself in a strange speech (*parole*) that may end in madness; it is this speech itself, the truth of being anterior

MITCHELL FRANKLIN / 517

to (though expressed by) the distinction between the subjective self and the objective world.[128]

The impure intention of the superstructure may be ironic or ambiguous or infected with what Sartre has called bad faith, depending on the hidden intention or guile (as Ricoeur has called it) of the infrastructure. The impure intention of the superstructure is vulnerable to such *Verstellung* because of the deactualization produced by bracketing. The impure intention of the superstructural legal methodology in relation to the superstructural *Grundnorm* issues as a superstructural reciprocal double idealism. The superstructural *Grundnorm* is an objective idealism; legal method as art is a subjective idealism. In relation to method, superstructural *Grundnorm* may be subject or object; and, reciprocally, superstructural method may be subject or object. Whether superstructural *Grundnorm* or superstructural method is subject or object is determined by the impure intentionality which conceals the pure, distanced intentionality of the infrastructure. Because of the bracketing, ironic, impure intentionality is both subject and object. Following a different path, Muralt says the concrete subject is intentionality itself.[129] This also was the outcome of nineteenth-century German romanticism, which had its *centrum* where subject-object became indifference. At least in part, such a Schelling-like or Savigny-like *centrum* seems to be related to Husserl today by Landgrebe. He writes:

There is no doubt of course that it was the aim of Husserl's phenomenological analyses to comprehend the world as a structure (*Gebilde*), to demonstrate that the world owes its origin to the experiential operations and achievements of the community of subjects. Man's "being-in-the-world" therefore has for him a dual meaning: it signifies (1) that man lives already within his horizons, that he is an individual of this particular time and this particular community and therewith—as a human being "in this world"—within a definitely limited horizon. . . . Man's "being-in-the-world" means (2) that he is a center of intentional operations and performances and that he knows himself as a being who builds upon the foundations laid by others and thus transforms

128. Mikel Dufrenne, *The Notion of the A Priori,* trans. Edward S. Casey (Evanston, Ill.: Northwestern University Press, 1966), p. 35.
129. André de Muralt, *L'Idée de la phénoménologie: L'Exemplarisme husserlien* (Paris: Presses Universitaires de France, 1958), p. 327.

the already given world for himself and for others. . . . And so it would seem as if Husserl's analysis of the world and its constitutive origin terminates once again in the traditional path of transcendental idealism. The difference lies in the fact that the central question concerns no longer the production of the object by virtue of the creative intellectual functions of the subject but —in a much more profound sense—*the central question concerns now the production of the world as the "wherein"* (das Worin) *of all possible objects, as* the horizon within which all individual entities stand out, so that they can be grasped and comprehended as objects.[130]

However, Landgrebe does not rest here. Later he says:

Husserl's analyses had already shown that the world cannot be understood as an isolated system of interrelated existing entities but must be conceived as having its center in a "zeropoint" (*Nullpunkt*).[131]

Several aspects of Husserl's situation in general may be gathered here into a unity: (1) Because Husserl has deactualized the world, Husserl's intentionality theory in which intention is an ironic or ambiguous subject-object is, to cite Hegel, impure or historically unjustified intentionality. (2) Because the impure intentionality conceals an idealist infrastructure or infrastructural *Grundnorm* or *centrum*, it justifies legal method as the ironic art of the jurist. (3) Because Husserl does not acknowledge the material, historic infrastructures of law, his historical conceptions are entirely superstructural. Thus, in the *Crisis* he conceives that his present situation as a philosopher is not a relationship to the reality of nazism, but rather a relationship to Greek philosophy, also conceived as superstructure. (4) Husserl's idealistic thinking is justified both by unhistoric conceptions of natural law (physiocratic philosophy of law) and by an undialectical Kantian distinction between "is" and "ought," the untenability of which had been shown by Hegel. (5) As phenomenological philosophy of law is a science subordinate to irrationalism, it is not *Wissenschaft*, but *Scheinwissenschaft*. *Schein* shines, but it also blinds. Phenomenology of law is a

130. Landgrebe, *Major Problems in Contemporary European Philosophy*, p. 73.
131. *Ibid.*, p. 79.

repetition of a deeply rooted movement in the history of law. Thus, Savigny created the science of Roman law, but subordinated it to the irrationalism of *Volksgeist* theory. (6) Because impure intentionality is ironic subject-object, Fink's multiplicity of egos, discussed earlier, weakens under the attack of Sartre's *Transcendence of the Ego.* (7) Phenomenological impure intentionality theory is a futility, designed to preclude the reversal into materialism of earlier idealisms, including Hegel's.

Because of the bracketing or deactualization of the natural world, Husserl's basic norm appears as objective idealism, the jurist is veered into subjective idealism, and the norms may collapse into nothingness, masked as being, as arbitrariness may require.

It is necessary here to mention Sartre's attack on dialectic in *Being and Nothingness.* He writes: "Nothingness *is not.* If we can speak of it, it is only because it possesses an appearance of being, a borrowed being. . . . Nothingness is not, Nothingness 'is made-to-be.' " [132] What Sartre should have said is that if being does not acknowledge non-being, that is, mediation or negation, there is non-being and its equal non-being which is masked as "borrowed" being. Sartre then introduces motion through the *pour-soi.* Hence he writes: "Nothingness does not nihilate itself; Nothingness 'is nihilated.' It follows therefore that there must exist a Being (this can not be the In-Itself) of which the property is to nihilate Nothingness. . . . But how can this Being be related to Nothingness so that through it Nothingness comes to things? We must observe first that the being postulated can not be passive in relation to Nothingness, can not receive it; Nothingness could not come to this being except through another Being. . . . Man presents himself at least in this instance as a being who causes Nothingness to arise in the world, inasmuch as he himself is affected with non-being to this end." [133] This "man" may be the existential jurist who may veer between norm as non-norm and non-norm as norm. This ambiguity is the irony of Husserl's "non-normative" methodology which dominates the norms or structures, which because of Husserl's bracketing are nothings that may have "borrowed" being. So far as this may be said to touch Sartre, Hartmann says:

132. Sartre, *Being and Nothingness,* p. 22.
133. *Ibid.,* pp. 22, 24.

Sartre's ontological scheme covering being and subject is restricted to the notions of being-in-itself and being-for-itself. He rejects a dialectical determinative process; accordingly, there can be no mediation between being and nothingness. . . . Being-for-itself, by itself a dialectical mediation of being and negation, is retained as a fixed opposite to being. . . . Negation is ontologically unique: an event rather than a logical relation. . . . Hegel's tripartite division of being into pure being, determinate being, and being-for-itself is replaced by a duality of *being* and *being-with-negation,* or of being-in-itself and being-for-itself. . . . [O]nly the human subject is a for-itself, just as in Heidegger only man is a being in the mode of *Dasein.* . . .

Consistently, the for-itself is given a non-logical and undialectical foundation. . . . Sartre conceives of a regressive analysis, designed to establish the necessity of a negative ground . . . from negative phenomena. The for-itself must be a negative, but one requiring being for its support, so that it is in fact a dialectical unity, a type of being of its own. . . .

The collapsing of different subjective structures in the notions of the for-itself and the in-itself entails, furthermore, that these notions become ambiguous not only as to specific content but as to their dialectical import, in such a way that their meaning reverses itself abruptly. . . . Sartre cannot, like Hegel, mediate these shifts of emphasis between the positive and the negative. . . . Positive and negative constitute an antithesis for Sartre, and yet they collapse into each other. Similarly, being-in-itself displays an abrupt dialectic. . . . [I]n Sartre . . . shifts from the positive to the negative are not made plausible dialectically; his notion of being is abruptly ambiguous in view of the missing mediation.[134]

This presentation omits the role of the *Grundnorm* which appears in Husserl's *Logical Investigations* and in Kelsen. With Sartre, the legal method may infect the structure or norm. Like Kant's categorical imperative as "ought" and Fichte's "yearning," Sartrean legal method justifies irony or *Verstellung* or agility but does so too feebly for the actuality of the unbracketed social world. Sartre establishes the liberty of the jurist, but its *Zweck* or purpose is vague because the bourgeois unhappy consciousness, of which Sartre is see-er, is divided between capitalism and socialism. Sartre's theory of the will in *Being and Nothingness* reveals the divided consciousness. Like Pfänder, he discusses, ap-

---

134. Klaus Hartmann, *Sartre's Ontology* (Evanston, Ill.: Northwestern University Press, 1966), pp. 132–33, 134.

parently without realizing its legal implication, the question of the role of *motif* and *mobile* in the theory of the will. These words seem to suggest different degrees of the will as self-determined will. In truth, the distinction between *motif* and *mobile* should be taken to mean a distinction between the will as self-determined and the will as other-determined, that is, it should be taken to mean a distinction between self-determined volition and volition determined or appropriatively alienated by the legal methodology of the bourgeois jurist. This is a distinction between the role of subjective idealism and objective idealism in the theory of volition as alienation. It is reflected in the history of the alienation theory of *causa* or presupposition in Roman law and to a certain extent in Anglo-American contract law insofar as the latter has become a bourgeois theory of "bargain." The role of such alienation in the modern theory of the *Rechtsgeschäft* or *acte juridique* emerges in the theory of presupposition as the latter appears in the modern Italian Civil Code and in some American theory. It appears as an aspect of historical materialist theory of law, but not as an alienation conception, in the USSR and the DDR. It appears in French legal history in the theory of *cause* of Domat, who was close to Pascal. Schutz's discussion of both *mobiles* and *motifs* seems to preserve the volition theory of the Roman consensual contracts and the *Zweck* or *ut* theory of the Roman innominate contracts (*do ut des, facio ut facias, etc.*). As Sartre's theory of existential freedom is threatened by the problem of *motif-mobile,* he seems somewhat uncertain of himself in *Being and Nothingness* and turns toward the psychoanalytical theory of Freud. Today this is a feature of certain phenomenology and existentialism. Although Husserl's transcendental phenomenology is regarded as a subjective idealism, it seems that, because he relates methodology, as displacement, to the basic norm in *Logical Investigations* and because Fink stated a hierarchical "tension" of the *egos,* objective idealism also enters into the structure of phenomenology of law. If so, there issues a new ambiguity, new possibilities, in which there are multiple subjects and multiple objects which may exchange positions.

The matter of legal methodology has several aspects. There is the methodological problem of interpretation of the force of the norm or of the text. There is the problem of the *lacuna* or of prolongation of the norm or text in new historical situations. There is the problem of the overcoming of the norm or text in novel situations. These three problems are perhaps regarded as hermeneutic in general, though they are not the same. The first of these will not be considered now. The second problem, that of the *lacuna* or gap, will be studied.

As an objective idealist, Savigny was theorist for romantic, counterrevolutionary German feudalism. His theory of analogy derived from his feudal theory of the *Volksgeist* or so-called national spirit, which explained the positivity of law. The *Volksgeist*, or, so to speak, the *Grundnorm,* justified prolongation of the feudal law by analogy. Savigny's theory of analogy was not dialectical, probably because of his hostility to the dialectic of his colleague, Hegel, whose orientation was bourgeois. The problem of analogy in law should be considered dialectically as a recognized struggle to negate the particular in the norm or in the text and thus to state or to posit the universal or general of the particular as negation through which the universal or general becomes posited as law. Justice Douglas has recently opened new paths in American constitutional law. He has justified the development of the texts of the Bill of Rights, consecrated in the first eight amendments, beyond the particularism of such texts. This he did on the authority of the Ninth Amendment, which had been narcotized for almost two centuries. However, Justice Douglas invoked Neo-Platonic ideas (such as "emanation") and not dialectic.

As has been indicated, Husserl's ideas as to legal method or legal technique present the problem of the development of the particularism of the norm or text, so that the general or universal within the particular text reveals itself. Because the natural world has been bracketed by him, the revelation disclosed to him through the *lacuna* or possibility of the gap may or may not be justified. Because Husserl does not truly acknowledge the history of the natural world, he cannot justify the validity of the dialectical process historically. The historic particular is in unity with its opposite, historic generality. History necessitates the eruption of the particular into the actuality of real possibility. If the general possibility is strong enough to establish the actuality of its actuality, the new general both preserves and overcomes the old particular. This struggle can only be regarded as abstract, hidden or distanced, if law is bracketed. The truth of the actuality of the analogy resides in the struggle of human social forces through the art of legal method to accept or to reject the new general legal idea. If there is bracketing of the social world, impure bourgeois alienation-intentionality, reflecting the struggles outside the bracketing, that is, within the infrastructure, in truth determines the fate of the analogy within the bracket, unless the struggling forces within the infrastructure are no longer completely alienated by the bourgeois force, which may be weak or weakened by the course of the history of the infrastructure. The theory of analogy of Savigny, who is related to the objective idealism of Schelling, presents analogy as justified by the silently working innerness of the feudal *Volksgeist*. This objective idealism is not dialectical and merely announces its accomplishment. Referring to present-day thought, the bourgeois justification of the analogy, so as to realize a new positivity, is really grounded on sedimentation as posited or on the practico-inert as acquired right. Savigny, a feudal rather than a bourgeois thinker, justifies analogy on acquired or vested right, as established by the long-continued domination of Europe through feudal conquest thereof. Because Husserl has bracketed the natural world, this process is related to the legal things themselves and to the art of "non-normative" legal method as intended by the secretive, bracketed, distanced *Grundnorm*. As this crisis of bracketing is perceivable, the *coupure* of Husserl today leads, it seems, to the infiltration of Freud into phenomenology. Ricoeur may be mentioned here.

The third problem of the art of legal method should also be considered. It may not be intended that the activism of legal method or legal technique should unfold the norm or text, as required by the basic norm. This aspect of legal method does not interest Savigny, whose concern was the protection and furthering of the positivity of feudalism historically. Nevertheless, the infrastructural intention may be to destroy the norm, not by shattering the limit of particularism, but by replacing the fettered particular with a new norm which owes nothing to the old norm. This may be explained dialectically if the infrastructural *Grundnorm* requires it or becomes questioned historically. But as Husserl has bracketed the natural world he cannot really explain the intention of the superstructural *Grundnorm*. This again may be considered as the problem of the "ought," understood either as Kantian or as natural law. But Husserlian methodology, as presented in the *Logical Investigations*, is a mystification, because the "ought" may lead to two directly opposed fulfillments: one the development of the positive law by analogy; the other the destruction of the posited law, so as to justify a new content which, despite masking, owes nothing or little to the old content. Here the art of legal method is destructive in the sense attributed by Ricoeur, for example, to Nietzsche, Heidegger, and mistakenly to Marx.

Thus the outcome of Husserl's methodology may be legal ambiguity. There may be either "unfolding" or "destruction." Because he has bracketed the natural world, he cannot scientifically relate theory to the praxis of the external world. Historically both processes at different times have been called equity. Although equity is ordinarily considered, especially in the English legal world, as "destructive," it has had both meanings in Roman law. The general problem would be better discussed as that of a relation between law and paralaw.

The outcome of Husserl's thought, in this discussion, is that it masks and justifies the hegemony and the arbitrariness in the legal superstructure of the bracketed social hegemony which obtains in the infrastructure. The historical negation of this outcome, insofar as it concerns a historical period in which such social hegemony is weakening, may be found in the principle of unanimity or of *intercessio* which obtained in early Roman law. Here contradictory social forces, which have been forced through struggle to recognize each other, make determinations on the basis of unanimity. It must be emphasized that the contradictory social forces recognize their coequality, after the struggle, in the sense of recognition which appears in Hegel's discussion of domination and oppression presented in the *Phenomenology*, save that in *intercessio* domination is excluded by the unanimity principle. Hence the recognized self-determined social forces must concur both in the formulation and in the interpretation of legal norms and legal texts. Legal method becomes either genuine legal science or rival methodological arts in concurrence. Intentionality as impure intentionality, in Hegel's sense of impurity, is overcome. The most important recent manifestation is the unanimity principle which prevails among the permanent members of the Security Council of the United Nations. The unanimity principle overcomes the hegemony of the external mediator, whether he is called the neutral judge or the existential jurist who realizes his freedom through his choices among possibilities. Husserl's "non-normative" methodology or legal technique is thus laid to rest as a principle which met the needs within the state or in the international law of nineteenth- and twentieth-century imperialism.

HUSSERL'S RELATION TO THEORY OF LEGAL METHOD

HUSSERL'S INFLUENCE on the philosophy of law is not justified by the content of his legal thought, though he dominates vast sectors of bourgeois philosophy of law. This means that the content of his legal thought must be distinguished from phenomenological method or technique in general as well as from phenomenological legal method or technique. Toulemont has examined the materials of the legal thought in Husserl's unpublished writings,[135] but these need not be reviewed here, save to indicate some interest by Husserl in what should be called appropriative alienation and in the anthropology of space or distance, the latter a matter of importance in the imperialistic Germany of Husserl's time. To this, Carl Schmitt, the Nazi "crown jurist," devoted himself fully.

The important problem in phenomenological philosophy of law is its relation to phenomenology in general. Husserlian philosophy of law should be understood as influenced by Malebranchean physiocratic legal theory. Moreover, such legal theory should be understood as an interiorization of the God of Malebranche. Merleau-Ponty has suggested this. Physiocratic legal theory culminates in the hegemony of the corporealized natural law or jurist. In opposition to such mandarinist magistrature, Mably asks Le Mercier de la Rivière why it is these mandarins, and not the legislatures, that have the power of *évidence*.[136] Mably could ask the same question of phenomenological philosophers of law. The discussion of Husserl by Heise, Zweiling, and Oiserman here becomes of significance. "Husserl," they say, affirmed "that the correctness of the law of contradiction is not psychological, but possesses another founding, deeper, and what is most important, a founding independent of human subjectivity." They continue:

Husserl rejects not only the psychological, but also the empiric, sensuous materialist foundation of logic. Indeed, he especially

135. René Toulemont, *L'Essence de la société selon Husserl* (Paris: Presses Universitaires de France, 1962), pp. 182, 183, 206.
136. Mably, *Doutes proposés*, p. 50.

does not include the materialist reflection theory. . . . He declares that the objectivity of truth consists in its ideality. . . . He submits that the area of the logical is independent of nature as well as of man. . . . Husserl interprets in an idealist manner the fact that the logical forms are equal in all men and that the laws of thought are independent of their will and consciousness. . . . Logical forms are naturally objective (and therein exists the gnoseological root of the phenomenological conception of Husserl), but only in the sense that the relations existing independently of thought reflect actual things. Hegel approached an understanding of this problem. Dialectical materialism disclosed clearly the objective foundation of logical forms and relations. But Husserl and his followers of the "phenomenological school" produced by him, declared the logical forms and relations to be a special type of "ideal" being. . . . As Husserl separated the logic from mankind, opposed logic as ideal being to real, empirical true being and also to the psychic life of mankind (insofar as it is bound with real being) . . . he . . . presupposed "scientific knowledge of the essence of consciousness." [137]

The problem of whether Husserl's antidialectical general theory of phenomenology embraces phenomenology of law has been discussed by Schapp. In 1968 he wrote:

Edmund Husserl had already in 1910 indicated in his famous article "Philosophy as Rigorous Science" the possibility of phenomenological legal research. In this essay E. Husserl differentiated between religion as culture-formation and religion as idea . . . between art as culture-formation and valid art, between historical and valid law. . . . Isay truly errs respecting this, when he thinks, in his criticism of Reinach, that E. Husserl himself had already turned fundamentally away, that the essence-learning of phenomenology had no meaning for law and knowledge of it, because through the "phenomenological reduction," among others, law also was excluded. The work of E. Husserl cited by Isay in the *"Ideen"* (S. 56) only says that law as the actuality of the natural world and the social-human sciences as sciences which the natural attitude needs, decline exclusion. However, according to the conception of E. Husserl, the method which leads us from historical law to valid law is thereby sketched. . . . Reinach had at that time set out the comprehensive elaboration of an a priori

137. W. Heise, K. Zweiling, and T. I. Oiserman, in Dynnik, *Geschichte der Philosophie,* V, 464.

legal doctrine in the work, *Die apriorischen Grundlagen des bür-gerlichen Rechts*, which appeared in 1913.[138]

To the writer it seems that Husserl's discussion of method or of technique in the first volume of *Logical Investigations* embraces phenomenology of law as phenomenological legal methodology, as distinguished from the content of law (though Husserl's expression may not be sufficiently precise at times). Such thought is strengthened because in the Foreword to the second edition of the work, written in 1913, Husserl said: "I must express my heartfelt thanks for much friendly assistance, and, in the first place, to the Privatdozent Dr Adolf Reinach, who helped me with his zeal and knowledge when, two years ago, I first went thoroughly into deliberations concerning the possibilities of revision." [139]

This should not be taken to mean that in "Philosophy as Rigorous Science," published in 1910–11 (in the same volume in which Struve mentioned Husserl), Husserl advanced into the realm of law without certain caution. There are two important aspects to "Philosophy as Rigorous Science." One is an attack on Hegel, seemingly related to the antidialectical Neo-Kantian–Neo-Hegelianism which was prominent then and (in a hidden manner) today. The other is Husserl's dialogue with Dilthey, the leader of Neo-Hegelianism.

In encountering Dilthey, Husserl was encountering the then most recent stage in the history of *Verstehen* (comprehension or "understanding") theory. Neo-Kantianism developed two theories of knowledge. *Erklärung* was causal, and the theory of knowledge of the natural sciences. *Verstehen* was anticausal, and the activist theory of knowledge of the Neo-Kantian social and human sciences. The latter was designed to overcome the law-governed social dialectic of Hegel and of Marx. The well-known work of the Neo-Kantian jurist, Stammler, was directed against the law-governed historical materialism of Marx and Engels. However, as anticausal, activist *Verstehen* theory was individuating and subjectivist, it failed as a rival of Marxist social dialectic. Among others, Dilthey sought to strengthen activist Neo-Kantian *Verstehen* theory by uniting Neo-Kantianism with

138. Jan Schapp, *Sein und Ort der Rechtsgebilde* (The Hague: Nijhoff, 1968), p. 26.
139. Husserl, *Logical Investigations*, I, 50.

an activist objective idealism from which Hegel's dialectic was weakened or eliminated. This did not solve the problems of Neo-Kantian–Neo-Hegelianism either, because it created an activist double or divided idealism, that is, idealism as both subjective and objective, in which through irony, *Verstellung*, *déplacement*, ambiguity, hypocrisy, or bad faith each activist idealism was reciprocally both subject and object, and each was readily placed or displaced by the other. Such activist double idealism justified external mediation, or was external mediation. This is the situation in which Husserl condemns Hegel and encounters Dilthey in "Philosophy as Rigorous Science." In this essay Husserl committed himself to the idea that there was phenomenology of the social and human sciences, including law. On his side, Dilthey was influenced by Husserl's phenomenological thinking. The reciprocal influence of Dilthey and Husserl later culminates in Heidegger.

The above may serve as the foundation for some review of Husserl's discussion of Dilthey in "Philosophy as Rigorous Science." It may indicate that the phenomenology of law is founded in the problems of ironic, double idealism of Neo-Kantian–Neo-Hegelianism, that is, the problem of subjects which may be veered into objects and of objects which may be veered into subjects. However, such ambiguity or *Verstellung* is already present in Husserl's *Logical Investigations*, in which he discussed method or technique.

Early in "Philosophy as Rigorous Science," Husserl prepares the way for his discussion of Dilthey with an attack on Hegel, who was accused of weakening the impulse toward the production of rigorous philosophical science. Moreover, on the same page Hegel is related to idealist romanticism and then is also said to have given an impetus to "naturalism . . . which invalidated all absolute ideality and objectivity." This "largely determined the *Weltanschauung* and philosophy of the last decades." [140]

Husserl states that "All physically real properties are causal." [141] This is inspired by the Neo-Kantian idea of *Erklärung* of the natural sciences. Later, in turning to the social and human sciences, described as "historicism" and "*Weltanschauung* phi-

---

140. "Philosophy as Rigorous Science," in Husserl, *Phenomenology and the Crisis of Philosophy*, trans. Quentin Lauer (New York: Harper Torchbooks, 1965), p. 77.
141. *Ibid.*, p. 104.

MITCHELL FRANKLIN / 529

losophy," Husserl acknowledges structure and typology, but says that "Therein there are no enduring species and no constructions of the same out of enduring organic elements. Whatever seems to be enduring is but a stream of development." [142] Then Husserl enters the realm of *Verstehen* theory:

> If by interior intuition we enter vitally into the unity of spirit-life, we can get a feeling for the motivations at play therein, and consequently "understand" the essence and development of the spiritual structure in general, in its dependence on a spiritually motivated unity and development. In this manner everything historical becomes for us "understandable," "explicable," in the "being" peculiar to it, which is precisely "spiritual being," a unity of interiorly self-questioning moments of a sense and at the same time a unity of intelligible structuration and development according to inner motivation. Thus in this manner also art, religion, morals, etc. can be intuitively investigated, and likewise the *Weltanschauung* that stands so close to them and at the same time is expressed in them. . . . With a view to such a philosophy there arises the enormous task of thoroughly investigating its morphological structure and typology as well as its developmental connections and of making historically understandable the spiritual motivations that determine its essence, by reliving them from within.[143]

Thus Husserl moves through Neo-Kantian *Verstehen* or anti-causal theory to Neo-Kantian *Erlebnis* or reliving *Weltanschauung* theory, an accomplishment requiring both subjective and objective idealism. At this point Husserl praises Dilthey, "especially the most recently published study on the types of *Weltanschauung*" [144] (the thought of which, it may be mentioned, is indebted in part to Schelling's objective idealism and to Savigny's juridical theory of *Volksgeist*).

The Neo-Kantian–Neo-Hegelian role of reliving, *Erlebnis* and *Nacherlebnis*, as an aspect of *Verstehen* theory is acknowledged by Husserl. His considerations relative to Dilthey in effect emphasize general phenomenological and subsequently general existential theory of interpretation or hermeneutics. This is the great problem of legal method and of all philosophy of law, including twenty-six centuries of Roman law. Husserl writes in "Philosophy as Rigorous Science":

142. *Ibid.*, p. 122.
143. *Ibid.*, p. 123.
144. *Ibid.*

[I]f knowledge theory will nevertheless investigate the problems of the relationship between consciousness and being, it can have before its eyes only being as the correlate of consciousness, as something "intended" after the manner of consciousness: as perceived, remembered, expected, represented pictorially, imagined, identified, distinguished, believed, opined, evaluated, etc. It is clear, then, that the investigation must be directed toward a scientific essential knowledge of consciousness, toward that which consciousness itself "is" according to its essence in all its distinguishable forms. At the same time, however, the investigation must be directed toward what consciousness "means," as well as toward the different ways in which—in accord with the essence of the aforementioned forms—it intends the objective, now clearly, now obscurely, now by presenting or by presentifying, now symbolically or pictorially, now simply, now mediated in thought, now in this or that mode of attention, and so in countless other forms, and how ultimately it "demonstrates" the objective as that which is "validly," "really." [145]

Closer examination of the general matter of legal interpretation is reserved for further discussion in this paper. It is now sufficient to recall that phenomenological philosophy of law is mandarinist in that interpretation in all its forms is subordinated to the exclusive power of the methodology of the jurist. This hegemony, as has been shown, was challenged by Mably in his attack on physiocratic legal theory of *évidence*. Against Mably, it may be suggested that Heidegger would justify the hegemony of the methodology of the jurist relative to interpretation by invoking his distinction between authentic and inauthentic, the jurist being authentic. To this, Hegel, in the *Philosophy of Law*, would reply that through legal power of interpretation the "subjects" of law are appropriated or alienated by the methodology of the jurist, and veered into objects of law; and that Hegel justifies himself by relating the power of the authenticity of the jurist to his dialectic of oppressor and oppressed in the *Phenomenology*. Moreover, because infrastructural alienation is hidden in phenomenological and existentialist interpretation of law, Hegel would condemn Husserl's intentionality as impure intentionality.

What is important to note at this point is that Husserl, through Dilthey, draws the *Geisteswissenschaften*, or the social

145. *Ibid.*, p. 89.

and human sciences, within the scope of phenomenological method. He explicitly mentions philosophy of law among the sciences which may become subject to phenomenological method.[146]

In his discussion of Dilthey, certain of the problems and characteristics of phenomenology of law emerge, in addition to the general problem of interpretation or hermeneutics. In his considerations of *Verstehen* theory and of the problem of relating subjective idealism to the objective idealism of *Weltanschauung*, Husserl mentions motivation. "If by interior intuition," he writes "we enter vitally into the unity of spirit-life, we can get a feeling for the motivations at play therein, and consequently 'understand' the essence and the development of the spiritual structure in question, in its dependence on a spiritually motivated unity and development." [147] He adds later: "Of course, *Weltanschauung* and *Weltanschauung* philosophy are cultural formations that come and go in the stream of human development, with the consequences that their spiritual content is definitely motivated in the given historical relationships. But the same is true of the strict sciences. Do they for that reason lack objective validity?" [148] After some pages, Husserl writes: "Experience as a personal habitus is the residue of acts belonging to a natural experimental attitude, acts that have occurred during the course of life. This habitus is essentially conditioned by the manner in which the personality, as this particular individuality, lets itself be motivated by acts of its own experience, and not less by the manner in which it lets experiences transmitted by others work on it by agreeing with it or rejecting it." [149] Husserl's problem here is whether he is truly unifying *motifs* (used by this writer in the sense of subjective idealism) and *mobiles* (used by this writer in the culture sense of objective idealism), or whether he has ironically and ambiguously collapsed into doubled or divided idealism. What Husserl is saying here is reminiscent of the feudal romantic legal and social theory of F. Schlegel, save that the latter's habitus was God. F. Schlegel, who also attacked the dialectic of Hegel, justifies through revelation the play of the sedimented old and of the new. He writes:

146. *Ibid.*, pp. 126, 137, 144.
147. *Ibid.*, p. 123.
148. *Ibid.*, p. 124.
149. *Ibid.*, p. 131.

532 / *Phenomenology and Legal Theory*

[T]here is another characteristic by which we may distinguish a genuine from a spurious mission from God. Although it is both external and negative, still, as being historical, it deserves to be here adduced. It is this: a genuine revelation is in the doctrine which it promulgates at the same time both old and new. It is new in regard to its novel application to life and its fulfillments . . . but old in so far as invariably referring to an earlier revelation and to a still older source.[150]

Having replaced dialectical negation of the negation with divine revelation, F. Schlegel may now acknowledge contradictions in thought, law, and social life, because such contradictions are at the mercy of the subjective irony or "equity" of the genius, including the genius-jurist, or, by way of anticipation of the twentieth century, of the authenticity of the jurist. The quarrel between Husserl and F. Schlegel relates to the *habitus*, or, perhaps better, the *Ort*. With the feudal F. Schlegel, it is God. With the bourgeois Husserl, it is interiorized, as Merleau-Ponty said of phenomenology in relation to Malebranche. With both F. Schlegel and Husserl, the *centrum* or *Ort* or *habitus* is subject to the ambiguity or irony of *placement* and *déplacement*.

In his dialogue with Dilthey, Husserl, who perceived the rivalry of the *Weltanschauungen*, ultimately subordinates him to phenomenology. The rivalries of *Weltanschauungen* he sums up as the "contraries of validity," and adds that "the scientific decision concerning validity itself and regarding its ideal normative principles is in no way the affair of empirical science." He says that "The science of history, or simply empirical humanistic science in general, can of itself decide nothing, either in a positive or in a negative sense, as to whether a distinction is to be made . . . between historical and valid law." [151] But these contraries, or rival world-views, or rival legal outlooks, are Kantian antinomies. This means that as there is no internal unity-in-opposition among antagonistic forces, a dialectical negation of the negation is excluded, and the external mediation of phenomenological method becomes justified. A justification for bracketing is claimed here, and there is also a recollection, it seems, of the Husserl of *Logical Investigations*, in that the methodology of the jurist as art or as legal aesthetics is not to be

150. F. Schlegel, *Philosophy of Life*, trans. A. J. W. Morrison (London: Bohn, 1881), p. 329.
151. Husserl, "Philosophy as Rigorous Science," p. 126.

condemned as unscientific. Husserl writes: "If, however, we have admitted science as a valid idea, what reason would we still have not to consider similar differences between the historically worthwhile and the historically valid as at least an open possibility— whether or not we can understand this idea in the light of a critique of reason?" [152] After saying that "If the sceptical criticism of naturalists and historicists dissolves genuine objective validity in all fields into nonsense . . . if unclear and disagreeing concepts, even though naturally developed concepts and consequently equivocal and erroneous problems impede the understanding of actuality . . . then there is only one remedy for these and all similar evils: a scientific critique and in addition a radical science. . . . *Weltanschauungen* can engage in controversy; only science can decide and its decision bears the stamp of eternity." [153] Husserl reiterates his domination over the objectively idealist *Weltanschauungen:* "To the extent that this is intended as a reconciliation calculated to erase the line of demarcation between *Weltanschauung* philosophy and scientific philosophy, we must throw up our defense against it. . . . There are no compromises here." [154]

Thus Husserl has accepted Dilthey and yet has subordinated him to the bracketing methodology of phenomenology in law as well as in other social and human sciences. Husserl's effort is Kantian in that the separated or distanced contradictions lead to the external mediation of a higher or more profound objective idealism, presented as an unknowable thing-in-itself.

Perhaps certain of the thoughts considered here may be gathered into a unity. What Husserl is seeking to strengthen is (1) the Neo-Kantian unity of the reliving subject and what is relived; (2) the Neo-Kantian defeat of materialism and the Neo-Kantian–Neo-Hegelian justification for two idealisms, subjective and objective; and (3) the Neo-Kantian justification of *Verstehen* (comprehension or "understanding") through the defeat of law-governed ("causal") dialectic of negation and of negation of the negation. The crisis from which Husserl emerges explains the importance for phenomenology of bracketing and of impure intentionality. But phenomenology is futile. "Pure insight and intention, operating negatively, can only be—since its very

152. *Ibid.*
153. *Ibid.,* p. 141.
154. *Ibid.,* p. 142.

principle is all essentiality and there is nothing outside it—the negative of itself," Hegel writes in the *Phenomenology*. "As insight, therefore it passes into the negative of pure insight, it becomes untruth and unreason; and as intention it passes into the negative of pure intention, becomes a lie and sordid impurity of purpose. It involves itself in this contradiction by the fact that it engages in a strife and thinks to do battle with some alien external other. It merely imagines this, for its nature as absolute negativity lies in having that otherness within its own self." [155]

The Theory of Interpretation of Phenomenological Philosophy of Law

It is necessary to develop further the consideration of the theory of interpretation of phenomenological philosophy of law, though it is difficult to avoid taking account of the development thereof into existentialism. Bourgeois juridical interpretation is mandarinist, authentic (in Heidegger's usage of the word), distancing, or appropriative alienation of meaning. Insofar as interpretation is bourgeois, legal interpretation masks impure intentionality. Beyer relates Heidegger's theory of hermeneutics to distance, that is, to appropriative alienation theory. Throughout the *Phenomenology*, Hegel relates appropriative alienation not only to work but also to language. The problem of juridical interpretation is essentially a problem of the interpretation of language.

If phenomenological philosophy of law is an area or region of a fundamental phenomenology which brackets, disguises, separates, or deactualizes actuality, and if phenomenology of law justifies the authenticity or mandarinism of juridical method, then appropriative alienation of social actuality by phenomenological-existential theory of interpretation of legal structures, sources (in the legal sense), forms (in the legal sense), content, texts, "monuments" of law in general, becomes possible through such legal research into juridical meaning and force.

As has been said, the role of hermeneutics in Roman law is approximately twenty-six centuries old. Savigny was the first to attempt systematic study of legal method, but his effort appeared

155. Hegel, *Phenomenology of Mind*, p. 565.

as late as 1840. He subordinated legal method as science to the unscientific, objective idealist *Volksgeist,* and he justified legal irony or *Verstellung,* though he is sparing in his reference to Roman praetorian law or Roman equity. Windscheid later spoke of legal method or theory of interpretation as an "art." The French *projet* of a civil code of the Year VIII (1800) ambiguously attempted to give content to what was legal form or legal method, but such texts almost vanish in the final formulation. However, this formulation of legal method was received in the Louisiana Civil Code. The BGB (German Civil Code of 1900) is silent in regard to methodology of legal texts. Nevertheless the content of the BGB has been appropriated by mandarinist legal method as a priori. The BGB has had several histories, though the text or posited material as such has been little altered. This text appeared in 1900 as a bourgeois type of code, but its meaning was affected by the struggle between the Romanist and Germanist rivalries which obtained in German legal history of that time. Under the Nazis the BGB acquired a fascist meaning, and today in the BRD (German Federal Republic) it perhaps is a *Zwischen* or interim code. In the DDR (German Democratic Republic), the text of the BGB of 1900, insofar as the text has not been changed or repealed, has become a socialist civil code, without phenomenological bracketing of social actuality, following the overthrow of fascism there. In general, a principle of anticolonial and antibourgeois legal theory is this: the civil code of the metropolis or of the old bourgeois state is retained, but its meaning becomes explicitly anticolonial or socialist without bracketing. Such history shows the role of theory of legal meaning. Bourgeois legal meaning masks subjectivity and arbitrariness in legal phenomenology and legal existentialism, because the latter are legal theories of interpretation which are distancing or appropriative theories of legal method in bourgeois regimes which purport to be bound by the rule of law and hence are free from distancing and arbitrariness. This is possible because phenomenology consecrates bracketing or because existentialism separates beings and Being. In phenomenology and existentialism there is no theory of dialectical negation, which would justify establishing the truth and meaning of the legal texts in their otherness, that is, in the social infrastructure. The intentionality is impure.

What is involved in interpretation is the dialectic of form and content, in which the content appears as prior to form or method.

The unity-in-opposition of form and content may explode, through historic change in the infrastructure, so that the form or method itself becomes a force which further develops the regularities of the content or inner relation of the content and form in order to meet new historical requirements of the infrastructure. But when the new historical infrastructural relations become themselves rent by infrastructural contradictions, the unity of form and content is torn asunder, so as to require new meaning or new content which is hostile to the old or original positing or regularity or continuity. Form or legal method thus may become formalism. This connotes that a new and hidden content is at work, hostile to the old content and to the old form itself. Bracketing of social actuality conceals this destructiveness.

The problem today in philosophy of law is to bring forward the rivalry among philosophical conceptions of interpretation, especially the rivalry between dialectical and phenomenological-existential theories of interpretation, and to consider the solution of the problem of interpretation in bourgeois societies in which bourgeois power is either weakened or threatened by antibourgeois social forces. The problem of interpretation in such societies has driven certain phenomenological and existential thought toward Freudianization of meaning. Among philosophers, Ricoeur has been prominent in this direction. In bourgeois states in which Marxism is strong, it may be expected that structuralist legal theory will develop. In France, Althusser has redirected attention to Montesquieu. If Montesquieu's theory of separation of powers is understood as a theory of structuralist rivalry of social forces, a theory may develop justifying antipositivist meaning of posited law. Such a conception of Montesquieuan ideas justifies the struggles within the Supreme Court of the United States since the period of President Roosevelt. A Spanish theorist has asked whether a structuralist theory of law is possible.[156] In his discussion of hermeneutics, Beyer regards de Saussure and Betti as very important representatives of present-day bourgeois thought. De Saussure dominates the history of contemporary structuralism.[157] The emergence of a structuralist theory of in-

---

156. Vladimiro Lamsdorff-Galagane, *Estructuralismo en la filosofía del derecho?* (Santiago de Compostela: Porto y Cia. Editores, 1969).

157. Wilhelm Raimond Beyer, in *Philosophisches Wörterbuch*, 2 vols., 7th ed. (Berlin: Europäischer Buch, 1970), I, 473, 474.

terpretation of law, of what may be called a Neo-Montesquieuan conception of interpretation, ultimately would have to be related to the *intercessio* or unanimity principle of Roman law, to which reference already has been made.

It already has been said that some phenomenological and existential theory of interpretation of law has invoked the protection of Freud. The problem of theory of interpretation of phenomenology and of existentialism derives from the obvious subjectivity of the Neo-Kantian conception of *Verstehen*. This required the additional support of *Erlebnis* or reliving theory of interpretation, which also was subjectivist. The dialogue between Dilthey and Husserl issued, so far as Husserl was concerned, in his phenomenological theory of interpretation, which required both bracketing of actuality and impure intentionality, the latter smuggling infrastructural actuality into interpretation although the bracketing seemed to exclude actuality. This development may be described as a double idealism, seeking to unify subjective and objective idealism into a totality. Throughout the history of Neo-Kantianism and its problems, the idea in philosophy of law has been to assert that interpretation is free of infrastructural influence and yet to preserve and to mask the activist ambiguity, hypocrisy, equivocation, *Verstellung*, or *déplacement* which bourgeois social relations require, because the bourgeoisie is not the universal class which the Enlightenment claimed it was.

Heidegger, more powerfully than Husserl, states the problem of methodology of interpretation as activist or as *projet*. This statement concerning the activism of phenomenological and existentialist theory of legal interpretation may be put in the context of the first of Marx's "Theses on Feuerbach," where he wrote:

> The chief defect of all hitherto existing materialism (that of Feuerbach included) is that the thing, reality, sensuousness is conceived only in the form of the *object or of contemplation*, but not as *sensuous human activity*, practice, not subjectively. Hence, in contradiction to materialism, the *active* side was developed abstractly by idealism—which, of course, does not know real, sensuous activity as such. Feuerbach wants sensuous objects, really distinct from the thought objects, but he does not conceive human activity itself as *objective* activity.[158]

158. Marx, "Theses on Feuerbach," p. 599.

Heidegger's activism is idealist and alienating, intended to subdue inauthentic men, the objects of Nietzsche's pathos of distance. In *Dog Years,* Grass writes of the German soldiers of World War II, "We wanted to set out for the Eastland with Hölderlin and Heidegger in our knapsacks." Allemann regards Grass's *Dog Years* as a "travesty" of Heidegger, but this is an aspect of the effort, after the war, to restore the influence of Heidegger over his inauthentic or alienated men, victims of the pathos of distance.[159]

Beyer, who is a philosopher and a philosopher of law, in writing of hermeneutics in the DDR, says: "To the modern trait of hermeneutics: Dilthey has brought the self-comprehension of man in his historicity. He characterized the knowability function within the social sciences as '*Verstehen,*' knowledge in the natural sciences, on the contrary, as *causal Erklären.* Hermeneutics here becomes *subsequent consummating seizure of strange signification-form.* . . . The utmost precision and stylistically careful speech gives contemporary hermeneutics an especially scientific appearance. This epistemological trait guarantees its distance." Here Beyer quotes Heidegger that the fundamental propositions of hermeneutics get their meaning from *"earlier"* appearances. "The advantage for the present remains a pretty, rhetorical '*Verstehen.*' " [160]

Heidegger's conception of interpretation, in accordance with general or fundamental phenomenological methodology, must also be a concept of juridical interpretation.[161] It already has been shown that Heidegger seeks to unite methodology of art and methodology of science. This, too, appears in German legal romanticism of the early nineteenth century. Thus, Savigny, who subordinated legal science to the legal aesthetics of method, and to the silently working *Volksgeist,* is known as the poet-jurist. Before him, Schelling wrote that reason developed out of the unreason of the darkness of the womb.

Although Heidegger does not pretend to be a jurist, his theory of interpretation must embrace or be the foundation of all existentialist interpretation, including law. Beyer accords importance to Heidegger's *Was heisst Denken?,* originally published

159. Beda Allemann, "Martin Heidegger und die Politik," in *Heidegger,* ed. Otto Pöggeler (Cologne: Kiepenheuer & Witsch, 1969), p. 246.
160. Beyer, *Philosophisches Wörterbuch,* p. 474.
161. *Ibid.*

in 1954, and translated into English in 1968 as *What Is Called Thinking?* [162] Beyer, who is referring here to the work of the later Heidegger, says that "According to Heidegger neither a thinker nor a poet comprehends himself." This establishes the way to the alienating force of objective idealism, through legal method, over the content of law.

The discussion of Heidegger's theory of interpretation may begin with the double or ambiguous idealism of the earlier Heidegger of *Being and Time*. He writes:

> With the question of the meaning of Being, our investigation comes up against the fundamental question of philosophy. This is one that must be treated *phenomenologically*. Thus our treatise does not subscribe to a "standpoint" or represent any special "direction"; for phenomenology is nothing of either sort, nor can it become so as long as it understands itself. The expression "phenomenology" signifies primarily a *methodological conception*. This expression does not characterize the what of the objects of philosophical research as subject-matter, but rather the *how* of that research. The more genuinely a methodological concept is worked out and the more comprehensively it determines the principles on which a science is to be conducted, all the more primordially is it rooted in the way we come to terms with the things themselves. [163]

Thus phenomenology justifies the universality of methodology as the weapon with which to know the thing, which thing may be the thing of all science, including juridical science. Hegel has something important to say here. In the small *Logic*, he writes: "We ought, says Kant, to become acquainted with the instrument, before we undertake the work for which it is to be employed; for if the instrument be insufficient, all our trouble will be spent in vain. . . . But to seek to know before we know is as absurd as the wise resolution of Scholasticus, not to venture into the water until he had learned to swim." [164] Hegel is here saying that methodology which is not based on the unity of theory and social praxis is vulnerable. This appears in the second and eighth of Marx's "Theses on Feuerbach."

162. *Ibid.* Martin Heidegger, *What Is Called Thinking?*, trans. J. Glenn Gray and F. Wieck (New York: Harper & Row, 1968).
163. Martin Heidegger, *Being and Time*, trans. John MacQuarrie and Edward Robinson (New York: Harper & Row, 1962), pp. 49–50.
164. G. W. F. Hegel, *The Logic of Hegel*, trans. William Wallace, 2d ed. (Oxford: Clarendon Press, 1892), p. 17.

Although the methodology of existentialism does not bracket or distance or deactualize actuality, as in the phenomenology of Husserl, it maintains otherwise separation or *coupure*. Heidegger writes:

> Phenomenology is our way of access to what is to be the theme of ontology, and it is our way of giving it demonstrative precision. . . .
>
> "Behind" the phenomena of phenomenology there is essentially nothing else; on the other hand, what is to become a phenomenon can be hidden. And just because the phenomena are proximally and for the most part *not* given, there is need for phenomenology. Covered-up-ness is the counterconcept to "phenomenon." [165]

Heidegger proceeds:

> The way in which Being and its structures are encountered in the mode of phenomenon is one which must first of all be *wrested* from the objects of phenomenology. Thus the very *point of departure* for our analysis requires that it be secured by the proper method. . . .
>
> Because phenomena, as understood phenomenologically, are never anything but what goes to make up Being, while Being is in every case the Being of some entity, we must first bring forward the entities themselves if it is our aim that Being should be laid bare; and we must do this in the right way. . . . Our investigation itself will show that the meaning of phenomenological description as a method lies in *interpretation*.[166]

Though Husserl's theory of bracketing seems clumsier than Heidegger's theory, both men are Neo-Kantian in that, as idealists, they deny Kant's unknowable-thing-in-itself, which was Kant's vague connection with the mechanical materialism of the eighteenth century. To this Heidegger adds, for the sake of ambiguity, Nietzsche's ideas of the role of the mask, disguise, incognito, and so on. Husserl's bracketing yields nothingness disguised as idealistic essence. Heidegger's hiddenness gives beings masking the nothingness of idealistic Being. These are all disguised nothings in that the objects are relationless objects which do not have their being or truth, through negation, in the

---

165. Heidegger, *Being and Time*, p. 60.
166. *Ibid.*, p. 61.

respective others. Marx and Hegel realized that reality does not immediately present itself as truth, and hence that science was the necessity of knowledge. Dialectically, knowledge is historical (requiring the unity of theory and social praxis). They say that the Kantian unknowable-thing-in-itself is knowable; and that knowledge is wrested through the mediation or negation of the unity-in-opposition of appearance and reality.

Beyer suggests that there is a relation between the latter-day Heidegger and Schleiermacher, who says that "One of the basic missions of hermeneutics reads: to comprehend [zu verstehen] a writer *better* than he comprehends himself." [167] With Schleiermacher, Hegel said: "Dialectic is the last thing to arise and to maintain its place." [168] With Heidegger, too, there is no dialectic. He passes in *Being and Time* from one "moment" to another (universal-particular) without necessitated negation:

> In explaining the tasks of ontology we found it necessary that there should be a fundamental ontology taking as its theme that entity which is ontologico-ontically distinctive, Dasein, in order to confront the cardinal problem—the question of the meaning of Being in general. Our investigation itself will show that the meaning of phenomenological description as a method lies in *interpretation*. . . .
>
> Being, as the basic theme of philosophy, is no class or genus of entities; yet it pertains to every entity. Its "universality" is to be sought higher up. Being and the structure of Being lie beyond every entity and every possible character which an entity may possess. . . . And the transcendence of Dasein's Being is distinctive in that it implies the possibility and the necessity of the most radical *individuation*.[169]

Heidegger concludes this discussion in *Being and Time* by relating his thought to *Logical Investigations*, holding, however, that his own position is more activist or more possibilist than Husserl's.[170] However, this is formal possibility, not Hegel's dialectical real possibility, in which actuality-possibility are a unity of opposites. On the contrary, Heidegger's theory of possibility, *Entwurf* or *projet,* is related to the earlier German

167. Beyer, *Philosophisches Wörterbuch*, p. 474.
168. Hegel, *Lectures on the History of Philosophy*, III, 508.
169. Heidegger, *Being and Time*, pp. 61–62.
170. *Ibid.*, p. 62. See Paul Ricoeur, *Le Conflit des interprétations: Essais d'herméneutique* (Paris: Seuil, 1969), p. 11.

romantic idea of subjective irony or ambiguity. He says that "in our everyday Being-with-one-another . . . ambiguity has already established itself in the understanding as a potentiality-for-Being, and in the way Dasein projects itself and presents itself with possibilities." [171]

Heidegger's theory of interpretation in *Being and Time,* which is activist and possibilist, is a development of prior Neo-Kantian theory of *Verstehen.*[172] Heidegger writes:

> As understanding, Dasein projects its Being upon possibilities. This *Being-towards-possibilities* which understands is itself a potentiality-for-Being, and it is so because of the way these possibilities, as disclosed, exert their counter-thrust upon Dasein. The projecting of the understanding has its own possibility—that of developing itself. This development of the understanding we call "interpretation." . . . In it the understanding appropriates understandingly that which is understood by it. In interpretation, understanding does not become something different. It becomes itself. Such interpretation is grounded existentially in understanding; the latter does not arise from the former. Nor is interpretation the acquiring of information about what is understood; it is rather the working-out of possibilities projected in understanding. In accordance with the trend of these preparatory analyses of everyday Dasein, we shall pursue the phenomenon of interpretation in understanding the world—that is, in inauthentic understanding, and indeed in the mode of its genuineness.[173]

There seems a sharpening between Heidegger's double or ambiguous idealist *Verstehen* theory of interpretation in *Being and Time* and his objective idealist *Verstehen* theory of interpretation in the more recent writing. Beyer's presentation of the more recent position of Heidegger may be deepened. Beyer refers to Schleiermacher's fundamental principle of hermeneutics as that of comprehending a writer *better* than he does himself. "According to Heidegger," Beyer writes, "neither a thinker nor a poet comprehends himself. An 'other' actualizes the possibility of *Verstehen* of the pretended phenomenon. Hermeneutics exhausts itself therein. Every *Verstehen* precedes a process of interpretation." [174]

171. Heidegger, *Being and Time,* p. 217.
172. Beyer, *Philosophisches Wörterbuch,* p. 474.
173. Heidegger, *Being and Time,* pp. 188–89.
174. Beyer, *Philosophisches Wörterbuch,* p. 474.

In *What Is Called Thinking?* Heidegger writes:

It is remarkable that we must clarify something like laying. . . . The thing that matters when we lay something . . . is this: what must be laid lies there, and henceforth belongs to what *already* lies before us. And what lies before us is primary, especially when it lies there *before* all the laying and setting that are *man's* work, when it lies there prior to all that man lays out, lays down or lays in ruin. To the Greeks, telling is laying. Language has its essential being in the telling. . . . When man finds himself among what so lies before him, should he not respond to it in all purity by letting it lie before him just as it lies? And this letting-lie, would it not be that laying which is the stage for all the other laying that man performs? Thus laying would now suddenly emerge as a relatedness that pervades man's stay on this earth from the ground up—though we have never asked where this relatedness originates.[175]

Thus, Heidegger, restated profanely, has prepared the way for appropriating the positive law or the posited texts of the law through interpretation or "laying." The appropriation is by an objective idealism, which is an unknowable-thing-in-itself. The instrument for achieving the submission to the interpretation is poetic-scientific method or poetic-scientific technique of legal method.

After Heidegger, the most important theorist of the phenomenology of legal interpretation is Emilio Betti, as he has emerged during the history of the anticausalist Neo-Kantian *Verstehen* theory of the twentieth century. Betti flourishes at the University of Rome, and has been one of the great Romanist scholars of this period. His massive two-volume general theory of interpretation was published in 1955.[176] In 1967 it was translated into German in the BRD and discussed in the DDR not only as philosophy of law but as philosophy. This work was reviewed and attacked in *Deutsche Zeitschrift für Philosophie* in 1970 by Lothar Kreiser and Wolfgang Lorenz.[177] These scholars perceive in Betti an

175. Heidegger, *What Is Called Thinking?*, p. 205.
176. Emilio Betti, *Teoria generale della interpretazione*, 2 vols. (Milan: Dott. A. Giuffrè, 1955). See also Betti, "Falsa impostazione della questione storica, dipendente da erronea diagnosi giuridica," in *Studi in onore de Vincenzo Arangio-Ruiz* (Naples: Jovene, 1953), IV, 81–125.
177. Kreiser and Lorenz, review of *Allgemeine Auslegungslehre als Methodik der Geisteswissenschaften* by Emilio Betti, *Deutsche Zeitschrift für Philosophie*, XVIII, no. 8 (1970), 1004.

attempt to delimit the irrationalism of Dilthey and the existentialism of Heidegger by strengthening objective idealism. Of course, it has already been indicated that Heidegger himself turned toward objective idealism during the period in which Betti published his major work. It may be mentioned that Betti publishes frequently.

Betti describes interpretation as triadic. Beyer, writing of Betti in German, states that the triadic interpretation process has the following character: "Indication [*Deutung*] (thought production) of a sign, a task, a role, never resulting in the opposition of subject-object, but, instead, mediated through an 'inner linking' with strange spirit, and, indeed, 'through the mediation of meaningful stable forms in which this has objectivized itself.' " [178] Betti's own Italian text, of which *"Deutung"* is presumably the translation of *"a intendere il senso,"* could be translated into English as "to comprehend the meaning." [179] The "inner linking" with other spirit in interpretation which Betti mentions shows the presence of double idealism, and his theory of mediation indicates the place of legal method in authentic meaningful stable form.

In his considerations on the recent bourgeois hermeneutics theory, Beyer perceives both distance and pathos. [180] This may be restated as the perception of appropriative alienation of speech by the hidden or "downward" infrastructure through the impure instrumentality of legal method.

Beyer turns from Heidegger and Betti to Sartre's *Critique de la raison dialectique,* the first volume of which appeared in 1960 and which was translated into German in 1967. Sartre is given great significance because he makes the moment of praxis the cardinal point in hermeneutics. [181] Therewith the distinction between *Verstehen* and *Erklärung* is overcome. Sartre points toward the theory of knowledge of dialectical materialism. For him, the moment of praxis in the use of speech must appear in *"every"* definition. Sartre is quoted by Beyer as writing that "I therefore call *Erklärung* all temporal and dialectical *Evidenzen,* in so far as they must be able to totalize *all* practical realities, and I de-

---

178. Beyer, *Philosophisches Wörterbuch,* p. 474.
179. Betti, *Teoria generale della interpretazione,* I, 71.
180. Beyer, *Philosophisches Wörterbuch,* p. 474.
181. *Ibid.,* p. 475.

limit the concept *Verstehen* by the totalizing inclusion of all praxis in so far as it is intentionally produced." [182] The unanimity or tribunitial juridical principle achieves the unity of theory and praxis in interpretation. This is called the tribunitial principle because the Roman patricians recognized the power of the plebeian tribunes to concur in or to veto patrician juridical and other determinations affecting plebeians.

PHENOMENOLOGICAL PHILOSOPHY OF LAW AS APPROPRIATIVE ALIENATION

SEVERAL TIMES IN THIS ESSAY it has been necessary to suggest that legal phenomenology and legal existentialism represent efforts to unite the subjective idealism of Neo-Kantianism and the objective idealism of Neo-Hegelianism, while at the same time rejecting Hegelian dialectic. Mougin long ago discussed Sartre's "double idealism." [183] Marcuse has written that "We have seen how, in Sartre's philosophy, the concept of 'pour-soi' vacillates between that of the individual subject and that of the universal *Ego* or consciousness." [184]

The problem of double or divided idealism appears in the discussion of volition in the theory of intentionality. So far as interpretation of law is concerned, it should be mentioned that the idea of hermeneutics affects not only the force of the legal texts, such as the constitution or the civil code, but also acts of the "private" will. Volition is discussed generally in the modern Roman law as the *Rechtsgeschäft* or *acte juridique*. There is no similar Anglo-American legal conception, but the problem of volition of course exists there also, and must be studied for purposes of phenomenological and existential theory of volition. A *Rechtsgeschäft* is subject to interpretation, whether it be a contract or a testament.

Insofar as phenomenology and existentialism purport to justify ideas of human freedom, as they do prominently with

182. *Ibid.*
183. Henri Mougin, *La Sainte famille existentialiste* (Paris: Editions sociales, 1947), p. 166.
184. Herbert Marcuse, "Existentialism: Remarks on Jean-Paul Sartre's *L'Etre et le néant,*" *Philosophy and Phenomenological Research,* VIII (1947), 334.

Sartre, phenomenological and existential intentionality become involved in the problem of contradiction between *motifs* and *mobiles*. The question is whether such contradiction conceals appropriative alienation, and whether volition is self-determined or other-determined. It must be mentioned that bourgeois theory of freedom of the will began as a theory of abstract self-determination. This may be felt as far back as Bodin. Even Hegel, in his *Philosophy of Law,* based his theory of punishment for crime on the supposed self-determination of the accused to suffer the sanction. But this involved objective idealism, too. Bourgeois ideas of freedom of will, that is, of will which is not subject to appropriation, was not the legal theory of the bourgeoisie following its victory over feudalism. Thus, if there were a discrepancy between subjective will and exteriorized or objective will, it was the latter which was the legal will. For instance, if X apparently offered to sell an object for $46, whereas he had internally intended to state a price of $64, this usually would be taken to be an offer to sell for $46. Thus the will of the declarant was alienated or appropriated and veered against him. He is distanced from his own will, which has become his enemy. His objectivized will becomes the subject of which the declarant is the object. He is the intention of such distanced enemy. Marx's *Economic and Philosophic Manuscripts of 1844* is addressed to such appropriation in its most general form, and largely to work rather than to speech. Hegel once said that only a stone is innocent, meaning that appropriation lurks in bourgeois social life and that there is a responsibility to negate such alienation.

Another instance of the absence of freedom of will in volitional theory appears in civil law ideas of the suppletive will. Here the jurist is justified by the law in supplementing the supposedly free will of the subject of law. For instance, if nothing is agreed as to the place of delivery in a sale, the sale will not collapse, for the civil code supplies the missing elements. Likewise, legal ideas determine the effect of nonfulfillment or of defective fulfillment of contracts in such a way that the position of the victim of the defective fulfillment is not necessarily determined by the original speech of the contracting subjects of law. Indeed, Marx in the *Grundrisse* perceived sale not as social "solidarity" but as social eruption.[185]

185. Karl Marx, *Grundrisse der Kritik der politischen Ökonomie* (Berlin: Dietz, 1953), p. 68.

Probably it may be said that it is in private international law (conflict of laws) that volition as particular or "private" self-determination has collapsed. To mention a very primitive instance in American law, a hit-run motorist who wills to pass from one state to another is held, after he has fled the state of injury, to will his own submission to the competence of the second state over him for delicts or torts ("accidents") which he has caused in the second state, even though he never willed such consequence of his freedom to move from one state to another and back.

It is not possible here to review what seems to be the chaos or ambiguity of American private international law (conflict of laws) from the point of view of phenomenological or existential philosophy of law. Insofar as these movements have been influenced by Freud, ambiguity or irony in this area of law may reflect the opaqueness or concealment which Freudianism offers to double or divided idealisms based on phenomenological or existential legal theory. Insofar as private international law (conflict of laws) may be influenced by bracketed or deactualized existential spatial ideas of distance and nearness, Heidegger's thought has juridical importance. Likewise, Carl Schmitt, the most important Nazi jurist, developed theory of public international law based on existential theory of nearness and distance. Günter Grass, who criticizes Heidegger repeatedly in *Dog Years*, recalls Nazi anthropological distance theory: "A horseman rides through German lands, proclaiming: 'The Reich is bigger than its borders.' " [186]

What must be pursued here is the phenomenology of volition, or, to be more precise, the contradiction between *motifs* and *mobiles*. For dialectical reasons the writer prefers to indicate that freedom of will is supposedly governed by the idea of *motifs*, and that alienation of freedom of will is governed by activist or possibilist *mobiles;* the latter connote other-determination. The ideas of *mobiles* and *motifs* appear freely in French law, but they emerge in phenomenology vividly in Sartre's *Being and Nothingness*. Schutz, Pfänder, and Jeanson are also important theorists of phenomenological volition theory.[187] Schutz is detailed in his

186. Grass, *Dog Years*, trans. Ralph Manheim (New York: Harcourt Brace, 1965), p. 398.
187. Alfred Schutz, *Collected Papers*, 3 vols. (The Hague: Nijhoff, 1962–66), Vol. III, ed. Ilse Schutz (1966), pp. 27, 30, 123, 125; Vol. I, ed.

discussions, which seem to be a reworking of academic juridical thought. Pfänder's work as edited initiates phenomenological consideration of the problems, which include discussion of the English translation of Sartre's *mobiles-motifs* in *Being and Nothingness*. There is mentioned the difficulty of translating these words as "cause" and "motives"—a weakness which the translator of Sartre also discusses.[188] Insofar as phenomenology is based on *Verstehen* theory, the word "cause" should not be used. Jeanson is important as a critic of Sartre's discussion of *mobiles* and *motifs*.

These theorists, including Sartre himself, show the bourgeois weakness of considering *mobiles-motifs* in bourgeois terms, a weakness which is forced on them by the difficulty of Husserlian thought in really justifying the actuality of the "other." Sartre has been chosen for consideration here because through him the crisis of Husserlian thinking may be perceived. This crisis Sartre seeks to overcome in *Being and Nothingness* by invoking Freud.

Sartre's discussion of *mobiles-motifs* is part of his presentation of existential freedom. The problem of *mobiles-motifs* is really not important from the point of view of vulgar bourgeois subjectivity, because such theory usually collapses into a discussion of two degrees or levels of "motives," efficient or teleological, one near and one distant. But this should be sufficient to suggest that the problem of appropriative alienation is really latent in the distinction between the two. One such "motive" suggests freedom of will, and the other such "motive" suggests that freedom of will is grounded in will or structure determined by an other.

Although Sartre discusses an opposition between *mobile* and *motif*, he rejects both because existence precedes essence, forcing him to recoil from accepting permanently any conception which may weaken his theory of intentionality or of activist *projet*. In other words, Sartre seems to preserve the purity of the motion or activism in *Verstehen* theory. Nevertheless, he finally makes a

Maurice Natanson (1962), pp. 19, 69, 88. Alexander Pfänder, "Motives and Motivation," in *Phenomenology of Willing and Motivation*, trans. Herbert Spiegelberg (Evanston, Ill.: Northwestern University Press, 1967), pp. 12, 13, n. 8. See also Hans Welzel, *Vom Bleibenden und vom Vergänglichen in der Strafrechtswissenschaft* (Marburg: Elwart, 1964), p. 30. Francis Jeanson, *Le Problème moral et la pensée de Sartre* (Paris: Seuil, 1965), pp. 233, 235.
188. Sartre, *Being and Nothingness*, p. 435, n. 2.

distinction between "profound" intention and intention, leading him into a discussion of *Weltanschauung*. It will be recalled that Husserl discussed this in his reflections on Dilthey. It will also be recalled that Hegel condemned impure intentionality.

Having moved to *Weltanschauung*, Sartre then veers toward Freud in order to find the meaning which refers only to itself. He writes:

> We are not attempting to disguise how much this method of analysis leaves to be desired. This is because everything remains still to be done in this field. The problem indeed is to disengage the meanings implied by an act—by every act—and to proceed from there to richer and more profound meanings until we encounter the meaning which does not imply any other meaning and which refers only to itself. . . . A gesture refers to a *Weltanschauung* and we *sense* it. But nobody has attempted a systematic disengagement of the meanings implied by an act. There is only one school which has based its approach on the same original evidence as we, and that is the Freudian. For Freud as for us an act can not be limited to itself; it refers immediately to more profound structures. And psychoanalysis is the method which enables us to make these structures explicit. Freud like us asks: under what conditions is it possible that this particular person has performed this particular act? Like us he refuses to interpret the action by the antecedent moment. . . . The act appears to him *symbolic;* that is, it seems to him to express a more profound desire which itself could be interpreted only in terms of an initial determination of the subject's libido. Freud . . . aims at constituting a vertical determinism. In addition because of this bias his conception necessarily is going to refer to the subject's past. Affectivity for Freud is at the basis of the act in the form of psycho-physiological drives. But this affectivity is originally in each of us a *tabula rasa;* for Freud the external circumstances and, so to speak, the *history* of the subject will decide whether this or that drive will be fixed on this or that object.[189]

With Sartre, Freudian profound meanings should suggest distancing or rupture in appropriative alienation in bourgeois society. Elsewhere in this discussion Sartre invokes Husserl's bracketing in order to lay the foundation for "profound" meaning. He writes of the voluntary act: "To adopt Husserl's famous expression, simple voluntary reflection by its structure as re-

189. *Ibid.*, pp. 457–58.

flectivity practices the *epochē* with regard to the cause; it holds the cause in suspense, puts it within parentheses." [190] This rupture, this distancing, is really the path of the other, the objective idealism. Sartre states:

> If the given cannot explain the intention, it is necessary that the intention by its very upsurge realize a rupture with the given, whatever this may be. . . . Moreover, this rupture is necessary for the *appreciation* of the given. The given, in fact, could never be a *cause* for an action if it were not appreciated. But this appreciation can be realized only by a withdrawal in relation to the given, a putting of the given into parentheses, which exactly supposes a break in continuity. In addition, the appreciation if it is not to be gratuitous, must be effected in the light of something. And this something which serves to appreciate the given can be only the end. Thus the intention by a single unitary upsurge posits the end, chooses itself, and appreciates the given in terms of the end. Under these conditions the given is appreciated in terms of something which does not yet exist; it is in the light of non-being that being-in-itself is illuminated. There results a double nihilating coloration of the given; on the one hand, it is nihilated in that the rupture makes it lose all efficacy over the intention; on the other hand, it undergoes a new nihilation due to the fact that efficacy is returned to it in terms of a nothingness appreciation. Since human reality is act, it can be conceived only as being at its core a rupture with the given. It is the being which causes *there to be* a given by breaking with it and illuminating it in the light of the not-yet-existing.[191]

This, of course, is founded on the activism of *Verstehen* theory. It recalls Hegel's condemnation of impure intentionality as this has been restated through Dilthey's effort to unite subjective and objective idealism in which the objective idealism is an unknowable-thing-in-itself, which recent bourgeois thought requires because of the hidden actuality of its contradictions and the opaqueness of the future toward which it is groping. The intentionality of volition is the volition of an objective idealist unknowable-thing-in-itself. Here Sartre, too, seems to be justifying Kierkegaard. Sartre here seems to veer toward Heidegger's idea of destiny or *Geschick* through Husserl and through Freud, among others. Such an unknowable-thing-in-itself is nothingness,

190. *Ibid.*, p. 451; see also p. 439.
191. *Ibid.*, p. 478.

which masks what Sartre himself in this discussion calls "appropriation." "We shall see," he writes, "what is the meaning of the word *having* and to what extent *doing* is a method of *appropriating*." [192] Distancing (with Sartre, Freudian distancing) is the outcome of his discussion of *mobiles* and *motifs*. But distancing is appropriative alienation.

Nevertheless, Sartre accuses Heidegger of bad faith in the latter's theory of distance. For Heidegger, Sartre writes, "Man is a 'being of distances.' In the movement of turning inward which traverses all of being, being arises and organizes itself as the world without there being either priority of the movement over the world, or the world over the movement. But this appearance of the self beyond the world—that is, beyond the totality of the real—is an emergence of 'human reality' in nothingness." [193] Here Sartre in effect accuses Heidegger of double idealism in order to justify *Verstellung* or hypocrisy or ambiguity. This is the so-called third way in philosophy. More accurately, Heidegger justifies both *Entfernung* and *Ent-fernung,* that is, alienation as both distancing and nearness in order to justify both objective and subjective idealism. In legal phenomenology and in legal existentialism this means alienation both as the distancing of state power or of ownership or of *dominium* and as the nearness of state power or of legal possession or *possessio* of the instruments or means of production. Sartre apparently here believes Heidegger's distancing to be a threat to his own phenomenology of freedom. Thus he writes:

> Heidegger's *transcendence* is a concept in bad faith: it aims, to be sure, at surpassing idealism. . . . But the idealism thus surpassed is only a bastard form of idealism, a sort of empirical-critical psychologism. Undoubtedly Heidegger's human-reality "exists outside itself." But this existence outside itself is precisely Heidegger's definition of the *self*. It resembles neither the Platonic (Neo-Platonic?) ekstasis where existence is really alienation, existence in an Other, nor Malebranche's vision in God, our own conception of the ekstasis and of the internal negation. Heidegger does not escape idealism; his flight outside the self, as an *a priori* structure of his being, isolates him as surely as the Kantian reflection on the *a priori* conditions of our experience. In fact what human-reality rediscovers at the inaccessible limit of

192. *Ibid.*, p. 455.
193. *Ibid.*, pp. 17–18.

this flight outside itself . . . is a flight toward the self, and the world appears as the pure distance between the self and the self.[194]

As Marcuse suggests, Sartre himself is guilty of bad faith or ambiguity in that he, too, offers a double or divided idealism. Sartre truly justifies both freedom and *Weltanschauung*, both *motifs* and *mobiles* and the rejection of each; he masks his difficulty with an appeal to Freud. Dufrenne, stating his own thought, writes, "The genius yielding to inspiration no longer belongs to himself . . . his 'I' is an other." [195] Husserl, in the *Crisis*, says what the philosopher is *"truly seeking"* is a "will coming *from* the will and *as* the will of his spiritual forefathers." [196]

Ricoeur writes that Marx, Nietzsche, and Freud are three great "destroyers," but complains that Marxists are stubbornly insistent on the "reflex" theory.[197] This may focus the discussion on the relation of *mobiles* and *motifs* in historical materialism. Marxist reflection theory is the Marxist materialist conception of the dialectic of consciousness in relation to infrastructure. This means that there may be a valid distinction between *mobiles* and *motifs,* one indicating social consciousness, which is the truth of particular or individual consciousness mediated by historic social theory and social praxis. This is not the exclusively subjective consciousness, which becomes ultimately the consciousness of phenomenology and existentialism, nor is it exclusively the objective consciousness which is ultimately the consciousness of contemporary structuralism. Nor is it the ironic or ambiguous consciousness, which veers between two idealisms. *Motifs* and *mobiles* are a dialectical unity of opposites, that is, of the historic general and the historic particular, in which the historic general is primary, and in which the historic particular reflects such historic general and its eruption as its inner necessity through praxis.

However, as has been said, the opposition between *mobiles* and *motifs* has been understood by bourgeois jurists as a problem in antidialectical degrees or hierarchy of idealized volition. Probably Scheler and N. Hartmann could be mentioned here as theorists of degrees or levels of idealistic value ideas. Gurvitch, too, may be mentioned.

194. *Ibid.*, p. 249.
195. Dufrenne, *Notion of the A Priori*, p. 35.
196. Husserl, *Crisis*, p. 71.
197. Ricoeur, *Freud*, pp. 33–34.

Probably the most important juridical discussion of this problem is still that by Josserand, in his book, *Les Mobiles dans les actes juridiques du droit privé*, published in 1928. "[M]obiles unmask intention," Josserand writes, "whereas the latter does not suffice to reveal *mobiles*." [198] This could be led back to Hegel's discussion of impure intentionality. A merit of Josserand's presentation is that he considers *mobiles* in relation to wars of aggression,[199] and it may be mentioned in passing that French legal writing concerning responsibility under the Nürnberg charter brought forward the theory of *mobiles*.

If the problem of *mobiles-motifs* is considered dialectically, that is, in the Marxist conception of infrastructure and superstructure, it may be related to Marx's discussion of consciousness and ideology. Moreover, the dialectic of *mobiles-motifs* may be related to Marxist and Hegelian conceptions of crisis responsibility. Insofar as the discussion is limited to bourgeois law, the contradiction of *mobiles-motifs* becomes a weapon for attaining bourgeois impure intention through appropriative alienation.

It should be clear from what has been said that theory of volition which does not take account of the historicity of the contradiction, *mobiles-motifs,* is abstract or formal volition, or volition as a thing-in-itself, which being relationless is nothingness masked as being. This leads to a brief discussion of the role of *causa* in Roman law theory of volition, and, to a certain extent, to the role of consideration in Anglo-American law.

The theory of *causa* has been a battlefield of Roman and civilian thought for centuries. Instead of consecrating theory of freedom of will, as Sartre hoped to justify it in the presentation above, the *code civil*, in general, requires *causa* in order to justify volition. Bourgeois jurists tend to discuss the matter tautologically, that is, in terms of "empty intentions" (to generalize the purport of the phrase used by Sartre in discussing Husserl's intentionality theory).[200] However, the requirement of *causa* is legitimated if it is the means by which the bourgeois infrastructure may assert itself in the legal superstructure. Hence *causa* may or may not justify the validity of the volition, and it may or may not determine, furthermore, the legal history of the fulfill-

198. L. Josserand, *Les Mobiles dans les actes juridiques du droit privé* (Paris: Dalloz, 1928), p. 21.
199. *Ibid.,* p. 15.
200. Sartre, *Being and Nothingness*, p. 26.

554 / Phenomenology and Legal Theory

ment of a valid volition. Bourgeois intention theory, in general, justifies or fails to justify the appropriation or alienation of the particular volition, but it masks the power of the infrastructure therein. Perhaps such appreciation of the theory of *causa* is, within limits, acknowledged in the present Italian Civil Code.

Causa theory appears in the French Civil Code, mediating in effect between the particular wills of the bourgeoisie in civil society and the supposedly universal will of the bourgeois state. Although Marx early destroyed the idea of the bourgeoisie as the universal class, the importance of *causa* as a dialectical idea in a socialist state, based on a real universal class, has turned the USSR and DDR toward socialized *causa* theory.[201] This is significant, because the DDR has retained the BGB (German Civil Code of 1900), and codification in the USSR has been formulated under the influence of a socialist meaning of the BGB. However, the BGB itself, speaking generally, does not acknowledge *causa*. This means that in the USSR and DDR the French theory of volition justified by socialist *causa* has been preferred to the abstractness of the bourgeois meaning of the BGB.

Anglo-American law does not know *causa*, but insofar as it does consecrate the idea not of volition as such, but of "bargain" as such, "bargain" theory is *mobile* theory in the infrastructural sense advanced in this essay. Although he is not a jurist, Mac-Pherson, in his work, *The Political Theory of Possessive Individualism*, published in 1962, helps to show, so far as Anglo-American theory of contract based on "bargain" is con-

201. See D. M. Genkin, S. N. Bratus, L. A. Lunz, and I. B. Nowizki, *Sowjetisches Zivilrecht*, German trans. (Berlin: VEB Deutscher Zentral, 1953), I, 253; G. Dornberger, H. Kleine, G. Klinger, and M. Posch, *Das Zivilrecht der Deutschen Demokratischen Republik, Allgemeiner Teil* (Berlin: VEB Deutscher Zentral, n.d.), pp. 272, 286. See the important discussion of German legal history in Hans Kleine, *Die historische Bedingtheit der Abtraktion von der Causa* (Berlin: VEB Deutscher Zentral, 1953). See also J. Dabin, *La teoría de la causa*, trans. Francisco de Pelsmalker (Madrid: Librería general de Victoriano Suarez, 1929), p. 15 (conception of Domat); K. Wolff, *Grundriss des österreichischen bürgerlichen Rechts* (Vienna: Springer, 1948), pp. 6, 46, 61 (*Beweggrund*); R. Merle and A. Vitu, *Traité de droit criminel* (Paris: Cujas, 1967), p. 436 (*mobiles* in criminal law); G. Ripert, *La Règle morale dans les obligations civiles*, 3d ed. (Paris: Librairie générale de droit et de jurisprudence, 1935), p. 66 (*cause* and materialism; theory of Capitant); J. Dabin, "General Theory of Law," in *The Legal Philosophies of Lask, Radbruch, and Dabin*, pp. 225, 293 (intention, *cause*, "soul of the group," materialism, Josserand).

cerned, an unbracketed, infrastructural concept of volition which is grounded in "profound" bourgeois intentionality.

Such theory, founded on the actuality and real possibility of the infrastructure, avoids the hiddenness of the vice of what Hegel called "impure" intentionality.

The problem of appropriative alienation in *mobiles* and *motifs*, including *causa*, is not solved by legal phenomenology and legal existentialism and was not solved by objective idealism, which preceded them. The writer has said:

> There has been developing in the thought of some important American judges . . . the idea of "presupposition" as the justification for the enforcement and fulfillment of promises. This is reminiscent of Windscheid's individualistic theory of *causa* as *Voraussetzung* or presupposition. But if Windscheid's theory were restated as a theory of state alienation in possessive market society or as a theory of bourgeois presupposition, and if the American theory of presupposition were also restated as a theory of alienation, as it must be in the bourgeois state, American theory and certain civilian theory might coincide in a doctrine of what could be called possessive-market-society-cause. . . . Williston recognizes the "basis" of the contract. . . . These may be the same as Windscheid's theory of presupposition and likewise should be understood as justification for appropriative state alienation of the volition or promises of the subjects of the private law. The idea of "basis" may be an inadvertent echo of Leibniz's theory of "ground" as considered by Hegel, who may have felt in the idea of basis or ground a dialectical-causal idea explaining the passage from a fundamental social level, that is, from social life under certain determinate conditions, to the superstructural reflection of such social life. Hegel wrote: "Leibniz especially opposed the sufficiency of ground to causality in its strict meaning of mechanical efficacy. The latter is an external activity, restricted in content to one determinateness, and consequently the determinations which it posits become connected externally and contingently; partial determinations are comprehended by their causes, but their relation—and this it is which constitutes the essential part of an existence—is not contained among the causes with which mechanism operates." [202]

202. Mitchell Franklin, "A *Précis* of the American Law of Contract for Foreign Civilians," *Tulane Law Review*, XXXIX (1965), 681. See Henri Batiffol, "La 'Crise du contrat' et sa portée," *Archives de philosophie du droit*, XIII (1968), 13, 17.

Husserl's phenomenology was to have been presupposition-less. Because of his bracketing, Husserl's presuppositionless phenomenology is a methodology or an a priori which separates history from essence or presupposition. This is contrary to Hegel's conception of essence, which is historical. Even if Husserlian essence yielded the thing-in-itself, the thing-in-itself is a nothingness masked as essence because a relationless or pre-suppositionless thing-in-itself is nothingness. Sartre's discussion of intention and profound intention, which finally was abandoned to Freud, suggests that Husserlian bracketing or deactualization leads to presuppositionless nothingness or to impure intentionality. Sartre knows that he must confront the dialectic of *mobiles-motifs* in discussing human will, but in truth he brackets the contradiction buried in them. The objective idealists of the nineteenth century still haunt Sartre as he disappears into Freud. However, in 1965, this writer said that "it may be anticipated that phenomenological or existential theories of presupposition will in due course emerge." [203] This is suggested by the persistence of the presence of double or divided idealism, by Sartre's early, pre-Freudian profound intentionality, and by Heidegger's relation of *Denken* or "thinking" and speech. But such idealist theory will not openly confront or overcome appropriative alienation.

Bracketing and the Anthropology of Space as Appropriative Alienation

There is a dialectic of negations from hermeneutics to *mobiles-motifs* to *Entfernung* or distance as bourgeois appropriative alienation. Husserl's bracketing and its outcome in the activist chiaroscuro effects of existentialism are described variously in philosophical literature. What must be emphasized is that such bracketing is a theory of distancing and of separation. Gotesky has given a valuable account of many conceptions of distance in his essay, *Aloneness, Loneliness, Isolation, Solitude.*[204] These words suggest the secondary or passive, as opposed to the active, moment of distance.

Distancing conceals bourgeois alienation or *Entfremdung,*

203. Franklin, "A *Précis*," p. 685.
204. In James M. Edie, ed., *An Invitation to Phenomenology* (Chicago: Quadrangle, 1965), p. 211.

alienation being understood as appropriation, seizure, or, in terms of Roman law, either *occupatio* or *usucapio*. *Occupatio* connotes ownership, justified by gaining the possession of the other, e.g., the slave, the wild animal. Without mentioning certain details, *usucapio* connotes private property claims justified by long-continued possession of the property of another. The history of such theory of successive appropriative alienations, as the history of consciousness, is the true force of Hegel's *Phenomenology;* this establishes the philosophic importance of that writing, in which Hegel discusses the appropriation or alienation of work and of language. This perhaps ultimately explains the importance of speech in contemporary idealist philosophy and its increased prominence in the more recently published writings of Heidegger, especially his *Letter on Humanism* and *What Is Called Thinking?* Idealistic distance becomes anthropological, though at times distancing originates in geopolitical spatial theory and then is veered into an anthropological conception of social distance or appropriative alienation. Of course, this is not always true, because feudal and religious ideas of distance, including ideas of revealed religion, are not spatial. It is assumed that Kant's idealistic theory of space has assumed some role in the history of the development of the anthropological space or distance theory. Insofar as Husserl has interiorized the God of Malebranche, as Merleau-Ponty suggests, he seems to have negated religious distancing by nearness; but insofar as Husserl has bracketed the external world, he has, so to speak, negated the negation, by justifying profane, anthropological distance based on the intentionality of the appropriating force in relation to the means of production. As phenomenological method is offered as the method of all science, including human and social science, Husserl through his bracketing has created a philosophical justification for distancing or appropriative alienating juridical theory. Much phenomenological philosophy of law is therefore devoted to theory of property and of legal transactions, and of aggression against or injury to them, that is, to criminal and delictal (tort) law. The idea of such alienation or distance as "past" (to use Hegel's word) is prominent in German distance theory. It appears in the nostalgia of Husserl and the "home-sickness" of Heidegger, and seems to be a reworking of the nostalgia for feudalism with which early-nineteenth-century German romanticism opposed the French Revolution. Although phenomenology and existentialism are activist and possibilist, nostalgia is also apparent in ideologies as a mask for bourgeois futurism. What may be suspected here is the influence of Tönnies, with his distinction between feudal *Gemeinschaft* and bourgeois *Gesellschaft*. This was possible because of the rivalry between German feudal and bourgeois forces, which, while terminating in the victory of the German bourgeoisie, left it with a patina of feudalism, so that it could mask itself as nostalgic or feudal. This occurred because nineteenth-century Germany became bourgeois without following the revolutionary path of the French bourgeoisie. Nazi imperialism exploited *Volksgemeinschaft* theory. Its juridical theorist was Höhn, who, together with Carl Schmitt, was a leading Nazi jurist. However, nostalgic "distance" or nostalgic appropriative alienation thus became a weapon not of feudalism against the bourgeoisie but of the German bourgeoisie against historical materialism, and, indeed, a weapon of recent German bourgeois legal and social ideas against the historically progressive legal and social ideas of the early German bourgeoisie. Hegel's thought, if carefully considered, is not involved in this development, which reflects the German bourgeois situation first in the face of feudalism and later in the face of Marxism. But Hegel, too, pursues a method which is progressive-regressive, though with him this is an aspect of the dialectic of the abstract-concrete and of the concrete-abstract.

It is very important to understand distance as appropriative alienation and not to delimit it merely to this or that particular historical form of hegemony, such as space, revealed religion, historic nostalgia, etc. The specific historic mask and the specific ambiguity of distancing as the justification for juridical activism appear in the history of bourgeois law. Because the recent bourgeoisie requires legal conceptions different from or destructive of early bourgeois conceptions, it may be realized that Husserlian bracketing phenomenology with its theory of the role of method, including interpretation or hermeneutics, has reopened the door to a revival of natural law based on the nature of the things themselves. The justification of such methodology as destruction is the task of the *Logical Investigations*, which already has been discussed. Moreover, Husserl's bracketing also makes it possible to restore for the purposes of the recent bourgeoisie Kant's undialectical distinction between "is" and "ought," which

Hegel condemned, and thus to create a new, unholy alliance between natural law and Kant.

There are two aspects of Hegel's conception of distance in the *Phenomenology* which should be mentioned. The first of these is Hegel's acknowledgment of the role of distance and of negation of distance in the dialectical intentionality of the abstract-concrete.[205] This has already been adverted to. It should be studied in connection with E. G. Ballard's excellent essay, "The Visual Perception of Distance," published in 1970.[206] Because of his bracketing, Husserl cannot achieve the dialectic of abstract-concrete, in part because he has no theory of social praxis. Hegel's second discussion of distance is in connection with revealed religion in his treatment of the struggle of the Enlightenment with superstition. These are presented by Hegel as aspects of his theory of impure and similar intentionality. Unlike intentionality discussed in the dialectic of the abstract-concrete, the idea of impure intentionality is presented pejoratively by Hegel. "The conditions, 'past' and 'distance,'" he writes, "are, however, merely the imperfect form in which the immediateness gets mediated or made universal; this is merely dipped superficially in the element of thought." [207] Insofar as Hegel is considering "past" as "distance," he seems to be condemning the feudal, romantic German historical school of law, founded by the jurist Hugo and later headed by the jurist Savigny, which confronted the French Revolution with a theory of feudal, appropriative alienation justified by distant, long-continued enjoyment.

After Hegel, Marx condemned anthropological alienation or distancing. In *The Economic and Philosophic Manuscripts of 1844*, he writes that "atheism and communism are no flight from, no abstraction from, no loss of the objective world created by man as his essential capacities objectified." [208] What Marx is here considering is the unbracketed relation between appropriative alienation and distance. He writes: "It is now time to grasp the *positive* aspects of the Hegelian dialectic within the realm of estrangement. . . . Supersession as an objective movement of *retracting*

---

205. Hegel, *Phenomenology of Mind*, p. 156.
206. In *Phenomenology in Perspective*, ed. F. J. Smith (The Hague: Nijhoff, 1970), p. 187.
207. Hegel, *Phenomenology of Mind*, p. 763.
208. Marx, *Economic and Philosophic Manuscripts of 1844*, p. 187.

the alienation *into self*. This is the insight, expressed within the estrangement, concerning the *appropriation* of the objective essence through the supersession of its estrangement; it is the estranged insight into the *real objectification* of man, into the real appropriation of his objective essence through the annihilation of the *estranged* character of the objective world, through the supersession of the objective world in its estranged mode of being." [209] This leads to the fourth of Marx's "Theses on Feuerbach," in which he discusses religion as alienation through distancing.

In 1960 the writer discussed the passive or secondary aspect of appropriative alienation in distancing, that is, the passive aspect of *Entfremdung* as *Entfernung:*

> [I]dealistic existential conceptions of alienation in general connote separation and distance. They conceive that *Entfremdung* means *Entfernung.* . . . Naville gives an account . . . of the idealistic alienation ideas of alienation. . . . "Numerous novelists express the sentiment of being 'strangers in the world,' . . . [T]his type of alienation terminates by becoming the contrary of that described by Hegel and criticized by Marx. . . . This form of alienation is therefore quite removed from that which with Marx engenders *struggle.* . . ." Hegel's conception of alienation is directly opposed to that of existentialism. . . . [W]ith Hegel the basic alienation is the alienation of labor and language. Labor and language are externalized, and both passed to and appropriated by the other. In the present historic period this process of alienation may have as its reflex the kind of distancing estrangement described by existentialism.[210]

What is prominent in the above texts relating to distance or *Entfernung* is the victimization of the alienated. But in German military law *Entfernung* means desertion, and this idea is responsive to Hegel's idea of responsibility, which in his theory of alienation means that the alienated-dominated force has a responsibility to struggle to alienate the alienation, to negate the negation. But through his concept of the pathos of distance, Nietzsche justifies the appropriating power of the dominant power. He writes:

209. *Ibid.*
210. Mitchell Franklin, "On Hegel's Theory of Alienation and Its Historic Force," *Tulane Studies in Philosophy,* IX (1960), 53.

The cleavage between man and man, status and status, the plurality of types, the will to be oneself, to stand out—what I call the *pathos of distance*, that is characteristic of a strong age. The strength to withstand tension, the width of the tensions between extremes, becomes ever smaller today. . . . The decline of life, the decrease in the power to organize, that is, to separate, tear open clefts, subordinate and super-ordinate—all this has been formulated as the ideal in contemporary sociology. Our socialists are decadents.[211]

The writer cannot say whether Nietzsche's conception of pathos is borrowed from Hegel.[212] For the latter, pathos connotes not only movement, but movement which is internal and so should establish an inner unity-in-separation between the dominating and the dominated. Moreover, for particular persons the activist, distancing relation of pathos connotes the unity-in-opposition of particular and general. Hegel is suggesting the clash of general forces through particular men. The distinction between *motifs* and *mobiles,* between human will and the ground of human will, should be recalled, as well as Hegel's theory of responsibility to change what can be changed.

It is not the purpose of this paper to indicate the literature of distancing. However, very important American writing has recently been published, by such men as Natanson, Jarrett, Casebier, and Ballard.[213] Attention should also be directed to the import of Hegel's discussion of political distance as measure in the small *Logic*.[214] Here Hegel related the internal nature of the constitution to the measure of the state. He considers the problem, much discussed during the Enlightenment, of the possibility of a republican constitution in a state of great space. Probably he did not know that this problem had been discussed in the United

211. Friedrich Nietzsche, *Twilight of the Idols,* in *The Portable Nietzsche,* ed. and trans. Walter Kaufmann (New York: Viking, 1954), pp. 540–41.
212. G. W. F. Hegel, *The Philosophy of Fine Art,* trans. F. P. B. Osmaston (London: Bell, 1920), I, 308, 313.
213. Maurice Natanson, "Man as an Actor," *Philosophy and Phenomenological Research,* XXVI (1966), 327; James L. Jarrett, "On Psychical Distance," *The Personalist,* LII, no. 1 (1971), 61; Allen Casebier, "The Concept of Aesthetic Distance," *The Personalist,* LII, no. 1 (1971) 70; Edward G. Ballard, "The Visual Perception of Distance," in Smith, *Phenomenology in Perspective,* p. 187.
214. Hegel, *Logic,* p. 203.

States, with its vast distances, during the formative period resulting in the Philadelphia constitution.

It is necessary to focus the development of distance theory of alienation on Heidegger, and even beyond. Simmel must be mentioned because he reifies, corporealizes, fetishizes, and "defuses" the relations of social distance. He writes:

> The firmer and the more technically articulated the organization of the group, the more objectively and firmly do the patterns of superordination and subordination present themselves. . . . This by no means applies to hierarchies of governmental positions alone. Money economy creates a very similar societal formation in the spheres which are dominated by it. The possession or lack of a particular sum of money entails a certain social position. . . . Money has carried to its extreme the separation emphasized a moment ago, between man, as a personality, and man as the instrument of a special performance or significance.[215]

Carl Schmitt, the Nazi "crown jurist," said in 1932 that "The specific political discrimination of which political affairs and motives permit themselves to be reduced, is the discrimination between friend and foe." [216] This, understood as a conception of geopolitical distance, was also a conception of anthropological distance. "The concepts of friend and foe," Schmitt writes, "are received in their concrete, existential sense, not as metaphors or symbols, nor mixed and weakened through economic, moral and other presentations." [217] Schmitt's existential conception of friend and foe justifies not only Nazi aggression, but also that aggression within Germany itself. After World War II, Schmitt stated his thought as a theory of international law in *Der Nomos der Erde*.[218]

What has been said prepares the way for consideration of Heidegger's theory of the structure of social space. If the ironic "prettiness" of Heidegger (to recall Beyer's description) is to be negated or "destroyed" (to use Heidegger's own methodology), section 23 of *Being and Time* is a text in which Heidegger's theory of appropriative alienation is concealed or masked. In section 23

---

215. Kurt H. Wolff, ed. and trans., *The Sociology of Georg Simmel* (Glencoe, Ill.: Free Press, 1964), p. 293; see also p. 411.
216. Carl Schmitt, *Der Begriff des Politischen* (Munich: Duncker & Humblot, 1932), p. 14.
217. *Ibid.*, p. 15.
218. (Cologne: Greven, 1950).

he makes a spatial distinction between *Entfernung* as remoteness and *Ent-fernung* as closeness. This conceals his conception of social space as social appropriative alienation. The social meaning of space is Heidegger's meaning of the ontology of space. This may be Heidegger's narcotization of Hegel's dialectic of the dissatisfied, unhappy, appropriated, feudal consciousness which veered between heaven and earth, between remoteness and nearness. Heidegger seems to reify or to corporealize social relations in the anthropology of space. However, he never discovers that *Entfernung* or social distance or *Ent-fernung* or social nearness should have involved him also in a discussion of these concepts as a theory of social responsibility to negate appropriative alienation as justified by his theory of social or ontological spatiality. It already has been said that in German military law *Entfernung* means desertion from responsibility. The secularization of this meaning of *Entfernung* should have led Heidegger to a theory of the negation or social appropriation of the social appropriation hidden in his theory of social space. This is the meaning of Hegel's *Phenomenology* and his *Philosophy of Law,* both of which are devoted to the history of consciousness of historical social responsibility through necessity.

But what Heidegger really gives in his theory of social space is the passive acceptance hierarchically of the appropriation of the reified appropriated force through the activism or possibilism or futurism of the dominant social force. Alienation becomes existential passivity or perhaps merely resentment or social flight. Heidegger's conception both of *Entfernung* as remoteness and of *Ent-fernung* as nearness in reality and in their totality serves the goals of appropriative alienation. In section 23, Heidegger says, "That which is presumably 'closest' is by no means that which is at the smallest distance 'from us.' " [219] The play of *Entfernung* or remoteness and *Ent-fernung* or closeness, means three things: (1) Heidegger is justifying both objective idealism (*Entfernung*) and subjective idealism (*Ent-fernung*). (2) Heidegger is justifying both the Tönnies-like role of the feudal *Volksgemeinschaft* or community, which is remote and nostalgic, and the bourgeois *Rechtsgemeinschaft* or society (perhaps, civil society), which is near. Höhn, who, along with Schmitt, was a leading Nazi jurist, demanded the restored hegem-

219. Heidegger, *Being and Time,* p. 141.

ony of the *Volksgemeinschaft* over the *Rechtsgemeinschaft*. The force of this is clear if existential possibility is prior to actuality, that is, if the *projet* or *Entwurf* of activist *Verstehen* theory may bracket or deactualize actuality. Alfred Rosenberg's activist theory of the Nazi subjectivity-free myth was that of a type to-be-created out of "our entire history." [220] (3) But Heidegger, like Nietzsche and Simmel, is also justifying bourgeois, as bourgeois, appropriative alienation. *Ent-fernung* states the nearness or closeness of the owner as legal possessor of the tools with which the worker produces. *Ent-fernung* apparently reifies or "choosifies" the relationship. Juridically, both in Roman and Anglo-American law the worker only has *detentio* or custody of the means of production, but the owner has the legal *possessio* or possession. In the history of Roman law, Savigny justified an *animus domini* theory of possession. But in lay usage, possession suggests the nearness of the social space among the possessor, the thing possessed, and the worker, especially if the social spatiality is reified so that the relation between the possessor and the worker is fetishized in the tool. But *Entfernung* indicates the remoteness of the social space between the oppressor and the oppressed. *Entfernung,* justified by state power, indicates the social remoteness of ownership (as distinguished from the lay idea of possession) of the means of production. The idea of *dominium* or of ownership reifies in the tool the social remoteness of the owner of the means of production from the worker. The worker is bracketed or deactualized through such reification. This reification-alienation states remoteness or *Entfernung* between the owner and the worker. This seems reminiscent of Nietzsche's pathos of distance and is close to Simmel.

In section 27 of *Being and Time,* Heidegger masks the relationship of domination by making the alienating force distant. In a note to their French translation of *Being and Time,* Boehm and de Waelhens write: "Distancing, or more precisely, the constant care of distance toward the other (toward the 'one') is a proof of the domination of the other (the 'one'). Said otherwise, distancing is a consequence of this domination." [221] In section 23,

---

220. Alfred Rosenberg, *Der Mythus des 20. Jahrhunderts* (Munich: Hoheneichen, 1935), p. 531; see also p. 481.
221. Heidegger, *L'Etre et le temps,* trans. Rudolf Boehm and Alphonse de Waelhens (Paris: Gallimard, 1964), p. 299. See William A. Luijpen, *Phenomenology of Natural Law,* trans. Henry J. Koren (Pittsburgh: Du-

where he has been discussing spatiality, Heidegger, continuing his use of "pretty" speech, says ironically, "Though we may know these distances exactly, this knowledge still remains blind." [222] Perhaps Nietzsche is being heeded here. "[B]eware, my dear philosopher," Nietzsche said, "of telling the truth." Lukács refers to the incognito as an element in the thought of Heidegger, Carl Schmitt, and Ernst Jünger; and Bloch, in his writing on natural law, refers to the role of the mask. [223] The reference to Jünger is important, because he became an important link between Heidegger and the Nazi theory of work.

The force of Heidegger's "pretty" language of anthropological space in section 23 of *Being and Time* is deepened by the later Heidegger's speech in *Discourse on Thinking*, [224] the English translation of *Gelassenheit*, published in 1959. In this text Heidegger restates the theory of nearness-closeness, brings forward very prominently the problem of objective idealism as an unknowable-thing-in-itself in relation to subjective idealism, defends alienation, emphasizes the aleatory activism or possibilism of methodology (which may be poetic with Heidegger), and very firmly rejects dialectic. Heidegger in some respects is reminiscent here of F. Schlegel's effort, as a romanticist, to unite the new with the old, so that there is an activist indifference between new-old. Heidegger's presentation is in conversational form:

Scientist: If any examination which focuses on what is a part of history is called historical, then the methodological analysis in physics is, indeed, historical.
Scholar: Here the concept of the historical signifies a mode of knowing and is understood broadly . . .
Teacher: The historical rests in that-which-regions, and in what occurs as that-which-regions. It rests in what, coming to pass in man, regions him into his nature. [225]

This leads to Heidegger's consideration of alienating objective idealism as an unknowable-thing-in-itself:

quesne University Press, 1967), pp. 224–25, for Welzel on Heidegger's subject of law as "inauthentic."
222. Heidegger, *Being and Time*, p. 141.
223. See Lukács, *Die Zerstörung der Vernunft*, p. 666; and Ernst Bloch, *Naturrecht und menschliche Würde* (Frankfurt am Main: Suhrkamp, 1961), p. 172.
224. Martin Heidegger, *Discourse on Thinking*, trans. John M. Anderson and E. Hans Freund (New York: Harper & Row, 1966).
225. *Ibid.*, p. 79.

Scientist: Now authentic releasement consists in this: that man in his very nature belongs to that-which-regions, i.e., he is released to it . . .
Scholar: . . . prior to everything . . .
Scientist: Thus man's nature is released to that-which-regions in what is prior to thought . . .
Teacher: It appropriates man's nature for its own regioning . . .
Scholar: Evidently the nature of man is released to that-which-regions because this belongs to it so essentially, that without man that-which-regions can not be a coming forth of all natures, as it is.[226]

Then the problem emerges for Heidegger's method of the relation of activism and alienation or appropriation:

Scientist: We have just characterized that-which-regions as the hidden nature of truth. If . . . we say truth in place of that-which-regions, then the statement of the relation of human nature to that-which-regions is this: human nature is given over to truth, because truth needs man. Yet now the distinguishing characteristic of truth . . . is . . . to be what . . . is independent of man . . .
Teacher: The nature of man is released to that-which-regions . . . for this reason alone—that man of himself has no power over truth and it remains independent of him. Truth's nature can come forth independently of man only because the nature of man . . . is used by that-which-regions. . . . Evidently truth's independence *from* man is a relation *to* human nature.[227]

Then Heidegger indicates cryptically his theory of method as bourgeois alienation by stating it as an activist theory of distance-nearness, that is, of the active relation of the superstructure, which is near, and the infrastructure, which is distant:

Scientist: All the same I can no longer hold back the confession that while its nature has neared, that-which-regions itself seems to me to be further away than ever before.
Scholar: You mean to say that you are near to its nature and yet are distant from that-which-regions itself? [228]

This leads Heidegger to the following:

226. *Ibid.,* p. 82.
227. *Ibid.,* p. 83.
228. *Ibid.,* p. 85.

Scientist: Then that-which-regions itself would be nearing and distancing.

Scholar: That-which-regions itself would be the nearness of distance, and the distance of nearness . . .

Scientist: . . . a characterization which should not be thought of dialectically.

Teacher: But how?

Scientist: In accordance with the nature of thinking so far as determined solely by that-which-regions . . .

Teacher: Yet what then would be the nature of thinking if that-which-regions is the nearness of distance? . . .

Scholar: The Greek word translates as "going toward."

Scientist: I regard this word as an excellent name for designating the nature of knowledge; for the character of advancing and moving toward objects is strikingly expressed in it.[229]

Then Heidegger states that the activist force of the dialogue is methodological:

Scientist: Actually, one could use this Greek word to make clear the fact that scientific research is a kind of attack on nature, but one which allows nature to be heard.[230]

RELATION OF PHENOMENOLOGICAL PHILOSOPHY OF LAW TO
IDEALISTIC REVIVED NATURAL LAW AND IDEALISTIC
KELSENISM

THERE IS AN INNER DISPUTE among practitioners of legal phenomenology as to whether it is a school of natural law. The phenomenological movement itself today is infected with eclecticism. Phenomenological philosophy of law is also eclectic. In reviewing the position of the phenomenologists of law, Peschka concludes that this legal movement is an epistemological natural law movement masked as ontology.[231] If the relation of phenomenology to Malebranche is recalled, this is justified. Peschka, too, suggests that phenomenology of law is natural law from the point of view of historical materialism, which regards law as that which signifies an ensemble of norms created or sanctioned by the superstructural state.

229. *Ibid.*, p. 86.
230. *Ibid.*, p. 88.
231. Peschka, "La Phénoménologie," p. 277.

568 / Phenomenology and Legal Theory

However, the theory of natural law itself is historical. The natural law of scholasticism is an objective idealism. The mechanical materialistic natural law which developed from one side of Descartes was, in the language of Husserl, "naturalistic" and so subject to condemnation. Because mechanical materialistic natural law eventually required the mediation of external mediation, it too concealed idealism. However, Husserl's thought does not develop in this direction. Even if he had accepted mechanical materialistic natural law, his theory of deactualization or of bracketing questions the validity of the subject of such natural law.

This subject, the essence of man or human nature, is deactualized by Husserl. But both Marx and Hegel surpass Husserl's destruction of the subject of eighteenth-century natural law. With both Hegel and Marx, the essence of mankind is his self-making through history. Marx regarded the force of Hegel's *Phenomenology* as the history of the self-making of mankind by labor. In the *Philosophy of Law,* Hegel wrote: "In [abstract] right, what we had before us was the person; in the sphere of morality, the subject; in the family, the family-member; in civil society as a whole, the burgher or *bourgeois*. Here at the standpoint of needs . . . what we have before us is the composite idea which we call *man*. Thus this is the first time, and indeed properly the only time, to speak of *man* in this sense." [232] In the sixth of Marx's "Theses on Feuerbach," he writes: "Feuerbach resolves the religious essence into the *human* essence. But the human essence is no abstraction inherent in each individual. In its reality it is the ensemble of the social relations." [233] However, although he is an existentialist, the latter-day Heidegger in the *Discourse on Thinking* writes both of "the nature of man" and of "the nature of thinking."

Husserl himself directed attention to the things themselves. In this sense he has strengthened idealistic natural law theory, which is now perhaps interested in the nature of the things rather than with the nature of mankind. However, natural law based on the so-called nature of the thing, indeed, is not new in the history of natural law theory.

232. Hegel, *Philosophy of Right* [Law], p. 127.
233. Marx, "Theses on Feuerbach," p. 660.

Although phenomenology has become intertwined with the revival of natural law theory, Kelsen, the Neo-Kantian opponent of natural law, also has been seized by theorists of phenomenological philosophy of law. Felix Kaufmann, in *Logik und Rechtswissenschaft*, as early as 1922, directed attention both to Husserl and to Kelsen.[234] So far as this writer knows, Kelsen has discussed Husserl in a long footnote; but he has directed his fire against the philosophy of law of existentialism, especially against Georg Cohn, the author of *Existentialismus und Rechtswissenschaft*.[235] However, if it were not for the title, Cohn's work could be understood as if it were written by an American legal realist.

Contemporary natural law, founded on the nature of the things themselves, is related to or united in an unholy alliance with Kant's undialectical distinction between the "is" and the "ought." This distinction appears in effect in Husserl's discussion of methodology in the *Logical Investigations*. If Husserl's work as a theory of meaning of structures collapses into a Kantian distinction between "is" and "ought," the so-called radical meaning of Husserl's school may be questioned. Kant's distinction between the "is" and the "ought" is overcome by Hegel's conception of the unity-in-opposition of actuality and of real possibility.

Because with Kant himself the edifice of natural law crumbles, the basis for unity between Kant and natural law must be stated otherwise. Both ironic natural law and ironic Kantian theory may justify rivalry between law and paralaw. Paralaw connotes law which purports to accept positive law, although in truth it destroys the force of such positive law. But this characterizes only one side of the history of natural law, because natural law may also defend and develop the positive law. The justification for such contradictory missions of natural law must be determined by the crises of the historic infrastructures.

The basic problems of philosophy of law cannot be stated or

234. (Tübingen: Mohr, 1922). For a recent discussion, see Poulantzas, *Nature des choses*, p. 57.
235. Hans Kelsen, "Existentialismus in der Rechtswissenschaft?" (1957), reprinted in Klecatsky, *Die Wiener Rechtstheoretische Schule*, I, 763. Georg Cohn's book was published in Basel by Helbing and Lichtenhahn in 1955; English translation by George H. Kendal, *Existentialism and Legal Science* (Dobbs Ferry, N.Y.: Oceana, 1967).

solved within the framework of the categories of natural law–positive law. The fundamental problems of philosophy of law relate to the struggle between materialism and idealism and cryptoidealism, and between dialectical and antidialectical conceptions of law.

Bibliography

IT IS NOT POSSIBLE to provide a comprehensive bibliography for this work; that would take far more space than is available. I have attempted, however, to bring together various strands which may be of interest and use to the reader. The following list includes many of the essential titles in the field, some references not already cited in the essays, some marginal but suggestive sources, and a representative sampling of the writings of our contributors (including an occasional book which is not related to phenomenology). Wherever possible, English translations have been cited. A number of the contributors have made helpful suggestions for this bibliography, though it remains the responsibility of the editor. It is hoped that despite its incompleteness and at times seemingly arbitrary inclusions and exclusions, this list will lead the reader back through the chapters of our work and forward to what is yet to be written.

Amselek, Paul. "L'Etonnement devant le droit." *Archives de philosophie du droit*, XIII (1968), 163–83.
———. *Méthode phénoménologique et théorie du droit*. With a Preface by Charles Eisenmann. Paris: Librairie générale de droit et de jurisprudence, 1964.
Arendt, Hannah. *The Human Condition*. Chicago: University of Chicago Press, 1958.
Ballard, Edward G. "Husserl's Philosophy of Intersubjectivity in Relation to His Rational Ideal." *Tulane Studies in Philosophy*, XI (1962), 3–38.
Berger, Gaston. *The "Cogito" in Husserl's Philosophy*. Translated

by Kathleen McLaughlin with an Introduction by James M. Edie. Evanston, Ill.: Northwestern University Press, 1972.

——. *Phénoménologie du temps et prospective*. With a Preface by Edouard Morot-Sir. Paris: Presses Universitaires de France, 1964.

Berger, Peter L., and Luckmann, Thomas. *The Social Construction of Reality: A Treatise in the Sociology of Knowledge*. Garden City, N.Y.: Doubleday, 1966.

Bidney, David. "On the Philosophical Anthropology of Ernst Cassirer and Its Relation to the History of Anthropological Thought." In *The Philosophy of Ernst Cassirer*, edited by Paul Arthur Schilpp (Library of Living Philosophers), pp. 465–544. New York: Tudor, 1949.

——. *Theoretical Anthropology*. New York: Schocken, 1967.

——, ed. *The Concept of Freedom in Anthropology*. The Hague: Mouton, 1963.

Boas, Franz. *The Mind of Primitive Man*. Rev. ed. New York: Collier, 1963.

Boehm, Rudolf. "La Phénoménologie de l'histoire." *Revue internationale de philosophie*, LXVII, nos. 71–72 (1965), 55–73.

Brand, Gerd. *Gesellschaft und persönliche Geschichte: Die mythologische Deutung sozialer Prozesse*. Stuttgart: Kohlhammer, 1972.

——. *Die Lebenswelt: Eine Philosophie des konkreten Apriori*. Berlin: de Gruyter, 1971.

Brecht, Arnold. *Political Theory: The Foundations of Twentieth-Century Political Thought*. Princeton, N.J.: Princeton University Press, 1967.

Bruzina, Ronald. *Logos and Eidos: The Concept in Phenomenology*. The Hague: Mouton, 1970.

Cairns, Dorion. "The Ideality of Verbal Expressions." *Philosophy and Phenomenological Research*, I, no. 4 (June, 1941), 453–62.

Cicourel, Aaron V. *Method and Measurement in Sociology*. New York: Free Press, 1964.

Cossio, Carlos. *La teorie egologica del derecho*. Buenos Aires: Abeledo-Perrot, 1964.

Davis, Murray S. "That's Interesting! Towards a Phenomenology of Sociology and a Sociology of Phenomenology." *Philosophy of the Social Sciences*, I, no. 4 (December, 1971), 309–44.

Derrida, Jacques. *Speech and Phenomena: And Other Essays on Husserl's Theory of Signs*. Translated by David B. Allison. Evanston, Ill.: Northwestern University Press, 1973.

Descartes, René. *A Discourse on Method and Selected Writings*. Translated by John Veitch. New York: Scribner, 1951.

Donius, Charles. "Existentialisme, phénoménologie et philosophie

du droit." *Archives de philosophie du droit*, III (1957), 221–31.
Douglas, Jack D., ed. *Understanding Everyday Life: Toward the Reconstruction of Sociological Knowledge*. Chicago: Aldine, 1970.
Dreyfus, Hubert L. *What Computers Can't Do: A Critique of Artificial Reason*. New York: Harper & Row, 1972.
Dufrenne, Mikel. *La Personnalité de base: Un Concept sociologique*. 2d ed. Paris: Presses Universitaires de France, 1966.
Edie, James M. "Expression and Metaphor." *Philosophy and Phenomenological Research*, XXIII, no. 4 (June, 1963), 538–61.
———. "Husserl's Conception of 'The Grammatical' and Contemporary Linguistics." In Lester E. Embree, ed., *Life-World and Consciousness: Essays for Aron Gurwitsch*, pp. 233–61.
———, ed. *Phenomenology in America: Studies in the Philosophy of Experience*. Chicago: Quadrangle, 1967.
———, Parker, Francis H., and Schrag, Calvin O., eds. *Patterns of the Life-World: Essays in Honor of John Wild*. Evanston, Ill.: Northwestern University Press, 1970.
Elveton, R. O., ed. *The Phenomenology of Husserl: Selected Critical Readings*. Chicago: Quadrangle, 1970.
Embree, Lester E., ed. *Life-World and Consciousness: Essays for Aron Gurwitsch*. Evanston, Ill.: Northwestern University Press, 1972.
Eucken, Walter. *The Foundations of Economics*. Translated by T. W. Hutchison. Chicago: University of Chicago Press, 1951.
Fackenheim, Emil L. *Metaphysics and Historicity*. Milwaukee, Wis.: Marquette University Press, 1961.
Farber, Marvin. *The Foundation of Phenomenology: Edmund Husserl and the Quest for a Rigorous Science of Philosophy*. 3d ed. Albany, N.Y.: State University of New York Press, 1967.
———, ed. *Philosophical Essays in Memory of Edmund Husserl*. Cambridge, Mass.: Harvard University Press, 1940; reprinted, New York: Greenwood Press, 1968.
Filmer, Paul; Phillipson, Michael; Silverman, David; and Walsh, David. *New Directions in Sociological Theory*. London: Collier-Macmillan, 1972.
Fink, Eugen. *Studien zur Phänomenologie: 1930–1939*. The Hague: Nijhoff, 1966.
Firth, Raymond. *Human Types*. London: Nelson, 1938.
Franklin, Mitchell. "Aspects of the History of Theory of Alienated Consciousness." *Philosophy and Phenomenological Research*, XX, no. 1 (September, 1959), 25–37.
———. "On Hegel's Theory of Alienation and Its Historic Force." *Tulane Studies in Philosophy*, IX (1960), 50–100.
Friedmann, Wolfgang. *The Changing Structure of International Law*. New York: Columbia University Press, 1964.

———. *Law in a Changing Society*. Baltimore, Md.: Penguin, 1964.

———. *Legal Theory*. 5th ed. New York: Columbia University Press, 1967.

Friedrich, Carl J. *Constitutional Government and Democracy*. Rev. ed. New York: Blaisdell, 1950.

———. *Man and His Government: An Empirical Theory of Politics*. New York: McGraw-Hill, 1963.

———. *Philosophy of the Law in Historical Perspective*. Rev. ed. Chicago: University of Chicago Press, 1963.

Frostig, Jakób. *Das schizophrene Denken: Phänomenologische Studien zum Problem der widersinnigen Sätze*. Leipzig: Thieme, 1929.

Funke, Gerhard. "Geschichte als Phänomen." *Zeitschrift für philosophische Forschung*, XI, no. 2 (April–June, 1957), 188–234.

———. *Phänomenologie: Metaphysik oder Methode?* Bonn: Bouvier, 1966.

———. *Zur transzendentalen Phänomenologie*. Bonn: Bouvier, 1957.

Garfinkel, Harold. *Studies in Ethnomethodology*. Englewood Cliffs, N.J.: Prentice-Hall, 1967.

Geertz, Clifford. *Person, Time and Conduct in Bali: An Essay in Cultural Analysis*. Southeast Asia Studies, Cultural Report Series, no. 14. New Haven, Conn.: Yale University, 1966.

Gendlin, Eugene T. *Experiencing and the Creation of Meaning: A Philosophical and Psychological Approach to the Subjective*. New York: Free Press, 1962.

Giorgi, Amedeo. *Psychology as a Human Science*. New York: Harper & Row, 1970.

Goyard-Fabre, Simone. *Essai de critique phénoménologique du droit*. Paris: Klincksieck, 1972.

Grathoff, Richard H. *The Structure of Social Inconsistencies: A Contribution to a Unified Theory of Play, Game, and Social Action*. The Hague: Nijhoff, 1970.

Gunnell, John G. *Political Philosophy and Time*. Middletown, Conn.: Wesleyan University Press, 1968.

———. "Social Science and Political Reality: The Problem of Explanation." *Social Research*, XXXV, no. 1 (Spring, 1968), 159–201.

Gurvitch, Georges. *Les Tendances actuelles de la philosophie allemande: E. Husserl, M. Scheler, E. Lask, M. Heidegger*. With a Preface by Léon Brunschvicg. Paris: Vrin, 1949.

Gurwitsch, Aron. *The Field of Consciousness*. Pittsburgh, Pa.: Duquesne University Press, 1964.

———. *Studies in Phenomenology and Psychology*. Evanston, Ill.: Northwestern University Press, 1966.

Gusdorf, Georges. *Introduction aux sciences humaines*. Paris: Société d'édition, 1960.

Habermas, Jürgen. *Knowledge and Human Interests.* Translated by Jeremy J. Shapiro. Boston: Beacon, 1971.

——. *Zur Logik der Sozialwissenschaften.* Tübingen: Mohr, 1967.

Hartmann, Nicolai. *Ethics.* Translated by Stanton Coit with an Introduction by J. H. Muirhead. 3 vols. New York: Macmillan, 1932.

Hayek, Friedrich A. *The Counter-Revolution of Science: Studies on the Abuse of Reason.* Glencoe, Ill.: Free Press, 1952.

——. *Individualism and Economic Order.* London: Routledge & Kegan Paul, 1949.

Hegel, Georg W. F. *The Phenomenology of Mind.* Translated by J. B. Baillie with an Introduction by George Lichtheim. New York: Harper & Row, 1967.

Heidegger, Martin. *Being and Time.* Translated by John Macquarrie and Edward Robinson. New York: Harper, 1962.

——. *Existence and Being.* Edited with an Introduction by Werner Brock. Chicago: Regnery, 1949.

——. "The Idea of Phenomenology." Translated by John N. Deely and Joseph A. Novak with the assistance of Eva D. Leo. *New Scholasticism,* XLIV, no. 3 (Summer, 1970), 325–44.

——. On *"Time and Being."* Translated by Joan Stambaugh. New York: Harper & Row, 1972. (Note: Includes a translation of "My Way to Phenomenology.")

——. "Der Zeitbegriff in der Geschichtswissenschaft." *Zeitschrift für Philosophie und philosophische Kritik,* CLXI, no. 1 (1916), 173–88.

Heilbroner, Robert L., ed. *Economic Means and Social Ends: Essays in Political Economics.* Englewood Cliffs, N.J.: Prentice-Hall, 1969.

Heron, John. "The Phenomenology of Social Encounter: The Gaze." *Philosophy and Phenomenological Research,* XXXI, no. 2 (December, 1970), 243–64.

Hohl, Hubert. *Lebenswelt und Geschichte: Grundzüge der Spätphilosophie E. Husserls.* Munich: Alber, 1962.

Holzner, Burkart. *Reality Construction in Society.* Rev. ed. Cambridge, Mass.: Schenkman, 1972.

Hülsmann, Heinz. "Zur Theorie der Sprache bei Edmund Husserl." *Salzburger Studien zur Philosophie,* IV (1964), 1–255.

Husserl, Edmund. *Cartesian Meditations: An Introduction to Phenomenology.* Translated by Dorion Cairns. The Hague: Nijhoff, 1960.

——. *The Crisis of European Sciences and Transcendental Phenomenology: An Introduction to Phenomenological Philosophy.* Translated with an Introduction by David Carr. Evanston, Ill.: Northwestern University Press, 1970.

——. *Experience and Judgment.* Translated by James Spencer

Churchill and Karl Ameriks, with a Foreword by Ludwig Land-grebe and an Afterword by Lothar Eley. Evanston, Ill.: North-western University Press, 1973.

————. Formal and Transcendental Logic. Translated by Dorion Cairns. The Hague: Nijhoff, 1969.

————. The Idea of Phenomenology. Translated by William P. Als-ton and George Nakhnikian with an Introduction by George Nakhnikian. The Hague: Nijhoff, 1964.

————. Ideas: General Introduction to Pure Phenomenology. ("Ideas I.") Translated by W. R. Boyce Gibson. New York: Macmillan, 1931.

————. Ideen zu einer reinen Phänomenologie und phänome-nologischen Philosophie. Vol. II: Phänomenologische Untersuchun-gen zur Konstitution. Edited with an Introduction by Marly Biemel. The Hague: Nijhoff, 1952. Vol. III: Die Phänomenologie und die Fundamente der Wissenschaften. Edited by Marly Biemel. The Hague: Nijhoff, 1952.

————. Logical Investigations. Translated with an Introduction by J. N. Findlay. 2 vols. New York: Humanities Press, 1970.

————. The Paris Lectures. Translated with an Introduction by Peter Koestenbaum. The Hague: Nijhoff, 1964.

————. "Phenomenology." In Encyclopaedia Britannica, 14th ed. London: 1927. Complete new translation by Richard E. Palmer, Journal of the British Society for Phenomenology, II, no. 2 (May, 1971), 77–90.

————. "Phenomenology and Anthropology." Translated by Richard G. Schmitt. In Realism and the Background of Phenomenology, edited by Roderick M. Chisholm, pp. 129–42. Glencoe, Ill.: Free Press, 1960.

————. The Phenomenology of Internal Time-Consciousness. Trans-Rigorous Science and Philosophy and the Crisis of European Man. Translated with an Introduction by Quentin Lauer. New York: Harper Torchbooks, 1965.

————. The Phenomenology of Internal Time-Consciousness. Trans-lated by James S. Churchill and edited by Martin Heidegger with an Introduction by Calvin O. Schrag. Bloomington, Ind.: Indiana University Press, 1964.

Husserl. Cahiers de Royaumont, Philosophie No. III. With an Avant-Propos by M.-A. Bera. Paris: Minuit, 1959.

Husserl et la pensée moderne. With an Avant-Propos by H. L. Van Breda and J. Taminiaux. The Hague: Nijhoff, 1959.

Husserl, Gerhart. Person, Sache, Verhalten: Zwei phänomenologische Studien. Frankfurt a.M.: Klostermann, 1969.

————. Der Rechtsgegenstand: Rechtslogische Studien zu einer Theorie des Eigentums. Berlin: Springer, 1933.

———. *Recht und Welt*. Frankfurt a.M.: Klostermann, 1964.
———. *Recht und Zeit: Fünf rechtsphilosophische Essays*. Frankfurt a.M.: Klostermann, 1955.
Jakobson, Roman. "Linguistics." In *Main Trends of Research in the Social and Human Sciences*, pt. I, pp. 419–63. The Hague: Mouton-UNESCO, 1970.
Janssen, Paul. *Geschichte und Lebenswelt: Ein Beitrag zur Diskussion von Husserls Spätwerk*. The Hague: Nijhoff, 1970.
Jaspers, Karl. *General Psychopathology*. Translated by J. Hoenig and Marian W. Hamilton. Chicago: University of Chicago Press, 1963.
———. *Von der Wahrheit*. Munich: Piper, 1947.
Jonas, Hans. *The Phenomenon of Life: Toward a Philosophical Biology*. New York: Harper & Row, 1966; New York: Dell, 1966.
Jordan, Robert Welsh. "Husserl's Phenomenology as an 'Historical Science.'" *Social Research*, XXXV, no. 2 (Summer, 1968), 245–59.
Jung, Hwa Yol. "The Political Relevance of Existential Phenomenology." *Review of Politics*, XXXIII, no. 4 (October, 1971), 538–63.
———, ed. *Existential Phenomenology and Political Theory: A Reader*. With a Foreword by John Wild. Chicago: Regnery, 1972.
Kaufmann, Felix. *Kriterien des Rechts*. Tübingen: Mohr, 1924.
Kaufmann, Fritz. "Cassirer, Neo-Kantianism, and Phenomenology." In *The Philosophy of Ernst Cassirer*, edited by Paul Arthur Schilpp (Library of Living Philosophers), pp. 799–854. New York: Tudor, 1949.
———. "The Phenomenological Approach to History." *Philosophy and Phenomenological Research*, II, no. 2 (December, 1941), 159–72.
———. "Phenomenology of the Historical Present." In *Proceedings of the 10th International Congress of Philosophy*, edited by E. W. Beth, H.-J. Pos, and J. H. A. Hollak, I, 967–70. Amsterdam: North-Holland, 1949.
Kelkel, L. "Le Problème de l'autre dans la phénoménologie transcendentale de Husserl." *Revue de métaphysique et de morale*, LXI, no. 1 (January–March, 1956), 40–52.
Kelsen, Hans. "Eine phänomenologische Rechtstheorie." *Österreichische Zeitschrift für öffentliches Recht*, XV (1965), 353–409.
Kersten, Frederick I. "The Constancy Hypothesis in the Social Sciences." In Lester E. Embree, ed., *Life-World and Consciousness: Essays for Aron Gurwitsch*, pp. 521–63.
———, and Zaner, Richard M., eds. *Phenomenology: Continuation and Criticism: Essays in Memory of Dorion Cairns*. The Hague: Nijhoff, 1973.
Kockelmans, Joseph J. *Edmund Husserl's Phenomenological Psy-*

chology: A Historico-Critical Study. Translated by Berndt Jager and revised by the author. Pittsburgh, Pa.: Duquesne University Press, 1967.

——. A First Introduction to Husserl's Phenomenology. Pittsburgh, Pa.: Duquesne University Press, 1967.

——, ed. Phenomenology: The Philosophy of Edmund Husserl and Its Interpretation. Garden City, N.Y.: Doubleday, Anchor Books, 1967.

Kracauer, Siegfried. Soziologische Wissenschaft: Eine erkenntnis-theoretische Untersuchung. Dresden: Sibyllen, 1922.

Kraft, Julius. "Die wissenschaftliche Bedeutung des phänomenologischen Rechtsphilosophie." Kantstudien, XXXI (1926), 286–96.

Kroeber, Alfred Louis. The Nature of Culture. Chicago: University of Chicago Press, 1952.

——, and Kluckhohn, Clyde. Culture: A Critical Review of Concepts and Definitions. Peabody Museum of American Archaeology and Ethnology, Papers, Vol. XLVII, no. 1. Cambridge, Mass.: Harvard University, 1952; New York: Random House, Vintage, 1963.

——. Definitions. Peabody Museum of American Archaeology and Ethnology, Papers, Vol. XLVII, no. 1. Cambridge, Mass.: Harvard University, 1952; New York: Random House, Vintage, 1963.

Lachmann, Ludwig M. "Methodological Individualism and the Market Economy." In Roads to Freedom: Essays in Honour of Friedrich A. Von Hayek, edited by E. Streissler, pp. 89–103. New York: Kelley, 1969.

Laguna, Grace A. de. On Existence and the Human World. New Haven, Conn.: Yale University Press, 1966.

Landgrebe, Ludwig. Phänomenologie und Geschichte. Gütersloh: Mohn, 1968.

——. Phänomenologie und Metaphysik. Hamburg: Schröder, 1949.

——. "The World as a Phenomenological Problem." Translated by Dorion Cairns. Philosophy and Phenomenological Research, I, no. 1 (September, 1940), 38–58.

Lanteri-Laura, Georges. La Psychiatrie phénoménologique: Fondements philosophiques. Paris: Presses Universitaires de France, 1963.

Lawrence, Nathaniel, and O'Connor, Daniel, eds. Readings in Existential Phenomenology. Englewood Cliffs, N.J.: Prentice-Hall, 1967.

Lee, Edward N., and Mandelbaum, Maurice, eds. Phenomenology and Existentialism. Baltimore, Md.: Johns Hopkins Press, 1967.

Levinas, Emmanuel. En découvrant l'existence avec Husserl et Heidegger. Paris: Vrin, 1949.

————. *La Théorie de l'intuition dans la phénoménologie de Husserl.* Paris: Alcan, 1930. English translation by André Orianne, *The Theory of Intuition in Husserl's Phenomenology.* Evanston, Ill.: Northwestern University Press, forthcoming.

————. *Totality and Infinity.* Translated by Alphonso Lingis. Pittsburgh, Pa.: Duquesne University Press, 1969.

Lowe, Adoph. *On Economic Knowledge: Toward a Science of Political Economics.* New York: Harper & Row, 1965.

Lowe, Donald M. *The Function of "China" in Marx, Lenin, and Mao.* Berkeley, Calif.: University of California Press, 1966.

Lowie, Robert H. *Culture and Ethnology.* New York: McMurtrie, 1917.

Luckmann, Thomas. "The Constitution of Language in the World of Everyday Life." In Lester E. Embree, ed., *Life-World and Consciousness: Essays for Aron Gurwitsch,* pp. 469–88.

————. "On the Boundaries of the Social World." In Maurice Natanson, ed., *Phenomenology and Social Reality: Essays in Memory of Alfred Schutz,* pp. 73–100.

McBride, William L. *Fundamental Change in Law and Society: Hart and Sartre on Revolution.* The Hague: Mouton, 1970.

Mannheim, Karl. *Essays on the Sociology of Knowledge.* Edited by Paul Kecskemeti. New York: Oxford University Press, 1952.

Marcuse, Herbert. "On Science and Phenomenology." In *Boston Studies in the Philosophy of Science,* Vol. II: *In Honor of Philipp Frank,* edited by Robert S. Cohen and Marx W. Wartofsky, pp. 279–90. New York: Humanities Press, 1965. (Note: A "Comment on the Paper by H. Marcuse" by Aron Gurwitsch follows on pp. 291–306.)

Marrou, Henri-Irénée. *The Meaning of History.* Translated by Robert J. Olsen. Baltimore, Md.: Helicon, 1966.

Merleau-Ponty, Maurice. *Les Aventures de la dialectique.* Paris: Gallimard: 1955. English translation by Joseph Bien, *Adventures of the Dialectic.* Evanston, Ill.: Northwestern University Press, 1973.

————. *Phenomenology of Perception.* Translated by Colin Smith. New York: Humanities Press, 1962.

————. *The Primacy of Perception: And Other Essays on Phenomenological Psychology, the Philosophy of Art, History and Politics.* Edited with an Introduction by James M. Edie and translated by William Cobb et al. Evanston, Ill.: Northwestern University Press, 1964.

————. *Sense and Non-Sense.* Translated with an Introduction by Hubert L. Dreyfus and Patricia Allen Dreyfus. Evanston, Ill.: Northwestern University Press, 1964.

————. *Signs.* Translated with an Introduction by Richard C. Mc-

Cleary. Evanston, Ill.: Northwestern University Press, 1964. (Note: See, in particular, chap. 3, "The Philosopher and Sociology," and chap. 4, "From Mauss to Claude Lévi-Strauss.")

———. *The Structure of Behavior.* Translated by Alden J. Fisher with a Foreword by John Wild. Boston: Beacon, 1963.

———. *Themes from the Lectures at the Collège de France, 1952–1960.* Translated by John O'Neill. Evanston, Ill.: Northwestern University Press, 1970.

Minkowski, Eugène. *Lived Time: Phenomenological and Psychopathological Studies.* Translated by Nancy Metzel. Evanston, Ill.: Northwestern University Press, 1970.

Mohanty, J. N. *Edmund Husserl's Theory of Meaning.* The Hague: Nijhoff, 1964.

Natanson, Maurice. *The Journeying Self: A Study in Philosophy and Social Role.* Reading, Mass.: Addison-Wesley, 1970.

———. *Literature, Philosophy, and the Social Sciences: Essays in Existentialism and Phenomenology.* The Hague: Nijhoff, 1962.

———. "Philosophy and Social Science: A Phenomenological Approach." In *The Handbook of Political Science,* edited by Donald M. Freeman. New York: Free Press, forthcoming.

———, ed. *Essays in Phenomenology.* The Hague: Nijhoff, 1966.

———, ed. *Phenomenology and Social Reality: Essays in Memory of Alfred Schutz.* The Hague: Nijhoff, 1970.

———, ed. *Philosophy of the Social Sciences: A Reader.* New York: Random House, 1963.

Neisser, Hans P. "The Phenomenological Approach in Social Science." *Philosophy and Phenomenological Research,* XX, no. 2 (December, 1959), 198–212.

Nota, John H. *Phenomenology and History.* Translated by Louis Grooten and the author. Chicago: Loyola University Press, 1967.

O'Malley, John B. *Sociology of Meaning.* London: Human Context Books, 1972.

O'Neill, John. *Perception, Expression, and History: The Social Phenomenology of Maurice Merleau-Ponty.* Evanston, Ill.: Northwestern University Press, 1970.

———. *Sociology as a Skin Trade: Essays Towards a Reflexive Sociology.* London: Heinemann, 1972.

Ortega y Gasset, José. *Man and People.* Translated by Willard R. Trask. New York: Norton, 1957.

Orth, Ernst W. *Bedeutung, Sinn, Gegenstand: Studien zur Sprachphilosophie E. Husserls und R. Hönigswalds.* Bonn: Bouvier, 1967.

Paci, Enzo. *The Function of the Sciences and the Meaning of Man.* Translated with an Introduction by Paul Piccone and James E. Hansen. Evanston, Ill.: Northwestern University Press, 1972.

Parsons, Talcott. *The Structure of Social Action.* 2d ed. New York: Free Press, 1949.

Peschka, Vilmos. "La Phénoménologie dans la philosophie du droit moderne." *Archives de philosophie du droit,* XII (1967), 259–86.

Polin, Raymond. *La Création des valeurs.* 2d ed. Paris: Presses Universitaires de France, 1952.

Pos, H.-J. "Phénoménologie et linguistique." *Revue internationale de philosophie,* I, no. 2 (January, 1939), 354–65.

Poulantzas, Nicos. *Nature des choses et droit.* Paris: Librairie générale de droit et de jurisprudence, 1965.

Psathas, George. "Ethnomethods and Phenomenology." *Social Research,* XXXV, no. 3 (Autumn, 1968), 500–520.

————, ed. *Phenomenological Sociology: Issues and Applications.* New York: Wiley, forthcoming.

Rauhala, Lauri. *Intentionality and the Problem of the Unconscious.* Turku, Finland: Turun Yliopisto, 1969.

Recaséns Siches, Luis; Cossio, Carlos; Llambías de Azevedo, Juan; and García Máynez, Eduardo. *Latin-American Legal Philosophy.* Translated by Gordon Ireland, Milton R. Konvitz, Miguel A. de Capriles, and Jorge Roberto Hayzus, with an Introduction by Josef L. Kunz. Cambridge, Mass.: Harvard University Press, 1948.

Reichling, Anton Joannes Bernardus Nicolaas. *Het Woord: Een studie omtrent de grondslag van taal en taalgebruik.* Zwolle: Tjeenk Willink, 1967.

Reinach, Adolf. *Zur Phänomenologie des Rechts.* Munich: Kösel, 1953. (Note: Originally published as *Die apriorischen Grundlagen des bürgerlichen Rechtes.* Halle: Niemeyer, 1913.)

Richardson, William J. *Heidegger: Through Phenomenology to Thought.* With a Preface by Martin Heidegger. 2d ed. The Hague: Nijhoff, 1967.

Ricoeur, Paul. *Freedom and Nature: The Voluntary and the Involuntary.* Translated with an Introduction by Erazím V. Kohák. Evanston, Ill.: Northwestern University Press, 1966.

————. *History and Truth.* Translated with an Introduction by Charles A. Kelbley. Evanston, Ill.: Northwestern University Press, 1965.

————. *Husserl: An Analysis of His Phenomenology.* Translated by Edward G. Ballard and Lester E. Embree. Evanston, Ill.: Northwestern University Press, 1967.

Rothbard, Murray N. "In Defense of 'Extreme Apriorism.'" *Southern Economic Journal,* XXIII, no. 3 (January, 1957), 314–20.

————. "Ludwig von Mises." In *International Encyclopedia of the Social Sciences,* edited by David L. Sills, XVI, 379–82. New York: Macmillan and Free Press, 1968.

————. *Man, Economy, and State: A Treatise on Economic Principles.* 2 vols. Princeton, N.J.: Van Nostrand, 1962.

Santayana, George. *Realms of Being.* New York: Scribner, 1942.

Sartre, Jean-Paul. *Being and Nothingness: An Essay on Phenomenological Ontology.* Translated with an Introduction by Hazel E. Barnes. New York: Philosophical Library, 1956.

————. *Critique de la raison dialectique.* Vol. I: *Théorie des ensembles pratiques.* Paris: Gallimard, 1960.

————. *Imagination: A Psychological Critique.* Translated with an Introduction by Forrest Williams. Ann Arbor, Mich.: University of Michigan Press, 1962.

————. *The Psychology of Imagination.* Translated by Bernard Frechtman. London: Rider, 1949.

————. *The Transcendence of the Ego: An Existentialist Theory of Consciousness.* Translated and annotated with an Introduction by Forrest Williams and Robert Kirkpatrick. New York: Farrar, Straus, Noonday Press, 1957.

Scheler, Max. *Der Formalismus in der Ethik und die materiale Wertethik: Neuer Versuch der Grundlegung eines ethischen Personalismus.* Edited by Maria Scheler. 5th ed. Bern: Francke, 1966. English translation by Manfred Frings and Roger Funk, *Formalism in Ethics and Non-Formal Ethics of Values: A New Attempt toward the Foundation of an Ethical Personalism.* Evanston, Ill.: Northwestern University Press, 1973.

————. *Man's Place in Nature.* Translated with an Introduction by Hans Meyerhoff. Boston: Beacon, 1961; New York: Farrar, Straus, Noonday Press, 1963.

————. *The Nature of Sympathy.* Translated by Peter Heath with an Introduction by W. Stark. New Haven, Conn.: Yale University Press, 1954.

————. "Problems with a Sociology of Knowledge." Translated by Ernest Ranly. *Philosophy Today,* XII, no. 1 (Spring, 1968), 42–70.

————. *Ressentiment.* Edited with an Introduction by Lewis A. Coser and translated by William W. Holdheim. New York: Free Press, 1961.

————. *Die Wissenformen und die Gesellschaft.* Edited by Maria Scheler. 2d ed. Bern: Francke, 1960.

Schrag, Calvin O. "Existence and History." *Review of Metaphysics,* XIII, no. 1 (September, 1959), 28–44.

————. *Experience and Being: Prolegomena to a Future Ontology.* Evanston, Ill.: Northwestern University Press, 1969.

Schutz, Alfred. "Choice and the Social Sciences." In Lester E. Embree, ed., *Life-World and Consciousness: Essays for Aron Gurwitsch,* pp. 565–90.

————. *Collected Papers*, Vol. I: *The Problem of Social Reality.* Edited with an Introduction by Maurice Natanson and a Preface by H. L. Van Breda. The Hague: Nijhoff, 1962. Vol. II: *Studies in Social Theory.* Edited with an Introduction by Arvid Brodersen. The Hague: Nijhoff, 1964. Vol. III: *Studies in Phenomenological Philosophy.* Edited by Ilse Schutz with an Introduction by Aron Gurwitsch. The Hague: Nijhoff, 1966.

————. *The Phenomenology of the Social World.* Translated by George Walsh and Frederick Lehnert with an Introduction by George Walsh. Evanston, Ill.: Northwestern University Press, 1967.

————. *Reflections on the Problem of Relevance.* Edited and annotated with an Introduction by Richard M. Zaner. New Haven, Conn.: Yale University Press, 1970.

————, and Luckmann, Thomas. *The Structures of the Life-World.* Translated by Richard M. Zaner and H. Tristram Engelhardt, Jr. Evanston, Ill.: Northwestern University Press, 1973.

Shiner, L. E. "Husserl and Historical Science." *Social Research,* XXXVII, no. 4 (Winter, 1970), 511–32.

Shmueli, Efraim. "Critical Reflections on Husserl's Philosophy of History." *Journal of the British Society for Phenomenology,* II, no. 1 (January, 1971), 35–51.

Sokolowski, Robert. *The Formation of Husserl's Concept of Constitution.* The Hague: Nijhoff, 1964.

Solomon, Robert C., ed. *Phenomenology and Existentialism.* New York: Harper & Row, 1972.

Spiegelberg, Herbert. *Gesetz und Sittengesetz: Strukturanalytische und historische Vorstudien zu einer gesetzesfreien Ethik.* Zurich: Niehans, 1935.

————. *The Phenomenological Movement: A Historical Introduction.* 2 vols., 2d ed. The Hague: Nijhoff, 1965.

————. *Phenomenology in Psychology and Psychiatry: A Historical Introduction.* Evanston, Ill.: Northwestern University Press, 1972.

Stein, Edith. *On the Problem of Empathy.* Translated by Waltraut Stein with a Foreword by Erwin W. Straus. The Hague: Nijhoff, 1964.

Strasser, Stephan. *The Idea of Dialogal Phenomenology.* Translated by Henry J. Koren. Pittsburgh, Pa.: Duquesne University Press, 1969.

————. *Phenomenology and the Human Sciences: A Contribution to a New Scientific Ideal.* Translated by Henry J. Koren. Pittsburgh, Pa.: Duquesne University Press, 1963.

————. *The Soul in Metaphysical and Empirical Psychology.* Translated by Henry J. Koren. Pittsburgh, Pa.: Duquesne University Press, 1957.

Straus, Erwin W. *Phenomenological Psychology: Selected Papers.* Translated, in part, by Erling Eng. New York: Basic Books, 1966.
———. "Psychiatry and Philosophy." Translated by Erling Eng. In *Psychiatry and Philosophy*, edited by Maurice Natanson, pp. 1–83. New York: Springer, 1969.
———, ed. *Phenomenology, Pure and Applied: The First Lexington Conference.* Pittsburgh, Pa.: Duquesne University Press, 1964.
Taylor, Charles. "Interpretation and the Sciences of Man." *Review of Metaphysics*, XXV, no. 1 (September, 1971), 3–51.
Theunissen, Michael. *Der Andere: Studien zur Sozialontologie der Gegenwart.* Berlin: de Gruyter, 1965.
Thévenaz, Pierre. *What Is Phenomenology? And Other Essays.* Edited with an Introduction by James M. Edie and translated by James M. Edie, Charles Courtney, and Paul Brockelman, with a Preface by John Wild. Chicago: Quadrangle, 1962.
Tibbetts, Paul, ed. *Perception: Selected Readings in Science and Phenomenology.* Chicago: Quadrangle, 1969.
Tiryakian, Edward A. "Existential Phenomenology and the Sociological Tradition." *American Sociological Review*, XXX, no. 5 (October, 1965), 674–88.
———. *Sociologism and Existentialism: Two Perspectives on the Individual and Society.* Englewood Cliffs, N.J.: Prentice-Hall, 1962.
Toulemont, René. *L'Essence de la société selon Husserl.* Paris: Presses Universitaires de France, 1962.
Tran Duc Thao. *Phénoménologie et matérialisme dialectique.* Paris: Minh-Tan, 1951.
Tymieniecka, Anna-Teresa. *Phenomenology and Science in Contemporary European Thought.* With a Foreword by I. M. Bochenski. New York: Farrar, Straus, Noonday Press, 1962.
Urban, Wilbur M. *The Intelligible World.* London: Allen & Unwin, 1929.
———. *Language and Reality.* New York: Macmillan, 1939.
Van Breda, H. L., ed. *Problèmes actuels de la phénoménologie.* Paris: Desclée de Brouwer, 1952.
van Peursen, Cornelius A. *Phenomenology and Analytical Philosophy.* Translated by Rex Ambler and amended by Henry J. Koren. Pittsburgh, Pa.: Duquesne University Press, 1972.
Verhaar, John W. M. "Philosophy and Linguistic Theory." *Language Sciences*, no. 14 (February, 1971), 1–11.
———. *Some Relations between Perception, Speech, and Thought.* Assen: Van Gorcum, 1963.
von Mises, Ludwig. *Epistemological Problems of Economics.* Princeton, N.J.: Van Nostrand, 1960.

————. *Human Action: A Treatise on Economics*. New Haven, Conn.: Yale University Press, 1949.

Waelhens, Alphonse de. *Existence et signification*. Louvain: Nauwelaerts, 1958. (Note: See especially the essays "La Philosophie du langage selon M. Merleau-Ponty" and "Réflexions sur les rapports de la phénoménologie et de la psychoanalyse.")

Wagner, Helmut R., ed. *Alfred Schutz on Phenomenology and Social Relations: Selected Writings*. Chicago: University of Chicago Press, 1970.

Wahl, Jean. *Husserl*. 2 vols. Cours de Sorbonne. Paris: Centre de documentation universitaire, 1958.

————. *L'Ouvrage posthume de Husserl: La Krisis: La Crise des sciences européennes et la phénoménologie transcendentale*. Cours de Sorbonne. Paris: Centre de documentation universitaire, 1958.

Waldenfels, Bernhard. *Das Zwischenreich des Dialogs: Sozialphilosophische Untersuchungen in Anschluss an Edmund Husserl*. The Hague: Nijhoff, 1971.

Wann, T. W., ed. *Behaviorism and Phenomenology: Contrasting Bases for Modern Psychology*. Chicago: University of Chicago Press, 1965.

White, Leslie. *The Science of Culture*. New York: Grove, 1949.

Wild, John. *Existence and the World of Freedom*. Englewood Cliffs, N.J.: Prentice-Hall, 1963.

Würtenberger, Thomas, ed. *Phänomenologie, Rechtsphilosophie, Jurisprudenz: Festschrift für Gerhart Husserl zum 75. Geburtstag*. Frankfurt a.M.: Klostermann, 1969.

Zaner, Richard M. "Theory of Intersubjectivity: Alfred Schutz." *Social Research*, XXVIII, no. 1 (Spring, 1961), 71–93.

————. *The Way of Phenomenology: Criticism as a Philosophical Discipline*. New York: Western Publishing, Pegasus, 1970.

Zeltner, Hermann. "Das Ich und die Anderen: Husserls Beitrag zur Grundlegung der Sozialphilosophie." *Zeitschrift für philosophische Forschung*, XIII, no. 2 (April–June, 1959), 288–315.

List of Contributors

PAUL AMSELEK is Professor in the Faculty of Law and Political Science and Director of the Center of Municipal Public Law at the University of Strasbourg. In addition to his phenomenological studies, he has written a book entitled *Le Budget de l'état sous la Ve république*.

DAVID BIDNEY is Professor of Anthropology at Indiana University. He has been a Research Associate of the Wenner-Gren Foundation for Anthropology and a Guggenheim Fellow. The focus of much of his work has been theoretical anthropology and its relationship to philosophy.

MITCHELL FRANKLIN is Professor of Law and Professor of Philosophy at the State University of New York at Buffalo. Before that, he was Irby Professor of Law at Tulane. He was educated at Harvard and has held Rosenwald and Guggenheim fellowships. He has written on Hegel and alienation, and is a contributing editor of the *Tulane Law Review*.

WOLFGANG FRIEDMANN (1907–72) was Professor of International Law and Director of International Legal Research at Columbia University. He held degrees from the Universities of Berlin, London, and Melbourne and had taught in England, Australia, and France. His publications include *International Financial Aid* and *Joint International Business Ventures*.

CARL J. FRIEDRICH is Professor Emeritus of Government at Harvard, where he was Eaton Professor of the Sciences of Govern-

[587]

ment. He is a past President of the American Political Science Association and an editor of *Public Policy* and *Nomos*. His latest book is *Tradition and Authority*.

GERHARD FUNKE is Professor of Philosophy at the University of Mainz. In addition to his works on phenomenology, he has published studies of Maine de Biran and Leibniz, and has edited a volume on *Die Aufklärung*. He also serves as an editor of *Kant-Studien*.

EUGENE T. GENDLIN is Associate Professor of Psychology at the University of Chicago. He has been a member of the Wisconsin Psychiatric Institute at the University of Wisconsin, and was given the Distinguished Professional Psychology award in 1970 by the American Psychological Association.

JOHN G. GUNNELL is Professor of Political Science at the State University of New York at Albany. He received his Ph.D. from the University of California, and is presently completing a book on *Political Science and Philosophy*. He is interested in Anglo-American as well as Continental philosophy.

HWA YOL JUNG is Professor of Political Science at Moravian College. He has done postdoctoral research at the University of Chicago, Northwestern University, and Yale, and has contributed to journals in philosophy as well as political science. He is especially concerned with existential phenomenology.

JOSEPH J. KOCKELMANS is Professor of Philosophy at Pennsylvania State University. He has been a visiting professor at the New School for Social Research and at the University of Pittsburgh. In addition to books on Husserl's phenomenology, he has written on the natural sciences and on Heidegger.

DONALD M. LOWE is Professor of History at San Francisco State University. Previously, he taught at the University of California at Riverside and City University of New York. He is presently preparing a book of *Essays in the History of Perception*.

THOMAS LUCKMANN is Professor of Sociology at the University of Constance. He has also taught at the University of Frankfurt and at the New School for Social Research. His publications are in the fields of sociology of religion and language as well as philosophical anthropology.

MAURICE MERLEAU-PONTY (1908–61), whose ideas have had a major impact on contemporary philosophical thought, was educated at the Ecole Normale Supérieure, where he later taught. After 1952 he lectured at the Collège de France. At the time of his death, he was at work on *The Visible and the Invisible.*

MAURICE NATANSON is Professor of Philosophy and Fellow of Cowell College at the University of California at Santa Cruz. He is the author of a forthcoming book on *Edmund Husserl,* research for which was done as a National Endowment for the Humanities Senior Fellow.

JOHN O'NEILL is Professor of Sociology at York University. He received his Ph.D. from Stanford in the History of Social Thought and continues to combine work in sociology, philosophy, and economics. He is a member of the editorial board of *Philosophy of the Social Sciences.*

ERNST WOLFGANG ORTH is Professor of Philosophy at the University of Trier. Earlier, he taught at the University of Mainz. Philosophy of language is one of his central concerns and the field in which he has published.

MURRAY N. ROTHBARD is Professor of Economics at Polytechnic Institute of Brooklyn. Trained at Columbia University, he has been a consultant for the William Volker Fund and the Princeton Panel. He has also taught at the City College School of Business in New York.

EDWARD A. TIRYAKIAN is Professor of Sociology at Duke University. Before that, he taught at Harvard and Princeton. Much of his work is concerned with problems of theoretical sociology. He is an advisory editor of *Cahiers internationaux de sociologie* and editor of a reader on *The Phenomenon of Sociology.*

JOHN W. M. VERHAAR, S.J., is Extraordinary Professor of Linguistics at the University of Djakarta and Managing Editor of the journal *Foundations of Language*. He has also taught in the United States and in the Philippines. Among his published works is a four-part study of *The Verb "Be" and Its Synonyms*, which he edited.

Index

(Note: roman numerals refer to volume numbers)

[591]